Wiley
CMAexcel Learning System
Exam Review 2021

About IMA® (Institute of Management Accountants)

IMA®, the association of accountants and financial professionals in business, is one of the largest and most respected associations focused exclusively on advancing the management accounting profession.

Globally, IMA supports the profession through research, the CMA® (Certified Management Accountant) program, continuing education, networking, and advocacy of the highest ethical business practices.

IMA has a global network of more than 125,000 members in 150 countries and 300 professional and student chapters. Headquartered in Montvale, N.J., USA. IMA provides localized services through its four global regions: The Americas, Asia/Pacific, Europe, and Middle East/ India. For more information about IMA, please visit www.imanet.org.

Wiley CMAexcel Learning System Exam Review 2021

Self-Study Guide

Part 1: Financial Planning, Performance, and Analytics

The Association of Accountants and Financial Professionals in Business

Library of Congress Cataloging-in-Publication Data

ISBN 978-1-119-72314-1 (Part 1)
ISBN 978-1-119-72363-9 (Part 1 ePDF)
ISBN 978-1-119-72369-1 (Part 1 ePub)
ISBN 978-1-119-72364-6 (Part 2)
ISBN 978-1-119-73431-4 (Part 2 ePDF)
ISBN 978-1-119-72368-4 (Part 2 ePub)

Printed in the United States of America

SKY10021287_091720

Contents

Acknowledgments of Subject Matter Experts

The Wiley CMAexcel Learning System (WCMALS) content is written to help explain the concepts and calculations from the Certified Management Accountant (CMA) exam Learning Outcome Statements (LOS) published by the Institute of Certified Management Accountants (ICMA).

Wiley would like to acknowledge the team of subject matter experts who worked with us to produce this version of the WCMALS. IMA would also like to acknowledge this team of subject matter experts, who worked together in conjunction with IMA staff to produce this version of the WCMALS.

Content Contributors for 2021 Edition

Marjorie E. Yuschak, CMA, MBA, is fortunate to have enjoyed multiple careers. She had a 21-year career at Johnson & Johnson developing expertise in cost/managerial accounting, financial reporting, and employee stock option programs while working in the consumer, pharmaceutical, and corporate segments of the business. Following that she was an adjunct professor of accounting and faculty advisor to Beta Alpha Psi at the Rutgers Business School, New Brunswick. Marj continues to facilitate the CMA Review courses at Villanova University, which she has done for over ten years and is currently an adjunct professor of accounting at The College of New Jersey. She has a consulting business providing coaching for accounting, communication skills, and small business management. Marj is a member of the Raritan Valley Chapter of the IMA in New Jersey. In addition, she is a Certified Trainer in both AchieveGlobal and DDI (Development Dimensions International) and a member of ATD (the Association for Talent Development).

Michael G. Solomon, Ph.D., CISSP, PMP, CISM, PenTest+, is a security, privacy, blockchain, and identity management author, consultant, and speaker who specializes in leading teams in achieving and maintaining secure and effective IT environments. An IT professional and consultant since 1987, Dr. Solomon has led project teams for many Fortune 500 companies and has authored and contributed to over 25 books and numerous training courses. He is a Professor of Cyber Security and

Global Business with Blockchain Technology at the University of the Cumberlands, and holds a PhD in Computer Science and Informatics from Emory University.

Prior Content Contributors

William G. Heninger, PhD, CPA, is an Associate Professor in the School of Accountancy at Brigham Young University (BYU). He received a Bachelor of Science in Accounting and a Master of Accountancy from BYU and a Ph.D. in Accounting from the University of Georgia. Professor Heninger teaches accounting information systems, data communications, data analytics, and financial and managerial accounting at both undergraduate and graduate levels. He has taught Executive MBA courses at the State University of New York (SUNY) at Buffalo, the Singapore Institute of Management, and the International Graduate School of Business and Algebra University in Zagreb, Croatia. His research interests include online financial disclosures, online group decision making, earnings management, and ERP systems. He is the SAP Campus Coordinator for BYU. He has served as editor and associate editor for the *Accounting Information Systems Educator Journal*. Prior to entering academia, he worked as an auditor for Ernst & Young and as a systems administrator for Cyprus Minerals Corporation.

Kip Holderness, PhD, CPA, CMA, CFE, is an associate professor of accounting at West Virginia University. Dr. Holderness graduated from Brigham Young University with a Bachelor of Science degree in Accounting and a Master's of Accountancy degree. He earned a PhD in Accounting from Bentley University.

He teaches managerial and forensic accounting, and works extensively with doctoral students conducting various research projects. Dr. Holderness' research focuses primarily on the impact of fraud and employee deviance on individuals and organizations, as well as improving detection methods. He also examines the effects of personality and generational differences in the workplace.

He has published in practitioner and academic journals in the areas of fraud and forensics, auditing, managerial accounting, information systems, and accounting education. In addition, Dr. Holderness has received numerous research grants from the Institute for Fraud Prevention and the Institute of Management Accountants.

Meghann Cefaratti, Ph.D., is an associate professor in the Department of Accountancy at Northern Illinois University. She completed her Ph.D. in Accounting at Virginia Tech. Professor Cefaratti teaches financial accounting, assurance services, and internal auditing. Her primary research interest involves auditors' fraud risk assessment judgments. Her research has received awards from the American Accounting Association's Forensic Accounting Section and the Accounting and Information Systems Educators Association and has been published in the Journal of Information Systems, Journal of the Association for Information Systems, Journal of Forensic Accounting Research, and Internal Auditor. Professor Cefaratti is a member of the Illinois CPA Society Audit and Assurance Services Technical

Committee. She is a former auditor for the Air Force Audit Agency (AFAA) where her audit coverage included Andrews Air Force Base, MD, the Pentagon and various Air National Guard installations. Prior to working with the AFAA, she worked as a tax associate for PricewaterhouseCoopers in Baltimore, MD.

Gary Cokins, CPIM, is an internationally recognized expert, speaker, and author in enterprise and corporate performance management (EPM/CPM) systems. He is the founder of Analytics-Based Performance Management LLC (www.garycokins. com). He began his career in industry with a Fortune 100 company in CFO and operations roles. Then for 15 years he was a consultant with Deloitte, KPMG, and EDS (now part of HP). From 1997 until 2013 Gary was a Principal Consultant with SAS, a business analytics software vendor. His most recent books are *Performance Management: Integrating Strategy Execution, Methodologies, Risk, and Analytics* and *Predictive Business Analytics*. He graduated from Cornell University with a Bachelor of Science degree in industrial engineering/operations research and went on to earn his MBA from Northwestern University Kellogg.

Daniel J. Gibbons, CPA, Associate Professor of Accounting, has been employed by Waubonsee Community College since 2001. Prior to starting his career in education, he worked in Accounting and Finance for approximately 21 years. He has a Bachelor of Science degree in Accounting from Northeastern Illinois University and a Master of Science degree in Finance from Northern Illinois University. He is a resident of Naperville, IL.

Joseph Kastantin, CPA, CMA, MBA, ACCA, is a Professor of Accountancy at the University of Wisconsin-La Crosse and an alum of KPMG Central and Eastern Europe having worked from 1997 to 2008 in both full time and part time capacities with KPMG Central Europe in the department of professional practice and training. Kastantin served on the board of directors and audit committee of the North Central Trust Company (now Trust Point) for three years and as chairman of the board of La Crosse Funds, Inc. for four years. Additionally, he served as president and board member for several not-for-profit entities, as CEO of a small manufacturing company, business manager for an auto dealership, controller for a textile wholesaler, and as sole practitioner in public accounting. He has more than 30 published journal articles and books. His most recent publications are on fraud and a practical guide to impairments under IFRS and US GAAP. He served nearly ten years on active duty with the US Army (SFC E-7) with tours in Korea and Vietnam and was an instructor and MOS test writer at the US Army AG School.

Candidate Study Information

CMA Certification from ICMA

The Certified Management Accountant (CMA) certification provides accountants and financial professionals with an objective measure of knowledge and competence in the field of management accounting. The CMA designation is recognized globally as an invaluable credential for professional accountancy advancement inside organizations and for broadening professional skills and perspectives.

The two-part CMA exam is designed to develop and measure critical thinking and decision-making skills and to meet these objectives:

- To establish management accounting and financial management as recognized professions by identifying the role of the professional, the underlying body of knowledge, and a course of study by which such knowledge is acquired.
- To encourage higher educational standards in the management accounting and financial management fields.
- To establish an objective measure of an individual's knowledge and competence in the fields of management accounting and financial management.
- To encourage continued professional development.

Individuals earning the CMA designation benefit by being able to:

- Communicate their broad business competency and strategic financial mastery.
- Obtain contemporary professional knowledge and develop skills and abilities that are valued by successful businesses.
- Convey their commitment to an exemplary standard of excellence that is grounded on a strong ethical foundation and lifelong learning.
- Enhance their career development, salary qualifications, and professional promotion opportunities.

The CMA certification is granted exclusively by the Institute of Certified Management Accountants (ICMA).

CMA Learning Outcome Statements (LOS)

The Certified Management Accountant exam is based on a series of Learning Outcome Statements (LOS) developed by the Institute of Certified Management Accountants (ICMA). The LOS describe the knowledge and skills that make up the CMA body of knowledge, broken down by part, section, and topic. The Wiley CMAexcel Learning System (WCMALS) supports the LOS by addressing the subjects they cover. Candidates should use the LOS to ensure they can address the concepts in different ways or through a variety of question scenarios. Candidates should also be prepared to perform calculations referred to in the LOS in total or by providing missing components of a calculation. The LOS should not be used as proxies for exact exam questions; they should be used as a guide for studying and learning the content that will be covered on the exam.

A copy of the ICMA Learning Outcome Statements is included in Appendix A at the end of this book. Candidates are also encouraged to visit the IMA Web site to find other exam-related information at www.imanet.org.

CMA Exam Format

The content tested on the CMA exams is at an advanced level—which means that the passing standard is set for mastery, not minimum competence. Thus, there will be test questions for all major topics that require the candidate to synthesize information, evaluate a situation, and make recommendations. Other questions will test subject comprehension and analysis. However, compared to previous versions, this CMA exam will have an increased emphasis on the higher-level questions.

The content is based on a series of LOS that define the competencies and capabilities expected of a management accountant.

There are two exams, taken separately: Part 1: Financial Planning, Performance, and Analytics; and Part 2: Strategic Financial Management. Each exam is four hours in length and includes multiple-choice and essay questions. One hundred multiple-choice questions are presented first, followed by two essay questions. All of these questions—multiple-choice and essay—can address any of the LOS for the respective exam part. Therefore, your study plan should include learning the content of the part as well as practicing how to answer multiple-choice and essay questions against that content. The study plan tips and the final section of this WCMALS book contain important information to help you learn how to approach the different types of questions.

Note on Candidate Assumed Knowledge

The CMA exam content is based on a set of assumed baseline knowledge that candidates are expected to have. Assumed knowledge includes economics, basic statistics, and financial accounting. Examples of how this assumed knowledge might be tested in the exam include:

- How to calculate marginal revenue and costs as well as understand the relevance of market structures when determining prices
- How to calculate variance when managing financial risk
- How to construct a cash flow statement as part of an analysis of transactions and assess the impact of the transactions on the financial statements

Please note that prior courses in accounting and finance are highly recommended to ensure this knowledge competency when preparing for the exam.

Overall Expectations for the CMA Candidates

Completing the CMA exams requires a high level of commitment and dedication of up to 170 hours of study for each part of the CMA exam. Completing the two-part exam is a serious investment that will reap many rewards, helping you to build a solid foundation for your career, distinguish yourself from other accountants, and enhance your career in ways that will pay dividends for a lifetime.

Your success in completing these exams will rest heavily on your ability to create a solid study plan and to execute that plan. IMA offers resources to support you during this process—we encourage you to register as a CMA candidate as soon as you begin the program to maximize your access to these resources and tools and to draw on these benefits with rigor and discipline that best supports your unique study needs. We also suggest candidates seek other sources if further knowledge is needed to augment knowledge and understanding of the ICMA LOS.

For more information about the CMA certification, the CMA exams, or the exam preparation resources offered through IMA, visit www.imanet.org.

Standard and pronouncement changes in authoritative literature have an issuance date, an effective date, and possibly an early adoption date. These changes will be eligible for testing on the CMA examinations one year after the effective date. The contents of this curriculum reflect standards that are currently eligible for testing.

Updates and Errata Notification

Please be advised that our materials are designed to provide thorough and accurate content with a high level of attention to quality. From time to time there may be clarifications, corrections, or updates that are captured in an Updates and Errata Notification.

To ensure you are kept abreast of changes, this notification will be available on Wiley's CMA update and errata page. You may review these documents by going to www.efficientlearning.com/cma/support/updates.

How to Use the
Wiley CMAexcel Learning System

This product is based on the CMA body of knowledge developed by the Institute of Certified Management Accountants (ICMA). This material is designed for learning purposes and is distributed with the understanding that the publisher and authors are not offering legal or professional services. Although the text is based on the body of knowledge tested by the CMA exam and the published Learning Outcome Statements (LOS) covering the two-part exams, the Wiley CMAexcel Learning System (WCMALS) program developers do not have access to the current bank of exam questions. It is critical that candidates understand all LOS published by the ICMA, learn all concepts and calculations related to those statements, and have a solid grasp of how to approach the multiple-choice and essay exams in the CMA program.

Some exam preparation tools provide an overview of key topics; others are intended to help you practice one specific aspect of the exams such as the questions. The WCMALS is designed as a comprehensive exam preparation tool to help you study the content from the exam LOS, learn how to write the CMA essays and practice answering exam-type questions.

Study the Book Content

The **table of contents** is set up using the CMA exam content specifications established by ICMA. Each section, topic, and subtopic is named according to the content specifications and the **Learning Outcome Statements (LOS)** written to correspond to these specifications. As you go through each section and major topic, refer to the related LOS found in Appendix A. Then review the WCMALS book content to help learn the concepts and formulas covered in the LOS.

The **Topic Questions** and **Practice Questions** are a sampling of the type of exam questions you will encounter on the exam and may involve extensive written and/or calculation responses. Use these questions to begin applying what you have learned, recognizing there is a much larger sample of practice questions available in the Online Test Bank (described in the next section).

The WCMALS also contains a **Bibliography and References** in case you need to find more detailed content on an LOS. We encourage you to use published academic sources. While information can be found online, we discourage the use of open-source, unedited sites such as Wikipedia.

Suggested Study Process Using the WCMALS

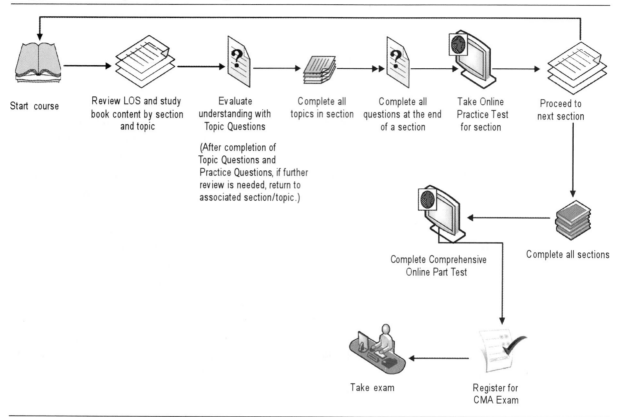

Start course → Review LOS and study book content by section and topic → Evaluate understanding with Topic Questions → Complete all topics in section → Complete all questions at the end of a section → Take Online Practice Test for section → Proceed to next section

(After completion of Topic Questions and Practice Questions, if further review is needed, return to associated section/topic.)

Complete all sections → Complete Comprehensive Online Part Test → Register for CMA Exam → Take exam

WCMALS Book Features

The WCMALS books use a number of features to draw your attention to certain types of content:

Key terms are **bolded** where they appear in the text with their definition, to allow you to quickly scan through and study them.

 Key formulas are indicated with this icon. Be sure you understand these formulas and practice applying them.

 Topic Questions at the end of each topic are representative of exam questions and enable you to test your understanding and mastery of the topic.

Study tips offer ideas and strategies for studying and preparing for the exam.

 Practice questions are presented at the end of each section; these questions help you solidify your learning of that section and apply it to the type of questions that appear on the exam.

 LOS icons appear in the body of the sections to highlight where each Learning Outcome Statement is addressed within the text.

Online Test Bank

Included with your purchase of the Wiley CMAexcel Learning System Part 1 book is an Online Test Bank made available to you through www.wileycma.com. This test bank includes a pool of nearly 1900 questions that can be used to create section-specific tests. All the multiple-choice questions provide feedback in response to your answers.

It is suggested that you integrate the Online Test Bank throughout your study program instead of leaving it until the end. The test bank is designed for you to practice questions related to the section content—read and learn a section and then practice online questions related to that section. This also will help you identify whether further study of the section content is required before moving to the next section.

In addition, sample essay questions are provided for each section that simulate the testing environment. The correct answer is provided which will enable you to self-score your answer.

The comprehensive Part 1 test is designed to help you simulate taking the actual CMA exam. Try the comprehensive Part 1 test after you have studied all the Part 1 content. It is recommended that you set up your own exam simulation—set aside four hours in a room without interruption, do not have any reference books open, and work through the comprehensive part exam as if you were taking the real exam. This will prepare you for the exam setting and give you a good idea of how ready you are.

You are strongly encouraged to make full use of all online practice and review features as part of your study efforts. Please note that these features are subscription based and available only for a specific number of months from the time of registration.

Learn to Write the CMA Essays

The four-hour CMA exam will test your understanding of each part's content using both multiple-choice and essay questions. This means you must learn to write two types of tests in one sitting. The WCMALS books contain tips, instruction, and examples to help you learn to write an essay exam. Be sure to study the Essay Exam Support Materials section so that in addition to practicing with the Online Test Bank, you also learn to respond to the content in essay format.

Create a Study Plan

E ach part of the two-part CMA exam uses a combination of a multiple-choice format and an essay format to test your understanding of the part concepts, terms, and calculations. Creating and managing your plan is critical to achieving success. The next tips and tactics are included to help you prepare and manage your study plan.

Study Tips

There are many ways to study, and the plan you create will depend on things such as your lifestyle (when and how you can schedule study time), your learning style, how familiar you are with the content, and how practiced you are at writing formal essays. Only you can assess these factors and create a plan that will work for you. Some suggestions that other exam candidates have found helpful follow.

- Schedule regular study times and stay on schedule.
- Avoid cramming by breaking your study times into small segments. For example, you may want to work intensely for 45 minutes with no interruptions, followed by a 15-minute break during which time you do something different. You may want to leave the room, have a conversation, or exercise.
- Highlight key ideas when reading, especially unfamiliar ones. Reread later to ensure comprehension.
- Pay particular attention to the terms and equations highlighted in this book, and be sure to learn the acronyms in the CMA body of knowledge.
- Create personal mnemonics to help you memorize key information. For example, CRCIM to remember the five COSO Internal Control framework components: Control Environment, Risk Assessment, Control Activities, Information and Communication, and Monitoring.
- Create study aids such as flash cards.
  - Use index cards, and write a question on one side and the answer on the other. This helps reinforce the learning because you are writing the information as well as reading it. Examples: What is ____? List the five parts of ____.
  - Make flash cards of topics and issues that are unfamiliar to you, key terms and formulas, and anything you highlighted while reading.

- Keep some cards with you at all times to review when you have time, such as in an elevator, while waiting for an appointment, and so on.
- Use a flash card partner. This person does not need to understand accounting. He or she only needs the patience to sit with you and read the questions off the flash card.
- Start to eliminate the flash cards you can easily answer from your stack as test time approaches so you can concentrate on the more challenging topics and terms.
- Tap into other resources, such as the Internet, library, accountant colleagues, or professors, to augment your understanding when particular topics are difficult.
- Use your study plan—treat it as a living document and update it as you learn more about what you need to do to prepare for the exam.
- Use the Topic Questions in the book to assess how well you understand the content you just completed.
- Use the Online Test Bank to test your ability to answer multiple-choice practice questions on each section's content as you finish it. After completing 40–50 questions, review areas in the book that you were weak on in the practice questions. Then try another section test.
  - Learn how to take a multiple-choice question exam—there are many online resources with tips and guidance that relate to answering multiple-choice exams.
  - Make an attempt to answer all questions. There is no penalty for an incorrect answer—if you don't try, even when you are uncertain, you eliminate the potential of getting a correct answer.
- Learn to write an effective essay answer.
  - Use the Essay Exam Support Materials section of this book. This content shows a sample grading guide and includes a sample of a good, a better, and a best answer in addition to some helpful tips for writing an essay answer.
  - Learn how points are awarded for an essay answer so that you can ensure you get the most points possible for your answers, even when you are very challenged by a question.
  - Practice essay responses using the questions in this WCMALS book as well as the Online Test Bank.
- Access the Online Test Bank and its Essay Questions until you are comfortable with the content.
- Simulate an actual exam by setting aside four uninterrupted hours and take the full Part 1 Online Practice Exam as if you were taking the actual exam.

Ensure you are both well rested and physically prepared for the exam day as each exam is four hours in length with no break for meals. Learning how to answer a multiple-choice and essay exam and being mentally and physically prepared can improve your grade significantly. Know the content and be prepared to deal with challenges with a focused, confident, and flexible attitude.

Introduction

Welcome to Part 1: Financial Planning, Performance, and Analytics of the Wiley CMAexcel Learning System.

This Part 1 textbook is composed of six sections:

Section A: External Financial Reporting Decisions (15%) covers the four financial statements (balance sheet, income statement, statement of changes in equity, and statement of cash flows) as well as recognition, measurement, and valuation.

Section B: Planning, Budgeting, and Forecasting (20%) looks at basic budgeting concepts and forecasting techniques that provide the information a company can use to execute its strategy and pursue its short- and long-term goals.

Section C: Performance Management (20%) deals with the methods of comparing actual financial performance to the budget. It also describes tools that incorporate both financial and nonfinancial measures to aid an organization in matching its planning to its overall strategy.

Section D: Cost Management (15%) describes various costing systems that can be used to monitor a company's costs and provide management with information it needs to manage the company's operations and performance.

Section E: Internal Controls (15%) begins with a discussion of the assessment and management of risk. Understanding risk provides the basis for internal auditing activities and the means of ensuring the security and reliability of the information on which the company bases its decisions.

Section F: Technology and Analytics (15%) was a new section for the 2020 CMA exam, and encompasses emerging topics in the management accounting field. As you develop in your professional life, it will be increasingly critical that you understand information systems and can apply new technologies and methodologies including data governance, technology-enabled finance transformation, and data analytics.

Many of these subjects, tested in the Part 1 CMA exam, provide a foundation for the concepts and methodologies that will be the subject of the Part 2 exam.

External Financial Reporting Decisions (15%)

To perform their duties, management accountants must understand the four external financial statements—the balance sheet, income statement, statement of changes in equity, and statement of cash flows—and the concepts underlying these statements. Concepts underlying the four financial statements include recognition, measurement, and valuation as well as an understanding of the key differences between U.S. generally accepted accounting principles (GAAP) and International Financial Reporting Standards (IFRS).

Topics covered in this section include the financial statements themselves, asset and liability valuation, income taxes, leases, equity transactions, revenue and expense recognition, income measurement and determination, and U.S. GAAP and IFRS differences.

Financial Statements

LOS
§1.A.1.f

LOS
§1.A.1.e

THE FOUR FINANCIAL STATEMENTS DISCUSSED in this topic are required by the Securities and Exchange Commission (SEC) for all publicly traded companies and are useful for presenting a financial picture of any company. The four required financial statements include the income statement, the statement of changes in equity, the balance sheet, and the statement of cash flows.

The four financial statements are integrally related. The balance sheet is connected to the income statement (net income) through the change in retained earnings shown in the statement of changes in shareholders' equity. The balance sheet change in cash and other changes in financial position are presented in the statement of cash flow. Changes in capital received in the balance sheet are shown in the statement of changes in shareholders' equity.

The way in which various financial transactions affect the elements of each of the financial statements and the proper classification of the various financial transactions is covered in Topic 2: Recognition, Measurement, Valuation, and Disclosure.

The financial statements displayed for this topic are for a fictitious organization, Robin Manufacturing Company. They are for a given year. The linkages between the various statements are illustrated with notes and by the amounts themselves.

Most entities provide their prior years' financial statement information located next to the current year's information for comparison. For example, income and cash flow statements usually show the results of three consecutive years. This allows analysts to compare past financial performance to present performance which can provide an indication for the company's future performance.

This topic ends with a discussion of Integrated Reporting <IR>. The integrated report itself is a voluntary report on the part of both public and private global companies.

READ the Learning Outcome Statements (LOS) for this topic as found in Appendix A and then study the concepts and calculations presented here to be sure you understand the content you could be tested on in the CMA exam.

Income Statement

LOS §1.A.1.b

The income statement, commonly called a profit and loss (P&L) statement, measures the earnings of an entity's operations over a given period of time, such as a quarter or a year. The income statement is used to measure profitability, creditworthiness, and investment value of an entity. When its information is combined with information from the other statements, they collectively help assess the amounts, timing, and uncertainty of future cash flows.

Income and Other Comprehensive Income

The financial statement elements reported on the income statement are revenues, expenses, gains, and losses. Financial Accounting Standards Board (FASB) Accounting Standards Codification (ASC) Topic 220, *Comprehensive Income* (formerly SFAS No. 130), requires firms to report certain unrealized gains and losses outside of net income as components of other comprehensive income. **Comprehensive income** is the sum of net income plus (or minus) the items of other comprehensive income.

Firms have the option of presenting the calculation of comprehensive income either as part of an income statement (appended at the end) or as a separate statement of comprehensive income.

Format of Financial Information

The two most common formats are single-step income statements and multiple-step income statements.

Single-Step Income Statement

A single-step income statement subtracts total expenses and losses from total revenues and gains in a single step. No attempt is made to categorize expenses and revenues or to arrive at interim subtotals. However, despite the inherent simplicity of the single-step income statement, the multiple-step income statement is more popular because it provides more information to explain a firm's financial performance.

Figure 1A-1 shows a single-step income statement for Robin Manufacturing Company, Year 1.

Figure 1A-1 Single-Step Income Statement

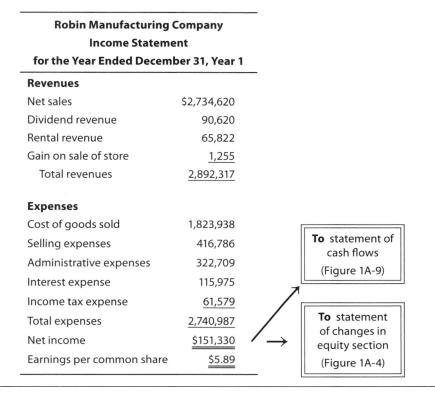

Robin Manufacturing Company	
Income Statement	
for the Year Ended December 31, Year 1	
Revenues	
Net sales	$2,734,620
Dividend revenue	90,620
Rental revenue	65,822
Gain on sale of store	1,255
Total revenues	2,892,317
Expenses	
Cost of goods sold	1,823,938
Selling expenses	416,786
Administrative expenses	322,709
Interest expense	115,975
Income tax expense	61,579
Total expenses	2,740,987
Net income	$151,330
Earnings per common share	$5.89

To statement of cash flows (Figure 1A-9)

To statement of changes in equity section (Figure 1A-4)

Multiple-Step Income Statement

The multiple-step income statement separates information into operating and non-operating categories. The sections in the statement that do not relate to operations are called other revenues and gains and other expenses and losses. These categories can include gains and losses from the sale of equipment, interest revenue and expense, or dividends received.

The multiple-step income statement has subcategories, such as cost of goods sold (COGS); operating (selling and administrative) expenses; and other revenues, expenses, gains, and losses. These subcategories allow users to compare a company's results over time or to evaluate its financial performance relative to its competitors. Such comparisons become more useful as more years of income statements are compared.

The multiple-step income statement often reports subtotals for gross profit and income from operations, which are useful for financial statement analysis purposes. For example, gross profit can be used to compare how competitive pressures have affected profit margins.

Figure 1A-2 shows a multiple-step income statement.

Figure 1A-2 Multiple-Step Income Statement

LOS §1.A.1.f   LOS §1.A.1.g

Robin Manufacturing Company
Income Statement for the Year Ended December 31, Year 1 (Y1)

Sales Revenue

Sales			$2,808,835
Less: Sales discounts		$22,302	
Less: Sales returns and allowances		51,913	74,215
Net sales revenue			2,734,620

Cost of Goods Sold

Merchandise inventory, Jan. 1, Y1		424,321	
Purchases	$1,830,518		
Less: Purchase discounts	17,728		
Net purchases	1,812,790		
Freight and transportation—in	37,363	1,850,153	
Total merchandise available for sale		2,274,474	
Less: Merchandise inventory, Dec. 31, Y1		450,536	
Cost of goods sold			$1,823,938
Gross profit on sales			910,682

Operating Expenses

Selling expenses

Sales salaries and commissions	186,432		
Sales office salaries	54,464		
Travel and entertainment	45,025		
Advertising expense	35,250		
Freight and transportation—out	37,912		
Shipping supplies and expense	22,735		
Postage and stationery	15,445		
Depreciation of sales equipment	8,285		
Telephone and Internet expense	11,238	416,786	

Administrative expenses

Officers' salaries	171,120		
Office salaries	56,304		
Legal and professional services	21,823		
Utilities expense	21,413		
Insurance expense	15,667		
Building depreciation	16,614		
Office equipment depreciation	14,720		
Stationery, supplies, and postage	2,645		
Miscellaneous office expenses	2,403	322,709	739,495
Income from operations			171,187

Other Revenues and Gains

Dividend revenue		90,620	
Rental revenue		65,822	
Gain on sale of store		1,255	157,697
			328,884

To statement of cash flows (Figure 1A-9)

Other Expenses and Losses

Interest on bonds and notes			115,975
Income before income tax			212,909
Income tax			61,579
Net income for the year			$151,330
Earnings per common share			$5.89

To statement of changes in equity (Figure 1A-4)

Additional Income Statement Presentation Items

Occasionally, companies will experience an unplanned event that requires separate reporting displayed below the income from continuing operations line.

- **Discontinued operations.** When an entity disposes of a business component that has clearly distinguishable operations and cash flows from the continuing business, then the item is recorded in a separate section of the income statement located after continuing operations. Discontinued operations are shown net of tax.

Figure 1A-3 shows how net income is determined when these items are included.

Figure 1A-3 Multistep Income Statement with Additional Income Statement Items

Net sales

− Cost of goods sold

Gross profit on sales

− Operating expenses

Operating income

+/− Other gains and losses

Earnings before tax

− Tax expense

Income from continuing operations

+/− Discontinued operations, net of tax

Net income

Statements of Change in Equity

When a balance sheet is issued, the FASB requires disclosure of the changes in each separate shareholder's equity account. This requirement satisfies the FASB's suggestion that complete financial statements should include investments by and distributions to owners during the period. The required statements of change in equity is intended to help external users assess how changes in the company's financial structure may affect its financial flexibility.

Major Components and Classifications

Shareholders' equity commonly includes these five components: 1) capital stock (par value of preferred and common shares), 2) additional paid-in capital, 3) retained earnings, 4) accumulated other comprehensive income, and 5) treasury stock. The first two categories combine to form contributed capital, also called paid-in capital.

1. Capital stock is the par value (or face value) for the shares,
2. Additional paid-in capital is the amount paid for the shares in excess of par.
3. Retained earnings can be subdivided into general earnings retained for company use and appropriated earnings set aside for some purpose.

Format of Financial Information

The statement of changes in equity usually lists information in the following general order:

- Beginning balance for the period
- Additions
- Deductions
- Ending balance for the period

Figure 1A-4 shows a sample statement of changes in equity. This example shows the statement listed in a columnar format for a company with only common stock outstanding.

Figure 1A-4 Statement of Changes in Equity

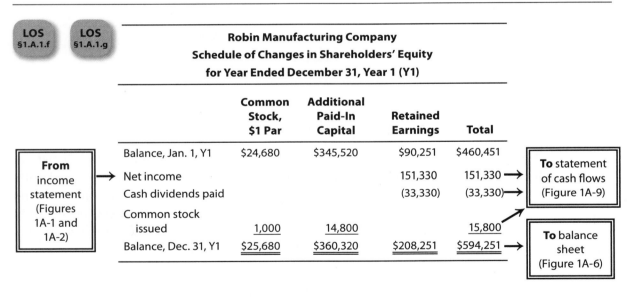

		Common Stock, $1 Par	Additional Paid-In Capital	Retained Earnings	Total	
	Balance, Jan. 1, Y1	$24,680	$345,520	$90,251	$460,451	
	Net income			151,330	151,330	
	Cash dividends paid			(33,330)	(33,330)	
	Common stock issued	1,000	14,800		15,800	
	Balance, Dec. 31, Y1	$25,680	$360,320	$208,251	$594,251	

Robin Manufacturing Company
Schedule of Changes in Shareholders' Equity
for Year Ended December 31, Year 1 (Y1)

LOS §1.A.1.f   LOS §1.A.1.g

From income statement (Figures 1A-1 and 1A-2)

To statement of cash flows (Figure 1A-9)

To balance sheet (Figure 1A-6)

Balance Sheet

LOS §1.A.1.b

The balance sheet (sometimes called a statement of financial position) is an essential tool in assessing the amounts, timing, and uncertainty of prospective cash flows. It is referred to as the balance sheet because of the balance expressed by the accounting equation:

$$Assets = Liabilities + Shareholders' \ Equity$$

Alternatively, the accounting equation can tell us that equity equals assets less liabilities, which is also known as net assets. The balance sheet provides a snapshot of the company's assets and the claims on those assets at a specific point in time.

While the balance sheet does not claim to show the value of the entity, it should allow external users to make their own estimates of the entity's value when used in conjunction with the other financial statements and other relevant information. An example of "other relevant information" could be forecasts of future periods' cash flows.

The balance sheet helps users evaluate the capital structure of the entity and assess the entity's liquidity, solvency, financial flexibility, and operating capability.

The balance sheet is also essential in understanding the income statement because revenues and expenses reflect changes in assets and liabilities, so an analyst must evaluate both statements together.

Major Components and Classifications

LOS
§1.A.1.c

The balance sheet is divided into three sections: assets, liabilities, and shareholders' equity. These classifications are designed to group similar items together so they can be analyzed more easily. Assets are listed with the most liquid items first and the least liquid ones last. Liabilities are listed in the order in which their dates for payment become due. In the case of equity, the items that have the most claim to the equity are listed before items with less claim. Figure 1A-5 summarizes the general subdivisions of each category.

The components of assets, liabilities, and equity are more thoroughly discussed in Topic 2 of this section.

Figure 1A-5 Balance Sheet Components

Assets	Current assets (cash, accounts receivable [A/R], inventory, etc.)	Intangible assets (patents, goodwill, etc.)
	Long-term investments	Other assets
	Property, plant, and equipment (PP&E)	
Liabilities	Current liabilities (accounts payable [A/P], interest payable, current portion of long-term debt, etc.)	Long-term liabilities (bonds, mortgages, etc.)
		Other liabilities
Shareholders' equity	Capital stock	Accumulated other comprehensive income
	Additional paid-in capital	
	Retained earnings	Treasury stock

Format of Financial Information

The two most common formats for the balance sheet are the account form and the report form. All styles of balance sheets subdivide the assets, liabilities, and shareholders' equity into the categories listed in Figure 1A-5 (current assets, etc.). The account form lists assets on the left side and liabilities and shareholders' equity on the right side. The report form, shown in Figure 1A-6, lists assets at the top and liabilities and shareholders' equity at the bottom. Outside the United States, other balance sheet formats are used, such as the financial position form, which deducts current liabilities from current assets to show working capital.

In Figure 1A-6, the assets and liabilities are also categorized by their levels of financial flexibility and adjustability. For example, current assets are shown separately from fixed assets.

LOS §1.A.1.f   LOS §1.A.1.g

Figure 1A-6 Balance Sheet

Robin Manufacturing Company
Balance Sheet
December 31, Year 1

Assets

Current assets:	
Cash and short-term investments	$24,628
Trade receivables, net of $30K allowance	552,249
Other receivables	18,941
Note receivable—related party	80,532
Inventory	252,567
Prepaid insurance	7,500
Total current assets	936,417
Fixed assets:	
Property and equipment	209,330
Less: Accumulated depreciation	(75,332)
Net fixed assets	133,998
Total assets	$1,070,415

→ To statement of cash flows (Figure 1A-9)

Liabilities and Equity

Current liabilities	
Accounts payable	$175,321
Accrued expenses	2,500
Current portion of long-term debt	36,000
Line of credit	145,000
Total current liabilities	358,821
Long-term debt	117,343
Total current and long-term liabilities	476,164
Shareholders' equity:	
Common stock, $1.00 par	25,680
Additional paid-in capital	360,320
Retained earnings	208,251
Total shareholders' equity	594,251
Total liabilities and shareholders' equity	$1,070,415

From statement of changes in equity (Figure 1A-4)

Statement of Cash Flows

Cash is a company's most liquid resource, and therefore it affects liquidity, operating capability, and financial flexibility. FASB ASC Topic 230, *Statement of Cash Flows* (formerly SFAS No. 95), states that a statement of cash flows "must report on a company's cash inflows, cash outflows, and net change in cash from its operating, financing, and investing activities during the accounting period, in a manner that reconciles the beginning and ending cash balances." The statement helps interested parties determine if an entity needs external financing or if it is generating sufficient positive cash flows to meet its obligations and pay dividends. Keep in mind that a company could have high income but still have negative cash flow. It is not unusual for new companies to quickly grow sales but become bankrupt due to insolvency.

Components and Classifications

Cash receipts and cash payments are classified in the statement of cash flows as related to operating, investing, or financing activities.

Operating Activities

Cash flows from operating activities are those related to the normal course of business. Any transaction that is reported on the income statement is included in operating activities. Examples of cash inflows include cash receipts from sales of any kind, collection of A/R, collection of interest on loans, and receipts of dividends. Cash outflows include cash paid to employees, suppliers, contractors, the Internal Revenue Service (IRS), and to lenders for interest.

To determine operating cash flows, FASB ASC Topic 230, *Statement of Cash Flows*, allows entities to use either the indirect method or the direct method.

Indirect Method

Statements that are compliant with generally accepted accounting principles (GAAP) use accrual accounting, so net income includes noncash revenues (e.g., uncollected credit sales) and noncash expenses (e.g., unpaid expenses). Other items that are included in accrual accounting are depreciation, depletion, amortization, and other costs that were incurred in prior periods but are being charged to expenses in the current period. These items reduce net income but do not affect cash flows for the current period. Therefore, these items are added back when determining net cash flow from operating activities.

Examples of noncash expense and revenue items that require adjustments to net income include those listed next.

- Depreciation expense and amortization of intangible assets
- Amortization of deferred costs, such as bond issue costs
- Changes in deferred income taxes

- Amortization of a premium or discount on bonds payable
- Income from an equity method investment

The indirect method, or reconciliation method, is the most popular method of converting net income to net cash flow from operating activities. It starts with net income and then adjusts it by adding back noncash expenses and paper losses and subtracting noncash revenues and paper gains that have no effect on current period operating cash flows. Additional adjustments are made for changes in current asset and liability accounts related to operations by adding or subtracting amounts, as shown in Figure 1A-7. For example, an increase in A/R (a current asset) would be subtracted from net income to arrive at operating cash flows because it means that the amount of cash collected from customers is less than the amount of accrual revenue reported. See Figure 1A-7 for an example of the indirect method.

LOS
§1.A.1.g

Figure 1A-7 Cash Flows from Operating Activities—Indirect Method

Net income
+ Noncash expenses (typically depreciation and amortization expenses)
− Gains from investing and financing activities
+ Losses from investing and financing activities
+ Decreases in current assets
− Increases in current assets
+ Increases in current liabilities
− Decreases in current liabilities
+ Amortization of discounts on bonds
− Amortization of premiums on bonds

Operating cash flow

Direct Method

In the direct method, or income statement method, net cash provided by operating activities is calculated by converting revenues and expenses from the accrual basis to the cash basis. The direct method is not tested on the CMA Exam, but is shown here as it is an alternative method to the indirect method under FASB. Figure 1A-8 shows how a direct method statement is formatted. (The figure includes sample amounts for illustration.)

Investing Activities

Most items in the investing activities section come from changes in long-term asset accounts. Investing cash inflows result from sales of PP&E, sales of investments in another entity's debt or equity securities, or collections of the principal on loans to another entity. (Interest is included in operating cash flows.) Investing

Figure 1A-8 Cash Flows from Operating Activities—Direct Method

Cash received from customers	$100,000
Cash paid to suppliers	(40,000)
Cash paid for interest	(5,000)
Cash paid for taxes	(10,000)
Cash paid for operating expenses	(25,000)
Cash provided by operating activities	$20,000

cash outflows result from purchases of PP&E, purchases of other companies' debt or equity securities, and the granting of loans to other entities.

Financing Activities

Most items in the financing activities section come from changes in long-term liability and equity accounts. Financing cash inflows come from the sale of the entity's equity securities or issuance of debt, such as bonds or notes. Cash outflows consist of payments to stockholders for dividends and payments to reacquire capital stock or redeem a company's outstanding debt. In other words, investing activities involve the purchase or sale of fixed assets and investments in another company's securities, while financing activities involve the issuance and redemption of a company's own equity and debt securities.

Footnotes

The statement of cash flows requires footnote disclosure of any significant noncash investing and financing activities, such as the issuance of stock for fixed assets or the conversion of debt to equity. In addition, when the indirect method for cash flow from operations is used, both interest paid and income taxes paid need to be disclosed.

Example of a Statement of Cash Flows

The statement of cash flows shown in Figure 1A-9 illustrates the more commonly used indirect method for calculating operating cash flows. Cash flows from each category (operating, investing, and financing) are separately classified and totaled. The sum of cash inflows (or outflows if negative) from these three categories equals the net increase or decrease in cash for the period. This net cash inflow (outflow) is added to (subtracted from) the cash balance at the beginning of the year to obtain the cash balance at the end of the year (highlighted in gray). Thus the cash flow statement explains the net change in the amount of cash and cash equivalents (short-term, highly liquid investments that are close to maturity) from the beginning to the ending balance sheet.

Figure 1A-9 Statement of Cash Flows—Indirect Method

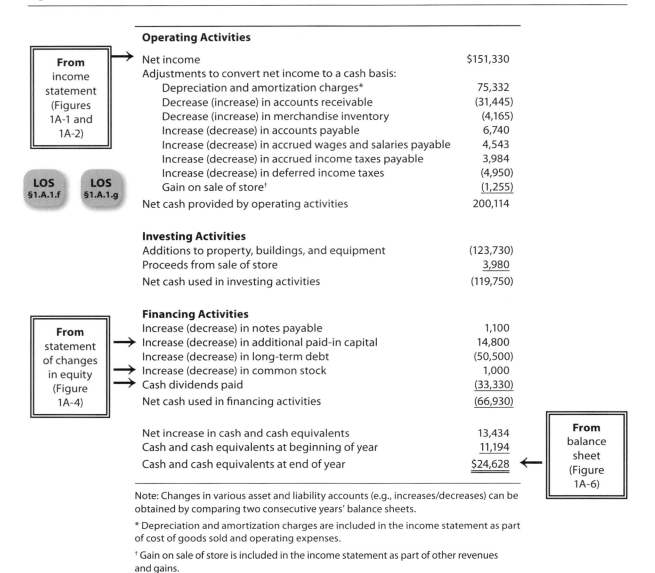

Operating Activities	
Net income	$151,330
Adjustments to convert net income to a cash basis:	
Depreciation and amortization charges*	75,332
Decrease (increase) in accounts receivable	(31,445)
Decrease (increase) in merchandise inventory	(4,165)
Increase (decrease) in accounts payable	6,740
Increase (decrease) in accrued wages and salaries payable	4,543
Increase (decrease) in accrued income taxes payable	3,984
Increase (decrease) in deferred income taxes	(4,950)
Gain on sale of store†	(1,255)
Net cash provided by operating activities	200,114
Investing Activities	
Additions to property, buildings, and equipment	(123,730)
Proceeds from sale of store	3,980
Net cash used in investing activities	(119,750)
Financing Activities	
Increase (decrease) in notes payable	1,100
Increase (decrease) in additional paid-in capital	14,800
Increase (decrease) in long-term debt	(50,500)
Increase (decrease) in common stock	1,000
Cash dividends paid	(33,330)
Net cash used in financing activities	(66,930)
Net increase in cash and cash equivalents	13,434
Cash and cash equivalents at beginning of year	11,194
Cash and cash equivalents at end of year	$24,628

From income statement (Figures 1A-1 and 1A-2)

LOS §1.A.1.f   LOS §1.A.1.g

From statement of changes in equity (Figure 1A-4)

From balance sheet (Figure 1A-6)

Note: Changes in various asset and liability accounts (e.g., increases/decreases) can be obtained by comparing two consecutive years' balance sheets.

* Depreciation and amortization charges are included in the income statement as part of cost of goods sold and operating expenses.

† Gain on sale of store is included in the income statement as part of other revenues and gains.

LOS §1.A.1.d

Limitations of the Financial Statements

The following items describe the limiting characteristics of financial statements.

- *Historical cost.* Most asset accounts of a nonfinancial nature are reported at historical cost. While historical cost measures are considered reliable because the amounts can be verified, they are also considered less relevant than fair value or current market value measures would be for assessing a firm's current financial position. For example, a company may purchase a raw material such as steel at a price. If three months later the price of the steel is substantially increased (e.g., 20%) then that inventoried asset arguably can appear to have been a good investment.

- *Different accounting methods.* Employing different accounting methods will yield different net incomes. Each choice of two or more accounting methods will further change the results reported, making the task of comparing different entities very difficult, even when these methods are disclosed.
- *Omit nonobjective items of value.* Financial statements exclude valuable assets that are of financial importance but cannot be objectively expressed in numbers. For example, the value of human resources, intangibles such as brand recognition and reputation, or the value of the entity's customer base cannot be exactly or reliably estimated, so they are not included on the balance sheet. Therefore, the balance sheet does not pretend to measure the value of the company as a whole.
- *Use of estimates and judgments.* Financial statements incorporate the use of numerous estimates and professional judgments. Differences in estimates mean that the income statements for two or more entities may be difficult to compare. Common estimates include the amount of receivables allocated to an allowance for doubtful accounts and the useful life and salvage value of a piece of equipment.
- *Off–balance sheet information.* Transactions may be recorded in a way that avoids reporting liabilities and assets on the balance sheet, for example, with the factoring of accounts receivable. The Sarbanes-Oxley Act of 2002 (SOX) requires publicly traded firms to disclose off–balance sheet information in their filings with the SEC.
- *Noncash transactions.* The statement of cash flows omits noncash transactions, such as the exchange of stock for a property, exchanges of nonmonetary assets, conversion of preferred stock or debt to common stock, or issuing equity securities to retire a debt. Disclosure of any noncash transactions that affect assets or liabilities would be reported in a note or a supplemental schedule.

Users of Financial Statements

Financial statements are intended to aid in decision making. The most efficient companies will more successfully attract investors or will be granted credit first from banks. They will also be more likely to produce a higher return on investment. Moreover, a company becomes efficient partly through the proper allocation of its internal resources to those areas, including product or standard service lines, most likely to produce a profit. Financial statements are an integral part of the decision-making process for users both internal to the organization and external to it.

Internal and External Users

Internal Users

Internal users need financial statements and other sources of information for internal decision making. The information is used to plan and control operations on both a short-term and long-term basis. The quality of these decisions will have an impact on how internal resources are allocated, the profits that are realized, and, ultimately, whether the organization will survive. Internal users of financial statements include executives, managers, management accountants, and other employees including those with stock options or investments in the organization. Unlike external users, internal users may request or generate any type of information that is available in their accounting system. Internal users may even make alternative assumptions that are different from GAAP rules such as applying different indirect and shared expense allocations to products for more accurate product profit margin analysis. The potential for misuse of such information requires an organization to place internal controls on the use and access to such information, but not to the extent that the internal decision makers cannot access the information needed in a timely manner.

External Users

External users are any interested parties who must rely on the published financial statements and other publicly available information of an entity when making decisions. Some external users, such as lending institutions, may be in a position to demand additional information from an entity that is not publicly available. As mentioned earlier, the FASB defines external users as current and potential investors and creditors and their advisors who have a reasonable understanding of business and economics and who are willing to study the information with reasonable diligence. Investors, creditors, unions, analysts, financial advisors, competitors, and government agencies are all external users of information. Investors include individuals and other corporations. Creditors include lending institutions and suppliers of raw materials and other goods.

Other users of financial statements include stock exchanges (for rule making, listings, and cancellations), unions (for negotiating wages), and analysts (for advising others).

Needs of External Users

Creditors and investors comprise the two main sources of capital for publicly traded entities, so the primary focus of financial statements is the needs of these two types of users. According to the FASB, financial reporting should provide information that is useful to external users in making reasoned choices among alternative investment, credit, and similar decisions. Users cannot absorb infinite amounts of data, and too much information may obscure the most relevant measures of the success of a business. Therefore, the goal of financial accounting is to summarize the vast amount of information into understandable reports and disclosures. Its purpose is for "valuation." The FASB's statements are intended to require a minimum level of disclosure, but it is still up to each entity to make this information user friendly. In contrast, the goal of managerial accounting is to facilitate investigation and ask questions to lead to better internal business decisions. Its purpose is "to create financial value."

Needs of Investors and Creditors

Financial information must be relevant for it to be useful. To be relevant, the information must be presented in a timely fashion. Investors and lenders are interested in both a return *of* their investment and a return *on* their investment. They receive a return of their investment only if the organization can maintain its capital. They receive a return on their investment through dividends and interest.

Investors in the stock market receive a return on their investment if the market perceives that the company is doing well. Actual or potential investors who have or are considering a direct ownership stake in an entity need financial information primarily to decide whether to initiate or continue this relationship (i.e., buy, hold, or sell the firm's securities).

Actual or potential creditors are interested in the ability of the entity to comply with debt covenants. The four decisions they are concerned with are to extend credit, maintain credit, deny credit, or revoke credit. Creditors are also interested in financial statements to determine the risk level of their loan. Lending institutions expect a higher return on investment for more risky endeavors and will make low-return investments only when the risk is similarly low. Therefore, the entity's credit rating is of particular importance. The credit rating is based primarily on the entity's liquidity, solvency, and financial flexibility, all of which are determined from the entity's financial statements and other disclosures.

Integrated Reporting <IR>

Integrated reporting <IR> will begin being tested effective with the 2020 CMA exam testing windows. The concept of <IR> started with ideas put forth in 1999. It was developed over the years until the International Integrated Reporting Council (IIRC) published and copyrighted the ideas and concepts in 2013. <IR> might be new to you because it is not a mandatory report, as the annual report of a publicly traded company in the United States is. The hope of the IIRC is that <IR> will be adopted by both public and private companies on a global basis. The IIRC defines <IR>, integrated thinking, and an integrated report as follows:

LOS
§1.A.1.h

Integrated reporting <IR>: A process founded on integrated thinking that results in a periodic integrated report by an organization about value creation over time and related communications regarding aspects of value creation.*

Integrated thinking: The active consideration by an organization of the relationships between its various operating and functional units and the capitals that the organization uses or affects. Integrated thinking leads to integrated decision-making and actions that consider the creation of value over the short, medium, and long term.*

Integrated report: A concise communication about how an organization's strategy, governance, performance and prospects, in the context of its external environment, lead to the creation of value in the short, medium and long term.*

The symbol used to abbreviate integrated reporting is <IR>. The less-than symbol means that the integrated report is less-than an entire annual report or 10K. The report should be concise, or short and "to the point". The greater-than symbol means that the integrated report is greater-than the annual report because it has a broader scope. This comes from the reporting of the six capitals: financial, manufactured, intellectual, human, social and relationship, and natural.

The primary purpose of <IR> is to provide information to the external users of the financial statements and specifically to the providers of financial capital. The belief is that when this is done, there will be more efficient and productive allocation of capital.

Value is created over the short, medium, and long term. Part of the foundation of <IR> is to focus not only on short-term results but to develop strategies and make decisions with both the medium and long terms in mind. This supports the going-concern principle that a company is in business today and expects to be in business for the long term and to pay back all of its debts and obligations. Value should be created for all internal and external stakeholders of the company.

Internal stakeholders are the employees of the company. External stakeholders are identified as customers, suppliers, business partners, creditors, communities, and others. The creation of value is done through the six different capitals. Figure 1A-10 provides information about the six capitals.

Figure 1A-10 Six Capitals

Capitals	Description	Examples
1. Financial	Funds available to a firm to produce goods or provide services	From: debt or equity financing; generated by operations; grants; investments
2. Manufactured	Physical objects available to a firm to produce goods or provide services	Buildings; equipment; infrastructure that includes roads, parts, bridges; waste and water treatment facilities
3. Intellectual	Knowledge-based intangibles	Patents; copyrights; software; licenses; rights
	Organizational	Knowledge; systems; processes; procedures
4. Human	Competencies, capabilities, experiences, motivations for innovation from the people	People align with and support a firm's governance and ethical values; ability to understand, develop, and implement a firm's strategy; to be loyal and motivated; to be able to lead, manage, and collaborate
5. Social and relationship	The relationships within and among institutions, communities, and groups of stakeholders	Shared norms, values, and behaviors; key stakeholder relationships based on trust and willingness; a firm's brand and reputation
	Ability to share information for both individual and collective well-being	
6. Natural	Renewable and nonrenewable environmental resources; processes that support a firm's past, current, and future prosperity	Land; water; air; minerals; forests; biodiversity; ecosystem health

These six capitals are integral to the value creation process. The process takes the six capitals and uses them throughout the firm's business model to create inputs that are transformed through the business activities to create outputs that provide desired outcomes. The firm's mission and vision drive the business model. But it is the responsibility of those people who are accountable for governance to create the oversight structure that results in value creation. Value creation is impacted by risks and opportunities, strategy and resource allocation, performance, and outlook. Value creation is also impacted by the external environment, which includes the economy, changing technology, environmental issues, and societal issues.

The outcomes should create overall value that result in the increase, decrease, or transformation of the six capitals. The value creation process is explained in Figure 1A-11.

Figure 1A-11 Value Creation Process

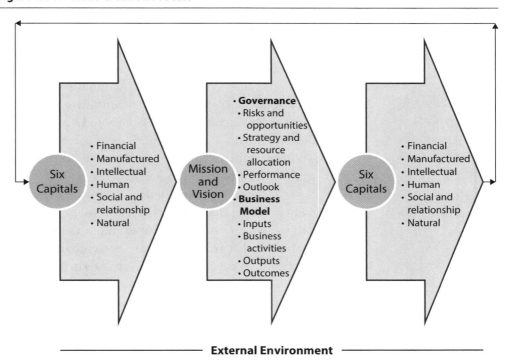

As with any successful process, the outcomes that are achieved must be compared to expectations. Feedback is provided and incorporated back into the beginning six capitals through appropriate decision making.

In many ways, the integrated report uses concepts that are incorporated in Generally Accepted Accounting Principles (GAAP). These include, but are not limited to: being reliable and complete; being free from material error; using a cost/benefit analysis of what is included in the integrated report; consistency; comparability; and materiality.

LOS
§1.A.1.k

Guidelines provided by the IIRC prescribes content elements of the integrated report that are intended to answer questions such as:

- What does the firm do and what are the circumstances of its operations?
- How does the firm's governance structure support value creation?

- What is the firm's business model?
- What is the extent to which the firm achieved its strategic objectives?
- What is the firm's outlook in terms of challenges and uncertainties it faces in pursuit of its strategy?
- Where does the firm want to go, and how does it plan on getting there?

In essence, the integrated report reports on all of the elements contained within the value creation process.

The IIRC does not prescribe a specific reporting format for the integrated report. The report can be standalone or included as a distinguishable part of another report or communication made by the firm. The IIRC provides general reporting guidance:

1. *Disclosure of material matters* including an explanation of the matter and the impact it has on strategy, business model, or capitals. The key information about the material matters should include (but are not limited to): relevant interactions and interdependencies, the firm's view on the matter, actions to manage the matter and their effectiveness, and quantitative and qualitative disclosures.
2. *Disclosures about the capitals* using quantitative indicators to aid comparability, relevance, and consistency. They should be reported with targets (forecasts) and presented for multiple periods of three or more years. Disclosures should include qualitative information that will provide context and enhance the meaningfulness of the quantitative data.
3. *Time frames for short, medium, and long term* are determined by the firm and will usually be longer than some other forms of reporting. Time frames can be influenced by industry or sector. For example, the technology industry might have time frames that are significantly shorter than those used by the automobile industry, which covers two model-cycle terms that span between eight and ten years.
4. *Aggregation and disaggregation* is determined by the firm and can include by country, subsidiary, or division.

LOS §1.A.1.l

Benefits and Challenges of Adopting <IR>

The adoption of <IR> by any company has both benefits and challenges. The main benefits are that <IR> aims to improve the quality of information available to the providers of financial capital and to promote a more cohesive and efficient approach to corporate reporting based on the ability of the company to create value over time. Integrated reporting can enhance the accountability and stewardship of the six capitals employed by the company.

The challenges begin with the fact that there are no reporting standards for the integrated report itself. Integrated reporting is complex for organizations with diverse operations and causes added burdens for small and medium-size organizations due to the creation of additional costs. The use of qualitative and forward-looking information, which includes targets and forecasts, can create litigation risks.

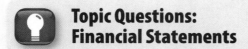

Topic Questions:
Financial Statements

Directions: Answer each question in the space provided. Correct answers and explanations appear after the topic questions.

1. An accountant is preparing the statement of cash flows using the indirect method. She found on the balance sheet that the prior year's balance of equipment was $295,700 and the current year's balance of equipment is $304,000. Depreciation expense during the current year was $22,400. During the year, the company sold equipment for $40,000, resulting in a gain of $21,600. On the statement of cash flows, what is the cash outflow for the purchase of equipment this year?

    ☐ **a.** $4,300

    ☐ **b.** $49,100

    ☐ **c.** $52,300

    ☐ **d.** $79,700

2. Which one of the following would **not** be classified as a current liability?

    ☐ **a.** Security deposits received from renters for a one-year lease

    ☐ **b.** Rent for the current year received on January 2 of the current year

    ☐ **c.** Undistributed stock dividends

    ☐ **d.** Ten-year bonds sold 110 months ago

3. A company received an invoice in January for the electricity used by its warehouse in December, and it recorded the expense in January. The company uses the accrual basis of accounting. What is the impact to the company's December financial statements?

    ☐ **a.** Current liabilities were understated, and retained earnings were overstated.

    ☐ **b.** Operating expenses were overstated, and retained earnings were overstated.

    ☐ **c.** Cash and cash equivalents were overstated, and retained earnings were understated.

    ☐ **d.** Accrued expenses were overstated, and retained earnings were understated.

Topic Question Answers: Financial Statements

1. An accountant is preparing the statement of cash flows using the indirect method. She found on the balance sheet that the prior year's balance of equipment was $295,700 and the current year's balance of equipment is $304,000. Depreciation expense during the current year was $22,400. During the year, the company sold equipment for $40,000, resulting in a gain of $21,600. On the statement of cash flows, what is the cash outflow for the purchase of equipment this year?

    ☐ **a.** $4,300

    ☒ **b.** $49,100

    ☐ **c.** $52,300

    ☐ **d.** $70,700

The book value for the equipment sold for the year must be calculated first. The book value can be calculated as cash received less any gain recognized on the sale. In this case, the book value of the equipment sold during the year equals $18,400 ($40,000 − $21,600).

The formula to calculate the current year's balance of equipment is the prior year's balance minus depreciation minus book value of any equipment sold plus purchases. Rearranging this formula, the cash outflow for the purchase of equipment equals $49,100 ($304,000 − $295,700 + $22,400 + $18,400).

2. Which one of the following would **not** be classified as a current liability?

    ☐ **a.** Security deposits received from renters for a one-year lease

    ☐ **b.** Rent for the current year received on January 2 of the current year

    ☒ **c.** Undistributed stock dividends

    ☐ **d.** Ten-year bonds sold 110 months ago

The undistributed stock dividends would not be classified as a current liability. Current liabilities are the obligations that a company has that are to be paid within one year. A stock dividend occurs when a company distributes shares of its stock to its shareholders instead of paying a cash dividend. A stock dividend is accounted for on the balance sheet as a reclassification of the amounts in the equity portion of the balance sheet, and it does not affect the company's liabilities.

3. A company received an invoice in January for the electricity used by its warehouse in December, and it recorded the expense in January. The company uses the accrual basis of accounting. What is the impact to the company's December financial statements?

    ☑ **a.** Current liabilities were understated, and retained earnings were overstated.

    ☐ **b.** Operating expenses were overstated, and retained earnings were overstated.

    ☐ **c.** Cash and cash equivalents were overstated, and retained earnings were understated.

    ☐ **d.** Accrued expenses were overstated and retained earnings were understated.

This company's current liabilities were understated, and retained earnings were overstated. Under the accrual basis of accounting, expenses are recorded in the period that the expense is incurred, not when the expense is paid. This company should have recorded the electricity expense and an associated liability on the December financial statements; therefore, the company's current liabilities and expenses were understated for the year. Because the expenses were understated, the net income and therefore the retained earnings were overstated.

Recognition, Measurement, Valuation, and Disclosure

This topic covers the recognition, measurement, valuation, and disclosure requirements of accounting transactions and specific accounts within a company's financial statements. The topic concludes with a comparison of International Financial Reporting Standards (IFRS) and U.S. generally accepted accounting principles (GAAP) as they relate to key financial statement accounts and transactions.

The new FASB Accounting Standards Codification (ASC) 842, *Leases*, started being tested with the January 2020 testing window.

 READ the Learning Outcome Statements (LOS) for this topic as found in Appendix A and then study the concepts and calculations presented here to be sure you understand the content you could be tested on in the CMA exam.

Accounts Receivable

LOS §1.A.2.a

Companies may have several different types of receivables on their balance sheet. A receivable is an asset that represents a promise to pay from another entity to the company. Receivables may include trade accounts receivable (often referred to as accounts receivable), interest receivable, and receivables from an insurance claim or successful lawsuit. Trade accounts receivables are created when sellers extend credit to buyers. Receivables are considered liquid, but not as liquid as cash.

Types of Receivables

Receivables are classified as current or noncurrent. Current receivables are due to be collected within one year or the current operating cycle, whichever is longer. Noncurrent receivables are due after one year or the current operating cycle, whichever is longer.

Trade Accounts Receivables

Trade accounts receivables are the most common form of receivables because they arise from an entity's normal operations: credit sales of goods and services.

- **Accounts receivable (A/R)** are an asset that represents customers' promises to pay for goods or services delivered. Most have 30- or 60-day net payment terms, so they are usually classified as current assets.
- **Notes receivable** are more formal trade receivables because they are supported by a written promise to pay on a specified date. They can be either current or noncurrent, depending on when they are due.

Nontrade Receivables

Nontrade receivables include all types of receivables other than those involved in daily operations, including interest and dividends receivables, damage deposits and other guarantee deposits, advances to officers or to subsidiaries, and claims against insurance companies, common carriers, lawsuit defendants, the government, and vendors for returned, lost, or damaged goods. Nontrade receivables are usually reported as separate items on the balance sheet.

Impact of Sales Practices on A/R Balances

Accounts receivable may be subject to trade discounts and cash discounts. In addition, they may be affected by sales returns and allowances if customers are not satisfied with their purchases.

Trade Discounts

Trade discounts (also called volume or quantity discounts) allow a business to list a single price for a given item in its catalog and then sell the item to various wholesale and retail customers at different discounts from the list price. A sale that is subject to a trade discount is simply recorded at the negotiated price.

Cash Discounts

Cash discounts are incentives for prompt payment. Buyers can apply this type of discount automatically if they make payment by the specified deadline. Cash discounts are expressed in shorthand, such as 2/10, n/30. This means a 2% discount can be taken if payment is made within 10 days. If not, the net amount (any unpaid balance) is due within 30 days. A discount of 2/10, net 30 that is not taken represents an opportunity cost to the customer of 37.25%.

$$\text{Effective Cost of Discount} = \frac{\text{Discount \%}}{(1 - \text{Discount \%})} \times \frac{365}{(\text{Net Period} - \text{Discount Period})}$$

$$= \frac{0.02}{(0.98)} \times \frac{365}{30 - 10} = 0.02041 \times 18.25 = 37.25\%$$

Because the customer can probably borrow funds for less than this rate, it would be cheaper to borrow funds to pay within the discount period than to use the extended payment period.

Receivables with cash discounts can be recorded at either their gross amount or net amount.

- **Gross method** records each receivable and sale at the gross or undiscounted amount. Sales discounts (a contra revenue account) are recognized if payment is received by the end of the discount period. On the income statement, the balance in this account must be subtracted from gross sales in the computation of net sales.
- **Net method** assumes that all discounts will be taken, so receivables and sales are recorded at their net amounts. This follows the matching principle because it matches discounts to sales in the same period, thus recording the sales at closer to their net realizable value. To account for any unused sales discounts, an additional revenue account called sales discounts forfeited is used to record adjusting entries.

Sales Returns and Allowances

Sales returns and allowances is a contra revenue account that is used to reduce the net value of sales revenue when customers are dissatisfied with the merchandise that they receive.

If the seller offers an allowance and the buyer agrees to keep the goods, both sales revenue and accounts receivable must be reduced by the amount of the allowance.

However, if the customer actually returns goods, the seller needs a second journal entry to recognize the restocking or scrapping of the goods and the reduction in cost of goods sold (COGS).

Some companies experience such high rates of returns that they routinely record sales net of an estimate for the expected returns and establish an allowance for sales returns as a contra asset account to accounts receivable.

Valuation of Trade Receivables

Trade receivables are initially recorded at the sales invoice value.

The trade receivables must be valued and reported on the balance sheet at their net realizable value (NRV). The **NRV for trade receivables** is the net amount of cash that the company expects to receive, that includes an estimate of uncollectible amounts (bad debt) and expected returns (if there is a return policy). In other words, accounts receivable is presented net of the allowance for uncollectible accounts (i.e., A/R minus allowance) on the balance sheet.

Valuation and Uncollectible Accounts

LOS
§1.A.2.a

When sales are made on account, there is always a possibility that the firm may not be able to collect the full amount of its accounts receivable. There are several ways to account for the resulting bad debt expense.

Allowance Method

In an allowance method, the firm estimates the expected uncollectible amounts from all credit sales or from all outstanding receivables. The allowance for doubtful accounts (contra asset) is subtracted from accounts receivable to determine the net realizable value of the receivables. This is the amount the company expects to collect. Bad debt expense is reported as an operating expense on the income statement. Under the allowance method, there are two ways to estimate and recognize expected future bad debt.

- **Balance sheet approaches.** These methods focus on the relationship between accounts receivable and the allowance for doubtful accounts on the balance sheet.

  1. *Percentage of outstanding A/R.* This method assesses the historical relationship between actual bad debts and accounts receivable over time. The resulting percentage is multiplied by the current accounts receivable at the end of the period to determine the required ending balance in the allowance for doubtful accounts. For example, if a company has $100,000 in accounts receivable at the end of a period and estimates that 4% of receivables will result in bad debts, the desired ending balance in the allowance for doubtful accounts should be ($100,000 × 4%) = $4,000. Thus, the net realizable value of the accounts receivable would be $100,000 − $4,000 = $96,000.

     If the allowance for doubtful accounts had an existing balance of $1,000, the amount necessary to adjust the balance in the allowance account to the desired level would be $3,000:

Allowance for Doubtful Accounts		
	Debit	**Credit**
Existing balance		1,000
Adjustment		**3,000**
Desired ending balance		4,000

   Similarly, if the allowance for doubtful accounts had a $1,000 *debit* balance, then the amount needed to adjust the balance in the allowance account to the desired level would be a credit of $5,000.

Allowance for Doubtful Accounts		
	Debit	**Credit**
Existing balance	1,000	
Adjustment		**5,000**
Desired ending balance		4,000

  2. *Aging of A/R.* Accounts receivable become harder to collect over time. An aging schedule can be used to categorize A/R by the length of time the debts have been outstanding. The older the debts are, the higher the estimated percentage of doubtful accounts. Figure 1A-12 shows an example of an aging schedule. The amount of the adjusting journal entry would be calculated the same way as shown in number 1.

Figure 1A-12 Accounts Receivable Aging Schedule

		Bounce Sporting Goods Company Aging Schedule				
Customer	Balance Dec. 31	Under 60 Days	61–90 Days	91–120 Days	Over 120 Days	Required Balance in Allowance
East Side Sport Supply	$54,880	$44,800	$10,080			
Rockford Gyms & Courts	179,200	179,200				
Freedom Tennis Supply	30,800				$30,800	
Broadway Sporting Goods	41,440	33,600		$7,840		
Total	$306,320	$257,600	$10,080	$7,840	$30,800	
Estimated uncollectible %		× 5%	× 15%	× 20%	× 25%	
Estimated future bad debt		$12,880	$1,512	$1,568	$7,700	$23,660

Write-offs and Collection of Write-offs

In the allowance method, when it is clear that a specific account receivable (e.g., for $1,200) is uncollectible, the accounts receivable is written off (reduced) and part of the allowance for bad debt is used up (the allowance is also reduced). No expense associated with the specific account being written off is recognized in the period the account is written off because the expense was recognized when the allowance for bad debt was booked. In other words, the expense and the allowance were created to absorb the future write-off.

Thus, the net carrying value of accounts receivable on the balance sheet is not affected.

Factoring of Receivables

LOS §1.A.2.b

Factoring is a way for firms to sell receivables to generate cash without additional borrowing or issuing more stock. In factoring, a bank or finance company called a factor buys receivables and often takes on the billing and collection functions. Firms that use factors get immediate cash and can eliminate their credit departments because factors usually do the credit reviews, extend or deny credit, and take payments directly from customers. The factor remits the cash collected minus a fee to the company. The company continues normal activities directly with its customers. Allowing the factor to make credit decisions mitigates some of the factor's risk, which reduces service costs, but the firm must accept the factor's credit decisions, so some credit sales may not be approved.

Most factors pay only 80% to 90% of the value of the receivables to allow for sales returns and allowances and bad debts. In addition, factors charge a commission depending on the gross amount of receivables transferred and the perceived risk of noncollection. The company records the factor's commission as an expense or a loss. There are two types of factoring arrangements: sales with recourse and sales without recourse.

Sale with Recourse

In a sale *with* recourse, the seller must pay the factor for any bad debts in the receivables sold. Because the seller has continuing involvement with the receivable, the transaction is recorded using the financial components approach, which requires the seller to recognize only the assets and liabilities it controls after sale with recourse.

For example, a firm sells $500,000 of accounts receivable with recourse and estimates that the recourse obligation (estimated bad debt in the receivables sold) has a fair value of $6,000. The factor assesses a 3% finance charge and retains another 5% for possible bad debt. The computation of loss on the sale of receivables with recourse is shown in Figure 1A-13.

Figure 1A-13 Calculating Net Proceeds

Loss on sale of receivables:		
Finance charge (3% × $500,000)	15,000	
Recourse obligation	6,000	
Loss on sale of receivables		$21,000

The journal entry to record this transaction would be:

Dr. Cash		460,000	
Dr. Due from factor	(5% × $500,000)	25,000	
Dr. Loss on sale of receivables		21,000	
Cr. Accounts receivable			500,000
Cr. Recourse liability			6,000

On the balance sheet, the $25,000 "Due from factor" is a current asset that will be returned to the firm if there are no bad debts in the receivables factored, and the $6,000 "Recourse liability" represents the firm's estimation of the fair value of possible bad debts in the receivables sold. On the income statement, the $21,000 "Loss on sale of receivables" is reported as an operating expense if the firm factors its receivables as part of its normal operations or under "Other expenses and losses" if this is not a common business activity.

Sale without Recourse

Factoring can also be a sale *without* recourse, which means that the purchaser assumes the risk of bad debts. Since the sale transfers title, it is considered an outright sale in form, and because the sale transfers control of credit granting and collection, it is also an outright sale in substance. If the $500,000 of receivables from the previous example had been sold to the factor without recourse, the company would not recognize any recourse liability, and the journal entry would be:

Dr. Cash	460,000	
Dr. Due from factor	25,000	
Dr. Loss on sale of receivables	15,000	
Cr. Accounts receivable		500,000

In this scenario, the balance sheet would show the $25,000 "Due from factor" as a current asset that will be returned to the firm if there are no bad debts in the receivables factored. There would be no current liability for bad debts in the receivables sold since the seller has no further obligation in a sale without recourse. The income statement would include the $15,000 "Loss on sale of receivables" either under operating expenses or under "Other expenses and losses," depending on the frequency of this type of transaction.

Inventory

Inventory includes assets that are held for sale in the normal course of business, work in the process of being produced for sale, or raw materials used to produce salable goods. Items that are not sold in the usual course of business are not inventory.

Inventory is classified by its use. Retailers often have only one category, called merchandise, which includes retail goods that were purchased ready for sale. Manufacturers often have three categories: raw materials, work in process, and finished goods. Costs of direct materials, labor, overhead, and storage are traced or allocated to these categories as appropriate. Manufacturers may also need inventory categories for other materials used internally, such as manufacturing supplies, indirect materials, parts inventory, or factory supplies.

Inventory Valuation

**LOS
§1.A.2.c**

Inventory valuation is the process of determining what items to include in inventory, what costs should be included in inventory, and which cost flow assumption should be used. There are two systems of accounting for inventory: the perpetual system and the periodic system. There are four cost flow assumptions from which a company may choose: specific identification, weighted-average, FIFO, and LIFO.

The overall cost of goods is allocated between the goods sold and the goods still on hand. The **cost of goods available for sale or use** is the cost of goods on hand at the start of the period plus the cost of goods acquired or produced throughout the period. The **cost of goods sold** is the cost of goods available for sale or use minus the cost of goods on hand at the end of the period, that is, ending inventory. These calculations are shown in Figure 1A-14.

Figure 1A-14 Cost of Goods Sold Calculation

Beginning inventory, January 1	$350,000
Cost of goods acquired or produced during the year	670,000
Total cost of goods available for sale	1,020,000
Less: Ending inventory, December 31	400,000
Cost of goods sold during the year	$620,000

Which Goods to Include in Inventory

Purchases of inventory generally are recorded when the goods are received by the buyer, even though ownership legally transfers when the title passes to the buyer. Exceptions to this practice include:

- *Consigned goods.* Consignment is a way for the retailer (consignee) to mitigate the risk of unsalable inventory by allowing the wholesale seller (consignor) to retain ownership of the goods until a sale is made. The wholesaler receives payment for the goods from the retailer, who takes a commission for holding, marketing, and selling the goods. The consignor keeps the goods on its inventory until the sale to a third party. The consignee never records the goods as inventory.

- *Goods in transit* are items that have been shipped but have not yet reached their destination. Ownership of goods in transit is determined by the shipping terms. Under FOB (free or freight on board) shipping point, title transfers as soon as the seller delivers the item to a common carrier serving as an agent of the buyer. Under FOB destination, title transfers only when the goods arrive at the buyer's warehouse. Title is important because damages to the goods are the owner's responsibility. Before title transfers, the goods are the property of the seller; after transfer, they must be accounted for on the books of the buyer.

- *Sale agreements* may involve a transfer of title at a different point from the transfer of the risks of ownership. Sales with high rates of return are common in the publishing, sporting goods, music, and other seasonal industries, where customers are permitted to return unsold inventory for a full or partial refund. If the number of returns can be reasonably estimated, the goods should be considered sold and a sales return and allowances account established. However, when such an estimate is impossible, the seller should not record a sale until the amount of returns is known.

- *Sales with buyback agreements* are a type of swap in which a firm sells its inventory and agrees to repurchase the inventory at a specific price and at a specific time. Such a transaction is called a parking transaction because the seller "parks" inventory on the buyer's balance sheet for a short time. Effectively, the seller is financing its inventory and retaining the risks of ownership, but transfers title to the goods. As customer orders are received, the firm buys back the inventory and ships it to the customer. When a repurchase agreement has a set price that covers all of the buyer's costs plus the cost of the inventory, the inventory and the liability under the repurchase agreement should remain on the seller's balance sheet.

What Costs to Include in Inventory

The types of costs to be included or excluded in the determination of inventory value are discussed next.

- *Manufacturing overhead costs.* For entities that make their own goods for sale, the cost of inventory should include all direct and indirect costs incurred in production. Acquisition and production costs are included. Overhead is allocated to goods manufactured using either the traditional or activity-based approach. For example, a line manager's salary would be part of the fixed overhead pool attributable to a specific product line.

- *Product costs.* Product costs include freight-in, labor costs, and all direct and indirect costs of acquisition, production, and processing and are included in the inventory value.
- *Cash discounts.* As discussed earlier, cash discounts are discounts for early payment and are included in the inventory value. The gross method records all purchases at the gross price, and discounts are recorded only if taken. The net method records all purchases net of discounts. Purchase discounts lost are then charged to an expense account.
- *Period costs.* Items not included as part of inventory, such as are selling, general and administrative expenses, are called period costs and are expensed in the period in which they are incurred. These costs are generally unrelated to production. Interest costs related to the preparation of inventory are also treated as period costs. Under GAAP, only interest costs for internally constructed assets or discrete projects, such as ships or real estate for sale or lease, can be capitalized. Financing costs for routine manufacture of inventory are not capitalized.

Perpetual and Periodic Inventory Systems

There are two basic approaches to inventory record keeping: perpetual and periodic. The perpetual system relies on computers and bar code scanners to update inventory records continuously as purchases and sales are made. The periodic system evolved before computers were used to track inventory.

Perpetual Inventory System

The perpetual inventory system tracks changes in the inventory account as they occur. Sophisticated databases record sales, purchases, conversions, and transfers in real time. Retail systems recognize inventory changes directly at the point of sale, updating both inventory and COGS. All purchases, returns and allowances, discounts, and freight-in are also updated.

When a firm uses a perpetual inventory system, a journal entry is made with each sale to reduce inventory and increase COGS. However, some goods may be stolen, accidentally shipped without an invoice, or damaged and discarded without being recorded. Therefore, inventory recorded on the books generally will be higher than the amount actually on hand, although overages can also occur. Firms using the perpetual system must periodically compare their physical inventory count to their records and write off any difference. Since the difference between actual and recorded inventory can be measured, management can determine the amount of such losses each year.

The basic formula for the perpetual system is:

> Beginning Inventory + Purchases (Net) – COGS = Ending Inventory

Note to candidate: The basic formula to calculate Ending Inventory or COGS is helpful when analyzing the effects of inventory errors. Remember that COGS is an expense and impacts the income statement and net income, while ending inventory is an asset and impacts the current assets section on the balance sheet and may also impact the current ratio of a company.

Periodic Inventory System

By contrast, the periodic system does not track cost of goods sold during the period, so COGS must be computed at the end of the period once the physical inventory count is complete. The basic formula for the periodic system is:

> Beginning Inventory + Purchases (Net) – Ending Inventory = COGS

The periodic inventory system is becoming obsolete as more companies adopt inventory tracking databases and technologies.

This system does not record an increase to cost of goods sold or a decrease to inventory at the time of sale. Instead, this amount must be computed at the end of the accounting period:

```
  Purchases
– Purchase discounts
– Purchase returns and allowances
+ Freight in
  Cost of goods purchased
```

```
  Cost of goods purchased
+ Merchandise inventory (beginning balance)
  Cost of goods available for sale
```

```
  Cost of goods available for sale
– Merchandise inventory (ending physical count)
  Cost of goods sold
```

Since cost of goods sold is determined only once a year, the information is not timely. To deal with this problem, companies can use a modified perpetual inventory system that keeps a detailed record of quantities (but not prices) in a memorandum account off the books. Another drawback of the periodic system is that it cannot measure losses due to theft or damage. Instead, these losses are included in COGS.

Lower of Cost or Market Rule

**LOS
§1.A.2.e**

The amendments in the updated FASB ASC Inventory ***do not apply to*** inventory measured using last-in, first-out (LIFO), or the retail inventory method. This inventory will continue to be measured at the *lower of cost or market (LCM)* just as they have been.

The *lower of cost or market (LCM) rule* now applies only when inventory that is valued using the last-in, first-out (LIFO) or the retail inventory method of cost flow becomes obsolete or declines in value (e.g., foreign competition brings prices down). In such situations, inventory is valued at either its cost or its market value, whichever is lower. Market is still defined as a replacement cost of the inventory based on the current inventory's utility. Thus, it is the value in the purchase market, not in the sales market. Inventory is written down in the period when the value declines, not the period when the item is sold. This method assumes that a decline in the replacement cost of an item normally means that the item's selling price will also drop to stay competitive.

Lower of Cost or Market Ceiling and Floor

Two constraints limit replacement cost as a measure of market value:

1. *Ceiling.* Market value should not be greater than the inventory's net realizable value.
2. *Floor.* Market value should not be less than the inventory's net realizable value less an allowance for a normal markup or profit margin.

The ceiling (upper limit) is designed to make sure that the inventory is not over-stated and the loss understated, thus avoiding the need to recognize further losses in future periods. The floor (lower limit) is designed to make sure that the loss is not overstated and the inventory is not understated, preventing the recognition of excessive future profits.

Applying Lower of Cost or Market

The lower of cost or market rule may be applied to individual items, to categories of items, or to the total inventory as long as it's consistently applied year to year. When applying LCM to categories or the total inventory, increases in market price for some items tend to offset decreases in the market price for other items, generally leading to a smaller restatement than if LCM is applied to individual items. Item-level LCM is the most common, and it is generally required for taxes. Item-level LCM produces the most conservative (lowest) inventory value and largest holding loss, because for each item the lower of cost or market is chosen. Figure 1A-15 shows how LCM can be applied in various ways.

Figure 1A-15 Applying LCM

Alternative Methods to Apply Lower of Cost or Market Rule					
Inventory	**Cost**	**Market**	**By Item**	**By Category**	**In Total**
Rubber products department:					
Tennis balls (box)	$120	$ 84	$ 84		
Racquet balls (box)	144	156	144		
	$264	$240		$240	
Racquet department:					
Tennis racquet 1	$192	$230	192		
Tennis racquet 2	240	211	211		
	$432	$441		432	
Inventory valuation	$696	$681	$631	$672	$681
Loss recognition*			$ 65	$ 24	$ 15

*By item: $696 − $631 = $65

By category: $696 − $672 = $24

In total: $696 − $681 = $15

Recording Lower of Cost or Market

Inventory is initially recorded at historical cost, but if it declines in value due to obsolescence, damage, or price level changes, then the inventory should be written down to its current value.

The difference is recognized as a loss in the current period and reported in the income statement. The journal entry to record the loss would be:

Dr. Loss or Cost of Goods Sold	X	
Cr. Inventory or allowance account		X

Lower of Cost and Net Realizable Value (NRV)—The Updated Standard

The amendments in the update **apply to** inventory measured using either the first-in, first-out (FIFO) or average cost method. The entity will apply the new standard "prospectively to the measurement of inventory after the date of adoption." During the transition to the updated standard, the entity will "disclose the nature of and reason for the change in accounting principle in the first interim and annual period of adoption." In addition, if the firm has written down inventory using the FIFO or average cost method to below its cost prior to the adoption, the reduced amount is considered to be the *cost* upon adoption.

Due to the fact that NRV is an estimate, there is inherent risk that users of the financial statements should be aware of. There should be disclosure in the financial statements when there are substantial and unusual losses resulting from the subsequent measurement of inventory.

The definition of NRV is:

Net Realizable Value (NRV) is "the estimated selling prices in the ordinary course of business, less reasonably predictable costs of completion, disposal, and transportation."

When the NRV of inventory is lower than its cost, the difference is recognized as a loss in earnings in the period when it occurs. The purpose is to fairly reflect the income for the period. The loss may be required due to damage, physical deterioration, obsolescence, or changes in price levels. Another way of saying this is that there has been diminished utility of the goods since their acquisition.

The cost and accompanying NRV can be applied directly to each item, components of a major category, or to the total inventory. This is similar to the LCM method. Please refer back to Figure 1A-15 Applying LCM. This same type of figure is used for the updated standard; the title would be changed to Applying Lower of Cost and NRV; the second title would be changed to Alternative Methods to Apply Lower of Cost and NRV; the third column labeled "Market" would be changed to "NRV" and the appropriate NRV amounts would be reported.

Cost Flow Assumptions

Cost flow assumptions are methods to account for inventory costs, but they do not represent the actual physical flow of goods. The four cost flow assumptions currently in use are specific identification, average cost, FIFO (first in, first out), and LIFO (last in, first out). For example, LIFO (last in, first out) does not imply that the newest inventory is sold first. Instead, the cost flow assumption simply determines which costs are allocated to inventory on the balance sheet and which are allocated to cost of goods sold on the income statement. In addition:

LOS §1.A.2.f

LOS §1.A.2.i

- *Specific identification* tracks the cost of each individual item and records the item in cost of goods sold or inventory depending on whether that item was sold. This method is feasible only if all items are uniquely tagged, so it works best with small numbers of expensive items, such as jewelry or automobiles, with special orders, or with products manufactured using a job costing system.
- *Average cost* is a method that determines an average cost for all similar inventory items and uses that cost during the period to assign costs to cost of goods sold and ending inventory.
  - In the **perpetual inventory system,** this method is called the moving average method, because a new average cost must be calculated after each purchase, and that average is used until another purchase is made and a new average cost is calculated. Figure 1A-16 shows the moving average costs for a month. The total of the July 31 ending inventory balance of $62,400 when added to the cost of goods sold of $65,600 equals $128,000. This is the total amount of the costs to be accounted for. This holds true for Figures 1A-16, -17, -18, -19, and -20.

Figure 1A-16 Moving Average Inventory Cost Flow Assumption

Bounce Sporting Goods Company Moving Average Inventory Cost Flow Assumption (Perpetual Inventory System)		
July 1, beginning inventory	1,000 units @ $40	$40,000
July 7, purchases	1,000 units @ $60	60,000
July 7, balance	2,000 units @ $50	$100,000
July 15, sales	(1,000) units @ $50	(50,000)
July 15, balance	1,000 units @ $50	$50,000
July 20, purchases	500 units @ $56	28,000
July 20, balance	1,500 units @ $52	$78,000
July 28, sales	(300) units @ $52	(15, 600)
July 31, balance (ending inventory)	1,200 units @ $52	$62,400
Cost of goods sold (1,300 units)	$50,000 + $15,600	$65,600

- **In the periodic system,** the weighted-average method is used. Divide the total cost of the goods available for sale (beginning inventory + purchases) by the total number of units available to find a weighted-average cost per unit. Multiply the units in ending inventory by the average cost to determine the value of ending inventory. To find cost of goods sold, subtract ending inventory from the cost of goods available for sale or multiply the units sold by the average cost.

The average cost method is objective and simple, so firms may choose to use it for practical reasons.

- *First in, first out (FIFO)* recognizes older inventory costs in cost of goods sold and more recent inventory costs as ending inventory.

   When costs are increasing, FIFO yields a lower cost of goods sold because it includes the older, lower costs, whereas ending inventory is relatively high because it includes higher, newer cost. If costs were going down, the converse would be true.

   Using the data from Figure 1A-16, the cost of goods sold and the ending inventory are calculated as shown in Figure 1A-17 under the perpetual method. When a quantity sold exceeds the number of units obtained at the earliest price, the price of the next most recent purchase is used. Cost of goods sold is always based on the earliest costs.

Figure 1A-17 Perpetual FIFO

Bounce Sporting Goods Company

FIFO Inventory Cost Flow Assumption

(Perpetual Inventory System)

Cost of goods sold (1,300 units):

July 15	1,000 units @ $40	$40,000
July 28	300 units @ $60	18,000
Total		$58,000

Ending inventory (1,200 units):

Beginning Inventory + Purchases – Cost of Goods Sold = Ending Inventory

$40,000 + $88,000 – $58,000 = $70,000

	700 units @ $60	$42,000
	500 units @ $56	28,000
		$70,000

If the periodic system is used, ending inventory is calculated using the most recent costs. The cost of goods available for sale minus the ending inventory equals the cost of goods sold. **FIFO perpetual and FIFO periodic will always yield the same results because the same costs are always the first in.** Figure 1A-18 shows periodic FIFO valuation.

FIFO approximates the actual flow of inventory. When the oldest goods are sold first, FIFO approximates the specific identification method and FIFO ending inventory values are approximate inventory replacement costs. However, FIFO does not match current costs with current revenues on the income statement. Since the oldest costs are matched with revenue, FIFO can distort net income and produce phantom profits.

Figure 1A-18 Periodic FIFO

Bounce Sporting Goods Company	
FIFO Inventory Cost Flow Assumption	
(Periodic Inventory System)	

Ending inventory (1,200 units):

700 units @ $60	$42,000
500 units @ $56	28,000
Total	$70,000

Cost of goods sold (1,300 units):

Beginning Inventory + Purchases – Ending Inventory = Cost of Goods Sold

$40,000 + $88,000 – $70,000 = $58,000

- *Last in, first out (LIFO)* assigns the cost of the newest goods to cost of goods sold and the cost of the oldest goods to ending inventory. When costs are increasing, LIFO produces the highest cost of goods sold and the lowest ending inventory.

  In the **perpetual inventory system,** which records events in the order they actually occur, the LIFO cost of goods sold must be determined after each sale. Using data from Figure 1A-16, Figure 1A-19 shows the perpetual LIFO method.

Figure 1A-19 Perpetual LIFO

Bounce Sporting Goods Company		
LIFO Inventory Cost Flow Assumption		
(Perpetual Inventory System)		

Cost of goods sold (1,300 units):

July 15	1,000 units @ $60	$60,000
July 28	300 units @ $56	16,800
Total		$76,800

Ending inventory (1,200 units):

Beginning Inventory + Purchases – Cost of Goods Sold = Ending Inventory

$40,000 + $88,000 – $76,800 = $51,200

1,000 units @ $40	$40,000
200 units @ $56	11,200
	$51,200

Unlike FIFO, the LIFO perpetual inventory system and the LIFO periodic system will yield different costs of goods sold and ending inventory figures. This happens because the periodic system measures LIFO cost as of the end of the accounting period, whereas the perpetual method measures LIFO cost as of the date of each sale.

When using LIFO in the **periodic system,** the cost of goods sold is calculated by subtracting the ending inventory from the cost of goods available for sale. Figure 1A-20 shows how inventory is valued using the periodic LIFO method.

LIFO has the advantage of providing a better measure of current earnings because it matches recent costs against current revenues. LIFO also allows

Figure 1A-20 Periodic LIFO

Bounce Sporting Goods Company

LIFO Inventory Cost Flow Assumption

(Periodic Inventory System)

Ending inventory (1,200 units):

	1,000 units @ $40	$40,000
	200 units @ $60	12,000
Total		$52,000

Cost of goods sold (1,300 units):

Beginning Inventory + Purchases – Ending Inventory = Cost of Goods Sold

$40,000 + $88,000 – $52,000 = $76,000

income tax deferrals when costs are rising and inventory levels remain stable because cost of goods sold will be higher and net income lower compared to other methods. Lower taxes increase a company's cash flows. LIFO can also hedge against price declines because it rarely requires markdowns to market value as a result of price decreases, which might be needed under FIFO. However, the lower reported earnings that reduce taxes under LIFO are a disadvantage to firms that wish to report higher income. LIFO also distorts the balance sheet by understating inventory values and working capital.

Figure 1A-21 is a summary of inventory cost flow assumptions. The up and down arrows in FIFO and LIFO assume there is inflation.

Figure 1A-21 Inventory Cost Flow Assumptions

Valuation Method	Description	EI	COGS	NI	Perpetual	Periodic	LCM	LCNRV
Specific ID	Tracks cost of each unique item for inventory & COGS	n/a			n/a	n/a	n/a	n/a
Average Cost	Averages cost of similar items for inventory & COGS	Inventory & COGS results are between FIFO & LIFO			Moving average-average cost recalculated with each purchase	Weighted average		x
FIFO	Cost of first in goes to COGS	↑	↓	↑	Results in same amount reported for both inventory & COGS			x
LIFO	Cost of last in goes to COGS	↓	↑	↓	Layers calculated with each purchase & subsequent sale	Layers determined for the time period, then COGS is calculated	x	
Retail Inventory Method	Calculate a cost-to-retail ratio, then apply the ratio to EI at retail to estimate the cost of EI	n/a			n/a		x	

EI: Ending Inventory

COGS: Cost of Goods Sold

NI: Net Income

LCM: Lower of Cost or Market

LCNRV: Lower of Cost or Net Realizable Value

Cost-to-Retail Ratio: Cost of goods available for sale divided by retail value of goods available for sale

LIFO Liquidation

LIFO records inventory in layers separated by different purchase times and costs. The oldest costs are called the base layer. If sales exceed purchases during a period, LIFO liquidation occurs. **LIFO liquidation** is the sale of multiple layers of inventory, causing a firm to recognize revenues at current prices but costs at a mix of current and old prices. When prices are rising, LIFO liquidation results in higher reported income and likely higher taxes as well.

One solution to the problem of LIFO liquidation is to use *dollar-value LIFO*, which measures increases and decreases in cost pools by their total dollar value instead of physical quantities. This allows pools to be more broadly defined, reducing the chance of LIFO liquidation.

LIFO Reserve

LIFO has tax advantages, but it is less useful internally because it does not approximate the physical flow of goods and is cumbersome for interim reporting. Therefore, *many firms use LIFO for taxes and external reporting but average cost or FIFO internally.* In addition, it is difficult for external users of financial statements to compare a LIFO firm to a firm using FIFO or weighted average since the choice of an inventory cost flow assumption has significant balance sheet and income statement effects. Therefore, **GAAP requires LIFO firms to report the difference** *between LIFO and FIFO in an allowance account called the LIFO reserve* that reduces the FIFO inventory value to its LIFO value. Changes in the LIFO reserve balance are called the LIFO effect.

Firms using different inventory methods cannot be compared directly. An external user of financial statements must convert one method to the other method for a true comparison. Since companies using LIFO are required to disclose their LIFO reserve, it is easier for external users to convert LIFO to FIFO. Selected data from a LIFO-basis company is shown in Figure 1A-22.

Figure 1A-22 Partial Financial Statements of Company using LIFO

	Year 2	Year 1
Excerpts from balance sheet:		
Inventories (approximate FIFO cost)	$338,757	$307,566
Less: LIFO reserve	$32,231	$11,820
LIFO cost	$306,526	$295,746
Excerpts from income statement:		
Cost of goods sold (COGS)	$2,590,650	
Net income	$108,690	

The LIFO reserve increased by ($32,231 − $11,820) = $20,411. Therefore, if the firm had used FIFO, its COGS would have been lower and its net income higher, as shown in Figure 1A-23. The example assumes a 40% tax rate.

The LIFO reserve is an accumulation of total cost differences between LIFO and FIFO since the LIFO method was adopted. Multiplying the current LIFO reserve by the tax rate gives the amount of income tax saved by using LIFO. In this example: 40% × $32,231 = $12,892. Thus, the firm had $12,892 more capital to invest in its operations over the long term.

Effect on Income and Assets from Different Cost Flow Assumptions

When costs are rising, LIFO minimizes income, which results in lower income taxes. LIFO also follows the matching principle by matching recent costs (approximates replacement costs) with current revenues.

Figure 1A-23 Converting from LIFO to FIFO

LIFO-basis COGS		**$2,590,650**
Change in LIFO reserve:		
LIFO reserve, Year 2	$32,231	
LIFO reserve, Year 1	11,820	
Less: Increase in LIFO reserve		20,411
FIFO-basis COGS		**$2,570,239**
Net income under LIFO		**$108,690**
Increase in pretax income due to reduced COGS under FIFO		+ $20,411
Difference in taxes		
Change in pretax income	$20,411	
Tax rate	× 40%	
Taxes on increase in pretax income under FIFO		− $8,164
Net income under FIFO		**$120,937**

The effects of FIFO, average cost, and LIFO methods are compared in Figure 1A-24 using the data from the preceding examples.

Figure 1A-24 Comparing Perpetual Inventory Cost Flow Assumptions

Cost Flow Assumption	Cost of Goods Available for Sale	Cost of Goods Sold	Ending Inventory
FIFO, perpetual	$128,000	$58,000	$70,000
Moving average, perpetual	$128,000	65,600	62,400
LIFO, perpetual	$128,000	76,800	51,200

All of these cost flow assumptions are permitted under GAAP. The fact that so many inventory valuation methods, each resulting in a different net income level, are allowed makes comparing financial statements from different firms more difficult; therefore, companies must disclose the cost flow assumption that they use in the notes to the financial statements.

Effect of Converting from LIFO to FIFO

When a firm switches inventory accounting methods, there is always a reason. In times of inflation, a firm would report higher cost of goods sold and lower pretax income and lower income taxes if it chooses LIFO instead of FIFO. Thus, firms seeking to minimize their taxes choose LIFO. By contrast, firms that seek to maximize their reported income would choose FIFO.

The International Accounting Standards Board (IASB) does not accept LIFO for inventory valuation. As the IASB and the FASB move toward convergence, it is likely that inventory valuation methods could be affected.

Figure 1A-25 summarizes the advantages and disadvantages of the different inventory valuation methods.

LOS
§1.A.2.i

Figure 1A-25 Inventory Valuation Methods

Inventory Valuation Method	Advantages	Disadvantages
Specific Identification	• Accurate cost of inventory & COGS	• Tracks the cost of individual items so it does not work well for large number of inventory items and homogenous products
Average Cost	In periodic system: • Simple to use • Objective • Requires one average cost calculation at the end of the time period	In perpetual system: • Requires new average cost to be calculated after each purchase
FIFO	• Periodic & perpetual systems report the same results • Allowed globally, no need for inventory valuation using different methods for different countries • Inventory values approximate inventory replacement cost • Approximates actual physical flow of goods	• Higher taxes in times of inflation decrease cash flows • Does not match current costs with revenues and can distort net income by producing phantom profits
LIFO	• Is better measure of current earnings • Lower taxes in times of inflation increase cash flows in the U.S. • Matches current costs with revenues providing better measurement of earnings • Hedges against price declines so it rarely requires markdowns to market value	• Periodic & perpetual systems report different results • Distorts balance sheet by understating inventory values & working capital • GAAP requires reporting of LIFO reserve • Not allowed under IASB • Periodic & Perpetual systems report different results

Effects of Inventory Errors

LOS
§1.A.2.g

Two main types of inventory errors are misstatements in ending inventory and misstatements in purchases.

- *Misstated ending inventory.* When items are incorrectly omitted from ending inventory, the balance sheet understates inventory, which in turn understates retained earnings, working capital, and possibly the current ratio. In addition, income is understated because the cost of goods sold is overstated. If the error is not corrected in the following period, the opposite effect will result, so the two periods' statements viewed together will result in the same total income as if no error had occurred. However, the net income for each year will be misstated when viewed individually. When ending inventory is overstated, the opposite occurs: Net income, inventory, retained earnings, working capital, and the current ratio are overstated while the cost of goods sold is understated.

For example, Figure 1A-26 shows the effects of overstating ending inventory by $10,000 in Year 1 and the reversal of this error in Year 2. Increases or decreases are represented by up or down arrows.

Figure 1A-26 Correcting an Inventory Misstatement

	Timing	Change
Ending inventory misstated	Year 1	↑ $10,000
Cost of sales	Year 1	↓ $10,000
Operating income	Year 1	↑ $10,000
Tax expense (40% tax rate)	Year 1	↑ $4,000
Net income	Year 1	↑ $6,000
Retained earnings	Year 1	↑ $6,000
Beginning inventory	Year 2	↑ $10,000
Cost of sales	Year 2	↑ $10,000
Operating income	Year 2	↓ $10,000
Tax expense (40% tax rate)	Year 2	↓ $4,000
Net income	Year 2	↓ $6,000
Ending inventory	Year 2	Correct
Retained earnings	Year 2	Correct

- *Misstated purchases.* When a purchase is not recorded or included in ending inventory, the balance sheet understates inventory and accounts payable. The current ratio will be overstated or understated depending on what the original current ratio was. On the income statement, both purchases and ending inventory are understated, so the cost of goods sold is correct. Therefore, net income is not affected. The current ratio will be overstated if the original current ratio is greater than 1 to 1 because reducing the size of both current assets and current liabilities yields a higher ratio. For example, if current assets are $200,000 and current liabilities are $100,000, the current ratio is 2 to 1. However, if both sums are reduced by a $50,000 error, the ratio would be 3 to 1, an overstatement. However, if the original current ratio is less than 1 to 1 the current ratio will decrease and be understated. When the current assets are decreased to $75,000 and the current liabilities are kept at $100,000, the current ratio is .75 to 1. Now when both sums are reduced by a $50,000 error, the ratio would be .5 to 1, an understatement. When both purchases and inventory are overstated, the opposite is true in each of these situations.

Fair Value Standards and Measurements

Fair value is commonly used by corporations reporting their investments in other companies' debt or equity securities.

Definition   Fair value is defined as the price that would be received for the sale of an asset or the price paid to transfer a liability in an orderly transaction between market participants at the measurement date, under current market conditions. Sometimes the fair value is referred to as the market value or the fair market value. All of these terms indicate the same concept of fair value. Fair value measurement assumes that the asset or liability is exchanged in an orderly transaction between market participants on the measurement date.

- For example, the fair value of an asset is the amount a market participant is willing to pay to purchase the asset.
- When a principal market exists, fair value is defined as the price in that market. The principal market is the one with the greatest volume and level of activity for the asset or liability in which the entity could sell the asset or transfer the liability.
- In the absence of a principal market, the price in the most advantageous market (maximizes the amount received for assets or minimizes the amount paid to transfer liabilities) should be used to determine fair value. For example, there may be multiple markets for a car dealer including the market to customers or to other dealers but the most advantageous market may be the market to other dealers.
- Fair value measurement assumes the "highest and best use" of a nonfinancial asset by market participants (i.e., the use that would maximize the asset's value) and is based on the use of the asset by market participants even if the firm's intended use is different. For example, if land in a prime residential area is acquired to build a warehouse, the fair value of the land would be its value if it were used for residential purposes. The highest and best use concept is only relevant to nonfinancial assets.

Fair Value Measurement   There are three valuation techniques that can be used to estimate fair value: market approach, income approach, and cost approach. The **market approach** uses prices or other relevant information from market transactions that involve the identical or similar assets or liabilities. The **income approach** uses valuation techniques to convert future amounts to a single discounted present value. The **cost approach** is based on the replacement value of the asset.

To increase consistency and comparability, a fair value hierarchy prioritizes the inputs to valuation techniques used to measure fair value, and the financial statement disclosures must classify the information for each major category of assets and liabilities into these three levels:

Level 1 is the most certain measure of fair value. An active market exists for the identical asset that the company is measuring and the company has access to the fair value information on the date of measurement (usually at year end or period end). For example, if a company holds one share of Disney stock, the company can easily figure out the fair value of that share of stock because there is an active market for

Disney stock and the information is readily available. Level 2 is less certain in measurement of fair value than Level 1. A Level 2 measurement of fair value occurs when an active market exists for an asset that is similar (but not identical) to the asset the company owns. A Level 3 measurement of fair value is the least certain measure. An active market does not exist for the asset nor for an asset similar to the one the company is measuring (i.e. no Level 1 or Level 2 fair value measurement is available). The company can measure the fair value of a Level 3 asset by using a financial model such as discounted cash flows to estimate the fair value.

Advantages and Disadvantages of Using Fair Value Compared to historical cost, fair value provides more current information about the valuation of assets. Many financial institutions and investors rely on fair values to make decisions about financial assets and liabilities. The disadvantages of using fair value include increased volatility in the reported value and uncertainty as to the reliability of estimates particularly with assets valued using a Level 3 measure.

IFRS requirements for fair value disclosure are similar to that of U.S. generally accepted accounting principles (GAAP).

The various fair valuation techniques are summarized in Figure 1A-27.

Figure 1A-27 Fair Valuation Techniques

Fair Valuation Techniques		Level	Reliability of Estimate
Market Approach	Price or other relevant info from market transactions for identical or similar assets	1	Most
Cost Approach	Replacement value of asset	2	Somewhat
Income Approach	Converts future amounts to single discounted present value	3	Least

Asset Fair Value	Market	Identical Asset	Similar Asset
Level 1	Active	Yes	Yes
Level 2	Active	No	Yes
Level 3	No	No	No

Asset Valuation

Assets are valued and presented on the balance sheet in order of liquidity: the ability and/or management's intent to convert the asset to cash. An asset is reported as a current asset if the firm expects the asset to convert to cash or be used up during the year or its operating cycle, whichever is longer. Current assets typically include cash, short-term investments, accounts receivable, inventory, supplies, and prepaid expenses. Assets that will be held for more than one (1) year are classified as long-term assets and would include investments; property, plant, equipment; and intangibles.

Investments

This section covers accounting for investments in debt securities and equity securities issued by other companies.

Debt Securities

A **debt security** is a form of loan from one entity to another, including federal and municipal government securities, commercial paper, corporate bonds, securitized debt instruments, and convertible debt. They are used to preserve capital and generate income. Debt securities are categorized and accounted for as shown in Figure 1A-28:

Figure 1A-28 Debt Security Investments

Categories	Held to Maturity	Available for Sale	Trading
Criteria	Management intent and ability to hold to maturity	Management intent to sell sometime in future	Management intent to sell in near term
Valuation	Amortized cost: acquisition cost plus any unamortized premium or minus any unamortized discount	Fair value	Fair value
Record unrealized holding gains or losses	None	Other comprehensive income—Equity	Income
Record interest income	Income	Income	Income

On the balance sheet, firms should report individual investments as either current or noncurrent, depending on when management expects to sell the debt investment and convert it to cash. For securities classified as available for sale and held to maturity, the aggregate fair value, gross unrealized holding gains and losses, and amortized cost basis must be disclosed.

A valuation allowance account is used to adjust trading and available-for-sale portfolios to market value. At each balance sheet date, the valuation allowance account is adjusted so that the sum of the portfolio (at cost) and the valuation allowance equal the fair value of the securities, and an unrealized gain or loss is recognized. When a security is sold, the cost is removed from the portfolio and a realized gain or loss is recorded.

Held to Maturity

Debt securities can be held to maturity because the contract has a stated maturity date. To classify securities as held to maturity, the reporting entity must have both the positive intent and the ability to hold the securities to maturity (i.e., to the maturity date of the security when the principal investment is returned to the investing company, the investor).

Thus, sales of held-to-maturity securities should be rare. When they are sold, the amortized cost of the security, the related gain or loss, and the circumstances leading to the decision to sell or transfer the security must be disclosed in the notes to the financial statements.

Any unamortized discount or premium is deducted from or added to the acquisition cost to determine the carrying value. Unrealized gains and losses are not recognized because the assets are not recorded at fair value. The effective interest method is used to compute interest income. In this method:

- For bonds purchased at a premium:
  Carrying Value × Effective Rate = Interest Revenue
  Face Value × Stated Rate = Cash Interest
  Cash Interest – Interest Revenue = Premium Amortized
  Old Carrying Value – Premium Amortized = New Carrying Value
- For bonds purchased at a discount:
  Carrying Value × Effective Rate = Interest Revenue
  Face Value × Stated Rate = Cash Interest
  Interest Revenue – Cash Interest = Discount Amortized
  Old Carrying Value + Discount Amortized = New Carrying Value

Available for Sale

Available-for-sale securities include all securities held with the intent to sell sometime in the future. These securities have no definite holding time and are not being actively traded to take advantage of temporary differences in market prices. The portfolio is reported at fair value, and any unrealized gains or losses resulting from marking the securities to market at the balance sheet date are reported in other comprehensive income, as a separate component of stockholders' equity, until realized by a sale.

Figure 1A-29 shows how an available-for-sale portfolio is adjusted to fair value. In this example, there was an unrealized loss of $14,257 last year. Since the $12,000 unrealized loss at the end of the current year is $2,257 less than last year, the value of the portfolio has actually increased, so an unrealized gain is recorded. The debit side of the entry is made to the debt investment valuation adjustment account for the amount of the securities fair value adjustment.

Dr. Debt valuation allowance	2,257	
Cr. Unrealized holding gain or loss—equity		2,257

Figure 1A-29 Calculation of Debt Securities' Fair Value Adjustment—Available for Sale

Investments	Amortized Cost	Fair Value	Unrealized Gain (Loss)
Available-for-Sale Debt Security Portfolio for Year Ended December 31, Year 1			
X Corporation 10% bonds (total portfolio)	$300,000	$288,000	$(12,000)
Previous securities fair value adjustment balance—credit			(14,257)
Securities fair value adjustment—debit			$2,257

The financial statement presentation for the available-for-sale portfolio in Figure 1A-29 is illustrated in Figure 1A-30.

Figure 1A-30 Available-for-Sale Debt Securities on the Balance Sheet and Income Statement

Balance Sheet (partial)	
Current assets	
Interest receivable	$ xxx
Investments	
Available-for-sale securities, at fair value	288,000
Stockholders' equity	
Accumulated other comprehensive loss	12,000
Statement of Comprehensive Income	
Net income	$ xxx
Other comprehensive income	
Unrealized holding gain (loss) on available-for-sale debt securities	2,257
Total other comprehensive income	xxx
Comprehensive income	$ xxx

Trading

Trading securities are intended to be sold in the short term, generally within 90 days or 3 months of the financial statement date, to generate income from short-term differences in price. At acquisition, each security is recorded at its purchase price including commissions, fees, and taxes. Since the firm's intention is to trade these securities, the portfolio is reported at fair value. Any unrealized holding gain or loss on the portfolio resulting from marking the securities to market (fair value) at the balance sheet date is included in income. Interest revenue recognized but not received is treated as a receivable.

Figure 1A-31 shows a sample trading portfolio including the cost, fair value, and unrealized gain or loss.

Figure 1A-31 Computation of Debt Securities' Fair Value Adjustment—Trading

Trading Debt Security Portfolio			
for Year Ended December 31, Year 1			
Investments	**Cost**	**Fair Value**	**Unrealized Gain (Loss)**
X Corporation 12% bonds	$54,386	$64,860	$10,474
Y Corporation 10% bonds	228,445	216,248	(12,197)
Z Corporation 8% bonds	107,086	114,600	7,514
Total of portfolio	$389,917	$395,708	5,791
Previous securities' fair value adjustment balance—debit			3,201
Securities' fair value adjustment—debit			$2,590

Equity Security Investments

LOS §1.A.2.k

The issuance of Accounting Standards Update (ASU) 2016-01, *Recognition and Measurement of Financial Assets and Financial Liabilities*, amended the accounting for equity investments in another entity with the issuance of Accounting Standards Codification (ASC) 321, *Investments–Equity Securities*.

The most significant change was to eliminate the categories of "Available for Sale" and "Trading" securities for holdings that are less than 20% of equity ownership. This means that all fair value adjustments resulting in unrealized holding gains or losses made on the financial statement date must be reported on the income statement. These unrealized gains or losses can no longer be reported in other comprehensive income in equity.

Equity securities represent ownership in another entity. They include common stock, preferred stock (excluding redeemable preferred stock), stock warrants, and stock options. They do not include convertible debt. When an investor acquires the investee's stock, the percentage of voting stock acquired determines the method of accounting for the security. Figure 1A-32 summarizes the accounting and reporting of equity security investments:

Figure 1A-32 Equity Security Investments

Holdings	**< 20%**	**≥ 20% – 50%**	**> 50%**
Influence or interest	Passive	Significant	Controlling
Accounting method	Cost	Equity	Equity or cost
Valuation	*If readily determinable fair value:* use fair value *If no readily determinable fair value:* use cost minus any impairment	Equity unless fair value option is elected	None

Figure 1A-32 Equity Security Investments *Continued*

Record unrealized holding gains or losses	Income	Income	None
Balance sheet presentation	Current *or* noncurrent investment, based on management intent to sell	Usually noncurrent investment	Consolidated financial statements
Record dividend income	Income	Investment account	Investment account

Holdings of Less than 20%—Fair Value (Cost) Method

Equity securities that represent less than 20% ownership have no maturity date, so they cannot be classified as held-to-maturity securities. Investors with less than 20% interest generally have little or no influence over the investee.

Under the fair value (cost) method, equity investments are initially recorded at their purchase price including fees, such as transfer fees or brokerage fees. Securities acquired in a noncash exchange (such as for services or land) are recorded at the fair value of the consideration given or the fair value of the security received, whichever is more readily determinable.

The investor reports cash dividends declared by the investee as dividend income. At year-end, the portfolio is adjusted to its fair value, with any net unrealized gain or loss calculated as shown in Figure 1A-33.

Figure 1A-33 Calculation of Equity Securities' Fair Value Adjustment

Equity Security Portfolio for Year Ended December 31, Year 1			
Investments	**Cost**	**Fair Value**	**Unrealized Gain (Loss)**
X Corporation	$228,536	$242,000	$ 13,464
Y Corporation	279,400	267,520	(11,880)
Z Corporation	124,388	91,520	(32,868)
Total of portfolio	$632,324	$601,040	(31,284)
Previous securities fair value adjustment balance—credit			(1,000)
Securities fair value adjustment—credit			$(30,284)

The net unrealized gain or loss on the portfolio is recognized on the income statement.

When a stock in the portfolio is sold, a realized gain or loss is calculated by deducting the acquisition cost from the net proceeds from sale. A realized gain or loss is recognized at the date of the sale in income. Also, the unrealized gain or loss account balance on the securities account is removed along with any fair value adjustment account. Sales and purchases of equity securities during the year will change the cost basis of the investment account.

Holdings between 20% and 50%—Equity Method

The equity method of accounting, described in ASC Topic 323, *Investments—Equity Method and Joint Ventures*, is required for any investor who can exercise significant influence over an investee's operating and financial policies. The term "significant influence" is not limited to a minimum percentage of ownership of 20% but also can be determined by the amount of representation on the board of directors, material intercompany transactions, and other factors.

However, unless evidence demonstrates otherwise, a 20% or greater investment is presumed to create significant influence.

Equity Method Accounting

In the equity method, an investment is initially recorded at its purchase price plus fees. Subsequently, the investment's carrying value is increased (or decreased) by the investor's percentage share of the investee's income (or losses) and is decreased by the investor's percentage share of any dividends received/declared by the investee.

An investor using the equity method will recognize and report changes in the investment to reflect the changing value of the investee's equity accounts, including:

- *Results of operations.* The investor reports its proportional share of the investee's income or loss excluding its share of any intercompany profits/losses in assets.
- *Investee's items of other comprehensive income.* The investor reports its proportionate share of items of other comprehensive income that result in changes to equity and would increase the investment account and other comprehensive income for the investor assuming the items increase equity.
- *Investee dividends.* The investor will recognize its proportionate share of investee dividends as a decrease in the investment account and an increase to cash or dividends receivable.
- *Difference in investee book value and investment cost/fair value.* The differential is generally attributed to identifiable assets and liabilities or goodwill. The proportionate share of the difference between fair values and book values of the investee's fixed assets should be depreciated. Goodwill, however, is not depreciated but is tested for impairment.

For example, ABC, Inc. (investor) purchases a **30% share in XYZ, Inc**. (investee) for $20 million. On the date of the investment, XYZ's book value is $50 million. The excess of purchase price over the proportionate share of the book value acquired is: $20 million – (30% of $50 million) = $5 million. In this example, the difference is allocated among goodwill ($2.5 million), finite-lived intangibles ($1.5 million), and undervalued depreciable assets of the investee's company ($1 million). The intangibles are amortized over five years, and the assets are depreciated over ten years.

At the end of the first year when XYZ releases its results, ABC must account for its share of XYZ's results of operations, including other comprehensive income. In this example, XYZ reported $4.6 million in net income and declared and paid a $1.4 million year-end dividend. ABC must also account for the amortization and depreciation resulting from the allocation of the excess purchase price. ABC's year-end entries are shown in Figure 1A-34.

Figure 1A-34 Year-End Accounting Entries for Equity Securities—Equity Method

Dr. Investment in XYZ stock	1,380,000	
Cr. Income from investment		1,380,000
To record share of XYZ net income		($4,600,000 × 0.3)
Dr. Cash	420,000	
Cr. Investment in XYZ stock		420,000
To record dividend received ($1,400,000 × 0.3) from XYZ		
Dr. Income from investment (ordinary income)	400,000	
Cr. Investment in XYZ stock		400,000
To record amortization of investment cost in excess of book value:		
Undervalued depreciable assets ($1 million/10 years)		$100,000
Unrecorded intangibles ($1.5 million/5 years)		300,000
Total		$400,000

The carrying value of the investment is calculated in Figure 1A-35, assuming that XYZ declared a June dividend of $700,000 and ABC has recognized its 30% share ($210,000) of that dividend in June.

Figure 1A-35 Calculation of Investment Carrying Value

ABC's Investment in XYZ at the End of Year 1		
Acquisition cost, 1/1/Year 1	$20,000,000	
Add: Share of Year 1 income before dividends and amortization	1,380,000	$21,380,000
Less:		
Dividends received 6/30	(210,000)	
Dividends received 12/31	(420,000)	
Amortization of undervalued depreciable assets	(100,000)	
Amortization of unrecorded intangibles	(300,000)	(1,030,000)
Carrying value, 12/31/Year 1		$20,350,000

Holdings of Greater than 50%

When a firm achieves a controlling interest (more than 50% of the investee's stock), each firm continues to maintain separate accounting records. Financial statements are prepared using the equity method, and the investment is treated as a long-term investment. At the end of the accounting period, the parent company consolidates its results with those of the subsidiary. On the consolidated balance sheet, the investment account is eliminated to avoid double-counting and is replaced with the individual assets and liabilities of the subsidiary. Consolidated statements treat the separate entities as a single accounting entity.

Business Combinations

A business combination is a transaction or event in which the acquirer obtains control of one or more businesses where control is generally indicated by ownership of more than 50% of the outstanding voting shares of another company. If an acquisition qualifies as a business combination, GAAP requires the use of the acquisition method.

The acquisition method requires the following four steps:

1. Determine the acquisition date.
2. Recognize and measure identifiable assets, liabilities assumed, and noncontrolling interest in the acquireee.
3. Recognize and measure goodwill or a gain from a bargain purchase.
4. The consideration transferred in the acquisition is measured at fair value on the acquisition date, and may include assets transferred, liabilities assumed, and equity interest issued by the acquirer.

Acquisition-related costs are generally expensed as incurred.

The net assets of the acquired firm are recorded in the consolidated financial statements at their fair value. Any difference between the amount paid and the fair value of the acquired firm's net assets is recorded as goodwill, which must be tested annually for impairment and written down if impaired.

If the acquired firm remains a separate legal entity, it is considered a subsidiary of the acquiring (parent) firm and keeps its own set of books. The parent firm carries the subsidiary on its books in an investment in a subsidiary (asset) account. After acquisition, this account is adjusted annually. If the parent company has 20% to 50% control, it usually tracks its investment in the subsidiary using the equity method. If the parent company has a controlling interest (usually greater than 50% ownership), the equity method and consolidated financial statements are required.

For example, Acme Diversified purchases **60% of Abco Inc.'s stock** for $3.84 million. The $3.84 million investment exceeded Abco's book value by $480,000. Of this, $240,000 was considered goodwill and $240,000 was considered an excess of market value over book values for depreciable assets (amortized over five years). In Year 1, Abco reported income of $432,000 and a dividend of $144,000. Income of $432,000 minus the dividend leaves $288,000 of income after dividends. Figure 1A-36 compares the journal entries under the cost and equity methods for Year 1, and Figure 1A-37 shows how the investment account balances are determined.

Figure 1A-36 Cost Method versus Equity Method—Acme the Parent Company's Books

Cost Method—Year 1		Equity Method—Year 1	
Dr. Investment in Abco	3,840,000	Dr. Investment in Abco	3,840,000
Cr. Cash	3,840,000	Cr. Cash	3,840,000
To record initial investment		*To record initial investment*	
Dr. Cash	86,400	Dr. Cash	86,400
Cr. Dividend income	86,400	Cr. Investment in Abco	86,400
To record dividends received (0.6 × $144,000)		*To record dividends received (0.6 × $144,000)*	
		Dr. Investment in Abco	259,200
		Cr. Equity in subsidiary income	259,200
		To record equity in subsidiary income (0.6 × $432,000)	
		Dr. Equity in subsidiary income	48,000
		Cr. Investment in Abco	48,000
		To adjust equity in subsidiary income for excess depreciation ($240,000/5 years)	

Figure 1A-37 Investment Accounts: Cost versus Equity Methods

Cost Method			Equity Method		
Investment in Abco			**Investment in Abco**		
Year 1 cost	3,840,000		Year 1 cost	3,840,000	
			Dividends		86,400
			Income	259,200	
			Depreciation		48,000
Year 1 ending balance	3,840,000		Year 1 ending balance	3,964,800	

This comparison between the two methods indicates that:

- The investor's share of dividends paid or declared by the investee is considered income under the cost method, but it decreases the investment under the equity method.
- The investor's share of the investee's income increases the investment under the equity method, but it is not recorded under the cost method.
- Additional depreciation expense for assets marked up during acquisition is included in the equity method but not in the cost method.

Depreciation Methods for Long-Term Assets

The goal of depreciation is to follow the matching principle by recognizing a portion of the cost of a tangible asset as an expense in each period when the asset helps to generate revenues. Depreciation is a method of cost allocation, not a method of asset valuation, so the fair value of an asset might not equal its book value. In order to calculate depreciation, the following must be known:

- Depreciable base
- Useful life
- Method of depreciation

An asset's depreciable base is its original cost minus its salvage (residual) value, which is the estimated value of the asset at the end of its useful economic life. An asset's useful economic life may be shorter than its actual physical life if, for example, it is expected to become obsolete before it actually wears out.

When assets are purchased or sold during a year, the annual depreciation expense is calculated and then prorated for the partial year. For example, if a full year's depreciation is $120,000 and the asset was purchased on April 1, then depreciation in the first year would be (9/12 × $120,000) = $90,000.

In the following examples, several depreciation methods are used to depreciate a machine that cost $1,000,000 and has an estimated salvage value of $150,000 at the end of its estimated life of 70,000 units or seven years.

Activity Method

The activity method depreciates an asset by the amount that it is used. An asset's use can be measured by input units (e.g., number of hours used) or output units (e.g., number of items produced).

The depreciation charge for a year is calculated as:

$$\text{Depreciation Charge} = \frac{\text{Depreciable Base} \times \text{Units Produced or Hours Used}}{\text{Total Units of Production or Total Hours Usable Over Life}}$$

The machine in this example has a depreciable base of $1,000,000 (cost) – $150,000 (salvage value) = $850,000. If the machine actually produces 9,500 units in the first year, the depreciation charge for the first year is calculated as:

$$\frac{\$850,000 \times 9,500}{70,000} = \$115,357.14$$

An alternative calculation is to first determine a rate, in this case based on the number of units. Take the $850,000 and divide it by the 70,000 total units to get $12.1428/unit. Then apply that rate to the actual activity. Take the 9,500 and multiply it by $12.1428 to get the first year depreciation expense of $115,356.60. The difference between this amount and the one previously calculated is due to rounding.

The activity method is suitable for equipment and vehicles, but it is not useful for buildings because they depreciate due to time rather than to use. The activity method produces lower depreciation during periods of low use and higher depreciation during periods of high use, so it matches costs with revenues for assets whose utility declines with use. Therefore, the activity method is considered the best approach under GAAP for items that depreciate through wear or use.

Straight-Line Method

The straight-line method of depreciation is simple and widely used. This is a time-based method that allocates equal amounts of depreciation to each time period.

It is most appropriate when obsolescence is a primary cause of depreciation. It is also appropriate for assets that generate consistent revenues over their useful life. Depreciation is calculated as follows:

$$\text{Annual Depreciation Charge} = \frac{\text{Depreciable Base}}{\text{Estimated Useful Service Life}}$$

In this example:

$$\text{Annual Depreciation Charge} = \frac{\$850,000}{7} = \$121,428.57$$

This method assumes that the asset's usefulness is the same every year and that repair costs are also the same each year, which may be unrealistic. Another problem with this method is that, as the depreciation reduces the asset's book value, if the revenue produced from use of the asset is steady each year, then the rate of return from the asset will increase over time.

Accelerated Depreciation Methods

Accelerated depreciation (decreasing charge) methods depreciate an asset more in the earlier years and less in the later years of the asset's life. The logic behind such methods is that assets lose the majority of their value in the first years of use and that repair costs will generally increase over the life of the asset. Repair costs increase as depreciation charges decrease, so the total asset-related expenses are smoothed out. These methods are also conceptually appropriate for assets that generate more revenue in their earlier years than in their later years.

Depreciation is a noncash expense that reduces a company's operating income and its tax liability. Hence, methods that record higher depreciation expenses early in the life of the asset will reduce the firm's tax liability sooner, which results in a better cash flow in the earlier periods.

- *Sum-of-the-years'-digits method* multiplies the depreciable base (cost less salvage value) by a fraction that decreases each year. The fraction is determined as follows:

$$\text{Depreciation Fraction} = \frac{\text{Years of Useful Life Remaining}}{\text{Sum of All Years of Useful Life}}$$

$$\text{First Year of 7-Year Life} = \frac{7}{7 + 6 + 5 + 4 + 3 + 2 + 1} = \frac{7}{28}$$

or

$$\text{Sum of All Years of Useful Life} = \frac{n(n+1)}{2} = \frac{7(7+1)}{2} = 28$$

(where n = number of years of useful life)

Figure 1A-38 shows how this method is applied in this example.

Figure 1A-38 Sum-of-the-Years' Digits Method

Year	Depreciable Base	Years of Life Remaining	Depreciation Fraction	Depreciation Expense	Year-End Book Value
0					$1,000,000*
1	$850,000	7	7/28	$212,500	787,500
2	850,000	6	6/28	182,143	605,357
3	850,000	5	5/28	151,786	453,571
4	850,000	4	4/28	121,429	332,142
5	850,000	3	3/28	91,071	241,071
6	850,000	2	2/28	60,714	180,357
7	850,000	1	1/28	30,357	150,000†
Total		28	28/28	$850,000	

*Book value at date of purchase (i.e., cost).

†Salvage value. Final book value should always equal salvage value.

- *Declining balance method* is applied using a percentage of the straight-line depreciation rate. In the straight-line method, an asset with a 10-year life is depreciated at 1/10 = 10% per year. The declining balance method is usually applied at 150% ("one-and-a-half declining balance") or 200% ("double-declining balance") of the straight-line rate.

  The declining-balance method calculates depreciation based on the asset's book value without regard to salvage value. As the asset's book value declines, applying the constant percentage rate of depreciation results in a lower amount of depreciation recognized each year.

  The machine in this example has a life of seven years, so its straight-line depreciation rate would be 1/7, or 14.29% per year.

  If 150% declining balance is used, the rate is 1/7 × 1.5 = 1.5/7 = 21.43%
  The double-declining-balance rate is 1/7 × 2 = 2/7 = 28.57%

  Depreciation schedules using both 150% declining-balance and double-declining-balance rates are shown in Figure 1A-39. Note that when the asset's salvage value is reached, the depreciation stops. As a result in this example, the normal declining-balance computation requires an extra year under the 150% declining-balance rate and the depreciation is settled a year early using the double-declining balance.

Figure 1A-39 Declining-Balance Depreciation Methods

Bounce Sporting Goods Company
Declining-Balance Depreciation Methods

Year	Book Value of Asset at Beginning of Year	Rate	Depreciation Charge	Book Value at End of Year
150% Declining Balance				
1	$1,000,000	21.43%	$214,300	$785,700
2	785,700	21.43%	168,376	617,324
3	617,324	21.43%	132,293	485,031
4	485,031	21.43%	103,942	381,089
5	381,089	21.43%	81,667	299,422
6	299,422	21.43%	64,166	235,256
7	235,256	21.43%	50,415	184,841
8*	184,841		34,841	150,000
			$850,000	

* In Year 8, the depreciation charge is adjusted to reach the $150,000 salvage value.

Year	Book Value of Asset at Beginning of Year	Rate	Depreciation Charge	Book Value at End of Year
Double-Declining Balance				
1	$1,000,000	28.57%	$285,700	$714,300
2	714,300	28.57%	204,076	510,224
3	510,224	28.57%	145,771	364,453
4	364,453	28.57%	104,124	260,329
5	260,329	28.57%	74,376	185,953
6*	185,953		35,953	150,000
7				
			$850,000	

* In Year 6, the machine is fully depreciated to its $150,000 salvage value.

To ensure that the asset is not depreciated below its salvage value or to complete depreciation on schedule, some firms switch to a straight-line method near the end of the asset's useful life. For example, in Year 5 of the 150% declining-balance example, the book value is $299,422, and the depreciable base is ($299,422 – $150,000) = $149,422. The asset has two years left, so ($149,422/2) = $74,711 could be recorded as depreciation for Years 6 and 7.

Selecting a Depreciation Method

LOS
§1.A.2.m

A firm can select different depreciation methods for different classes of assets. For example, buildings that provide constant benefits over their useful life might be depreciated using straight line, whereas equipment that loses more utility in its early years might be depreciated using the declining-balance method.

Figure 1A-40 compares the effects of straight-line and accelerated depreciation methods on depreciation expense, operating income, tax expense, and book value.

Figure 1A-40 Comparison of Depreciation Methods

	Straight-Line Method	Sum-of-Years'-Digits Method	150% Declining Balance	Double-Declining Balance
Depreciation expense				
In Year 1	$121,429	$212,500	$214,300	$285,700
In Year 7	$121,429	$30,357	$50,415	$0
Effect on operating income				
In Year 1	–	↓ $91,071	↓ $92,871	↓ $164,271
In Year 7	–	↑ $91,072	↑ $71,014	↑ $121,429
Effect on taxes (40%)				
In Year 1	–	↓ $36,428	↓ $37,148	↓ $65,708
In Year 7	–	↑ $36,429	↑ $28,406	↑ $48,571
Effect on book value				
In Year 1	–	↓ $91,071	↓ $92,871	↓ $164,271
In Year 7	–	↑ $91,072	↑ $71,014	↑ $121,429

For tax purposes, firms usually compute depreciation using the modified accelerated cost recovery system (MACRS) of the Internal Revenue Service (IRS), which sets different depreciation rates and methods, depending on the asset's useful life.

Differences in depreciation methods for financial reporting and tax purposes often create deferred tax liabilities. For example, assume that the firm in the previous discussion (Figure 1A-40) used the straight-line method for financial reporting and the sum-of-the-years'-digits method for tax reporting and has operating income of $1,000,000 in Year 1 before depreciation is deducted.

Under the straight-line method, pretax income is ($1,000,000 – $121,429) = $878,571, and the firm would owe ($878,571 × 40%) = $351,428 in taxes.

For tax reporting under the sum-of-years'-digits method, income before taxes is ($1,000,000 – $212,500) = $787,500, and the firm would owe ($787,500 × 0.40) = $315,000 in taxes.

This creates a deferred tax liability of ($351,428 – $315,000) = $36,428. The firm pays less tax now but will owe more tax later.

If the asset is retained for all seven years, the tax liability would be offset by corresponding increases in taxes owed (e.g., $36,428 in Year 7), removing this temporary difference. Most companies prefer to pay lower taxes in earlier years, making more money available to reinvest in their business.

Impairment

Property, plant, and equipment (PP&E) is carried at historical cost, and increases in fair market value are not recognized. However, when the book value of PP&E cannot be recovered through sale or use, the asset is considered to be impaired, and the carrying value must be written down to fair value.

PP&E should be tested for impairment in the following circumstances:

- Significant decrease in the market value of an asset
- Significant adverse change in the extent or manner in which an asset is used or its physical condition
- Significant adverse change in legal factors or business climate that could affect an asset's value
- Accumulation of costs significantly in excess of the amount originally expected to acquire or construct an asset
- A current-period operating or cash flow loss combined with a history of such losses or a forecast of continuing losses associated with an asset
- The expectation that an asset is likely to be sold or retired before the end of its previously estimated useful life

When one of these situations exists, a two-step recoverability test is used to determine whether impairment has occurred.

Step 1. If the sum of the undiscounted future net cash flows expected from the use and disposition of the asset is less than its carrying value, the asset is impaired. If the undiscounted cash flows are greater than or equal to the carrying value, the asset is not impaired.

Step 2. If impairment exists, the asset is written down to its fair value, and the write-down is recorded as an impairment loss. The fair value is the price that would be acceptable to the firm and another party for the transfer of the asset, if determinable; otherwise, the present value of the expected future net cash flows is used.

For example, an asset cost $1,000,000 and has accumulated depreciation of $200,000, so the carrying value is $800,000. If the undiscounted expected future net cash flows from use and disposition of the asset are $700,000, the asset is impaired. If the fair value of the asset is estimated to be $650,000, then an impairment loss of ($800,000 − $650,000) = $150,000 must be recorded.

The impairment loss is recorded as part of income from continuing operations under other expenses and losses. Any recognized impairment loss should be disclosed, including information about the assets impaired, the reason for the impairment, the amount of the loss, and the method of determining fair value.

Intangibles

LOS
§1.A.2.n

Many intangible assets, such as customer lists or contracts, copyrights, or patents, are difficult to value, so they are not reported on the financial statements. However, the balance sheet does include the value of acquired intangible assets, which are measured at amortized cost. This section covers the characteristics of intangibles and then discusses valuation, amortization, testing for impairment, and accounting for goodwill and research and development (R&D).

Characteristics of Intangibles

Intangible assets are defined by two main characteristics: They lack physical substance and are not financial instruments. Other factors that distinguish intangible assets from tangible assets include:

- Their values may fluctuate due to competitive conditions.
- They may be valuable only to the company possessing them.
- Their future benefits may not be readily determinable.
- They may have indeterminate lives.

Intangible assets typically are classified as noncurrent assets.

Types of Intangibles

ASC Topic 805, *Business Combinations*, defines six categories of intangible assets:

1. **Marketing intangibles** are assets used to market or promote a business, including trademarks, trade names, company names, Internet domain names, and agreements not to compete. They include words or symbols that identify products, services, or companies. The U.S. Patent and Trademark Office will grant an indefinite number of 10-year renewals for registered marks, but common law protects even unregistered marks. Acquired marketing intangibles are capitalized at their acquisition price. Internally developed marketing intangibles are capitalized for the amount of legal fees, registration fees, design and consulting fees, and other costs, excluding R&D. Most marketing intangibles have indefinite lives, so their cost cannot be amortized.

2. **Customer intangibles** include customer lists, order or production backlogs, and other customer contracts and relationships. Most customer intangibles are amortized over their finite lives.

3. **Artistic intangibles** include copyrights on books, movies, plays, poems, music, photos, and audiovisual information. Copyrights granted to individuals for artistic intangibles are currently good for 70 years past the life of the creator and cannot be renewed. The costs to purchase and defend a copyright are amortized over the period of expected benefit, which may be shorter than the legal life of the copyright.

4. **Contract intangibles** are the rights granted by contract arrangements, such as construction permits, broadcast rights, franchises or licensing agreements, and service contracts. For example, the initial costs of securing a franchise (such as legal fees or an advance payment) are recorded in an intangible asset account and amortized over the life of the franchise if it is limited. However, annual payments required under a franchise agreement are expensed as incurred.

5. **Technological intangibles** include patents for technology, trade secrets, and other innovations. Product and process patents have a legal life of 20 years. Acquired patents are capitalized at the acquisition price plus any legal fees paid to successfully secure or defend the patent. However, R&D costs related to the patented product or process must be expensed as incurred. The capitalized cost of a patent is amortized over the shorter of its legal life or its useful life.

6. **Goodwill** is the difference between the price paid to acquire a business and the fair market value of its underlying identifiable assets. This topic is discussed later.

Valuation of Intangibles

Intangibles are recorded differently depending on whether they were purchased or created internally.

- *Acquired intangibles* are recorded at acquisition cost plus any additional costs, such as legal fees. If intangibles are acquired in exchange for stock or noncash assets, the exchange is recorded at the more reliable of the fair value of consideration given or the intangible asset received. If they are part of a basket purchase, the lump-sum price is allocated among the assets received based on relative fair values.
- *Intangibles created internally* are expensed immediately if they are not specifically identifiable, have indeterminate values, or are inherent in a continuing business and related to the entity as a whole. The only costs related to internally developed intangible assets that are capitalized are registration and legal fees paid to external parties. R&D costs incurred to develop a patent internally are expensed as incurred.

Amortization

Indefinite-life intangibles are not amortized but are tested for impairment annually. The cost of limited-life intangible assets is amortized over the period of expected benefit, which is estimated using the following factors:

- Expected use of the intangible
- Legal, regulatory, or contractual limits placed on an intangible's life
- Extension rights or other provisions for renewal
- Provisions that allow renewal or extension of the asset's life without substantial cost
- Effects of technological change, obsolescence, consumer demand, competition, and other economic factors
- Expected useful life of other assets related to the intangible asset
- Levels of maintenance costs required to obtain the expected future benefits from the asset (suggests limited life if these costs are material)

When an intangible asset has a limited life, the capitalized cost minus any residual (salvage) value is amortized over that life. Residual value is usually zero unless the firm believes that the intangible can be sold at the end of the amortization period (e.g., a purchase commitment for a mailing list). Intangible assets are usually amortized on a straight-line basis. The journal entry is a debit to amortization expense and a credit either to the intangible asset account or to a separate accumulated amortization account.

Goodwill

This section deals with recording goodwill and testing it for impairment. In business combinations, goodwill is measured as the excess of (a) over (b):

- **a.** The aggregate of the following:
  1. The consideration given by the acquirer (e.g., cash, stock, debt), measured at fair value on the acquisition date
  2. The fair value of any noncontrolling interest in the acquiree firm
  3. The fair value at the acquisition date of the acquirer's previously held equity interest in the acquiree (if being acquired in stages)

b. The net value of the identifiable assets and liabilities obtained from the acquiree at the acquisition date

In essence, goodwill is the excess of the cost of an acquired firm over the net values assigned to assets acquired and liabilities assumed in a business acquisition.

Recording Goodwill

Only acquired goodwill is capitalized, and only when an entire business is acquired. It cannot be separated from the business as a whole but is an integral part of the going concern. Internally created goodwill is never reported as an asset.

When one company acquires another company, a price is determined based on the fair value (not book value) of the new subsidiary's assets and liabilities. An audit is usually conducted to arrive at the fair value of the subsidiary's net assets. Once the fair value is determined, the negotiators settle on an acquisition price that usually accounts for intangibles that cannot be valued, such as management expertise and reputation. Therefore, the acquisition price is often materially higher than the fair value. In rare instances, negative goodwill occurs if the acquisition price is less than the fair value. Also known as *bargain purchase*, this situation is rare because the seller is more likely to sell off the pieces of the business separately to get their market value.

For example, a parent company acquires another firm as a subsidiary. The net fair market value for the underlying assets and liabilities is $35 million, but the acquisition price is $40 million. The $5 million difference is treated as goodwill. Figure 1A-41 shows the allocation of the acquisition price.

Figure 1A-41 Calculation of Goodwill

Purchase price		$40,000,000
Less:		
Cash	$2,500,000	
Receivables	5,000,000	
Inventories	9,000,000	
Property, plant, and equipment	22,000,000	
Patents	1,500,000	
Liabilities	(5,000,000)	
Fair value of identifiable net assets		35,000,000
Goodwill		$ 5,000,000

Impairment Testing of Goodwill

Goodwill is not amortized but is tested for impairment at least annually and is written down when impairment has occurred.

A potential impairment of goodwill exists when the fair value of the reporting unit is less than its carrying value including goodwill. In that case, the loss (if any) must be measured. An impairment loss is recognized for the excess of the carrying value of the reporting unit goodwill over the implied fair value of that goodwill. To measure implied goodwill, the fair value of the reporting unit is allocated to identifiable net assets, and any excess is considered implied goodwill.

For example, if a subsidiary has a fair value of $40 million including goodwill and the value of its net identifiable assets (excluding goodwill) is $36 million, the implied goodwill would be $4 million. If the goodwill recorded on the parent company's books is $5 million, it must be written down by $1 million.

Dr. Impairment loss	1,000,000	
Cr. Goodwill		1,000,000

An impairment loss cannot exceed the carrying value of goodwill, and after a loss is recognized, it cannot be reversed.

Accounting for Impairment of Intangible Assets

Intangible assets other than goodwill also are tested annually for impairment.

Impairment Testing for Limited-Life Intangibles

Intangible assets that are subject to amortization are reviewed for impairment in the same way as property, plant, and equipment. (See the "Property, Plant, and Equipment" section for details on the recoverability test.) An impairment loss is recognized if the carrying value of an intangible asset is not recoverable and its carrying value exceeds its fair value. Once an intangible asset has been written down, any recovery in value cannot be recognized.

Impairment Testing for Indefinite-Life Intangibles

Intangibles that are not subject to amortization should be tested for impairment at least annually by comparing the fair value of the intangible asset with its carrying value. If the carrying value exceeds the fair value, an impairment loss is recognized for the excess. Once a loss is recognized, it cannot be reversed.

Accounting for Liabilities

Short-Term Obligations

Accounts payable are amounts owed to suppliers for goods purchased on credit. A discount may be allowed for early payment, based on the invoice terms. Cash discounts, expressed in terms such as 2/10, net 30, were covered previously under "Accounts Receivable." Accounts payable should be recorded when title to the goods passes or the services have been received, so special attention must be paid to transactions near the end of the accounting period. Accounts payable are valued at the amount owed.

Notes payable are more formal, written agreements to pay a certain sum on a certain date. Notes can be short or long term, interest bearing or zero interest bearing. Interest-bearing notes are recorded at the initial cash received from the lender. Interest expense and interest payable are recorded over the period during which the note is outstanding. At maturity, the borrower pays back the face value of the note plus interest. With zero-interest-bearing notes, the face value of the note represents the total amount that the borrower must repay on the due date, but the borrower receives only the present value of that amount when the note is signed. The difference represents the implied interest.

Short-Term Obligations Expected to Be Refinanced

Many companies prefer to classify liabilities as noncurrent rather than current to improve their reported liquidity position and reduce the perceived immediate riskiness of the firm. There are definite criteria which must be met before a liability due within one year of the balance sheet date can be reclassified as noncurrent. According to GAAP, if a company has both the intent and ability to refinance a short-term obligation with a long-term obligation, then the debt can be reported as non-current. The intent must be proven (e.g., board of directors' meeting minutes) and the ability must be demonstrable before the financial statements are issued. There are three ways a company can meet the ability criteria: the company must actually refinance the liability on a long-term basis, enter into a noncancelable financing agreement with a viable lender, and issue equity securities to replace the debt. If the short-term debt is greater than the financing in place or arranged, only the portion of the debt that will be covered by the arrangement may be classified as long-term debt.

Warranties, Premiums, and Coupons

Based on the matching principle, costs for attached product warranties, coupons, and premiums are reported as expenses and liabilities in the period when the related product is sold. Experience serves as a basis for estimating the expected costs to repair or replace products under warranty, fulfill cash rebates, or deliver premiums in exchange for box tops. When the product under warranty actually is repaired, the cash rebate is paid, or the premium is delivered, the estimated liability is reduced. Warranties, coupons, and premiums are types of loss contingencies.

Accounting for Warranty Costs Under the New Revenue Recognition Standard

The FASB issued Accounting Standard Update No. 2014-09 Revenue from Contracts with Customers (Topic 606) in May of 2014. This new revenue recognition standard requires the firm to distinguish between warranties representing assurance of a product's performance and service-type warranties.

To assess whether a warranty provides a customer with a service-type warranty in addition to the assurance warranty that the product complies with the agreed-upon specifications, three factors should be considered:

1. Whether the warranty is required by law: If required by law to provide a warranty, it is not a performance obligation and only an assurance warranty
2. Length of the warranty coverage period: The longer the coverage period, it is most likely a performance obligation and therefore a service-type warranty
3. Nature of tasks to be performed: If the entity needs to perform specified tasks to provide assurance, it is not a performance obligation. An example is return shipping service for a defective product.

Assurance warranties continue to be accounted for under the cost-accrual guidance in ASC 460-10, *Guarantees*.

The cash basis is required if it is *unlikely* that a liability will be incurred or if the liability cannot be reasonably estimated. This method may also be used if warranty costs are immaterial or the warranty period is brief. In this method, no estimated warranty liability is recognized in the period of sale, and warranty expense is recognized only when the warranty is exercised. The cash basis is required for income taxes.

The accrual method is required when it is probable that warranty claims will be made and the firm can make a reasonable estimate of the costs.

The journal entry to accrue the warranty expense is based on the number of units multiplied by the estimated warranty cost per unit.

Dr. Assurance warranty expense	x,xxx	
Cr. Assurance warranty liability		x,xxx

When a warranty claim is made, the actual cost of honoring the warranty is journalized as:

Dr. Assurance warranty liability	x,xxx	
Cr. Cash		x,xxx

Service-type warranties exist based on the three criteria mentioned earlier. The defining criteria is when the customer has the option to buy it. This type of warranty is accounted for as a separate performance obligation.

Sales revenue from the extended warranty is deferred and may be recognized on a straight-line basis over the life of the warranty.

If a firm offers a two-year extended warranty for $100 and sells 100 of these extended warranties in Year 1, the journal entry for the sale of the service-type warranty would be:

Dr. Cash or accounts receivable	10,000	
Cr. Unearned warranty revenue		10,000

At the end of Years 2 and 3, warranty revenue is recognized using straight-line amortization ($10,000 / 2 = $5,000 per year):

Dr. Unearned warranty revenue	5,000	
Cr. Warranty revenue		5,000

Alternatively, the warranty revenue can be recognized as units are repaired over the two-year extended warranty.

The actual cost to fulfill the extended warranty claim is expensed in years 2 and 3 as the costs are incurred. The journal entry is:

Dr. Service warranty expense	x,xxx	
Cr. Cash or another account		x,xxx

Deferred Income Taxes

LOS §1.A.2.q **LOS §1.A.2.r** **LOS §1.A.2.s**

Since the IRS tax code differs from GAAP, pretax financial income often differs from taxable income. **Pretax financial income** (or income before taxes) is the income derived for financial reporting under GAAP. **Taxable income** is a term in the IRS tax code denoting the base amount of income (after all allowed deductions) that is used to calculate income tax payable.

Temporary Differences

A **temporary difference** is a difference between pretax financial income under GAAP and taxable income for the IRS that will reverse in a later period, resulting in the same net tax being paid. Such differences require interperiod tax allocation whenever items are recorded in different periods for tax accounting and financial reporting. A firm records income tax expense based on its pretax financial income under GAAP but records its income tax payable based on taxable income under IRS code. Any difference becomes a deferred tax asset (DTA) or a deferred tax liability (DTL).

For example, a company accrues warranty expense in the period when a product is sold for financial reporting but deducts the repair costs for tax purposes only when warranty service is provided. In the year of sale, taxable income under IRS code is greater than pretax financial income under GAAP, so the company debits a deferred tax asset for the additional tax paid in that year:

Dr. Income tax expense	GAAP amount	
Dr. Deferred tax asset	Difference	
Cr. Income tax payable		IRS amount

In the future when the warranty work is done, pretax financial income under GAAP will be higher than taxable income under IRS code, so the company will credit (use up) the deferred tax asset:

Dr. Income tax expense	GAAP amount	
Cr. Deferred tax asset		Difference
Cr. Income tax payable		IRS amount

Since the ability to realize the benefit of deferred tax assets is uncertain, an allowance may be used to reduce deferred tax assets to the extent that it is more likely than not that they will not be used.

Other differences between GAAP and the IRS code may cause pretax income under GAAP initially to be larger than taxable income for the IRS. For example, a firm uses straight-line depreciation for financial reporting, but uses MACRS for tax reporting. GAAP-based income will be larger than IRS-based income, which creates a deferred tax liability in the early years of the life of the depreciable asset when the installment sales are made:

Dr. Income tax expense	GAAP amount	
Cr. Deferred tax liability		Difference
Cr. Income tax payable		IRS amount

In the future when the firm reports depreciation in the later years of the life of the depreciable asset, taxable income for the IRS will be greater than GAAP-based income, so the firm will recognize fulfillment of the liability:

Dr. Income tax expense	GAAP amount	
Dr. Deferred tax liability	Difference	
Cr. Income tax payable		IRS amount

According to ASC Topic 740, *Income Taxes*, deferred taxes are measured using the asset and liability method. This method measures the tax effects that arise when the carrying values of assets and liabilities differ for financial reporting and tax purposes. Examples of temporary differences include:

- *Installment sales method*—Recognized by the IRS but usually not permitted under GAAP
- *Long-term construction contracts*—Cash basis for the IRS but the Output Method or the Input Method under the new Revenue Recognition
- *Depreciation*—Different methods for the IRS and GAAP
- *Goodwill*—Amortized over 15 years for the IRS but tested for impairment and not amortized under GAAP
- *Estimated costs*—Not recorded until paid for the IRS but accrued under GAAP (e.g., warranty expense)
- *Unearned revenue*—Part of taxable income when received for the IRS but a liability until earned under GAAP
- *Accounting for investments*—Cost method for the IRS, but GAAP permits the equity method
- *Net capital loss*—Carried forward to offset future capital gains for the IRS but recognized in the current period under GAAP
- *Deferred compensation*—Not a deduction until paid for the IRS but accrued over the employee's employment period for GAAP
- *Contingent liabilities*—Cannot be deducted for the IRS until fixed and determinable but recognized under GAAP if they are likely and can be estimated
- *Excess charitable contributions*—Carried over to future years for the IRS but recognized in the current period under GAAP
- *Income recognition*—Modified cash basis for the IRS but the accrual basis under GAAP

Permanent Differences

A number of differences between GAAP and tax accounting will never be reversed because certain items affect one method but never the other method. Examples of permanent differences include:

- *Changes in effective tax rate.* If the tax rate changes, a portion of a temporary difference could become permanent. For example, if a 40% tax rate changes to 35%, the 5% change would be a permanent difference because it would not need to be paid when the temporary difference reverses.
- *Deduction for dividends received.* Depending on the extent of ownership, part of dividends received may be nontaxable, but the tax must be recognized for financial reporting.
- *Municipal interest income.* Hundred percent exclusion from taxes is allowed for qualified municipal securities but the income is not excluded from financial reporting.
- *Percentage depletion.* Excess of percentage depletion over cost depletion is allowable as a deduction for taxes but not for financial reporting.
- *Government tax exemptions.* Governments may pass laws that exempt certain revenues from taxes, permit special deductions above what is allowed by GAAP,

or add special taxes on types of businesses to discourage their growth. In such situations, a company's effective tax rate will differ from the statutory tax rate (used for financial reporting), and that difference will be permanent.

Illustration of Temporary and Permanent Difference

The following example illustrates the difference between the accounting treatment for temporary and permanent tax differences.

Acme, Inc. reported pretax financial income of $100,000 for Year 1, $110,000 for Year 2, and $120,000 for Year 3. The firm has a 40% tax rate and received municipal interest income of $20,000 in each of the three years, which is entirely deductible for taxes but not for financial reporting. The company also sold a $15,000 asset on installment, recognizing the entire sale in Year 1 for financial reporting but only a third of the amount per year for tax purposes. Figure 1A-42 shows how to calculate income taxes payable each year.

Figure 1A-43 shows the journal entries for each of these years and reflects how temporary differences require a deferred tax liability account but permanent differences impact the effective tax rate, but have no deferred tax consequences.

Figure 1A-42 Calculating Income Taxes Payable with Temporary and Permanent Differences

	Year 1	Year 2	Year 3
Pretax financial income	$100,000	$110,000	$120,000
Permanent difference			
Tax-exempt income	($20,000)	($20,000)	($20,000)
Temporary difference			
Installment sale*	($10,000)	$5,000	$5,000
Taxable income	$70,000	$95,000	$105,000
Income tax payable (40%)	$28,000	$38,000	$42,000

*Installment sale in Year 1: ($15,000) for GAAP + $5,000 for tax = ($10,000)

Figure 1A-43 Acme Company Journal Entries for Income Taxes in Years 1, 2, and 3

December 31, Year 1		
Dr. Income tax expense [$28,000 + ($10,000 × 40%)]	32,000	
Cr. Deferred tax liability ($10,000 × 40%)		4,000
Cr. Income tax payable		28,000
To record income payment of income taxes		
December 31, Year 2		
Dr. Income tax expense [$38,000 – ($5,000 × 40%)]	36,000	
Dr. Deferred tax liability ($5,000 × 40%)	2,000	
Cr. Income tax payable		38,000
December 31, Year 3		
Dr. Income tax expense [$42,000 – ($5,000 × 40%)]	40,000	
Dr. Deferred tax liability ($5,000 × 40%)	2,000	
Cr. Income tax payable		42,000

Although the statutory tax rate for each year is 40%, the effective tax rates differ in each year:

$$\text{Effective Tax Rate} = \frac{\text{Total Income Tax for Period}}{\text{Pretax Financial Income}}$$

$$\text{For Year 1} = \frac{\$32,000}{\$100,000} = 32\% \quad \text{For Year 2} = \frac{\$36,000}{\$110,000} = 32.73\% \quad \text{For Year 3} = \frac{\$40,000}{\$120,000} = 33.33\%$$

The recording of both the receivable and the DTA is an income tax benefit. For the DTA to be recognized in full, there must be more than a 50% chance of it being realized; a valuation allowance (contra DTA) would be recognized for any part of the DTA not meeting this requirement.

Example. The taxable income history for XCEL Inc. is as follows:

Year	Income (Loss)	Taxable Income Tax Rate
20x5	($200,000)	30% ($200,000 Net Operating Loss (NOL) in current year)
20x4	60,000	25%
20x3	100,000	28%
20x2	70,000	32%

Assume no temporary or permanent differences, and the tax rate after 20x5 has not been changed as of 12/31/x5.

Option 1	Option 2
12/31/x5 Tax accrual entry:	12/31/x5 Tax accrual entry:

Tax refund receivable 43,000*
 DTA 12,000**
   Income tax benefit 55,000
	DTA 60,000*
	   Income tax benefit 60,000
	
	 *$200,000(.30)

*$100,000(.28) + $60,000(.25)	
**$40,000(.30) $160,000 of the NOL is first used to absorb the previous two years' income, leaving $40,000 of the NOL remaining to carryforward. 20x3 income is exhausted before moving to 20x4. 20x2 is not available as it is outside the two-year carryback period.	In this option, XCEL decides not to apply for the refund available in favor of carrying forward the entire NOL in the expectation of higher tax rates. A DTA is recognized for the entire expected tax benefit.
The refund receivable is the amount of tax paid in the previous two years and will be received in 20x6. The DTA is the anticipated tax reduction in future years.	Net income under this option is ($140,000), which is the $200,000 NOL less $60,000 benefit.
The value of the $200,000 NOL in this case is $55,000, the tax savings caused by the NOL.	The benefit is higher for this option because the tax rates for the refund were less than 30%.

Option 1	Option 2
The source of the DTA is the same as for any deductible future difference: an item that reduces future taxable income relative to future book income.	The classification of the DTA depends on the period of realization. The portion of the DTA related to the amount of the NOL expected to be used in 20x6 to absorb taxable income is classified as current at 12/31/x5; the remainder is noncurrent.
The income tax benefit increases net income (reduces the loss) to ($145,000), which is the $200,000 NOL less $55,000 benefit.	
If the NOL were less than $160,000, then no DTA is recognized because nothing would remain after the carryback of the NOL.	20x6, assume $260,000 taxable income
20x6, assume $260,000 taxable income	
The remaining $40,000 of NOL absorbs that much taxable income, leaving $220,000 subject to tax.	The $200,000 NOL carryforward absorbs the first $200,000 of 20x6 taxable income, leaving only $60,000 subject to tax.
12/31/x6 tax accrual entry:	12/31/x6 tax accrual entry:

Income tax expense 78,000
    Income tax payable 66,000*
    DTA 12,000
	Income tax expense 78,000
	    Income tax payable 18,000*
	    DTA 60,000

*($260,000 – $40,000).30	*($260,000 – $200,000).30
There is no remaining DTA balance because there is no remaining NOL to carryforward after 20x6.	Instead, if 20x6 taxable income had been only $180,000 and the tax rate in future years was changed to 35% before 12/31/x6, then the 20x6 tax accrual entry would be:
	Income tax expense 53,000 DTA 53,000
	Beginning DTA balance: 60,000 Ending DTA balance: ($200,000 – 180,000).35 (7,000) Decrease in DTA 53,000

Leases

A **lease** is a contract between a lessor (the one that owns the asset) and a lessee (the one that rents the asset for use). The lessor gives the lessee the right to use the lessor's property for a period of time in exchange for periodic rent payments. The lessor retains the title to the property, so the form of a lease agreement is different from a sale. Sometimes the substance of the lease is comparable to a sale if the lease transfers substantially all risks and benefits of ownership to the lessee.

The lease section in this edition reflects the new CMA testing guidelines beginning January 1, 2020. The new lease standard is from the Financial Accounting Standards Board (FASB) and is Accounting Standards Update (ASU) 2016-02 Accounting Standard Codification (ASC) Topic 842, *Leases.*

According to Topic 842, a lease is a contract that conveys the right to control the use of an identified asset such as property, plant, or equipment, for a period of time in exchange for consideration. The consideration is usually regular rent payments made by the lessee (the one using the asset) to the lessor (the one who owns the asset).

The critical determination for the lessee is whether a contract is, or contains, a lease because lessees are now required to recognize a lease asset and lease liabilities for both finance and operating leases. Lessees can enter into three types of leases:

1. Short-term lease
2. Operating lease
3. Finance lease

The **short-term lease** has a term of 12 months or less. The lessee is allowed to make an accounting policy election to recognize the lease or rent expense on a straight-line basis over the term of the lease. There is no recording of a lease asset or lease liability.

The determination for a lease is to be accounted for as an **operating lease** or a **finance lease** is based on the FASB lease classification tests. The lessee classifies a lease as a finance lease if the lessee effectively obtains control of the underlying asset as a result of the lease. The lessee obtains control of the underlying asset when the lease meets *any* of the following criteria at the commencement of the lease:

1. The lease transfers ownership of the underlying asset to the lessee by the end of the lease term.
2. The lease grants the lessee an option to purchase the underlying asset that the lessee is reasonably certain to exercise.
3. The lease term is for the majority of the remaining economic life of the underlying asset. A reasonable approach to "majority" is if:
   a. 75% or more of the remaining economic life of the underlying asset is a major part of the remaining economic life of that underlying asset.
4. The sum of the present value (PV) of the lease payments and the present value of any residual value guaranteed by the lessee amounts to substantially all of

the fair value of the underlying asset. A reasonable approach to "substantially all" is:

a. 90% or more of the fair value of the underlying asset amounts to substantially all of the fair value of the underlying asset.

5. The underlying asset is of such a specialized nature that it is expected to have no alternative use to the lessor at the end of the lease term.

One additional thing to consider is if the lease is cancelable or not. When the lease is noncancelable, it is automatically classified as a financing lease.

Both *operating and finance leases* will be capitalized with the creation on the balance sheet (aka statement of financial position) of both a right-of-use (ROU) asset and a capitalized lease liability. This is recorded at the lease inception at the present value (PV) of the total lease payments using the imputed interest rate of the lease. Most often this rate is only known by the lessor. So the interest rate that commonly is used is the incremental borrowing rate of the lessee. The lessee records the following at the lease inception:

Dr. Right-of-use asset	PV of payments
Cr. Capitalized lease liability	PV of payments

When the lease is determined to be an *operating lease*, the recording of the liability activity is based on the actual cash payment to be made and the difference between the PV of the payments at inception and the PV of the payments in the next year. This difference and the actual cash payment is the amount journalized to rent expense. The recording of the liability activity is shown next.

Dr. Rent expense	Imputed Interest $
Dr. Capitalized lease liability	Difference
Cr. Cash	Lease payment $

The entry to record the asset activity is the amortization of the ROU asset using the straight-line method. This is debited to rent expense and credited to the ROU asset. The asset activity is recorded as:

Dr. Rent expense	Amortization $
Cr. Right-of-use asset	Amortization $

The result is a total rent expense that is equal to the actual cash payments made during the time period, over the term of the lease.

When the lease is determined to be a *financing lease*, the initial recording of the ROU and the capitalized lease liability are determined the same way as under an operating lease. The difference from the operating lease is that the amortization expense portion of the regular payments is calculated using the straight-line method. The interest expense portion of the financing lease expense is calculated using the effective interest method. This results in a front loading of the interest expense, which makes the rent expense higher in the first years of the term of the lease. There will be a crossover point that results in a lower rent expense in the later years, as the interest decreases from year to year. This is due to the interest being calculated on the remaining balance of the lease liability under the financing lease method.

The end result is that the total rent expense recognized over the life of the lease will be exactly the same for both operating and finance leases.

The financial statement presentation of leases is as follows:

On the Balance Sheet:

Noncurrent assets:

ROU Asset

Long-term liabilities:

Capitalized Lease Liability

On the Income Statement:

Operating expenses:

Rent expense

In summary, the new FASB guidelines for leases require the capitalization of any lease longer than 12 months as either an operating lease or a finance lease. The determination of a lease as being operating or finance is based on FASB's five criteria. Companies are no longer able to categorize a lease that is longer than 12 months as off-balance sheet financing.

Equity Transactions

Corporate Capital

LOS
§1.A.2.v

Equity in a corporation is called corporate capital, stockholders' equity, or shareholders' equity and has two main components: paid-in capital and retained earnings. **Paid-in capital** represents the total amount paid by investors for equity securities. Retained earnings result from profitable operations and are generally available for shareholder dividends.

There are two major classes of stock: (1) Common Stock and (2) Preferred Stock. Each type of stock typically has a par value assigned to it. **Legal capital** is defined as the par value of the capital stock. **Par values** are nominal amounts printed on the shares, unrelated to fair market values. However, an investor who buys stock for less than par value (an infrequent event) would have a contingent liability to the corporation's creditors in the event of bankruptcy. Par values are typically low to avoid this problem. Shares can also be issued without a par value. In that case, they may be assigned a stated value, which is similar to par value but does not trigger the same contingent liability.

Common Stock

Capital stock is divided into common stock and preferred stock. If a corporation has only one type of stock, it is always common stock.

A corporation can issue stock after it has been granted a charter or certificate by the state of incorporation and can sell its shares directly or through an underwriter.

Par Value Stock

When par value common stock is sold, the par value is credited to the common stock account, but any amount received in excess of par is credited to additional paid-in capital. This distinction is important because the par value is legal capital that must be safeguarded to protect creditors in the case of bankruptcy, whereas the additional paid-in capital can be invested in the growth of the firm. For example, the issuance of 1,000 shares of $6 par value stock for $10,000 would result in $6,000 (1000 shares @ $6 par value each) of common stock recorded at par and $4,000 of additional paid-in capital recorded ($10,000 issue price minus the $6,000 par value assigned to the common stock).

Dr. Cash	10,000
Cr. Common stock (1,000 shares × $6/share)	6,000
Cr. Paid-in capital in excess of par	4,000

Preferred Stock

Preferred stock grants certain preferences compared to common stock, but preferred shareholders usually do not have the right to vote. Preferred stock typically has par value just like common stock does. Additional paid-in capital for preferred stock is computed in the same manner as discussed above for common stock (issue price minus par value equals additional paid-in capital). Some preferred stock is convertible into common stock; other preferred stock is callable at the option of the company for a specified price. Preferred stock may be issued instead of debt when an entity's debt to equity ratio is too high. Features that distinguish preferred stock include:

- *Dividend preference.* Preferred shareholders receive dividends before common shareholders. Before declaring a dividend, the board of directors must confirm that the company has sufficient retained earnings and cash to fund the dividend.

  The dividend rate on preferred stock is expressed as a percentage of par value. For example, 10% preferred stock with a $50 par value will pay an annual dividend of $5 per share if declared by the board of directors. With cumulative preferred stock, dividends that are not declared during a year accumulate and must be paid before dividends can be declared on common stock. These dividends "in arrears" are not considered a liability but are disclosed in the notes to financial statements.

Participating preferred stock calls for preferred and common shareholders to share in a total dividend declared based on a stated allocation.

- *Voting rights*. Preferred stock usually does not allow any voting rights.
- *Liquidation preference*. If the corporation is liquidated, assets are distributed first to creditors, then to preferred stockholders, and last to common shareholders.

Treasury Stock

Shares that have been issued and are later reacquired are called **treasury stock**. A firm may choose to reacquire its own shares for several reasons:

- To reduce the number of stockholders or prevent takeover attempts
- To have shares available to fulfill employee stock options
- To increase earnings per share and return on equity
- To stabilize or increase the stock price
- To distribute cash to shareholders at favorable capital gains rates

Treasury stock is reported as a reduction of stockholders' equity, not an asset because an entity cannot own itself. Shares held as treasury stock have no voting or dividend rights. Treasury stock not intended to be retired is accounted for by either the cost method or the par value method. The cost method is more commonly used in practice.

Retiring Treasury Stock

Sometimes a firm decides to retire treasury shares instead of holding them. When the shares are retired, an appropriate amount must be removed from the relevant accounts. Ordinarily, shares are repurchased and retired at the same time, using the par value method (except common stock is debited instead of treasury stock). The following examples assume the company already repurchased shares and later decided to retire the repurchased shares. For example, 10,000 shares of $5 par common stock are retired from the treasury. The shares had originally sold for $8 per share and had been repurchased as treasury stock at $9 per share.

The journal entry to record the repurchase using the cost method is:

Dr. Treasury stock	$90,000	
Cr. Cash		$90,000

When the cost method was used to originally record the repurchase, the journal entry for this event is:

Dr. Common stock ($5 × 10,000 shares)	50,000	
Dr. Additional paid-in capital—common stock ([$8 – $5] × 10,000 shares)	30,000	
Dr. Retained earnings	10,000	
Cr. Treasury stock ($9 × 10,000 shares)		90,000

The journal entry to record the repurchase using the par value method is:

Dr. Treasury stock	$50,000	
Dr. Additional paid-in capital-common stock	$30,000	
Dr. Retained earnings	$10,000	
Cr. Cash		$90,000

When the par value method is used to originally record the repurchase, the later retirement eliminates the common stock and treasury stock at par. The journal entry is:

Dr. Common stock ($5 × 10,000 shares)	50,000	
Cr. Treasury stock ($5 × 10,000 shares)		50,000

Paid-in Capital

Paid-in capital, or contributed capital, is recorded whenever capital stock is issued, but it can also be affected by other transactions:

- Sale of treasury stock at above or below cost
- Revision of capital structure to absorb a deficit (quasi-reorganization)
- Conversion of convertible bonds or preferred stock to common stock

Balance Sheet Presentation of Paid-in Capital

Capital stock and additional paid-in capital are reported in the stockholders' equity section of the balance sheet. Disclosures include the rights and privileges of each type of outstanding stock. Changes in these account balances during the year are reported in the statement of stockholders' equity. An example of the stockholders' equity section of the balance sheet is shown in Figure 1A-44.

Figure 1A-44 Contributed Capital

Bounce Sporting Goods Company Contributed Capital for Year Ended December 31, Year 1	
Stockholders' Equity	
Contributed capital:	
Preferred stock, $70 par (9%, cumulative, convertible, 10,000 shares authorized, 5,500 shares issued and outstanding)	$ 385,000
Common stock, $4 par (70,000 shares authorized, 46,500 shares issued)	186,000
Treasury stock, at cost (1,000 shares common)	(18,400)
Additional paid-in capital	652,093
Total contributed capital	$1,204,693

Retained Earnings

Retained earnings represent all income earned by the firm but not distributed to shareholders as dividends. Thus, profitable operations are the primary source of retained earnings. Other transactions that can affect retained earnings include prior-period adjustments (error corrections and certain changes in accounting principle), dividends of all types, some treasury stock transactions, and quasi-reorganizations.

Stock Options, Warrants, and Rights

Stock options, warrants, and rights give the holder the right to buy shares of stock at a set price. Since these are equity instruments, accounting for them affects paid-in capital. It is helpful to think of the stock options, warrants, and rights as pieces of paper that grant the holder the chance to purchase stock of a company at a given price (i.e., the strike price) within a set period of time (i.e., the life of the option, warrant, or right).

Stock Options

Effectively, stock options are a contract (think of them as pieces of paper) that may be awarded to employees and gives the employee the option to purchase a share of the company's stock for a stated price (i.e., the exercise or strike price) within a given time period (i.e., the life of the option). Stock options are typically good for (i.e., have a life of) 5 to 10 years before they expire. Shares may be issued to employees who exercise stock options granted to them as a form of additional compensation.

- At the date that stock options are granted to employees, the fair value of the options is usually measured using an option pricing model. The fair value of the options is recorded as additional paid-in capital and as compensation expense over the service period. The service period is the period during which the employee renders services in exchange for the compensation and frequently is the period between the date of grant and the date that the options first become exercisable. For example, an executive is granted options for the purchase of 1,000 shares of $8 par common stock at $20 per share. There is a four-year service period before the options become exercisable. At the date of grant, the options are determined to have a fair value of $6 each. Compensation expense and the equity account named Paid-in Capital—Stock Options will be increased evenly over the service period as the executive earns the options. The fair value of the options at the date of the grant is $6,000 (1,000 options @ $6 fair value each). Because the service period is four years, the compensation expense and increase to Paid-in Capital—Stock Options will be recognized as $1,500 per year over the next four years ($6,000 fair value of the options at the date of the grant divided by the service period of four years).

When the option is exercised, the executive has to hand two things over to the company. First, he/she has to turn in the options that he/she is exercising; this reduces Paid-in-Capital—Stock Options because those options are no longer outstanding. The executive also has to turn in the cash required to exercise the options. The cash required is calculated by multiplying the number of options times the strike price. The company then issues common stock to the executive and records additional paid-in-capital for the value of the Paid-in-Capital—Stock Options plus Cash that exceeds the par value of the stock being issued.

Warrants and Rights

Warrants allow the holder to acquire shares of stock at a set price within a stated time. Stock options are a specific form of stock warrants that are associated with compensation. Warrants may be bundled with other securities, such as bonds or preferred stock. When the stock price rises above the exercise price, the holder can make a profit by exercising the warrant and selling the shares or by selling the warrant itself. No entry is recorded when the warrants are issued. When the warrants are exercised, the receipt of cash and the issuance of the shares will be recorded as for any other sale of shares.

Preemptive rights give current stockholders the right to purchase any new shares issued in proportion to their current holding, preventing their ownership and voting rights from being diluted.

Dividends

Dividends are a distribution of wealth from the company to its stockholders. There are four primary forms of dividends.

1. A cash dividend, the most common form, distributes an amount of cash per share from the company to its shareholders.
2. Property dividends distribute an asset that is something other than cash to shareholders.
3. Liquidating dividends are typically completed in the form of cash sent to shareholders, but liquidating dividends represent a return of capital (i.e., the shareholder's investment). Cash, Property, and Liquidating dividends all reduce **total** stockholders equity by reducing retained earnings and possibly paid-in capital (in the case of liquidating dividends).
4. Stock dividends are the only form of dividend that does not reduce total stockholders' equity. Stock dividends simply reclassify retained earnings into common stock and, in the case of small stock dividends, additional-paid-in capital.

LOS
§1.A.2.v

Dividend distributions typically are made from retained earnings. Some firms try to maintain a steady record of dividends over time to meet investors' expectations, but new firms often pay no dividends because they have no retained earnings or because they want to retain their earning to fund their growth.

Cash Dividends

Cash dividends on preferred stock are fixed either as a percentage of par or as a per-share amount. Dividends on common stock vary at the discretion of the board of directors. Cash dividends become a current liability on the date they are declared by the board of directors. The dividends are payable to stockholders who own shares as of the record date and are distributed on the payment date. For example, the board declares a $1/share dividend on 200,000 shares outstanding. This dividend results in a distribution (reduction) of retained earnings of $200,000 (200,000 shares times $1 per share dividend).

Property Dividends

Dividends payable in property, merchandise, or investments are called property dividends and are accounted for at the fair value of the assets transferred. At the date of declaration, a gain or loss is recognized for the difference between the asset's cost and its carrying value.

For example, a company declares a property dividend of securities held as an investment. These securities have a cost and carrying value of $1,000,000 and a fair market value of $1,300,000. Because there is a difference between the market value of the property to be distributed and the carrying value (i.e., the amount the asset is carried at on the books), the process to record the property dividend is a two-step process. First, write-up (i.e., recognize a gain) or write-down (i.e., recognize a loss) the asset from its carrying value to its fair market value. At this point, the asset is on the books at its fair market value. Second, record the dividend at the fair market value of the property to be distributed. The result is a decrease to retained earnings for the fair value of the property to be distributed. When the property dividend is distributed, the asset is removed from the company's books.

Liquidating Dividends

A dividend that reduces paid-in capital rather than retained earnings is a liquidating dividend because it is a return of invested capital, not a return on investment. Liquidating dividends typically occur when a firm is ceasing operations Companies must notify shareholders when a dividend is a liquidating dividend. The company must also identify how much of the dividend is considered a return of capital (coming from additional paid-in capital) and how much is a distribution of wealth (coming from retained earnings).

For example, if a firm with a $750,000 balance in retained earnings declares a $1,000,000 dividend, then $750,000 is considered a distribution of wealth out of retained earnings and $250,000 ($1,000,000 dividend minus $750,000 stemming from retained earnings) is considered a return of capital from the company's additional paid-in capital account.

Cumulative Dividends

If preferred stock is cumulative, a corporation that fails to pay a dividend in a given year owes the preferred dividend "in arrears" and must pay the dividends in arrears plus the current year's dividend before it can pay any dividends to common shareholders. Unless preferred stock is labeled noncumulative, it is legally considered to be cumulative. Like common stock, noncumulative preferred stock carries no obligations to pay dividends.

Stock Dividends

LOS §1.A.2.w

Unlike cash or property dividends, stock dividends do not affect total assets or shareholders' equity. Instead, they reclassify retained earnings as paid-in capital. This capitalization of earnings retains them in the corporation permanently. Effectively, a stock dividend moves a balance of value from retained earnings to common stock and, in the case of small stock dividends, additional-paid-in-capital as well. Small stock dividends are the distribution of less than 20% to 25% of the number of shares outstanding and reduce retained earnings by the **market value** of the shares to be issued. By contrast, large stock dividends involve the transfer of more than 20% to 25% of the number of shares outstanding and reduce retained earnings by the **par value** of the shares to be issued.

For example, a firm has 100,000 of its $1 par value shares issued and outstanding. The market value is $15 per share. When the firm declares a 10% stock dividend and fulfills the dividend, this stock dividend is considered a small stock dividend because it is less than 20 to 25%. The firm reclassifies the fair value of the stock dividend (100,000 shares times 10% dividend times $15 market price per share = $150,000) from retained earnings and into common stock for the par value of the shares (10,000 shares @ $1 par equals $10,000 par value). The additional amount above par value ($150,000 minus $10,000 par equals $140,000 additional) is reclassified as additional paid in capital.

Using the same fact pattern as above, but assuming the firm had issued a 30% stock dividend (i.e., a large stock dividend) instead, the impact on retained earnings would be for the par value of the stock dividend as opposed to the fair value used in a small stock dividend. The number of shares issued in the 30% stock dividend would be 100,000 shares times 30% or 30,000 shares. The par value of those shares (30,000 @ $1 par or $30,000) would be reclassified from retained earnings to common stock. There is no additional paid in capital when issuing a large stock dividend.

Stock dividends often are issued when a firm wants to give something to shareholders without using its cash. The company can reinvest its cash, and shareholders can sell these extra shares on the open market. Although shareholders maintain their same proportional ownership in the company after the stock dividend, there are more shares outstanding, which will cause book value per share and market price per share to adjust downward. This effect is more noticeable for large stock dividends, which (like stock splits) are often used to decrease the stock price to a more marketable level. Therefore, the market usually treats large stock dividends as if they were stock splits.

Stock Splits

A **stock split** reduces the market price per share of stock without changing ownership by issuing a specific number of new shares for each old share outstanding and reducing the par value per share by the same proportion. For example, a 4-for-1 stock split on 100,000 shares of stock trading at $400 per share results in 400,000 shares of stock trading at about $100 per share. Thus, there is no net change to stockholders' equity. Stock splits are used to make the stock more affordable, increasing overall trading. No entry is recorded for a stock split, but a memorandum notes the changed par value of the shares as well as the new number of shares outstanding.

A **reverse split** reduces the number of outstanding shares and proportionally increases the per-share price. For example, a 1-for-20 reverse stock split would transform 200,000 shares at $1 per share into 10,000 shares at approximately $20 per share.

Revenue Recognition—Accounting Standards Update

Revenue recognition under U.S. Generally Accepted Accounting Principles (GAAP) has always been different from International Financial Reporting Standards (IFRS). For this reason, the Financial Accounting Standards Board (FASB) and the International Accounting Standards Board (IASB) got together to develop a common revenue standard that would:

1. Remove inconsistencies and weaknesses in revenue requirements.
2. Provide a more robust framework for addressing revenue issues.
3. Improve comparability of revenue recognition practices across entities, industries, jurisdictions, and capital markets.
4. Provide more useful information to users of financial statements through improved disclosure requirements.
5. Simplify the preparation of financial statements by reducing the number of requirements to which an entity must refer.

The FASB created the new Accounting Standards Update (ASU) 2014-09, *Revenue from Contracts with Customers (Topic 606),* that was issued on May 28, 2014. This new Topic 606 supersedes the revenue recognition requirements in Topic 605, *Revenue Recognition*, including the cost guidance in Topic 605-35, *Revenue Recognition – Construction-Type and Production-Type Contracts.* The guidance in this Update is largely principles-based instead of being rules-based as the previous standard was.

The effective date for a public entity was for annual reporting periods beginning after December 15, 2016. This includes the interim periods within the annual reporting period. Early application of this Topic was not permitted. The effective date for nonpublic entities was for annual reporting periods beginning after December 15, 2017, including interim periods within any annual period beginning after December 15, 2018. A retrospective approach is used for any prior period statements included in the annual report for comparison purposes.

The IASB issued IFRS 15, *Revenue from Contracts with Customers*, and it was implemented on January 1, 2018. Now the FASB and IASB standards are in sync.

The New FASB Guidelines

LOS
§1.A.2.y

The Update states that an entity should recognize revenue to show the transfer of promised goods or services to customers in an amount reflecting the consideration the entity expects to be entitled to in exchange for those goods and services.

To achieve this, an entity should apply the following five steps:

1. Identify the contract(s) with a customer.
2. Identify the performance obligations in the contract.
3. Determine the transaction price.

4. Allocate the transaction price to the performance obligations in the contract.
5. Recognize revenue when (or as) the entity satisfies a performance obligation.

Step 5 is critical to the new Topic 606 due to a change in the wording that is used. As you read the following, pay attention to the use of **control**. The transfer of a good or service all has to do with who has control, the seller or the buyer.

> "An entity should recognize revenue when or as it satisfies a performance obligation by transferring a promised good or service to a customer. A good or service is transferred when (or as) the customer obtains control of that good or service."

Each performance obligation is evaluated to determine whether the entity **satisfies** the obligation over time **by transferring control of the good or service over time**. If the performance obligation **is not satisfied over time**, then the obligation **is satisfied at a point in time.**

When an entity **transfers control** of an asset **over time,** the performance obligation and revenue are recognized over time. Transfer of control occurs if one of the following three is met:

1. The customer simultaneously receives and consumes the benefits provided by the entity's performance as it is performed by the entity.
2. The entity's performance creates or enhances an asset (i.e., work in process) that the customer controls as the asset is created or enhanced.
3. The entity's performance does not create an asset with an alternative use to the entity *and* the entity has an enforceable right to payment for the performance completed to date.

If one of the above three criteria is not met, the performance obligation is considered to be satisfied at a **point in time**. The entity must consider indicators of the transfer of control to be able to determine the point in time when a customer obtains control of a promised asset and the entity satisfies a performance obligation. These indicators include, but are not limited to, the following five:

1. The entity has a present right to payment for the asset.
2. The customer has legal title to the asset.
3. The entity has transferred physical possession of the asset.
4. The customer has the significant risks and rewards of ownership of the asset.
5. The customer has accepted the asset.

The guidance in this Topic applies to all contracts with customers **except** for the following:

- Lease contracts under Topic 842, *Leases*
- Insurance contracts under Topic 944, *Financial Services-Insurance*
- Financial instruments under various Topics regarding receivables, investments, liabilities, debt, derivatives and hedging, financial instruments, and transfers and servicing.

- Guarantees under Topic 460, *Guarantees*. This *excludes product or service warranties* which are covered under the Update.
- Nonmonetary exchanges between entities in the same industry, such as oil companies

When performance obligations are satisfied over time, the entity can recognize revenue over time by measuring the progress toward complete satisfaction of the performance obligation. This is done by allocating the transaction price to the performance obligation based on a reasonable measure. The objective of the allocation is for the amount to depict the amount of consideration the entity expects to be entitled to, in exchange for the transfer of promised goods or services to the customer. The transaction price of each performance obligation identified in the contract will be allocated based on a relative standalone selling price. The best evidence of the *standalone selling price* is the observable price of a good or service when the entity sells the good or service separately, in similar circumstances, to similar customers.

If the standalone selling price is not observable under the above circumstances, the Update includes methods for estimating the standalone price. These methods include, but are not limited to, the following:

a. **Adjusted market assessment approach:** Evaluate the market that the entity sells the goods or services in and estimate the price that a customer in that market would be willing to pay. This could include starting with a price a competitor of the entity charges and adjusting it to reflect the entity's costs and margins.

b. **Expected cost plus a margin approach:** Forecast the expected costs of satisfying a performance obligation and then add an appropriate margin.

c. **Residual approach:** Estimate the standalone selling price of one or more of the goods or services by subtracting the sum of the observable standalone selling prices from the total transaction price. An entity can use this approach *only if one* of the following criteria is met:

   1. The entity sells the same good or service to different customers for a broad range of prices.
   2. The entity has not established a price for that good or service, and the good or service has not previously been sold on a standalone basis.

Methods for Measuring Progress toward Complete Satisfaction of a Performance Obligation

Topic 606 defines two methods that can be used to measure an entity's progress toward complete satisfaction of a performance obligation that is satisfied over time. These two methods are:

1. Output Methods
2. Input Methods

1. **Output Methods:** Figure 1A-45 provides the information to select the output method for the allocation, specific output methods that can be used and how to evaluate the method, and the disadvantages of using the output method.

Figure 1A-45 Output Methods

Criteria	Recognize revenue on the basis of **direct measurement of the value to the customer** of the goods or services transferred to date, relative to the remaining goods or services promised in the contract
Output Methods	• Surveys of performance completed to date • Appraisals of results achieved • Milestones reached • Time elapsed • Units produced or units delivered
Evaluation of Output Methods	Consider whether the output selected faithfully depicts performance toward complete satisfaction of the **performance obligation**
Practical Expedient	If the entity has a right to consideration from a customer, in an amount corresponding directly with the value to the customer of the entity's performance completed to date, revenue can be recognized in the amount the entity has a right to invoice
Disadvantages	• The outputs used may not be directly observable • The information required to apply the outputs used may not be available without undue cost

The FASB provided examples of output methods, some of which are summarized here.

LOS §1.A.2.x

Example 1A Customer simultaneously receives and consumes the benefits of performance obligations satisfied over time

A firm enters into a *contract to provide monthly payroll processing services* to a customer for a one year time period. In this example, the payroll processing services are accounted for as a single performance obligation satisfied *over time* because the customer simultaneously receives and consumes the benefits of the firm's performance in processing each payroll transaction as and when each transaction is processed.

Therefore, the firm would recognize revenue over time by measuring the progress toward complete satisfaction of the performance obligation.

Example 1B Allocating the transaction price

Assume a firm enters into a contract with a customer to sell Products A, B, and C in exchange for $100. The performance obligation will be satisfied for each of the products at a different point in time. The firm regularly sells Product A separately, which means the standalone selling price is *directly observable*. The standalone selling prices of Products B and C are not directly observable. This means the firm must estimate them.

The firm decides to use the *adjusted market assessment approach* for Product B and the *expected cost plus a margin approach* for Product C.

Product	Estimated Standalone Selling Price	Method
A	$ 50	Directly observable
B	25	Adjusted market assessment approach
C	75	Expected cost plus a margin approach
Total	$150	

The customer ends up with a discount by purchasing the bundle of goods based on the sum of the standalone selling price of $150, as compared to the promised consideration of $100. In this situation, the $50 discount is allocated proportionately across the three products to get the allocated transaction price as follows:

Product	Allocated Transaction Price	
A	$ 33	($50 ÷ $150) × $100
B	17	($25 ÷ $150) × $100
C	50	($75 ÷ $150) × $100
Total	$100	

The allocated transaction price would be recognized as revenue upon the transfer of control as each of the products is delivered.

Example 1C Allocating a Discount Cases I, II, and III

A firm regularly sells Products A, B, and C individually and establishes the following standalone selling prices:

Product	Standalone Selling Price
A	$ 40
B	55
C	45
Total	$140

Case I: A firm enters into a contract with a customer to sell Products A, B, and C in exchange for $100. This contract includes a discount of $40 from the standalone selling price. Normally, this would be allocated proportionately to all 3 performance obligations. However, because the firm regularly sells Products B and C together for $60 and Product A for $40 there is evidence that the entire discount should be allocated to the promises to transfer Products B and C.

If they transfer control of Products B and C at the same point in time, then the firm can account for the transfer of these products as a single performance obligation. This means the entity would allocate $60 of the transaction price to the single performance obligation. Revenue of $60 would be recognized when Products B and C are transferred to the customer at the same time.

However, if the contract requires the transfer of control of Products B and C at different points in time, the original standalone prices are used to allocate the $60 transaction price.

Product	Standalone Selling Price	Allocated Transaction Price	
B	$ 55	$ 33	($55 ÷ $100) × $60
C	45	27	($45 ÷ $100) × $60
Total	$100	$ 60	

Case II is an example of when the *residual approach is appropriate*. The firm enters into a contract with a customer to sell Products A, B, and C as described in Case I. The contract also includes a promise to transfer Product D. The total consideration for the contract is $130. The standalone price for Product D is highly variable because the firm sells Product D to different customers over a range of $15 to $45. Therefore, the firm chooses to estimate the standalone selling price of Product D using the *residual approach*.

First, the firm has to determine if any discount should be allocated to the other performance obligations. As in Case I, the firm regularly sells Products B and C together for $60 and Product A for $40; observable evidence shows that $100 should be allocated to those three products and a $40 discount should be allocated to the promises to transfer Products B and C. Using the residual approach, the firm estimates the standalone selling price of Product D to be $30 as follows:

Product	Standalone Selling Price	Method
A	$ 40	Directly observable
B and C	60	Directly observable with discount
D	30	Residual approach
Total	$ 130	

Case III is an example of when the *residual approach is not appropriate*. Assume all the same facts in Case II except the transaction price is $105 instead of $130. The use of the residual approach would result in Product D having a standalone selling price of $5. Because this is out of the range of Product D's standalone selling price range of $15 to $45, the firm concludes that $5 does not faithfully depict the amount of consideration the firm should expect to be entitled to. In this Case, the firm would review the observable data, including sales and margin reports, to estimate the standalone selling price of Product D using another method. The entity decides to allocate the transaction price of $105 to Products A, B, C, and D using the relative standalone selling prices that totaled $130 in Case II.

2. **Input Methods:** Figure 1A-46 provides the information to select the input method for the allocation, specific input methods that can be used and how to evaluate the method, and a disadvantage of using the input method.

Figure 1A-46 Input Methods

Criteria	Recognize revenue on the basis of the **entity's efforts or inputs** to the satisfaction of a performance obligation
Input Methods	• Resources consumed • Labor hours expended • Costs incurred • Time elapsed • Machine hours used
Evaluation of Output Methods	If the entity's efforts or inputs are expended evenly throughout the performance period, it may be appropriate to recognize revenue on a straight-line basis
Disadvantage	• There may not be a direct relationship between an input and the transfer of control of goods or services to a customer

The FASB provided examples of input methods that are summarized here.

Example 2A Measuring progress when making goods or services available

A firm, the owner and manager of health clubs, enters into a contract with a customer for one year of access to any of its health clubs. The customer has unlimited use of the health clubs and promises to pay $100 per month. In this example, the promise to the customer is to provide the service of making the health clubs available for the customer to use as and when they wish. The extent to which the customer uses the health clubs does not affect the amount of the remaining services they are entitled to. Therefore, the customer simultaneously receives and consumes the benefits of the performance obligation as the firm is making the health clubs available. This is a performance obligation that is satisfied over time. It can also be determined that the customer benefits from the service evenly throughout the year.

Therefore, the best measure of progress toward complete satisfaction of the performance obligation over time is a *time-based measure*. The firm would recognize revenue on a straight-line basis throughout the year at $100 per month.

Example 2B—Uninstalled materials

During November Year 1, a firm contracted with a customer to refurbish a 3-story building and install new elevators for a total amount of $5 million. In this case, the promised refurbishment service, including the installation of the elevators, is considered to be a single performance obligation satisfied over time.

Transaction price		$5,000,000
Expected costs:		
Elevators	1,500,000	
Other costs	2,500,000	4,000,000
Profit		$1,000,000

In this example, satisfaction of the performance obligation will use an input method based on *costs incurred* to measure progress.

The customer obtains control of the elevators when they are delivered to the site during December Year 1. However, the elevators will not be installed until June Year 2. Notice that the cost to purchase the elevators at $1.5 million is significant relative to the total expected costs of $4 million. The firm concludes that including the costs to procure the elevators in the measure of progress would overstate the extent of the entity's performance.

As of December 31 Year 1:

- Other costs incurred, excluding the elevators, are $500,000
- Performance is 20% complete: $500,000 ÷ $2,500,000

At December 31 Year 1, the firm would recognize the following:

Revenue	$2,200,000[a]
Cost of Goods Sold	2,000,000[b]
Profit	$ 200,000

(a) Revenue is calculated as (20% × ($5,000,000 transaction price − $1,500,000 cost of the elevators)) + $1,500,000

(b) Cost of goods sold is $1,500,000 (the cost of the elevators) + $500,000 (other costs incurred)

The New Terminology

The new terminology that is used, as well as some familiar terminology, is defined by FASB in the Update as follows:

- **Contract:** Agreement between two or more parties that creates enforceable rights and obligations.
- **Contract Asset:** An entity's right to consideration in exchange for goods or services that the entity has transferred to a customer, when that right is conditioned on something other than the passage of time. An example is the entity's future performance.
- **Contract Liability:** An entity's obligation to transfer goods or services to a customer, from whom the entity has received consideration, or the amount due, from the customer.
- **Customer:** A party that has contracted with an entity to obtain goods or services, that are an output of the entity's ordinary activities, in exchange for consideration.
- **Receivables:** Represents the unconditional right for the entity to receive consideration (payment) in exchange for goods or services that the entity has transferred to a customer.

The exact name to be used for these accounts is up to the entity. In a way, this has not changed very much because the entity can still use the account called "unearned revenue" when a customer makes a deposit for a service or product to be provided in the future.

Major Changes from the Old Standard and Terminology No Longer Used

The new standard is principles-based rather than being rules-based. In addition, it no longer specifies rules and guidelines based on a specific industry such as construction. Figure 1A-47 that follows summarizes these major changes and the terminology that is no longer used. When taking the exam, *block these from your mind*.

Figure 1A-47 Summary of Old and New Terminology

Old Standard Guidance	Terms No Longer Used	New Term if Applicable
Industry guidance no longer applies	Software, Real Estate, Telecommunications, and Construction	Recognize revenue *over time* based on transfer of control. Two methods allowed: **1.** Output Method **2.** Input Method
Revenue Recognition before Delivery	**1.** Completion of Production Basis **2.** Percentage-of-Completion Method	
Revenue Recognition after Delivery	**1.** Installment Sales Method **2.** Cost Recovery Method **3.** Deposit Method	
Accounting for Long-Term Construction Projects	**1.** Percentage-of-Completion Method **2.** Completed-Contract Method	
Point-of-Sale	Point-of-Sale	Recognize revenue at a *point in time*

Gains and Losses

A **gain** is the excess of revenue over cost for a transaction outside the normal course of business (e.g., from the sale of fixed assets or investments, or from early retirement of debt). A **loss** occurs when cost exceeds revenues for a transaction outside the normal course of business (e.g., fire loss, loss on sale of fixed assets or investments, loss on early debt retirement). Gains and losses are shown below operating income on the income statement.

Disposition of Property, Plant, and Equipment

PP&E can be sold or exchanged, involuntarily converted, or abandoned. The company should depreciate the asset to the date of the disposal and then remove all related accounts from the books. At the time of disposition, any difference between the depreciated book value and the asset's disposal value must be recognized as a gain or loss. Gains or losses on dispositions of plant assets are reported as part of income from continuing operations unless the disposal is related to a discontinued operation.

Sale

When PP&E is sold, depreciation must be recorded from the date of the last depreciation entry to the date of disposal. This brings the book value of the asset up to date in order to measure the gain or loss from the sale of the asset.

For example, a firm has a machine that originally cost $34,000 and has recorded $3,400 in depreciation annually for the past seven years. On April 1 of Year 8, the machine is sold for $10,000. To determine the gain or loss on the sale, the firm must first account for the depreciation from January through March of Year 8, which is ($3,400 × 3/12) = $850. The firm records this amount in a journal entry with a debit to depreciation expense and a credit to accumulated depreciation. This brings the balance in accumulated depreciation to:

$$[(\$3,400/\text{year} \times 7 \text{ years}) + \$850] = \underline{\$24,650}$$

The net book value of the machine is the difference between its cost and its accumulated depreciation: $34,000 − $24,650 = $9,350

The gain (loss) on the sale is the difference between the selling price and the net book value: $10,000 − $9,350 = $650

Involuntary Conversion

Flood, fire, earthquake, theft, and condemnation are types of involuntary conversions of assets.

Even if the converted asset is replaced immediately by another asset, a gain or loss on disposal (i.e., involuntary conversion) must be recognized.

For example, a plant was purchased for $1,600,000 and had $600,000 of accumulated depreciation when it was destroyed by fire; therefore, the book basis of the asset at the time of the fire was $1,000,000 ($1,600,000 cost minus $600,000 accumulated depreciation). The insurance company paid the firm $1,700,000 in settlement, and the company will record a $700,000 gain on the disposal of the asset because the insurance settlement exceeded the book basis by $700,000 ($1,700,000 insurance settlement minus $1,000,000 book basis).

Abandonment

Abandoned or scrapped items that do not result in any recovery of cash produce a loss equal to the book value of the asset. If any scrap value is received, a gain or loss is recognized for the difference between the asset's scrap value and its book value. Fully depreciated assets that are still in use should be disclosed in the notes to financial statements.

Expense Recognition

LOS
§1.A.2.z

The accrual basis of accounting is used for external financial reporting because it is a better predictor of a firm's future financial performance than the cash basis.

Accrual accounting is based on expense recognition principle that is based on the matching principle.

LOS
§1.A.2.cc

The matching principle requires expenses to be matched against the revenues that they help to generate. Thus, the cost of inventory is initially capitalized as an asset on the balance sheet and cannot be recognized as an expense (COGS) until it is sold to generate sales revenue. Similarly, property, plant, and equipment (PP&E) is capitalized as an asset and then depreciated over time or use in order to match its cost to the revenue that it helps to generate in each period. Interest expense is recognized in each period when the borrowed funds are available to help the firm generate revenues, and wage expense is recognized in each period when employees' work helps the firm to generate revenues. Selling and administrative costs and research and development (R&D) are expensed in the period incurred, rather than being capitalized as assets, because their future revenue-generating ability is unmeasurable or uncertain. Recognizing estimated future bad debt and estimated future warranty costs are also examples of following the matching principle because they match these costs to the underlying revenues they helped to generate.

Comprehensive Income

LOS
§1.A.2.dd

FASB defines comprehensive income as "the change in equity [net assets] of a business enterprise during a period from transactions and other events and circumstances from non-owner sources. It includes all changes in equity during a period except those resulting from investments by owners and distributions to owners." These changes result from the effects of exchange transactions, the entity's productive efforts, price changes, and peripheral transactions.

Thus, comprehensive income includes all revenues, expenses, gains, and losses that affect a business during the period, including both realized gains and losses that are included in net income and unrealized gains and losses that are reported as part of other comprehensive income. The main items of other comprehensive income are:

- Unrealized gains and losses on investments in available-for-sale debt securities
- Unrealized gains and losses on certain derivative financial instruments
- Pension losses that result from the pension liability adjustment
- Certain foreign currency translation adjustments

Other Comprehensive Income

Comprehensive income includes all events that affect stockholders' equity except for transactions with the stockholders. Per-share amounts are not reported for comprehensive income.

Net income is closed to retained earnings and other comprehensive income is closed to accumulated other comprehensive income, so each is accumulated separately as a component of shareholders' equity. To avoid double-counting when a gain or loss previously reported in other comprehensive income is later realized and reported in net income, a reclassification adjustment is required. This adjustment removes the effect of the gain or loss, once it has been realized, from accumulated other comprehensive income.

Comprehensive income can be presented either in a single combined financial statement or in two separate and sequential financial statements.

- *Single combined statement of income and comprehensive income.* A company can choose to present net income as a subtotal, followed by the items of other comprehensive income, with comprehensive income as the total. Although straightforward, this approach gives less prominence to net income. Figure 1A-48 illustrates a single combined statement of comprehensive income.

Figure 1A-48 Combined Income Statement—Comprehensive Income

Bounce Sporting Goods Company	
Statement of Income and Comprehensive Income	
for Year Ended December 31, Year 1	
Sales revenue	$1,120,000
Cost of goods sold	840,000
Gross profit	280,000
Operating expenses	126,000
Net income	154,000
Unrealized holding gain, net of tax	42,000
Comprehensive income	$196,000

- *Two-statement approach.* The first statement (statement of income) is presented first and reports net income, followed by the statement of comprehensive income. The second statement, the statement of comprehensive income, starts with net income and then adds (subtracts) the items of other comprehensive income to arrive at the second statement, the total comprehensive income statement. This presentation clarifies the relationship between net income and other comprehensive income. Figure 1A-49 illustrates the two separate statements of income and comprehensive income.

Figure 1A-49 Separate Income Statement and Comprehensive Income Statement

Bounce Sporting Goods Company Income Statement for Year Ended December 31, Year 1		Bounce Sporting Goods Company Comprehensive Income Statement for Year Ended December 31, Year 1	
Sales revenue	$1,120,000	Net income	$154,000
Cost of goods sold	840,000	Other comprehensive income	
Gross profit	280,000	Unrealized holding gain, net of tax	42,000
Operating expenses	126,000	Comprehensive income	$196,000
Net income	$154,000		

Discontinued Operations

LOS §1.A.2.ee

A goal of financial reporting is to help investors and creditors to predict the future. Since a business segment that has been (or will be) discontinued has little predictive value, its impact on the firm's income statement is reported separately as an irregular item below income from continuing operations. When a business segment is being discontinued, there are two components:

1. Any operating income or loss for the segment that has been sold during the year or is being held for sale would be reported under *discontinued operations*, net of tax.
2. Any losses or gains related to sale or impairment of the segment's assets are also reported under *discontinued operations*, net of tax.

Operations that will be discontinued are transferred from the held-and-used category to the held-for-sale category on the balance sheet.

Accounting Issues

A discontinued operation is when a component or group of components of an entity are 1) disposed for by sale or other than sale, or classified as held-for-sale, and 2) the disposal represents a strategic shift that has or will have a major effect on an entity's operation and financial results.

When a company decides to discontinue a major component or part of its business, we refer to this as "discontinued operations." The date of this decision becomes the decision date. On or after the decision date, the operation is officially classified as held for sale. When the operation is officially disposed of, this becomes the disposal date.

Calculating the Gain or Loss on Disposal

Two basic amounts must be known to calculate the gain or loss on operations: the loss or gain from operations of the discontinued operation (net of tax) and the loss or gain on disposal of the discontinued operation (net of tax). The total of these amounts equals the loss or gain on the discontinued operation. The loss from operations is calculated by summing these items:

- Income (or loss) from the discontinued operation for the year is reported.
- Gain (or loss) on the disposal is reported.

The gain or loss on disposal is determined by comparing the net proceeds to the carrying value of the operation. The formula for the gain (loss) on disposal is:

> Gain (Loss) on Disposal = (Amount Received − Costs to Dispose of the Assets) − Carrying Value of Component's Net Assets

The first step in calculating a gain or loss on disposal of an operation is to determine the costs to sell the asset. These costs are deducted from the fair value of the asset. Incremental direct costs of transacting the sale (costs that arise directly from the decision to sell) include:

- Brokers' commissions and other selling fees
- Fees for fair value assessment of operation
- Legal fees
- Title transfer fees
- Closing costs

The next step in calculating the gain or loss on the disposal of an operation is to calculate the carrying value of the operation. This should include capitalization of interest and other costs. Generally, all material costs needed to get the asset ready for its initial use, including any interest costs from financing the asset, should be capitalized to show a more accurate initial investment cost.

Once the carrying value of the operation is determined, the fair value of the operation is assessed by an actuary. If the total carrying value is greater than the fair value less these costs, then a loss on disposal is recognized in the period in which the asset is classified as held for sale. The component is considered impaired, a loss is recognized, and the carrying value is written down to fair value less cost to sell. Subsequently, gains may be recognized based on increases in fair value less cost to sell but not in excess of the total loss previously recognized. However, if there is a gain on disposal, it is not recognized until the period of actual sale.

Financial Statement Impact

The results of discontinued operations, less applicable income tax effect, are reported as a separate component of income after income from continuing operations. Figure 1A-50 illustrates the presentation of discontinued operations on the income statement.

Figure 1A-50 Income Statement—Discontinued Operations

Income from continuing operations		$8,000,000
Discontinued operations		
Loss from operation of discontinued division (net of tax)	$120,000	
Loss from disposal of division (net of tax)	200,000	320,000
Net income		$7,680,000

Future-Period Adjustments

Future losses from the end of the fiscal year until the anticipated date of sale are recognized in the periods when they occur. In addition, amounts reported in discontinued operations may need to be adjusted in later periods by classifying them separately in discontinued operations for the current period, and disclosing the nature and amount of the adjustments.

Differences in Financial Results: IFRS versus GAAP

LOS
§1.A.2.ff

The International Accounting Standards Board (IASB) is responsible for the approval of International Financial Accounting and Reporting Standards (IFRS). A key objective of the IASB is to bring about convergence of accounting standards, so the IASB has been working closely with the FASB to harmonize the international standards with U.S. GAAP.

The IASB's focus is to require similar transactions and events to be accounted for in ways that are similar to each other but different from the accounting for other types of transactions and events, both within an entity and among entities across industries and geographical boundaries. To that end, the IASB seeks to reduce the number of alternative treatments for similar transactions or events. The next discussion covers some common financial statement elements for which the IFRS differs from U.S. GAAP. Candidates for the CMA exam should review the current pronouncements from the IASB and FASB by visiting their Web sites (www.iasb.org and www.fasb.org) in preparation for the exam.

Figure 1A-51 compares IFRS and U.S. GAAP and shows the relevant International Accounting Standard (IAS) for each item.

Figure 1A-51 IFRS–GAAP Differences

Topic	IFRS	U.S. GAAP	IAS/IFRS
Expense recognition: Share-based payments and employee benefits	Compensation cost is recognized on an accelerated basis.	Compensation cost can be recognized on a straight-line basis or over an accelerated basis.	IAS No. 19, *Employee Benefits* IFRS No. 2, *Share-Based Payment*
Intangible assets: Development costs and revaluation	Development costs may be capitalized; revaluation permitted if the asset trades in an active market.	Generally, development costs are expensed as incurred; revaluation is prohibited.	IAS No. 38, *Intangible Assets*

Figure 1A-51 (Continued)

Topic	IFRS	U.S. GAAP	IAS/IFRS
Inventories: Costing methods	LIFO is prohibited.	LIFO is permitted.	IAS No. 2, *Inventories*
Inventories: Valuation	Inventory is carried at the lower of cost or net realizable value.	Inventory is carried at the lower of cost or market for LIFO or retail inventory; lower of cost or NRV for FIFO or weighted average.	IAS No. 2, *Inventories*
Inventories: Write-downs	Previous write-downs of inventory can be reversed if the impairment no longer exists.	Any write-downs of inventory become the new cost basis and cannot be reversed.	IAS No. 2, *Inventories*
Leases:	Lessee accounts for all leases as a financing lease unless the asset cost is $5,000 or less.	Lessee accounts for leases as short term (< 12 months), operating, or financing.	IFRS No. 16, *Leases*
Long-lived assets: Revaluation, depreciation, and capitalization of borrowing costs	Long-lived assets are recorded at historical cost or a revalued amount (fair value).	Long-lived assets are recorded at historical cost. Revaluation is prohibited.	IAS No. 16, *Property, Plant, and Equipment*
Impairment of assets: Determination, calculation, and reversal of loss	Impairment is recorded when an asset's carrying value exceeds the discounted present value of the asset's expected future cash flows and fair value less costs to sell.	Impairment is recorded when an asset's carrying value exceeds the expected future cash flows on an undiscounted basis.	IAS No. 36, *Impairment of Assets*
Consolidation: Control	The basis for consolidation is whether control exists or not. Control can be achieved even when less than 50% of the voting rights are held by an investor. Control exists when the investor has **all** three of the following characteristics: power over the investee; exposure (or rights) to variable returns from its involvement with the investee; and the ability to exercise its power over the investee to affect the amount of the investor's return.	Under U.S. GAAP, generally a controlling financial interest exists if the investor owns (directly or indirectly) a majority voting interest (> 50% voting interest) in another investee. With control of that investee, the investor would need to consolidate the investee.	IFRS No. 10, *Consolidated Financial Statements*

Intangibles

IAS No. 38, *Intangible Assets*, prescribes accounting treatment for intangible assets and specifies how to measure the carrying value and the required disclosures.

The standard identifies intangible assets as items that are capable of being separated or divided from the entity and sold, transferred, licensed, rented, or exchanged either individually or together with a related contract. An intangible asset can also be created by contractual or other legal rights. To recognize an item as an intangible asset, the firm must have control over the asset and be able to obtain the future economic benefit arising from that asset.

The IASB recognizes capitalization of expenditure on in-process research and development projects if the following conditions are met:

- The technical feasibility of completing the project has been established.
- The firm has demonstrated the ability to use or sell the intangible.

- The firm intends to complete the project.
- Adequate technical, financial, and other resources are available to complete the development of the product.
- The expenditure attributable to the asset during its development can be reliably measured.

Inventory

IAS No.2, *Inventories,* prescribes accounting treatment for inventories. The primary issue in accounting for inventories is the amount of cost to be recognized as an asset and carried forward until the inventory is sold and the related revenues are recognized.

The standard requires that "cost of inventories that are not ordinarily interchangeable and goods or services produced and segregated for specific projects shall be assigned by using specific identification of their individual costs." Specific identification should be used when items are segregated for specific projects. When specific identification cannot be used, the cost of inventories "shall be assigned using either the first-in, first-out (FIFO) or weighted-average cost formulas." Unlike U.S. GAAP, the standard does not permit the use of LIFO.

Leases

IFRS and the new U.S. GAAP lease accounting have converged from the accounting perspective of the lessee. Under the new FASB guidelines, the lessee must report a lease of more than twelve months as either an operating or financing lease, based on a set of criteria. Under IFRS, the lessee has to report a lease of more than $5,000 as a financing lease. For both an operating and financing lease based on FASB and a financing lease based on IFRS, a leased asset and the related lease liability are recognized on the balance sheet.

Property, Plant, and Equipment

IAS No. 16, *Property, Plant, and Equipment,* prescribes the accounting treatment for PP&E and the related accounting for depreciation expense and impairment losses. It defines PP&E as tangible items that are held for use in production or supply of goods or services and are expected to be used for more than one accounting period. Its recognition criteria are similar to U.S. GAAP in that it requires two conditions: future economic benefit and the cost can be measured reliably.

The standard specifies costs that can be capitalized and those that must be excluded. For example, cost to transport the asset to its location and estimated costs to dismantle and remove the asset can be capitalized. Costs that cannot be capitalized as part of PP&E include the costs to open a new facility or conduct business at a new location.

The standard allows the choice of either the cost model or the revaluation method for valuing PP&E after initial acquisition. The cost method recognizes the value of PP&E at its cost less accumulated depreciation. By contrast, the revaluation method requires periodic estimation of the fair value, and the asset is carried at the fair value less any accumulated depreciation from the date of remeasurement. Thus, the cost method measures accumulated depreciation from the date of purchase, whereas the revaluation method values it from the date of re-measurement.

The standard allows for a variety of depreciation methods to allocate the cost of the asset over its useful life. These methods include the straight-line method, the diminishing-balance method, and the units-of-production method.

Consolidated Financial Statements: Control

IFRS is generally more principles-based while U.S. GAAP is generally more rules-based. U.S. GAAP generally requires consolidation when the investor owns, directly or indirectly, greater than 50% of the voting shares of the investee because the investor is considered to have control of that investee. If the investee entity is a variable interest entity (VIE), then the controlling entity is the VIE's primary beneficiary. IFRS does not have separate guidance on control for consolidating a VIE.

Under IFRS No. 10, *Consolidated Financial Statements*, like under U.S. GAAP, the ability of one entity (investor) to control another entity (investee) requires that the controlled entity be consolidated with the investor. However, under IFRS the definition and determination of control specifies that control can be achieved even when less than 50% of the voting rights are held by an investor.

Under IFRS, an investor has control of the investee when the investor has the following three characteristics: power over investee; exposure, or rights, to variable returns from its involvement with the investee; and the ability to affect the amount of the investor's return through its power. Power over the investee comes from existing rights of the investor. Such rights that give the investor the ability to direct the relevant activities of the investee (e.g., voting rights, decision-making rights, rights embedded in contractual arrangements, etc.). The exposure, or rights, to variable returns from the investor's involvement must have the potential to vary due to investee performance (return may be positive, negative, or both).

Business Combinations: Acquisition Method

In an acquisition, many of the acquired items have different accounting principles under IFRS compared to U.S. GAAP (e.g., inventory, property, plant and equipment, etc.). To note here, goodwill and goodwill impairment acquired in an acquisition have different treatment under U.S. GAAP and IFRS. Under U.S. GAAP, acquired goodwill is allocated to the reporting units while under IFRS it is allocated to the acquirer's cash generating units (CGU). Under U.S. GAAP, when testing goodwill for impairment, the entity may perform a qualitative assessment and then a two-step impairment test for goodwill. Under IFRS, the impairment test is a one-step test: compare the recoverable amount (higher of the fair value less costs to sell and value in use of the CGU) to the carrying amount of the CGU.

Topic Questions: Recognition, Measurement, Valuation, and Disclosure

Directions: Answer each question in the space provided. Correct answers and explanations appear after the topic questions.

1. Majesty Amusement Park recently installed a new thrill ride. Although this attraction has an average life of 40 years, Majesty estimates that the ride will be popular for 15 years, at which point it will be disassembled and replaced with a different ride. Park attendance is based on the local economy, which is difficult to predict. The method Majesty should use to depreciate this ride is:

    ☐ **a.**   declining balance.

    ☐ **b.**   straight line with a 15-year life.

    ☐ **c.**   straight line with a 40-year life.

    ☐ **d.**   units of output.

2. The purpose of interperiod income tax allocation is to:

    ☐ **a.**   reconcile the tax consequences of permanent and tempo-rary differences that appear on the company's current financial statements.

    ☐ **b.**   recognize a tax asset or liability for the tax consequences of tempo-rary differences that exist at the date of the balance sheet.

    ☐ **c.**   adjust the income tax expense on the income statement to be con-sistent with the income tax liability shown on the balance sheet.

    ☐ **d.**   provide proper disclosure of a distribution of earnings to a taxing authority.

3. Which one of the following statements correctly describes the accounting treatment of research and development costs (R&D) under U.S. GAAP and IFRS?

    ☐ **a.**   Both U.S. GAAP and IFRS allow for costs of R&D to be capitalized.

    ☐ **b.**   Neither U.S. GAAP nor IFRS allow for costs of R&D to be capitalized.

    ☐ **c.**   U.S. GAAP allows for the capitalization of the costs of R&D, and IFRS requires R&D costs to be expensed.

    ☐ **d.**   U.S. GAAP requires R&D to be expensed, and IFRS requires research costs to be expensed but allows for the capitalization of develop-ment costs.

Topic Question Answers: Recognition, Measurement, Valuation, and Disclosure

1. Majesty Amusement Park recently installed a new thrill ride. Although this attraction has an average life of 40 years, Majesty estimates that the ride will be popular for 15 years, at which point it will be disassembled and replaced with a different ride. Park attendance is based upon the local economy, which is difficult to predict. The method Majesty should use to depreciate this ride is:

   ☐ **a**. declining balance.
   ☑ **b**. straight line with a 15-year life.
   ☐ **c**. straight line with a 40-year life.
   ☐ **d**. units of output.

Depreciation is recognized over the period of time that long-term assets provide benefit to the organization. Straight-line depreciation recognizes an equal amount of depreciation over the asset's useful life. Because Majesty estimates that the ride will be replaced in 15 years, and it can be assumed that it will provide an equal amount of benefit each year, Majesty should use the straight-line method with a 15-year life.

2. The purpose of interperiod income tax allocation is to:

   ☐ **a**. reconcile the tax consequences of permanent and temporary differences that appear on the company's current financial statements.
   ☑ **b**. recognize a tax asset or liability for the tax consequences of temporary differences that exist at the date of the balance sheet.
   ☐ **c**. adjust the income tax expense on the income statement to be consistent with the income tax liability shown on the balance sheet.
   ☐ **d**. provide proper disclosure of a distribution of earnings to a taxing authority.

The purpose of interperiod income tax allocation is to recognize a tax asset or liability for the tax consequences of temporary differences that exist at the balance sheet date. Temporary differences arise when there are differences between pretax financial income under GAAP and taxable income for the IRS that will reverse in a future period.

3. Which one of the following statements correctly describes the accounting treatment of research and development costs (R&D) under U.S. GAAP and IFRS?

☐ **a.** Both U.S. GAAP and IFRS allow for costs of R&D to be capitalized.

☐ **b.** Neither U.S. GAAP nor IFRS allow for costs of R&D to be capitalized.

☐ **c.** U.S. GAAP allows for the capitalization of the costs of R&D, and IFRS requires R&D costs to be expensed.

☑ **d.** U.S. GAAP requires R&D to be expensed, and IFRS requires research costs to be expensed but allows for the capitalization of the development costs.

U.S. GAAP and IFRS treat R&D costs differently. Under GAAP, R&D costs are expensed as incurred except for software development costs, which are treated as under IFRS standards. Under IFRS, research costs are expensed as they are incurred; development costs for internally developed intangible assets can be capitalized once the project has established technological feasibility and certain conditions have been met.

Practice Questions:
External Financial Reporting Decisions

Directions: This sampling of questions is designed to emulate actual exam questions. Read each question and write your response on another sheet of paper. See the "Answers to Section Practice Questions" section at the end of this book to assess your response. Validate or improve the answer you wrote. For a more robust selection of practice questions, access the **Online Test Bank** at www .wileycma.com.

Question 1A1-W001
Topic: Financial Statements

The income statement for Harrington Technologies Inc.:

Net sales		$2,000,000
Less:	Cost of goods sold	890,000
Gross profit		1,110,000
Less:	Transportation and travel	45,000
	Depreciation	68,000
	Pension contributions	21,000
Operating income		976,000
Less:	Discontinued operations	76,000
Income before taxes		900,000
Less:	Tax expense @ 30%	270,000
Net Income		$630,000

Glen Hamilton analyzed the company's financial statements and concluded that the real net income should be $683,200 instead of $630,000. Which of the following arguments is **most likely** to support his conclusion?

- ☐ **a.** $53,200 due from a client was written off as irrecoverable after the finalization of accounts for the current period.

- ☐ **b.** The company valued its inventory using the specific identification method, whereas the financial analyst used the LIFO method for the current period.

- ☐ **c.** The company might have liquidated its LIFO reserve.

- ☐ **d.** The company has included expenses in relation to discontinued operations as part of income from continued operations.

Question 1A1-W003

Topic: Financial Statements

The cash flows and net income from four business segments for Taylor Laboratories Inc. have been provided.

	Segment 1	Segment 2	Segment 3	Segment 4
Cash flow from operations	$3,000	$(250)	$(3,000)	$2,000
Cash flow from investing activities	(4,000)	6,000	8,000	(3,000)
Cash flow from financing activities	1,080	(1,000)	(1,000)	1,080
Net income	1,500	1,750	2,375	1,500

Based on the information, which segment should be discontinued by the company?

☐ **a.** Segment 3, because cash used in operations is high and cash inflow is predominantly from investing activities.

☐ **b.** Segment 1, because net income is lowest and requires high investments.

☐ **c.** Segment 4, because net income and cash inflow from operations are low.

☐ **d.** Segment 2, because cash used in operations is low and cash flow from investing activities is not properly utilized.

Question 1A1-W004

Topic: Financial Statements

The cash flow from operations for Charlene Energy Inc. is $25,000 for the current year. If the amortization expense increases by $5,000 and other factors remain the same, under which of the following assumptions will the cash flow from operations remain unaffected?

☐ **a.** A change in amortization method will not have a retrospective effect.

☐ **b.** The company has an infinite life.

☐ **c.** The company is operating in a tax-free environment.

☐ **d.** The company can change the depreciation method in between a financial year.

Question 1A1-W005

Topic: Financial Statements

The following information is extracted from the latest financial information of Hines Materials Inc.

Tax rate	30%
Net Income	$15,000
Cash flow from operations	$45,000

Additional information:

1. The tax rate for next year is expected to increase by 2%.

2. The company is planning to purchase equipment worth $500,000 in the first quarter of next year.

3. A 15% increase in capacity is expected with the use of new equipment.

Considering the given factors, which of the following would be an ideal strategy to decrease the tax liability for the next year?

☐ **a.** Defer the purchase of equipment to next year to take advantage of tax-loss carryforward.

☐ **b.** Depreciate the asset using the double-declining-balance method to show higher cash flows from operations in initial years.

☐ **c.** Prepare the cash flow statement using the direct method to show lower cash from operations and lower net income.

☐ **d.** Defer the purchase of equipment to next year if a deferred tax liability can be reasonably estimated.

Question 1A1-W006

Topic: Financial Statements

The financial accountant of Eva Wolfe Corp. has ascertained the cash flows from operations as follows:

Net income	$15,000
Depreciation on equipment	2,500
Dividend income	2,500
Interest income	5,000
Increases in current assets	8,000
Increases in current liabilities	6,500
Cash flow from operations	$16,000

The company's management accountant argues that the cash flow from operations should be $8,500. Which of the following statements, if true, will support the management accountant's calculation?

- ☐ **a.** The company operates in a tax-free environment.
- ☐ **b.** The company uses IFRS to ascertain cash flow from operations.
- ☐ **c.** Cash flow from operations is ascertained using the direct method.
- ☐ **d.** Depreciation on equipment should not be added back to net income for calculating cash flows from operations.

Question 1A1-W007

Topic: Financial Statements

The management of Arthur Energy recognized a contingent liability of $50,000 in the current year. However, before the annual report was issued, the company resolved the issue, making a lump-sum payment of $42,000. The board of directors has decided to incorporate the transaction in the subsequent year's financial statements. Which of the following provisions of US GAAP, if applicable, is likely to prove the management decision wrong?

- ☐ **a.** Loss contingencies must be recognized when it is both probable that a loss has been incurred and the amount of the loss is reasonably estimable.
- ☐ **b.** Whenever GAAP or industry-specific regulations allow a choice between two or more accounting methods, the method selected should be disclosed.
- ☐ **c.** If an event alters the estimates used in preparing the financial statements, then the financial statements should be adjusted.
- ☐ **d.** If an event provides additional evidence about conditions that existed as of the balance sheet date and alters the estimates used, then the financial statements should be adjusted.

Question 1A1-W008

Topic: Financial Statements

Shelton Devin Corp. has two stock investments in which the corporation owns 30% of the outstanding stock. The CEO of the company is not in favor of presenting consolidated financial statements. Based on the information, which of the following is **most likely** true?

- ☐ **a.** The decision of the CEO is correct because companies are required to issue consolidated statements only when the ownership exceeds 50%.

- ☐ **b.** The decision of the CEO is wrong because companies are required to issue consolidated statements when the ownership exceeds 20%.

- ☐ **c.** The decision of the CEO is wrong because companies are required to issue consolidated statements only if a company holds more than ten subsidiaries.

- ☐ **d.** The decision of the CEO is correct because companies are required to issue consolidated statements only when a company has three or more subsidiaries.

Question 1A2-W002

Topic: Recognition, Measurement, Valuation, and Disclosure

Claire Enterprises has $150,000 in accounts receivable at the end of the current year. It estimates its bad debts to be 5% of the receivables, so the accountant reports $7,500 as bad debts and the net realizable value as $142,500. Under which of the following circumstances will the amount of bad debts reported **most likely** reduce?

- ☐ **a.** If the company shortens the credit period allowed.

- ☐ **b.** If the company lengthens the credit period allowed.

- ☐ **c.** If the allowance for doubtful accounts has a credit balance of $1,500.

- ☐ **d.** If the allowance for doubtful accounts has a debit balance of $1,500.

Question 1A2-W003
Topic: Recognition, Measurement, Valuation, and Disclosure

The financial statements of Darlene Properties show 140,000 outstanding shares, par value $10. The current market value is $25 per share. At the beginning of this year, the company reacquired 10,000 shares at $4 per share. The company uses the cost method to account for treasury stock. The current year's books of accounts show the value of outstanding shares as follows:

Common stock, $10 par	$1,400,000
Less: Treasury stock	100,000
Net common stock, $10 par	$1,300,000

The company's CFO did not approve the financial statements. The **most likely** reason for CFO's disapproval is that:

- □ **a.** The treasury stock is incorrectly valued based on par value, instead of valuing at the acquisition price.
- □ **b.** The treasury stock is incorrectly valued based on par value, instead of valuing at the current market rate.
- □ **c.** The par value of the treasury stock should be presented as a deduction from par value of issued shares of the same class
- □ **d.** The treasury stock should be reported as an asset.

Question 1A2-W004
Topic: Recognition, Measurement, Valuation, and Disclosure

Rogers Electronics is planning to make a market in the company's stock. The company's CFO suggests the reacquisition of shares. Which of the following is **most likely** to happen if the CFO's suggestion is implemented?

- □ **a.** The risk of takeovers by competitors will increase.
- □ **b.** This will hinder exercise of employee stock options.
- □ **c.** The stock price will increase.
- □ **d.** This could serve as an indication of the company's negative outlook about its future performance.

Question 1A2-W006

Topic: Recognition, Measurement, Valuation, and Disclosure

Calvin Software has invested in 35% of the voting stock of BioTech Corp. The CFO suggests acquiring more stock of BioTech. Based on the information, which of the following will be true?

- ☐ **a.** Additional acquisitions beyond 15% will require Calvin Software to issue consolidated financial statements.
- ☐ **b.** Calvin's total value will decrease as incidental costs of acquisition must be subtracted when holdings exceed 35%.
- ☐ **c.** The circumstances leading to the decision to acquire additional shares shall be disclosed in the notes to the financial statements.
- ☐ **d.** Any additional acquisition of assets up to 20% should be classified as held to maturity.

Question 1A2-W007

Topic: Recognition, Measurement, Valuation, and Disclosure

Warner Machines missed recording purchases worth $10,000 in the current year's income statement. While finalizing the financial statements, the company's accountant detected the error and partially corrected it. Under which of the following situations will the company report lower than actual net income?

- ☐ **a.** If the accountant has reduced cash by $10,000.
- ☐ **b.** If the accountant has added the missing purchases worth only $10,000 to the cost of goods sold.
- ☐ **c.** If the accountant has increased accounts payable only by $10,000.
- ☐ **d.** If the accountant has reduced inventory by $10,000.

Question 1A2-W008

Topic: Recognition, Measurement, Valuation, and Disclosure

Sandra Bellucci is analyzing inventory of companies from four different industries: consumer goods, sports goods manufacturers, electronics, and aircraft manufacturers. Assuming the inventory valuation methods reflect the actual flow of inventory and the inventory includes only finished goods, which of the following industries will **most likely** have zero LIFO reserve?

- ☐ **a.** Consumer goods
- ☐ **b.** Sports goods manufacturers
- ☐ **c.** Electronics
- ☐ **d.** Aircraft manufacturers

Question 1A2-New

Topic: Recognition, Measurement, Valuation, and Disclosure

An entity has determined that a performance obligation within a contract is satisfied over time because the transfer of control of the goods to the customer is satisfied over time. Which of the following is an allowed method to measure an entity's progress toward complete satisfaction of the performance obligation?

- ☐ **a.** Installment input method
- ☐ **b.** Output method
- ☐ **c.** Cost recovery method
- ☐ **d.** Through-put method

To further assess your understanding of the concepts and calculations covered in Part 1, Section A: External Financial Reporting Decisions, practice with the **Online Test Bank** for this section.

REMINDER: See the "Answers to Section Practice Questions" section at the end of this book.

Planning, Budgeting, and Forecasting (20%)

How do some companies become great successes while others flounder? Successful companies have a strategy that is based on accurate information from both external and internal sources. They match their internal strengths to the best external opportunities available. But a good strategy is not enough. Companies need to convert an overall strategy into action. This is the purpose of a budget. A budget is a detailed plan for executing both long-term and short-term goals. A successful budget not only provides cost controls but also makes sure that day-to-day operations take the company where it wants to be in the future.

This section covers strategic planning as well as basic budgeting concepts and forecasting techniques that provide the assumptions on which budgets are based. It discusses various budget methodologies and their applications and explores the master budget in detail. It demonstrates, with case study examples, how a company can use components of a master budget to analyze its performance and operations.

Strategic Planning

S TRATEGY SETS FORTH THE GENERAL direction an organization plans to follow to achieve its goals. It represents the collective soul of an organization. Strategies are developed by evaluating how the enterprise can use its core competencies to respond to opportunities and/or threats.

Strategic planning (sometimes referred to as **long-range planning**) involves a comprehensive look at an organization in relation to its industry, competitors, and environment. An organization charts its destination, assesses barriers to be overcome to reach that destination, and identifies approaches for moving forward and dealing with the barriers. Although traditionally the responsibility of top management, all organizational members should be involved in the process. Effective strategic planning can help an organization adeptly navigate through changing times—both good and bad.

 READ the Learning Outcome Statements (LOS) for this topic as found in Appendix A and then study the concepts and calculations presented here to be sure you understand the content you could be tested on in the CMA exam.

LOS
§1.B.1.a

Strategy and Strategic Planning

Every well-managed organization formulates both strategies and strategic plans to some degree. Executives and managers typically spend considerable time thinking about strategies to achieve organizational goals; these strategies are then formally incorporated in a strategic plan.

Strategy

Strategy is a broad term. Organizations generally develop strategies at different levels. Figure 1B-1 shows three levels for which firms commonly develop organizational strategies:

Figure 1B-1 Levels of Strategy

Corporate (or multibusiness)	• Looks at all opportunities the corporation has and includes geographical expansion, mergers and acquisitions, and product expansion or contraction • Defines the organization's values • Centers on identifying and building or acquiring key resources and capabilities • Involves decisions about which industries the organization will compete in and how the business units will be linked • Determines how organizational resources will be allocated among the firm's business units • Determines constraints on what the firm will and will not do
Competitive (or business unit)	• Defines how an organization competes in a given industry—how the firm creates value in that industry • Involves a vision of the customers the organization serves and how it delivers value to them • Aligns organizational activities so all efforts consistently reinforce the potential advantage of the firm's competitive positioning • Reinforces the organization's competitive strategy
Functional (within a business)	• Includes plans and objectives for marketing, finance, research, technology, operations, and other business functions • Focuses on coordination among the business functions • Defines activities and processes to help the organization maximize its competitive position • Clarifies if and how the organization's functions fit with its competitive strategy

Corporate strategy considers the big picture, determines the appropriate mix of businesses, and identifies where and in what markets the firm competes. **Competitive and functional strategies** are more tactically focused on how the organization will compete in a given industry or market. Although the outcomes differ for the various levels of strategy, they all must be consistent and aligned. Goal congruence is a key to success. It is important to formulate and communicate strategies so the company's managers share the same vision.

Strategies will naturally differ among organizations. For example, Dell, IBM, and Toshiba each compete for market share in the same business sector, but each company is driven by a different strategy.

Organizational strategies must be dynamic in today's competitive environment. The strength of an organization's strategy is not determined by the firm's initial move but rather by how well it:

- Anticipates competitors' actions.
- Anticipates and/or influences changing customer demands.
- Capitalizes on advantages in a changing competitive environment (regulations, technology, the economy, global opportunities and events).
- Reacts to, chooses, and executes alternative competitive strategies.

Anticipation and preparation are key to an effective strategy. Every eventuality with competitors and customers and other influencing factors must be met and addressed with rapid moves and countermoves.

Strategic Planning

A conceptual representation of strategic planning is shown in Figure 1B-2.

Figure 1B-2 Key Elements of Strategic Planning

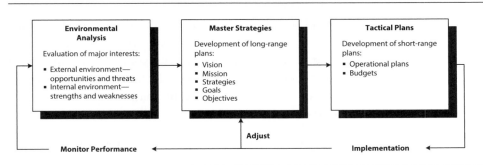

Keep in mind that the representation shown here is conceptual. It is intended to provide a general view of the strategic planning process. In practice, strategic planning terminology and approaches differ among organizations. An organization devises its own operational models that elaborate on the specifics of its strategic planning process.

What is the appropriate time frame for strategic planning? There is no set rule as to how often strategic plans will be prepared. The time frame for strategic planning is normally five to ten years. It may, however, be longer or shorter, depending on the industry, the level of competition (new entrants), and how fast products or services change. For example, technology-focused businesses prepare strategic plans at shorter time intervals to address the rapid changes and competitive pressure of their markets.

In the end, the resulting strategic plan yields insights into how an organization can position itself for sustainable competitive advantage.

The Relationship Between Strategy and Strategic Planning

In practice, strategy formulation and strategic planning overlap. But the two processes have important conceptual differences.

On a fundamental level, **strategy formulation** results in new strategies and **strategic planning** addresses how to implement the strategies. Additional distinctions can be made:

- Strategy formulation leads to organizational goals.
- Strategic planning is typically a systematic process with a timetable and some measure of prescribed procedures.

- Strategies are continually reevaluated based on changes to both internal and external factors.

Regardless of the overlap or distinctions in terms and processes, strategy formulation and strategic planning both address the following core elements at some level:

1. **External factors.** Recognition of business environment opportunities, limitations, and threats
2. **Internal factors.** Recognition of organizational strengths, weaknesses, and competitive advantages
3. **SWOT (Strengths, Weaknesses, Opportunities, and Threats) analysis.** Identification and evaluation of elements that will help or hinder the organization
4. **Long-term vision, mission, and goals.** Development of the overall organizational vision and mission and the formulation of long-term business goals
5. **Tactics to achieve long-term goals.** Development of short-term plans and tactics

Subsequent content looks at each of these elements in more detail.

1. Analysis of External Factors Affecting Strategy

Before creating strategies, the firm must first assess the organization's business environment.

The specific external factors affecting an organization's strategy are determined by its industry and broader environment. Typically a variety of external factors make up an organization's business environment. Examples of key external factors shaping organizational strategy include:

a. Legal and regulatory factors.
b. Market forces, industry trends, and competition.
c. Technological changes.
d. Stakeholder groups and their social concerns.
e. Globalization trends, emerging markets, and nongovernment organizations (United Nations, World Bank, etc.).

All of these external factors need to be examined during the strategic planning process.

a. Legal and Regulatory Factors

Legal and regulatory factors affect every business in some way.

Legal Factors

Legal factors are rules of conduct promulgated by legal entities (federal, state, county/provincial, or city laws). They are enforced by the threat of punishment.

Legal factors can impact how successful a product/service will be. Examples of legal factors include:

- Patents
- Copyrights
- Trademarks
- Antitrust laws
- Trade protectionism
- Product/service liability issues
- Environmental liability concerns
- Employment law and litigation
- Compliance with the Sarbanes-Oxley Act (SOX)

Regulatory Factors

Regulatory factors (or regulations) are principles or rules designed to control or govern behavior. Agencies under legal entities as well as nongovernmental entities (industry self-regulating bodies and professional societies) typically set regulations and sanctions. Unlike legal factors, which are always enforced by the threat of punishment, regulatory factors are enforced most often by some form of self-regulation, which may include the threat of fines and/or disenfranchisement.

General examples of regulatory factors that can affect an organization's strategy include:

Social Regulations

This is an economics term for government rules that restrict behaviors that are a direct threat to public health, safety, or well being.

Examples include but are not limited to:

- Environmental Protection Agency (EPA) standards restrict pollution of air, water, and land.
- Occupational Safety and Health Administration (OSHA) standards protect the safety and health of American workers.
- Federal Trade Commission (FTC) regulations protect consumers, require truthful advertising by businesses, and prohibit acts of collusion, such as price fixing and allocating markets.
- The Consumer Product Safety Commission (CPSC) can order a product recall and sets the requirements for product "label content."

Industry Regulations

These are defined as government regulation of an entire industry.

Examples include but are not limited to:

- Federal Aviation Administration (FAA) requirements for airports, air traffic control, safety issues, and routes.
- Federal Communications Commission (FCC) regulations for radio and television frequencies.

- Food and Drug Administration (FDA) requirements for safety in the food and drug industry and in medical device manufacturing.

Linkage of Legal and Regulatory Factors to Strategic Planning

The influence of legal and regulatory factors on an organization's strategy can be quite pervasive. The following are a few examples of how legal and regulatory factors can affect an organization:

Legal or Regulatory Factor	Impact
Antitrust law and licensing requirements	Influences how a firm chooses to compete
Trade protectionism	Limits global operations
Tax and patent laws	Promotes or thwarts technology innovations
Equal employment opportunity and antidiscrimination laws, wage and price controls, Family and Medical Leave Act, etc.	Human resource practices
FTC controls	Restrict marketing campaigns
EPA controls	Force environmental accountability
Required technical capabilities to meet government requirements	Increase capital requirements

The legal and regulatory factors already noted can directly affect management accounting due to significant cost incurrence implications. For example, changes in EPA or OSHA regulations can require significant capital investments.

Consider these additional factors that have specific implications for management accounting:

- Securities and Exchange Commission (SEC) laws and rules to protect investors and maintain the integrity of the securities markets
- The Sarbanes-Oxley Act changes regarding internal controls
- The Internal Revenue Service (IRS) code
- Congressional changes to minimum wage requirements and/or overtime compensation
- State-regulated insurance and banking commissions regulate how business is conducted and how various financial transactions are to be accounted for

b. Market Forces, Industry Trends, and Competition

A critical part of strategic planning is an industry analysis—a thorough assessment of the competitive environment that includes the competitors the organization must face and the structure and/or boundaries of that environment.

Michael Porter recognized three generic strategies to gain competitive advantage:

1. **Cost Leadership Strategy.** The firm gains market share by having the lowest prices. This appeals to the cost-conscious consumer. This strategy works best for large firms that have economies of scale and large production volumes.

2. **Differentiation Strategy.** The firm uses unique resources or capabilities to create and market products that command a market premium. This strategy is appropriate in saturated markets or when the market is not price sensitive. This strategy is generally unsuitable for small firms.

3. **Focus Strategy.** The firm focuses on a few target or niche markets. This strategy works best for small firms looking to avoid competing with large firms.

Most industry analyses consider the following factors:

1. Entry of new competitors
2. Threat of substitutes
3. Bargaining power of buyers
4. Bargaining power of suppliers
5. Rivalry among existing competitors

Michael Porter developed a model examining these five forces and their collective role in determining the strength of competition and profitability. The discussion of Porter's five forces that follows is synthesized from two of Porter's books, *Competitive Strategy: Techniques for Analyzing Industries and Competitors* (1980) and *Competitive Advantage: Creating and Sustaining Superior Performance* (1985), and the collaborative text *Wharton on Dynamic Competitive Strategy* (Day and Reibstein, 1997). Figure 1B-3 depicts Porter's model.

LOS
§1.B.1.i

Figure 1B-3 Five Forces Driving Industry Profitability

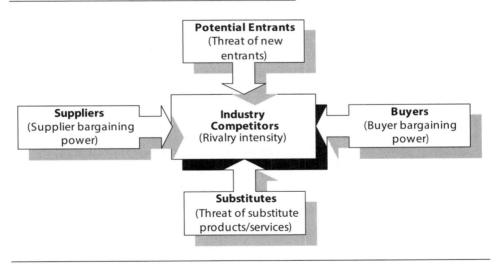

Source: Adapted from Michael Porter, *Competitive Advantage—Creating and Sustaining Superior Performance.*

1. Entry of New Competitors

A new entrant in a marketplace generally brings with them new and additional capacity and resources. The profitability for an incumbent, the largest company in a specific industry, in the marketplace will be reduced if the barriers to entry are low.

The threat of new competitors depends on the magnitude of the entry and exit barriers and if they create an advantage or a disadvantage for prospective entrants. Examples of entry barriers include these items:

- **Incumbent cost advantages.** This occurs when incumbents have advantages such as low labor or capital costs, preferred access to raw materials, government subsidies, favorable locations, proprietary technology and product designs, and accumulated learning experience.
- **Economies of scale.** These are defined as a decline in unit costs as volume increases. Economies of scale can deter an entrant. Facilities, research, marketing, sales force coverage, and distribution are all examples of areas of economies of scale that potentially require significant entry investments.
- **Product/service differentiation.** *Differentiation* refers to the brand identification and existing customer loyalties of an incumbent. Entrants will need to invest time and money to build their own brand name.
- **Switching costs.** If a buyer considers changing from an existing supplier's product or service to that of a new entrant, the one-time switching costs can be a deterrent to entry. Some switching costs are considered to be sunk costs.
- **Channel crowding.** Many distribution channels have limited capacity or exclusive relationships with manufacturers that restrict the number of product lines. Intense selling efforts generally are required to convince a distributor to take on a new product line.
- **Expected incumbent reactions.** Entry barriers may be raised or lowered depending on how aggressively incumbents have defended their positions in the past. Incumbents with deep pockets, staying power, and who have demonstrated a willingness to take a short-term reduction in profits to defend market share will discourage entrants.

2. Threat of Substitutes

When an acceptable substitute product or service is available—one that provides the same functions and offers the same benefits—the average price that can be charged will be determined by the market. The resulting profit margin is usually reduced.

The way electronic surveillance and alarm systems have impacted the use of security guards is one example of industry threats posed by the availability of substitutes. The key in this situation is to account for similarities while looking for differentiation opportunities beyond product or service similarities.

3. Bargaining Power of Buyers

Buyers (customers) and sellers (suppliers) of goods and services can have a wide range of relationships. They may involve tightly integrated, just-in-time manufacturing systems, or they may be at the other end of the spectrum, with mass marketing. Buyer power is enhanced or deterred depending on bargaining leverage and price sensitivity.

Bargaining Leverage

In general, leverage is any strategic or tactical event that can be exploited to an advantage. A buyer's bargaining leverage is enhanced by the following factors:

- **Large-volume purchases made by a few key customers.** In this situation, the seller becomes dependent on the key buyers. Market share would decrease significantly if the relationship were severed.
- **Ability for customers to easily switch.** Customers may change suppliers if there is little product or service differentiation, low switching costs, or readily available low-cost substitutes.
- **Ability to backward-integrate.** Current prices and/or other terms can make an alternative more attractive than continuing to buy externally. Examples include the purchase of an upstream supplier or the ability to bring back in house something that was previously outsourced.
- **Customer insider knowledge.** Bargaining leverage is gained if customers know the supplier's costs and profits or learn that the supplier needs their business to offset excess capacity or other mitigating circumstances.

Price Sensitivity

Price sensitivity is an indicator of how important lower prices are to customers. Price sensitivity is heightened by the following factors:

- **Product or service impact on end product quality.** A buyer pays more attention to price if the consequences of product or service failure are more severe than in situations where the product/service failure has little impact on the quality of the end product.
- **Price of the product or service relative to a customer's total costs.** Big-ticket items tend to incur greater purchasing scrutiny; smaller incidental items often escape analysis of cost alternatives.
- **Buyer's profits.** When customers are suffering from poor profitability, they often seek price concessions from suppliers. The pressure for concessions can become intense if survival is at stake.

Price sensitivity is intensified further if buyers perceive little difference among competing suppliers.

4. Bargaining Power of Suppliers

A supplier's ability to withstand bargaining by customers tends to mirror those conditions making buyers powerful. A supplier's bargaining power depends on the following items:

- **Size of the supplier relative to the customer.** A larger supplier can have a distinct advantage and leverage in dealing with a small, dispersed customer base.

- **Customer's reliance on the supplier's product or service.** Reliance is influenced to the extent that a customer cannot buy an equivalent, the input is not storable (so the buyer cannot stockpile inventory), or switching costs are high.
- **Threat of forward integration.** If suppliers can sell directly to end users, customers will have less leverage to get better prices.

5. Rivalry Among Existing Competitors

In some environments, rivals coexist. In other environments, direct rivals constantly jockey for market share with tactics such as temporary price cuts, special promotions, advertising blitzes, aggressive new product launches, and increased customer service and extended warranties. Value often erodes as competitors match moves.

Telecommunication providers are notorious for price cutting in their efforts to secure new customers and cover fixed costs. Yet such actions often decrease profits and leave market share unchanged. The following factors typically influence the status of competitor relations.

- **Structure of competition.** Rivalry is generally most intense when there are a few balanced competitors or several small players serving the same market.
- **Structure of costs.** Capacity utilization is emphasized when fixed costs are high. Any excess capacity often leads to price cutting and a cycle of price matching.
- **Product or service differentiation.** Product differentiation can foster buyer preferences and loyalties to particular suppliers. Therefore, rivalry is subdued when customers develop preferences and brand loyalty due to large perceived differentiation. In the absence of differentiation, customers often focus on price and terms, which will intensify any rivalry.
- **Customer switching costs.** Costs that tie a buyer to one supplier provide good protection against raids by rivals. Changing a computer operating system is an example of a situation in which a customer typically would incur a general disruption of operations and increased costs.
- **Diversity of competitors' strategies and objectives.** It is much easier for competitors to anticipate another's intention or accurately anticipate reactions to market moves when all competitors have similar strategies, cost structures, and management philosophies. When competitors come from diverse backgrounds, such as foreign-owned, government-owned, or small owner-operated firms, the actions and activities are much less predictable.
- **High exit barriers.** Exit barriers can keep players trapped even when profits are depressed. Firms may choose to endure the drain on profits caused by excess capacity rather than sell or close the business. Management may resist an economically justified exit decision based on an emotional rationale, such as loyalty to a particular business or employees.

Linkage of the Five Forces to Strategic Planning

Porter's five forces determine the intensity of industry competition and profitability. The collective strength of the five competitive forces determines the ability of firms to earn rates of return on investment in excess of the cost of capital.

In industries where the strength of the five forces is favorable (pharmaceuticals), profits are attractive. In industries where the strength of one or more of the forces is under fire (airlines), few firms have good returns in spite of management efforts. Porter notes that industry profitability is not a function of what a product looks like or whether a service incorporates high technology or low technology. Rather, it is determined by industry structure. That is why a product that looks mundane (an automotive aftermarket part) may be extremely profitable whereas a more glamorous high-tech product (a cellular handset) may not be highly profitable for all of the market players.

To a large extent, the five forces are moving targets. In this respect, they:

- Can vary from industry to industry.
- Can change as an industry evolves.
- Are not equally important in any one industry.
- Are vulnerable to high growth and market demand (if a surplus of competitors is attracted, leading to overcrowding).

Naturally, different firms will have unique strengths and weaknesses that influence their ability to deal with or even alter industry structure. Understanding industry structure is a critical starting point during strategy formulation. The strongest force or forces assume increased importance during strategic planning and strategy formulation.

c. Technological Changes

No industry is immune to the strategic implications of technology. Consider the following points as proof:

- Technology can result in the creation of industry substitutes, such as wireless phones versus land lines.
- Technology can reduce the need for large-scale distribution and open a market up to new entrants, as when web-based e-commerce technology disrupted traditional distribution channels.
- Technology can accelerate new product designs and facilitate short production runs in manufacturing-based industries, leading to either intense rivalry or monopoly.
- Technology can create a shift in the balance of power between an organization and a supplier or buyer, depending on where the technology is developed and exploited.
- Technology can change industry structure and thereby either improve or degrade average profitability.

Those firms savvy in recognizing and exploiting technological changes are generally more adept at gaining and sustaining competitive advantage. To a degree, technological change is both an external factor and an internal factor. Technology impacts what products and services an organization offers, how products and services are made, how customers are serviced, and with whom the firm must compete. Therefore, technology must reinforce a firm's strategic intent and competitive strategy.

Characteristics of a Technology Assessment

Technology cuts across all of the business units and activities of an enterprise. Given the span of technology and its importance to market success, an organization needs to assess its technology capabilities on an ongoing basis. *The Portable MBA* (Bruner et al., 1998) outlines a five-step process for a technology assessment:

1. Identify key technologies.
2. Analyze the potential changes in current and future technologies.
3. Analyze the competitive impact of technologies.
4. Analyze the organization's technical strengths and weaknesses.
5. Establish the organization's technology priorities.

Step 1. Identify Key Technologies

This initial phase in a technology assessment identifies all technologies that impact the organization.

General categories that should be considered include:

- Product technology
- Manufacturing and/or service process technology
- Technology used by support functions, such as sales, customer service, finance and accounting
- Information management technology
- Technologies used by competitors
- Technologies used by suppliers or buyers of the organization's products, and services

Consideration should be given to technologies not currently used by the enterprise, especially if they might have future implications. For example, a small business not currently using e-commerce might well explore how the technology is used in other industries and how it could impact the firm's current products and processes.

Step 2. Analyze the Potential Changes in Current and Future Technologies

This next step involves evaluating short- and long-term changes in all the important technologies identified. Complex technologies may have many layers of subtechnologies. The evaluation must consider all of the subtechnologies.

In regard to analyzing potential changes, note that:

- People with expertise in the technologies should conduct the technology evaluation.
- Evaluations should be constructively examined and challenged by others to preclude the possibility of a forecast based on unquestioned conventional wisdom.
- The effort applied to technology development varies. A technology that is critical to a competitor will most likely evolve more quickly than technologies that are necessary but not an important source of competitive advantage.
- Mature technologies do not always change slowly, especially if the need for progress or replacement of the technology exists. Mature technologies will also change rapidly when a new technology offers opportunities for new entrants.

Step 3. Analyze the Competitive Impact of Technologies

The intent of this step is to answer the following key questions:

- What technologies or technological changes can give the organization the greatest source of competitive advantage?
- What technologies or technological changes would be the greatest threat in the hands of a competitor?
- What technologies or technological changes could significantly change the industry structure?

The competitive impact of different technologies generally is classified by base, key, or pacing characteristics.

- **Base technologies** are widely used throughout an industry. As such, they are well understood and considered necessary. They do not provide a competitive advantage.
- **Key technologies** are critical to competitive advantage. They help an organization differentiate its products or services. In some instances, they enable the firm to compete with lower costs.
- **Pacing technologies** are those that have the potential to redefine an industry or change the whole basis of competition. Pacing technologies often replace key technologies. When firms that are not the market leader develop a pacing technology, the opportunity to change industry leadership exists.

Step 4. Analyze the Organization's Technical Strengths and Weaknesses

Managers must assess the organization's strengths and weaknesses for each technology classification as well as the potential costs of developing each technology. The evaluation should compare findings with competitors' strengths and weaknesses (both current and future scenarios).

Just as in the overall organizational SWOT analysis, pride and unwillingness to acknowledge the organization's weaknesses or the strengths of a competitor can skew this assessment. To help ensure objectivity, it is best to have a team of technical specialists who understand the technologies and managers who are operations and market focused perform the assessment together.

Step 5. Establish the Organization's Technology Priorities

Based on findings from the technology assessment process, a tentative set of priorities for the acquisition, development, and use of product, service, and process technologies can be created. A technology assessment should also consider the pros and cons of having highly integrated technology systems.

- **Integration benefits.** Integration facilitates the simultaneous updating of databases. This makes the current data available for decision making. The costs of data entry and processing are lower than would be for standalone applications.
- **Integration concerns.** System integration typically requires huge financial investments, comprehensive designs, and careful project management and execution. It also requires timely training on system features and the transition process. Integration requires a big commitment of resources.

Linkage of a Technology Assessment to Strategic Planning

Insights gained from the technology assessment should evolve into an organizational technology strategy through a process of interaction between the firm's leaders and managers representing all the functional areas of the organization.

Characteristics of a sound technology strategy include:

- Enhancement of technology's strategic role in the organization.
- Support of the organization's corporate and competitive strategies.
- Plans for attaining short-term and long-term objectives and major projects, including goals and milestones.
- Resource allocation.
- Alignment to the organization's financial plan and budget.
- Metrics for measuring accomplishment.

A technology strategy should be easily understood and well communicated. The commitment of key people must be secured.

The technology strategy establishes preliminary organizational priorities and commitments to innovation and technology development, always keeping the firm's strategic positioning in mind. It is in this manner that a technology assessment leads to a technology strategy and ultimately provides inputs for strategic plans.

d. Stakeholder Groups and Their Social Concerns

Stakeholders include people, departments, groups, organizations, or other bodies that have a "stake"—an investment or interest—in the success of, or actions taken by, an organization. Thus, stakeholders include:

- Executives
- Managers and employees (including their families)

- The organization's board of directors
- Shareholders (stockholders)
- The industry in which the organization operates
- Customers
- Competitors
- Suppliers
- Business partners
- Consulting and advisory services
- Creditors
- Special interest groups—industrial, political, consumer, and so on
- Unions
- Regulating government bodies
- The community in which the organization operates
- The nation
- The environment—plants, animals, ecosystems, natural resources
- Educational institutions
- The media
- Future generations

During strategic planning, it is important to identify the various stakeholders to understand their expectations and potential influences on the enterprise. This ensures that their needs and interests are addressed. If not on board, stakeholders can withhold resources and support, which will potentially undermine the legitimacy of the enterprise.

Maximizing Shareholder Value While Being Socially Responsible in Business

The idea of maximizing shareholder value is associated with for-profit corporations and generally refers to the market valuation of a firm. The idea of profit maximization requires consideration of marginal costs and a demand curve. Certainly, an organization must earn a profit that is at least equal to its cost of capital based on the risk. Although critical to organizational success, profit maximization and optimizing shareholder value are not the only goals for organizations.

The social responsibility approach in business implies that organizations should act as good corporate citizens and adopt socially responsible practices that will be a positive force for change and help improve the quality of people's lives. The premise behind this approach is that corporations have societal obligations that must complement—and not compete for—profit maximization. This philosophy suggests that corporate actions should balance the claims of all stakeholders and not focus only on the shareholders.

Organizations naturally encounter a host of challenges in attempts to be socially responsible. Consider a few common examples:

- Accounting practices—insider trading
- Advertising—accurate and truthful product/service representation
- Corporate restructuring—layoffs
- Diversity issues—race, ethnicity, gender, sexual orientation

- Employee privacy issues—drug testing, chemical dependency, AIDS
- Harassment issues—gender or age discrimination
- Environmental issues—pollution, animal rights
- International operations—conduct encountering bribery, nepotism, and other issues acceptable in other countries that challenge the organization's ethics
- Competition—predatory pricing, antitrust actions

Stakeholder Analysis

Most organizations use some type of model for stakeholder analysis to assess ethical challenges and how best to be socially responsible. Stakeholder analysis provides an organization with a framework for weighing all the various claims and stakeholder concerns to reach a socially responsible decision.

A common method of stakeholder analysis uses a matrix. The main steps of this type of stakeholder analysis are listed in Figure 1B-4.

Figure 1B-4 Steps in a Stakeholder Analysis Framework

Step 1.	Identify stakeholders; brainstorm a list of the main participants.
Step 2.	Determine stakeholder needs; collect input through interviews, focus groups, surveys, and so on.
Step 3.	Develop a matrix of the organization's objectives and the stakeholders' needs.
Step 4.	Identify the effect of the organization's objectives versus the stakeholders' needs (using a plus or minus sign or question mark).
Step 5.	Make a decision based on the effects recorded.

A stakeholder analysis done in this manner sets the stage for decisions to change the organization's objectives, satisfy stakeholder demands, mitigate potential conflict, and pass if compatible or acceptable.

Figure 1B-5 shows an example of a stakeholder analysis. In this analysis, a produce distributor plans to build automated warehouses and install pricey high-tech

Figure 1B-5 Stakeholder Analysis Example—Automating a Produce Warehouse

(+ or −)	Organization	Employees	Consuming Public	Suppliers	Government Inspectors
Harm and benefits	− Higher costs + Higher profits	+ More free time − Fewer hours/ potential layoffs	+ Lower prices + Quick time to market; less spoilage	− New hardware	+ Power and influence
Rights and responsibilities	+ Value + Profits for owners and shareholders	+ Competitive market position	? Possible quality concerns ? Public good	? Ability to meet demand	+ Protect the public + Regulate industry

gear. The matrix shown considers the stakeholders. The analysis points out that there is no one "right" way; differences in the weighting shown here can exist. The point of stakeholder analysis is to tackle such stakeholder issues and make informed and thoughtful decisions that are consistent and defensible.

Other methods are available for conducting a stakeholder analysis. Some organizations do a stakeholder analysis by answering a series of guiding questions, such as:

- Who are the main stakeholders?
- What are the most important values of each stakeholder? (For example, what are the harm and benefits to each?)
- What rights and duties are at issue?
- What principles and rules are relevant?
- What are some relevant parallel cases?
- What should be done?

Linkage of a Stakeholder Analysis to Strategic Planning

Stakeholder analysis helps an organization frame its corporate social responsibility and identifies the role good citizenship plays in a business. Through stakeholder analysis, a firm learns:

- How people feel about the organization and the industry it is in.
- What issues the organization should rethink/reevaluate its position on.
- What the organization should do differently to improve its position.

e. Globalization

Globalization describes an organization's migration to international operations. Globalization is a reflection of organizational strategy and an integrated progression of worldwide operations.

Although globalization is prevalent and a goal on which many organizations set their sights, an organization does not simply become a global entity overnight. The migration from domestic to global operations typically evolves through a series of relatively predictable stages.

- **Export.** This is the initial stage of globalization for most organizations. Firms begin to export their products or services abroad through direct sales to customers, import/export firms, and independent agents or distributors. Sales from exports generally represent a small portion of total revenue.
- **International division and sales subsidiaries.** As international sales grow in importance, the organization is likely to establish a separate international division and/or sales subsidiaries. At this stage of globalization, increased communication and coordination is required between domestic and international operations.

  A sales subsidiary generally involves a branch operation in a country or countries where sales have become significantly large. Subsidiaries range from a relatively modest office to operations such as stores, service centers, or manufacturing plants, depending on the volume and the nature of the business.

- **Multinational corporation (MNC).** As sales volume and the number of countries significantly increase, an organization evolves to the stage of an MNC. The MNC generally operates in several countries and treats each one as a relatively separate entity. It often maintains global coordination of some functions such as finance, staffing, and marketing. In contrast, the firm may move to a regional structure with more regional headquarters and coordination.

- **Global organization.** A global organization views the whole world as one market where national boundaries are seamless. The organization's headquarters may be located anywhere.

    The global organization is characterized by features that include:

    - Global strategic planning
    - Products and services designed and marketed worldwide
    - Pursuit of technology and innovation worldwide
    - Sharing of global technology and innovation between all operations
    - Product and service development wherever cost, quality, and cycle time are favorable and demand is sufficient
    - Pursuit of resources (such as money, materials, parts, insurance, and people) in locations where the best quality for the cost can be found
    - Employees moving freely between countries

- **Alliances, partnerships, joint ventures.** This stage of globalization does not necessarily replace the MNC or global organization, but it does offer an organization a channel to capitalize on resources (such as research and design, technology, personnel, manufacturing facilities) that would not otherwise be available. Two examples of this level of globalization are:

    - A large telecommunications firm subcontracting for technology resources in other countries, including from a major competitor
    - Two international electronics companies pooling resources to design and develop sophisticated computer chips and distribute them in more than 120 countries

Linkage of Globalization to Strategic Planning

The stages of globalization are sometimes named or categorized slightly differently than those just described. And, obviously, not every organization passes through each stage in exactly the same way. Some can move at an accelerated pace due to mergers and acquisitions. Others evolve slowly in a deliberate manner and may take years to move from export to MNC and global. Regardless of the nomenclature, the number of stages, and the time frame it takes for an organization to go global, it is helpful to recognize that globalization follows a progression.

An enterprise needs to acquire additional skills and competence as it moves towards globalization. Various activities and functions evolve as an organization becomes a full-fledged multinational or global organization. For example, international financial skills and tax knowledge become increasingly important along the globalization spectrum.

To compete successfully in the global arena, organizations must make considerable investments in resources, and these investments should be carefully crafted during strategic planning.

2. Analysis of Internal Factors Affecting Strategy

To complement the assessment of external factors affecting strategy, an organization must conduct an internal capability analysis. Together these two assessments help an organization to establish its current capabilities and close the gap between current capabilities and those needed for industry success.

What to Assess in Internal Capability Analysis

In particular, an internal capability analysis helps to ensure that the organization has the resources, skills, and processes to reach its strategic and tactical goals.

- **Resources.** An internal assessment of resources looks at the finances, facilities, equipment, and other infrastructure issues that can support or impede organizational initiatives. Assessing resources requires review of financial statements, along with additional analytical work and quantitative information such as capital investment analysis, value chain analysis, and review of activity-based costing (ABC) information. (Note: Additional information on value chain analysis is found in Section D, Topic 5: Business Process Improvement.)
- **Skills.** Skills assessments examine the current education levels of employees, the core knowledge and skills required, and the specific technical or organizational skills required. As organizations face competitive pressures, employees must be prepared. A commitment to training should be made as needed.
- **Processes.** Cycle time and a variety of capacity issues are considered when assessing the organizational processes necessary to gain competitive advantage. (Note: Process analysis is discussed further in Section D, Topic 5: Business Process Improvement.)

How to Assess Internal Resources, Skills, and Processes

Organizations may choose from a variety of tools and techniques to analyze their internal capabilities, including:

- Baldrige National Quality Program Criteria for self-assessment
- ISO 9001 quality system and ISO 14000 environmental management system requirements for gap analysis
- Benchmarking processes to understand best-in-class
- Competitive analysis of the five forces to understand competitors' businesses, market share, etc.

- Employee competency assessments to determine current knowledge, skills, experience, and aptitude
- Training needs analysis to identify training needs that can support organizational initiatives
- Employee surveys to determine if employees understand the organization's focus and to assess conditions and/or issues in the current work environment, compensation approaches, management, etc.
- Audits to verify that processes are working within established limits

No matter how an organization chooses to assess internal factors, internal issues should not be given a lower priority than the challenges the organization faces in the external environment. Without the internal capabilities in place, an organization is hard pressed to address external business issues. An internal gap can constrain an organization's ability to fulfill strategic external initiatives.

Linkage of Internal Capability Analysis to Strategic Planning

Internal capability analysis has two phases. The first phase is establishing a snapshot of the present state and identifying gaps. The second phase involves making decisions about closing the critical gaps to the desired state. Some gaps may be fairly simple and straightforward to address while others may require costly capital expenditures and time. The cost of developing any new capabilities must be weighed against the potential payoffs.

Different capabilities can provide sources of competitive advantages. An organization's future success often depends on the capabilities it develops. Capabilities that require financial investments can be risky because returns are uncertain. But not investing can be just as risky as it may cause an organization to fall behind competitors, fail to sustain profits, or compromise existing capabilities, leading to lost opportunities.

Strategic planning should involve an understanding of the internal requirements and capabilities needed prior to the operational plans being made. In the end, due diligence in assessing internal capabilities and addressing them appropriately helps the organization position itself to take advantage of future opportunities.

3. SWOT Analysis

SWOT is the acronym for **s**trengths, **w**eaknesses, **o**pportunities, and **t**hreats. A **SWOT analysis** provides a means to organize the data gathered in detailed internal and external analyses. Strengths and weakness are identified from an internal analysis of the organization; opportunities and threats are part of an external analysis of the environment in which the organization operates. SWOT analysis is also referred to as a current state analysis.

Figure 1B-6 SWOT Diagram

	Help Achieve Objectives	**Don't Help Achieve Objectives**
Internal	**S**trengths	**W**eaknesses
External	**O**pportunities	**T**hreats

Strengths

Strengths are the skills, capabilities, and core competencies that an organization has and that gives them the ability to achieve its goals and objectives, and sustain its competitive position.

Organizational strengths might be any of the following:

- Strong leadership
- Financial soundness
- Organizational learning
- Research and development (R&D)
- Innovative product designs
- Breakthrough technology
- Product development
- Product assembly
- Strong distribution channel
- Strong market position

One or more strengths can provide a competitive advantage and help an organization differentiate itself in the marketplace. For example, if a company is exceptional at R&D, it might focus efforts on in-house product development to build or strengthen a competitive advantage.

Weaknesses

Weaknesses are the skills, capabilities, and competencies that the organization lacks and prevents it from achieving its goals and objectives. Weaknesses may be thought of as opportunities for improvement.

When faced with a deficiency, an organization generally has three choices:

1. Modify the goal and objective into something achievable.
2. Invest the necessary capital to acquire the knowledge, skill, or resource required.
3. Find another organization that has the expertise needed and outsource that requirement.

For example, consider a small manufacturing company that does not have the funds or plant floor space for heat-treating furnaces. It would either have to outsource this "weakness" or invest capital funds if this capability was deemed critical for operations.

Opportunities

Opportunities generally are described as those external events and trends that can help an organization meet goals and grow to new levels. Examples of opportunities include the chance to:

- Expand the customer base—based on growth in customer numbers due to demand, favorable demographic population shifts, and so on.
- Provide new avenues of customer access—such as distribution channels or bundling of services.
- Increase customer appeal of the product/service offering—new media for advertising or methods of packaging to entice customers to switch from competitors.
- Exploit a competitor's weakness—capitalize on windows of opportunity to strengthen customer acceptance of the firm's product/service.

Threats

Threats are external barriers to an organization's growth. They are created mostly by events, trends, or competitor actions. Examples of threats include situations that:

- Reduce the size of a firm's customer base—due to economic downturns, unfavorable demographic population shifts, or in-sourcing by customers.
- Make customer access more difficult or costly—due to changes in customer buying practices or doing business with smaller numbers of suppliers.
- Reduce the customer appeal of a firm's product/service—price wars or other activities that can entice the customer to choose alternatives.
- Surpass the organization's product/service offering—price cutting or new offerings that provide significant improvements.

Overall, an organization should look to capitalize on opportunities and minimize threats.

Example of a SWOT Weighted Average

A weighted average can be useful in implementing SWOT analysis data.

Example

This example shows one way to select strategies using a weighted average in conjunction with SWOT data.

ABC Company has identified the following factors that can impact market attractiveness and business strength for a product. Each item has a different proportionate weight, that sum to 1.0. The rating scale ranges from 1 (the highest) to 5 (the lowest).

Market Attractiveness	Weight	Rating (1–5)
Market size	0.3	4
Market profitability	0.4	5
Distribution structure	0.2	4
Government regulations	0.1	2

Business Strength	Weight	Rating (1–5)
Unit costs	0.4	3
Customer loyalty	0.5	2
Brand reputation	0.1	4

The calculated weighted average for market attractiveness is 4.2, and the calculated weighted average for business strength is 2.6, as shown below. Because the highly attractive market will presumably entice others to enter, planning strategies to build on the lower business strength (rather than attempting to exploit the higher market attractiveness) could be a more beneficial plan.

Market attractiveness = $(0.3 \times 4) + (0.4 \times 5) + (0.2 \times 4) + (0.1 \times 2) = 4.2$

Business strength = $(0.4 \times 3) + (0.5 \times 2) + (0.1 \times 4) = 2.6$

Linkage of a SWOT Analysis to Strategic Planning

A SWOT analysis will generate a series of lists that an organization will then need to sort through. Organizations will be faced with a number of questions, such as:

- What interrelationships exist among the strengths, weaknesses, opportunities, and threats?
- Does the organization have the necessary resources and capabilities to seize the opportunities and neutralize the threats?
- How many competitors already have the same resources and competencies?
- Are there barriers to market entry?
- Could the organization gain a source of competitive advantage?
- Will acquiring a particular resource or capability create a cost disadvantage for the firm?
- Are substitutes available?
- Does the organizational structure allow the firm to take full advantage of its resources and capabilities and support potential growth/change?

The challenge in evaluating all the strengths, weaknesses, opportunities, and threats is to prioritize them and then identify appropriate actions. The basic idea is to:

- Build on strengths.
- Eliminate or deal with weaknesses.
- Exploit opportunities.
- Minimize threats.

In addressing strengths and weaknesses, the outlook can change quickly. What is true or feasible now may differ in time. For example, something that is considered a strength today can be immediately neutralized by a technological innovation or a change in a government regulation.

A SWOT analysis is an important part of strategic planning because it incorporates both internal and external assessments about an organization into one summary that is practical and usable. The opportunities and limitations identified provide information for reasonable goals and action plans in the strategic planning process.

4. Long-Term Vision, Mission, Goals, and Objectives

Organizational goals and strategies cannot be left to chance and intuition. They must be explicitly stated and clearly communicated to those in the organization responsible for their implementation. For that reason, an important step during strategic planning is to formally write out the organization's vision, mission, goals, and objectives. Referring back to Figure 1B-2 Key Elements of Strategic Planning will be helpful with the following section.

Vision

An organization's **vision statement** is a guiding image of future success and achievement articulated in terms of the organization's contribution to society. It is a succinct statement of what an organization will do for future generations and how it wants to be perceived.

Consider the vision statement example shown in Figure 1B-7.

Figure 1B-7 Vision Statement Example

Hilton Worldwide

To fill the earth with the light and warmth of hospitality.

PepsiCo

Our vision is put into action through programs and a focus on environmental stewardship, activities to benefit society, and a commitment to build shareholder value by making PepsiCo a truly sustainable company.

A clear vision statement is compelling and unites everyone in the organization. It will reflect organizational values and inspire and challenge management and employees to action.

Mission

A **mission statement** provides the guiding compass for an organization. A mission statement answers this question: Why are we in business? In answering this question, a mission statement must be accurate, easily understood, motivating, and transferable into action. It expresses how the organization will continuously move toward its vision and provides a clear view of what the firm is trying to accomplish for its customers and other stakeholders.

Figure 1B-8 shows an example of corporate mission statements.

Figure 1B-8 Corporate Mission Statement Example

Hilton Worldwide

To be the preeminent global hospitality company—the first choice of guests, team members, and owners alike.

PepsiCo

Our mission is to be the world's premier consumer products company focused on convenient foods and beverages. We seek to produce financial rewards to investors as we provide opportunities for growth and enrichment to our employees, our business partners and the communities in which we operate. And in everything we do, we strive for honesty, fairness and integrity.

Goals

Goals are the targets that an organization hopes to achieve in order to fulfill its mission and achieve its vision. Goals serve as general guidelines and tend not to be specific or quantifiable. A goal states the desired end result and the benefits of that result. It does not state the implementation plan. Organizations typically develop both strategic and tactical goals.

Strategic Goals

Strategic goals are established at the highest levels of an organization. Strategic goals are long range in nature. Examples of strategic goals are business diversification, the addition or deletion of product lines, and the penetration of new markets. The achievement of strategic goals requires the establishment and achievement of tactical goals.

Tactical Goals

Tactical goals generally are established by strategic business units (SBUs) or by functional departments at middle and lower levels of an organization. Tactical goals are short range, usually spanning one year or less. An example of a tactical goal is "to increase product line profits by 10% in the next year."

Concepts Applying to Strategic and Tactical Goals

Just as organizational strategies must be dynamic, so too must strategic and tactical goals. New things are always on the competitive horizon. Therefore, goals need to be modified or changed to reflect the internal and external changes taking place. At a minimum, goals should be evaluated on an annual basis.

Objectives

Objectives provide the details or actions required to support the goals. Well-conceived objectives specify the quantitative measures that will be used to track progress and performance—the desired action, the timing of the action, the level of performance desired, and the function or individual responsible for the action. Multiple objectives may support one goal. In this situation, all the objectives must be completed to realize the benefit of the goal. One objective alone cannot ensure fulfillment of the goal. Expanding on the previous example, "to increase product line profits by 10% in the next year," the supporting objective might include the following:

- Marketing team member A determines customer quality perceptions of product X within 30 days. Team member A prioritizes these customer perceptions and assigns a relative weight to each.
- Production team member B develops a process flow diagram of product X within 30 days, including all equipment involved.
- Accounting team member C conducts a profitability analysis of product X within 30 days, determining the profit margin percentage and the investment return.

In total, all the objectives would support the goal of increasing product line profits by 10% in the next year.

The acronym **SMART** is often applied as a reminder of an objective's requirements. Objectives should be:

Specific
Measurable
Attainable
Realistic
Timely

5. Alignment of Tactical Plans with Long-Term Strategic Goals

As noted earlier, a **strategic plan** tends to have a long-range planning horizon. This can be between one and ten years, depending upon the nature of the business. In contrast, an **operational plan** focuses on the fiscal year ahead and involves more tactical issues. A strategic plan precedes an operational plan because the strategic plan provides the foundation upon which the more detailed operational plan is developed. Therefore, strategic plans are "macro" plans and operational plans are "micro" plans. An overview comparing strategic and operational plans is shown in Figure 1B-9.

Linkage of Budgets to Strategic Plans

Strategic plans and operational plans lead to the formation of budgets. A **budget** represents a quantitative expression of proposed management actions for a defined period of time. Budgets have numerous advantages no matter what type or size an organization is. Budgets can:

- Provide a blueprint for the organization to follow in an upcoming time period, identifying the resources and commitments required to meet organizational goals and objectives.

Figure 1B-9 Comparison of Strategic and Operational Plans

	Strategic Plan	**Operational Plan**
Focus	Underlies both long- and short-run planning; provides the basis for the budget	Formulates specific goals for each business with detailed revenue and expense budgets
Issues Examined	Identifies and analyzes issues such as: • New global market entrants • Economic conditions • Plans for diversification	Identifies and analyzes issues such as: • Quarterly earnings • Inventory levels • Major capital expenditures • Marketing plans • Productions plans
Development	Flows from top down; reflects a comprehensive analysis of external and internal factors	Flows from bottom up; recommends specific options for the upcoming year
Control	Reviewed annually and updated as needed to reflect high-level changes	Reviewed and updated/modified periodically throughout the year to address changing needs such as lagging product sales or competitors' new pricing structures

- Help to identify potential bottlenecks/problems and facilitate smoother operations across businesses.
- Serve as a communication device, indicating expected performance for all divisions and all employees for the specified time period.
- Provide a frame of reference with guidelines for operations and criteria for monitoring and control.
- Facilitate performance evaluation of divisions and employees through the comparison of expected operations with actual results.

Budgets quantify management expectations regarding income, cash flows, and financial position. An organization prepares a variety of operational budgets (production, research and design, marketing, distribution, administration, etc.). A master budget coordinates all these individual budgets into a comprehensive organization-wide budget on an annual basis.

Organizational strategies and the strategic plan provide the basis and starting point for preparing the annual master budget. Naturally, the master budget must be congruent with the strategic plan and contribute to the achievement of the organization's long-term strategic vision, mission, and goals.

How strategy flows from strategic planning through the budgeting process is shown in Figure 1B-10. Strategy starts with a broad perspective. At the budget level, the focus becomes very specific and detailed.

Figure 1B-10 Flow of Organizational Strategy

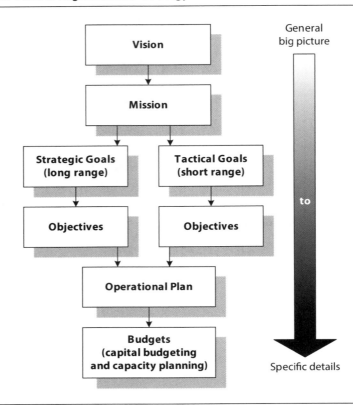

Characteristics of Successful Strategic/Tactical Planning

LOS
§1.B.1.g

Organizations and the industries they compete in are complex moving targets for strategists. Enterprises continually shift in response to anything that can upset the competitive balance.

The strategic planning process—no matter how large or small the organization or how formal or informal the methodology—offers several benefits in helping a firm frame its competitive strategy. It also has some limitations. Understanding both the advantages and disadvantages helps to recognize what constitutes successful strategic planning.

Benefits of Strategic Planning

Strategic planning provides the following benefits:

- A systematic approach to analyzing threats and opportunities and examining why some organizational strategies have better competitive and profit prospects than others
- A sound framework for developing an effective operating budget
- An organizational learning opportunity for managers to think about strategies and how to best implement them

- An exercise to align management decision making and actions with corporate strategies (to gain the buy-in of managers and show how their decisions and actions support corporate programs)
- A basis for both financial and nonfinancial performance measures
- A channel of communication among all levels of management about strategies, objectives, operational plans, and so on
- Guidance for approaching new situations

Limitations of Strategic Planning

Strategic planning is not the end-all panacea to all organizational woes. Some of the key shortcomings of strategic planning include:

- The effort, time, and expense involved in the process
- The fact that planning based on predictions is not an exact science; due to a variety of factors, plans may prove to be incorrect and fail
- The potential for resistance to change resulting from entrenched ways of doing things
- The risk that planning can become a bureaucratic exercise devoid of fresh ideas and strategic thinking

LOS
§1.B.1.i

Contingency Planning

Well-conceived strategic plans are based on events that are likely to occur but should also include the uncertainties that are so prevalent in today's business environment.

Contingency Planning Defined

Strategic plans often include contingency plans to help cope with turbulent conditions that could lead to serious difficulty for the enterprise.

Contingency plans are preparations for the what-if situations that might occur and are used for a specific unintended event. The purpose of contingency planning is to allow a faster reaction time and to provide guidance to managers when they are faced with unexpected developments and crises.

Subjects of Contingency Plans

Typical conditions for contingency planning include:

- Lower sales or profit levels
- New entrants that can capture market share
- Government regulations
- Loss of a key executive or manager/succession planning for key employee replacement
- Damage to a critical facility
- Computer system hacking/information security issues

- Disaster recovery
- Sudden changes in interest rates
- Shrinking capital availability
- Union activity
- Mergers, acquisitions, and takeovers

Realistically, contingency plans cannot cover every possible scenario. Most organizations prepare contingency plans for the most critical events, based on how critical the event could be to operations and the probability the event will occur.

Steps in Contingency Planning

In most companies, contingency plans are prepared after the strategic plan is completed. The strategic planning process provides valuable data for developing the contingency plans. Contingency plans typically deal with short-range tactical strategies rather than long-range strategies.

Figure 1B-11 outlines basic steps for contingency planning.

Figure 1B-11 Steps in Contingency Planning

Step 1.	Identify potential scenarios needing contingency plans (events, what-ifs).
Step 2.	Estimate the potential impact of the events identified (in financial terms, competitive position, etc.).
Step 3.	Develop strategies and tactical plans to deal with each possible occurrence.
Step 4.	Specify trigger points or warning signals.
Step 5.	Store plans off-site.
Step 6.	Routinely review plans and revise as warranted (at least as often as strategic planning).

No standard format for a contingency plan exists. Ideally, a contingency plan should be succinct but include enough detail to guide actions if needed. The more critical the threat, the more detail is warranted.

A few simple examples of accounting-related contingency plans are shown in Figure 1B-12.

Figure 1B-12 Examples of Accounting-Related Contingency Plans

Subject	Plan
Loss of a computer system during a general ledger (GL) close	Identification of off-site (outsourcing) location/service for computer usage
	Identification of company-trained associates who could work at the remote site
Loss of a chief financial officer or another key financial associate	Succession plan
	Identification of key associates to train
	Identification of backup personnel from another division
	Provisions/steps for an outside search
Declining major product/service sales	Identification of areas for analysis and/or change
	Plans for the alternate use of resources
	Layoff considerations

Other Planning Tools and Techniques

There are several other important tools and techniques an organization might use in its strategic planning efforts. These tools and techniques include situational analysis, scenario planning, competitive analysis, and the BCG Growth-Share matrix.

Situational Analysis

Situational analysis refers to a collection of methods that an organization uses to analyze its internal and external environment in order to enhance understanding of the organization's capabilities, customers, and business environment. The situational analysis looks at both the macroenvironmental factors that affect many organizations within the environment and the microenvironmental factors that specifically affect the organization. The purpose of the analysis is to identify the organization's position and to provide an assessment of the organization's ability to survive within the environment. Organizations must be able to summarize opportunities and problems within the environment so they can understand their capabilities within the market.

The methods used in conducting a situational analysis might include a SWOT analysis, Porter's Five Forces analysis, as well as a 5C analysis. The 5C analysis is considered the most useful and common way to analyze the market environment because of the extensive information it provides. It consists of five mini-analyses focused around the 1) **c**ompany, 2) **c**ompetitors, 3) **c**ustomers, 4) **c**ollaborators, and 5) the **c**limate, meaning business climate.

The *company analysis* evaluates the organization's objectives, strategy, and capabilities. The *competitor analysis* assesses competitor position within the industry and the potential threat it may pose to other businesses. The *customer analysis* is extensive, focusing on customer demographics (wants and needs, motivation to buy, quantity and frequency of purchase, target advertising, etc.). *Collaborator analysis* deals with identifying other key "middlemen" that might help increase the organization's likelihood of gaining more business opportunities. Collaborators include agencies, suppliers, distributors, and other business partners. Finally, a *climate analysis* focuses on researching factors within the business climate and environment that can have an effect on the organization. This analysis is also referred to as a **PEST analysis**, which includes conducting analyses of the following:

- **Political and regulatory environment**. How actively the government regulates the market with its policies and how this might affect the production, distribution, and sale of goods and services
- **Economic environment**. Analyzing trends regarding macroeconomics, such as exchange rates and inflation rate
- **Social/cultural environment**. Focuses on interpreting societal trends, which include the study of demographics, education, and culture
- **Technological analysis**. Assessing current technological state and technological advances in order to be able to stay competitive and gain advantage over competitors

Scenario Planning

Scenario planning, also called scenario thinking or scenario analysis, is a strategic planning methodology designed to assist the organization in developing flexible strategic plans. It involves simulating or gaming the expected behavior of what are called STEEEPA trends. STEEEPA is an acronym for plausible alternative:

Social
Technical
Economic
Environmental
Educational
Political
Aesthetic trends

These are the key driving forces in the organization's environment. Again, the focus is on assessing opportunities and threats and developing coping mechanisms.

Competitive Analysis

Competitive analysis, or competitor analysis, focuses on understanding an organization's competition. It includes recognizing who the competition really is, rather than who the organization thinks it is. It involves profiling competitors regarding history, products and services, financial condition, corporate and marketing strategies, facilities, and personnel. It also encourages the organization to scan the environment for potential new customers. The steps in competitor analysis involve:

- Determining the organization's industry and its scope and nature
- Determining who the organization's real competitors are
- Determining the organization's customers and their needs
- Determining critical success factors (CSFs) or key performance indicators (KPIs) for the organization's industry
- Ranking the KPIs
- Ranking the organization's competition in relation to the KPIs

BCG Growth-Share Matrix

The **BCG Growth-Share matrix** is a chart/matrix created by the Boston Consulting Group (BCG) in 1970 to help organizations analyze their business units and/or product lines to enable the firm to allocate resources appropriately. The chart/matrix is an effective analytical tool in brand marketing and in product and strategic management. An example of the BCG Growth-Share Matrix is shown in Figure 1B-13.

Figure 1B-13 BCG Growth-Share Matrix

		Relative Market Share (RMS)	
		High	Low
Market Growth Rate (MGR) — High		Stars	Question Marks
Market Growth Rate (MGR) — Low		Cash Cows	Dogs

Through the matrix, an organization ranks its business units or products on the basis of their relative market share (RMS) and market growth rate (MGR) and places them into one of the following four quadrants:

1. **Cash cows.** These business units or product lines have high RMS, but low MGR. They have a positive net cash flow and do not need cash for expansion.
2. **Dogs.** These business units or product lines have low RMS and low MGR. They have a modest net cash flow and cash should not be put towards them for expansion.
3. **Stars.** These business units or product lines have high RMS and high MGR. Their net cash flow is usually modest. However, cash should be put into them for expansion. These are the units or brands the firm would want to build.
4. **Question marks.** These business units or product lines have low RMS but a high MGR. Their net cash flow is usually poor. The firm would put cash towards expansion if they are believed to have potential. If not, the firm should divest them.

Bruce Henderson of BCG has quoted the following with regard to the practical use of the matrix: "To be successful, a company should have a portfolio of products with different growth rates and different market shares. The portfolio composition is a function of the balance between cash flows. High-growth products require cash inputs to grow. Low-growth products should generate excess cash. Both kinds are needed simultaneously."

Topic Questions: Strategic Planning

Directions: Answer each question in the space provided. Correct answers and explanations appear after the topic questions.

1. In strategic planning, PEST analysis is best described as evaluating which of the following factors?

    ☐ **a.** Political, economic, social, and technological

    ☐ **b.** People, environment, sustainability, and tactics

    ☐ **c.** Process, efficiency, scale, and timing

    ☐ **d.** Products, employees, strengths, and threats

2. What type of plan is formulated at the highest levels of management, takes the broadest view of the company and its environment, is the least quantifiable, and determines the future nature of the firm, its products, and its customers?

    ☐ **a.** Short-range plan

    ☐ **b.** Long-range plan

    ☐ **c.** Strategic plan

    ☐ **d.** Future plan

3. A company has developed and implemented a wireless charging feature into one of its flashlights. No other competitor in the marketplace currently offers this feature. In a marketing research study, the vast majority of consumers indicated that they would pay a premium for this feature. Which one of the following is the best strategy to bring this product to the market?

    ☐ **a.** Porter's cost strategy

    ☐ **b.** Porter's focus strategy

    ☐ **c.** Porter's differentiation strategy

    ☐ **d.** Porter's segmentation strategy

Topic Question Answers: Strategic Planning

1. In strategic planning, PEST analysis is best described as evaluating which of the following factors?

    ☑ **a.** Political, economic, social, and technological

    ☐ **b.** People, environment, sustainability, and tactics

    ☐ **c.** Process, efficiency, scale, and timing

    ☐ **d.** Products, employees, strengths, and threats

The PEST analysis is a specific tool used to analyze external and internal conditions. The acronym stands for Political, Economic, Social, and Technological.

2. What type of plan is formulated at the highest levels of management, takes the broadest view of the company and its environment, is the least quantifiable, and determines the future nature of the firm, its products, and its customers?

    ☐ **a.** Short-range plan

    ☐ **b.** Long-range plan

    ☑ **c.** Strategic plan

    ☐ **d.** Future plan

A strategic plan addresses how to implement new strategies that result from the strategy formulation process. Strategic planning addresses the following core elements at some level: external factors, internal factors, strengths, weaknesses, opportunities, and threats (SWOT) analysis, long-term vision, mission and goals, and tactics to achieve long-term goals.

3. A company has developed and implemented a wireless charging feature into one of its flashlights. No other competitor in the marketplace currently offers this feature. In a marketing research study, the vast majority of consumers indicated that they would pay a premium for this feature. Which one of the following is the best strategy to bring this product to the market?

    ☐ **a.** Porter's cost strategy

    ☐ **b.** Porter's focus strategy

    ☑ **c.** Porter's differentiation strategy

    ☐ **d.** Porter's segmentation strategy

The best strategy to bring this product to the market is Porter's differentiation strategy because the wireless charging feature makes the product unique and more attractive to customers.

Budgeting Concepts

PLANNING IS THE PROCESS OF mapping out the organization's future direction to attain desired goals. Strategy is the organization's plan to match its strengths with the opportunities in the marketplace to accomplish its desired goals over the short and long term. A budget provides the foundation for planning, because a successful budget is created by a process of aligning the company's resources with its strategy.

This topic introduces the concepts underlying budgeting, the processes used, the people involved, and their roles. It also examines the standards that may be employed in developing budget expectations and evaluating performance against these expectations. This topic provides an overview of the elements of a budget that are explored in greater detail in subsequent topics.

 READ the Learning Outcome Statements (LOS) for this topic as found in Appendix A and then study the concepts and calculations presented here to be sure you understand the content you could be tested on in the CMA exam.

Fundamentals: Terminology, Budget Cycle, and Reasons for Budgeting

These budget terms are used in this section.

Budget. A budget is an operational plan and a control tool for an entity that identifies the resources and commitments needed to achieve the entity's goals over a time period. Budgets are primarily quantitative, not qualitative. They set specific goals for income, cash flows, and financial position.

Budgeting. Budgeting is undertaking the steps involved in preparing a budget. Along with clear communication of organizational goals, the ideal budget also contains budgetary controls.

Budgetary control. Without a formal system of control, a budget is little more than a forecast. Budgetary control is a management process to help ensure that a budget is achieved by:

- instituting a systematic budget approval process
- coordinating the efforts of all involved parties and operations
- analyzing variances from the plan and providing appropriate feedback to responsible parties

The goals identified in the budget must be perceived by employees as realistic if those employees are to be motivated to achieve the goals.

Pro forma statement. A pro forma statement is a budgeted financial statement based on historical documents and appropriate forecasting techniques that is adjusted for events as if they had occurred. Budgeted balance sheets, budgeted statements of cash flows, and budgeted income statements are forecasts of goals for a future period that assist in the allocation of resources.

Budget Cycle

A budget cycle usually involves six key considerations:

1. A budget is created that addresses the entity as a whole, as well as its subunits. Senior management gives their managers a set of specific expectations for the budget.
2. All the managers of the subunits agree to fulfill their part of the budget. A critical aspect of the budgeting process is subunit management affirmation and commitment to adopting and fulfilling their part of the budget in support of the achievement of overall company objectives. This management buy-in aligns subunits with overall company strategies.
3. Once finalized, the budget becomes the company's performance benchmark. As such, actual results are measured against budgeted expectations.
4. All variations from budget are closely analyzed to determine the root cause of the variance.
5. Management uses the variance analysis to take all necessary corrective action to re-direct future results to budget expectations wherever possible.
6. Further evaluation of performance is closely monitored. If conditions cannot be altered to re-direct future results to budget expectations, management will determine appropriate plans which identify future expectations given those conditions. Since these revised plans consider significant changes in the business and economic environment, they are often used in the development of subsequent budgeting.

Figure 1B-14 shows how these steps revolve back to the beginning to form a cycle.

Figure 1B-14 Budget Cycle

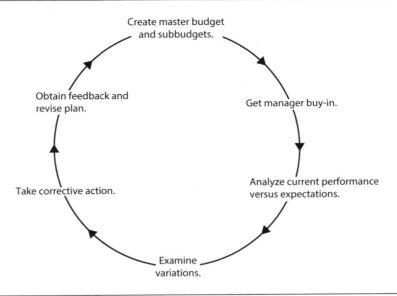

Reasons for Budgeting

There are four main reasons a company creates a budget: planning, communication and coordination, monitoring, and evaluation.

1. Planning

One of the major benefits of budgeting is that it forces the organization to examine the future. Expectations must be established for income, expenses, personnel needs, future growth or contraction, and so on. Both strategic and operational planning allow for the input of ideas from multiple sources and viewpoints within the organization. The planning process may generate new ideas for the organization's direction, or it may provide insight into better ways to achieve goals that have already been established. Budgets, an output of the planning process, provide a framework to achieve the goals of the organization. Without the budget framework, individual managers would improvise decisions and operate in a reactive rather than a proactive manner. As a result, there would be a lack of both direction and coordination of activities.

LOS
§1.B.2.f

2. Communication and Coordination

Budgeting also promotes the communication and coordination of efforts within the organization. The different business functions of the organization (production, marketing, materials management, etc.) must communicate their plans and needs to each other during the budget process so that all can evaluate the effect that the plans and needs of others have on their own. Each part of the organization must coordinate its activities to attain the budgeted goals and objectives. For example, if a new product is to be developed, funds must be provided for development, the purchase of materials for production of the product, promoting and selling the new product, and additional storage space, shipping, and distribution. Budgeting also allows the organization to communicate its goals to everyone in the organization, including those not involved in the budget process. Budgeting sets the stage for everyone in the organization to work toward the goals of the organization.

3. Monitoring

The budget sets standards, or performance indicators, by which managers can monitor the organization's progress in meeting its goals. By comparing the actual results for a time period to the budgeted results for that period, managers can see whether the organization is on track to achieving its goals. Breaking down the organization's master budget to divisional and departmental levels allows each level of the organization to be evaluated. The organization as a whole may be meeting its goals while individual divisions and departments are not. A variance is considered to be **favorable** or **unfavorable**, depending on its impact on Net Income. An increase in Sales and a decrease in an expense are considered favorable variances. Both will increase Net Income. But a decrease in Sales and an increase in expenses are considered unfavorable variances. Both of these will decrease Net Income.

4. Evaluation

Budgets also serve as a way to evaluate employees. Once the budget is set and managers have been advised of their responsibilities in relation to budget performance, they can be held responsible for their portion of the budget. A manager's performance can be evaluated by comparing actual results to the budget for a given period. Having unfavorable results does not necessarily mean that a manager is not performing well, but provide an indication of where to find the root cause of the variance. Likewise, favorable results do not necessarily mean that a manager is performing well. Macroeconomic changes can have a sizable effect on the manager's ability to meet budgets. For instance, weather, conflict, and consumer tastes can drastically change the selling price of a company's goods or the price of raw materials. Performance evaluations allow an organization to motivate employees by rewarding them for good performance. This can be done through performance-based bonuses and/or by including performance evaluations in the decision process for future compensation or promotion decisions. To the extent possible, performance-based pay should be tied to metrics that are controllable by the employee and should disregard factors that are uncontrollable.

Economic Considerations in the Budgeting Process

There are a significant number of interrelationships among economic conditions, industry situations, organizational plans, and the budgeting process. Budgeting is most effective when the budgeting process is linked to the overall strategy of the organization. Managers should build their strategy and organizational objectives to focus on all economic factors, including the financial impact of decision-making and understanding the factors of competition.

When developing an organizational strategy, managers should ask these questions:

- What are our organizational objectives?
- How can we relate our organizational objectives to the budgeting process?
- Who are our competitors, and how can we differentiate ourselves from them?
- How are we affected by the competition and trends in the marketplace?
- What organizational risks exist that may impact the budgeting process?
- What organizational opportunities exist that may impact the budgeting process?

Operations and Performance Goals

A prerequisite for budget development is a strategic analysis that matches an entity's capabilities with available marketplace opportunities. Strategy addresses the objectives of the organization; locates potential markets; considers the impact of events, competitors, and the economy; addresses the structure of the organization; and evaluates the risks of alternative strategies. Strategic analysis is the basis for both long-term and short-term planning. These plans lead, respectively, to long-term and short-term budgets (as summarized in Figure 1B-15), and these budgets in turn lead to the creation of a master budget and its components.

Figure 1B-15 Strategy, Planning, and Budgets

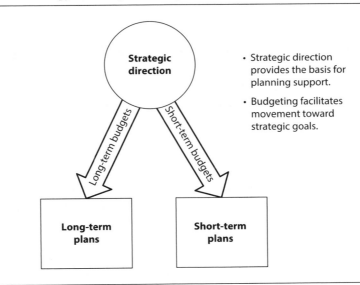

LOS
§1.B.2.d

Budgets play a role in measuring performance against established goals. When using past performance solely to evaluate present results, the mistakes and problems that occurred in the past are automatically factored in to the benchmark that is being used.

For example: A company reports poor sales because of a new and inexperienced sales force. If current-year data is used as the benchmark for next year's sales, the mark would be set lower than necessary and the sales team would not be motivated to work as hard. However, if the benchmark is set too high, employees may not strive to achieve amounts they view as unrealistic.

Employing a forecasted budget as a plan allows for the use of the expected results as the benchmark. Another benefit of using a budget instead of historical results is that past performance is not always indicative of future results. Relying only on historical data leads to a sense that the past year must always be improved on, no matter the circumstances.

Costs are considered "controllable" or "discretionary" when the purchaser or manager has the discretion to incur the charge or alter the level of the charge within a short amount of time. Variable costs and other costs directly under the control of the manager are called controllable costs. The manager can cut workers' hours, use cheaper materials, or otherwise restrict such controllable costs. A division manager can control maintenance and advertising costs to a certain degree.

Fixed costs, such as administrative salaries or rent, usually are not controllable by the manager. They are called "committed" or noncontrollable costs.

Controllable costs are the most useful for performance evaluation.

- Rating a manager's use of funds based on divisional net revenue less controllable costs will be perceived, by those being evaluated, as a more reasonable approach. Managers should not be held accountable for noncontrollable costs, as this can be very unmotivating.
- Focusing on controllable costs places the emphasis where the most benefit can be achieved from the effort of budgeting.

Characteristics of Successful Budgeting

No single factor developed in isolation can lead to a successful budget. Many of the following factors must be considered together to develop a successful budget:

- The budget must be aligned with the corporate strategy.
- The budget process should be kept separate from, but should flow from, the strategic planning and forecasting processes.
- **Strategic plans** are higher level, longer term, and structured in companywide terms, such as product lines, rather than responsibility centers. However, early budgeting steps can be used to refine the strategic direction of the company because they use more current information.
- Budgets must use the forward-looking information from more comprehensive forecasts. Therefore, the forecasts directly used in the budgeting process, such as the sales forecast, will have a high level of accountability.
- The budget should be used to alleviate potential bottlenecks and to allocate resources to those areas that will use the funds most efficiently and effectively.
- The budget must contain technically correct and reasonably accurate numbers and facts.
- Management (including top management) must fully endorse the budget and accept responsibility for reaching the budget goals.
- Employees must consider the budget as a planning, communication, and coordinating tool, and not as a pressure or blame device.

- The budget must be characterized as a motivational tool to help employees work toward organizational goals.
- The budget must be seen as an internal control device, where internal-use budgets base employee evaluations on controllable or discretionary costs.
- Sales and administrative budgets need to be detailed in order that key assumptions can be better understood.
- A higher authority than the team that developed the budget must review and approve the budget.

The final budget should not be easily changed, but must be flexible enough to be useful. Budgets should compel planning, promote communication and coordination, and provide performance criteria. The budget process must balance input from those who will need to follow the budget against a thorough and fair review of the budget by upper management.

Characteristics of a Successful Budget Process

Whether the organization and its budget are very simple or highly complex, the characteristics of a successful budget process include: the budget period, the participants in the budget process, the basic steps in budgeting, and the use of cost standards.

Budget Period

LOS §1.B.2.i

The time period for a budget is the length of time appropriate for the purpose of the budget. Short-term budgets are prepared for a one-year time period that coincides with the entity's fiscal year. A master budget is usually for a one-year time period. This can be broken down to quarterly, monthly, and weekly budgets as needed. Long-term budgets are often prepared for three-, five-, and ten-year time periods. This is appropriate for a strategic plan. The shorter the time period, the more detailed the budget will be. Budgets can be prepared as continuous (rolling) budgets. A continuous budget has a monthly, quarterly, or yearly basis. As each period ends, the upcoming period's budget is revised by adding an additional budget time period to the end of the budget. Software is available for implementing continuous budgets.

Budget Process

LOS §1.B.2.j

LOS §1.B.2.k

Methods of budget preparation differ among companies, but all fall somewhere on a continuum between entirely authoritative and entirely participative. In an **authoritative budget** (top-down budget), top management sets everything from strategic goals down to the individual items of the budget for each department. Lower-level managers and employees are expected to adhere to the budget and meet the goals. In a **participative budget** (bottom-up or self-imposed budget), managers at all levels and certain key employees cooperate to set budgets for their areas. Top management usually retains final approval. The ideal budget process combines the features of each and falls somewhere between these methods.

Figure 1B-16 Comparison of Authoritative, Combined, and Participative Budgeting

Authoritative Approach	Combination Approach	Participative Approach
Top management incorporates strategic goals into its budgets.	Strategic goals are communicated top down and implemented bottom up.	Strategic goals do not receive priority in the budgetary process.
Better control over decisions.	Control retained and expertise gained at cost of a slightly longer process.	Expertise leads to informed budget decisions.
Dictates instead of communicates.	Two-way communication: Top management understands participants' difficulties and needs. Participants understand management's dilemmas.	Communicates lower-level perspective (of product/service or market) to management.
Employees: Resentful Unmotivated	Personal control leads to acceptance, which leads to greater personal commitment.	Employees: Involved Empowered
Stringent budgets may not be strictly followed at lower levels.	Ownership of budget and thorough review leads to tight budgets that get followed.	Easy or abdicated approval can lead to loose budgets and budget slack.
Not a recommended approach but could work in small or slow-changing environments.	Best for most companies; provides balance between strategic and tactical inputs.	Best for responsibility centers with highly variable situations where area manager has best data.

Figure 1B-16 lists benefits and limitations of purely authoritative and participative budgeting and shows how a combined approach provides the greatest number of checks and balances over the budgetary process. Note that the combination approach sometimes is considered to be a form of the participative approach.

The five steps in a combined approach include:

1. Budget participants are identified, including representatives of all levels of management, as well as key employees with expertise in particular areas.
2. Top management communicates the strategic direction to budget participants.
3. Budget participants create the first draft of their budget.
4. Lower levels submit budgets to the next higher level for review in an iterative process stressing communication in both directions.
5. Rigorous but fair review and budget approval sets the final budget.

Budget Participants

Three groups make or break a budget: the board of directors, top management, and the budget committee. Middle and lower management also play a significant role, because they create detailed budgets based on upper management's plan. Depending on the size of the company and the type of budget being created, a budget coordinator and process experts may be involved in budget development.

Board of Directors

The board of directors does not create the budget, but it cannot abdicate its responsibility to review the budget and either approve or send it back for revision. The board usually appoints the members of the budget committee.

Top Management

Top management is ultimately responsible for the budgets, and the primary means top managers have of exercising this responsibility is to ensure that all levels of management understand and support the budget and the overall budget control process. If top management is not perceived to endorse a budget, line managers will be less likely to follow the budget precisely. Also, top managers should pay close attention to how they are affecting each line manager's budget, because insensitive policies could result in creative budgeting on the part of staff.

Top managers should give their subordinates incentives for making truthful and complete budgets, such as rewarding accuracy. A common problem that needs to be avoided is budget slack. **Budget slack** occurs when budgeted performance differs from actual performance because the manager built in some extra money in the budget to deal with the unexpected. Budget slack is built-in freedom to fail, and cumulative budget slack at each sublevel can result in a very inaccurate master budget. Budgetary slack works against goal congruence because the manager is budgeting without taking the organization's goals in to account.

However, rigid enforcement of budgets will, in some situations, cost an organization more in the long run than if some flexibility is allowed. For example, a manufacturer could lose thousands of dollars if the maintenance manager refuses to approve overtime for its mechanics to make an urgent repair because "it would use up too much of the maintenance budget."

Budget Committee

Large corporations usually need to form a budget committee composed of senior management and often led by the chief executive officer (CEO) or a vice president. The size of the committee will vary depending on the organization. The committee directs budget preparation, approves budgets, rules on disagreements, monitors the budget, reviews results, and approves revisions.

Middle and Lower Management

Once the budget committee sets the tone for the budget process, many others in the organization have a role to play. Middle and lower management do much of the specific budgeting work. These managers follow budget guidelines, which are general guidelines for responsibility centers preparing individual budgets set by either top management or the budget committee. A responsibility center, cost center, or strategic business unit is a segment of a company in which the manager is vested with the authority to make cost, revenue, and/or investment decisions and therefore also set budgets. The budget guidelines are formed around the company's strategy and long-term plans. The guidelines govern preparation methods, layout, and events that should be considered, such as new downsizing needs or changes in the economy.

Budget Coordinator

The more people who are involved in a budget process, the greater the need for an individual or team who can identify and resolve discrepancies between the budgets of the various responsibility centers and between various portions of a master budget.

Process Experts

When participative budgeting is used, often certain key nonmanagerial employees are added to the team. Team participants tend to be those who have a detailed understanding of the costs for a particular area, especially those areas that are extremely complex or variable. Such participants will not only bring more focus to a budget but will also take ownership of the budget and increase its likelihood of being followed at the operational level.

Budgeting Steps

The steps that responsibility centers take in preparing their budgets include the initial budget proposal, budget negotiation, review and approval, and revision.

Budget Proposal

After the CEO decides on the company strategy, a memo or directive is sent to all line managers or responsibility centers so they can start aligning their budget process with the strategic plan (i.e., a top-down implementation). With this strategy in mind, each responsibility center prepares an initial budget, taking both internal and external factors into account. Internal factors include: changes in price, availability, and manufacturing processes; new products or services; changes in related or intertwined responsibility centers; and staff changes. External factors include changes in the economy and the labor market, the price and availability of goods and services, industry trends, and actions of competitors.

Budget Negotiation

When the initial budget proposal is submitted to a superior or to the budget committee, the budget is reviewed to see if it meets the organization's strategic goals, falls within an acceptable range, and is consistent with similar budgets. Reviewers also determine if the budget is feasible and if it fits within the goals of units the next level up. Negotiations take up the bulk of time in budget preparations because pushback from a superior will result in renegotiation of priorities for both the superior and the responsibility center.

Budget Review and Approval

Budgets are reviewed and approved up the chain of command to the level of the budget committee. The combined budgets become the master budget, after review for consistency with the budget guidelines, short- and long-term goals, and strategic plans. Once the committee and the committee leader approve the plan, it is submitted to the board of directors for final approval.

Budget Revision

The rigidity of a budget varies from organization to organization. Some budgets must be followed absolutely; others can be revised only under specific circumstances; and others are subject to continuous revision. Rigidly following a budget in the face of changing circumstances has the potential for disaster. Management should not be required to rely on the budget as the sole operational guideline. Regular revisions may provide better operating guidelines. However, this may lead managers to anticipate regular changes and not prepare budgets as carefully as they should. Organizations that allow regular revisions should make sure that the threshold for revision is set high enough to keep employees working as efficiently as possible. When regular revisions occur, a copy of the original budget should be kept for comparison with actual results at the end of the period.

Cost Standards

Organizations set different types of standards that they strive to achieve. A **standard** is any carefully determined price, quantity, service level, or cost. Standards in manufacturing are usually set on a per-unit basis. A standard cost is how much an operation or service should cost, or the cost an entity expects to incur assuming that all goes as planned (expected time and capacity). Budget planners use standard costs to prepare budgets and then update standard costs as circumstances change. In practice, there is not a precise dividing line between a budgeted amount and a standard amount. Within shorter time frames, there is little distinction between a budgeted amount and a standard amount.

Types of Standards

Standards can be set in either an authoritative or participative way.

Authoritative Standards

Authoritative standards are determined solely by management. They are more speedily set and can closely match overall company goals, but they may be a cause for resentment or may not be followed at all.

Participative Standards

Participative standards are set by holding a dialogue between management and all involved parties. They are more likely to be adopted than authoritative standards, but they take more time because they require negotiation to ensure that operating goals are still met.

Specific types of standard costs include ideal standards and reasonably attainable standards.

Ideal Standards

An ideal standard is a forward-looking goal that is currently attainable only if all circumstances result in the best possible outcome. Ideal standards work into a continuous improvement strategy and total quality management philosophies. They allow for no work delays, interruptions, waste, or machine breakdown. Ideal standards require a level of effort that can be attained only by the most skilled and efficient employees working at their best efficiency all of the time. Some firms use progress toward an ideal standard instead of deviations from the ideal to measure and reward success. However, ideal standards are very difficult to attain, and their frequent use can become frustrating. If difficult-to-attain ideal standards are constantly required, they can be a disincentive to productivity, because workers may not even attempt to meet such "impossible" goals.

Reasonably Attainable Standards

A reasonably attainable standard is closer to a historical standard because it sets goals at a level that is attainable by properly trained individuals operating at a normal pace. The standard is expected to be reached most of the time, and it allows for normal work delays, spoilage, waste, employee rest periods, and machine downtime. These practical standards can be attained by efficient efforts from an average worker. Variances from practical standards represent deviations caused by abnormal conditions.

Standard Costs for Direct Materials and Labor

Direct cost items, such as direct materials and direct labor, are measured by determining the number of units of each type of input required to get one unit of output. This amount is multiplied by the standard cost per input unit.

For example: If three input units are allowed for producing one output unit and an input unit costs $10, then the standard cost would be $30 per output unit. For direct labor, if 0.7 manufacturing labor hours of input are allowed for producing one output unit and labor hours cost $10, then the standard cost would be $7 per output unit.

A total standard cost for one unit of output is developed by adding together multiple direct materials and labor costs. More specific guidelines for determining the prices for direct materials and labor are described next.

Standard Costs for Direct Materials

Standard costs are determined based on quality, quantity, and price. Quality must be determined first, because it affects all the other variables. Quality level is determined by the product's targeted market niche. The standard is developed by engineers, production managers, and management accountants working together based on the production facilities, the quality of the product, the costs of manufacturing, and the equipment to be used. Direct material usage standards should allow for losses, spoilage, scrap, and waste normally expected in the production process. A price is set as a combination of all prior work done, including quality, quantity, and supply chain costs. Determining supply chain costs includes such considerations as whether to select the lowest-cost vendor each time (costs will vary) or to establish a relationship with one reliable vendor (costs will be more stable).

Standard Costs for Direct Labor

Product complexity, personnel skill levels, the type and condition of equipment, and the nature of the manufacturing process will all affect the direct labor costs. Management accountants, engineers, production managers, labor unions, human resources, and others affect the direct labor standards. Labor efficiency standards should consider normally expected equipment downtime and worker breaks that slow the production process. The cost of direct labor is based on gross base pay that includes fringe benefits, not net base pay. Overtime and shift premiums are normally considered labor-related overhead costs and reported as indirect labor.

Sources for Standards Setting

Several sources are often used simultaneously when setting standards: activity analysis, historical data, market expectations, strategic decisions, and benchmarking.

Sources for Standards Setting			
Source	How are standard costs determined?	Pros	Cons
Activity Analysis	Interviewing personnel and detailed analysis of operations	Most thorough costing method	Very expensive to implement
Historical Data	Previous company performance	Relative inexpensive	Can perpetuate past inefficiencies and fails to account for technological improvements
Market Expectations/ Strategic Decisions	The cost is determined by what the market will bear	Useful when a company is a price taker in the market	It may take considerable time to determine and achieve target cost
Benchmarking	Best practices of the company or industry	Can lead to continuous improvement as best practices change	May prevent company from being innovative

Activity Analysis

An activity analysis is part of activity-based costing (ABC) that identifies, codifies, and analyzes the activities needed to finish a job or operation. (ABC is discussed in more detail in Section D: Cost Management.) The most efficient combination of resources and other inputs is derived by interviewing personnel directly involved with various aspects of the operation. Engineers are involved in calculating the product ingredients and determining the specific steps required in the process. Management accountants help analyze the direct costs of the inputs and allocate an appropriate amount of the indirect costs (lighting, rent, repairs, etc.) to the operation. Such analyses also evaluate the skill levels required of those who perform the tasks. The activity analyses required in activity-based costing result in the most thorough costing method but are the most expensive to implement.

Historical Data

Relying on historical data for determining costs is relatively inexpensive but is less reliable than activity analysis. When reliable, historical data can be used to find the average or median historical cost for an operation. To implement continuous improvement, the best performance recorded could be used as the standard.

However, historical data can perpetuate past inefficiencies or fail to take into account the impact of new technologies.

Market Expectations and Strategic Decisions

Market expectations and strategic decisions can determine a maximum cost level that is allowed for a product, as is the case when using target costing. Target costing is a technique in which the product's target operating income is subtracted from the target price to determine the target cost. This is most useful when a company is a price taker in the market. Strategic objectives, such as a program of continuous improvement or zero defects, will help to accomplish the target cost.

Benchmarking

The company would compare its processes to the processes of other companies or the industry it is operating in. Benchmarking is discussed in more detail in Section D: Cost Management.

Resource Allocation

All entities have a finite amount of resources and want to make the most of their capital. The allocation of scarce resources among competing opportunities is accomplished through implementation of a strategy.

Strategy

A company analyzes external factors to identify opportunities and threats, and it analyzes internal factors to identify competitive advantages and weaknesses. When a company sees how it can match its strengths to market opportunities, it has a strategy that can be applied to the budget.

When a budget exists without consideration of strategy, it usually begins with the prior year's budget and misses opportunities to change the direction of the company, causing stagnation. Many once-great companies have met their demise because they failed to change in response to market demands. Implementing the strategy requires formulation of long-term plans, and long-term plans are implemented using a budget process.

Master Budget

A master budget is a plan based on a company's strategy for controlling its operations for a specific period of time. A key point is that master budgets are fixed at an expected level of business activity.

Long-Term Planning

While a strategy is the starting point for achieving organizational goals, a long-term plan is needed to ensure that the strategy is implemented. A long-term plan is usually a five- to ten-year plan of actions required to achieve the company's goals. Planning for the long term can involve discontinuing certain operations over time, arranging for equity or debt financing, and allocating resources gradually to new branches of business. Such major reorganizations can be accomplished only over a period of time and usually involve the use of capital budgeting (part of the master budget). Capital budgeting is the process of allocating resources to an entity's proposed long-term projects in the form of buildings, equipment, and hiring and training staff. These are extremely expensive and the decision to invest in them must be made in accordance with strategy.

LOS §1.B.2.c

Short-Term Objectives

Short-term objectives are the variations in the long-term plan that result from capital budgeting, the operating results of past periods, and expected future results caused by the current economic, social, industrial, and technological environment. These variations are fed into each year's master budget.

Components of a Master Budget

The **master budget** is the overall plan of operations for a company or business unit over a year, an operating period, or a shorter duration. The master budget sets quantitative goals for all operations, including detailed plans for raising the required capital. Figure 1B-17 shows how the factors behind a master budget relate to it.

Figure 1B-17 Strategic Goals, Long-Term Objectives, Budgets, and Operations

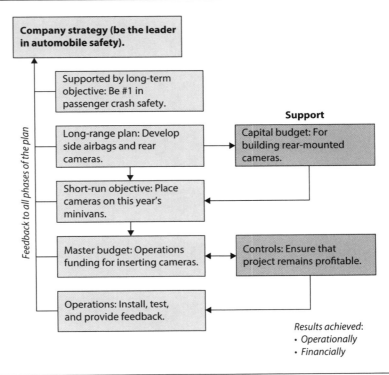

The master budget is a map showing where the company is heading. If it is properly designed, it will show the company heading in the same direction as the strategy and the long-term plan. The budget is more precise and of shorter duration than long-term plans. It is more focused on responsibility centers than longer-term planning tools.

A master budget is broken down into an operating and a financial budget.

LOS
§1.B.2.h

- An **operating budget** identifies resources that are needed for operations and is concerned with the acquisition of these resources through purchase or manufacture. Operating budgets include production budgets, purchasing budgets, sales promotion budgets, and staffing budgets. These budgets culminate in the preparation of the income statement.
- A **financial budget** matches sources of funds with uses of funds in order to achieve the goals of the firm. This includes budgets for cash inflows and outflows, financial position, and capital expenditures. A **capital budget** is used to plan how resources will be used to support significant investments in projects that have long-term implications. These projects could include the purchase of new equipment or investment in new facilities.

Topic Questions: Budgeting Concepts

Directions: Answer each question in the space provided. Correct answers and explanations appear after the topic questions.

1. Which one of the following best describes a reason why a company's budgeting should be based on the company's strategic plans?

   ☐ **a.** Helps control costs so that products can be sold profitably.

   ☐ **b.** Identifies resources needed to reach strategic goals.

   ☐ **c.** Identifies the external factors that have changed from the prior year and those that remain the same.

   ☐ **d.** Establishes standards to measure employee performance.

2. An advantage of participatory budgeting is that it

   ☐ **a.** minimizes the cost of developing budgets.

   ☐ **b.** yields information known to management but not to employees.

   ☐ **c.** encourages acceptance of the budget by employees.

   ☐ **d.** reduces the effect on the budgetary process of employee biases.

3. A company uses participative budgeting. In order to more easily meet budgetary goals, the controller underestimates the amount of revenue and overestimates fixed selling and administrative expenses. This is an example of

   ☐ **a.** Flexible budgeting

   ☐ **b.** Budgetary slack

   ☐ **c.** Zero-based budgeting

   ☐ **d.** Budgetary variance

Topic Question Answers: Budgeting Concepts

1. Which one of the following best describes a reason why a company's budgeting should be based on the company's strategic plans?
   - ☐ **a.** Helps control costs so that products can be sold profitably.
   - ☑ **b.** Identifies resources needed to reach strategic goals.
   - ☐ **c.** Identifies the external factors that have changed from the prior year and those that remain the same.
   - ☐ **d.** Establishes standards to measure employee performance.

A budget that is based on the company's strategic plans can help the company identify resources needed to reach strategic goals because the money that an organization spends and resources the organization invests represent the organization's strategy; therefore, an effective budget can identify spending that will help the company meet their goals and spending that is not effective to implementing their strategy.

2. An advantage of participatory budgeting is that it
   - ☐ **a.** minimizes the cost of developing budgets.
   - ☐ **b.** yields information known to management but not to employees.
   - ☑ **c.** encourages acceptance of the budget by employees.
   - ☐ **d.** reduces the effect on the budgetary process of employee biases.

In a participative budget (bottom-up or self-imposed budget), managers and employees at all levels work together to set budgets for their areas. This budget process does encourage acceptance of the budget by employees because they are involved and empowered in the process.

3. A company uses participative budgeting. In order to more easily meet budgetary goals, the controller underestimates the amount of revenue and overestimates fixed selling and administrative expenses. This is an example of
   - ☐ **a.** Flexible budgeting
   - ☑ **b.** Budgetary slack
   - ☐ **c.** Zero-based budgeting
   - ☐ **d.** Budgetary variance

Budgetary slack occurs when a company utilizes a participative budgeting process and the managers involved set easily attainable targets for themselves and their business entities. Budgetary slack can occur for many reasons, including job security or meeting bonus goals if performance is tied to the achievement of budgeted numbers.

Forecasting Techniques

A VITAL FUNCTION OF MANAGING any business is planning for the future. Experienced judgment, intuition, and awareness of economic conditions may give business leaders a rough idea of what may happen in the future. However, this experience must be supported by various quantitative methods that can be used to forecast such outcomes as next quarter's sales volume or the viability of introducing a new product line. In addition, a degree of uncertainty needs to be incorporated into the decision-making process.

This topic looks at a number of forecasting techniques that companies can use to plan for future financial performance. The quantitative methods discussed here are regression analysis, learning curve analysis, and expected value.

READ the Learning Outcome Statements (LOS) for this topic as found in Appendix A and then study the concepts and calculations presented here to be sure you understand the content you could be tested on in the CMA exam.

Quantitative Methods

When planning for the future, a company faces some degree of uncertainty and will rely on a variety of quantitative methods to help it make better decisions. This content focuses on quantitative methods in three areas:

Data analysis involves analyzing a given set of data to establish the relationship and/or pattern in the data. These analyses can be used to predict the outcome based on a given set of conditions such as regression analysis or based on an established pattern.

Model building involves creating a mathematical model that establishes the relationship between different factors. Learning curve analysis is one type of model that is used to determine how the amount of time required to produce a product changes as the number of units produced changes.

Decision theory deals with uncertainty by looking at various potential outcomes that can happen in the future and the likelihood of these outcomes occurring. Expected value is one method to deal with uncertainty.

Regression Analysis

Linear regression analysis is a statistical method used to determine the impact one variable (or a group of variables) has on another variable. It provides the best linear equation and unbiased estimate of the relationship between the dependent variable (Y) and one or more independent variables (X or X's). Linear regression is used by management accountants to analyze and forecast cost behavior (i.e., determine the fixed and variable portions of a total cost) or to forecast future amounts such as sales dollars.

The assumptions underlying linear regression are:

- The relationship between the dependent variable and the independent variable(s) is **linear**. This relationship is valid over a relevant range.
- The process underlying the relationship is **stationary** and does not change over time. This assumption is also called the constant process assumption.
- The differences between the actual values of the dependent variable and its predicted values (the error or residual terms) are normally distributed with a mean of zero and a constant standard deviation. In other words, the dependent variable is not correlated with itself; meaning, it is not autocorrelated or serialcorrelated.
- The independent variables (X's) in multiple regression analysis are independent of each other. There is no multi-colinearity.

There are two main types of regression analysis: a **simple regression analysis**, which uses only one independent variable, and a **multiple regression analysis**, which uses two or more independent variables.

Regression analysis equations systematically reduce estimation errors. Therefore, it is also called least square regression. Regression analysis fits a line (the regression line) through a set of data points—this line minimizes the difference between the line (prediction) and the data point (actual).

Simple Linear Regression

Let's use a simple linear regression analysis to analyze the relationship between sales (the dependent variable) and marketing costs (the independent variable).

For example: A retail firm called Build and Fix is trying to forecast sales and believes that store sales depend on marketing costs. To forecast sales for year 4, Build and Fix management collects data about its past sales and marketing expenditures. Figure 1B-18 summarizes the data.

Figure 1B-18 Data on Marketing Costs and Sales for Build and Fix

Quarter	Marketing Costs ($000)	Sales ($000)	Marketing Costs ($000)	Sales ($000)	Marketing Costs ($000)	Sales ($000)
	Year 1		Year 2		Year 3	
Q1	$50	$48,000	$100	$89,000	$40	$62,000
Q2	30	40,000	90	105,000	90	130,000
Q3	40	62,000	80	73,000	70	80,000
Q4	60	75,000	110	105,000	50	50,000

Figure 1B-19 shows the data from Figure 1B-18 on a scatter diagram. First the data points are plotted on the graph. Next, the regression line is drawn as an estimate of the linear relationship between sales and marketing costs. Notice that the line is upward sloping. This indicates that there is a positive relationship between sales and marketing costs.

Figure 1B-19 Marketing Costs as a Predictor of Sales

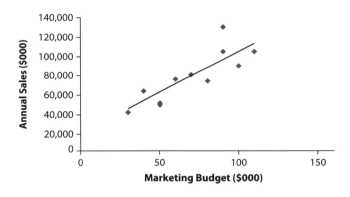

The dependent variable (y), is always plotted on the vertical axis and represents sales. The independent variable (X) is plotted on the horizontal axis. In this example, it represents marketing costs. A mathematical expression of the original data points is then developed and can be used to forecast sales (y) based on a given marketing budget. The regression line is a straight line that is represented mathematically as the next equation:

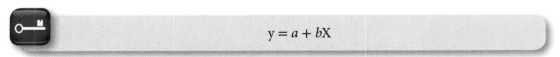

$$y = a + bX$$

where:

LOS
§1.B.3.c

y = annual sales; this is the dependent variable to be forecast. An observed value uses a capital Y.

a = amount of y when X = 0. This value is also called the y intercept, because when X = 0, y = a.

b = slope of the line, also known as the regression coefficient. It represents the "impact" X has on y. For every 1 unit change in X, y is expected to change by b units.

X = value for the independent variable (in this case, marketing costs) or the driver for the dependent variable.

Figure 1B-20 represents the results of the simple linear regression analysis performed on the given set of sales and marketing data in Figure 1B-18.

Figure 1B-20 Regression Values for Marketing Costs as Predictor of Sales

	Coefficients	t-Value	Standard Error
Intercept	$18,444,808.74	1.48	$12,460,200.96
Marketing costs	$861.31	4.98	$172.93

In the example shown in Figures 1B-19 and 1B-20, the regression equation is:

$$y = \$18{,}444{,}809 + \$861(X)$$

where X represents the marketing budget. This formula can be used to go beyond the table and forecast sales with a marketing budget of $75,000.

$$y = \$18{,}444{,}809 + \$861(75{,}000) = \$83{,}019{,}809 \text{ Forecast Sales}$$

Regression analysis also provides a number of objective benchmarks that allow users to evaluate the reliability of the regression equation. Three common measures are goodness of fit, statistical reliability of each independent variable, and standard error of the estimate (SE).

1. Goodness of Fit

The goodness of fit measures the reliability of the regression. R-squared is the quantitative measurement of the degree that a change in the dependent variable is predicted by the change in the independent variable. This number will be between zero and 1. The closer the number is to 1, the more reliable the regression is.

Let's assume the R-squared value for Build and Fix's sales and marketing costs is 0.7127. This means that approximately 71.27% of the variation in sales is accounted for by the variation in marketing costs.

2. Statistical Reliability of Each Independent Variable

Another quantitative measure of reliability is the statistical reliability of each independent variable. This measure is called the t-value. It measures if an independent variable (X) has a valid, long-term relationship to the dependent variable (y). A good rule of thumb is that the t-value should be greater than 2. A lower number indicates that there is little or no statistical relationship between the variables.

For Build and Fix, the T-value is greater than 2 for the marketing costs, which indicates that the impact marketing cost has on sales is statistically significant.

3. Standard Error of Estimate

The standard error of estimate (SE) measures the accuracy of y, the regression's estimate. It is a measurement of the dispersion around the regression line. A relatively small SE is better than a large one. It implies that the actual value will lie in the range of the estimate of y, plus or minus the SE.

Multiple Linear Regression

In the Build and Fix example, a simple linear regression analysis was used to estimate the impact that the amount of money spent on marketing would have on the company's sales. Using a simple regression analysis, it is assumed that marketing expenditures are the only factor that explain (or have an impact on) a company's sales level. Based on the results of the analysis, the R-squared is 0.7127. That means only 71.27% of the variation in sales can be explained by changes in marketing expenditures. The remaining 28.73% (100% – 71.27%) is explained by changes in other factors that are not included in the regression model.

In forecasting sales, an organization would want to take into consideration not only its marketing efforts but other factors, such as the economic conditions, its competitors' actions, its pricing strategy, etc. All of these other factors can be incorporated into a multiple regression model and become the additional independent variables that can help to explain the other 28.73% in sales variation that is not explained by marketing expenditures. As Build and Fix learns more about what impacts sales, they improve their ability to improve sales. Better yet, the company will have a greater opportunity to focus their efforts on those independent variables that will yield increased sales.

A multiple regression model looks very similar to a simple regression model, except that it has two or more independent variables (X_1, X_2, etc). The regression "line" for a multiple regression model is represented mathematically as follows:

$$y = a + b_1X_1 + b_2X_2 + b_3X_3 + \dots b_nX_n$$

In addition to the R-squared, t-value, and standard error of the estimate (SE), a multiple regression requires the user to evaluate the correlation between the independent variables (X's) to assure there is a lack of multi-colinearity. As a general rule of thumb, as long as the correlation between any two independent variables is 0.7 or below then all the independent variables can be included in the regression. If the correlation between two of the independent variables is 0.7 or above, then one of them must be eliminated from the regression equation.

Benefits and Shortcomings of Regression Analysis

Regression analysis gives management accountants an objective measure to use in evaluating the precision and reliability of estimations.

It is important to prepare a graph of the data prior to using regression analysis and to determine whether any unusual data points, called outliers, are present. Regression analysis can be influenced strongly by outliers, which may result in an estimation line that is not representative of most of the data. If present, each outlier should be reviewed to determine whether it is due to a data recording error, a normal operating condition, or a unique and nonrecurring event. Regression analysis requires an adequate collection of data points—preferably 30 or more—to be accurate.

Regression analysis also assumes that past relationships between dependent and independent variables will hold true into the future. When using regression analysis as a forecasting tool, it is important to evaluate or make adjustments for changes in the relationship between the variables over time.

When using the results of a regression analysis to make any prediction, it is important to remember that the dependent variables used for the prediction must fall within the range of the data set used to establish the regression line. For the Build and Fix sales and marketing costs, the marketing costs used to estimate the regression line fall in the relevant range of $30,000 and $110,000. The company can reliably predict its sales for any marketing cost that falls within this range. It cannot rely on the result if the marketing cost used in the prediction is outside this range.

One caveat regarding regression analysis is that the user must evaluate the reasonableness of the relationship between the dependent and independent variables. Does it make sense that X causes y to change? Any numbers can be input as X and y variables and will result in an equation, but whether the equation makes sense is based on the user's judgment.

LOS §1.B.3.d

Learning Curve Analysis

Learning curve analysis is a systematic method for estimating labor costs based on increased learning by an individual person performing a task, such as the assembly of a widget. As the person makes more units, they become more efficient at completing the task. The result is that costs will decrease as learning increases. The learning curve concept has been called the experience curve when applied to different business functions along the value chain. Calculation of the learning curve is based on a learning rate. As output doubles, the average time will decrease from the previous level based on a constant percentage. For example, a learning curve for a 20% reduction in time is called an 80% learning curve; a 10% reduction occurs from a 90% learning curve.

The learning curve can be measured using the **cumulative average-time learning model** (also called the Wright method or traditional method). This is the generally accepted model. The model calculates the cumulative total time by multiplying the incremental unit produced by the cumulative average time per unit.

For example: Assume that a new worker can assemble the first widget in 10 hours and there is an 80% learning curve. As output doubles, the cumulative average time decreases to 8 hours. Therefore, the first two units take a cumulative total time of 16 hours, made up of 10 hours spent on the first unit and 6 hours spent on the second unit. Figure 1B-21 shows these calculations.

LOS
§1.B.3.e

Figure 1B-21 Cumulative Average-Time Learning Model

	Learning Curve 80% at each Doubling	Cumulative Average-Time Model	
X	Cumulative Average Time per Widget* (c)	Cumulative Total Time (c × X)	Individual Time for xth Widget
1	10 (value of c)	10 (10 × 1)	10
2	8 (10 × 0.8)	16 (8 × 2)	6 (16 − 10)
4	6.4 (8 × 0.8)	25.6 (6.4 × 4)	4.54[†]
8	5.12 (6.4 × 0.8)	40.96 (5.12 × 8)	3.55[†]

*Each c = rate (0.8 here) x the preceding value of the variable c.

[†]Calculated by a formula not shown here.

Figure 1B-22 shows the results plotted on a graph. Notice that the curve is a nonlinear cost function. Also note that the curve shows that costs decrease to a certain point and then they level off. This depicts the fact that labor costs will decrease; however, they will not go away due to increased learning.

Figure 1B-22 Cumulative Average-Time Learning Curve

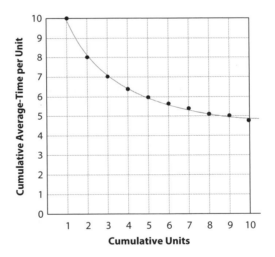

LOS
§1.B.3.f

Benefits and Limitations of Learning Curve Analysis

A company can use learning curve analysis when evaluating performance, because an individual's productivity should increase as the individual learns the given task. Learning affects quality and improves productivity. Other factors contribute to the learning curve besides production output. These include job rotation, work teams, and total quality management. The use of learning curve analysis is a viable way to forecast labor costs.

The limitations of learning curve analysis are:

- The learning curve approach is not as effective when machinery performs repetitive tasks, such as robotics. It is most appropriate for labor-intensive processes that involve repetitive tasks and long production runs.
- The learning rate is assumed to be constant in the calculations, but the actual declines in labor time are not usually constant.
- Conclusions might be unreliable because observed changes in productivity may actually be due to factors other than learning, such as a change in the labor mix, the product mix, or a combination of both.

LOS
§1.B.3.g

Expected Value

Expected value is the weighted average of a set of possible outcomes. One use of expected value is to forecast cash flows for the coming year. The actual results can vary based on possible economic conditions. For example, if the economy is in a recession then the company's cash flows will be lower.

To start, create cash flows forecasts based on different economic conditions. Boom, average, and recession are used in this example. Next, assign a probability to each condition. Remember, the probabilities have to add to 1.0. An example for Hardware Haven is presented in Figure 1B-23.

LOS
§1.B.3.i

Figure 1B-23 Hardware Haven Cash Flows Forecasts Based on Economic Conditions

Economic Condition	Cash Flows Forecast	Probability
Boom	$3,000,000	0.1
Average	$2,000,000	0.8
Recession	$600,000	0.1

The company can now forecast the expected value of cash flows by using the following formula:

$$\text{Expected Value (EV)} = \Sigma \,(\text{rp})$$

where:
    EV = expected value
    Σ = sum of the variables that follow in the equation
    r = result of the outcome
    p = probability associated with the outcome

To calculate the expected value, simply multiply the outcome of each possible economic condition by the probability associated with that condition. Then, add them all together. The expected value of the cash flows in Figure 1B-24 is calculated as follows:

LOS §1.B.3.i

Figure 1B-24 Hardware Haven Cash Flows Forecast

Economic Condition	Cash Flows Forecast	Probability	Expected Outcome
Boom	$3,000,000	0.1	$300,000
Average	$2,000,000	0.8	1,600,000
Recession	$600,000	0.1	60,000
		Total	$1,960,000

This is stated as: The company expects its cash flows to be $1,960,000 for the coming year, based on the identified economic conditions.

Another use for expected value is to choose between two or more alternative courses of action.

For example: An organization may be presented with a choice of two investment options. Option A has a 60% chance of making a profit of $300,000 and a 40% chance of incurring a loss of $500,000. Option B has a 70% chance of making a profit of $200,000 and a 30% chance of incurring a loss of $250,000. The calculation of the expected value of these investments is shown in Figure 1B-25.

Option A is expected to lose $20,000, while Option B is expected to have a profit of $65,000. Given this information, the best choice for the organization is to invest in Option B because it has the higher expected profit.

Figure 1B-25 Decision Making Using Expected Value

	Option A			Option B		
	Profit	Probability	Expected Value	Profit	Probability	Expected Value
Option A	$300,000	0.6	$180,000	$200,000	0.7	$140,000
Option B	(500,000)	0.4	(200,000)	(250,000)	0.3	(75,000)
Expected Profit			$(20,000)			$ 65,000

LOS §1.B.3.h

Benefits and Limitations of Expected Value

It's important to remember that the expected value calculation is only as good as the estimated potential outcomes for each scenario and the probability assigned to each scenario. If any of these assumptions is unreliable, then the calculated expected value cannot be trusted in making a sound decision.

Expected value analysis assumes that the decision maker is risk neutral. If the decision maker is either a risk taker or risk averse, then the expected value model may not be appropriate.

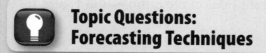

**Topic Questions:
Forecasting Techniques**

Directions: Answer each question in the space provided. Correct answers and explanations appear after the topic questions.

1. An accountant estimated the repair costs for the company's plant facilities for next year's operating budget. The accountant has determined the following probability distribution after analyzing historical repair costs.

Probability	Repair costs
15%	$2,000,000
45%	2,500,000
30%	3,500,000
10%	5,000,000

    What is the estimated repair cost that the accountant should project for next year's operating budget?

    ☐ **a.** $1,850,000

    ☐ **b.** $1,925,000

    ☐ **c.** $2,975,000

    ☐ **d.** $3,250,000

2. A software company recently established a customer service department. After the first week, the average time required to handle one customer call was 15 minutes. The manager of the customer service department estimates an 80% learning curve. Under the cumulative average-time learning model, the cumulative average time required to handle one customer call by the fourth week will be:

    ☐ **a.** 7.7 minutes.

    ☐ **b.** 9.6 minutes.

    ☐ **c.** 12.0 minutes.

    ☐ **d.** 15.0 minutes.

3. An accountant for a biotechnology company is working on a projection of next year's maintenance expenditures for the company's laboratory equipment used in research and development. By analyzing past maintenance expenditures, the accountant was able to determine that future maintenance expenditures can be expressed by the following simple regression equation: $y = \$20{,}000 + (\$50 \times X)$. The variable X is the number of hours the laboratory equipment has been in service. For the previous year, the variable X was determined to be 4,500 hours. If the accountant is projecting that X will be 5,000 hours next year, how much should the accountant project for next year's maintenance expenditures?

☐ **a.** $225,000.

☐ **b.** $245,000.

☐ **c.** $250,000.

☐ **d.** $270,000.

Topic Question Answers: Forecasting Techniques

1. An accountant estimated the repair costs for the company's plant facilities for next year's operating budget. The accountant has determined the following probability distribution after analyzing historical repair costs.

Probability	Repair costs
15%	$2,000,000
45%	2,500,000
30%	3,500,000
10%	5,000,000

What is the estimated repair cost that the accountant should project for next year's operating budget?

- ☐ **a.** $1,850,000
- ☐ **b.** $1,925,000
- ☑ **c.** $2,975,000
- ☐ **d.** $3,250,000

The formula for the expected value of a set of possible outcomes is: EV = Σ(rp) where r = result of the outcome, and p = probability of the outcome. The expected value of the repair costs in this scenario equals $2,975,000 ((15% × $2,000,000) + (45% × $2,500,000) + (30% × 3,500,000) + (10% × $5,000,000)).

2. A software company recently established a customer service department. After the first week, the average time required to handle one customer call was 15 minutes. The manager of the customer service department estimates an 80% learning curve. Under the cumulative average-time learning model, the cumulative average time required to handle one customer call by the fourth week will be:

- ☐ **a.** 7.7 minutes.
- ☑ **b.** 9.6 minutes.
- ☐ **c.** 12.0 minutes.
- ☐ **d.** 15.0 minutes.

The cumulative average-time learning model assumes that as output doubles, the cumulative average time or cost of the total output is reduced by a constant percentage. The manager in this problem estimates an 80% learning curve; therefore, there is a 20% reduction in the average time required to handle one customer call every time the department's experience in handling the calls doubles. After two weeks, the average time required to handle one customer call will be reduced from 15 minutes to 12 minutes (15 × 80%). After four weeks, the average time is reduced again to 9.6 minutes (12 × 80%).

3. An accountant for a biotechnology company is working on a projection of next year's maintenance expenditures for the company's laboratory equipment used in research and development. By analyzing past maintenance expenditures, the accountant was able to determine that future maintenance expenditures can be expressed by the following simple regression equation: y = $20,000 + ($50 × X). The variable X is the number of hours the laboratory equipment has been in service. For the previous year, the variable X was determined to be 4,500 hours. If the accountant is projecting that X will be 5,000 hours next year, how much should the accountant project for next year's maintenance expenditures?

☐ **a.** $225,000.

☐ **b.** $245,000.

☐ **c.** $250,000.

☑ **d.** $270,000.

A simple regression analysis only uses one independent variable. To project the maintenance expenditures for next year, the accountant should use the formula provided and set X equal to the number of projected hours that the laboratory equipment will be used next year (5,000 hours). The projected maintenance expenditures for next year equals $270,000 ($20,000 + ($50 × 5,000 hours)).

Budgeting Methodologies

IN ORDER FOR A COMPANY to use its budget as an effective planning and management tool, a company must choose a budget methodology that supports and reinforces its management approach. A firm looking to continuously improve and reinvent its operations may not be well served by an incremental budget system. For a stable operation with a few products, the investment in an activity-based budget effort may not be worth the effort. However, the availability of a range of budget methods enables an organization, and its constituent departments and divisions, to create budgets that are meaningful and appropriate to their requirements.

This topic covers the different types of budget systems including annual/master budgets, project budgets, activity-based budgets, incremental budgets, zero-based budgets, continuous (rolling) budgets, and flexible budgets.

 READ the Learning Outcome Statements (LOS) for this topic as found in Appendix A and then study the concepts and calculations presented here to be sure you understand the content you could be tested on in the CMA exam.

Annual/Master Budget

 LOS §1.B.4.a, b, c, d

An organization's **master budget**, also known as an annual business plan or profit plan, is a comprehensive budget for one year or less. Every aspect of the company's revenue and cost flows is projected, starting with the sales forecast and ending with a set of pro forma financial statements. The benefits of having a master budget are numerous and the drawbacks are few. Virtually every company needs some form of master budget.

Depending on the type of business, organizational structure, complexity of operations, and management philosophy, a company can choose different approaches in formulating its master budget. The company can even adopt different approaches for different pieces of its master budget. Six different budgeting systems that a company can use to create its budgets are:

1. *Project budgeting.* Used for creating a budget for specific projects rather than for an entire company
2. *Activity-based budgeting.* Focuses on classifying costs based on activities rather than based on departments or products
3. *Incremental budgeting.* Starts with the prior year's budget or actual results and makes minor changes to come up with the next year's budget
4. *Zero-based budgeting.* Starts each new budgeting cycle from scratch as though the budgets are prepared for the first time
5. *Continuous (or rolling) budgeting.* Allows the budget to be continually updated by removing information for the period just ended (March of this year) and adding estimated data for the same period next year (March of next year)
6. *Flexible budgeting.* Serves as a control mechanism that evaluates the performance of managers by comparing actual revenue and expenses to the budgeted amount for the actual level of activity, and not the original budgeted level of activity

These budgeting systems are not mutually exclusive; in fact, a company can choose to adopt several of them simultaneously. They are summarized in the table on page 192 and explained in detail below.

LOS §1.B.4.a, b, c, d

1. Project Budgeting

Project budgets are used when a project is completely separate from other elements of a company. Examples include:

1. A motion picture has a crew and costs that are related solely to that movie
2. A ship, a road, an aircraft
3. Major capital asset

The time frame for a project budget is simply the duration of the project. A multiyear project could be broken down by year. Successful past project budgets for similar projects can be used as benchmarks when developing project budgets. Project budgets are developed using the same techniques and components as shown for developing a master budget, except that the focus will be solely on costs related to the project instead of the company as a whole. Allocations for the variable and fixed overhead costs will also be included in the project's budget. This accomplishes a reporting of the total costs for the project.

One advantage of a project budget is the ability to contain all of a project's costs so that its individual impact can be easily measured. Also, project budgets work well on both large and small scales. Project management software can facilitate developing and tracking these budgets. A potential limitation of project budgets occurs when projects use resources and staff that are committed to the entire organization rather than dedicated to the project. In such situations, the budget will contain links to these resource centers, and affected individuals may be reporting to two or more supervisors. Care must be taken in measuring costs and lines of authority.

2. Activity-Based Budgeting

An **activity-based budget (ABB)** focuses on activities instead of departments or products. Each activity is matched with the most appropriate cost driver, which is any volume-based (labor hours or square feet) or activity-based (number of parts to assemble for a machine) unit of measure of the cost of a job or activity needed to sustain operations. Costs are divided into cost pools, such as unit, batch, product, and facility. Cost pools include homogeneous costs that all vary in the same proportion to the rise and fall of production. Fixed costs are in one pool, and different levels of variable costs are in their own pools. The accuracy of these groupings should be evaluated each time a master budget is prepared. The concept of activity-based costing (ABC) is discussed in greater detail in Section D: Cost Management.

While traditional budgeting focuses on input resources and expresses budgeting units in terms of functional areas, ABB focuses on value-added activities and expresses budgeting units in terms of activity costs. Traditional budgeting places emphasis on increasing management performance; ABB places emphasis on teamwork, synchronized activity, and customer satisfaction.

Proponents of ABB believe that traditional costing obscures the relationships between costs and outputs by oversimplifying the measurements into one category such as labor hours, machine hours, or output units for an entire process or department. Instead of using only volume drivers as a measurement tool, ABB uses activity-based cost drivers, such as number of setups, to make a clear connection between resource consumption and output. ABB will also use volume-based drivers if they are the most appropriate measurement unit for a particular activity. If the relationships are made clear, managers can see how resource demands are affected by changes in products offered, product designs, manufacturing techniques, customer base, and market share. The cost implication of each planned activity is known if ABB is used. This enables a company using ABB to continuously improve their budgeting. Conversely, traditional budgets focus on past (historical) budgets and often continue funding items that would be cut if their cost-effectiveness were better known.

ABB can be used as the foundation of a master budgeting process. The resulting subbudgets would be based on different ways of measuring the costs, so the resulting proportions of costs would be weighted differently. For instance, some portion of the indirect materials or labor that would be part of overhead could be tracked more carefully and included in direct materials and direct labor amounts.

For example: Figure 1B-26 displays an overhead budget created for Bluejay Manufacturing Company using an activity-based approach. It shows overhead cost by activities, such as production setup, fabrication, assembly, quality control inspections, and engineering changes.

Figure 1B-26 Activity-Based Overhead Budget for Bluejay Manufacturing Company

Activity	Usage	Activity Rate	Activity Cost
Machine setup	80 setups	$4,000/setup	$320,000
Fabrication	1,700 DLH*	$5/DLH	8,500
Assembly	6,000 DLH	$12/DLH	72,000
Inspection	100 inspections	$2,500/inspection	250,000
Engineering changes	15 changes	$10,000/change	150,000
Total overhead cost			$800,500

* DLH = direct labor hours.

A key advantage of ABB is greater precision in determining costs, especially when multiple departments or products need to be tracked. This advantage comes at a cost, and a potential drawback to ABB can occur if the cost of designing and maintaining the ABB system exceeds the cost savings from better planning. Therefore, ABB is most appropriate in businesses that have products with varying complexity or other factors, such as setups. This is because the more complex a situation becomes, the less useful traditional costing is.

LOS
§1.B.4.a,
b, c, d

3. Incremental Budgeting

An **incremental budget** is a general type of budget that starts with the prior year's budget or actual results and uses projected changes in sales and the operating environment to adjust the individual items in the budget either upward or downward. It is the opposite of a zero-based budget. The primary advantage of incremental budgeting is its simplicity. Another advantage is that it fosters operational stability. The main drawback to using this type of budget (and the reason that some companies use zero-based budgets) is that the budgets tend to only increase in size over the years. Managers build in budgetary slack by forecasting too little revenue growth or excessive expenses. The result of budgetary slack most often is to have favorable variances, which makes the manager "look good."

LOS
§1.B.4.f

Consider the following example for preparing an incremental budget beginning with the company's actual amount. *For example*: A company using an incremental budgeting method would start with the prior year's actual results and use projected changes in sales and the operating environment to adjust individual items in the budget either up or down. If sales last year were $1,500,000 and management estimates that there will be a 10% increase in sales, the estimated budget for sales would be $1,650,000. The remaining components of the budget, such as selling, general, and administration, are derived using a similar logic.

LOS
§1.B.4.g

LOS
§1.B.4.a,
b, c, d

4. Zero-Based Budgeting

Some companies use zero-based budgeting in order to avoid situations where ineffective elements of a business continue to exist, simply because they were in the prior budget. As the name implies, the budget starts with zero dollars. A traditional budget focuses on changes to the past budget, while the **zero-based budget** focuses on constant cost justification of each and every item in a budget. Managers must conduct in-depth reviews of each area under their control to provide such justification.

The strength of the zero-based budget is that it forces review of all elements of a business. Zero-based budgets can create efficient, lean organizations and, therefore, are popular with government and nonprofit organizations. A zero-based budget is a way of taking a new look at the operations.

The first step in developing a zero-based budget is to have each department manager rank all department activities from most to least important and then assign a cost to each activity. Upper management reviews these lists, sometimes called decision packages, and cuts items that lack justification or are less critical. Upper management asks questions, such as "Should the activity be performed and if it is not, what will happen?" or "Are there substitute methods of providing this function such as outsourcing or customer self-service?" Managers may also use benchmark figures and cost-benefit analysis to help decide what to cut. Only those items approved will be in the budget. The cost of the accepted items may be arrived at through discussion and negotiation with the department managers. Once the budget figures are determined, the zero-based budget becomes the basis for a master budget.

Theoretically, zero-based budgets have the advantage of focusing on every line item instead of just the exceptions. This should motivate managers to identify and remove items that are more costly than the benefits they provide. These budgets are especially useful when new management is hired.

One drawback with zero-based budgeting is that the annual review process is time-consuming and expensive. As a result, the review may often be less thorough than it is intended to be. In addition, by not using prior budgets, the firm may be ignoring lessons learned from prior years. If used every year, a zero-based budget actually may become little more than an incremental budget with a little extra processing. Managers simply remember their old justifications and figures and use them the following year.

The time and expense of a zero-based budget can be mitigated by performing zero-based budgets on a periodic basis, such as once every five years, and applying a different budget method in the other years. Or, the firm might rotate the use of zero-based budgeting for a different division each year.

5. Continuous (Rolling) Budgets

A **continuous budget**, or rolling budget, adds a new period onto the budget at the end of each period so there are always the same number of periods planned for the future. This method keeps the budgets up-to-date with the operating environment. As with the other budget types, this budget becomes the master budget for an entity. However, while other budgets will expire at the end of the budgeted time period, the time frame for this budget always remains the same; that is, the company is always in the first month of an annual budget, no matter if it is viewed in January or July.

In a monthly budget meeting, managers report on the variances from the past month's budget and make projections for the next month. After review, a budget coordinator updates the master budget, performing the calculations not performed by line managers, such as depreciation or inventory valuation.

A continuous budget will be more relevant than a budget prepared once a year. It can reflect current events and changed estimates. It has the advantage of breaking down a large process into manageable steps. Because managers always have a full time period of budgeted data, they tend to view decisions in a longer-term perspective rather than what happens with a one-year budget, which will cover a shorter and shorter period of time as the year progresses.

Potential disadvantages of continuous budgets include the need to have a budget coordinator and/or the opportunity cost of having managers use part of each month working on the next month's budget. Continuous budgets are appropriate for firms that cannot devote a large block of time to a once-a-year budget process. These types of budgets are also useful for companies that want their managers to have a longer-term view of the firm.

6. Flexible Budgeting

Flexible budgeting establishes a base cost budget for a particular level of output (a cost-volume relationship), plus an incremental cost-volume amount that shows the behavior of costs at various levels of activity. Only the variable costs are adjusted; fixed costs remain unchanged. The most common use of a flexible budget is to show the budget that would have been made if the organization had met its sales forecast in units. Therefore, flexible budgets are used more as an analysis tool for determining variances from the plan than for creating the original budget.

The benefits of using a flexible budget include the ability to make better use of historical budget information to improve future planning. There are few disadvantages to using flexible budgeting, but there is the potential for the firm to focus principally on the flexible budget level of output and disregard the fact that the sales target was missed. However, most businesses use flexible budgets because they allow for extremely detailed variance analysis. The use of flexible budgeting in variance analysis is covered in Section D: Cost Management.

For example: Robin Manufacturing Company uses flexible budgeting to evaluate how closely its actual direct labor usage was to the budgeted amount using a variance analysis. For the month of July, the company has projected to produce 72,000 units requiring 0.5 direct labor hours per unit, with a budgeted hourly rate of $15. However, the actual production turns out to be only 68,000 units, and the actual hourly rate turns out to be $15.50. Figure 1B-27 presents the company's budgeted and actual cost of direct labor used.

Based on the information presented, it appears the company is $13,000 ($527,000 − $540,000) under its direct labor budget for the month of July. However, this is misleading because the company is not producing at its budgeted level of production. To truly evaluate its performance, the company needs to create a flexible budget

Figure 1B-27 Original Budget versus Actual for Robin Manufacturing Company

	Original Budget	Actual
Production (units)	72,000	68,000
DLH* per unit	× 0. 5	× 0. 5
DLH needed (or used)	36,000	34,000
Hourly rate	× $15.00	×$15. 50
Total direct labor cost	$540,000	$527,000

* DLH = direct labor hours.

where the standard cost per unit (and not the actual cost per unit) is applied to the actual production in units. Figure 1B-28 shows the company's flexible budget.

Figure 1B-28 Flexible Budget versus Actual

	Original Budget	Flexible Budget	Actual
Production	72,000	68,000 ←	68,000
DLH* per unit	× 0.5	× 0.5	× 0.5
DLH needed (or used)	36,000	34,000	34,000
Hourly rate	× $15.00 —→	× $15.00	$15.50
Total direct labor cost	$540,000	$510,000	$527,000

* DLH = direct labor hours.

From Figure 1B-28, it becomes clear that at the actual production level of 68,000 units, Robin Manufacturing Company is really $17,000 ($527,000 − $510,000) over its direct labor budget, not $13,000 under the budget.

Budgeting Systems

Budget Type	Sample Industry	Purpose	Time Frame	Application	Benefits	Limitations
Master Budget	Any	Develop a projection of every aspect of the company's revenue and cost flows.	One year or less	Starts with the sales budget and concludes with full set of pro forma financial statements. The next six budget systems can be used to create a master budget.	• Communication • Goal congruence	• Time to prepare
Project	Major Construction	Separate budget for each project rather than one for an entire company.	Duration of Project	Large projects such as a highway bridge that will generate significant revenue and costs perhaps over several years.	• Know full cost of project • Works for small and large projects	• Potential conflicts when resources and staff are not dedicated to the project
Activity-Based	Manufacturing	Classify costs based on activities rather than by departments or products.	Based on type of budget it's used for	Businesses with a complex number of products, departments, or other factors where traditional broad-brush costing is not useful.	• More accurate costing of cost objects • Focus on an activity's use of resources • Teamwork	• Cost to design and maintain the system
Incremental	Education	Use the prior-year budget and produce increments into the future based on the prior results and future expectations.	Based on type of budget it's used for	Traditional and efficient way to develop new budgets based on prior-year performance. Opposite of zero-based budgeting.	• Simple to do • Fosters operational stability	• Budgets tend to only increase over time
Zero-Based	Government	Start the budget cycle from scratch as if the budgets are prepared for the first time.	Based on type of budget it's used for	Focuses on annual cost justification of each item in the budget. Useful in creating lean organizations. Requires in-depth reviews, which can be time-consuming	• Focuses on every line item • Motivates managers to eliminate some costs	• Annual review is time consuming and expensive • By not looking at prior information, may lose benefit of a "lesson learned"
Continuous (Rolling)	Start-up	Allow the budget to be continually updated by removing information for the period just ended and adding estimated data for the same period next year.	One year or less	Better reflects current events and changes in estmates. Helps accomplish large projects in small steps. Provides better perspective than an annual budget.	• Keeps budgets up-to-date for operating environment • More relevant than budget prepared once each year • Breaks down large process to smaller steps • Encourages long-term perspective	• Might need a budget coordinator • Opportunity cost of manager spending time each month to develop the next budget
Flexible	Manufacturing Departments	Evaluate departmental performance by comparing actual revenue and expenses to the budgeted amount for the actual activities.	One year or less	Provides detailed variance analysis to reduce cost, increase output, and improve accuracy of future budgets.	• Analysis tool to determine detailed variances • Improves future planning	• Management might lose sight that sales forecast was missed

**Topic Questions:
Budgeting Methodologies**

Directions: Answer each question in the space provided. Correct answers and explanations appear after the topic questions.

1. Which one of the following types of budgets will allow management to best assess how costs will change based on changes in cost drivers such as direct labor hours or machine hours?

    ☐ **a.** Rolling budget

    ☐ **b.** Activity-based budget

    ☐ **c.** Production budget

    ☐ **d.** Cost budget

2. The controller of Allenwood Steel Company has tasked the newly-hired budget manager with restructuring the company's budget system. The controller would like her to gather information from each unit on their activities, and, with top management, examine each unit's contributions to the company as a whole. Then, with the objective of eliminating inefficiency and waste, each unit's budget for the following year will be determined without regard to past budgets and with little regard for past operating results. This method of budget development is called:

    ☐ **a.** activity-based budgeting.

    ☐ **b.** pro forma budgeting.

    ☐ **c.** flexible budgeting.

    ☐ **d.** zero-based budgeting.

3. A manufacturing firm has certain peak seasons, the summer season and the last two weeks of February. During these periods of increased output, the firm leases additional production equipment and hires additional temporary employees. Which one of the following budget techniques would best fit this firm's needs?

    ☐ **a.** Zero-based budgeting because it is based on manager input

    ☐ **b.** Project budgeting because discrete financial information is available

    ☐ **c.** Flexible budgeting because it allows for adjustments to the budget based on actual activity levels

    ☐ **d.** Static budgeting because it shows the changes in sales or production levels

**Topic Question Answers:
Budgeting Methodologies**

1. Which one of the following types of budgets will allow management to best assess how costs will change based on changes in cost drivers such as direct labor hours or machine hours?

   ☐ **a.** Rolling budget

   ☑ **b.** Activity-based budget

   ☐ **c.** Production budget

   ☐ **d.** Cost budget

Activity-based budgeting results in a more sophisticated and detailed view of the many activities that drive costs in most organizations. Core activities are identified and used throughout the organization to assign costs based on actual consumption relationships which results in more accurate cost planning, control, and evaluation results for management.

2. The controller of Allenwood Steel Company has tasked the newly-hired budget manager with restructuring the company's budget system. The controller would like her to gather information from each unit on their activities, and, with top management, examine each unit's contributions to the company as a whole. Then, with the objective of eliminating inefficiency and waste, each unit's budget for the following year will be determined without regard to past budgets and with little regard for past operating results. This method of budget development is called:

   ☐ **a.** activity-based budgeting.

   ☐ **b.** pro forma budgeting.

   ☐ **c.** flexible budgeting.

   ☑ **d.** zero-based budgeting.

This method of budget development is called zero-based budgeting. This approach takes all budgeting choices back to a "blank page" where all choices are reevaluated. Nothing is assumed to carry forward to next year's budget without going through a complete evaluation and approval process. This is a rigorous process that supports efficiency in the organization and is effective at controlling and reducing budgetary slack in the organization.

3. A manufacturing firm has certain peak seasons, the summer season and the last two weeks of February. During these periods of increased output, the firm leases additional production equipment and hires additional temporary employees. Which one of the following budget techniques would best fit this firm's needs?

- ☐ **a.** Zero-based budgeting because it is based on manager input
- ☐ **b.** Project budgeting because discrete financial information is available
- ☑ **c.** Flexible budgeting because it allows for adjustments to the budget based on actual activity levels
- ☐ **d.** Static budgeting because it shows the changes in sales or production levels

Flexible budgeting would best fit this firm's needs. Flexible budgeting is used by firms to examine possible future scenarios in sales volume.

Annual Profit Plan and Supporting Schedules

THE MASTER BUDGET, OR ANNUAL PROFIT PLAN, has many components and supporting schedules. Each of these pieces provides specific information that the organization can use to review its current operations and develop its plans for the short and long term. The forecasts and assumptions used in creating each component and the interplay of the components present an opportunity for effectively managing the organization toward its objectives.

This topic looks at the individual elements that come together to form the master budget. It describes the budgets for sales, production, direct materials, direct labor, overhead, cost of goods sold, and selling and administrative expenses. These are used to develop the operating budget and the pro forma income statement. It also discusses the cash budget, the capital expenditure budget, and the pro forma balance sheet and statement of cash flows that make up the financial budget.

 READ the Learning Outcome Statements (LOS) for this topic as found in Appendix A and then study the concepts and calculations presented here to be sure you understand the content you could be tested on in the CMA exam.

Master Budget

The master budget provides all of an entity's budgets and plans for the operating and financing activities of its subunits. It is the place where everything must add up, where strategy and long-term plans meet up with short-term objectives.

The master budget is made up of the quantitative projections of many different budgets for a company on an annual basis. Other shorter-duration time periods are also prepared. The master budget has two major components: the operating budget and the financial budget.

The operating budget includes the sales budget, the production budget, the direct materials budget, the direct labor budget, the overhead budget, and the selling and administrative (S&A) expense budget. All of these budgets culminate in the formation of the pro forma (or budgeted) income statement. The financial budget includes the capital expenditures budget, the cash budget, and the pro forma (or budgeted) balance sheet and statement of cash flows.

Figure 1B-29 shows how the components of the master budget are related.

Figure 1B-29 Master Budget

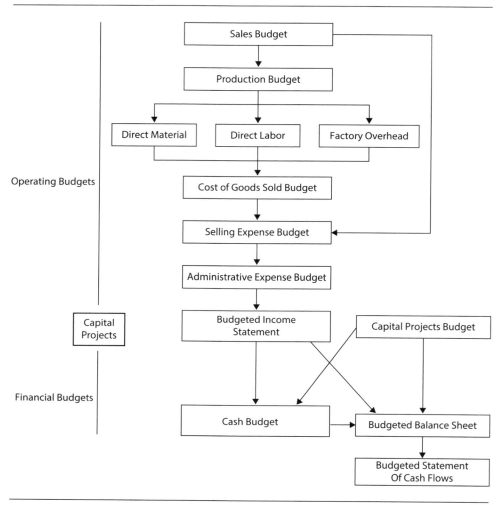

The operating budgets are prepared in the order shown. As they are prepared, each component provides information that is used to prepare the subsequent components of the operating budgets. It will also provide line items of the financial budgets. One example is the finished goods inventory amount on the balance sheet.

Operating Budget

In creating an operating budget, the various pieces are assembled, including, for instance, the sales budget, the production budget, the direct materials budget, the direct labor budget, the overhead budget, and the S&A expense budget. The individual operating budgets are then used to create the pro forma (or budgeted) income statement.

Sales Budget

An accurate sales forecast is needed to create the sales budget. A **sales forecast** is a subjective estimate of the entity's future sales for the upcoming period. Without an accurate sales forecast, all other budget elements will be inaccurate. Forecasters consider historical trends for sales, but also take into consideration economic and industry conditions and indicators, competitors' actions, rising costs, policies on pricing and extending credit, the amount of advertising and marketing expenditures, the number of unfilled back orders, and sales in the sales pipeline (unsigned prospects).

Sales forecasts should be prepared using statistical analysis techniques such as regression analysis and rely on sales managers' knowledge about their market and customer needs. Once a company has determined its forecasted sales level, based on its long- and short-term objectives, it forms a sales budget to accomplish its goals. The two key components of the sales budget are the projected number of sales units and the projected selling prices for the upcoming periods.

For example: Figure 1B-30 shows the sales budget of Robin Manufacturing Company for the third quarter.

Figure 1B-30 Sales Budget

		Robin Manufacturing Company Sales Budget for the Quarter Ended September 30, Year 1			
	July	August	September	Quarter	Ref #
Sales in units	70,000	72,000	77,000	219,000	1
Selling price per unit	$110.80	$110.80	$112.00	(varies)	
Total sales	$7,756,000	$7,977,600	$8,624,000	$24,357,600	2

It is important to note that the sales budget drives the operating budget because it impacts how many units will need to be produced (production costs), as well as the selling and administrative expenses needed to achieve those forecasted sales.

The development of the sales budget is extremely challenging because there are hardly any one-product companies. The real problem is that there may be so many products that it's not practical to develop forecasts by individual products. Instead, the forecasts are likely to be done at the level of product categories and then broken down into sales of individual products. If sales budgets are to be prepared at a grassroots level (such as sales territory), then there must be a reasonable way to eliminate over-/under-optimism from the budgets prior to rolling them up to higher levels of summation. Because the elapsed time to prepare the budget may be very long, and knowing that problems in the sales budgets trickle down to all the subsequent budget components, a company cannot afford to get to the pro forma income statement and discover that the forecasted sales level does not produce a satisfactory net income amount. A way to prevent this from happening is to project either contribution margin or gross profit using rules of thumb while preparing the sales budget. If the result looks likely to be unsatisfactory, determining other means to improve sales or to reduce costs must be considered.

Production Budget

The production budget is created next. The **production budget** is a plan for acquiring resources and combining them to meet sales goals and maintain a certain level of inventory. The budgeted production in units is calculated as shown next.

Budgeted Production = Budgeted Sales + Desired Ending Inventory − Beginning Inventory

Budgeted sales are the basis of what logistics managers use to plan resource needs for the coming year, develop manufacturing schedules, and create shipping policies. When actual sales either fall short or significantly exceed projected revenue, the entire inventory system is affected.

During the planning stages of a production budget, the production managers will complete a production schedule outlining how they will meet expected demand. The estimates should include the cost of production equipment, inventory, and personnel. Other factors that can affect the production budget include investment in new equipment, hiring necessary personnel, capacity constraints, and scheduling issues. *For example:* Figure 1B-31 shows a production budget for several months. The beginning and ending inventory in units will be either given in the problem or calculated based on a percentage of sales units.

Figure 1B-31 Production Budget

<table>
<tr><td colspan="7" align="center">**Robin Manufacturing Company**
Production Budget
for the Quarter Ended September 30, Year 1</td></tr>
<tr><td></td><td>**From**</td><td>**July**</td><td>**August**</td><td>**September**</td><td>**Quarter**</td><td>**Ref #**</td></tr>
<tr><td>Budgeted sales in units</td><td>1</td><td>70,000</td><td>72,000</td><td>77,000</td><td>219,000</td><td></td></tr>
<tr><td>Add: Desired ending inventory of finished goods</td><td></td><td>10,000</td><td>11,000</td><td>12,000 →</td><td>12,000</td><td></td></tr>
<tr><td>Total units needed</td><td></td><td>80,000</td><td>83,000</td><td>89,000</td><td>231,000</td><td></td></tr>
<tr><td>Less: Beginning inventory of finished goods</td><td></td><td>8,000</td><td>10,000</td><td>11,000</td><td>→ 8,000</td><td></td></tr>
<tr><td>Budgeted production in units</td><td></td><td>72,000</td><td>73,000</td><td>78,000</td><td>223,000</td><td>3</td></tr>
</table>

Many companies use materials requirements planning systems (MRP; also known as manufacturing resources planning) during the year in the execution phase of their operations. The MRP system can be fed a sales budget or a production plan as input, and the MRP system will produce outputs that suffice for the materials usage, materials purchases, and direct labor plans. Note that the production budget will be used to calculate the dollar amount of finished goods inventory on the balance sheet.

Direct Materials Budget

The **direct materials budget** (or the direct materials usage budget) determines the required amount of materials, based on the quality level of the materials needed to meet production. While the production budget specifies only the number of finished units to be produced, the usage budget specifies the amount and cost of materials needed for the production. The direct material purchases budget specifies the amount and cost of materials that must be purchased to meet the production requirement. This is determined as follows:

Direct Materials Purchased = Direct Materials Used in Production + Desired Ending Inventory of Direct Materials − Beginning Inventory of Direct Materials

For example: Figure 1B-32 illustrates Robin Manufacturing's direct materials usage budget. Figure 1B-33 illustrates the company's direct materials purchases budget.

The way the next two budget schedules have been structured shows how the two are interwoven with one another. The amount of raw material expected to be used is calculated in Figure 1B-32 and becomes the first input into Figure 1B-33. Then the bottom line of Figure 1B-33 flows back into the middle of Figure 1B-32.

Figure 1B-32 Direct Materials Usage Budget

Robin Manufacturing Company Direct Materials Usage Budget for the Quarter Ended September 30, Year 1						
	From	July	August	September	Quarter	Ref #
Production requirement						
Budgeted production in units	3	72,000	73,000	78,000	223,000	
Pounds of resin per unit of product		× 5	× 5	× 5	× 5	
Total pounds of resin required		360,000	365,000	390,000	1,115,000	4
Pounds of resin in beginning inventory		35,000	35,000	35,000	35,000	4a
Cost per pound		$13.00	$13.00	$13.00	$13.00	
Total cost of beginning inventory		$455,000	$455,000	$455,000	$455,000	
Total cost of resin purchases	6	4,680,000	4,745,000	5,135,000	14,560,000	
Cost of resin available for production		$5,135,000	$5,200,000	$5,590,000	$15,015,000	
Desired ending inventory in pounds		35,000	35,000	40,000	40,000	4b
Cost of desired ending inventory per pound		× $13.00	× $13.00	× $13.00	× $13.00	
Total cost of desired ending inventory		$455,000	$455,000	$520,000	$520,000	
Cost of resin used in production (Cost Available for Production – Cost of Desired Ending Inventory)		$4,680,000	$4,745,000	$5,070,000	$14,495,000	5

A standard cost system is used in this and subsequent calculations. For example, five (5) pounds of resin are needed to produce one (1) unit of finished product. The standard cost per pound of resin is $13.00.

Figure 1B-33 Direct Materials Purchases Budget

**Robin Manufacturing Company Direct Materials Purchases Budget
for the Quarter Ended September 30, Year 1**

	From	July	August	September	Quarter	Ref #
Total direct materials needed in production	4	360,000	365,000	390,000	1,115,000	
Add: Desired ending inventory	4b	35,000	35,000	40,000	40,000	
Total direct materials required		395,000	400,000	430,000	1,155,000	
Less: Direct materials beginning inventory	4a	35,000	35,000	35,000	35,000	
Direct materials purchases		360,000	365,000	395,000	1,120,000	
Purchase price per pound		$13.00	$13.00	$13.00		
Total cost for direct materials purchases		$4,680,000	$4,745,000	$5,135,000	$14,560,000	6

The direct materials purchases budget is used to calculate the dollar amount of raw materials on the balance sheet and as a cash disbursement in the cash budget.

Direct Labor Budget

The **direct labor budget** is prepared by the production manager and human resources manager. It specifies the direct labor needed to meet the production requirements. The direct labor requirement is determined by multiplying the expected production by the number of direct labor hours (DLH) required to produce one finished good unit. This number is then multiplied by the direct labor cost per hour to calculate the budgeted direct labor cost.

> Direct Labor Requirement = (Expected Production × Direct Labor Hours per Unit)
>
> Budgeted Direct Labor Cost = Direct Labor Requirement × Direct Labor Cost per Hour

Labor budgets are usually broken down into categories, such as skilled, semi-skilled, and unskilled.

For example: Figure 1B-34 illustrates a direct labor budget for Robin Manufacturing.

In addition to the cost of wages, an organization can estimate the cost of employee benefits. Employers match the Federal Insurance Contributions Act (FICA) contribution and may pay a share of health insurance, life insurance, or pension matching plans on behalf of their employees. Employee benefits can be included in direct labor costs or can be classified as overhead. Most often they are included in manufacturing overhead. The effect on cost of goods sold is the same regardless of whether it is classified as a direct labor cost or as overhead.

Figure 1B-34 Direct Labor Budget

Robin Manufacturing Company Direct Labor Budget for the Quarter Ended September 30, Year 1						
	From	**July**	**August**	**September**	**Quarter**	**Ref #**
Budgeted production	3	72,000	73,000	78,000	223,000	
DLH* required per unit		× 0.5	× 0.5	× 0.5		
DLH needed		36,000	36,500	39,000	111,500	7
Hourly rate		× $15	× $15	× $15		
Total wages for direct labor		$540,000	$547,500	$585,000	$1,672,500	8

* DLH = direct labor hours.

Overhead Budget (Factory Overhead Budget)

LOS §1.B.5.k

All other production costs that are not in the direct materials and direct labor budgets are in the **overhead budget**. Rent and insurance, for instance, remain stable even if production goes up or down. There are some overhead costs that do vary with production—variable costs such as batch setup costs, the costs of utilities, and fringe benefits. Fixed costs will not vary with production as long as production volume remains within the relevant range. Figure 1B-35 illustrates Robin Manufacturing's overhead budget.

LOS §1.B.5.l

Figure 1B-35 Factory Overhead Budget

Robin Manufacturing Company Factory Overhead Budget for the Quarter Ended September 30, Year 1							
	From	**Rate per DLH***	**July**	**August**	**September**	**Quarter**	**Ref #**
Total DLH	7		36,000	36,500	39,000	111,500	
Variable factory overhead							
Supplies		$0. 20	$7,200	$7,300	$7,800	$22,300	
Fringe benefits		4. 10	147,600	149,650	159,900	457,150	
Utilities		1. 00	36,000	36,500	39,000	111,500	
Maintenance		0. 50	18,000	18,250	19,500	55,750	
Total variable factory overhead		$5. 80	$208,800	$211,700	$226,200	$646,700	
Fixed factory overhead							
Depreciation			$20,000	$20,000	$20,000	$60,000	
Plant insurance			800	800	800	2,400	
Property taxes			1,200	1,200	1,200	3,600	
Salary supervision			10,000	10,000	10,000	30,000	
Indirect labor			72,000	72,000	72,000	216,000	
Utilities			4,000	4,000	4,000	12,000	
Maintenance			900	900	900	2,700	
Total fixed factory overhead		2.93**	$108,900	$108,900	$108,900	$326,700	
Total factory overhead		$8.73	$317,700	$320,600	$335,100	$973,400	9

* Direct labor hours (DLH) is assumed to be the cost driver for factory overhead in this example.

** $326,700 / 111,500 DLH = $2.93

Robin Manufacturing's management decided that direct labor hours is the most appropriate cost driver for the incurrence of variable overhead. Notice that each variable account is budgeted on the basis of dollars per budgeted direct labor hour; therefore, as direct labor hours increase, the budget for each of these four accounts increases. In practice, variable budgets are budgeted at the department-account level; this makes it possible to prepare responsibility report budgets at the department-account level of detail.

For Robin Manufacturing, employee benefits such as health and dental insurance, short-term and long-term disability insurance, and retirement benefits, are considered to be part of the overhead budget, and they are included in fringe benefits in Figure 1B-35.

Fixed Overhead Rate Determination

The fixed overhead budget is also prepared at the department-account level of detail. In order to convert the fixed overhead budget into the fixed overhead portion of Robin Manufacturing's overhead rate, it is necessary to divide by the denominator level of activity. Actual direct labor hours is considered to be the best overall measure of Robin's capacity, in addition to driving the incurrence of variable overhead. Several possible levels of activity could be considered as the denominator level of activity. These would include theoretical capacity (although this is really hard to rationalize), practical capacity, "normal" capacity (the average of what might be expected over the next three to five years), and the budget level of capacity. Robin Manufacturing's management chose the latter, which in this case is 111,500 direct labor hours. Dividing that into the total fixed overhead ($326,700/111,500) produces a value of $2.93 per DLH for the fixed overhead rate. Therefore, the total overhead rate is $8.73 per DLH.

Standard Cost Sheet Development

Now all the necessary information has been developed to make it possible to prepare the product standard cost sheet(s). A **standard cost sheet** shows the resources needed and the costs of those resources to manufacture one unit of a product. A cost sheet may be used to value inventory, to measure contribution margin, to set selling prices, and, as will be seen in a later topic, to measure the performance of departments within the purchasing and production functions.

Resources includes the physical units (such as pounds or linear feet or gallons) of each item of direct material required to produce one unit of product. The unit of measure used on the standard cost sheet can vary by industry and/or product. Examples include one dozen used for apparel and footwear or one case of shampoo where there are twelve (12) bottles in the standard case quantity. The cost sheet for the product is shown in Figure 1B-36.

Figure 1B-36 Product Cost Sheet

Cost Component	Units of Resource/Unit of Production	Cost/Unit of Resource	Cost/Unit of Production
Direct Material	5.00 lb/unit	$13.00/lb	$65.00/unit
Direct Labor	0.5 hr/unit	15.00/hr	7.50
Variable Overhead	0.5 hr/unit	5.80/hr	2.90
Total Variable Cost			$75.40/unit
Fixed Overhead	0.5 hr/unit	$2.93/hr	1.465
Total Cost			$76.865/unit

The cost sheet shows the product cost is $75.40 per unit in a variable costing income statement and $76.865 in an absorption costing income statement. Looking ahead to the pro forma income statement, it shows that Robin Manufacturing uses an absorption costing income statement to conform with GAAP. We know this because the income statement shows cost of goods sold rather than total variable and total fixed costs.

Cost of Goods Sold Budget

The **cost of goods sold budget** indicates the total cost of producing the product sold for a period. This budget is sometimes called the cost of goods manufactured and sold budget, because it often also includes items budgeted to be in inventory. This budget is created only after the production, direct materials, direct labor, and overhead budgets are formed, because it relies on all of these budgets.

For example: Figure 1B-37 illustrates a cost of goods sold budget for Robin Manufacturing.

Figure 1B-37 Cost of Goods Sold Budget

Robin Manufacturing Company Cost of Goods Sold Budget for the Quarter Ended September 30, Year 1						
	From	July	August	September	Quarter	Ref #
Beginning finished goods inventory, 7/1/Year 1 (8,000 units@$76.865)					$614,920	
Direct materials used (see Figure 1B-32)	5	$4,680,000	$4,745,000	$5,070,000	$14,495,000	
Direct labor used (see Figure 1B-34)	8	540,000	547,500	585,000	1,672,500	
Manufacturing overhead (see Figure 1B-35)	9	317,700	320,600	335,100	973,400	
Cost of goods manufactured		$5,537,700	$5,613,100	$5,990,100	$17,140,900	
Cost of goods available for sale					$17,755,820	
Less: Ending finished goods inventory (12,000 units@$76.865)					922,380	
Cost of goods sold					$16,833,440	10

A careful look at Figure 1B-37 shows that work-in-process inventories have been totally ignored in the planning process. Normally the three inputs—materials used, direct labor, and overhead—are added to the beginning balance of work-in-process inventory and the ending balance of work-in-process inventory would be subtracted to determine the cost of goods manufactured. Ignoring work-in-process inventories would be acceptable only if it can be safely assumed that the work-in-process inventory balance does not change. That is not a good assumption for many companies.

Next, it becomes apparent why the cost sheet(s) needed to be developed prior to determining the cost of goods sold budget. The planned units in the ending inventory are multiplied by the manufacturing cost per unit to arrive at the total inventory value for the ending inventory. The beginning finished goods inventory value also needs to be determined. Note that, were this being done for a full year, we still would have to estimate the number of units in the beginning inventory because the budget is being prepared late in the prior year, when that year's ending inventory is not known.

In Figure 1B-37, the cost of goods manufactured is made up of the cost of direct materials used, costs of direct labor used, and manufacturing overhead cost. This means that the cost of goods manufactured can be categorized into a **variable cost component** made up of the cost of direct materials used, the cost of direct labor used, and the variable overhead cost and a **fixed cost component** that is equal to the fixed overhead cost. Separating the costs of goods manufactured into the two components enables the calculation of the unit and total contribution margins of its product, as shown next.

Unit Contribution Margin = Price per Unit − Variable Cost per Unit

Total Contribution Margin = Total Revenue − Total Variable Cost

The contribution margin represents the portion of the revenue, less the total variable costs, that is used to recoup the fixed costs. Once the fixed costs have been recouped, the remaining contribution margin will go toward the company's operating income. When calculating both the contribution margins other nonmanufacturing-related variable costs, such as variable selling and administrative expenses, also need to be taken into consideration. For more information on calculating contribution margins, see Section D: Cost Management.

Selling and Administrative Expense Budget

Nonmanufacturing expenses are often grouped into a single budget called a selling and administrative (S&A) expense budget or nonmanufacturing costs budget. The selling expense components of this budget include salaries and commissions for the sales department, travel and entertainment, advertising expenditures, shipping, supplies, postage and stationery (related to sales), and so on. Sales expenses are included in this category because they are not allowed to be allocated to production. The administrative expense components of this budget, however, include management salaries, legal and professional services, utilities, insurance expense, non–sales-related stationery, supplies, postage, and the like. GAAP requires that both the selling and the administrative costs be expensed as incurred. These costs are often called operating expenses.

LOS
§1.B.5.o

Just as with overhead expenses, S&A expenses can be categorized into fixed costs and variable costs.

LOS
§1.B.5.p

The costs in this budget usually satisfy long-term goals, such as customer service. It is not easy to make cuts in these expense items. When using a contribution margin format for S&A expenses, all variable selling and administrative costs, as well as variable manufacturing costs, are deducted from net sales to find the contribution margin. This allows the budget to be used for internal performance measurement purposes.

For example: Robin Manufacturing Company's S&A expense budget is shown in Figure 1B-38.

Figure 1B-38 Selling and Administrative Expense Budget

Robin Manufacturing Company Selling and Administrative Expense Budget for the Quarter Ended September 30, Year 1					
	July	**August**	**September**	**Quarter**	**Ref #**
Research/design	$95,000	$95,000	$100,000	$290,000	
Marketing	240,000	280,000	290,000	810,000	
Shipping	135,000	140,000	150,000	425,000	
Product support	90,000	90,000	95,000	275,000	
Administration	185,000	190,000	192,000	567,000	
Total	$745,000	$795,000	$827,000	$2,367,000	11

LOS
§1.B.5.q

Pro Forma (or Budgeted) Income Statement

Various pieces of the operating budget that were developed are used to prepare the **pro forma (or budgeted) income statement**, which shows the profits for the company based on all the assumptions used throughout the budgeting process. A budgeted income statement is therefore a benchmark to be used in evaluating actual results.

For example: Figure 1B-39 shows the pro forma income statement for Robin Manufacturing Company compiled using information from the sales budget, the cost of goods sold budget, and the S&A expense budget. In addition, the company is expected to incur **interest expense of $140,361** and a **tax installment of $1,702,165** for the quarter.

Figure 1B-39 Pro Forma Income Statement

Robin Manufacturing Company
Pro Forma Income Statement
for the Quarter Ended September 30, Year 1

Sales (From 2)	$24,357,600
Less: Cost of Goods sold (From 10)	16,833,400
Gross margin	7,524,200
Less: S&A expenses (From 11)	2,367,000
Operating income	$5,157,200
Less: Interest expenses	140,361
Earnings before taxes	5,016,839
Less: Taxes	1,702,165
Net income	$3,314,674

Financial Budgets

Once a company completes the various pieces of the operating budget and creates the pro forma (or budgeted) income statement, it next develops the necessary financial budgets to identify the assets and capital (both debt and equity) needed to support the operation. These financial budgets include the capital expenditure budget, the cash budget, the pro forma (or budgeted) balance sheet, and the pro forma (or budgeted) statement of cash flows. Figure 1B-40 shows the flow of the financial budgets.

Figure 1B-40 Financial Budget Flow

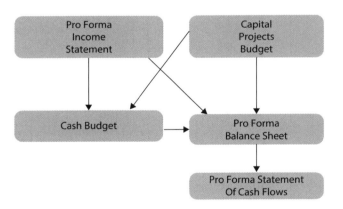

Capital Budget

The **capital budget** represents the amount of money the company plans to invest in selected long-term capital projects. This includes the purchases of property, plant, or equipment, as well as purchases of new businesses or operating capabilities. This budget often categorizes the capital projects by type (e.g., machines, buildings, etc.), the amount of funding, the timing of the funding need, and the reasons for investing in the capital projects (e.g., process improvement, replacement of obsolete equipment, etc.).

The capital budget is used for evaluating and selecting projects that require large amounts of funding, which will provide benefits far into the future. Because all businesses face a scarcity of resources, capital must be rationed. Therefore, capital budgets must first be aligned with the company strategy, and that strategy must be continually refined to take advantage of internal strengths and external opportunities.

Cash Budget

LOS
§1.B.5.t

Maintaining adequate liquidity is a requirement for staying in business. A cash budget is a plan to ensure liquidity. Financing can be planned in a strategic way to ensure that funding is available not only for capital projects, but also to pay current liabilities as they come due. Cash budgets are commonly prepared for monthly periods. Many companies find it useful to also prepare a cash budget for a weekly or quarterly time period.

Because cash is needed in all areas of operations, the cash budget gets data from all parts of the master budget. A cash budget is divided into four sections: the cash receipt section, the cash disbursement section, the cash excess or deficiency section, and the financing section.

Cash Receipts

Cash receipts are all collections in the current period from sales made in the current and prior periods (from collections of accounts receivable) and from other sources, such as interest income from investments.

Cash Disbursements

The cash disbursements section includes all outgoing cash payments. These include payments for purchases of materials, wages, operating expenses, taxes, and interest expenses.

Cash Excess or Deficiency

The cash excess or deficiency section is calculated as the beginning cash balance plus receipts and less disbursements and any minimum cash balance requirements. The result is either an excess or a deficiency of cash for the period. Excess cash can be invested per the company's policy, for temporary and short-term investments to make use of cash above a certain level. Most firms value capital preservation over returns on investment when choosing investments. So, they will choose relatively safe investments such as money market securities. Any deficiencies must be financed.

Financing

Financing includes finding sources of cash when liquidity levels fall below a point set by management or the board of directors.

The more complex aspects of the financing section involve calculating interest and loan repayments. If financing is needed in one month, the amount of financing must include enough for the minimum cash balance to be satisfied. Similarly, when calculating the amount of principal and interest that can be repaid, the minimum cash balance must be deducted first. In addition, it is important to note when the principal and interest are to be repaid (at the beginning or the end of a period), in order to determine the amount of principal the interest charge will be based on. Calculation of interest must consider the time frame of the budget to be able to properly calculate it for a monthly, quarterly, or annual time period.

Cash Budget Schedules

The cash receipts and cash disbursements sections of the budget are influenced by a number of factors. Companies generally create a pro forma schedule to estimate their cash receipts and another to estimate cash disbursements. The pro forma cash receipts schedule estimates percentages of collections for each period. The pro forma cash disbursements schedule can also use payment percentage patterns, but these are based on payment history instead of collection history. Often these disbursements are broken down by materials purchases, direct wages, general and administrative expenses, and income taxes.

An A/R collection pattern is a forecasting tool to estimate the timing of cash inflows and A/R levels resulting from sales made on credit. Companies use great care in analyzing historical collection trends and use these patterns as assumptions in forecasting cash collections.

For example: Figure 1B-41 shows an A/R sales collection history for Robin Manufacturing Company.

Figure 1B-41 A/R Sales Collection History

Robin Manufacturing Company A/R Sales Collection History	
Interval Since Month Sales	**Percentage Collected**
Month 0 (current month)	40%
Month 1 (next month)	30%
Month 2 (month after next)	20%
Month 3 (three months after)	10%

Using this information, the percentages can be applied to monthly sales to predict the timing of the cash collections for the upcoming time periods.

Figure 1B-42 shows Robin Manufacturing schedule of expected cash collections using the percentages from Figure 1B-41 and the formula that follows.

Figure 1B-42 Cash Collections Schedule

Robin Manufacturing Company
Schedule of Expected Collections (Cash Inflow) from Customers

Month	Sales	% Collected	July	% Collected	August	% Collected	September	Total % Collected
April	$9,500,000	10%	950,000					
May	9,032,000	20%	1,806,400	10%	903,200			
June	8,520,000	30%	2,556,000	20%	1,704,000	10%	852,000	
July	7,756,000	40%	3,102,400	30%	2,326,800	20%	1,551,200	90%
August	7,977,600			40%	3,191,040	30%	2,393,280	70%
September	8,624,000					40%	3,449,600	40%
Total Cash Inflow			**$8,414,800**		**$8,125,040**		**$8,246,080**	

Cash inflows from sales for the month are calculated using the next formula.

Cash Inflows for Month

$$= (\text{Month zero \% Collected} \times \text{Sales Current Month})$$
$$+ (\text{Month one \% Collected} \times \text{Sales Last Month})$$
$$+ (\text{Month two \% Collected} \times \text{Sales Two Months Ago})$$
$$+ (\text{Month three \% Collected} \times \text{Sales Three Months Ago})$$

For example: The cash inflow for the month of September is calculated as follows:

$$\text{For September} = + 0.4 \times \$8,624,000 = \$3,449,600 \text{ September}$$
$$+ 0.3 \times \$7,977,600 = \$2,393,280 \text{ August}$$
$$+ 0.2 \times \$7,756,000 = \$1,551,200 \text{ July}$$
$$+ 0.1 \times \$8,520,000 = \$852,000 \text{ June}$$
$$= \$8,246,080$$

Calculating accounts receivable for month end September uses the percentage remaining to be collected and multiplies it by the total sales for that specific month.

For example: Start with the total percentage collected found on Figure 1B-42 and subtract it from 100%. This is the percent remaining to be collected. Then multiply the percent remaining by the total sales for that month.

$$\text{A/R Balance} = + \$7,756,000 \times .10 = \$775,600 \quad \text{July}$$
$$+ \$7,977,600 \times .30 = \$2,393,280 \quad \text{August}$$
$$+ \$8,624,000 \times .60 = \$5,174,400 \quad \text{September}$$
$$= \$8,343,280$$

Note that the firm could have additional planned cash collections from nonsales sources, such as investment income. In this case, those cash receipts would be added to the cash receipts from sales to find total cash receipts. The next schedule to be prepared is the pro forma schedule of cash disbursements.

For example: Figure 1B-43 shows Robin Manufacturing's pro forma schedule of cash disbursements. In addition to the information stated previously in the direct materials, direct labor, and overhead budgets for Robin Manufacturing, assume that, in June, actual direct material purchases were $3,280,000, actual variable factory overhead was $188,500, actual fixed factory overhead (less depreciation of $20,000) was $88,900, and actual S&A expenses were $705,000. Half of Robin Manufacturing's direct materials purchases are paid in the same month as the purchase, and the other half are paid one month later. Direct labor is paid in the same month. Overhead is paid the next month. In the meantime, the company's interest expense on its long-term debt for the quarter of $120,000 will be paid in July, and its tax installment for the quarter of $1,702,165 will be paid in August. The company has also budgeted the capital expenditures: July, $880,000; August, $5,360,000: September, $51,000. The amounts calculated on this schedule are used in the cash budget.

Figure 1B-43 Pro Forma Schedule of Cash Disbursements

Robin Manufacturing Company Pro Forma Schedule of Cash Disbursements for the 3rd Quarter, Year 1				
	June Expected	July Expected	August Expected	September Expected
DM* purchases (see Fig. 1B-32)	$3,280,000	$4,680,000	$4,745,000	$5,135,000
Cash disbursements				
DM purchases—50% same month		$2,340,000	$2,372,500	$2,567,500
50% following month		$1,640,000	$2,340,000	$2,372,500
Direct labor paid same month (see Fig. 1B-34)		$540,000	$547,500	$585,000
Variable factory overhead paid following month (see Fig. 1B-35)		$188,500	$208,800	$211,700
Fixed factory overhead paid following month† (see Fig. 1B-35)		$88,900	$88,900	$88,900
S&A expenses paid following month (see Fig. 1B-38)		$705,000	$745,000	$795,000
Interest expense on long-term debt		$120,000		
Tax installment			$1,702,165	
Capital expenditure		$880,000	$5,360,000	$51,000
Total cash disbursements		$6,502,400	$13,364,865	$6,671,600

*DM = direct materials.

†Since depreciation is a noncash expense, the $20,000 of depreciation was removed from each month's fixed factory overhead.

Once the company has determined its cash receipts and cash disbursements, and with the beginning cash balance for the quarter, it can then put together its cash budget for the quarter. The cash budget will help the company determine if it has surplus cash or insufficient cash.

For example: It is assumed that Robin Manufacturing will not invest its surplus cash and it will borrow with short-term loans to bring its cash balance to the minimum required level if it has insufficient cash. It is assumed that the company has an established policy to keep its minimum cash balance at $250,000. Figure 1B-44 illustrates the cash budget for Robin Manufacturing Company for the quarter ended September 30.

Figure 1B-44 Cash Budget

Robin Manufacturing Company Cash Budget for the Quarter Ended September 30, Year 1				
	July	August	September	Quarter
Cash balance, beginning	$1,587,000	$3,499,400	$250,000	$1,587,000
Add cash receipts (see Fig. 1B-42)	8,414,800	8,125,040	8,246,080	24,785,920
Total cash available for needs	$10,001,800	$11,624,440	$8,496,080	$26,372,920
Deduct cash disbursements (see Fig. 1B-43)	6,502,400	13,364,865	6,671,600	26,538,865
Minimum cash needed	250,000	250,000	250,000	250,000
Total cash needed	$6,752,400	$13,614,865	$6,921,600	$26,788,865
Cash excess (deficiency)	3,249,400	(1,990,425)	1,574,480	($415,945)
Financing				
Borrowing (beginning balance)	–	–	1,990,425	–
Borrowing	–	1,990,425	–	1,990,425
Repayment (end of period)	–	–	(1,554,576)*	(1,554,576)
Interest expense	–	–	(19,904)†	(19,904)
Borrowing (ending balance)		$1,990,425	$435,849‡	$435,849
Total financing needs (adjusted for interest payments)	–	1,990,425	(1,574,480)	435,849
Cash balance, ending	$3,499,400	$250,000	$250,000	$250,000

* Only $1,554,576 could be paid back at this time.

† Interest on short-term borrowings.

‡ Note that interest for the following month will be $4,358.

General notes: Robin Manufacturing Company requires a cash balance of $250,000 at all times. In the month of August, the need to borrow almost $2 million was financed with a short-term loan at 12% per annum interest. Note also that the example assumes that excess cash is not being invested (see July).

LOS
§1.B.5.v

In Figures 1B-42, 1B-43, and 1B-44, the information from various pieces of the master budget is used to create the cash budget of Robin Manufacturing Company.

In the meantime, the cash budget is also influencing other pieces of the master budget. The financing portion of the cash budget will determine the borrowing needed (i.e., if the company has insufficient cash). This short-term borrowing will contribute to the current liabilities of the pro forma balance sheet, and the interest expense on the short-term borrowings will count toward the interest expense in the pro forma income statement. Similarly, any short-term investments made using surplus cash will contribute to the current assets of the pro forma balance sheet.

Pro Forma (or Budgeted) Balance Sheet

A pro forma balance sheet (also known as a budget balance sheet or statement of financial position) illustrates how operations affect the company's assets, liabilities, and stockholders' equity. The budgeted balance sheet is based in part on the budgeted balance sheet at the end of the current period. The effects of operations for the budget period are added to the data in the prior balance sheet.

Pro Forma (or Budgeted) Statement of Cash Flows

The pro forma statement of cash flows is usually the last statement created because it requires input from the pro forma income statement and balance sheet. A company's pro forma statement of cash flows represents its projected sources and uses of funds. Using information from the income statement and balance sheet, it groups the company's cash flows into one of three activities: operating, investing, and financing activities.

The operating activity portion tracks the cash flows generated by the operation itself. Cash flows that are included in this category include net income (after adding back depreciation, because it is a noncash expense) plus net changes to its noncash working capital accounts (i.e., accounts payable and receivable, inventory, accrued and prepaid expenses, and deferred taxes).

The investing activity portion tracks the cash flows associated with the buying and selling of capital assets.

The financing activity portion tracks the cash flows from the sale and repayment of the company's debt, both short term and long term, the sale and repurchase of its equity, both preferred and common stocks, and the payment of cash dividends. Note that the interest payments on debt appear in the operating activity portion and not in the financing activity portion.

Relationship Among Cash Budget, Capital Expenditure Budget, and Pro Forma Financial Statements

The cash budget combines the results of the operating, cash collections, and cash disbursements budgets to provide an overall picture of where an organization expects its cash to come from and be paid to for a given period. The capital expenditure budget is a line item that is included in the cash disbursements section of the cash budget. A pro forma income statement is completed to demonstrate that an acceptable level of income is possible. This estimated income and changes to the cash budget are used to create a pro forma balance sheet. The pro forma cash flow statement classifies all of the cash receipts and disbursements based on activity: that is, operating activities, investing activities, and financial activities.

Topic Questions:
Annual Profit Plan and Supporting Schedules

Directions: Answer each question in the space provided. Correct answers and explanations appear after the topic questions.

1. A steel company manufactures heavy-duty brackets for the shelving industry. The company has budgeted for the production and sale of 1,000,000 brackets, and has no beginning or ending inventory. Relevant operational, revenue, and cost data is as follows.

Unit selling price of a bracket	$22.50
Direct material required per unit	4 pounds
Direct labor required per unit	0.15 hours
Cost of material per pound	$1.75
Direct labor cost per hour	$9.00
Total variable selling costs	$2,250,000
Total fixed costs	$1,500,000

    Based on the data provided, what is the unit contribution margin per bracket?

    ☐ **a.** $14.15

    ☐ **b.** $11.90

    ☐ **c.** $10.60

    ☐ **d.** $10.40

2. A company is developing its annual budget. The company's products are made to order and shipped immediately. The controller has information on the following accounts:

    Raw materials

    Direct labor

    Advertising

    Research and development (R&D)

    Trade discounts

    Factory indirect labor

    Factory overhead

    Selling costs

Which of the above accounts should **not** be included in the cost of goods sold budget?

- ☐ **a.** Advertising, R&D, and selling costs, only
- ☐ **b.** R&D and trade discounts, only
- ☐ **c.** Advertising and selling costs, only
- ☐ **d.** Advertising, R&D, trade discounts, and selling costs, only

3. A company receives an order from a major customer on the first day of every quarter and has to produce an extra 10% to cover for product defects. Each finished product requires two pounds of direct material and three direct labor hours. Finished goods inventory as of January 1 is 300 units, which can be used to fulfill the order. The orders for the first quarter are shown below.

January   2,000 units

February   2,300 units

March   2,500 units

Budgeted direct labor hours for the first quarter are:

- ☐ **a.** 19,500.
- ☐ **b.** 20,400.
- ☐ **c.** 21,450.
- ☐ **d.** 22,440.

Topic Question Answers:
Annual Profit Plan and Supporting Schedules

1. A steel company manufactures heavy-duty brackets for the shelving industry. The company has budgeted for the production and sale of 1,000,000 brackets, and has no beginning or ending inventory. Relevant operational, revenue, and cost data is as follows.

Unit selling price of a bracket	$22.50
Direct material required per unit	4 pounds
Direct labor required per unit	0.15 hours
Cost of material per pound	$1.75
Direct labor cost per hour	$9.00
Total variable selling costs	$2,250,000
Total fixed costs	$1,500,000

Based on the data provided, what is the unit contribution margin per bracket?

- ☐ **a.** $14.15
- ☑ **b.** $11.90
- ☐ **c.** $10.60
- ☐ **d.** $10.40

The unit contribution margin is calculated as sales price per unit less total variable costs per unit. In this example the total variable costs per unit consist of direct materials of $7.00 per unit (4 pounds × $1.75), direct labor of $1.35 per unit (0.15 hours × $9.00), and total variable selling costs of $2.25 per unit ($2,250,000 ÷ 1,000,000 units). The unit contribution margin equals $11.90 ($22.50 − ($7.00 + $1.35 + $2.25)).

2. A company is developing its annual budget. The company's products are made to order and shipped immediately. The controller has information on the following accounts:

Raw materials

Direct labor

Advertising

Research and development (R&D)

Trade discounts

Factory indirect labor

Factory overhead

Selling costs

Which of the above accounts should **not** be included in the cost of goods sold budget?

- ☐ **a.** Advertising, R&D, and selling costs, only
- ☐ **b.** R&D and trade discounts, only
- ☐ **c.** Advertising and selling costs, only
- ☑ **d.** Advertising, R&D, trade discounts, and selling costs, only

The cost of goods sold budget can be computed by using the traditional income statement formula. This begins with direct materials purchased adjusted for beginning and ending inventory to compute the cost of direct materials used in production. That total is added to the direct labor and manufacturing overhead costs used in production. These total manufacturing costs are adjusted for the beginning and ending finished goods inventory to determine the cost of goods sold. Of the accounts listed that the controller has information for, advertising, R&D, trade discounts, and selling costs are not needed to calculate the cost of goods sold budget.

3. A company receives an order from a major customer on the first day of every quarter and has to produce an extra 10% to cover for product defects. Each finished product requires two pounds of direct material and three direct labor hours. Finished goods inventory as of January 1 is 300 units, which can be used to fulfill the order. The orders for the first quarter are shown below.

January	2,000 units
February	2,300 units
March	2,500 units

Budgeted direct labor hours for the first quarter are:

- ☐ **a.** 19,500.
- ☐ **b.** 20,400.
- ☑ **c.** 21,450.
- ☐ **d.** 22,440.

To compute the budgeted direct labor hours for the first quarter, the company must first determine how many units need to be produced in the quarter. The company must have 6,800 units to fulfill the orders, but it already has 300 units in finished goods inventory; therefore, it must produce 6,500 units plus an additional 10% to cover for product defects. The company must produce 7,150 total units during the first quarter ($6,500 \times 1.10$). Because each unit requires three direct labor hours, the budgeted direct labor hours for the first quarter total 21,450 hours ($7,150 \times 3$).

Top-Level Planning and Analysis

LOS
§1.B.6.a

THE MASTER BUDGET, OR ANNUAL profit plan, includes a set of pro forma financial statements. These financial statements are key elements in helping a company plan for the future. Based on these pro forma statements, a company can: determine if it is meeting its predetermined targets; estimate the amount of external funding needed to support its projected sales growth; and perform sensitivity analysis to identify the impacts of estimates, operating, and policy changes on selected financial ratios.

This topic traces the process of creating pro forma financial statements using the percentage-of-sales method, which builds a pro forma income statement and then a pro forma balance sheet. It includes an example of creating a pro forma statement of cash flows. Then it describes the process of assessing anticipated performance using pro forma financial statements, including performing sensitivity analyses.

READ the Learning Outcome Statements (LOS) for this topic as found in Appendix A and then study the concepts and calculations presented here to be sure you understand the content you could be tested on in the CMA exam.

Pro Forma Financial Statements and Budgets

The master budget is composed of the operating budgets and the financial budgets. The final product of the operating budget is the pro forma income statement, which shows a company's projected sales revenue, costs, and profit (i.e., net income). Once the company's dividend policy has been factored in to determine the amount of dividends to be paid, the amount of projected retained earnings will then be added to its current balance sheet to create the pro forma balance sheet. Information from the company's capital expenditure budget and cash budget will also be used to help formulate the pro forma balance sheet. Once the pro forma income statement and balance sheet are compiled, the information can then be used to create the pro forma statement of cash flows.

The relationships among the various pro forma financial statements and budgets are illustrated in Figure 1B-45.

Figure 1B-45 Relationships Among Pro Forma Financial Statements and Budgets

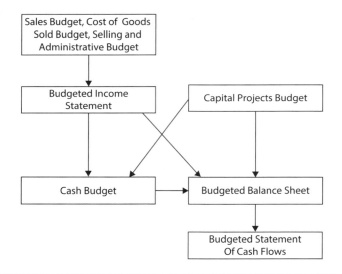

LOS
§1.B.6.e

Pro forma statements represent a company's projected financial statements. The process of creating pro forma statements should produce a plan that (a) is attainable, (b) that, if achieved, will be viewed as an acceptable result, and (c) is financially viable. The capital budget is particularly important for ensuring financial viability of a company's plans for the future. Pro forma statements are useful in the company's planning process because these statements support three major functions. They help a company to:

1. Assess whether its anticipated performance is in line with its established targets.
2. Anticipate the amount of funding needed to achieve its forecasted sales growth.
3. Estimate the effects of changes in assumptions of key numbers by performing sensitivity analysis (i.e., what-if analysis). Sensitivity analysis helps to identify potential conditions that could lead to major problems for the company. This enables the company to plan for appropriate actions in case such an event should occur. In addition, sensitivity analysis also provides the company with the opportunity to analyze the impact of changing its operating plans.

Creating a Pro Forma Income Statement with the Percentage-of-Sales Method

In Topic 5: Annual Profit Plan and Supporting Schedules, various pieces of the operating budget were projected and used to ultimately form the pro forma income statement. The process to complete these schedules is very complex and time consuming. Here a shortcut approach, known as the percentage-of-sales method, is used to create a pro forma income statement and a pro forma balance sheet.

The percentage-of-sales method is a simple approach that ties many of the items in the pro forma income statement and balance sheet to future sales revenue. It assumes that the relationship between sales revenue and these income statement and balance sheet items remains constant. This means that they grow proportionately with any sales growth. Any activity that is needed to directly support the operations and will generate the specific sales level is assumed to grow proportionately with sales. On the income statement, these items include the cost of goods sold (COGS) and selling and administrative (S&A) expense; on the balance sheet, it includes current assets, net fixed assets, accounts payables, and accruals.

None of the financing activities—namely, notes payable (short-term borrowing), long-term debt, and owners' equity—is assumed to grow proportionately with sales.

For example: Heavenly Furniture Company uses the percentage-of-sales method to forecast its pro forma financial statements. Based on historical financial statements, these relationships can be established between several items and sales:

- COGS is 80% of sales.
- S&A expense is 5% of sales.
- Cash and equivalent are 3% of sales.
- Account receivables are 18% of sales.
- Inventories are 25% of sales.
- Net fixed assets are 35% of sales.
- Accounts payables are 12% of sales.
- Accruals are 8% of sales.

The implication here is that the operating profit margin percentage is expected to remain unchanged at 15%.

Operating Profit Margin Percentage = Operating Income / Sales

Also implied is that the total asset turnover is expected to remain unchanged at 1.235.

Total Asset Turnover = Sales / Average Assets

Finally, the relationships between the *spontaneous liabilities* and sales is expected to remain unchanged. Spontaneous liabilities are those that arise naturally from the operations of the firm; accounts payable is a good example. If the volume of sales increases, then the volume of purchases must also increase. If vendor invoices continue to be paid the same number of days after the invoice date, then the level of accounts payable must increase in proportion to the increase in sales. It is important to note that spontaneous liabilities are non-interest-bearing liabilities.

Heavenly Furniture is projecting a sales revenue growth of 18% in the upcoming year. The company currently has 12,000 shares of common stock outstanding, and it plans on maintaining its dividend policy of paying out 40% of its net income as dividends. It is currently paying 8% interest on its notes payable and 10% on its long-term debt. The company has a 35% tax rate.

The process used is:

1. Create the pro forma income statement.
2. Create the pro forma balance sheet.
3. Create the pro forma statement of cash flows.

LOS
§1.B.6.b

Creating a Pro Forma Income Statement

To create the pro forma income statement, it is necessary to first estimate the sales revenue for the upcoming year. Given the current-year sales revenue of $100,000 and a projected growth rate of 18%, the upcoming-year sale revenue will be $118,000. The projected sales revenue is then used to determine COGS and S&A. Since COGS is assumed to remain at 80% of sales, the forecasted COGS is projected to be $94,400. S&A is assumed to remain at 5% of sales, so the upcoming S&A is projected to be $5,900.

To simplify the calculations, it is assumed that Heavenly Furniture's interest expense is calculated based on its beginning-of-period debt balance. Since the company is carrying a $5,000 note payable and $20,000 of long-term debt at the beginning of the upcoming year, the total interest expense is $2,400—the interest expense on the note payable is $400 ($5,000 note payable multiplied by the 8% annual interest rate), and the interest expense on the long-term debt is $2,000 ($20,000 long-term debt multiplied by the 10% annual interest rate).

These numbers are then used to create the upcoming year's pro forma income statement, presented along with the current year's income statement in Figure 1B-46.

Figure 1B-46 Heavenly Furniture Company Pro Forma Income Statement

	Current Year	%	Upcoming Year	%
Sales	$100,000	100	$118,000	100
COGS	80,000	80	94,400	80
Gross Margin	20,000	20	23,600	20
S&A Expenses	5,000	5	5,900	5
EBIT (Operating Income)	15,000	15	17,700	15
Interest	1,800		2,400	
EBT	13,200		15,300	
Taxes (35%)	4,620		5,355	
Net Income	$8,580		$9,945	
EPS	$0.72		$0.83	
Dividends (40%)	$3,432		$3,978	
Addition to retained earnings	$5,148		$5,967	

EBIT = earnings before interest and taxes; EBT = earnings before taxes; EPS = earnings per share.

Note that all the lines down to EBIT (operating income) increased by 18%. However, the interest expense calculation was independent of the growth in sales. Therefore, the remainder of the income statement lines increase by different percentages.

With a projected 18% sales growth, Heavenly Furniture expects to generate a net income of $9,945 and EPS of $0.83 (= $9,945/12,000 shares of common stock outstanding). Given the current dividend policy of paying out 40% of earnings as dividends, the company will be paying out $3,978 (= $9,945 × 0.40) in dividends and retaining $5,967 (= $9,945 − $3,978) in earnings.

Creating a Pro Forma Balance Sheet and Determining Additional Funding Needed

After creating the pro forma income statement for the upcoming year, Heavenly Furniture Company's pro forma balance sheet can be created. Once again, based on a projected sales revenue of $118,000 and the assumed relationships:

Cash and cash equivalents are projected to be $3,540 (3% of sales).

Accounts receivables are projected to be $21,240 (18% of sales).

Inventories are projected to be $29,500 (25% of sales).

Net fixed assets are projected to be $41,300 (35% of sales). (The percentage-of-sales method is a cruder method of estimating the cash requirement for fixed assets than is the use of the capital budget.)

Accounts payables are projected to be $14,160 (12% of sales).

Accruals are projected to be $9,440 (8% of sales).

In addition, based on the pro forma statement for the upcoming year, Heavenly Furniture Company is expected to retain $5,967 in earnings. The earnings will be added to the current year's retained earnings of $16,000 in the balance sheet to derive the upcoming year's retained earnings of $21,967.

Two iterations will be completed to derive Heavenly Furniture Company's pro forma balance sheet. In the first iteration, all financing activities (i.e., notes payables, long-term debt, and common stock) are assumed to remain at the current year's levels. This will help to determine if the company needs any additional external funding to support the projected sales growth. Once the level of external funding has been determined, it will be incorporated to create the final pro forma balance sheet in the second iteration.

Using the estimated balance sheet items calculated earlier, Heavenly Furniture's pro forma balance sheet (before any additional financing) is presented in Figure 1B-47.

Figure 1B-47 Heavenly Furniture Pro Forma Balance Sheet Before Additional Financing

	Current Year	Upcoming Year
Assets		
Cash and equivalents	$3,000	$3,540
Receivables	18,000	21,240
Inventories	25,000	29,500
Total Current Assets	46,000	54,280
Net Fixed Assets	35,000	41,300
Total Assets	$81,000	$95,580

Figure 1B-47 Heavenly Furniture Pro Forma Balance Sheet Before Additional Financing (*Continued*)

	Current Year	Upcoming Year
Liabilities and Equity		
Accounts payable	$12,000	$14,160
Accruals	8,000	9,440
Notes payable	5,000	5,000
Total Current Liabilities	25,000	28,600
Long-term debt	20,000	20,000
Total Liabilities	45,000	48,600
Common stock	20,000	20,000
Retained earnings	16,000	21,967
Total Equity	36,000	41,967
Total liabilities and equity	$81,000	$90,567
Additional Funding Needed		$5,013

Since the company needed $95,580 in assets to support its estimated sales revenue of $118,000 but only has $90,567 in financing (i.e., total liabilities and equity), the company will need $5,013 ($95,580 − $90,567) in external funding.

Heavenly Furniture Company has several options for raising the $5,013 of external funding it needs. The company can raise the funds using notes payable, long-term debt, common stock, or any combination of the three—such as $2,000 from notes payable and $3,013 from long-term debt. However, if the company is unwilling to seek that much external funding, it can lower its external funding need by increasing the amount of internal funding (i.e., retained earnings) available by altering its dividend policy. The company can lower its dividend payout ratio (e.g., from 40% to 30%) to reduce the amount of dividends paid out and to increase the amount of earnings retained. For every additional dollar of internal funding (in the form of retained earnings) raised, the company will need one less dollar of external funding.

In this scenario, it is assumed that Heavenly Furniture Company will acquire the $5,013 of external funding it needs by using notes payable. This will be added to the company's current $5,000 of notes payable for a total of $10,013. Figure 1B-48 shows the company's pro forma balance sheet after taking on the additional funding.

Figure 1B-48 Heavenly Furniture Pro Forma Balance Sheet After Additional Financing

	Current Year	Upcoming Year
Assets		
Cash and equivalents	$3,000	$3,540
Receivables	18,000	21,240
Inventories	25,000	29,500
Total Current Assets	$46,000	$54,280
Net Fixed Assets	35,000	41,300
Total Assets	$81,000	$95,580

	Current Year	**Upcoming Year**
Liabilities and Equity		
Accounts payable	$12,000	$14,160
Accruals	8,000	9,440
Notes payable	5,000	10,013
Total Current Liabilities	$25,000	$33,613
Long-term debt	20,000	20,000
Total Liabilities	$45,000	$53,613
Common stock	20,000	20,000
Retained earnings	16,000	21,967
Total Equity	36,000	41,967
Total liabilities and equity	$81,000	$95,580

It should be noted that the balance sheet for the upcoming year shows that Heavenly Furniture became more heavily leveraged. In the current year, the ratio of interest-bearing debt to equity was ($5,000 + $20,000) / ($20,000 + $16,000) =.694. For the upcoming year, that same ratio is expected to be ($10,013 + $20,000) / ($20,000 + $21,967) =.715. This increase in leverage could possibly increase the interest rate to be paid in the future. The increase in leverage may also increase the cost of equity capital. The likely effect would be an increase in the weighted average cost of capital. This should be a caution flag to warn that perhaps the 18% sales growth may not be a wise course of action because it is not attainable with the current funding or perhaps the dividend payout ratio should be decreased.

Creating a Pro Forma Statement of Cash Flows

Once Heavenly Furniture Company's pro forma income statement and balance sheet have been completed, that information can be used to create the company's pro forma statement of cash flows. There are two approaches to creating a statement of cash flows: the direct method and the indirect method. Heavenly Furniture Company's pro forma statement of cash flows will be created using the indirect method.

A key concept in dealing with cash flows is:

- Any increase in accounts receivables, inventories, net fixed assets, net income generated, and dividends paid represents a cash outflow, and vice versa.
- Any increase in accounts payables, accruals, and financing activities (i.e., notes payable, long-term debt, and common stock issued) represents a cash inflow, and vice versa.

For example: According to Figure 1B-48, Heavenly Furniture's accounts receivables increases by $3,240 (from $18,000 to $21,240). This represents a cash flow of −$3,240 (a cash outflow). Its accounts payable amount increases by $2,160 (from $12,000 to $14,160). This represents a cash flow of +$2,160.

A very useful formula appears in the next key box. This expression comes from the fundamental accounting equation that Assets = Liabilities + Stockholders' Equity and the idea that there are only two kinds of assets (cash and non-cash assets).

$$\Delta \text{ Cash} = \Delta \text{ Liabilities} + \Delta \text{ Stockholders' Equity} - \Delta \text{ Non-Cash Assets}$$

This is the process to be used when employing the indirect method to construct a cash flow statement. The process also helps project the effect on cash of any management decision affecting balance sheet accounts.

The pro forma statement of cash flows groups cash flows into three major categories of activities:

1. Cash flows from operating activities
2. Cash flows from investing activities
3. Cash flows from financing activities

For example: Using the information from the company's pro forma income statement and balance sheet (see Figures 1B-46 and 1B-48):

- Net cash provided by operating activities = $5,805
- Net cash used by investing activities   = ($6,300)
- Net cash provided by financing activities = $1,035

Heavenly Furniture's pro forma statement of cash flows is shown in Figure 1B-49.

Figure 1B-49 Heavenly Furniture Pro Forma Statement of Cash Flows

Net income	$9,945
Receivables	(3,240)
Inventories	(4,500)
Payables	2,160
Accruals	1,440
Net cash provided by operating activities	$5,805
Capital expenditure (net fixed assets)	$(6,300)
Net cash used by investing activities	$(6,300)
Notes payables	$5,013
Dividends	(3,978)
Net cash provided by financing activities	$1,035
Net change in cash flow	$540
Beginning cash	3,000
Ending cash	$3,540

The company's combined cash inflow for the upcoming year totals $540 (= $5,805 − $6,300 + $1,035). Together with the beginning cash balance of $3,000, the ending cash balance will be $3,540. This matches Heavenly Furniture Company's cash position in the pro forma balance sheet (see Figure 1B-48).

Assessing Anticipated Performance Using Pro Forma Financial Statements

LOS §1.B.6.c

Once a company creates its pro forma financial statements, the statements need to be analyzed to determine if the company is meeting its predetermined financial targets. This can be accomplished by calculating a variety of financial ratios and comparing them to predetermined targets and industry averages. These calculations can help answer questions such as:

- Is the company's leverage (as measured by its debt ratio) within an acceptable range?
- Is its return on equity (ROE) acceptable in relation to the industry average?

A more detailed discussion on financial statement analysis using additional ratios is covered in Part 2 of the Wiley CMAexcel Learning System Exam Review.

For example: Figure 1B-50 presents a few selected financial ratios for Heavenly Furniture, calculated using the current and pro forma income statement and balance sheets (Figures 1B-46 and 1B-48).

Figure 1B-50 Heavenly Furniture Selected Financial Ratios

	Current Year	Upcoming Year
Current ratio	1.8400	1.6149
Quick ratio	0.8400	0.7372
Return on assets (ROA)	0.1059	0.1040
Return on equity (ROE)	0.2383*	0.2370*
Gross profit margin	0.2000	0.2000
Operating profit margin	0.1500	0.1500
Net profit margin	0.0858	0.0843
Debt to total assets ratio	0.5556	0.5609
Times interest earned (TIE)	8.3333	7.3750
EPS	$0.72	$0.83

*Note that average equity was not used in these examples

The ratios shown are calculated using these formulas:

$$\text{Current Ratio} = \text{Current Assets} / \text{Current Liabilities}$$

$$\text{Quick (or Acid Test) Ratio} = \frac{\text{Cash} + \text{Marketable Securities} + \text{Accounts Receivable}}{\text{Current Liabilities}}$$

$$\text{ROA} = \text{Net Income} / \text{Average Total Assets}$$

$$\text{ROE} = \text{Net Income} / \text{Average Equity}$$

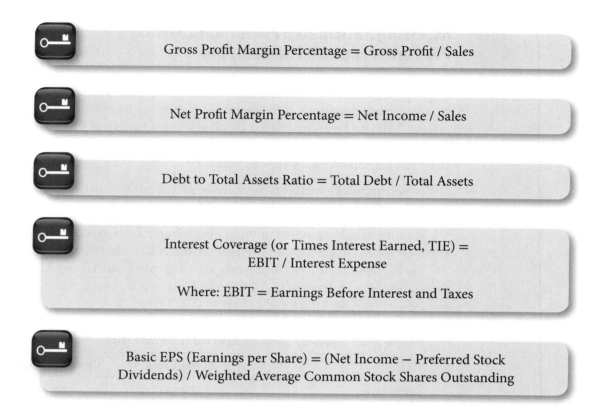

Gross Profit Margin Percentage = Gross Profit / Sales

Net Profit Margin Percentage = Net Income / Sales

Debt to Total Assets Ratio = Total Debt / Total Assets

Interest Coverage (or Times Interest Earned, TIE) = EBIT / Interest Expense

Where: EBIT = Earnings Before Interest and Taxes

Basic EPS (Earnings per Share) = (Net Income − Preferred Stock Dividends) / Weighted Average Common Stock Shares Outstanding

In order to support a projected 18% sales growth, Heavenly Furniture Company is raising $5,013 of external funding via notes payable. Because the company is tapping short-term borrowing for its external funding needs, its liquidity position will deteriorate as the current ratio and quick ratio are expected to decrease in the upcoming year. Its profit position, in terms of return on assets (ROA), return on equity (ROE), and net profit margin, is also expected to decrease in the upcoming year.

Because the company is relying on notes payable to raise its needed external funding, it is important that it pay close attention to its debt ratio and interest coverage (in terms of times interest earned [TIE]) to ensure that it has not violated any of its debt covenants. The company's debt ratio is expected to increase from 55.56% to 56.09%, and its TIE is expected to decrease from 8.333 to 7.3750. Both of these changes are relatively minor, so the company should be able to meet its debt covenants.

Earnings per share (EPS) is expected to increase from $0.72 to $0.83 (a 15.28% increase) as a result of the sales growth that is funded by additional debt.

The consequences cited earlier would all have been predicted by calculating the *sustainable growth rate*. The sustainable growth rate is the rate that a firm's sales might grow without increasing its leverage and without issuing any new common stock, given that its operating profitability remains the same and that its asset turnover remains the same.

Sustainable Growth Rate = Return on Equity × (1 − Dividends Payout Ratio)

The sustainable growth rate is discussed more fully in Part 2, Section A, Topic 3. When a firm tries to grow at a rate higher than the sustainable growth rate, it must (1) issue new shares of common stock, (2) issue debt at a level that will result in the firm becoming more leveraged, or (3) find ways to increase its return on invested capital. The current year's return on equity was calculated to be .2383 and (1.00 − payout ratio) is 0.6. Therefore, the sustainable growth rate is only 14.3%. Any sales growth rate above this will require additional funding, as was shown.

Performing Sensitivity Analysis

The pro forma statements in Figures 1B-46, 1B-47, 1B-48, 1B-49, and the selected ratios in Figure 1B-50 are based on Heavenly Furniture Company's assumptions of a projected 18% sales growth and certain assumed relationships between sales revenue and selected items in the income statement and balance sheet. Since the company is dealing with the future when projecting its pro forma statements, there is always a chance that these initial assumptions will change. What if the projected sales growth is 20% rather than 18%? What if the cost of production has increased and the COGS is actually 85% of sales rather than 80% of sales?

The company can analyze these alternatives by performing a series of sensitivity or what-if analyses. Doing this involves systematically changing one of the assumptions and analyzing the impact that these changes have on the pro forma statements and on the selected financial ratios.

For example: Heavenly Furniture Company is performing a sensitivity analysis to determine the effects of changing one or more of its initial assumptions. The original pro forma income statement and balance sheet (from Figures 1B-46 and 1B-47) and the selected ratios (from Figure 1B-50) serve as the base scenario.

Their first analysis focuses on changing two of the income statement–related assumptions: sales revenue growth rate and the relationship between COGS and sales.

Sensitivity Analysis Based on Growth Rate Changes

Heavenly Furniture Company initially projected a sales revenue growth rate of 18% for the upcoming year. However, this projected growth rate might be as high as 20% or as low as 16%, depending on the economic conditions in the upcoming year. The company can reproject its pro forma income statement and balance sheet first based on a 16% growth rate and then based on a 20% growth rate. All other variables are assumed to remain the same.

The 16% growth rate will lead to projected sales of $116,000. The 20% growth rate will lead to projected sales of $120,000. Using the methods discussed earlier in creating the initial pro forma financial statements, the pro forma income statement and balance sheet for the various growth rate assumptions are presented in Figure 1B-51.

Figure 1B-51 Sensitivity Analysis with Different Growth Rates

Heavenly Furniture Company Pro Forma Income Statement

	Growth = 16%	Base =18%	Growth = 20%	%
Sales	$116,000	$118,000	$120,000	100
COGS	92,800	94,400	96,000	80
Gross Margin	23,200	23,600	24,000	20
S&A Expenses	5,800	5,900	6,000	5
EBIT (Operating Income)	17,400	17,700	18,000	15
Interest	2,400	2,400	2,400	
EBT	15,000	15,300	15,600	
Taxes	5,250	5,355	5,460	
Net Income	$9,750	$9,945	$10,140	
EPS	$0.81	$0.83	$0.85	
Dividends	$3,900	$3,978	$4,056	
Addition to retained earnings	$5,850	$5,967	$6,084	
Assets				
Cash and equivalents	$3,480	$3,540	$3,600	
Receivables	20,880	21,240	21,600	
Inventories	29,000	29,500	30,000	
Total Current Assets	$53,360	$54,280	$55,200	
Net Fixed Assets	40,600	41,300	42,000	
Total Assets	$93,960	$95,580	$97,200	
Liabilities and Equity				
Accounts payable	$13,920	$14,160	$14,400	
Accruals	9,280	9,440	9,600	
Notes payable	8,910	10,013	11,116	
Total Current Liabilities	$32,110	$33,613	$35,116	
Long-term debt	20,000	20,000	20,000	
Total Liabilities	$52,110	$53,613	$55,116	
Common stock	20,000	20,000	20,000	
Retained earnings	21,850	21,967	22,084	
Total Equity	$41,850	$41,967	$42,084	
Total liabilities and equity	$93,960	$95,580	$97,200	

The sensitivity analysis for Heavenly Furniture Company was done by varying its projected sales growth within the range of 16% to 20%. The pro forma income statement and balance sheet will provide the company an opportunity to determine how various items in the income statement and balance sheet change as the projected growth rate changes.

For example: In Figure 1B-51, the company's EPS drops to $0.81 when the growth rate is 16%, but rises to $0.85 when the growth rate is 20%. This means that a 2% change in growth rate leads to a $0.02 change in EPS.

The new pro forma income statement and balance sheet can also be used to create new sets of financial ratios, as shown in Figure 1B-52. Once again, the company will be able to analyze how each financial ratio changes when the growth rate changes.

In addition to the financial ratios, the additional amounts of external funding needed for the various growth rates are also presented in Figure 1B-52. Since the company relies solely on the use of notes payable to meet its external funding need, the amount of external funding needed can be determined by subtracting the amount of notes payable in the current year ($5,000) from the amount of notes payable in the upcoming year. For instance, the amount of notes payable is $8,910 when the growth rate is 16%, so the amount of external funding needed is $3,910 (= $8,910 − $5,000). It is important for Heavenly Furniture to pay close attention to how the amount of external funding needed changes when the growth rate assumption changes. The company might not be comfortable raising the amount of external funding if the growth rate is higher than anticipated, or the company may need to arrange for a line of credit and be prepared to pursue other external funding options if needed.

Figure 1B-52 Selected Financial Ratio Sensitivity Analysis with Different Growth Rates

	Growth = 16%	Base = 18%	Growth = 20%
Current ratio	1.6618	1.6149	1.5719
Quick ratio	0.7586	0.7372	0.7176
ROA	0.1038	0.1040	0.1043
ROE	0.2330*	0.2370*	0.2409*
Gross profit margin	0.2000	0.2000	0.2000
Operating profit margin	0.1500	0.1500	0.1500
Net profit margin	0.0841	0.0843	0.0845
Debt to total assets ratio	0.5546	0.5609	0.5670
TIE	7.2500	7.3750	7.5000
Additional funding needed	$3,910	$5,013	$6,116

*Note that average equity was not used in these examples

**Topic Questions:
Top-Level Planning and Analysis**

Directions: Answer each question in the space provided. Correct answers and explanations appear after the topic questions.

1. A company makes one product that it sells for €125 per unit. The product has a contribution margin of 35% of sales. Direct materials account for 10% of sales. Variable manufacturing overhead is 5% of sales. Fixed costs are €200,000 per year. The controller wants to create a pro forma income statement where the sales increase from 10,000 units to 12,000 units. The average income tax rate is 25.71%. What is the change in operating income as a result of the increase in unit sales?

   □ **a.** €50,000

   □ **b.** €65,000

   □ **c.** €75,000

   □ **d.** €87,500

2. The pro forma income statement for a manufacturing company is built on projections of all of the following except:

   □ **a.** marketing costs.

   □ **b.** production overhead.

   □ **c.** cash balances.

   □ **d.** ending inventory.

3. What is the proper preparation sequencing of the following budgets?

   1. Budgeted Balance Sheet

   2. Sales Budget

   3. Selling and Administrative Budget

   4. Budgeted Income Statement

   □ **a.** 1,2,3,4

   □ **b.** 2,3,1,4

   □ **c.** 2,3,4,1

   □ **d.** 2,4,1,3

Topic Question Answers:
Top-Level Planning and Analysis

1. A company makes one product that it sells for €125 per unit. The product has a contribution margin of 35% of sales. Direct materials account for 10% of sales. Variable manufacturing overhead is 5% of sales. Fixed costs are €200,000 per year. The controller wants to create a pro forma income statement where the sales increase from 10,000 units to 12,000 units. The average income tax rate is 25.71%. What is the change in operating income as a result of the increase in unit sales?

    ☐ **a.** €50,000

    ☐ **b.** €65,000

    ☐ **c.** €75,000

    ☑ **d.** €87,500

The operating income is the income before interest and taxes. One way to calculate the change in operating income from the increase in unit sales is to multiply the increase in units of 2,000 units (12,000 − 10,000) by the unit contribution margin which is €43.75 (€125 × 35%). This formula can be used because the fixed costs of €200,000 will remain the same whether 10,000 or 12,000 units are produced; therefore, the increase in operating income will be €87,500 (2,000 units × €43.75).

2. The pro forma income statement for a manufacturing company is built on projections of all of the following except:

    ☐ **a.** marketing costs.

    ☐ **b.** production overhead.

    ☑ **c.** cash balances.

    ☐ **d.** ending inventory.

A pro forma income statement shows a company's projected sales revenue, costs, and profit. The pro forma income statement for a manufacturing company would be built on projections of marketing costs and production overhead because those both directly represent costs. Additionally, the pro forma income statement is built on a projection of ending inventory because even though it is a balance sheet item, ending inventory would be needed to calculate the cost of goods sold. A cash balance is a balance sheet item that would not be useful in calculating the company's revenue, costs, or profit.

3. What is the proper preparation sequencing of the following budgets?

   1. Budgeted Balance Sheet
   2. Sales Budget
   3. Selling and Administrative Budget
   4. Budgeted Income Statement

   ☐ **a.** 1,2,3,4
   ☐ **b.** 2,3,1,4
   ☑ **c.** 2,3,4,1
   ☐ **d.** 2,4,1,3

The budgeting process begins with the sales budget. The budgeted or pro forma financial statements are the last items to be prepared, with the income statement being prepared before the balance sheet; therefore, the correct sequence is 2,3,4,1.

Directions: This sampling of questions is designed to emulate actual exam questions. Read each question and write your response on another sheet of paper. See the "Answers to Section Practice Questions" section at the end of this book to assess your response. Validate or improve the answer you wrote. For a more robust selection of practice questions, access the **Online Test Bank** found on www.wileycma.com.

Question 1B5-CQ02

Topic: Annual Profit Plan and Supporting Schedules

Troughton Company manufactures radio-controlled toy dogs. Summary budget financial data for Troughton for the current year are shown next.

Sales (5,000 units at $150 each)	$750,000
Variable manufacturing cost	400,000
Fixed manufacturing cost	100,000
Variable selling and administrative cost	80,000
Fixed selling and administrative cost	150,000

Troughton uses an absorption costing system with overhead applied based on the number of units produced, with a denominator level of activity of 5,000 units. Underapplied or overapplied manufacturing overhead is written off to cost of goods sold in the year incurred.

The $20,000 budgeted operating income from producing and selling 5,000 toy dogs planned for this year is of concern to Trudy George, Troughton's president. She believes she could increase operating income to $50,000 (her bonus threshold) if Troughton produces more units than it sells, thus building up the finished goods inventory.

How much of an increase in the number of units in the finished goods inventory would be needed to generate the $50,000 budgeted operating income?

- ☐ **a.** 556 units
- ☐ **b.** 600 units
- ☐ **c.** 1,500 units
- ☐ **d.** 7,500 units

Question 1B5-CQ04

Topic: Annual Profit Plan and Supporting Schedules

Hannon Retailing Company prices its products by adding 30% to its cost. Hannon anticipates sales of $715,000 in July, $728,000 in August, and $624,000 in September. Hannon's policy is to have on hand enough inventory at the end of the month to cover 25% of the next month's sales. What will be the cost of the inventory that Hannon should budget for purchase in August?

- ☐ **a.** $509,600
- ☐ **b.** $540,000
- ☐ **c.** $560,000
- ☐ **d.** $680,000

Question 1B5-CQ06

Topic: Annual Profit Plan and Supporting Schedules

Tyler Company produces one product and budgeted 220,000 units for the month of August with these budgeted manufacturing costs:

	Total Costs	Cost per Unit
Variable costs	$1,408,000	$6.40
Batch setup cost	880,000	4.00
Fixed costs	1,210,000	5.50
Total	$3,498,000	$15.90

The variable cost per unit and the total fixed costs are unchanged within a production range of 200,000 to 300,000 units per month. The total for the batch setup cost in any month depends on the number of production batches that Tyler runs. A normal batch consists of 50,000 units unless production requires less volume. In the prior year, Tyler experienced a mixture of monthly batch sizes of 42,000 units, 45,000 units, and 50,000 units. Tyler consistently plans production each month in order to minimize the number of batches. For the month of September, Tyler plans to manufacture 260,000 units. What will be Tyler's total budgeted production costs for September?

- ☐ **a.** $3,754,000
- ☐ **b.** $3,930,000
- ☐ **c.** $3,974,000
- ☐ **d.** $4,134,000

Question 1B5-CQ08

Topic: Annual Profit Plan and Supporting Schedules

Savior Corporation assembles backup tape drive systems for home microcomputers. For the first quarter, the budget for sales is 67,500 units. Savior will finish the fourth quarter of last year with an inventory of 3,500 units, of which 200 are obsolete. The target ending inventory is 10 days of sales (based on 90 days in a quarter). What is the budgeted production for the first quarter?

- ☐ **a.** 75,000
- ☐ **b.** 71,700
- ☐ **c.** 71,500
- ☐ **d.** 64,350

Question 1B5-CQ09

Topic: Annual Profit Plan and Supporting Schedules

Streeter Company produces plastic microwave turntables. Sales for the next year are expected to be 65,000 units in the first quarter, 72,000 units in the second quarter, 84,000 units in the third quarter, and 66,000 units in the fourth quarter.

Streeter usually maintains a finished goods inventory at the end of each quarter equal to one half of the units expected to be sold in the next quarter. However, due to a work stoppage, the finished goods inventory at the end of the first quarter is 8,000 units less than it should be.

How many units should Streeter produce in the second quarter?

- ☐ **a.** 75,000 units
- ☐ **b.** 78,000 units
- ☐ **c.** 80,000 units
- ☐ **d.** 86,000 units

Question 1B5-CQ10

Topic: Annual Profit Plan and Supporting Schedules

Data regarding Rombus Company's budget are shown next.

Planned sales	4,000 units
Material cost	$2.50 per pound
Direct labor	3 hours per unit
Direct labor rate	$7 per hour
Finished goods beginning inventory	900 units
Finished goods ending inventory	600 units
Direct materials beginning inventory	4,300 units
Direct materials ending inventory	4,500 units
Materials used per unit	6 pounds

Rombus Company's production budget will show total units to be produced of:

- ☐ **a.** 3,700
- ☐ **b.** 4,000
- ☐ **c.** 4,300
- ☐ **d.** 4,600

Question 1B5-CQ11

Topic: Annual Profit Plan and Supporting Schedules

Krouse Company is in the process of developing its operating budget for the coming year. Given next are selected data regarding the company's two products, laminated putter heads and forged putter heads, sold through specialty golf shops.

	Putter Heads	
	Forged	**Laminated**
Raw materials		
Steel	2 pounds @ $5/pound	1 pound @ $5/pound
Copper	None	1 pound @ $15/pound
Direct labor	1/4 hour @ $20/hour	1 hour @ $22/hour
Expected sales	8,200 units	2,000 units
Selling price per unit	$30	$80
Ending inventory target	100 units	60 units
Beginning inventory	300 units	60 units
Beginning inventory (cost)	$5,250	$3,120

Manufacturing overhead is applied to units produced on the basis of direct labor hours. Variable manufacturing overhead is projected to be $25,000, and fixed manufacturing overhead is expected to be $15,000.

The estimated cost to produce one unit of the laminated putter head (PH) is:

- ☐ **a.** $42
- ☐ **b.** $46
- ☐ **c.** $52
- ☐ **d.** $62

Question 1B5-CQ12

Topic: Annual Profit Plan and Supporting Schedules

Tidwell Corporation sells a single product for $20 per unit. All sales are on account, with 60% collected in the month of sale and 40% collected in the following month. A partial schedule of cash collections for January through March of the coming year reveals these receipts for the period:

	Cash Receipts		
	January	**February**	**March**
December receivables	$32,000		
From January sales	$54,000	$36,000	
From February sales		$66,000	$44,000

Other information includes:
- Inventories are maintained at 30% of the following month's sales in units.
- Assume that March sales total $150,000.

The number of units to be purchased in February is

- ☐ **a.** 3,850 units
- ☐ **b.** 4,900 units
- ☐ **c.** 6,100 units
- ☐ **d.** 7,750 units

Question 1B5-CQ13

Topic: Annual Profit Plan and Supporting Schedules

Stevens Company manufactures electronic components used in automobile manufacturing. Each component uses two raw materials, Geo and Clio. Standard usage of the two materials required to produce one finished electronic component, as well as the current inventory, are shown next.

Material	Standard Usage per Unit	Price	Current Inventory
Geo	2.0 pounds	$15/pound	5,000 pounds
Clio	1.5 pounds	$10/pound	7,500 pounds

Stevens forecasts sales of 20,000 components for each of the next two production periods. Company policy dictates that 25% of the raw materials needed to produce the next period's projected sales be maintained in ending direct materials inventory.

Based on this information, what would the budgeted direct material purchases for the coming period be?

	Geo	Clio
☐ **a.**	$450,000	$450,000
☐ **b.**	$675,000	$300,000
☐ **c.**	$675,000	$400,000
☐ **d.**	$825,000	$450,000

Question 1B5-CQ14

Topic: Annual Profit Plan and Supporting Schedules

Petersons Planters Inc. budgeted these amounts for the coming year:

Beginning inventory, finished goods	$10,000
Cost of goods sold	400,000
Direct material used in production	100,000
Ending inventory, finished goods	25,000
Beginning and ending work-in-process inventory	Zero

Overhead is estimated to be two times the amount of direct labor dollars. The amount that should be budgeted for direct labor for the coming year is:

- ☐ **a.** $315,000
- ☐ **b.** $210,000
- ☐ **c.** $157,500
- ☐ **d.** $105,000

Question 1B5-CQ15

Topic: Annual Profit Plan and Supporting Schedules

Over the past several years, McFadden Industries has experienced the costs shown regarding the company's shipping expenses:

Fixed costs	$16,000
Average shipment	15 pounds
Cost per pound	$0.50

Shown next are McFadden's budget data for the coming year.

Number of units shipped	8,000
Number of sales orders	800
Number of shipments	800
Total sales	$1,200,000
Total pounds shipped	9,600

McFadden's expected shipping costs for the coming year are:

- ☐ **a.** $4,800
- ☐ **b.** $16,000
- ☐ **c.** $20,000
- ☐ **d.** $20,800

Question 1B5-CQ18

Topic: Annual Profit Plan and Supporting Schedules

In preparing the direct material purchases budget for next quarter, the plant controller has this information available:

Budgeted unit sales	2,000
Pounds of materials per unit	4
Cost of materials per pound	$3
Pounds of materials on hand	400
Finished units on hand	250
Target ending units inventory	325
Target ending inventory of pounds of materials	800

How many pounds of materials must be purchased?

☐ **a.** 2,475

☐ **b.** 7,900

☐ **c.** 8,700

☐ **d.** 9,300

Question 1B5-CQ22

Topic: Annual Profit Plan and Supporting Schedules

Given the next data for Scurry Company, what is the cost of goods sold?

Beginning inventory of finished goods	$100,000
Cost of goods manufactured	700,000
Ending inventory of finished goods	200,000
Beginning work-in-process inventory	300,000
Ending work-in-process inventory	50,000

☐ **a.** $500,000

☐ **b.** $600,000

☐ **c.** $800,000

☐ **d.** $950,000

Question 1B5-CQ23

Topic: Annual Profit Plan and Supporting Schedules

Tut Company's selling and administrative costs for the month of August, when it sold 20,000 units, were:

	Cost per Unit	Total Cost
Variable costs	$18.60	$372,000
Step costs	4.25	85,000
Fixed costs	8.80	176,000
Total selling and administrative costs	$31.65	$633,000

The variable costs represent sales commissions paid at the rate of 6.2% of sales.

The step costs depend on the number of salespersons employed by the company. In August there were 17 persons on the sales force. However, 2 members have taken early retirement effective August 31. It is anticipated that these positions will remain vacant for several months.

Total fixed costs are unchanged within a relevant range of 15,000 to 30,000 units per month.

Tut is planning a sales price cut of 10%, which it expects will increase sales volume to 24,000 units per month. If Tut implements the sales price reduction, the total budgeted selling and administrative costs for the month of September would be:

- ☐ **a.** $652,760
- ☐ **b.** $679,760
- ☐ **c.** $714,960
- ☐ **d.** $759,600

Question 1B5-CQ36

Topic: Annual Profit Plan and Supporting Schedules

Data regarding Johnsen Inc. 's forecasted dollar sales for the last seven months of the year and Johnsen's projected collection patterns are shown next.

Forecasted Sales

June	$700,000
July	600,000
August	650,000
September	800,000
October	850,000
November	900,000
December	840,000

Types of Sales

Cash sales	30%
Credit sales	70%

Collection pattern on credit sales (5% determined to be uncollectible)

During the month of sale	20%
During the first month following the sale	50%
During the second month following the sale	25%

Johnsen's budgeted cash receipts from sales and collections on account for September are:

- ☐ **a.** $635,000
- ☐ **b.** $684,500
- ☐ **c.** $807,000
- ☐ **d.** $827,000

Question 1B5-CQ37

Topic: Annual Profit Plan and Supporting Schedules

The Mountain Mule Glove Company is in its first year of business. Mountain Mule had a beginning cash balance of $85,000 for the quarter. The company has a $50,000 short-term line of credit. The budgeted information for the first quarter is shown next.

	January	February	March
Sales	$60,000	$40,000	$50,000
Purchases	$35,000	$40,000	$75,000
Operating costs	$25,000	$25,000	$25,000

All sales are made on credit and are collected in the second month following the sale. Purchases are paid in the month following the purchase while operating costs are paid in the month that they are incurred. How much will Mountain Mule need to borrow at the end of the quarter if the company needs to maintain a minimum cash balance of $5,000 as required by a loan covenant agreement?

- ☐ **a.** $0
- ☐ **b.** $5,000
- ☐ **c.** $10,000
- ☐ **d.** $45,000

Question 1B3-CQ05

Topic: Forecasting Techniques

Aerosub, Inc., has developed a new product for spacecraft that includes the manufacture of a complex part. The manufacturing of this part requires a high degree of technical skill. Management believes there is a good opportunity for its technical force to learn and improve as it becomes accustomed to the production process. The production of the first unit requires 10,000 direct labor hours. If an 80% learning curve is used, the cumulative direct labor hours required for producing a total of eight units would be:

- ☐ **a.** 29,520 hours
- ☐ **b.** 40,960 hours
- ☐ **c.** 64,000 hours
- ☐ **d.** 80,000 hours

Question 1B3-CQ18

Topic: Forecasting Techniques

Scarf Corporation's controller has decided to use a decision model to cope with uncertainty. With a particular proposal, currently under consideration, Scarf has two possible actions: invest or not invest in a joint venture with an international firm. The controller has determined this information:

Action 1: Invest in the Joint Venture

  Events and Probabilities:

   Probability of success = 60%

   Cost of investment = $9.5 million

   Cash flow if investment is successful = $15.0 million

   Cash flow if investment is unsuccessful = $2.0 million

   Additional costs to be paid = $0

   Costs incurred up to this point = $650,000

Action 2: Do Not Invest in the Joint Venture

  Events:

   Costs incurred up to this point = $650,000

   Additional costs to be paid = $100,000

Which one of the next alternatives correctly reflects the respective expected values of investing versus not investing?

- ☐ **a.** $300,000 and ($750,000)
- ☐ **b.** ($350,000) and ($100,000)
- ☐ **c.** $300,000 and ($100,000)
- ☐ **d.** ($350,000) and ($750,000)

To further assess your understanding of the concepts and calculations covered in Part 1, Section B: Planning, Budgeting, and Forecasting, practice with the **Online Test Bank** for this section.

REMINDER: See the "Answers to Section Practice Questions" section at the end of this book.

Performance Management (20%)

Once an organization has established a master budget, it is critical to compare actual financial performance against the master budget plan to determine variances. These variances help management determine their success in achieving goals. This financial measure comparison or feedback process allows an organization to confirm the overall vision of where it wants to be against actual results. Without this feedback, the budgeting process is not very useful.

This section reviews the process of how to:

- Break down variances from the master budget into subcategories so an organization can better assess the specific reasons for the variance.
- Utilize performance feedback from responsibility centers or strategic business units (SBUs) to help manage profitability.
- Understand the financial measures of profitability used in responsibility centers, products and product lines, customers, and in the organization as a whole.

After covering financial measures, this section also shows a balanced approach to performance measurement. The balanced scorecard measures both financial and nonfinancial aspects of an organization and is integrated with strategy so that reading the scorecard will tell anyone in the organization what the strategy is and how the organization plans to achieve it.

Cost and Variance Measures

ANALYZING ACTUAL PERFORMANCE AGAINST OPERATIONAL goals is a critical control that helps a company understand opportunities or threats to meeting their strategic goals. Differences between expected outcomes (budgets, forecasts, or set standards) and actual outcomes is referred to as a **variance**.

> **READ** the Learning Outcome Statements (LOS) for this topic as found in Appendix A and then study the concepts and calculations presented here to be sure you understand the content you could be tested on in the CMA exam.

Cost Flows

In Section B, detailed annual operating budgets were developed in order to prepare the pro forma income statement. These budgets included the production inputs that created the finished goods output. When sold, the cost is moved out of finished goods inventory into cost of goods sold on the income statement. The following diagram depicts this flow of costs:

Inputs:	**Output:**	**Income Statement:**
Direct Materials		
Direct Labor ⟶	Finished Goods ⟶	Cost of Goods Sold
Variable Overhead		
Fixed Overhead		

The operating plans and budgets are implemented at the start of the new year. Then the process of accounting for actual results begins. The actual results are compared to budget, which results in variances that enable management to evaluate performance.

The standard costs for each of the firm's products are established during the annual budget process. Then that standard is used as the basis for comparison. The standard costing system enables the management to measure performance on a current basis and to pinpoint the organizational function, department, or manager responsible for any variances from standard.

Bounce Sporting Goods is the example that will be used to demonstrate the development of a standard cost sheet for their tennis racquet. It will continue with a basic comparison of actual to budget and the development of initial variances. From there, the initial variances will be broken down into more meaningful variances that management can use to evaluate and investigate to determine why the variances occurred.

Developing a Standard Cost

During the annual planning process, the standard cost for the tennis racquet was created from the following information:

- Each unit is expected to use 1.0 pounds of titanium that will cost $60.00 per pound.
- The expected direct labor is 2.00 hours per unit, at a labor rate of $8.00 per hour.
- Variable overhead costs are expected to vary with the level of actual production, and machine hours are believed to drive the incurrence of the variable costs. It is expected to take 1.2 machine hours to form the racquet. The forming machine uses a great deal of power, and power is expected to cost $8.00 per machine hour. Material handlers are needed to bring materials to the forming machine and move the racquets to the next operation. Material handling is expected to cost $2.00 per machine hour, making the total variable overhead rate $10.00 per machine hour.
- The various fixed overhead accounts come to $300,000 per year. The cost driver is the anticipated production and sales volume for the year, which is 30,000 units. This makes the fixed overhead rate $10.00/unit ($300,000 divided by 30,000 units).

The standard cost sheet developed for the coming year is shown in Figure 1C-1.

Figure 1C-1 Product Cost Sheet for Tennis Racquet

Input	Units of Input/Unit of Prod.	Cost/Unit of Input	Cost/Unit of Prod.
Titanium	1.00 pound/unit	$60.00/pound	$60.00/unit
Direct Labor	2.00 DLH/unit	8.00/DLH	16.00
Variable Overhead	1.20 mach.-hr/unit	10.00/mach.-hr	12.00
Variable Cost			$88.00/unit
Fixed Overhead			10.00/unit
Total Cost			$98.00/unit

The tennis racquet's selling price has been set at $120 per racquet. Bounce's budgeted contribution margin per tennis racquet is $32.00/unit ($120 selling price minus $88 variable cost). In addition, the selling, general, and administrative expenses are considered to be fixed at $390,000 per year.

For management reporting purposes, Bounce uses variable costing, because management believes it will provide far more useful information for measuring performance and taking timely corrective action. However, variable costing (which will be described more fully in Section D, Topic 1: Measurement Concepts) cannot be used for reporting to outside stakeholders, because it does not comply with generally accepted accounting principles (GAAP). The financial statements that were reviewed in Section A used absorption costing which does comply with GAAP.

For reporting to the outside world, Bounce must use absorption costing. It is so named because fixed costs must be "absorbed" into inventory as goods are produced and then transferred to cost of goods sold (COGS) as goods are sold.

LOS
§1.C.1.c

Figure 1C-2 shows Bounce's actual results for the year, which are reported alongside the master budget for the year. It is important to recognize that all variances are shown as absolute dollar amounts, meaning parentheses are not used. Only the letters "U" for unfavorable and "F" for favorable are used. They relate to the effect the variance has on operating income. It is not uncommon in practice to see unfavorable variances expressed in parentheses and favorable variances without parentheses. They relate to the effect the variance has on operating income. Needless to say, Bounce's management was not pleased with the results. Operating income was off by more than $234,000.

Figure 1C-2 Bounce Income Statement for Year 1

	Actual	Master Budget	Total Variance	
Unit Sales	24,000	30,000	6,000	U*
Unit Selling Price/Unit	$125	$120	$5	F
Revenue	$3,000,000	$3,600,000	$600,000	U
Variable Cost of Goods Sold	2,280,240	2,640,000	359,760	F†
Contribution Margin	719,760	960,000	240,240	U
Fixed Manufacturing Cost	294,000	300,000	6,000	F
Fixed Selling, General, and Administrative Expense	390,000	390,000	–	
Operating Income	$35,760	$270,000	$234,240	U

*U = Unfavorable effect on operating income.
†F = Favorable effect on operating income.

LOS
§1.C.1.d

What can be learned from this initial comparison and variances? The number of units sold was significantly under plan. That could be expected to depress operating income, but by how much is not known. The revenue is significantly less than plan; however, whether this is simply the result of fewer units sold or deviations of actual selling price from planned selling price is not clear. The variable cost of goods sold was less than planned. But, it is not known if that suggests that cost control has been good or if that is simply the result of fewer units sold than planned. It is clear that fixed costs are under control. Selling, general, and administrative expenses (SG&A) are right on target, and fixed manufacturing costs are 2% under plan.

Flexible Budget

This analysis becomes more meaningful when the concept of flexible budgeting is introduced. **Flexible budgets** are a restatement of the original budgets that have been adjusted to the actual level of activity, in this case, it is the actual level of units sold. Flexible budgets help to measure actual performance in a manner that is fair to the organizational unit or individual whose performance is being measured and is consistent with standards of performance that have already been agreed to in the master budget. The standards for revenue, variable COGS, and contribution margin are $120/unit, $88/unit, and $32/unit as previously provided. Multiplying these unit values by the actual level of activity (24,000 units) produces the flexible budget values; the flexible budget values for fixed items are simply the values from the static budget, because fixed accounts are not affected by the level of activity.

This is illustrated in the income statement in Figure 1C-3, including the flexible budget. Variances between the actual results and flexible budget amounts have been calculated and displayed. These are called *flexible budget variances*. Note that the name is changed from "Master Budget" to "Static Budget."

Figure 1C-3 Bounce Income Statement for Year 1, Including Flexible Budget

	Actual (1)	Flexible Budget Variance (1-2)	Flexible Budget (2)	Sales Volume Variance (2-3)	Static Budget (3)
Unit Sales	24,000	–	24,000	6,000 U	30,000
Unit Selling Price/Unit	$125	$5 F	$120	$–	$120
Revenue	$3,000,000	$120,000 F	$2,880,000	$720,000 U	$3,600,000
Variable Cost of Goods Sold	2,280,240	168,240 U	2,112,000	528,000 F	2,640,000
Contribution Margin	719,760	48,240 U	768,000	192,000 U	960,000
Fixed Manufacturing Cost	294,000	6,000 F	300,000	–	300,000
Fixed Selling, General, and Administrative Expense	390,000	–	390,000	–	390,000
Operating Income	$35,760	$42,240 U	$78,000	$192,000 U	$270,000

Now we have an income statement that provides more detailed information about Bounce's performance for the year. We knew from Figure 1C-2 that Bounce fell short of its operating profit objective by about $234,240, or about 87%. Now we know that $192,000 was due to the sales volume variance, selling fewer units than planned. In addition, the flexible budget variances tell us that Bounce generated higher revenues due to an increase in the selling price that created a favorable $120,000 flexible budget variance. This is also called the sales price variance. However, this was more than offset by the unfavorable variance of $168,240 in the variable cost of goods sold line. This means that they were inefficient in their operations. Combined, there was an unfavorable variance of $42,240 at the operating income line. The combination of these two results—higher prices and fewer units sold—is typically considered the responsibility of the selling and marketing organizations. The two remaining causes of operating income erosion are the $168,240 of net unfavorable variable manufacturing variances and $6,000 net favorable fixed manufacturing overhead spending variances.

Now we need to consider the causes of the $168,240 variances. These variances must be attributable to some combination of direct material, direct labor, and variable overhead problems.

The next level of detail of the variances analyzes them into each of these three categories and breaks them down into price and efficiency components. Sometimes one part of the organization is responsible for the price component and another part is responsible for the efficiency component. The purchasing department is responsible for the direct material price variance and the forming (production) department is responsible for the direct material efficiency variance.

Assuming that 24,000 units were produced as well as sold, there should be no change in the level of finished goods inventory. This will make the detailed variance analysis easier to understand.

In a standard cost system, resources (most frequently cash) are expended when inventory is acquired or produced. However, the inventory is valued at standard cost. The difference between these two dollar amounts is what creates the variances.

Direct Labor Variances

Let us consider direct labor first, because it is the easiest to understand. When direct labor cost is incurred, the value of the resources expended becomes part of the cost of inventory and net favorable/unfavorable variances. The value of the resource expended is simply actual labor hours times actual average labor rate. The value of the inventory created is the number of units produced times the standard direct labor cost per unit. Standard direct labor cost per unit is taken from the cost sheet and is simply the standard direct labor hours per unit times the standard direct labor rate per hour.

Let us introduce a set of symbols to make the math statements as concise as possible:

A = actual

S = standard

H = hours

R = rate (usually dollars per hour)

Q = actual quantity produced

U = unit

It is important to understand that the term SH represents the number of hours that should have been used to produce the actual number of units produced. This is calculated by multiplying the actual number of units by the standard hours per unit.

There are two formulas used to determine the direct labor variances: (1) direct labor rate variance and (2) direct labor efficiency variance.

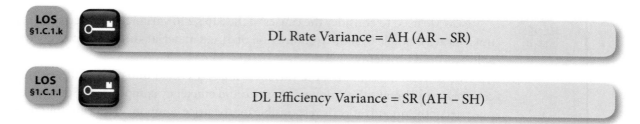

LOS §1.C.1.k

$$\text{DL Rate Variance} = AH\ (AR - SR)$$

LOS §1.C.1.l

$$\text{DL Efficiency Variance} = SR\ (AH - SH)$$

In the way these two equations are expressed, a positive value represents an unfavorable variance and a negative value represents a favorable variance.

You can also use your intuition to determine if the variance is favorable or unfavorable. If the actual rate is greater than the standard rate, the variance is unfavorable. The same is true for the efficiency variance; if the actual hours are greater than the standard hours, the variance is unfavorable. In both formulas, if the opposite is true then the variance will be favorable.

Now let us apply this to the situation at hand. Labor reporting records show that 52,800 direct labor hours, costing $475,200, were used to produce the 24,000 units. From this it can be determined that the actual average labor rate was $9.00 per hour. Caution: This actual average rate should have as many significant positions as there are in the actual dollar amount, which is 6. To round this rate prematurely can introduce rounding errors into the calculations. The value of the SH term is simply 24,000 units produced times 2.00 hours per unit, or 48,000 hours. Therefore,

DL Rate Variance = 52,800 hours ($9.00/hour – $8.00/hour) = $52,800 U

DL Efficiency Variance = $8.00/hour (52,800 hours – 48,000 hours) = $38,400 U

for total direct labor variance of $91,200 unfavorable.

Caution: Always use the appropriate units of measure to each numeric value and perform the appropriate math operation—multiply, divide, add, or subtract—to the units of measure. If you wind up with units of measure that are not what you expected, this is a signal that you have done something wrong and need to correct your work.

Now we can verify that we have done our work correctly. The resources expended for direct labor were $475,200, and the value that can be added to inventory for direct labor at standard is $384,000 (24,000 units times $16.00 per unit). The difference between these two amounts is exactly $91,200, and that is the sum of the two unfavorable direct labor variances.

Direct Materials Variances

LOS §1.C.1.k

This section considers **direct materials** (DM). There is an important difference between direct material and direct labor: Direct material costs can be stored in raw material inventory whereas labor costs cannot. They become part of the cost of work-in-process inventory. However, when direct material is acquired, it has value as an inventory of direct materials (raw materials and components). It can be used at a later time, and it should keep its value between the time of acquisition and the time of usage.

We skip the derivation of the formulas for the direct material variances because the logic is similar to that just demonstrated for direct labor, and go directly to the symbols that will be used and the definitions of the variances.

Many of the same symbols will be used:

A = actual

S = standard

Q_p = quantity of direct material purchased

Q_U = quantity of direct material used

P = price (usually dollars per some physical unit of measure)

Q = actual quantity produced

The direct material price variance is

$$\text{DM Price Variance} = Q_p \, (AP - SP)$$

The direct material efficiency variance, sometimes referred to as the usage, yield, or quantity variance, is

$$\text{DM Usage Variance} = SP \, (AQ_U - SQ)$$

Prices and quantities of direct material must be expressed in identical units of measure; for example, if the price is expressed in dollars per pound, then the quantities must be expressed in pounds. Again, the meaning of the term *standard quantity* is the amount of the direct material that should have been used to produce the actual quantity of product produced. The implication of the last two equations is that during any period of time, there could be an increase of the item in inventory (if quantity purchased exceeds the quantity used) or there could be a decrease of the item in inventory (if quantity used exceeds the quantity purchased).

Now we return to the Bounce illustration. Bounce acquired 25,000 pounds of titanium at a total cost of $1,839,840. It used 19,200 pounds in the production of the 24,000 units.

The variances are calculated next.

$$\text{DM Price Variance} = 25{,}000 \text{ Pounds } (\$73.5936/\text{Pound} - \$60.00/\text{Pound}) = \$339{,}840U$$

$$\text{DM Usage Variance} = \$60.00/\text{Pound } (19{,}200 \text{ Pounds} - 24{,}000 \text{ Pounds}) = \$288{,}000F$$

Once again, a relatively simple means of double checking the answers is available. The dollars expended for direct materials should be equal to the increase in direct materials inventory plus the value of the direct materials in the product produced plus the net unfavorable direct materials variances. This proves to be the case:

$$\$1,839,840 = (5,800 \text{ Pounds} \times \$60.00/\text{Pound}) + (24,000 \text{ Units} \times \$60.00/\text{Unit}) +$$
$$(\$339,840 - \$288,000) = \$348,000 + \$1,440,000 + \$51,840 = \$1,839,840$$

Variable Overhead Variances

Variable overhead is manufacturing overhead that varies as the level of activity varies. It has been determined that the level of activity that drives the spending for power and material handling is actual machine hours. Note that the actual machine hours are the hours that the forming machines in the forming department are actually in use forming products. The equations in this instance look very similar to those for direct labor, which were also based on hours and costs per hour. In the next formulas, H stands for hours or whatever is the measure of the cost driver of variable overhead. If hours are not the cost driver, then R must be expressed in dollars per appropriate unit of measure of the cost driver.

LOS §1.C.1.m

VOH Spending Variance = AH (AR − SR)

VOH Efficiency Variance = SR (AH − SH)

If a company has only a single product, variable overhead could be thought of as being driven by units produced. However, single-product companies exist primarily in textbook examples and CMA exam problems.

LOS §1.C.1.r

Here is the information that is relevant to Bounce's variable overhead. Actual machine hours for the period were 28,000. The total dollars spent for variable overhead were $313,200, consisting of $56,000 for material handling labor and $257,200 for power. Therefore, the actual variable overhead rate was $11.1857 per actual machine hour ($313,200/28,000 machine hours). Substituting values into the variable overhead spending variance formula:

VOH Spending Variance = 28,000 ($11.1857 − $10.00) = $33,200 U

The standard machine hours for the period were 24,000 units times 1.2 machine hours per unit, or 28,800 machine hours. The variable overhead efficiency variance is:

VOH Efficiency Variance = $10.00 (28,000 − 28,800) = $8,000 F

This variable efficiency variance is the responsibility of the forming department. The VOH spending variance can occur in any department that incurs variable overhead.

With the information provided, it can be determined that the power department incurred the entire amount of the unfavorable variable overhead spending variance in this illustration.

Fixed Overhead Variances

LOS
§1.C.1.m

Finally, there are two variances associated with fixed overhead—the fixed overhead spending variance and the production volume variance. The fixed overhead spending variance is the easiest of all the variances both to compute and to understand. Since fixed costs are not expected to vary with changes in the level of activity within the relevant range, a simple comparison of actual spending to the fixed overhead budget established during the planning process provides the amount of the fixed overhead spending variance.

Many people think production volume variance is the most difficult variance to compute and understand. The difficulty occurs because, in an absorption costing system, fixed overhead must be expressed on the basis of dollars per unit of activity, such as per unit or per standard hour, and the amount must be "absorbed" into inventory as product is produced. Yet it is known that fixed cost in total is not expected to vary as a result of changes in activity.

It is beneficial to look at the illustration in Figure 1C-4. The length of the line segments corresponds to the value of various terms and variances. At annual planning time, the firm determines the level of budgeted fixed expenses to be $300,000, which corresponds to line segments AB as well as E in the figure. The firm also determines the denominator level of activity, which corresponds to line segment 0A, to be 30,000 units. Finally, the firm divides the budgeted fixed expenses by the denominator level of activity, resulting in a rate of $10 per unit. If Bounce was a multiproduct company, the fixed overhead rate might

Figure 1C-4 Fixed Overhead Budgeted, Incurred, and Applied and Related Variances

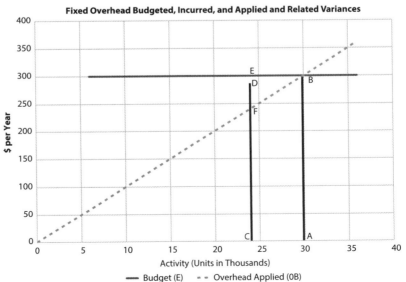

be expressed in dollars per direct labor hour, which would be $5.00/DLH. The result is the fixed overhead rate expressed in dollars of activity, such as dollars per unit or dollars per standard hour. This overhead rate is used to determine the fixed overhead component of product unit cost, as shown in cost sheets. And it is used during the year to absorb fixed overhead into inventory as production occurs. The applied overhead rate in the figure corresponds to the slope of the segment 0B and beyond.

During the year, fixed overhead will be incurred; this corresponds to segment CD, which must be plotted at the actual level of activity of $294,000. Fixed overhead is absorbed into inventory, which corresponds to segment CF. This amount is $240,000, calculated as 24,000 units times $10.

The following formula represents the spending variance.

> Fixed Overhead Spending Variance = Actual Fixed Overhead – Budgeted Fixed Overhead

The fixed overhead spending variance for Bounce is represented as DE and is calculated as: $294,000 minus $300,000 resulting in a $6,000 favorable variance. This amount can be measured for each department account that is budgeted on a fixed basis and summed across all department account combinations. This variance must be expensed in both variable costing and absorption costing.

The next formula is used to calculate the production volume variance.

> Production Volume Variance = Budgeted Fixed Overhead – Absorbed Fixed Overhead

The production volume variance for Bounce is represented as segment EF and is calculated as: $300,000 minus $240,000 resulting in a $60,000 unfavorable variance.

It is important to note that this variance appears only in absorption costing. Therefore, it is expensed in an absorption costing income statement. This variance is not a measure of any individual's or department's performance. It is simply the result of the actual level of activity varying from the level of activity used to establish the fixed overhead rate. If the actual level of activity is lower than the denominator level of activity, the production volume variance will be unfavorable. The unfavorable variance can be avoided by producing more units, but they are likely to sit in inventory and go unsold, if there isn't demand for them. They may even become obsolete and lose their value entirely. Thus, despite producing an unfavorable variance, the decision to produce less than planned may be the right business decision.

Management by Exception

LOS
§1.C.1.i

The combination of standard costing and flexible budgeting makes it possible to use the **management-by-exception** principle. Managers should analyze those variances that are likely to be the most fruitful in helping to produce improved results. Determining what should be investigated comes with experience. However, managers quickly learn to focus attention on the largest variances, both unfavorable and favorable, those that occur frequently, and what might be called "controllability." Labor efficiency can have significant variations from period to period, but consistency is expected in material purchase prices from period to period. The thresholds for which variances to investigate often are combinations of absolute amounts and a percentage of variance from budget. The acceptable percentage variation for labor efficiency might be set at a higher value than the acceptable percentage variation for material price. Management by exception could be described as employing the 80–20 rule (Pareto's principle). The Italian mathematician Vilfredo Pareto discovered that a small number of large items almost always account for a high percentage of total value in almost any mathematical distribution. For example, a large percentage of total invoice value is often accounted by a small percentage of the total of all invoices. This principle seems true of the distribution of variances as well.

LOS
§1.C.1.s

Different functional areas within the company have responsibility for the day-to-day operations, and therefore the variances from actual to budget. The following is a general guide to each variance and the functional area responsible for the variance. The manager of the functional area should be able to explain why the variance(s) occurred.

Variance	Functional Area/Department	Possible Explanation
Sales Price	Selling or Marketing	*Change in customer demand *Increase in production costs
Direct Labor Rate	Human Resources & Production	*Hired more skilled workers *Hired less skilled workers
Direct Labor Efficiency/ Usage	Production	*New inexperienced workers *Highly skilled workers *Machine breakdown
Direct Material Price	Purchasing	*Vendor increased or decreased their price *Purchased lower- or higher-quality materials
Direct Material Usage	Production	*Purchased lower- or higher-quality materials *New inexperienced workers
Variable Overhead Spending	Production	*Increased equipment repairs due to machine breakdowns *Decreased utility costs
Variable Overhead Efficiency	Production	*Used more or less of the cost driver than budgeted
Fixed Overhead Spending	Production	*Increased or decreased costs
Production Volume	Production	*Produced more or less units than budgeted

The difference between absorption costing and variable costing is covered in Section D, Topic 1: Measurement Concepts. We can illustrate the two income statements in Figure 1C-5 to bring this discussion to a logical conclusion.

Figure 1C-5 Bounce Income Statements for Year 1—Absorption and Variable Costing

Bounce Income Statement for Year 1 Absorption Costing			Bounce Income Statement for Year 1 Variable Costing		
Revenue	$3,000,000		Revenue	$3,000,000	
Standard Cost of Goods Sold	2,352,000		Standard Variable Cost of Goods Sold	$2,112,000	
Direct Labor Rate Variance	52,800	U	Direct Labor Rate Variance	52,800	U
Direct Labor Efficiency Variance	38,400	U	Direct Labor Efficiency Variance	38,400	U
Direct Materials Price Variance	339,840	U	Direct Materials Price Variance	339,840	U
Direct Materials Efficiency Variance	288,000	F	Direct Materials Efficiency Variance	288,000	F
Variable Overhead Spending Variance	33,200	U	Variable Overhead Spending Variance	33,200	U
Variable Overhead Efficiency Variance	8,000	F	Variable Overhead Efficiency Variance	8,000	F
Fixed Overhead Spending Variance	6,000	F			
Production Volume Variance	60,000	U			
Actual Cost of Goods Sold	$2,574,240		Actual Variable Cost of Goods Sold	$2,280,240	
Gross Profit	$425,760		Contribution Margin	$719,760	
			Actual Fixed Overhead Expense	294,000	
Selling, General, and Administrative Expenses	390,000		Selling, General, and Administrative Expenses	390,000	
Operating Profit (Absorption)	$35,760		Operating Profit (Variance)	$35,760	

Multiple Products and the Sales Mix Variance

When there are multiple products (as is the case in most companies) and when there is a meaningful unit of measurement in which all products can be expressed, the difference between actual revenue and the standard variable cost of the units actually sold is a measure of contribution margin that has not been affected by any manufacturing variances. Any erosion of this contribution margin from the level that was planned can be analyzed into the portions attributable to the overall quantity sold, changing product mix, and any pricing variations.

Let us assume a company sells both cans of tennis balls and cans of racquet balls. A can of tennis balls costs $4 per can and is expected to sell for $9 per can. A can of racquet balls costs $3 per can and is expected to sell for $6 per can. Overall, the company expects to sell 10,000 cans of balls per year, and the expected mix is 60% tennis balls and 40% racquet balls. Therefore, the planned contribution margin for the year is shown in Figure 1C-6. The expected average contribution margin per unit is $4.20.

Now assume that 9,600 cans were sold rather than 10,000. Assume that the mix of actual sales was 50% of each. The results for the year, assuming merchandise sold at regular prices, are shown in the Actual columns of Figure 1C-6. The actual average contribution margin per unit was $4.00.

Figure 1C-6 Sales Mix—Plan and Actual

	Plan			Actual			
	Tennis Balls	Racquet Balls	Total	Tennis Balls	Racquet Balls	Total	Variance
Units	6,000	4,000	10,000	4,800	4,800	9,600	400U
Revenue	$54,000	$24,000	$78,000	$43,200	$28,800	$72,000	$6,000U
Variable Cost	24,000	12,000	36,000	19,200	14,400	33,600	2,400F
Total Contribution Margin	$30,000	$12,000	$42,000	$24,000	$14,400	$38,400	$3,600U
CM/Unit	$5.00	$3.00	$4.20	$5.00	$3.00	$4.00	

The company expected to earn a contribution margin of $4.20 per each can sold. As a result of selling only 9,600 cans instead of the expected 10,000, the company lost $1,680 of contribution margin:

$$\text{Sales Volume Variance} = (\text{Actual Quantity} - \text{Planned Quantity}) \times \text{Planned CM/Unit}$$
$$= (9{,}600 \text{ Units} - 10{,}000 \text{ Units}) \times \$4.20/\text{Unit} = \$1{,}680 \text{ U}$$

LOS
§1.C.1.n

$$\text{Sales Mix Variance} = \text{Actual Quantity} \times (\text{Actual Standard CM/Unit} - \text{Planned Standard CM/Unit})$$
$$= 9{,}600 \text{ Units} \times (\$4.00/\text{Unit} - \$4.20/\text{Unit}) = \$1{,}920 \text{ U}$$

Thus, the company had planned to earn $42,000 CM and ended up earning only $38,400. The reasons for the shortfall in contribution can be summarized as follows:

Sales volume variance	$1,680 U
Sales mix variance	1,920 U
Total CM variance	$3,600 U

Management would next calculate and analyze the sales volume variance and the sales mix variance at the product level to determine which product or products was the cause of the total variance. These are calculated at the contribution margin level. The formula to calculate the sales volume variance by product is:

$$\text{Sales Volume Variance} = (\text{Total Planned Quantity} - \text{Total Actual Quantity}) \times \text{Planned Sales Mix \%} \times \text{Planned Standard CM/Unit}$$

First calculate the sales volume variance for Tennis Balls:

$$(10{,}000 - 9{,}600) \times 60\% \times \$5.00 = \$1{,}200 \text{ U}$$

Next calculate the sales volume variance for Racquet Balls:

$$(10{,}000 - 9{,}600) \times 40\% \times \$3.00 = \$480 \text{ U}$$

Now add the two sales volume variances together to get the total sales volume variance of $1,680 U that was calculated earlier. Now it is known that both products, albeit more from the Tennis Balls, caused the total unfavorable sales volume variance.

The following formula is used to calculate the sales mix variance by product:

Sales Mix Variance = (Actual Sales Mix % − Planned Sales Mix %) × Total Actual Quantity × (Individual Planned Standard CM/Unit − Total Planned Standard CM/Unit)

First calculate the sales mix variance for Tennis Balls:

$$(50\% - 60\%) \times 9,600 \times (\$5.00 - \$4.20) = (10\%) \times 9,600 \times \$0.80 = \$768 \text{ U}$$

Next calculate the sales mix variance for Racquet Balls:

$$(50\% - 40\%) \times 9,600 \times (\$3.00 - \$4.20) = 10\% \times 9,600 \times \$(1.20) = \$1,152 \text{ U}$$

Now add the two sales mix variances together to get the total sales mix variance of $1,920 U. This is the same variance as calculated before. In this analysis, the Racquet Balls was the largest cause for the total unfavorable sales mix variance.

Mix Variance When Raw Materials Are Substitutable

LOS §1.C.1.o

A somewhat similar situation can occur when two or more raw materials are blended together in proportions that can vary. They could, of course, simply be treated as two different raw materials, and direct material efficiency variances could be calculated for each.

However, a more elaborate method may be employed to calculate variances—in this case, a mix variance and a yield variance, which would be the equivalent of several usage variances.

Assume that tennis balls are made from a blend of synthetic and natural rubbers. Synthetic rubber is expected to cost $2.00 per pound, and natural rubber is expected to cost $3.00 per pound. A tennis ball would normally use 1.6 pounds of the blend, and the normal blend would consist of 62.5% of synthetic rubber and 37.5% of natural rubber. Therefore, the cost of the rubber in a tennis ball would be expected to be $3.80 per unit (1.00 pound of synthetic at $2.00/pound and 0.6 pounds of natural at $3.00/pound), and the weighted average cost of the blend of rubbers would be $2.375/pound (= $3.80/1.6 pounds).

Assume that 1,000 tennis balls are produced from a blend of 988 pounds of synthetic and 532 pounds of natural rubber. This makes the total actual pounds used $1,520 = 988 + 532. The yield variance would be calculated in the same manner as the normal material efficiency variance.

LOS §1.C.1.p

$$\text{DM Yield Variance} = SP(AQ_U - SQ) = \$2.375/\text{Pound}(1,520 \text{ Pounds} - 1,600 \text{ Pounds}) = \$190 \text{ F}$$

The actual mix is 65% synthetic and 35% natural rubber. The average cost per pound of that blend would be

$$.65 \times \$2.00/\text{Pound} + .35 \times \$3.00/\text{Pound} = \$2.35/\text{Pound}$$

The calculation of the mix variance would be

$$\text{DM mix variance} = AQ_U(AP - SP),$$

similar to a price variance. Substituting, the mix variance will be

$$1{,}520 \text{ pounds} \times (\$2.35/\text{Pound} - \$2.375/\text{Pound}) = \$38F$$

Variance Analysis in Nonmanufacturing Organizations

LOS
§1.C.1.q

It is no secret that variance analysis grew up in the manufacturing industries. But variance analysis is effective in service and merchandising organizations, as well. Service organizations have little or no direct materials, so the direct materials price and efficiency variances are likely to be of lesser value. That means that direct labor and overhead are a higher percentage of total cost. Consequently, direct labor rate and efficiency variances, variable overhead spending and efficiency variances, and fixed overhead spending variances are important.

Some organizations in the service industry have applied activity-based costing and activity-based management techniques. Frequently, one result has been that a greater percentage of total cost to be managed is variable costs rather than fixed costs.

The role of production volume variance in service industries has been problematic. Some industries, such as transportation and hospitality, have developed effective measures of capacity (e.g., available seat miles), measures of actual activity (e.g., revenue passenger miles), and measures of utilization of capacity (e.g., load factors). These adaptations make variations on the production volume variance concept useful.

Importance of Industry Knowledge

Tailoring variances to meet the needs of a specific industry can help management accountants create variances that are so actionable that significant money is saved with only modest effort.

Here are two examples:

In some states, the dairy industry is allowed to standardize in order to produce whole milk. In standardizing, raw milk of varying butterfat content is separated into skim milk and cream. It is reblended into milk with a target butterfat content of, say, 3.25%. One of the variances designed for a dairy company measured the cost of substituting butterfat pounds (the more expensive component of raw milk) for skim pounds (the less expensive component). At the end of the first month using the new reporting system, the company president saw that this variance was going to run more than $100,000 unfavorable for a year at the rate it was going. He pointed this out to the workers in the dairy and let them know that he would be watching this closely in the future. The workers did not need to be told more than once. In the future, the "whole milk" product and all other products (2%, 1%, etc.) were standardized much closer to standards, and the potential $100,000 variance was avoided.

In the apparel industry, fabric is spread out on long cutting tables until the spreader comes to the end of what should be one ply of fabric in a stack that may be more than 100 plies high. When spreading is complete, a marker (a pattern) is placed on top of the stack, and a long vertical knife is used to cut out the pieces that will be sewn together to make the garment. Fabric can be wasted in several ways:

- Fabric at the end of each bolt will be shorter than the marker; this is called an unusable end.
- There will be defects in the fabric as it comes from the mill. When a defect is encountered, it is cut out and a portion of that ply will have to be overlapped so there is at least one good piece for each part in the marker. This is called mill damage. If the damage exceeds some agreed-on maximum level, the apparel company may charge back the mill for the excessive damages.
- Finally, the material that extends beyond the ends of the marker will be wasted. This is called spreading waste. By reporting spreading waste as a separate variance, the system enabled management to track this waste and ultimately reduce it by about 1% of all fabric usage. Since fabric represents about 40% of the selling price of the garment, the pretax reduction in cost was about 0.4% of revenue. Since pretax operating profit was small (about 4% of sales), the net effect was a 10% improvement in profit.

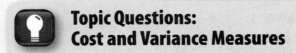

Topic Questions:
Cost and Variance Measures

Directions: Answer each question in the space provided. Correct answers and explanations appear after the topic questions.

1. A company's master budget projected the following information.

Sales (25,000 units)	$250,000
Manufacturing costs (1/3 fixed)	120,000
Other operating costs (all fixed)	100,000

    If the company actually sold 27,500 units, the operating income when using a flexible budget would be:

    ☐ **a.** $33,000.

    ☐ **b.** $43,000.

    ☐ **c.** $47,000.

    ☐ **d.** $51,000.

2. A company budgets to sell 4,000 units of its product. Actual sales are 4,200 units. The product has a standard price of $43 per direct labor hour. One direct labor hour is needed to produce one unit of product. When analyzing its direct labor flexible-budget variance for the period, the company determined that its direct labor efficiency variance was an unfavorable variance of $8,600. Which one of the following is closest to the actual price for direct labor if the total direct labor flexible-budget variance was an unfavorable variance of $4,400?

    ☐ **a.** $39 per unit

    ☐ **b.** $40 per unit

    ☐ **c.** $41 per unit

    ☐ **d.** $42 per unit

3. A paint manufacturing plant has two white pigments that are substitutable for the same product. Natural pigment costs $3/gallon, and artificial pigment costs $1/gallon. Standards call for 60% natural and 40% synthetic, but the actual ratio used was 50% of each. The actual total quantity of both ingredients was 30,000 gallons while the budgeted total quantity was 32,000 gallons. What is the mix variance for these ingredients?

    ☐ **a.** $6,000 favorable

    ☐ **b.** $17,400 favorable

    ☐ **c.** $17,400 unfavorable

    ☐ **d.** $6,000 unfavorable

Topic Question Answers:
Cost and Variance Measures

1. A company's master budget projected the following information.

Sales (25,000 units)	$250,000
Manufacturing costs (1/3 fixed)	120,000
Other operating costs (all fixed)	100,000

   If the company actually sold 27,500 units, the operating income when using a flexible budget would be:

   - ☐ **a.** $33,000.
   - ☐ **b.** $43,000.
   - ☑ **c.** $47,000.
   - ☐ **d.** $51,000.

The operating income is calculated as sales minus all operating costs before interest and taxes. When using a flexible budget, the sales price per unit and variable cost per unit must first be calculated in order to calculate the operating income. The sales price is $10 per unit ($250,000 ÷ 25,000 units) and the variable manufacturing costs per unit equal $3.20 because only 2/3 of the costs are variable (($120,000 × (2 ÷ 3)) ÷ 25,000 units). The total sales if the company actually sold 27,500 units would be $275,000 (27,500 units × $10), the total variable costs would be $88,000 (27,500 units × $3.20), the total fixed manufacturing costs would be $40,000 ($120,000 × (1 ÷ 3)) and the other operating costs would equal $100,000 because they are all fixed; therefore, the operating income would be $47,000 ($275,000 − ($88,000 + $40,000 + $100,000)).

2. A company budgets to sell 4,000 units of its product. Actual sales are 4,200 units. The product has a standard price of $43 per direct labor hour. One direct labor hour is needed to produce one unit of product. When analyzing its direct labor flexible-budget variance for the period, the company determined that its direct labor efficiency variance was an unfavorable variance of $8,600. Which one of the following is closest to the actual price for direct labor if the total direct labor flexible-budget variance was an unfavorable variance of $4,400?

   - ☐ **a.** $39 per unit
   - ☐ **b.** $40 per unit
   - ☐ **c.** $41 per unit
   - ☑ **d.** $42 per unit

Flexible-budget variances are composed of a price variance and an efficiency variance. Because the direct labor efficiency variance is $8,600 unfavorable (U) and the direct labor flexible-budget variance is $4,400 U, the direct labor price variance must be $4,200 favorable (F). This result is based on $8,600 U + Price variance = $4,400 U (computationally, this can be represented as $-8,600 + X = -4,400$; $X = 4,200$). Remember that Actual quantity × (Actual price – Standard price) = Price variance. Hence, we can compute the actual labor price as follows: 4,200 units × ($43 – X) = $4,200 F; X = $42.

3. A paint manufacturing plant has two white pigments that are substitutable for the same product. Natural pigment costs $3/gallon, and artificial pigment costs $1/gallon. Standards call for 60% natural and 40% synthetic, but the actual ratio used was 50% of each. The actual total quantity of both ingredients was 30,000 gallons while the budgeted total quantity was 32,000 gallons. What is the mix variance for these ingredients?

  ☑ **a.** $6,000 favorable

  ☐ **b.** $17,400 favorable

  ☐ **c.** $17,400 unfavorable

  ☐ **d.** $6,000 unfavorable

The mix variance is calculated as the difference between the standard costs at the actual mix ($\Sigma AQ \times A\%_i \times SP$) and standard costs at the standard mix ($\Sigma AQ \times S\%_i \times SP$). The standard cost at the actual mix and the standard cost at the standard mix are calculated as follows:

Standard cost at actual mix:
Natural pigment: $45,000 (30,000 × 50% × $3)
Artificial pigment: $15,000 (30,000 × 50% × $1)
Total: $60,000 ($45,000 + $15,000)

Standard cost at standard mix:
Natural pigment: $54,000 (30,000 × 60% × $3)
Artificial pigment: $12,000 (30,000 × 40% × $1)
Total: $66,000 ($54,000 + $12,000)

Because the standard cost is $6,000 ($66,000 – $60,000) less at the actual mix than at the standard mix, there is a $6,000 favorable mix variance for these ingredients.

Responsibility Centers and Reporting Segments

A CENTRALIZED ORGANIZATION ALLOWS MANAGERS very little free-dom to make decisions. In contrast, a decentralized organization spreads decision making to managers at different responsibility center levels. A responsibility center, also called a strategic business unit (SBU), is any portion of a business that grants the center's manager responsibility over costs, profits, revenues, or investments.

This topic covers different types of responsibility centers, including cost centers, profit centers, and investment centers. Reporting segments and contribution reporting are also discussed in this topic.

 READ the Learning Outcome Statements (LOS) for this topic as found in Appendix A and then study the concepts and calculations presented here to be sure you understand the content you could be tested on in the CMA exam.

Types of Responsibility Centers

Responsibility accounting is a method of defining segments or subunits in an organization as types of responsibility centers based on their level of autonomy and the responsibilities of their managers, and then basing performance evaluations on these factors. Responsibility centers are classified by their primary effect on the company as a whole. Revenue or profit centers sell their product or service to outside customers, generating revenues. Cost centers provide service to other parts of the organization and are not responsible for generating revenue through sales to outside customers. However, a cost center such as a service department may generate some revenues, but the department usually has a net cost. Investment centers not only generate revenues but also have authority on making investments.

Revenue Centers

Revenue centers are responsible for sales but not for the manufacturing costs of the sales. A revenue center obtains products from either a cost center or a profit center (discussed below). Revenue centers are evaluated on their ability to provide a contribution: sales less the direct revenue center costs. They are not responsible for the costs of the items obtained from cost or profit centers. A captive marketing division of a corporation would be an example of a revenue center. In the real world, most centers that would be responsible for revenues are likely to also be responsible for costs. Therefore, expect to see many more profit centers than revenue centers.

Cost Centers

A manager for a **cost center** is responsible for controlling costs in a department that generates little or no revenue. Therefore, the manager is not responsible for revenue or investments but is rewarded whenever he or she can minimize costs while maintaining an expected level of quality. Finance, administration, human resources, accounting, customer service, and help desks are all examples of cost centers. If the cafeteria is not expected to make a profit, it is also a cost center. Even plants and manufacturing facilities sometimes are considered cost centers, assuming that the profit center would then be the sales department or a different production department.

Managers of cost centers usually are responsible for direct material and labor efficiency variances as well as the variable overhead variance. Controlling unfavorable variances and analyzing favorable variances are often part of the manager's responsibility.

Profit Centers

Profit centers are responsible for both costs and revenues. Since profit is a function of both revenue and costs, a manager for a profit center is responsible for generating profits, managing revenue, and controlling costs. Managers of these departments usually do not have control over investments. Profit centers are often separate reporting segments. A grocery store that is part of a chain of stores could be a profit center and a separate reporting segment. Managers of profit centers would be evaluated based on actual profits versus expected profits.

Investment Centers

Managers for **investment centers** are responsible for investments, costs, and revenues in their department. Investment centers can be centered primarily on internal or external investments. Internal investment managers are responsible for reviewing and approving capital budgeting and other investments, such as in research and development. External investment managers are responsible for reviewing and approving temporary and long-term investments for capital maintenance, return on investment, and strategic investments. Managers in such centers would be evaluated not only by the center's profit but by relating the profit to its invested capital. Strategic investments would be evaluated for their fit with company strategy, while other investments would be judged on their return on investment and preservation of capital.

Figure 1C-7 provides a summary of the types of responsibility centers and what they are responsible for.

Figure 1C-7 Types of Responsibility Centers

Types of Responsibility Centers	Sales	Cost of Sales	Other Costs	Investments
Revenue Center	Yes	no	Yes	no
Cost Center	no	Yes	Yes	no
Profit Center	Yes	Yes	Yes	no
Investment Center	Yes	Yes	Yes	Yes

LOS
§1.C.2.b

For example: Consider an office supply store. Each product line, such as printers, is a revenue center responsible for the revenues from the product line's sales. Each department is a profit center, such as paper supplies, which accounts for the revenues and the expenses (i.e., the profitability) of that department. Finally, each store is an investment center, responsible for the revenues and expenses and also for the capital project budgets and the assets and liabilities of the store.

Contribution and Segment Reporting

Managing the performance of the various responsibility centers depends on an analysis of their costs and revenue contributions to the organization. Two approaches that are used to aid in this type of analysis are contribution reporting and segment reporting.

Contribution Reporting

The contribution approach to reporting an income statement is useful for internal decision making. It separates variable from fixed expenses, deducting variable expenses from revenue first to arrive at the contribution margin. The fixed expenses are deducted to arrive at net operating income. The **contribution margin** is the amount that contributes toward fixed expenses and profits. The contribution margin shows managers how profits are affected by changes in volume. Remember the fixed costs and operating capacity are constant over the relevant range.

The primary advantage of such an income statement format is that profit center managers can view the costs by their behavior (e.g., fixed or variable) instead of by departments, such as sales, administration, and production (cost of goods sold). Managers can use a contribution income statement when analyzing product lines, deciding on prices for goods, whether to expand a segment or discontinue it, or whether to make or buy a good.

Evaluating a contribution margin report often involves the use of cost-volume-profit (CVP) analysis such as the contribution margin, the contribution margin ratio, and breakeven sales in dollars. Alternatively, a balanced scorecard is a more comprehensive tool used in evaluating performance.

Management performance can be evaluated more easily using a contribution income statement because the items outside the manager's control are separated from the items within their control. However, many fixed costs are controllable, so managers often have them further divided into controllable fixed costs and uncontrollable fixed costs. Controllable fixed costs are those costs the manager makes decisions about. Uncontrollable fixed costs often come from a nonnegotiable corporate allocation of headquarters expenses. The controllable margin is the contribution margin less the controllable fixed costs.

Figure 1C-8 shows two versions of the same income statement, in traditional and contribution formats. If a prior period's statement showed that the uncontrollable fixed production costs were rising and the variable production costs were falling, a traditional statement would not show this fact. However, the contribution format would show that the manager has been successful at keeping costs relatively the same even in the face of rising fixed costs outside his or her control. Note also that the traditional income statement's cost of goods sold, selling, and administrative costs include both fixed and variable expenses, but there is no way to determine how the amounts are broken down.

**LOS
§1.C.2.c**

Figure 1C-8 Income Statements in Traditional versus Contribution Format

Traditional Approach (Costs Organized by Function)			Contribution Approach (Costs Organized by Behavior)		
Sales		$31,200	Sales		$31,200
Less cost of goods sold		15,600	Less variable expenses:		
Gross margin		$15,600	Variable production	$5,200	
Less operating expenses:			Variable selling expenses	$1,560	
Selling expenses	$8,060		Variable admin. expenses	1,040	$7,800
Administrative expenses	4,940	$13,000	Contribution margin		$23,400
Net operating income		$2,600	Less fixed expenses:		
			Fixed production	$10,400	
			Fixed selling	6,500	
			Fixed administrative	3,900	$ 20,800
			Net operating income		$2,600

**LOS
§1.C.2.e**

Segment Reporting

Reporting segments are portions of a business divided for reporting purposes along product lines, geographical areas, or other meaningful segments to provide individual information about that area. *For example:* Consider a grocery chain. Each store is a segment. Also, if the accounting and decision-making systems evaluate product lines separately, each product line (such as produce, dairy, meats, etc.) is a segment as well.

Segmented financial statements are the same as nonsegmented statements except that each segment has its own costs traced back to it so that the report shows how profitable each segment is by itself. The **segment margin** is the segment's contribution margin less all traceable fixed costs for the segment. The segment margin is a useful indication of a segment's profitability. If it is not positive, the segment may need to be discontinued unless it adds value to other segments.

Traceable fixed costs that are included in a segment's margin are costs that would not exist were it not for the segment. Administrative salaries for segment managers are an example of a fixed cost that can be traced directly to a segment. Similarly, building maintenance costs or insurance premiums for a specific business segment may be able to be traced to the segment.

Common Cost Allocation

LOS §1.C.2.f

Unlike traceable fixed costs, common fixed costs (such as the chief executive's salary) cannot be traced to a specific department because they are shared costs and must be apportioned between two or more departments using some allocation basis that may or may not provide an accurate allocation. Additionally, common costs are often uncontrollable by the segment manager to whom the cost is reported and thus make it more difficult to determine the profitability of an individual segment. A **common cost** is any cost that is shared by two or more segments or entities. When common costs are allocated to segments, the value of the segment margin on reporting profitability is diluted; therefore some businesses allocate common costs to segments only when all or most of the cost would disappear if the segment were to be discontinued. Two methods of allocating common costs are the stand-alone method and the incremental method.

LOS §1.C.2.g

Stand-alone cost allocation is a method that determines the relative proportion of cost driver for each party that shares a common cost and allocates the costs by those percentages.

For example: Company A has a new plant and an older plant, but both plants require some workers to be given on-site training. The traveling trainer's salary of $60,000 plus $10,000 travel and lodging expenses can be allocated based on the number of users who need to be trained at each location or some other cost driver, such as days spent at each location. If the old plant has 40 trainees and the new plant has 60 trainees, the old plant would receive $28,000 of the cost (40%) and the new plant would receive $42,000 of the cost. This method has the benefit of fairness and is easy to implement.

LOS §1.C.2.g

Incremental cost allocation is a method that allocates costs by ranking the parties by a primary user and incremental users, or those users who add an additional cost due to the fact that there is now more than one user of the cost.

For example: Company A, just described, hires a trainer because the new plant is being opened. The trainer is based in the new plant's city, so the new plant is the primary user of the trainer's time. If the trainer works at the new plant for three quarters of the time and at the old plant for one quarter of the time, the new plant is allocated $45,000 of the costs, while the old plant is allocated the remaining $15,000 plus all $10,000 of the travel expenses because these are an incremental cost of having the trainer travel to serve the incremental user.

Conversely, if management wanted to reduce start-up costs for the new plant, it could choose to designate the old plant as the primary user and allocate only a small amount of the costs to the new plant. Because this method allows managers to manipulate how costs are allocated, it is not as balanced as the stand-alone method. Also, when common costs are allocated in this manner, most of the segments want to be incremental users, so this method can cause interdepartmental contention.

Transfer Pricing Models

Allocating costs to a responsibility center or segment involves assigning prices for the goods and services that pass between segments. **Transfer pricing** sets prices for internally exchanged goods and services. An **intermediate product** is a good or service that is transferred between two segments of a company. Company strategy is greatly affected by choice of transfer prices. If the company wants the business units to behave independently and keep managers motivated to achieve company goals, transfer prices should be set at arm's length, as if the party were any other external client. When no external suppliers or customers exist for a product or service, the arm's-length price (an impartial or fair market price) is more difficult to determine. The amounts set for transfer prices require cooperation among many departments, including finance, production, marketing, and tax planning.

Firms that have a high degree of vertical integration will need to set transfer prices carefully. For example, a corporation that owns farms, food warehouses, distributors, and grocery stores will need to set prices for each service that will be considered fair by all segments and also allow each portion of the business to be financially viable.

Four models that can be used to set transfer prices are market price, negotiated price, variable cost, and full cost. Firms often combine various methods (dual pricing) to match their needs.

1. Market Price Model

The market price model is a true arm's-length model because it sets the price for a good or service at going market prices. This model can be used only when an item has a market; items such as work-in-process inventory may not have a market price. The market price model keeps business units autonomous, forces the selling unit to be competitive with external suppliers, and is preferred by tax authorities. Businesses that use this model should take into account the reduced selling and marketing costs in the price.

2. Negotiated Price Model

The negotiated price model sets the transfer price through negotiation between the buyer and the seller. When different business units experience conflicts, negotiation or even arbitration may be needed to keep the company as a whole functioning efficiently. Negotiated prices can make both buying and selling units less autonomous. There is also the issue that one business unit manager may simply be a better negotiator than the other.

3. Variable Cost Model

The variable cost model sets transfer prices at the unit's variable cost, or the actual cost to produce the good or service less all fixed costs. This method will lower the selling unit's profits and increase the buying unit's profits due to the low price. This model is advantageous for selling units that have excess capacity or for situations when a buying unit could purchase from external sources but the company wants to encourage internal purchases. Among the disadvantages of this method is the fact that it is not viewed favorably by tax authorities because it lowers the profits, and thereby taxes, for the location where the product was manufactured.

4. Full Cost (Absorption) Model

The full cost (absorption) model starts with the seller's variable cost for the item and then allocates fixed costs to the price. Some companies allocate standard fixed costs because this allows the buying unit to know the cost in advance and keeps the seller from becoming too inefficient due to a captive buyer that pays for the inefficiencies. Adding fixed costs is relatively straightforward and fair. However, it can alter a business unit's decision making.

Although fixed costs should not be included in the decision to purchase items internally or externally, often managers will purchase the "lower-cost" external item even though the internal fixed costs will still be incurred.

Figure 1C-9 provides a summary of the transfer pricing models, along with the determination of the amount that would be used.

Figure 1C-9 Transfer Pricing Models

Pricing Model	Price of Product or Service
Market Price	Current market price; true arm's-length model
Negotiated Price	Negotiated between seller and buyer (both internal)
Variable Cost	Variable cost
Full Cost (Absorption)	Variable cost, plus allocation of fixed costs

To illustrate: Hopkins Company has two operating divisions, North and South. One of the products of the North division is a raw material used in the South division. Income statements for the two divisions, excluding interdivisional operations, are shown in Figure 1C-10.

Figure 1C-10 North and South Division Income Statements

	North Division (30% Tax Rate)	South Division (40% Tax Rate)	Total Both Divisions
Sales			
10,000 units × $15 per unit	$ 150,000	–	$ 150,000
20,000 units × $18 per unit	–	$ 360,000	$ 360,000
Total sales	$ 150,000	$ 360,000	$ 510,000
Expenses			
Variable:			
10,000 units × $7 per unit	$ 70,000	–	$ 70,000
20,000 units × $10 per unit	–	$ 200,000	$ 200,000
Fixed:	50,000	65,000	$ 115,000
Total expenses	$ 120,000	$ 265,000	$ 385,000
Operating income	$ 30,000	$ 95,000	$ 125,000

Under the market price model, assuming that the North division is currently operating at full capacity and can sell all of the products it can produce, North will sell one unit to South for $15. This is the price at which all products of North are sold on the market.

Under the negotiated price model, assuming there is some excess capacity in the North division, if North sells to South at the market price of $15, South may prefer to purchase from an outside vendor. In this case, company profit may not be maximized. Therefore, North and South may negotiate a price between $15 (the market price) and $7 (the variable cost), which will provide some contribution toward North's fixed costs and contribute to overall company profits.

Under the variable cost model, North will sell to South at a price of $7 per unit (the variable costs).

Under the full cost (absorption) model, still assuming excess capacity, North will sell to South at a price of $12 per unit ($7 variable plus $5 fixed costs per unit).

Choosing Transfer Price Models

In general, the market price method is preferred in situations when the market price for a good or service is available. When a market price is not available, the negotiated price method is preferred. When neither is acceptable, companies may turn to one of the cost models. Cost-based methods are not recommended because they can lead to motivation problems between parties such as the seller not actively controlling costs because they are simply passed on to the buyer.

LOS
§1.C.2.k

The logic of choosing a transfer price model and setting transfer prices starts with a make-or-buy decision. If there are outside suppliers for a product or service, the market price model should be used. The company should compare the selling unit's variable costs to the market price for the external substitute. If the external market price is lower than the internal variable cost, the buyer should purchase externally to motivate the internal supplier to find ways to lower costs.

When the internal variable cost is less than the external market price, the buying unit should purchase internally, as long as the selling unit has excess capacity. The variable cost model is best for low-capacity utilization, and the market price model is best for high-capacity utilization. If the selling unit is at full capacity, the buying unit should purchase externally, as long as the selling unit can generate more profit from a sale to an external customer than will be lost if the buying unit pays the external market price for the item. When the opposite is true, the buying unit should purchase internally and pay market price for the item. The earlier reference to dual-pricing usually means the selling unit gets credited with a market price and the buying unit gets charged variable cost. This, obviously, creates an intercompany profit, which will need to be eliminated for external reporting.

Reporting of Organizational Segments

Performance measurement reports for various organizational segments are created for internal use and are focused on providing the information management needs to address problems and design improvements.

Performance Measurement Reports

Performance measurement reports should be tailored to the audience and level of management to which they are directed. Too much information can cloud an issue as easily as not enough information can, so the amount and timing of information delivery is critical to the success of each manager. Timing of performance measurement reports such as variance reports is critical; the information must be relevant for it to be useful. However, if a manager is flooded with information and cannot discern which information is important, reporting may be too frequent.

Effective performance measures lead to a desired strategic result by causing the manager and other employees to strive for organizational goals, simultaneously maximizing company goals and individual goals. The objectives of a performance evaluation system include:

- Goal congruence (e.g., aligning the individual's goals with those of the organization)
- Clear communication of expectations
- Opportunities to motivate the individual to perform in a way that will maximize organizational goals
- Providing communication between the individual and the organization
- Articulation of the organization's benchmarks

Improper motivation can occur when feedback is ineffective or when benchmarks are improperly matched with cost and/or revenue drivers of an operation, causing organizations to be counterproductive. Each performance measure selected needs to have these elements:

- A time period for performance measurement (e.g., view one year's results or several years' results simultaneously)
- Common definitions for items (e.g., assets are defined as total assets available regardless of function or usage)
- Definitions of specific measurement units used (e.g., historical cost, current cost)
- A target level of performance for each performance measure and each segment
- A feedback timing schedule (e.g., feedback supplied daily, weekly, quarterly)

Multinational Company Performance Measurement

The nonfinancial differences among countries—in economy, laws, customs, and politics—should play a part in evaluating a foreign division's results.

Multinational companies must account for additional concerns, such as how tariffs, exchange rates, taxes, currency restrictions, expropriation risk, and the availability and relative cost of materials and skills could affect performance evaluations. The use of transfer pricing by multinationals to gain tax and income advantages can conflict with the use of transfer pricing to evaluate performance or to create performance incentives.

For example: Some pharmaceutical companies produce their goods in Puerto Rico and sell the majority of the product in the mainland United States. Because Puerto Rico has a relatively lower tax status than the rest of the United States, the incentive is for the pharmaceutical company to charge the highest transfer price possible for drugs sold to their U.S. divisions (such as market price), thus retaining the profits in the territory that has a lower tax rate. Because the Puerto Rican subsidiary essentially has a captive market, it may not be as efficient as overall corporate management would like.

Conversely, if the producing country has relatively higher taxes than the primary country in which sales occur, the incentive will be to charge the lowest price possible (such as cost) for the goods so that the profits end up in the selling-country division. The resulting performance could be that the producing country fails to meet total demand. Also, if the price is actual cost, the producer will not have any incentive to control those costs because they are merely transferred to the other division. One solution to such a dilemma is to use standard costs instead of actual costs. (The standard could be made more stringent over time through continuous improvement efforts.) Another solution is to change the accountability structure of the segments, making them more centralized if decentralized transfer prices fail to create the desired incentives.

As with any performance evaluation, a multinational company should focus on separating controllable from noncontrollable costs, basing assessments only on costs that can be affected by the managers' choices. If a foreign currency becomes devalued, this will affect profits but is outside management's control. When foreign governments impose trade restrictions, such as tariffs, the performance measurement should take into account the reduced profits from such sources. When managers in foreign countries keep their books in a foreign country's currency, their supervisors should consider the effects of currency fluctuations, inflation, and differences in relative purchasing power in the foreign country. For example, a country with lower costs of labor and goods will also have to price goods for sale in that country much lower than in a country where labor and goods are more costly.

However, because performance evaluations should provide incentives for managers to improve overall operations, it is important to determine if any portion of a noncontrollable event actually could have been prevented or deflected. For example, if managers know they will not be held accountable for a devalued currency, they may not be as quick to move funds out of the country as if they were accountable for a portion of such losses. Managers evaluated in such a fashion might employ market analysts or economists specializing in currency exchange to help forecast such changes.

Another way of enhancing the value of performance measurement is by using benchmark values from other managers or companies in similar local environments. Each distinct area would have its own comparison group, which would provide an opportunity to evaluate performance across companies.

Finally, because profits can be so distorted by various international issues, performance evaluations could avoid focusing on profit and instead focus on more stable indicators, such as revenues, market share, or operating costs.

Topic Questions:
Responsibility Centers and Reporting Segments

Directions: Answer each question in the space provided. Correct answers and explanations appear after the topic questions.

1. The maintenance department of a hotel would be considered a(n):

   ☐ **a.** profit center.

   ☐ **b.** revenue center.

   ☐ **c.** cost center.

   ☐ **d.** investment center.

2. A company expects its plant manager to control manufacturing costs and to set prices for the products manufactured. The company's plant manager is evaluated as directing which type of responsibility center?

   ☐ **a.** Profit center

   ☐ **b.** Cost center

   ☐ **c.** Revenue center

   ☐ **d.** Investment center

3. A company has two operating segments. Segment A of the company has been operating at 70% capacity for the last two years. It produces a single product, which it sells to external customers for $17 per unit. Variable costs to produce one unit are $11, and the allocated fixed overhead costs are $3 per unit. Segment B purchases the same product produced by Segment A from an outside vendor for $15. Management is considering obtaining the product from Segment A. If Segment A begins to manufacture enough product to sell to its external customers as well as to Segment B, Segment A will be operating at 94% capacity. What is the minimum price that Segment A should charge Segment B?

   ☐ **a.** $11 per unit

   ☐ **b.** $14 per unit

   ☐ **c.** $15 per unit

   ☐ **d.** $17 per unit

Topic Question Answers: Responsibility Centers and Reporting Segments

1. The maintenance department of a hotel would be considered a(n):

   ☐ **a.** profit center.

   ☐ **b.** revenue center.

   ☑ **c.** cost center.

   ☐ **d.** investment center.

A cost center is an organizational unit whose manager is responsible only for costs. Cost centers often include service or staff departments that do not generate revenue. The maintenance department of a hotel is an example of a department that does not generate revenue.

2. A company expects its plant manager to control manufacturing costs and to set prices for the products manufactured. The company's plant manager is evaluated as directing which type of responsibility center?

   ☑ **a.** Profit center

   ☐ **b.** Cost center

   ☐ **c.** Revenue center

   ☐ **d.** Investment center

The company's plant manager is evaluated as directing a profit center. Because profit is a function of both revenue and costs, a profit center manager is responsible for generating profits, managing revenue, and controlling costs.

3. A company has two operating segments. Segment A of the company has been operating at 70% capacity for the last two years. It produces a single product, which it sells to external customers for $17 per unit. Variable costs to produce one unit are $11, and the allocated fixed overhead costs are $3 per unit. Segment B purchases the same product produced by Segment A from an outside vendor for $15. Management is considering obtaining the product from Segment A. If Segment A begins to manufacture enough product to sell to its external customers as well as to Segment B, Segment A will be operating at 94% capacity. What is the minimum price that Segment A should charge Segment B?

   ☑ **a.** $11 per unit

   ☐ **b.** $14 per unit

   ☐ **c.** $15 per unit

   ☐ **d.** $17 per unit

The minimum price that a business segment should charge another internal segment depends on whether the supplying segment has excess capacity or not. Because Segment A can manufacture enough product to sell to its external customers and Segment B, it has excess capacity. If a business segment has additional capacity to produce units for an internal segment, the minimum price that the supplying business segment should charge is the variable cost required to produce each unit, or $11 per unit in this problem.

Performance Measures

LOS
§1.C.3.a

PERFORMANCE MEASURES help ensure that overall profitability, business unit profitability, and customer profitability are all in alignment with company goals and strategies. Understanding the drivers of cost and revenue is critical to the management accountant's ability to direct or redirect specific measures that ultimately position the company toward achievement of their goals. Timely monitoring and corresponding corrective actions help keep performance on track to meeting overall goals, objectives, and strategic direction of the company.

LOS
§1.C.3.b

Assessing and evaluating performance can be looked at from different perspectives that lend insight into potential issues that can obstruct the achievement of performance objectives. This topic will explore performance analysis techniques that will help evaluate performance on a business unit, product, and customer profitability level. Additional monitoring techniques including the balanced scorecard will also be discussed.

> **READ** the Learning Outcome Statements (LOS) for this topic as found in Appendix A and then study the concepts and calculations presented here to be sure you understand the content you could be tested on in the CMA exam

Business Unit Profitability Analysis

LOS
§1.C.3.b

A **strategic business unit (SBU)** is an entity or operating unit within a larger organization. Assessing and evaluating business unit performance helps managers determine how the individual unit's profit contributions tie to overall profitability, company strategies, and objectives. Depending on the company focus for the particular business unit, performance measures could be assessed on the business unit's contribution margin, direct/controllable profit, income before taxes, or net income.

Figure 1C-11 provides an illustration of how each of these measures is calculated.

LOS
§1.C.3.c

Figure 1C-11 Business Unit Income Statement

Sales revenue	$780,000
Variable expenses	585,000
Contribution margin	**195,000**
Fixed expenses controllable by the profit center	19,500
Direct/controllable profit	**175,500**
Corporate charges allocated to the SBU	52,500
Income before taxes	**123,000**
Taxes	49,200
Net income	**$73,800**

Contribution Margin

A business unit's **contribution margin** will measure the SBU's ability to generate profitability to cover fixed costs. It is a useful performance measure because it includes the variable costs within the manager's control.

Direct/Controllable Profit

Deducting fixed costs that are controllable by the business unit manager, from the contribution margin, gives us the business unit's **Direct/Controllable Profit**. This measurement is particularly important when evaluating the manager's ability to manage performance of fixed costs, such as salaries. Fixed costs represented in this equation do not include allocated costs being passed down from the parent company level.

Income Before Taxes

Income before taxes is calculated by deducting company allocated costs from the direct/controllable profit. Typically, allocated costs represent various costs that are shared throughout an organization, which are allocated to the individual business units (legal fees, professional fees, company administrative costs). These allocated costs may be considered uncontrollable by the business unit manager, but can provide perspective in determining the level of profitability needed to make the business unit a profitable contributor to the overall business. This insight often plays a key role, making long-term decisions related to product pricing and productivity decisions.

Net Income

Calculated by deducting income taxes from income before taxes, **net income** is influenced by tax rates, inventory valuation methods, and depreciation methods. If determined at a parent company level, the impacts of accounting methods are not generally considered to be controllable by the business unit manager. However, if they are left to the discretion of the business unit, they can have a considerable impact on the net income.

Figure 1C-12 illustrates the impacts of specific accounting methods on net income:

Figure 1C-12 Impact of Select Accounting Methods on Net Income

Method	Assumption	Cost Impact	Causes Net Income To Be
FIFO Inventory	Oldest inventory prices used first. With inflation, newer inventory costs more.	Lower Cost of Goods Sold	Higher
LIFO Inventory	Newest inventory prices used first. With inflation, newer inventory costs more.	Higher Cost of Goods Sold	Lower
Straight-line Depreciation	Asset devaluation occurs consistently over the life of the asset.	Depreciation costs are spread evenly over the asset's life	Higher in the early years compared to the two other methods
Declining-balance Depreciation	Asset devalues greater in the earlier years of the asset life.	Depreciation costs are higher in the earlier years of the asset, but become lower as the asset matures.	Lower in the earlier years of the asset, but higher over time
Sum-of-the-Year's Digits	Asset devalues greater in the earlier years of the asset life.	Depreciation costs are higher in the earlier years of the asset, but become lower as the asset matures.	Lower in the earlier years of the asset, but higher over time

Product Profitability Analysis

LOS §1.C.3.b

Product profitability analysis is often used by business unit or product line managers to determine how specific product profitability contributes to the overall profitability of the business unit and/or overall company profitability. This type of performance measure can contribute to determining which products:

- Are the most profitable
- Require further cost or price evaluation
- Need support from marketing or promotional efforts
- Are unprofitable and should be considered for discontinuance

LOS §1.C.3.c

Before discontinuing an unprofitable product or product line, careful consideration should be given to the financial and non-financial impact of the decision. These considerations should include

- The impact of the decision on overall sales, or sales of other products
- Alternate solutions to making the product or product line profitable (such as price adjustment or increased marketing investments)
- The impact on absorption, joint, and by-product costing
- Determining if the product will become more profitable in the future
- Long-term impacts on company strategies
- Implications on company image or employee morale.

Customer Profitability Analysis

LOS §1.C.3.b

LOS §1.C.3.d

It's important to realize that although a particular customer may be profitable in terms of sales and the products they buy, the actual costs associated with maintaining that customer may make them an unprofitable contributor to overall business unit or company profitability. Special discounts, shared expenses (like co-op advertising), and special administrative costs (like human resources needed to maintain customer service or programs) are critical components of the **customer profitability analysis** used to determine ways to improve profitability and/or drop unprofitable customers and products.

LOS §1.C.3.c

LOS §1.C.3.d

Imagine a scenario where ABC Company offers to pay 20% of the customer's sales for all promotional materials that include ABC's products as co-op advertising costs. Figure 1C-13 illustrates the impact of Customer D purchasing newer, higher-margin merchandise, versus Customer E, who purchases only discontinued/clearance merchandise:

Figure 1C-13 Customer Profitability Analysis

	Customer D	Customer E
Units Sold	500	2,500
Customer Price per Unit	$500	$250
Customer Revenue	**$250,000**	**$625,000**
Cost of Goods Sold ($225 per unit)	112,500	562,500
Gross Customer Profit	**137,500**	**62,500**
Co-op Advertising Costs (20% of Sales)	50,000	125,000
Net Customer Profitability Before Taxes	**$87,500**	**$(62,500)**

As illustrated, although Customer E contributes to revenues and gross profit, the company's policy on co-op advertising creates a scenario where they are unprofitable overall. This type of analysis may lead management accountants to recommend applying the advertising discount only to customers purchasing specific products that yield higher margins.

Other cost considerations that go into customer profitability analysis may include:

- Costs associated with customer credit/payment terms
- Special discount arrangements
- Demurrage charges
- Penalties incurred for Electronic Data Interface (EDI) violations

Similar to the types of consideration given to evaluating the viability of discontinuing a product or product line, careful evaluation of financial and non-financial considerations must be given before dropping a customer based exclusively on their ability to contribute to net profitability.

Financial Profitability Analysis

Companies leverage several different financial analyses as effective company performance measures. This section will address key measures used in the overall evaluation of business unit and company performance.

LOS §1.C.3.e

LOS §1.C.3.f

Return on Investment

Return on investment (ROI) measures the profitability of the business unit based on the investment in assets made to attain that income.

The formula used by the ICMA for ROI is:

$$\text{Return on Investment} = \frac{\text{Income of a Business Unit}}{\text{Assets of a Business Unit}}$$

Note that Income means operating income unless otherwise noted.

The formula used for ROI has many variations for the definition of profit in the numerator and assets in the denominator. The formula shown here is the one that is tested on the CMA exam.

Sometimes the timeline for the net profit and the investment in assets is not always equal such as investing in bonds that generate interest over the next five years. When comparing two or more investment opportunities, it is important that the time horizons be the same for each project so that a fair comparison can be made. When using ROI for a cost-benefit analysis, it is important to account for any ongoing costs of the investment over the period that the benefits are tracked to determine the net benefit per year.

ROI can be measured for the short term (a single month or year) or the long term (investing in a computer system that will generate six years of benefits and six years of costs). When analyzing a long-term project, the use of a discounted cash flow model is more appropriate because these models consider the time value of money.

How a particular company calculates ROI may depend on industry conventions or internal company policy. Knowing the figures used to generate a ratio is the only way to be able to rely on those ratios. If the ratios for a firm are given without any context, it may be more reliable to recompute the ratios directly from the firm's financial statements. Doing this ensures that each ratio is computed using the same methodology and source data. Similarly, the disclosures to financial statements provide important information regarding the method the company used, for example, to account for inventory. The results will not be comparable unless data is converted to a common methodology. For example, companies using LIFO for inventory valuation will report a FIFO equivalent in their disclosures, and this amount can be used when comparing results to another company that uses FIFO.

ROI is expressed as a percentage. The greater the percentage, the greater the return on investment. ROI is a popular measure of profitability because it includes revenues, investments, and costs. Keep in mind that no financial ratio has meaning by itself. So, ROI should be used with other financial measures and should be compared to industry averages or to other possible investments.

For internal use, companies use various definitions of income (or profits) and investments. For external use, U.S. companies currently use the generally accepted accounting principles (GAAP) definitions. However, comparing business units may be difficult if the internal or external ratios were prepared using different methods to allocate common costs.

When ROI uses average total assets in its denominator, it becomes **return on assets (ROA)**, which shows how successful a company is at making a profit using the given level of assets available. Firms that are more efficient with their assets are more likely to be profitable.

When ROI uses ownership interest for the denominator, it is called **return on equity (ROE)**. ROE is calculated only for common equity because preferred stockholders have a set return, which is the preferred dividend rate.

In general, a company's ROE should be higher than its ROA because this implies that the funds borrowed (e.g., at 9%) were reinvested at a higher rate of return (e.g., 15% ROE). A firm uses financial leverage to achieve this difference, which is called trading on the equity. Financial leverage is calculated as shown:

$$\text{Financial Leverage Ratio} = \frac{\text{Assets}}{\text{Equity}}$$

Having more assets with less equity increases the financial leverage ratio. This occurs when a firm finances some of its assets through debt. From a shareholder's perspective, a higher financial leverage is preferable. For companies making profit above the financing costs, this would yield higher return on invested capital (equity). However, higher financial leverage also exposes the company to greater bankruptcy risk in situations in which the company earns less than the interest costs. When revenues increase, profits for shareholders increase at a faster rate, but when revenues decrease, profits shrink at a faster rate because interest costs must be paid regardless of profits.

For example, a sporting goods manufacturer analyzes ROI for two business units using operating income in the numerator and net assets in the denominator.

The tennis ball business unit has income of $100,000 and net assets of $400,000:

$$\text{ROI} = \frac{\$100,000}{\$400,000} = 25\%$$

The racquet ball business unit has income of $60,000 and net assets of $300,000:

$$\text{ROI} = \frac{\$60,000}{\$300,000} = 20\%$$

Residual Income

LOS §1.C.3.g

LOS §1.C.3.h

Residual income (RI) is the dollar amount of income minus the imputed cost of the investment. The formula used by the ICMA for RI is:

> Residual Income (RI) = Income of a Business Unit
> — (Assets of Business Unit × Required Rate of Return)
>
> Note that Income means operating income unless otherwise noted.

The imputed cost of an investment (assets of the SBU) is the required rate of return multiplied by that investment. This represents the opportunity cost of not being able to invest the funds elsewhere. The required rate of return is usually derived from the weighted average cost of capital adjusted for the riskiness of the potential investment.

For example, assume that the same sporting goods manufacturer from the ROI example decided that the required rate of return for tennis balls was 10% and the required rate of return for racquet balls was 12% due to greater risks involved in this business unit. The residual income of each business unit is calculated as shown:

RI, tennis balls = $100,000 − ($400,000 × 0.10) = $60,000

RI, racquet balls = $60,000 − ($300,000 × 0.12) = $24,000

RI implies that as long as the tennis ball unit earns more than $(0.10 \times \$400,000) =$ $40,000 RI and the racquet ball unit earns more than $(0.12 \times \$300,000) = \$36,000$ RI, the sporting goods manufacturer should continue to invest in assets to grow both operations. Using RI instead of ROI makes managers aim for an actual dollar amount rather than a percentage.

Like ROI, RI can measure a specific business segment's returns, in which case it uses segment income, segment investment, and a segment-specific required rate of return.

RI versus ROI

LOS §1.C.3.i

Financial ratios must be used in the context of the business and its industry. The nature of a company's business will affect how financial ratios such as ROI are perceived. For example, a particular industry may have lower average ROIs, so the market will view a slightly higher ROI favorably even though it is lower than ROIs for other industries. The maturity of the business also is considered. A firm in its first year of business is not expected to generate the same ROI as an established business. Firms entering new markets must set their expectations appropriately. For example, a firm that uses a particular ROI for its established television division would have to use different criteria for a new aerospace division. To get past these comparability issues, it is useful to compute the ratios for the company and for relevant benchmark firms (such as rivals or firms at the same maturity level) using the same methodology.

Focusing only on ROI is not a good business policy. Instead, firms should consider many factors that are both financial and nonfinancial. Perhaps for business development reasons, a firm might accept a low-ROI project because it promises to add a new long-term client and stronger long-term ROI.

When ROI is used as a primary performance evaluation tool, managers of business units with higher ROIs may reject capital investments that do not promise ROIs equal to or better than the current ROI ratio, even if the investment is strategically beneficial to the organization as a whole.

For example, Bounce's tennis ball unit might purchase a new machine for $100,000 that would produce $20,000 additional revenue. The machine's ROI of $(\$20,000 \div \$100,000) = 20\%$ would reduce the business unit's overall ROI of $(\$100,000 \div \$400,000) = 25\%$:

$$\text{ROI with machine} = \frac{(\$100,000 + \$20,000)}{(\$400,000 + \$100,000)} = 24\%$$

A manager compensated using ROI would be less likely to make this investment. By contrast, if the manager is evaluated using RI instead, the calculation (assuming a 10% required rate of return) is:

$$\text{RI without machine} = \$100,000 - (\$400,000 \times 10\%) = \$60,000$$

$$\text{RI with machine} = \$120,000 - (\$500,000 \times 10\%) = \$70,000$$

Since RI increases with this investment, a manager compensated based on RI would have the incentive to invest in the machine. As long as the investment earns the expected revenue, the manager will be rewarded for increasing RI.

RI gives managers the incentive to select any project that generates returns above the required rate of return. However, RI is a flat dollar amount, so it makes comparing business units of different sizes more difficult than using a percentage. For example, a large business unit, even with poor efficiency, can still have a larger RI than a small business unit with good efficiency. Therefore, the measure tends to favor large business units over smaller ones. RI is also sensitive to the required rate of return. As the investments become larger, this sensitivity becomes more pronounced.

The goal of maximizing ROI may induce managers of profitable subunits to reject projects that, from the viewpoint of the organization as a whole, should be accepted. This occurs whenever the subunit is operating at a higher ROI (22%) than the cost of capital for the organization (12%). In that case, a new project with an ROI of 18% would be beneficial to the organization but would be rejected by the subunit because it would reduce the ROI of the subunit. Conversely, a manager of an unprofitable subunit may accept a project that, from the viewpoint of the organization, should be rejected. For example, consider another subunit whose ROI is 8% when the organization has a cost of capital of 12%. The subunit manager will accept a project with ROI of 10% even though it will reduce residual income for the organization. Generally, goal congruence between subunits and the organization is promoted by using RI rather than ROI to measure a manager's performance.

There are other problems in using ROI and RI. Increasing either ROI or RI involves maximizing profits (maximizing sales while minimizing costs) and minimizing the investment base. Maximizing sales and minimizing costs promotes transfer price disputes among SBUs, because the transfer price is recorded as revenue to the seller SBU and as cost to the buyer SBU. Cost minimization also encourages SBUs to cut discretionary costs to reduce the unit's investment. The discretionary costs most likely to be cut in the short term are:

- Research and development
- Quality control
- Maintenance
- Human resource development
- Advertising and promotion

Cutting these costs will increase ROI or RI in the short run but may create long-term problems for the SBU and the organization.

Maximizing ROI or RI encourages SBU managers to reduce the investment base by not replacing old assets, not purchasing new assets or technology, or unwarranted disposal of assets. All of these actions tend to produce long-term problems.

Investment Base Issues

The key to performance measures is comparability. However, both ROI and RI are affected by the way that income and assets are measured. Therefore, using ROI or

RI as a performance measure may present challenges when comparing internal business units because each unit may use different approaches to measuring the revenues, costs, and assets that are the components of its assessed financial performance. Issues that make these comparisons less useful include:

- *Different revenue and expense recognition policies.* If internal business units operate in different industries, there may be inherent differences in their revenue and expense policies, reducing comparability. In addition, if one division supplies components to another division, the chosen transfer prices will affect the revenues of the producer division and the expenses of the user division, as well as each division's incentive to make the internal transfer.
- *Different inventory measurement policies.* Comparing business units that use different inventory policies can be complicated since the choice affects both income and assets in the ROI or RI computation.
- *Possession of joint or shared assets among business units.* Whenever units share an asset, the joint cost must be allocated. The choice of allocation method will affect the expenses and income recognized by each unit and the perception of each unit's performance.
- *Different choices on how to value assets.* Assets can be measured at their historical cost, their book value, or their replacement cost, and this choice can have a significant impact on both managers' decisions and perceived divisional performance. For example, using historical cost to compute ROI or RI favors divisions with older assets and discourages managers from replacing their divisional assets. By contrast, using replacement cost penalizes divisions with older assets and incentivizes managers to replace assets, even if the assets are still functioning well. Choosing book value means that ROI and RI will automatically increase each year as the assets are depreciated and book value decreases, even if there is no change in divisional income.

Balanced Scorecard

Traditionally, most companies analyze performance solely based on financial measures. Although these measures are objective and quantitative, they are historical in nature. Moreover, they are better at providing short-term forecasts than long-term predictions. Although these lagging indicators are important in tracking what has been done, companies should also focus on leading indicators (indicators of future success). The *balanced scorecard* (BSC) and similar holistic techniques provide this broader focus.

The BSC gives companies a simple tool that shows them specific financial and nonfinancial indicators. It is a strategic measurement and management system that translates a company's strategy into four balanced categories. The financial perspective measures the past performance of a firm. The customer, internal business process, and learning and growth perspectives drive future financial performance.

The BSC was created by Robert Kaplan and David Norton as a way to move organizations away from concentrating solely on financial data. The objective is to focus simultaneously on financial information and on creating the abilities and intangible assets required for long-term growth. This is done by translating a company's strategy into specific measures within each category. Companies use the BSC as a management tool to:

- Clarify and communicate strategy
- Align individual and unit goals to strategy
- Link strategy to the budgeting process
- Get feedback for continuous strategy improvement

Key Performance Indicators for a Balanced Scorecard

LOS
§1.C.3.l

To develop its strategies effectively, a firm needs to analyze its internal *strengths and weaknesses* and then analyze its external *opportunities and threats*. Combined, this effort is called a *SWOT analysis.*

Strengths include the organization's core competencies (special skills). Weaknesses are characteristics that place the company at some disadvantage. Opportunities are chances to increase revenues or profits, and threats are elements in the environment that may provide trouble for the company. Analysis of these factors helps a company determine its key performance indicators (KPIs).

KPIs are specific, measurable goals that must be met in order to achieve a firm's strategy. The BSC identifies KPIs and arranges them into the SWOT categories.

Figure 1C-14 presents an example of one company's KPIs.

Figure 1C-14 KPI Measurement

Factor	KPI	Measurement Examples
Financial	Sales	Sales forecast accuracy, return on sales, sales trends
	Liquidity	Asset, inventory, and receivables turnover; cash flow
	Profitability	ROI, residual income, economic value added
	Market value	Market value added, share price
Customer	Market share	Trade association analyses, market definitions
	Customer acquisition	Number of new customers, total sales to new customers
	Customer satisfaction	Customer returns, complaints, surveys
	Customer retention	Customer retention by category, percentage growth with existing customers
	Quality	Warranty expense
	Timeliness	Time from order to door, number of on-time deliveries
Internal business process	Productivity	Cycle time, effectiveness, efficiency, variances, scrap
	Quality	Defects, returns, scrap, rework, surveys, warranty
	Safety	Accidents, insurance claims, result of accidents
	Process time	Setup time, turnaround, lead time
	Brand management	Number of advertisements, surveys, new accounts
Learning and growth	Skill development	Training hours or trainees, skill improvement
	Motivation, empowerment	Suggestions per employee, suggestions implemented
	New products	New patents, number of design changes, research and development skills
	Competence	Employee turnover, experience, customer satisfaction
	Team performance	Surveys, number of gains shared with other teams, number of multi-team projects, percentage of shared incentives

After defining the KPIs, a measurement unit must be assigned to each one. According to Kaplan and Norton, "If you can't measure it, you can't manage it."

In developing KPIs, it is very possible that some measures may conflict with others. To avoid this, the BSC uses a process of integrating the KPIs into the firm's strategy.

The following chart in Figure 1C-15 shows how the company's vision and strategy are at the center of everything. The four BSC perspectives are linked to the company's vision and strategy, and the four BSC perspectives are also interrelated.

Figure 1C-15 Vision and Strategy are at the Center of the BSC

Effective Use of a Balanced Scorecard

Once the KPIs and their measurements are defined, they must be linked back to the firm's strategy. No set of measurement tools will be successful if managers are motivated to achieve their own goals at the expense of organizational goals. A successful BSC creates a shared understanding within the organization and how the individual contributes to strategic success. The elements of the BSC come from the organization's strategy, and the BSC should show what the strategy is. Linking the four perspectives to strategy requires understanding three principles: cause-and-effect relationships, outcome measures and performance drivers, and links to financial measures.

1. Cause-and-Effect Relationships

All KPIs should fit within an overall cause-and-effect relationship chain that ends with a relevant financial measure and the achievement of part of the company's strategy. Cause-and-effect situations can be hypothesized using if-then statements:

If the firm introduces a new product line, then the firm will attract a new customer base. If the firm attracts a new customer base, then all existing product lines will have new customers . . . and so on. These chains of cause-and-effect relationships should progress through each of the four areas where possible, and the net result of all of the chains should explicitly describe the company's strategy, how to measure each element, and how to provide feedback to the process. In the end, all KPIs should be incorporated into one of these cause-and-effect chains.

2. Outcome Measures and Performance Drivers

For the cause-and-effect chains of KPIs to be useful, they must be linked to a specific outcome and a performance driver that says how the outcome can be met. Outcome measures are lagging (historic) indicators of success, such as profitability, market share, employee skills, or customer retention. Outcome measures tend to be general measures of what must be achieved at the end of several cause-and-effect chains.

Performance drivers are leading indicators, or drivers that are specific to the strategy of a particular business unit, such as cycle times, setup times, or new patents. Performance drivers without outcome measures will show how to perform in the short term but will not indicate whether the strategy is successful in the long term. Outcome measures without performance drivers will indicate where the department or team needs to be, but they will not show the path to achieve the goal or give relevant information when it is needed.

3. Links to Financial Measures

No matter how focused an organization is on an initiative (e.g., total quality management or employee empowerment), it must be linked to the bottom line. Furthermore, the lack of a link to a tangible benefit from the program can disillusion managers because there is no way to measure program success. Therefore, all cause-and-effect chains need to be linked to financial outcome measures.

Nonfinancial Balanced Scorecard Measures

To drive future financial performance, the BSC requires assessment of customer, internal business process, and learning and growth measures.

Customer Measures

Because customers create a company's revenue, a company must identify customers and classify them into appropriate market segments. The customer perspective must include specific outcome measures and specific performance drivers. Since a company cannot target everyone without losing its focus on its core customers, a company must shape performance drivers (also known as value propositions) that are specific to market segments and their strategy.

The primary customer outcome measures include:

- Market share
- Acquisition

- Customer satisfaction
- Customer retention
- Customer profitability

These elements work together in a cause-and-effect relationship chain as shown in Figure 1C-16.

Figure 1C-16 Customer Outcome Measures

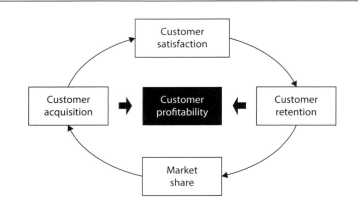

Market share is the proportion of customers that use a company's product or service out of the total users in that market segment. A subdivision of market share is account share. **Account share** is the proportion of a customer's business out of its total spending in the area the company represents. For example, a food distributor may measure the amount of purchases of its products over all of the targeted customers' food purchases as share of the pantry.

Data on the size of the total market segment for a business can be obtained from trade associations, industry groups, government studies, and customer surveys. The share of this market controlled by the company can be measured using metrics such as total number of customers, unit volume sold, or dollars spent. Account share is measured using surveys or approximation techniques that estimate the spending of an average user compared to the spending with the company itself. Companies with few customers can track individual customers, whereas companies with many customers must track customer segments.

Customer Acquisition

Companies with a growth strategy will focus strongly on the customer acquisition measure, but all companies need to add new customers because customer retention is never 100%. Customer acquisition measures the success of the funds spent to acquire the new customers, such as advertising and other marketing costs. Customer acquisition can be measured in absolute terms (number of new customers) or relative terms (net gain in customers). It can also be measured as total sales to customers or customer acquisition divided by customer market segment. Other measures focus on customer conversion rate, such as the number of new customers divided by the total number of prospect contacts.

Customer Satisfaction

Measures of customer satisfaction show how successfully a company has met the needs of its consumers. When a firm's customers are corporations, customer satisfaction can be measured by having the customer rank its vendors on a variety of factors. Retail customer satisfaction can be measured using surveys or customer complaints. The cost of customer surveys varies, depending on the medium used and the number of desired responses. Web-based surveys and Web tracking have made the data-gathering process relatively inexpensive.

Customer Retention

Customer retention is an ongoing process that can be measured directly by companies that maintain customer lists, such as magazines, auto dealerships, distributors, and banks. Customer retention can be further broken down into the percentage change in business with each customer. For retailers, some customer retention data can be gathered from credit card receipts. A major source of retention data for some retailers are loyalty programs that provide enrolled customers with discounts and enable the firm to track customer purchases precisely.

Customer Performance Drivers

Although outcome measures may be broadly defined for most industries, performance drivers are specific to each company's strategy and market. The performance drivers for customer acquisition, retention, and satisfaction are based on meeting the needs of customers. Examples of some common performance drivers include:

- Response time
- Delivery performance
- Defects
- Lead time

Internal Business Process Measures

After the financial and customer measures are created to meet company strategy, the internal business process measures can be designed to link to these metrics and create customer and shareholder value. Instead of creating measures that merely attempt to improve existing business processes, the BSC suggests that companies start with current and future customer needs, progressing through the cause-and-effect chain via operations, marketing, and other areas all the way to sales and service, keeping only the elements that add value to customers.

Internal business process measures go beyond simple financial variance to include output measures such as quality, cycle time, yield, order fulfillment, production planning, throughput, and turnover. However, improving such measures may not be enough to differentiate a company from its competitors if these firms are working toward the same goals. Entirely new internal processes may be needed to make the company a leader in all of these measures simultaneously. A SWOT analysis can help identify weaknesses that require new solutions rather than incremental improvements. For example, a business could radically improve cycle time by eliminating its warehouse and shipping goods directly to retail locations on a just-in-time basis.

The BSC identifies three business process areas that contribute to most companies' business strategies for internal business processes: innovation, operations, and postsale service.

1. Innovation

The innovation process starts with the SWOT analysis to identify customer needs that the company can satisfy. Research and development can be expensive, but becoming efficient and effective at producing new products can be at least as important as concentrating on the efficiency of ongoing production operations. Since the first company to introduce a new product has a distinct edge in market share, time to market is a key metric for evaluating the success of a new product introduction. Other measures include percentage of sales from new or proprietary products, new products versus competitors' new products, and variation from project budgets.

Product development processes can include performance measurements such as yield, cycle time, and cost. For example, research into new computer chips could test numerous materials, and the yield of materials that warrant further study can be judged against the total number tested. The firm can measure the time that materials spend in that phase (cycle time) and the overall cost of processing and research. Thus, the progress toward the outcome measurement of time to market and overall cost can be assessed.

2. Operations

The operations process is the area that has garnered the majority of performance measurements in the past, and it continues to be important in reducing costs or increasing capabilities. Using only financial measures for operations (e.g., variances and standard costs) can lead line managers to make decisions that run counter to the organization's strategy. For example, managers may create too much inventory in order to keep a financial ratio in line with expectations rather than adjusting inventory to fit customer demand. Financial measures are important, but the BSC recommends supplementing them with measures of quality, technological capabilities, and reducing cycle time to build the company's long-term strategy.

3. Postsale Service

Postsale service is a method of adding value to a product or service while simultaneously gaining feedback on customer satisfaction. Many companies that sell complex goods or services include postsale service in their strategic plans. Metrics such as response time for equipment failures and promptness of maintenance calls can be used to measure the success of post-sale service.

Learning and Growth Measures

A company develops learning and growth measures after identifying its financial, customer, and internal process strategic needs. If the company created its strategy based on ambition and innovation, it will need to achieve new capabilities through learning and growth. Although it is the last step designed in a BSC strategy, it will be the first step performed. Learning and growth measures are performance drivers for the desired strategic outcomes. Measuring learning and growth using financial measures alone tends to show only the short-term results. For example, training is unprofitable in the short term. However, the long-term consequences of not training employees can be devastating to the organization, so new measures must be introduced to guide managers' decisions in this area.

The learning and growth perspective can be broken down into three categories: (1) employee skill sets; (2) information system capabilities; and (3) empowerment, motivation, and organizational alignment.

1. Employee Skill Sets

The automation of repetitive tasks has transformed employee management from an industrial model to a knowledge-based model. Specific outcome measures of employee results include employee satisfaction, employee retention, and employee productivity. Satisfied employees produce satisfied customers. Employee satisfaction can be measured through employee annual reviews or surveys. Employee retention is measured by employee turnover or years of service. Employees with a greater investment in a company tend to be more satisfied. The employee productivity outcome measure results from performance drivers, such as employee training, autonomy in decision making versus results, and output versus numbers of employees needed to produce the output. Another common productivity measure is revenue per employee. This should not be used alone because focusing only on revenue can encourage employees to accept revenue even if the profit level is negative, such as sales personnel making sales by offering huge price discounts.

Employees needing new skill sets can be measured using the amount of training needed per employee, the proportion of the workforce needing training, or the training and experience required to advance from an unqualified to a qualified position. Such measures indicate the amount of work required to raise the organization's capabilities to the desired strategic level. The strategic job coverage ratio is another metric that tracks the number of employees qualified for a strategic job divided by total organizational needs. This ratio exposes gaps in organizational skill sets.

2. Information System Capabilities

Measures of the time needed to access or process business information can assess the capabilities of the current information systems and indicate the need for continued investment in such infrastructure. A strategic information coverage ratio can be used to measure current information system capabilities divided by anticipated system needs.

3. Empowerment, Motivation, and Organizational Alignment

Empowerment and motivation can be measured using metrics such as the number and impact of employee-initiated improvements and innovations. Empowerment and motivation can be enhanced when employees are encouraged to suggest improvements in the organization's products and processes. Organizational alignment, organizational learning, and teamwork measures include the goals set versus goals achieved for a department as well as the team-based measures coupled with team-based rewards. Linking personal goals and rewards to organizational outcomes is a key to achieving the overall company strategy. Performance drivers for organizational alignment include periodic surveys of employees to determine their level of motivation to achieve the KPIs in the BSC.

A Balanced Scorecard Example

Acme Company's BSC, shown in Figure 1C-17, gives the company's overall strategic goal and the associated targets. It then covers the specific objectives for each of the four perspectives. Each objective has a specific measurable tool and a target for each of the next two years. The "Programs" column is the result of a survey Acme performed that matched planned programs to particular strategic objectives. The targets were set under the assumption that these programs would go forward.

At the end of Year 1, the results were as shown in Figure 1C-18.

Figure 1C-17 Acme Company's Balanced Scorecard (Planned Results)

Overall goal: Grow sales by 20% over the next two years		Targets		
	Current Year (Y0)	Year 1 (Y1)	Year 2 (Y2)	
Revenues:	$400,000	$432,000	$484,000	
Perspective — Strategic Objectives	Measurements	Y1 Target	Y2 Target	Programs
Financial — F1: Maximize return on equity	Return on equity	9%	13%	
F2: Positive economic value added (EVA)	EVA	$20,000	$30,000	
F3: 10% revenue growth	% change in revenues	8%	12%	
F4: Asset utilization	Utilization rates	85%	88%	
Customer — C1: Price	Competitive comparison	−4%	−5%	
C2: Customer retention	Retention %	75%	75%	Implement customer relationship management (CRM) program
C3: Lowest-cost suppliers	Total cost relative to competition	−6%	−7%	Implement supplier relationship management (SRM) program
C4: Product innovation	% of sales from new products	10%	15%	
Internal business process — P1: Improve production work flow	Cycle time	0.3 days	0.25 days	Upgrade enterprise resource planning (ERP) system
P2: New product success	Number of orders	1,000	1,500	
P3: Sales penetration	Actual versus plan (variance)	0%	0%	
P4: Reduce inventory	Inventory as a % of sales	30%	28%	
Learning and growth — L1: Link strategy to reward system	Net income per dollar of variable pay (aggregate)	65%	68%	Implement CRM
L2: Fill critical competency gaps	% of critical competencies satisfied on tracking matrix	75%	80%	Tuition reimbursement
L3: Become customer-driven culture	Survey index	77%	79%	Implement CRM
L4: Quality leadership	Average ranking (on 10-point scale) of executives	8.9	9.2	Tuition reimbursement

Figure 1C-18 Acme Company's Balanced Scorecard (Actual Results)

Overall goal: Grow sales by 20% over the next two years				
		Y1 Target	**Y1 Actual**	**Variance***
Revenues:		$432,000	$424,000	$8,000 U
Perspective	**Strategic Objectives**			
Financial	F1: Maximize return on equity	9%	8%	1% U
	F2: Positive EVA	$20,000	$18,000	$2,000 U
	F3: 10% revenue growth	8%	6%	2% U
	F4: Asset utilization	85%	87%	2% F
Customer	C1: Price	–4%	–4%	0
	C2: Customer retention	75%	70%	5% U
	C3: Lowest-cost suppliers	–6%	–7%	–1% F
	C4: Product innovation	10%	8%	2% U
Internal business process	P1: Improve production work flow	0.3 days	0.25 days	0.05 days F
	P2: New product success	1,000 orders	800 orders	200 orders U
	P3: Sales penetration	0%	–7%	–7% U
	P4: Reduce inventory	30%	29%	1% F
Learning and growth	L1: Link strategy to reward system	65%	63%	2% U
	L2: Fill critical competency gaps	75%	75%	0
	L3: Become customer-driven culture	77%	74%	3% U
	L4: Quality leadership	8.9	8.9	0

*U = Unfavorable variance; F = Favorable variance.

What can Acme learn from the results of Year 1? It may have had trouble implementing its CRM program (poorly planned, project canceled, delayed, etc.) because each of the measures linked to that program had an unfavorable variance. A reexamination of that program may find ways to refocus on the customers' needs.

Acme's production costs and production efficiencies all have favorable variances, meaning that the SRM and ERP initiatives seem to be successful. Acme's workforce is progressing on pace, and its tuition reimbursement program is a likely aid to this success. However, although the workforce is strong in core competencies and leadership, its members have not become more customer-oriented, which is the primary reason for Acme's loss of customers and its inability to penetrate new markets and sell new products (which were likely designed with poor information on actual market needs). If Acme wants to turn things around and meet its goals, it must increase its investment in its CRM initiative, including training to change its employees' mind-sets toward a customer orientation.

Implementing the Balanced Scorecard

The following information on implementing the BSC was drawn from *The Strategy-Focused Organization* by Kaplan and Norton (Harvard Business Review Press, 2001). Execution is the key to implementing the BSC. Without execution, even the best vision remains a dream. In the past few decades, the average company has gone from about two-thirds of its value being based on tangible assets to about one-third. Thus, companies are moving from being able to describe and measure their success solely in financial terms to needing knowledge-based strategies that rely on more than just slow-reacting tools such as budgets. The BSC works well with strategy execution because the scorecard itself describes strategy in a way that can be implemented. A strategy-focused organization has these aspects:

- All financial and nonfinancial measures used in the BSC should be derived from the firm's vision and strategy.
- Processes become participative rather than directive.
- Change is not limited to cost cutting and downsizing, but includes repositioning the firm in a new or more specialized competitive market, or creating a customer focus, a performance mind-set, and so on.
- The organization must adopt new cultural values and priorities.

Kaplan and Norton developed the chart in Figure 1C-19 to demonstrate further the four perspectives and provide guidance for developing specific objectives for each.

Figure 1C-19 Balance Scorecard Framework

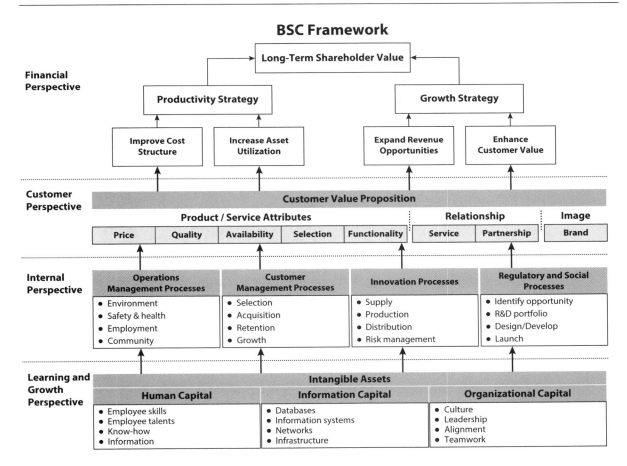

Aligning and Focusing Resources on Strategy

Rather than encouraging a general effort toward improvement or efficiency, the executive team, business units, information technology, human resources, budgets, and capital investments must all be aligned and focused toward specific and more intense (but not necessarily more capital-intensive) goals. To accomplish this, a firm must implement a continuous improvement cycle consisting of five steps:

1. Translate the strategy into operational terms.
2. Align the organization to the firm's strategy.
3. Make strategy everybody's everyday job.
4. Make strategy a continual process.
5. Mobilize change through executive leadership.

1. *Translate the strategy into operational terms using strategy maps and the BSC.* A **strategy map** gives a high-level view of the organization's strategy and associated priorities so that it can design metrics that will enable it to evaluate its performance against strategies.

   For example: Figure 1C-20 shows a strategy map that Mobil North America Marketing and Refining (NAM&R) created to address a new focus on the customer and on factors aimed at increasing customer use of Mobil stations and products.

2. *Align the organization to the firm's strategy using corporate scorecards as well as business unit and support unit synergies.* Synergies make the whole worth more than the sum of its parts. Firms should replace formal reporting structures with strategic priorities across business units (e.g., by having common themes across each unit's different scorecards). Examples of linked scorecards can be found in Kaplan and Norton's *The Strategy-Focused Organization.*

3. *Make strategy everyone's daily job using personal scorecards, strategic awareness, and balanced paychecks.* Replacing top-down direction with top-down communication means that every employee has a clear set of expectations that are aligned with strategy. The BSC becomes an educational tool showing how to measure success, but it may need to be backed up with more formal training (e.g., if employees must refine customer segments, they must first be taught about customer segmentation). Personal-level scorecards can be created by the end users based on an understanding of the higher-level priorities. Often this leads to additional synergies when an individual finds ways to help other areas of the company. This process helps create a strategic awareness at every level.

   Balanced paychecks link pay to the BSC measures, usually by business unit performance, not individual performance. Balanced paychecks apply financial and nonfinancial BSC measures, weighted by their importance. Some measures have components for both individual performance and unit performance, and most also tie the compensation to some external factors, such as an industry benchmark to compensate for factors outside of employees' control. Using some form of balanced paycheck raises all employees' interest in using the BSC. Employees may study the BSC to see what their compensation will be, but they

Figure 1C-20 Strategy Maps for Mobil NAM&R

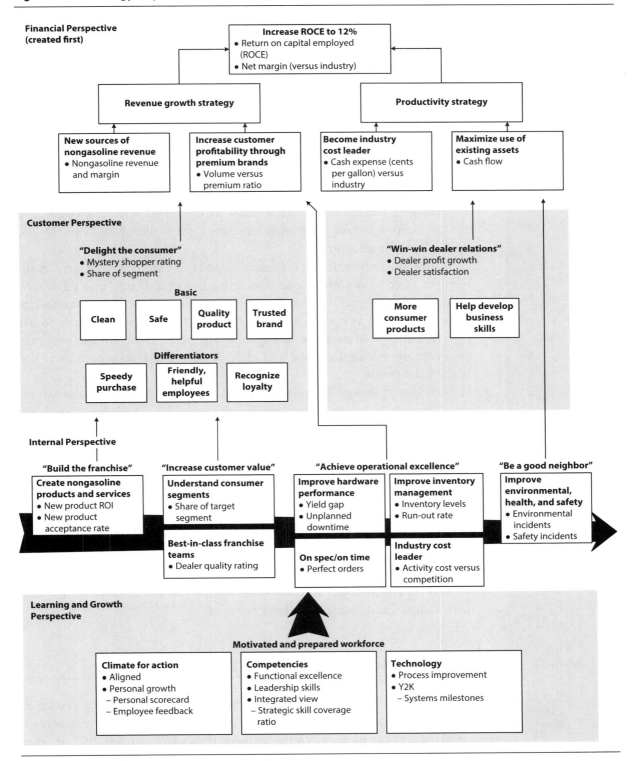

are simultaneously working to improve corporate goals through their diligence. In the Mobil example in Figure 1C-20, when truck drivers delivered gasoline to stations, they started reporting poor station conditions because they knew their own compensation was partly based on customer perceptions at the stations.

4. *Make strategy a continual process by linking strategy to budgeting, using analytical automation, holding strategy meetings, and implementing strategic learning.* Strategy is often neglected in favor of tactical decisions, such as setting a budget, so the BSC uses a double-loop process. For example, two budgets are created— a strategic budget and an operational budget—thus protecting the long-term objectives from suboptimization in the short term. Regular strategy meetings organized around the BSC allow input from a broader group of managers while keeping the meeting focused. Instead of talking about variances or other specifics, managers will use their BSCs to measure their own performance and will use the meeting to talk about what has gone right or wrong and what should be continued or discontinued.

    Automated analytical tools found in today's enterprise resource management systems can provide feedback to a broad audience, and a BSC can include such analysis. The firm must teach employees how to learn and adapt the strategy, such as by providing internal brochures explaining how to use a particular type of measure in a specific business context, or the firm may have employees use the cause-and-effect linkages in a scorecard and then analyze the results.

5. *Mobilize change through executive leadership using mobilization, governance processes, and a strategic management system.* Active executive involvement involves a focus on mobilization and momentum rather than on the metrics in the BSC itself. Governance processes involve how to manage the process once it has begun, using team-based approaches that break up old power structures and focus on executing strategy. In the final phase of implementing the BSC, governance becomes a strategic management system that incorporates the new methods and values into the new business culture. Governance processes reinforce positive changes, such as by determining when and how to link the executive level and other levels of the firm to the BSC. This last phase is dangerous, since the desire for stability can make future changes more difficult. However, this tendency toward setting standards is universal in organizations and so should be expected, embraced for a time, and then evaluated and changed as strategy evolves.

Performance Measures and Reporting Mechanisms

Management control systems, such as the BSC, aid in communicating and coordinating an organization's goals. If carefully designed and properly implemented, these systems also can motivate employee behavior. Implementing a BSC or other strategic mechanism requires developing a performance measurement system that supports the achievement of strategic goals and prevents dysfunctional behaviors that are not aligned with those goals. A well-designed management control system will measure and report both financial and nonfinancial performance measures.

Good performance measures must relate to the organization's goals. When performance measures are not aligned with these goals, they may induce suboptimal behavior. It is often said that "You get what you reward." Hence, when performance measures are not linked to organizational goals, employees receive a mixed message about what management wants.

Performance measures need to be reasonably objective and easy to measure. Overly complex performance measurement systems are not successful in practice. Employees should understand what is being measured, how the measurement system works, and how to relate the effects of their actions to those measures. This knowledge will help employees align their actions with the organization's goals.

Performance measures must also be applied uniformly. Inconsistent or irregular application of these measures reduces employees' morale and motivation.

While traditional performance measurement systems focus on financial measures, such as profits and cost variances, the emphasis is shifting toward the use of nonfinancial measures, such as those obtained from a BSC. Focusing on nonfinancial measures improves operational control. Moreover, such measures are more directly linked to the performance of lower-level employees.

Finally, the firm must consider the cost of collecting and analyzing data before implementing a performance measurement system. An expensive performance measurement system may report very accurate results, but the additional costs may not be justified. Hence, the performance measurement system is a trade-off between accuracy and cost.

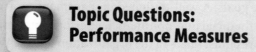

Topic Questions: Performance Measures

Directions: Answer each question in the space provided. Correct answers and explanations appear after the topic questions.

1. On a balanced scorecard, each of the following is an example of the customer perspective measure except:

   ☐ **a.** economic value-added.

   ☐ **b.** customer retention.

   ☐ **c.** time taken to fulfill orders.

   ☐ **d.** number of customer complaints.

2. A company has an 8% required rate of return. It is evaluating the following four mutually exclusive projects as possible investments.

	Estimated Operating Income	Assets
Project A	$1,250,000	$5,000,000
Project B	1,500,000	7,500,000
Project C	850,000	1,500,000
Project D	750,000	10,000,000

Using the residual income method, which one of the four projects should the company accept?

   ☐ **a.** Project A.

   ☐ **b.** Project B.

   ☐ **c.** Project C.

   ☐ **d.** Project D.

3. A company is considering three independent projects. Projected financial information is shown below.

	Riddler	Joker	Penguin
Sales	$5,000,000	$ 7,000,000	$10,000,000
Contribution margin	1,440,000	1,700,000	3,500,000
Operating income	1,000,000	1,650,000	2,520,000
Investment	9,000,000	10,000,000	14,000,000

The company's minimum rate of return for accepting projects is 15% and the total investment for new projects is a maximum of $20,000,000. The company's goal is to maximize its return on investment. Which project(s) should be accepted if the company uses return on investment to measure investment projects?

☐ **a.** Riddler only.

☐ **b.** Joker only.

☐ **c.** Joker and Penguin only.

☐ **d.** Penguin only.

Topic Question Answers:
Performance Measures

1. On a balanced scorecard, each of the following is an example of the customer perspective measure except:

   ☑ **a.** economic value-added.

   ☐ **b.** customer retention.

   ☐ **c.** time taken to fulfill orders.

   ☐ **d.** number of customer complaints.

   The customer perspective is the performance related to targeted customer and market segments. Economic value-added fits under the financial perspective.

2. A company has an 8% required rate of return. It is evaluating the following four mutually exclusive projects as possible investments.

	Estimated Operating Income	Assets
Project A	$1,250,000	$5,000,000
Project B	1,500,000	7,500,000
Project C	850,000	1,500,000
Project D	750,000	10,000,000

   Using the residual income method, which one of the four projects should the company accept?

   ☐ **a.** Project A.

   ☑ **b.** Project B.

   ☐ **c.** Project C.

   ☐ **d.** Project D.

   The residual income method measures the amount of estimated income minus the imputed investment cost and it is calculated as the Operating Income of a Business Unit − (Assets of the Business Unit × Required Rate of Return). The residual income for each of these projects is calculated as follows:

   Project A: $850,000 ($1,250,000 − ($5,000,000 × 8%))
   Project B: $900,000 ($1,500,000 − ($7,500,000 × 8%))
   Project C: $730,000 ($850,000 − ($1,500,000 × 8%))
   Project D: -$50,000 ($750,000 − ($10,000,000 × 8%))

   Because Project B has the largest residual income, the company should accept Project B.

3. A company is considering three independent projects. Projected financial information is shown below.

	Riddler	Joker	Penguin
Sales	$5,000,000	$ 7,000,000	$10,000,000
Contribution margin	1,440,000	1,700,000	3,500,000
Operating income	1,000,000	1,650,000	2,520,000
Investment	9,000,000	10,000,000	14,000,000

The company's minimum rate of return for accepting projects is 15% and the total investment for new projects is a maximum of $20,000,000. The company's goal is to maximize its return on investment. Which project(s) should be accepted if the company uses return on investment to measure investment projects?

- ☐ **a.** Riddler only.
- ☐ **b.** Joker only.
- ☐ **c.** Joker and Penguin only.
- ☑ **d.** Penguin only.

The Return on Investment (ROI) method is used to measure a business unit or project's profitability based on the investment required to obtain the associated income. The formula to calculate ROI is Income of the Business Unit or Project ÷ Assets of the Business Unit or Assets associated with the Project. The ROI for each individual project is calculated as follows:

Riddler: 11.1% ($1,000,000 ÷ $9,000,000)
Joker: 16.5% ($1,650,000 ÷ $10,000,000)
Penguin: 18.0% ($2,520,000 ÷ $14,000,000)

Joker and Penguin both have an ROI above the company's minimum rate of return. Because the company has a maximum total investment for new projects of $20,000,000, both projects cannot be accepted; therefore, the company should choose the project that has the largest ROI. This company should accept Penguin to maximize their return on investment and stay within the investment parameters provided.

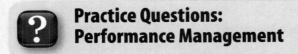

Practice Questions: Performance Management

Directions: This sampling of questions is designed to emulate actual exam questions. Read each question and write your response on another sheet of paper. See the "Answers to Section Practice Questions" section at the end of this book to assess your response. Validate or improve the answer you wrote. For a more robust selection of practice questions, access the **Online Test Bank** at www.wileycma.com.

Question 1C1-CQ16

Topic: Cost and Variance Measures

The following performance report was prepared for Dale Manufacturing for the month of April.

	Actual Results	Static Budget	Variance
Sales units	100,000	80,000	20,000 F
Sales dollars	$190,000	$160,000	$30,000 F
Variable costs	125,000	96,000	29,000 U
Fixed costs	45,000	40,000	5,000 U
Operating income	$20,000	$ 24,000	$ 4,000 U

Using a flexible budget, Dale's total sales-volume variance is:

☐ **a.** $4,000 unfavorable.

☐ **b.** $6,000 favorable.

☐ **c.** $16,000 favorable.

☐ **d.** $20,000 unfavorable.

Question 1C1-CQ17

Topic: Cost and Variance Measures

MinnOil performs oil changes and other minor maintenance services (e.g., tire pressure checks) for cars. The company advertises that all services are completed within 15 minutes for each service.

On a recent Saturday, 160 cars were serviced, resulting in the following labor variances: rate, $19 unfavorable; efficiency, $14 favorable. If MinnOil's standard labor rate is $7 per hour, determine the actual wage rate per hour and the actual hours worked.

		Wage Rate	Hours Worked
☐	a.	$6.55	42.00
☐	b.	$6.67	42.71
☐	c.	$7.45	42.00
☐	d.	$7.50	38.00

Question 1C1-CQ18

Topic: Cost and Variance Measures

Frisco Company recently purchased 108,000 units of raw material for $583,200. Three units of raw materials are budgeted for use in each unit of finished goods manufactured, and the raw material standard is set at $16.50 for each completed unit.

Frisco manufactured 32,700 finished units this period and used 99,200 units of raw material. If management is concerned about the timely reporting of variances in an effort to improve cost control and bottom-line performance, the materials purchase price variance should be reported as:

- ☐ a. $6,050 unfavorable.
- ☐ b. $9,920 favorable.
- ☐ c. $10,800 unfavorable.
- ☐ d. $10,800 favorable.

Question 1C1-CQ19

Topic: Cost and Variance Measures

Christopher Akers is the chief executive officer of SBL Contracting. Actual and budget information relating to the materials for a job include:

	Purchased and Used	Budget
Bricks — number of bundles	3,000	2,850
Bricks — cost per bundle	$7.90	$8.00

Which of the following is a **correct** statement regarding this job for SBL?

- ☐ **a.** The price variance was $285 favorable.
- ☐ **b.** The price variance was $300 favorable.
- ☐ **c.** The efficiency variance was $1,185 unfavorable.
- ☐ **d.** The flexible budget variance was $900 favorable.

Question 1C1-CQ20

Topic: Cost and Variance Measures

A company isolates its raw material price variance in order to provide the earliest possible information to the manager responsible for the variance. The budgeted amount of material usage for the year was computed as:

150,000 Units of Finished Goods × 3 Pounds/Unit × $2.00/Pound = $900,000

Actual results for the year were:

Finished goods produced	160,000 units
Raw materials purchased	500,000 pounds
Raw materials used	490,000 pounds
Cost per pound	$2.02

The raw material price variance for the year was:

- ☐ **a.** $9,600 unfavorable.
- ☐ **b.** $9,800 unfavorable.
- ☐ **c.** $10,000 unfavorable.
- ☐ **d.** $20,000 unfavorable.

Question 1C1-CQ21

Topic: Cost and Variance Measures

At the beginning of the year, Douglas Company prepared this monthly budget for direct materials:

Units produced and sold	10,000	15,000
Direct material cost	$15,000	$22,500

At the end of the month, the company's records showed that 12,000 units were produced and sold, and $20,000 was spent for direct materials. The variance for direct materials is:

- ☐ **a.** $2,000 favorable.
- ☐ **b.** $2,000 unfavorable.
- ☐ **c.** $5,000 favorable.
- ☐ **d.** $5,000 unfavorable.

Question 1C1-CQ22

Topic: Cost and Variance Measures

Cordell Company uses a standard cost system. Cordell budgeted $600,000 of fixed manufacturing overhead costs for 200,000 units of production for this year. During the year, the firm actually produced 190,000 units and incurred $595,000 of fixed manufacturing overhead. The production volume variance for the year was:

- ☐ **a.** $5,000 unfavorable.
- ☐ **b.** $10,000 unfavorable.
- ☐ **c.** $25,000 unfavorable.
- ☐ **d.** $30,000 unfavorable.

Question 1C1-CQ23

Topic: Cost and Variance Measures

Harper Company's performance report indicated this information for the past month:

Actual total overhead	$1,600,000
Budgeted fixed overhead	$1,500,000
Applied fixed overhead at $3 per labor hour	$1,200,000
Applied variable overhead at $.50 per labor hour	$200,000
Actual labor hours	430,000

Harper's total overhead spending variance for the month was:

- ☐ **a.** $100,000 favorable.
- ☐ **b.** $115,000 favorable.
- ☐ **c.** $185,000 unfavorable.
- ☐ **d.** $200,000 unfavorable.

Question 1C1-CQ24

Topic: Cost and Variance Measures

The JoyT Company manufactures Maxi Dolls for sale in toy stores. In planning for this year, JoyT estimated variable factory overhead of $600,000 and fixed factory overhead of $400,000. JoyT uses a standard costing system, and factory overhead is allocated to units produced using standard direct labor hours. The denominator level of activity budgeted for this year was 10,000 direct labor hours, and JoyT used 10,300 actual direct labor hours.

Based on the output for this year, 9,900 standard direct labor hours should have been used. Actual variable factory overhead was $596,000, and actual fixed factory overhead was $410,000 for the year. Based on this information, the variable overhead spending variance for JoyT for this year was:

- ☐ **a.** $24,000 unfavorable.
- ☐ **b.** $2,000 unfavorable.
- ☐ **c.** $4,000 favorable.
- ☐ **d.** $22,000 favorable.

Question 1C1-CQ25
Topic: Cost and Variance Measures

Johnson Inc. has established per-unit standards for material and labor for its production department based on 900 units of normal production capacity as shown:

3 pounds of direct materials @ $4 per pound	$12
1 direct labor hour @ $15 per hour	15
Standard cost per unit	$27

During the year, 1,000 units were produced. The accounting department has charged the production department supervisor with the following unfavorable variances:

Material Quantity Variance			Material Price Variance	
Actual usage	3,300 pounds		Actual cost	$4,200
Standard usage	3,000 pounds		Standard cost	4,000
Unfavorable	300 pounds		Unfavorable	$200

Bob Sterling, the production supervisor, has received a memo from his boss stating that he did not meet the established standards for material prices and quantity and that corrective action should be taken. Sterling is very unhappy about the situation and is preparing to reply to the memorandum explaining the reasons for his dissatisfaction.

All of the following are valid reasons for Sterling's dissatisfaction **except**:

- ☐ **a.** The material price variance is the responsibility of the purchasing department.
- ☐ **b.** The cause of the unfavorable material usage variance was the acquisition of substandard material.
- ☐ **c.** The standards have not been adjusted to the engineering changes.
- ☐ **d.** The variance calculations fail to reflect that actual production exceeded normal production capacity.

Question 1C3-AT35

Topic: Cost and Variance Measures

Teaneck Inc. sells two products, Product E and Product F, and had these data for last month:

	Product E		Product F	
	Budget	Actual	Budget	Actual
Unit sales	5,500	6,000	4,500	6,000
Unit contribution margin (CM)	$4.50	$4.80	$10.00	$10.50

The company's sales mix variance is:

- ☐ **a.** $3,300 favorable.
- ☐ **b.** $3,420 favorable.
- ☐ **c.** $17,250 favorable.
- ☐ **d.** $18,150 favorable.

Question 1C2-CQ17

Topic: Responsibility Centers and Reporting Segments

Manhattan Corporation has several divisions that operate as decentralized profit centers. At the present time, the Fabrication Division has excess capacity of 5,000 units with respect to the UT-371 circuit board, a popular item in many digital applications. Information about the circuit board includes:

Market price	$48
Variable selling/distribution costs on external sales	$5
Variable manufacturing cost	$21
Fixed manufacturing cost	$10

Manhattan's Electronic Assembly Division wants either to purchase 4,500 circuit boards internally or to buy them externally for $46 each. The Electronic Assembly Division's management feels that if the first alternative is pursued, a price concession is justified, given that both divisions are part of the same firm. To optimize the overall goals of Manhattan, the minimum price to be charged for the board from the Fabrication Division to the Electronic Assembly Division should be:

- ☐ **a.** $21.
- ☐ **b.** $26.
- ☐ **c.** $31.
- ☐ **d.** $46.

Question 1C3-CQ12

Topic: Performance Measures

Performance results for four geographic divisions of a manufacturing company include:

Division	Target Return on Investment	Actual Return on Investment	Return on Sales
A	18%	18.1%	8%
B	16%	20.0%	8%
C	14%	15.8%	6%
D	12%	11.0%	9%

The division with the **best** performance is:

- ☐ **a.** Division A
- ☐ **b.** Division B
- ☐ **c.** Division C
- ☐ **d.** Division D

Question 1C3-CQ13

Topic: Performance Measures

KHD Industries is a multidivisional firm that evaluates its managers based on the return on investment (ROI) earned by its divisions. The evaluation and compensation plans use a targeted ROI of 15% (equal to the cost of capital), and managers receive a bonus of 5% of basic compensation for every one percentage point that the division's ROI exceeds 15%.

Dale Evans, manager of the Consumer Products Division, has made a forecast of the division's operations and finances for next year that indicates the ROI would be 24%. In addition, new short-term programs were identified by the Consumer Products Division and evaluated by the finance staff, as shown.

Program	Projected ROI
A	13%
B	19%
C	22%
D	31%

Assuming no restrictions on expenditures, what is the optimal mix of new programs that would add value to KHD Industries?

- ☐ **a.** A, B, C, and D
- ☐ **b.** B, C, and D only
- ☐ **c.** C and D only
- ☐ **d.** D only

Question 1C1-AT03

Topic: Cost and Variance Measures

Franklin Products has an estimated practical capacity of 90,000 machine hours, and each unit requires two machine hours. The following data apply to a recent accounting period:

Actual variable overhead	$240,000
Actual fixed overhead	$442,000
Actual machine hours worked	88,000
Actual finished units produced	42,000
Budgeted variable overhead at 90,000 machine hours	$200,000
Budgeted fixed overhead	$450,000

Of the following factors, the production volume variance is **most** likely to have been caused by:

- ☐ **a.** acceptance of an unexpected sales order.
- ☐ **b.** a wage hike granted to a production supervisor.
- ☐ **c.** a newly imposed initiative to reduce finished goods inventory levels.
- ☐ **d.** temporary employment of workers with lower skill levels than originally anticipated.

Question 1C3-AT19

Topic: Performance Measures

Which one of the following **best** identifies a profit center?

- ☐ **a.** A new car sales division for a large local auto agency
- ☐ **b.** The information technology department of a large consumer products company
- ☐ **c.** A large toy company
- ☐ **d.** The production operations department of a small job-order machine shop company

Question 1C3-AT21

Topic: Performance Measures

The balanced scorecard provides an action plan for achieving competitive success by focusing management attention on key performance indicators. Which one of the following is **not** one of the key performance indicators commonly found in the balanced scorecard?

- ☐ **a.** Financial performance measures
- ☐ **b.** Internal business processes
- ☐ **c.** Competitor business strategies
- ☐ **d.** Employee innovation and learning

 To further assess your understanding of the concepts and calculations covered in Part 1, Section C: Performance Management, practice with the **Online Test Bank** for this section. REMINDER: See the "Answers to Section Practice Questions" section at the end of this book.

Cost Management (15%)

Cost management requires the ability to measure, accumulate, and assign all of the costs incurred in running a business enterprise. A costing system, such as job costing and process costing, is integral to accumulating the costs in the inventory accounts, determining the cost of goods manufactured, and ultimately determining the cost of goods sold. These may be supplemented by activity-based costing and life cycle costing. The true management of costs is much more involved as the actual costs are compared to forecasted amounts to determine operational efficiencies and evaluate performance.

The managers responsible for the costs of running the business balance providing customer value with the cost of resources used to accomplish this. This section will look to define the many cost terms that are used. In addition, the supply chain management and the methods used to contain costs will be reviewed.

Measurement Concepts

MEASUREMENT CONCEPTS MAKE USE OF cost behavior information to analyze the effect that changes in costs will have on the firm's profitability. Defining and classifying costs is essential to understanding how they can be used to measure performance.

This topic discusses the types and classifications of costs, including actual, normal, and standard costing; fixed, variable, and step costs; cost drivers; absorption and variable costing; and joint and by-product costing.

READ the Learning Outcome Statements (LOS) for this topic as found in Appendix A and then study the concepts and calculations presented here to be sure you understand the content you could be tested on in the CMA exam.

Actual, Normal, and Standard Costing

LOS
§1.D.1.e

There are three costing methods used to record the costs of production into the inventory accounts. Two of them are the "actual" and the "normal" methods. The third is the "standard" method can be used to record costs; however, this method is most often used for comparison to actual results to evaluate performance. The standard method was described in detail in Section C, Topic 1: Cost and Variance Measures.

The **actual costing method** uses the actual direct cost rate, multiplied by the actual quantity, for both direct materials and direct labor to record the actual cost of production. In addition, indirect costs are also recorded in the inventory accounts by multiplying the actual variable and fixed overhead rates by the actual quantity of the allocation base. This method works well for the direct costs, but it does not work well for the indirect costs.

For this reason, the **normal costing method** is used. The direct material and direct labor costs are calculated the same as in the actual costing method. However, the indirect variable overhead and fixed overhead will be calculated using a budgeted, or predetermined, overhead rate and will be multiplied by the actual quantity of the allocation base.

Actual Overhead Rates

The advantage of using actual overhead rates is the apparent precision obtained by doing so. Actual overhead costs are accumulated for the period into one or more overhead pools. The amounts of the activity base(s) that will be used to apply the overhead to jobs are also accumulated. The dollars in each pool are divided by the related allocation or activity base amount to determine the actual rate. Then that rate is multiplied by the activity base amount associated with each job in order to apply that overhead pool across all of the jobs. This process is then repeated for each overhead pool. When this process is completed, the amount of overhead applied to the jobs will be equal to the amount of overhead incurred.

The downside of this approach is a lack of timeliness. If "period" as used above means one year, all vital reports about cost control performance would be received only annually. This length of time, for all practical purposes, reduces the value of the information to zero. If "period" as used above means one month, there is still a loss of value due to lack of timeliness. However, another significant problem has been created. Overhead rates are likely to change from month to month due to seasonality or timing in the incurrence of some overhead costs and/or due to seasonality or timing in the levels of activity.

Normal Overhead Rates

Consequently, most companies will use *normal* costing, which uses predetermined overhead rates. These rates are determined as an integral part of the annual planning process. Therefore, the rates are available for use from the first day of implementation of the annual budget and throughout the year.

$$\text{Predetermined Factory Overhead Rate} = \frac{\text{Budgeted Factory Overhead Costs}}{\text{Estimated Cost Driver Activity Level}}$$

The only drawback to this approach is that the amount of overhead applied to all of the jobs will be different from the amount of overhead actually incurred. If the amount of overhead applied is greater than the overhead incurred, it is called *overapplied* overhead. There would be a net credit balance when adding the Factory Overhead Account (actual) balance to the Factory Overhead Applied account balance. The result is an increase in income from what would otherwise be reported. If the overhead applied is less than the overhead incurred, it is called *underapplied* overhead. Underapplied overhead has a net debit balance and results in a decrease to income from what would otherwise be reported.

Adjustments for Over-/Underapplied Overhead

How the over-/underapplied overhead is disposed of is based on the materiality of the dollar amount and management philosophy. It should be noted that the same issue applies to variances in a standard cost system. In a pure standard cost system, the sum of 1) the variable overhead spending variance, 2) the variable overhead efficiency variance, 3) the fixed overhead spending variance, and 4) the production volume variance will equal the total over-/underapplied overhead. In addition, there are direct labor and direct materials variances. Their disposition has the same set of concerns.

For example, assume that $1,530,000 of overhead was incurred and $1,490,000 of overhead was applied. This results in $40,000 of underapplied overhead that management considers to be immaterial. Cost of goods sold (COGS) would be increased by $40,000. See Figure 1D-1 for the associated journal entry. This journal entry brings to zero both the Factory Overhead Applied and Factory Overhead Incurred accounts as required by GAAP. Note that this amount cannot be associated with a specific product or customer.

Figure 1D-1 Journal Entry to Record Disposition of Underapplied Overhead

	COGS Method	
Cost of Goods Sold	$40,000	
Factory Overhead Applied	$1,490,000	
Factory Overhead Incurred		$1,530,000
To record the disposition of underapplied overhead.		

Now let's assume that the difference between overhead incurred and overhead applied is $100,000 and that this amount is considered to be material. Now an argument can be made that a more precise disposition is needed. The argument could be made that the majority of the variance should be allocated to COGS, but that some should also be allocated to finished goods and work-in-process inventories.

The next step is to calculate the adjustment needed to COGS, finished goods inventory, and work-in-process inventory. The amount to be adjusted is in proportion to the relative amounts of overhead in each of the three accounts. Let us assume that the overhead amount in each of the three accounts at year-end is:

Work-in-Process	$100,000	5%	$5,000
Finished Goods	$400,000	20%	$20,000
Cost of Goods Sold	$1,500,000	75%	$75,000
Total	$2,000,000	100%	$100,000

The journal entry to record the disposition is shown in Figure 1D-2:

Figure 1D-2 Journal Entry to Record Disposition of Underapplied Overhead

	Proration Method	
Factory Overhead Applied	$1,430,000	
Cost of Goods Sold	$75,000	
Finished Goods Inventory	$20,000	
Work-in-Process Inventory	$5,000	
Factory Overhead Incurred		$1,530,000

As seen in the first disposition example, these amounts are not directly associated with a specific product or customer.

Cost Behavior and Cost Objects

Figure 1D-3 Total Cost and the Effect of Capacity Limits

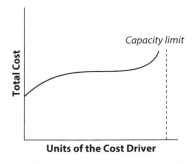

Figure 1D-3 is what economists tell us the total cost curve usually looks like. Notice the steep sections of the curve at the lowest and the highest levels of activity. The highest levels of activity show the effect of diminishing returns as capacity limits are approached. There is, however, a wide range of activity at which a straight line is a very good approximation of that portion of the curve. That is the portion of the curve known as the relevant range. The **relevant range** is the range of activity in which the company plans to operate.

A fixed cost remains constant in total over the relevant range and is expressed in dollars for the full time period. This is in contrast to variable costs, which vary in total in proportion to activity, volume, or some other cost driver. Variable costs are usually expressed in dollars per unit of activity. It is important to note that whenever fixed costs are expressed in dollars per unit, the information is incomplete. This value is valid at only one level of activity. The exam taker should immediately determine the one level of activity for which that value is valid and convert it into a total fixed cost dollar amount by multiplying the cost per unit by the related quantity at the level of activity.

For example: A manufacturing plant has fixed costs, such as rent and management salaries, and variable costs, such as production labor and material costs. The fixed costs will remain constant in total regardless of whether the plant has zero output or is at full production; however, on a per-unit basis, the fixed costs will change inversely to production changes. Variable costs, however, will not be incurred until production starts. Then the total variable costs will increase as production increases or decrease as production decreases. Again, it is important to note that the total variable costs are what change with production ups and downs; the variable costs on a per-unit basis remain constant over the relevant range.

Variable Costs

A **variable cost** includes changes in total for a cost object in proportion to each change in the quantity of a cost driver over a relevant range. Variable cost measured on a per-unit basis remains constant over a relevant range (e.g., $5/unit within a relevant range of 1 to 5,000 units). Direct materials and direct labor are both variable costs because more materials and labor are needed as more units of a product are produced. Some indirect costs are also variable costs, such as sealants and adhesives. These costs are difficult to trace to a cost object, but they must be accounted for as part of the product cost. In total, their usage will go up as production goes up.

Fixed Costs

Fixed costs are the portion of total costs that do not change when the quantity of a cost driver changes over a relevant range and duration. The duration is important because fixed costs may be constant one year and at a constant but higher level the next year. Fixed cost measured on a per-unit basis will decrease as quantities increase: At 100 units, a $1,000 fixed cost is $10/unit, but at 1,000 units, it is only $1/unit.

Fixed costs are also classified as discretionary or committed:

- **Discretionary costs**, which are also known as managed or budgeted fixed costs, can be included or excluded from the budget at the discretion of the managers. Examples of discretionary costs include advertising, training, or internships, as well as indirect manufacturing labor and selling and administrative labor.

- **Committed costs** are those costs that cannot be omitted due to strategic or operational priorities in the short run. An example is depreciation on equipment previously purchased. Committed fixed costs tend to be facilities related and result from prior capacity-related decisions.

Fixed costs include many indirect costs, such as depreciation, property taxes, employees paid on salary, insurance, and lease costs. These costs usually are fixed because regardless of the level of output within the relevant range, these costs will remain the same.

Figure 1D-4 Fixed and Variable Costs

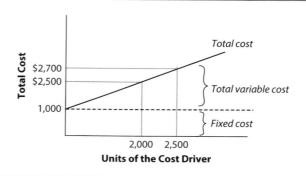

Figure 1D-4 shows fixed, variable, and total costs over a relevant range. While this "curve" does not look like the curve in Figure 1D-3, it does provide a very good approximation of it within the relevant range.

For a given output level, the next formula holds true:

 Total Cost/Unit for a Given Output Level = Fixed Cost/Unit + Variable Cost/Unit

Total cost per unit will decline as output increases because the fixed costs are being allocated over greater quantities.

Step Costs

Step costs are fixed costs with very narrow relevant ranges. For example, a maintenance employee might be added for each 2,000 hours of direct labor per month. A step cost function might look like that illustrated in Figure 1D-5. A step cost may be approximated as a variable cost if there are many steps and the cost remains the same over narrow ranges of the level of activity in each relevant range. It is a fixed cost if there are few steps and the cost remains the same over wide ranges of the level of activity in each relevant range. This cost identification would be done in order to be able to prepare an income statement in a contribution format.

Figure 1D-5 Example of Step Cost

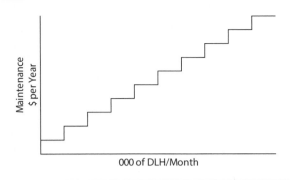

Total Cost and Mixed Cost

Total costs are all the fixed and variable costs for a cost object. Total costs are also called **mixed costs** when they include both fixed and variable components. Costs may also be classified as *product costs* or *period costs*. Costs required for manufacturing are product costs and must first be recorded in inventory then tracked through work-in-process to finished goods and then to cost of goods sold. SG&A expenses are period costs and are expensed in the period incurred.

Direct costs as well as indirect costs can also be fixed or variable. The only requirement to be a direct cost is that it can be traced directly to the cost object. Therefore, a fixed cost will be a direct cost if it can be traced directly to the cost object.

Capacity is based on the constraints or bottlenecks that keep a system from expanding in output or some other measure. Manufacturing capacity can be increased by adding manufacturing plants, employees, or equipment. Capacity relates to the relevant range because the capacity limits often are reached at the upper limit of the relevant range. Furthermore, as capacity limits are approached, operations lose efficiency and increase in cost. This leads to the need to define a company's **practical capacity**. This is the highest output level a resource, such as a plant, can achieve without increasing its costs significantly. When output exceeds the practical capacity, marginal costs begin to exceed marginal benefits. Practical capacity also takes into account normal operating conditions, such as the average number of errors or breakdowns, holidays and vacation time, and other real-world factors.

When such real-world factors are omitted, capacity is defined as **theoretical capacity**, or the upper limit of output assuming that nothing goes wrong, everything operates at full speed, and no holidays or other scheduling conflicts are included. Theoretical capacity is an ideal.

Capacity decisions made in the past generally will determine a company's present fixed costs. Fixed costs related to capacity choices include everything from the amount of space and resources devoted to each business unit and the size and cost

LOS
§1.D.1.d

of plants, to the amount of depreciation. These fixed costs are generally noncontrollable by division managers, who nevertheless feel the effect of these costs. If too much capacity is created, there will be opportunity costs and high fixed costs. If too little capacity is created, companies face other costs, such as overtime, lost sales, and higher wear and tear on facilities. Tracking the cost of excess capacity separately from the overall cost of an item can help show the cost of underutilized assets.

For example: Assume a plant's budgeted fixed overhead is $500,000, overhead is applied based on the units produced, and the plant has a practical capacity level of 5,000 units per period. The overhead would be applied at $100/unit. If the plant budgeted only 4,000 units at $100/unit, $400,000 would be allocated to production and the remaining $100,000 would be treated as a separate period expense; the cost of having excess capacity. It is important to match the manager's incentives to the plant's practical capacity so that any decisions made to increase output can be weighed against the costs of increasing that output, holding additional inventory, and the like.

Although the prior definitions of capacity hinged on output, when capacity is defined by the expected demand for output or budgeted demand, it is called capacity utilization. **Normal capacity utilization** is a level of capacity utilization that will meet the average customer demand over a period, including the seasonal and cyclical variations or trends. Normal capacity utilization is a long-term tool that often is used over a period of several years. **Master budget capacity utilization** is normal capacity utilization for the current budget period, that is usually one year. It is important to use the normal capacity utilization for long-term planning and the master budget capacity utilization for shorter-term planning. If not done this way, the end costs can be inaccurate. Each of these capacity levels can be used to allocate costs, but each will result in a different amount.

For example: In a plant with $500,000 in budgeted fixed overhead where the **theoretical** capacity is 8,000 units/period, the **practical** capacity is 5,000 units/period, the **normal** capacity utilization is 4,500 units/period, and the **master budget** capacity is 4,000 units/period, the budgeted fixed cost per unit would be $62.50, $100, $111, and $125, respectively. The best choice of capacity is therefore the key to cost analysis, management incentives, and performance evaluation decisions. All of these capacities, except for the master budget capacity, will result in the need to budget for anticipated over-/underapplied overhead if they are used to determine the overhead rates.

Cost Drivers

Firms manage their costs by determining how cost drivers affect a particular cost object. Performing cost analyses and developing an understanding of the firm's value chain are helpful in the selection of the cost drivers to be used. There are four types of cost drivers:

1. **Activity-based cost drivers** focus on operations that involve manufacturing or service activity, such as machine setup, machine use, or labor hours.

2. **Volume-based cost drivers** focus on output and involves aggregate measures such as units produced.
3. **Structural cost drivers** focus on company strategy and involves long-term plans for the scale, complexity, amount of experience in an area, or level of technical expertise.
4. **Executional cost drivers** focus on short-term operations and involves reducing costs through attention to workforce commitment and involvement, production design, and supplier relationships.

1. Activity-Based Cost Drivers

Firms use an activity analysis to determine a detailed description of each type of activity. These descriptions form the basis for the activity-based cost drivers. The intent is to determine how changing the steps in an activity will change the overall cost of the operation. The cost of each activity is determined and then used to determine the overall cost of a cost object. This detailed breakdown can help firms identify which activities add value for customers and which do not. When an activity costs more than is expected, the activity-based cost drivers will highlight this discrepancy.

For example, Figure 1D-6 illustrates a few of the activities and cost drivers for a retailer.

Figure 1D-6 Retailer Activities and Cost Drivers

Activity	Cost Driver
Accepting cash	Number of cash transactions
Processing of credit card	Number of credit transactions
Payment of credit card fee	Dollar size of transactions
Close-out and supervisor review of clerk	Number of close-outs
Consolidation and deposit of receipts	Number of deposits
Bank account reconciliation	Number of accounts
Updating of customer account balances via computer	Number of accounts updated
Investigation of unusual transactions	Number of transactions investigated
Processing of returns	Number of returns
Maintenance of computer equipment	Number of computer terminals
Training	Number of stores
Mailing of customer statements	Number of customer accounts

2. Volume-Based Cost Drivers

Volume-based cost drivers are activities that can be based on output volume.

Factors such as learning curves and efficient use of resources will cause costs to increase more slowly as production increases. This is called increasing marginal productivity, because the increasing output will use the inputs more efficiently.

At a certain level, the total costs will level off, and a rise in volume will have a proportional rise in cost within the relevant range. This will occur at the point at which the capacity of the persons or equipment will reach their limit. As the volume increases toward that limit, some costs will rise dramatically because of increased need for repairs, overtime, and other similar factors. This is called the law of diminishing marginal capacity. Estimating costs across the entire range of productivity is difficult and the reason why the relevant range is an important element of cost drivers.

Volume-based cost drivers ignore the differences in activities for different products, based on a product's complexity. For this reason, it is not a useful tool for management to make decisions, plans, and control.

3. Structural Cost Drivers

Structural cost drivers are long-term cost drivers based on the overall strategy of the company. The information from the use of this type of cost driver aids management to make plans and decisions that will have long-term effects on the company's costs. In addition, structural cost drivers can help a company develop competitive advantages. There are four types of structural cost drivers: scale, experience level, technology, and complexity.

(1) Scale

The scale of an investment project or the speed at which a company grows affects all of the costs to be incurred by the company. Deciding how many stores to open, how many employees to hire, or how much capital to devote to a project will affect costs directly.

(2) Experience Level

The experience level of the company for a particular strategic goal will affect the overall cost of achieving that goal. The areas in which the company has the most expertise will be the least costly to develop further. However, if the market no longer needs such expertise, developing a new area of expertise could be more cost effective in the long run.

(3) Technology

Changing the level of technology for a process can make that process more efficient and therefore less costly. The other benefit of investing in technology is that the products may be of higher quality. Therefore, the firm may be able to increase market share with a cheaper and better product.

(4) Complexity

The more complex a firm gets by virtue of the product lines and the more levels of hierarchy, the more it costs to sustain that complexity. Reducing complexity will reduce the costs of product development, production, distribution, and customer service. Strategic decisions related to complexity should be made to reduce overall complexity and cost. Conversely, a firm that has too few products or too small a staff may be missing out on market opportunities.

4. Executional Cost Drivers

Executional cost drivers are the short-term decisions that can be made to reduce operational costs. There are three types: workforce involvement, production process design, and supplier relationships.

(1) Workforce Involvement

The greater the commitment of the workforce, the lower the labor costs are in proportion to the amount of work that gets done. Many firms have been successful in improving quality and reducing labor costs by working to foster pride and commitment in the workplace through creative team building and an emphasis on consensus and employee input.

(2) Production Process Design

Analyzing and redesigning production processes and incorporating software applications to streamline workflow have been key factors in reducing production costs for many firms.

(3) Supplier Relationships

Close relationships with suppliers can reduce overall costs, especially inventory costs. With electronic data interchange (EDI) and similar applications, a firm can allow its supplier to view the company's inventory levels directly and automatically ship items as needed. This results in a more efficient production flow.

Absorption (Full) and Variable (Direct) Costing

Absorption costing, or full costing, is an inventory costing system that includes both variable and fixed manufacturing costs. Under absorption costing, inventory absorbs all costs of manufacturing. **Variable costing,** or direct costing, is an inventory costing method that includes only the variable manufacturing costs in the inventory costs and excludes fixed manufacturing costs. Variable costing expenses fixed manufacturing costs in the period in which the costs are incurred. Both methods expense all nonmanufacturing costs in the period in which they occur. Therefore, these two methods differ only in how they account for fixed manufacturing costs. This is illustrated in Figure 1D-7.

Figure 1D-7 Variable versus Absorption Costing

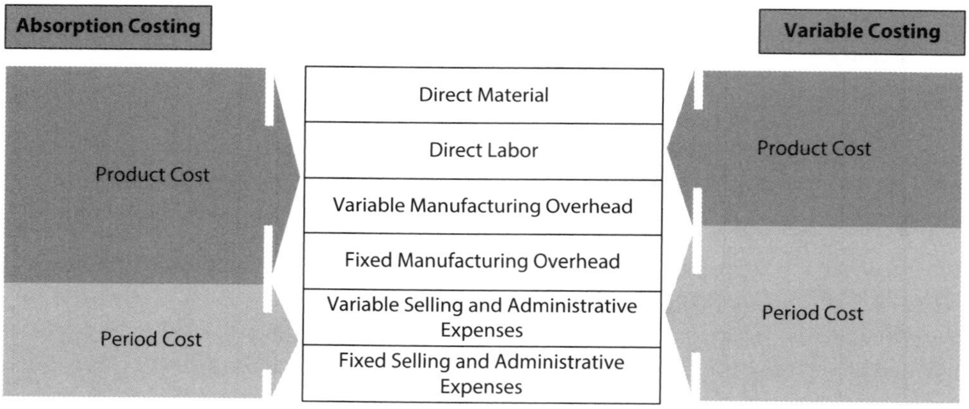

The difference between variable and absorption costing lies with the treatment of fixed manufacturing overhead. Absorption costing treats fixed manufacturing overhead as a product cost. Variable costing treats it as a period cost.

Looking carefully at this chart, the center column shows the six categories of costs that will appear in an income statement down to the operating income line. On the right is shown the treatment of each cost item in a variable costing income statement. On the left is shown the treatment of each cost item in an absorption costing income statement. As pointed out earlier, product costs are inventoried when incurred. Those costs flow from inventory to expense as cost of goods sold when the item is sold. Period costs, in contrast, are expensed as incurred. Only the treatment of the fixed manufacturing overhead differs between the two income statement formats. Fixed manufacturing overhead is expensed as incurred in variable costing. However, it is applied to inventory under absorption costing.

LOS §1.D.1.d

LOS §1.D.1.g

Income Statement Preparation Using Absorption and Variable Costing

Because variable costing and absorption costing have different objectives concerning the importance of the information presented on the income statement, each is usually presented in its own format. The variable costing method uses a contribution margin format that highlights the distinction between fixed and variable costs. The absorption method uses the gross margin format, which highlights the differences between manufacturing and nonmanufacturing costs. The variable manufacturing costs are accounted for in the same manner in both income statements. The absorption method is the format required by GAAP (generally accepted accounting principles) for external reporting and tax reporting.

When production does not equal sales, net income will differ between absorption and variable costing. If more units are produced than sold, absorption costing will have higher net income because the fixed costs are still in inventory. Variable costing will have lower net income because the fixed costs are not in inventory, but expensed. This means that when using absorption costing, fixed manufacturing

Figure 1D-8 Variable Costing versus Absorption Costing Example

Absorption Costing			Variable Costing		
Revenues:			**Revenues:**		
$200 × 500 units		$100,000	$200 × 500 units		$100,000
Costs of goods sold			**Variable costs**		
Beginning inventory	$0		Beginning inventory	$0	
+ Variable manufacturing costs: $30 × 700	+21,000		+ Variable manufacturing costs: $30 × 700	+21,000	
+ Fixed manufacturing costs: $25 × 700	+17,500		= Cost of goods available for sale	21,000	
= Cost of goods available for sale	38,500		− Ending inventory: $30 × 200	− 6,000	
− Ending inventory: ($30 variable + $25 fixed) × 200	−11,000		= Variable cost of goods Sold	15,000	
= Cost of goods sold		−27,500	+ Variable marketing costs: $20 × 500	+10,000	
			= Total variable costs		−25,000
= Gross margin		72,500	= Contribution margin		75,000
Operating costs			**Fixed costs**		
Variable marketing costs: $20 × 500	10,000		Fixed manufacturing costs: $25 × 700	17,500	
+ Fixed marketing costs	+14,000		+ Fixed marketing costs	+14,000	
+/− Adjustment for operating cost variances	0		+/− Adjustment for fixed cost variances	0	
= Total operating costs		−24,000	= Total fixed costs		−31,500
= **Operating income**		**$48,500**	= **Operating income**		**$43,500**

costs in ending inventory are deferred to future periods; variable costing expenses the entire amount of the fixed costs in the period in which the inventory is created.

LOS §1.D.1.i

For example, Figure 1D-8 shows each type of costing method and each type of format.

The data used for both sides of the table are the same.

- Units made: 700
- Units sold: 500
- Selling price per unit: $200
- Variable manufacturing costs per unit: $30
- Variable selling (marketing) costs per unit: $20
- Fixed manufacturing costs per unit: $25 ($17,500 in total)
- Fixed selling (marketing) costs: $14,000

LOS §1.D.1.h

In summary, when inventory increases, the net income under absorption costing will always be greater than under variable costing by the amount of the fixed cost related to the change in inventory (200 units × $25 = $5,000 in Figure 1D-8).

The key point is that the reconcilliation factor (difference between variable costing operating income and absorption costing operating income) can be predicted by

Reconciliation Factor = (Ending Inventory Units − Beginning Inventory Units) × Fixed Overhead/Unit

When inventory decreases, net income under absorption costing will be less than under variable costing by the amount of the change in inventory fixed cost. However, as methods such as just-in-time production and other inventory reduction methods increase in their use, the differences between variable and absorption costing may grow less material because inventory levels are less significant. In fact, if a company has zero inventory at the beginning and end of each accounting period, there is no difference between the results of these two methods of costing.

The income statements in Figure 1D-8 are, of course, correct but not very informative. The information content can be improved in these ways:

- Show the budget alongside the actual results so the statement user's attention can be drawn to significant variances.
- Separate variances, to the extent possible, so the statement user can use management-by-exception principles to discern problem areas. In a pure standard cost system using absorption costing, this would include eight different variances, which are defined in Section C, Topic 1.
- Eliminate the calculation of beginning inventory plus costs incurred minus ending inventory and replace it with units sold times standard cost per unit.
- Provide a statement format that has all the advantages of variable costing *and* still produces the absorption costing operating income to be in compliance with GAAP.

LOS
§1.D.1.i

Figure 1D-9 shows an income statement that does all of the above, except for the comparison to budget, which is not available. This income statement is called a hybrid income statement. It combines a variable costing income statement that converts to an absorption costing result by taking advantage of the reconciliation factor shown in the previous key formula, to convert variable costing operating income into absorption costing operating income.

All members of the management team would focus on the information down to the variable costing operating income line. A few members of management (usually the chief executive and chief financial officers and investor relations personnel) would need to fully understand the change in fixed costs in inventory (reconciliation factor) in order to be able to interpret the company's results to the company's stakeholders.

Note that the amount of fixed costs in inventory was needed to arrive at the absorption costing operating income. This hybrid income statement does not

Figure 1D-9 Variable Costing versus Absorption Costing—Enhanced Format

Hybrid Costing		Absorption Costing	
Revenue	$100,000	Revenue	$100,000
Variable Cost of Goods Sold	$15,000	Standard Cost of Goods Sold	$27,500
Variable Marketing Costs	10,000		
Variances	0	Variances	0
Total Variable Costs	$25,000	Actual Cost of Goods Sold	$27,500
Contribution Margin	$75,000	Gross Profit	$72,500
Fixed Manufacturing Costs	$17,500	Variable Marketing Costs	$10,000
Fixed Marketing Costs	14,000	Fixed Marketing Costs	14,000
Total Fixed Costs	$31,500	Total Marketing Costs	$24,000
Operating Income—Var.	$43,500	Operating Income	**$48,500**
Chg. in Fixed Cost in Inventory	5,000		
Operating Income—Abs.	**$48,500**		

include the production volume variance. The assumption is that the actual and standard unit costs are the same, in order to keep the example focused on the differences between variable and absorption costing.

Benefits and Limitations of Absorption and Variable Costing

LOS §1.D.1.f

Absorption costing is the standard method because both the U. S. Internal Revenue Service (IRS) and GAAP require its use. However, absorption costing allows managers to manipulate operating income simply by increasing production. If bonuses or other incentives are tied to operating income, managers might increase inventory even if no additional demand exists. Managers might choose to produce items that absorb the highest fixed manufacturing costs instead of products that absorb less. To fix this and other improper management incentives, the company could switch to variable costing for internal reporting as suggested earlier, allow managers less latitude in selecting what to produce, or provide a disincentive for accumulating excess inventory.

Variable costing is very effective in supporting internal decision making and is required for cost-volume-profit analysis.

Joint Product and By-Product Costing

LOS §1.D.1.j

Joint products and by-products arise in industries that process one raw material into two or more products.

LOS
§1.D.1.a

LOS
§1.D.1.b

LOS
§1.D.1.k

Joint products are considered the main products and have significantly higher sales values than do the by-products.

Consider this example. The cheesemaking industry is all about the processing of raw milk to make curds and whey. Curds would be the joint product because they become cheese when pressed and cured. Whey was at one time an unsellable by-product that cheesemakers disposed of or paid to have it hauled away. Today the liquid whey is processed further into food additives. So, the whey was once a by-product that has now become a joint product.

The cost of the raw milk, the labor, and overhead that go into the first process are called joint costs. The question is: How should joint costs be assigned to the multiple products that are identified at the split-off point? Additional processing may take place after the separation of the curds and the whey. The costs incurred in those processes are called *separable costs*. They are assigned to the one product whose value they enhance. When a product goes through one or more separable processes, it is possible for the product to be sold at any one of the intermediate points as long as there is a market for it.

An example from the paper industry illustrates the various methods for assigning joint costs to the joint products. Wood pulp is the input into the paper-making process. Assume that the joint cost for the process is $8,000 per day; that would be the cost of the pulp, labor, power, depreciation, and other items of overhead. Assume that there are two products at the split off point: fine-grade paper and semi-finished paper. The expected output is 2,000 pounds of fine-grade paper, which can be sold for $2.00 per pound, and 4,000 pounds of semifinished paper, which can be sold for $1.50 per pound. However, the fine-grade paper can be processed further through a separate finishing operation. Now let us assume there is no loss of weight of usable product and this product will sell for $3.50 per pound. The additional finishing operation will incur costs of $2,000 per day. The following diagram demonstrates the paper example.

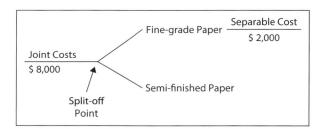

Market-Based Methods of Allocating Joint Costs to Joint Products

LOS
§1.D.1.l

There are several market-based methods used to assign costs to joint products. They are sales value at split-off, net realizable value, and constant gross profit percentage.

Sales Value at Split-off

This method can be used only when every product that goes through one or more separable processes can be sold in an intermediate market after the split-off point.

To apply this method, the sales value that would exist for each product at the split-off point is calculated.

Fine-grade paper	2,000 lb.	$2.00/lb.	$ 4,000	40%
Semifinished paper	4,000 lb.	$1.50/lb.	$ 6,000	60%
Total			$10,000	100%

Each product's sales value at split-off is calculated as a percentage of the total sales value at split-off. Note that these percentages must sum to 100%. Each product's percentage is multiplied by the total of the joint costs to determine the amount of joint cost to be assigned to that product. So 40% of the total joint costs of $8,000, or $3,200, would be assigned to fine-grade paper. The remaining 60%, or $4,800, would be assigned to the semifinished paper. A product's total cost is the sum of its joint costs and any additional separable cost. The total cost of the fine-grade paper would be $5,200 ($3,200 plus $2,000).

Net Realizable Value

The net realizable value (NRV) method of valuing joint products is not dependent on the existence of market values for intermediate products. Net realizable value is simply the end product sales value less any additional separable costs. Thus, the NRV for the fine-grade paper is its end product sales value of $7,000 (2,000 × $3.50) less the $2,000 of separable cost, or $5,000. The NRV for semifinished paper is its end product sales value of $6,000 that was used before. The allocation of joint costs to the two products uses the following percentages:

Fine-grade paper	$ 5,000	45.5%	$3,640
Semifinished paper	6,000	54.5%	4,360
Total	$11,000	100.0%	$8,000

Therefore, 45.5% of the joint costs of $8,000, or $3,640, is assigned to fine-grade paper and 54.5%, or $4,360, to semifinished paper.

Constant Gross Profit Percentage

As the name implies, this method simply forces each of the products to show the same gross profit percentage. The calculations are somewhat more complex than the two preceding methods. The total cost for the two products is the sum of the joint costs of $8,000 and the separable costs of $2,000 for a total of $10,000. The total end product sales are $13,000. The gross profit percentage is $3,000 divided by $13,000 for 23.1%. Therefore, the fine-grade paper needs to have a total production cost of $5,385 ($3,385 of joint cost and $2,000 of separable cost). The semifinished paper will have $4,615 of joint cost. Note that the total of the $5,385 and the $4,615 has to equal the total cost of $10,000.

Figure 1D-10 shows the results of these three cost allocation methods.

Figure 1D-10 Apparent Gross Profit Margin Based on Joint Cost Allocation Method

	Joint Cost		Sep. Cost	Total Cost		Revenue		Gross Profit %	
Method	Fine-Grade	Semi-Finished	Fine-Grade	Fine-Grade	Semi-Finished	Fine-Grade	Semi-Finished	Fine-Grade	Semi-Finished
Sales value at split-off	3,200	4,800	2,000	5,200	4,800	7,000	6,000	25.7%	20.0%
Net realizable value	3,640	4,360	2,000	5,640	4,360	7,000	6,000	19.4%	27.3%
Constant gross profit %	3,385	4,615	2,000	5,385	4,615	7,000	6,000	23.1%	23.1%

Physical Measure

The final method of allocating joint costs to joint products is the physical measure method. This method is not a market-based method. It simply measures the output at the split-off point in physical units. This means that all the units of measure must be the same. Frequently, the selected unit of measure is a measure of weight, such as pounds. Each joint product is allocated joint costs in proportion to its measure of physical output. Looking back at the weights of the joint products at the split-off point, they are 2,000 pounds of fine-grade paper and 4,000 pounds of semifinished paper, for a total of 6,000 pounds. This results in a 33%/67% allocation to the two paper products. Therefore, the total joint costs of $8,000 is allocated to fine-grade paper in the amount of $2,640 and to semifinished paper in the amount of $5,360.

The implication is that the semifinished paper will have $640 in gross profit, a small amount at 10.7%. Therefore, the three market-based methods appear to result in a more equitable allocation of joint costs.

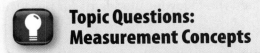

Topic Questions: Measurement Concepts

Directions: Answer each question in the space provided. Correct answers and explanations appear after the topic questions.

1. A dairy farm produces the following products jointly during the fiscal year for a total joint cost of €9,000,000.

Product	Kilograms
Milk	1,170,000
Butter	570,000
Yogurt	330,000
Cheese	930,000

Based on the information, which one of the following is most accurate regarding the allocation of the joint cost under the physical measure method?

- ☐ **a.** The milk product line should be allocated €1,710,000 of the joint costs.

- ☐ **b.** The butter product line should be allocated €990,000 of the joint costs.

- ☐ **c.** The yogurt product line should be allocated €3,510,000 of the joint costs.

- ☐ **d.** The cheese product line should be allocated €2,790,000 of the joint costs.

2. Which one of the following is true with respect to variable and absorption costing systems?

- ☐ **a.** Variable costing systems include fixed manufacturing overhead as period costs.

- ☐ **b.** Absorption costing systems include fixed manufacturing overhead as period costs.

- ☐ **c.** Variable costing systems include variable manufacturing overhead as period costs.

- ☐ **d.** Absorption costing systems include variable manufacturing overhead as period costs.

3. A company has determined the following standards for production of its dining tables:

   Square feet of oak per table: 10
   Price per square foot of oak: $3.50
   Number of screws per table: 12
   Price per screw: $0.50

   The company expects a 10% increase in the cost of oak and a 5% decrease in the cost of screws. What is the new standard cost per table?

   ☐ **a.** $40.88

   ☐ **b.** $43.05

   ☐ **c.** $44.20

   ☐ **d.** $45.10

Topic Question Answers:
Measurement Concepts

1. A dairy farm produces the following products jointly during the fiscal year for a total joint cost of €9,000,000.

Product	Kilograms
Milk	1,170,000
Butter	570,000
Yogurt	330,000
Cheese	930,000

   Based on the information, which one of the following is most accurate regarding the allocation of the joint cost under the physical measure method?

   ☐ **a.** The milk product line should be allocated €1,710,000 of the joint costs.

   ☐ **b.** The butter product line should be allocated €990,000 of the joint costs.

   ☐ **c.** The yogurt product line should be allocated €3,510,000 of the joint costs.

   ☑ **d.** The cheese product line should be allocated €2,790,000 of the joint costs.

Under the physical measure method, the joint costs can be allocated to the four products based on the percentage of kilograms of each product compared to the total amount of kilograms produced for all products. The total amount produced is 3,000,000 kilograms (1,170,000 + 570,000 + 330,000 + 930,000). The joint costs allocated to the cheese product line equals €2,790,000 (€9,000,000 × (930,000 ÷ 3,000,000)).

2. Which one of the following is true with respect to variable and absorption costing systems?

   ☑ **a.** Variable costing systems include fixed manufacturing overhead as period costs.

   ☐ **b.** Absorption costing systems include fixed manufacturing overhead as period costs.

   ☐ **c.** Variable costing systems include variable manufacturing overhead as period costs.

   ☐ **d.** Absorption costing systems include variable manufacturing overhead as period costs.

Under the absorption costing (full costing) method, both variable and fixed manufacturing costs are included in the inventory costs. Under the variable costing (direct costing) method, only the variable manufacturing costs are included in the inventory costs. The fixed manufacturing costs are expensed in the period in which they are incurred under the variable costing method; therefore, they are classified as period costs.

3. A company has determined the following standards for production of its dining tables:

   Square feet of oak per table: 10
   Price per square foot of oak: $3.50
   Number of screws per table: 12
   Price per screw: $0.50

   The company expects a 10% increase in the cost of oak and a 5% decrease in the cost of screws. What is the new standard cost per table?

   ☐ **a.** $40.88

   ☐ **b.** $43.05

   ☑ **c.** $44.20

   ☐ **d.** $45.10

The company can calculate the new standard cost per table by applying the projected price changes to each component and then adding the cost for each component together. Because the company expects a 10% increase in the cost of oak, the price per square foot of oak will increase from $3.50 to $3.85 ($3.50 × 1.10%). Each table requires 10 square feet of oak; therefore, the standard cost for the oak will be $38.50 per table ($3.85 × 10 square feet). The company expects the cost of the screws to decrease by 5%; consequently, the price per screw will decrease from $0.50 to $0.475 ($0.50 × 95%). The standard cost related to the screws will equal $5.70 per table ($0.475 × 12 screws). Adding the cost of the oak and the screws, the standard cost per table equals $44.20 ($38.50 + $5.70).

Costing Systems

OSTING SYSTEMS ARE USED TO accumulate costs and assign them to a particular cost object, such as a product or service. Costing systems and the cost data they contain provide strategic value by helping businesses manage costs and price their products and services appropriately. All retailing and manufacturing companies need to track costs from incurrence into the inventory accounts and will use either a job costing system or a process costing system.

This topic covers job order costing, process costing, activity-based costing (ABC), life-cycle costing, and other methods of cost accumulation.

READ the Learning Outcome Statements (LOS) for this topic as found in Appendix A and then study the concepts and calculations presented here to be sure you understand the content you could be tested on in the CMA exam.

Cost Flows in a Manufacturing Organization

It is important to understand how costs flow in a manufacturing organization. Certain inputs are fed into the cost of the product to determine the product's total cost. A representation of this cost flow is presented in Figure 1D-11.

Figure 1D-11 Cost Flows in a Manufacturing Organization

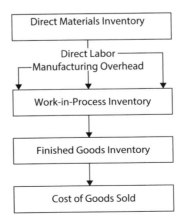

Job Order versus Process Costing

Companies typically adopt one of two basic types of costing systems when they need to assign costs to products or services:

1. **Job order costing (job costing)** assigns costs to a specific job (a customer, batch, or lot of a distinct unit of product or service).
2. **Process costing** accumulates product or service costs by process or department and then assigns them to a large number of nearly identical products by dividing the total costs by the total number of units produced.

LOS
§1.D.2.a

Job order costing is used when the product or service has costs that can be, and often need to be, tracked and assigned to a specific job or service. For example, job costing is used for capital asset construction (buildings, ships) in the manufacturing sector and for advertising campaigns, research and development, and repair jobs in the service sector. Costs for these products, projects, or services can be easily tracked to the product, project, or service because each of these is unique.

LOS
§1.D.2.a

Process costing is used for multiple, nearly identical units that can be organized into a flow. A process costing system would be suitable for products and services such as newspapers, books, and soft drinks in the manufacturing sector and for check processing and postal delivery in the service sector. These products tend to be homogeneous in nature, meaning they are all identical or very similar, and therefore it is not necessary to track costs to a specific unit of product or service.

Both costing systems share the overall purpose of assigning direct materials, direct labor, and manufacturing overhead to products. Both use the same accounts, including direct materials inventory, work-in-process (WIP) inventory, finished goods inventory, and cost of goods sold (COGS). Job costing differs from process costing in how costs are accumulated. In a job costing system, costs are accumulated by job in one WIP account. In a process costing system, costs are accumulated by department or process in separate WIP accounts. Job costing uses a job sheet or equivalent software to track specific items, whereas process costing uses a production cost report to track all department costs. Job costing computes unit cost by job when the job is completed. Under process costing, each department's costs are accumulated in its own WIP; unit costs are computed at the end of the accounting period, after total department costs are available. A few companies use a combination of the two methods, especially when they have some specific and some mass-produced products or services.

Job Order Costing

Actual, normal, and standard costing can be used in job order costing. Most often a company will use normal costing because the actual overhead rates would be determined at the end of the prior year. By waiting until the end of the year, the information is not available on a timely basis throughout the year for decision-making usefulness.

As part of the annual planning process management first identifies one or more pools from which overhead will be applied to jobs. Second, a cost allocation base is selected for each overhead cost pool identified. In the third and final step, the budgeted amount of the overhead dollars in the pool is divided by the quantity of the cost allocation base to determine the predetermined overhead rate. The assignment of overhead to cost objects can now be done monthly or as needed.

The basic steps in using job costing to assign costs to a job are:

1. Identify the job, typically with a unique identifier.
2. Trace the direct costs for the job (direct materials, direct labor).
3. Assign overhead to the job by multiplying the amount of each cost allocation base associated with the job by the related overhead rate.

For example: Smith Company is a shipbuilding firm that manufactures yachts. It uses actual costing for direct material and direct labor and predetermined rates for overhead.

1. The yacht to be made is identified as job number 123.
2. The direct costs for the job are $40,000 in direct materials and $60,000 in direct labor. Two thousand machine hours are incurred on the job, and 3,000 direct labor hours are incurred.
3. Overhead will be applied at the rates of $3.00 per machine hour and $4.00 per direct labor hour, the overhead rates determined during the annual planning process.
4. The following job cost report would be prepared.

Direct costs:	
Direct materials	$40,000
Direct labor	60,000
Total direct costs	100,000
Indirect costs:	
2,000 machine hours @ $3/MH	$6,000
3,000 direct labor hours @ $4/DLH	12,000
Total indirect costs	18,000
Total manufacturing costs	$118,000
Yacht selling price	$140,000
Less: total manufacturing costs	118,000
Gross profit	$22,000

Gross margin % = $22,000 / $140,000 = 15.7%

Spoilage, Rework, and Scrap in Job Costing

Companies want to reduce the amount of spoilage, rework, and scrap that is produced during the manufacturing process in order to maximize their profit.

Spoilage

Spoilage is any material or good that is considered unacceptable and is discarded or sold for its disposal value. Spoilage can be normal or abnormal.

Normal spoilage is any unit of production that is deemed unacceptable during the normal production process, assuming efficient operating conditions. Normal spoilage is considered part of the cost of operations and therefore is part of the cost of good units produced.

Abnormal spoilage is any unacceptable product that should not normally occur under efficient and normal operating conditions. Any spoilage over the amount considered normal is allocated to a loss from abnormal spoilage account. The transaction is to debit an abnormal spoilage account (an overhead account) and to credit the job on which the abnormal spoilage was generated. This is important to know for the CMA exam.

Rework

Rework is any finished product that must have additional work performed on it before it can be sold. If the units being reworked can be separately identified, then they can be reported either with a separate code indicating a rework operation or against a separate rework job number.

Scrap

Scrap is a portion of a product or leftover material that has little or no economic value. When scrap is sold, the accountant will credit (reduce) either WIP inventory or an overhead account by the amount received for the scrap. The latter is the more frequent case. Note that these costs are built into the standard cost of a product when using process costing.

Job Order Costing Benefits and Limitations

Job order costing can provide very detailed results of a specific job or operation so it is ideal for accounting for specific unique jobs. For large processes, job order costing is less valuable because it is impractical to assign individual costs to mass-produced items on a daily basis. Job order costing can accommodate multiple costing methods, such as actual, normal, and standard costing, so it is flexible enough to be used by a wide variety of companies.

Job order costing can have strategic value for a business because it gives a detailed breakdown of all of the different types of costs. The gross profit and gross profit margin can be used to compare the company's profitability across different jobs. For jobs that did poorly, the company can analyze whether the cost overruns were from direct labor costs and/or direct materials costs.

From the description, job costing sounds like a simple system to set up and operate. There is a need to know the cost of every in-process job. This can be found on the specific job's cost sheet. The sum of the costs on all in-process jobs must be equal to the balance in the Work-in-Process Inventory account. In many cases, additional capabilities will be built into the system so that jobs that have variances from budget can be identified early on and watched more carefully.

Process Costing

Process costing is recommended for companies that mass produce identical or nearly identical products. Such companies track their quantities and costs on a departmental production cost report and calculate the unit cost at the end of a period by dividing the total cost of an operation or department by the total units produced.

Process costing is good for any highly automated or repetitive process. Processes may be thought of as either batch or continuous. Examples of batch processes include products that have to be cooked or products that have to be fermented. A measured amount of material would be in a vat, either cooking or fermenting. Another example of a continuous process is a filling process where a liquid product is pumped or gravity-fed into a line that is continuously fed with empty containers. The filled containers emerge from the other end of the production line. The strategic value of process costing for such companies is that they can be in continuous operations while still receiving timely, accurate, and relatively inexpensive cost information each period. This is due in part to the use of equivalent units of production. Process costing also uses production cost reports, which have built-in checks, such as balancing units to be accounted for against units accounted for.

Equivalent Units in Process Costing

Unlike job costing, in which partially completed units have a cost already attached to them, process costing cannot easily determine values for partially completed units because the accounting determines the costs for processes or departments for a period, not a job or item. Therefore, process costing must find the combined cost for all units, including all units partially complete at the beginning and end of the accounting period. *Partially complete* means that the item is still in WIP inventory. Items that are considered complete by one department are not actually complete until they are moved to finished goods inventory. At the end of the period, either a production manager or an engineer gives an estimate of what percentage of units remains on the production line, i.e., in WIP inventory.

Because product cost is calculated by determining the cost per unit in each department, partially completed units must be factored into these calculations. At the end of an accounting period, a process costing system accounts for any WIP inventory as equivalent units. An **equivalent unit (EU)** is a measure of the amount of work done on partially completed units and expressed in terms of how many complete units could have been created with the same amount of work. EUs are necessary because a continuous process is being divided into artificial accounting time periods.

Engineers calculate EUs separately for direct materials and conversion cost because one category may be more complete than the other for the same product. Conversion cost is the combination of direct labor and overhead. The two costs are combined because the direct labor and overhead convert the direct materials into a finished good.

It should be noted that some overhead costs can be traced directly to a department because that department is responsible for controlling those costs. However, other overhead costs must be allocated to the production department because they are incurred and controlled by other departments.

For example: Taking the cooking process mentioned earlier, all the ingredients need to be present before the cooking can be started. Therefore, the direct materials are considered to be 100% complete. If we assume that 5 hours of cooking is required and only 2 hours has been completed at the cutoff date and time, then the conversion is considered to be 40% complete.

Process Costing Cost Flows

Unlike job costing, which moves costs through jobs directly, the cost flow in process costing is routed through processes and departments. In process costing, each department must have its own WIP inventory account. Because direct materials, direct labor, and overhead are incurred by each department involved, these charges must be made to the respective department incurring the cost. When departments complete their portion of work on a product, all of the costs are transferred to the next department's WIP inventory account with a debit to the transferred-in costs account on the next department's books. The direct materials, direct labor, and overhead that are needed and used are also debited to the department's WIP account. When goods are completed, the cost of goods completed is transferred to finished goods inventory.

For example: The accounting entries for two different departments working on the same product are shown in Figure 1D-12.

Figure 1D-12 T-Account Cost Flow Model Using Process Costing

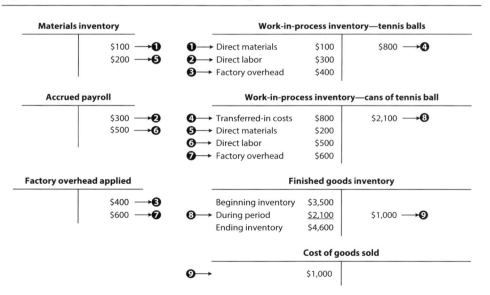

Note: Circled numbers indicate cost inputs and outputs of the process.

Steps in Preparing a Production Cost Report

Production cost reports contain the details of all physical units and EUs, and all the costs assigned to these units for each production department.

When using process costing, the production cost report can be prepared using the **first-in, first-out (FIFO) method** or the **weighted-average method**.

The FIFO costing method is an inventory valuation method that calculates the unit cost using only costs incurred and work performed during the current period. FIFO assumes that the units in the beginning WIP inventory are the first units to be completed during the current period. It is theoretically superior to the weighted-average method because it focuses on performance during the current period only. However, it is generally more complex.

The weighted-average inventory method creates an average of prior-period costs that is reflected in beginning WIP and current-period unit costs. Its advantage is its relative simplicity.

There are five steps in the preparation of the production cost report.

We offer a single set of facts that will be used to prepare production reports using each of the two methods. There are 100 units in the beginning WIP; they are judged to be 100% complete as to direct materials and 40% complete as to conversion costs. Seven hundred additional units are started during the period. Six hundred units are completed and transferred out of the department during the period. Therefore, it is assumed the first 100 units completed came from the beginning WIP; hence, 500 units must have been both started and completed during the period. There are 200 units in the ending WIP; they are judged to be 100% complete as to direct materials and 80% complete as to conversion costs.

Step #1

The first step in the preparation of the production report is called a materials balance. It is the same for both the weighted-average method and the FIFO method. Notice that the units to be accounted for and the units accounted for are equal. This would be true in a process in which there is no loss due to scrap or expected spoilage. More complex situations are not explained here because they will not be tested on the CMA exam. The materials balance is shown in Figure 1D-13.

Figure 1D-13 Materials Balance

Beginning WIP	100
Units started	700
Units to account for	800
Units completed from beginning WIP	100
Units started and completed	500
Units completed	600
Ending WIP	200
Units accounted for	800

Weighted-Average Method

Step #2 Determine the equivalent units.

The 600 units that were completed are considered to be 100% for both DM and conversion costs. The ending WIP units are multiplied by their respective percentage complete to determine the equivalent units for DM and conversion costs. For DM, they are 100% complete and for conversion costs they are 80% complete.

Step #3 Calculate total manufacturing costs.

The beginning WIP inventory amount is added to the values of the costs incurred during this period. These amounts are found in the general ledger accounts for this department. In this example, the beginning WIP is $5,200 ($3,000 for DM and $2,200 for conversion costs) and the costs incurred during the period is $52,998.80 for a total cost to be accounted for of $58,198.80.

Step #4 Calculate costs per equivalent unit.

Divide the total cost by the EUs for direct materials and conversion costs, respectively. Make sure to round the cost per EU out to five decimal places to avoid rounding errors in Step #5. The other cost amounts can be rounded to two decimal places.

The DM cost per EU is $41.24850 and the conversion cost per EU is $33.15789.

Step #5 Assign total manufacturing costs to units transferred out and to the ending WIP inventory.

The last step is to assign the DM and conversion costs by multiplying the EU by the cost per EU, to determine the total costs to be transferred out and the costs that will remain in WIP.

An example of the weighted-average method is shown in Figure 1D-14. Please study it carefully. Each of the five steps logically follows the previous one, in order to get from the given information to the two costs per EU, and the assignment of cost to completed units and those still remaining in WIP. You need to be prepared to do any part or all of this on the CMA exam. A part of it could make a reasonable multiple-choice question, while all of it could potentially be an essay question.

FIFO Method

Next, we use the same data to illustrate the production report preparation under the FIFO method. The FIFO method is illustrated in Figure 1D-15. Please study it carefully.

Step #2 Determine the equivalent units.

The FIFO method starts with calculating the direct materials and conversion costs needed to complete the 100 units in beginning WIP. These units were 100% complete for DM, so there is nothing to add in the current period. It is a different story for the conversion costs. They were 40% completed for conversion costs during the prior period. To complete them in the current period, we need to finish the other 60%. One hundred units times 60% says we must add the equivalent of 60 whole units of work during this period for conversion costs.

Next is to identify the 500 units both started and completed this period.

LOS
§1.D.2.f

Figure 1D-14 Production Report—Weighted-Average Method

Step #1

			Calculation of EU	
			DM	**CC**
Beginning WIP	100			
Units started	700			
Units to account for	800			

Step #2

			DM	CC
Units completed from beginning WIP	100			
Units started and completed	500			
Units completed	600		600	600
Ending WIP	200		200	160
Units accounted for	800		800	760

Step #3

		DM	CC
Costs to be accounted for:			
Beginning WIP	$5,200.00	$3,000.00	$2,200.00
Costs added during the period	52,998.80	29,998.80	23,000.00
Total costs to account for	$58,198.80	$32,998.80	$25,200.00

Step #4

	DM	CC
Cost per equivalent unit	$41.24850	$33.15789

Step #5

Costs transferred out	$44,643.84	(600 × $41.24850)	$24,749.10	(600 × $33.15789)	$19,894.74
Ending WIP	13,554.96	(200 × $41.24850)	8,249.70	(160 × $33.15789)	5,305.26
Total costs accounted for	$58,198.80		$32,998.80		$25,200.00

Similar to the weighted-average method, we determine the EUs in the ending WIP Inventory (units × % complete) based on the 200 units remaining in WIP at the end of the period.

Finally, sum the values on the three columns. Note that the FIFO EU will always be less than or equal to the weighted-average EU.

Step #3 Determine the relevant costs.

In the FIFO method, the only relevant costs are the current-period costs. These are DM costs of $29,998.80 and conversion costs of $23,000.00, for a total of $52,998.80.

Step #4 Calculate costs per equivalent unit.

Simply divide the current-period costs by the EUs for each of Direct Materials and Conversion Costs. Notice how this measures current-period performance only. The same caution about rounding applies here as it did in the weighted-average method.

Step #5 Assign total manufacturing cost to units transferred out and to ending WIP Inventory.

There are three components to the value of units transferred out. The first component is the value of the beginning WIP inventory. The second component is the

Figure 1D-15 Production Report—FIFO Method

Step #1

Beginning WIP	100
Units started	700
Units to account for	800

Step #2

		Calculation of EU	
		DM	CC
Units completed from beginning WIP	100	0	60
Units started and completed	500	500	500
Units completed	600		
Ending WIP	200	200	160
Units accounted for	800	700	720

Step #3

Costs to be accounted for:			
Beginning WIP	$5,200.00	$3,000.00	$2,200.00
Costs added during the period	52,998.80	29,998.80	23,000.00
Total costs to account for	$58,198.80	$32,998.80	$25,200.00

Step #4

Costs added during the period	$52,998.80	$29,998.80	$23,000.00
Equivalent units		700	720
Cost per equivalent unit		$42.85543	$31.94444

Step #5

Assignment of costs:					
Beginning WIP inventory	$5,200.00		$3,000.00		$2,200.00
Cost of completing units in WIP	1,916.67	(0 × $42.85543)	0.00	(60 × $31.94444)	1,916.67
Cost of started and completed units	37,399.93	(500 × $42.85543)	21,427.71	(500 × $31.94444)	15,972.22
Cost of units transferred out	$44,516.60		$24,427.71		$20,088.89
Ending WIP	13,682.20	(200 × $42.85543)	8,571.09	(160 × $31.94444)	5,111.11
Total costs accounted for	$58,198.80		$32,998.80		$25,200.00

cost to complete the units in the beginning WIP inventory. The third component is the cost per EU multiplied by the 500 EU of what was started and completed. Sum these three components to get the cost of the units transferred out.

Finally, the value of the ending WIP inventory is the cost per EU multiplied by the ending WIP EU.

Foot and cross-foot the results to demonstrate that the total costs have been properly accounted for. Again, here is where one would discover a rounding error or a procedural error.

This process works because a given dollar amount was divided by the sum of three EU values. That total was then multiplied by each of the three unit values, and the resulting dollar amounts were summed. It follows that the sum should be the same dollar amount that we started with.

Production Costing in a Multi-Department Company

Because most processes usually involve more than one department, a more complex example will help show how to deal with costs transferred in from a prior department. This example also illustrates how to calculate inventory values and the COGS in process costing using the weighted-average method.

Transferred-in costs are any costs accumulated by prior departments. These are charged to the current department upon transfer of the partially completed units. Each department is treated as a separate entity and the prior department is similar to a vendor that supplies a semifinished good for a price (cost).

With process costing, each production department will have its own WIP account. The completed production of a prior department is transferred to the next department's WIP account. This is different from job order costing where there is only one WIP account.

For example: Robusto Soup Company has three departments that operate in a continuous process. It starts with the mixing department, then goes to the cooking department, and finally goes to the canning department. When each department finishes its work (measured in cans' worth of finished product) and transfers the materials to the next department, it also transfers the costs of the batch to the next department as transferred-in costs.

Robusto Soup moves inventory between its accounts as shown in Figure 1D-16.

Figure 1D-16 Movement of Robusto's Inventory in Units for July

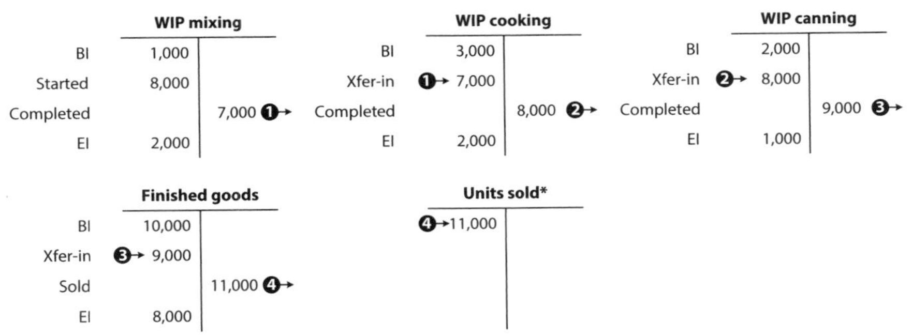

Key: BI = Beginning inventory   EI = Ending inventory
Xfer-in = Transferred in

* This account corresponds to cost of goods sold when viewed in dollars instead of in units.

Note: Circled numbers indicate flow of cost inputs and outputs.

Note that this figure shows movements in units and not in costs.

Figure 1D-17 shows a completed weighted-average method production cost report for the canning department.

Notice the third set of columns relating to transferred-in costs. Most times any units in WIP are 100% complete with regard to transferred-in costs. In all other respects, the production report is similar to those shown previously. Note, however, that the rounding "rule" was violated.

Also notice that the production report for the mixing department must be prepared before that of any other department. The production report for the cooking department must be prepared before the one illustrated for the canning department.

Figure 1D-17 Canning Department Production Cost Report—Weighted-Average Method

1. *Quantity Schedule and Equivalent Units (EUs)*

Quantity Schedule

Units to be accounted for:

Work in process, beginning	2,000	
Transferred in	8,000	
Total units	10,000	

	Transferred In		Materials		Conversion	
	EUs					
	Units	**%**	**Units**	**%**	**Units**	**%**
Units accounted for as follows:						
Units completed and transferred out	9,000	100%	9,000	100%	9,000	100%
Work in process, ending	1,000	100%	900	90%	800	80%
Total units and EUs of production	10,000		9,900		9,800	

(Quantity Schedule column: Units completed and transferred out 9,000; Work in process, ending 1,000; Total units 10,000)

2. *Costs per EU*

	Total Cost	**Transferred In**	**Materials**	**Conversion Costs**	**Whole Unit**
Cost to be accounted for:					
Work in process, beginning	$7,500	$6,250	$250	$1,000	
Cost added during the month	29,995	25,005	990	4,000	
Total cost (a)	$ 37,495	$ 31,255	$1,240	$5,000	
EUs of production (b)		10,000	9,900	9,800	
Cost per EU (a/b)		$3.125 +	$0.125 +	$0. 510 =	$3. 76

3. Cost Reconciliation

	Total Cost	EUs Transferred In	Materials	Conversion	Whole Units
Cost accounted for as follows:					
Goods completed and transferred out (9,000 × $3.76):	$33,840				9,000
Work in process, ending					
Transferred in (1,000 × $3.13)	3,130	1,000			
Direct materials (900 × $0.13)	117		900		
Conversion (800 × $0.51)	408			800	
Total work in process, ending	3,655				
Total Cost	$37,495				

Figure 1D-18 summarizes the data for Robusto Soup, showing the types of T-account transactions and journal entries that would coincide with the data from the weighted-average production cost report.

Separate production cost reports for the mixing department and the cooking department would also be prepared.

Note that each of the base accounts (raw materials, wages payable, and factory overhead) feeds not only into the first department but into all the other production departments. The costs transferred out by that department do not directly equal the costs added during the current period. However, beginning inventory plus the costs added in the current month always equal the ending inventory plus the costs transferred out.

Note also that each inventory account's beginning and ending inventory levels are broken down by direct materials, conversion costs, and transferred-in costs.

Spoilage in Process Costing

Process costing can have normal and abnormal spoilage as defined in the discussion of job costing. In the weighted-average method, cost per unit is calculated by dividing total cost by units to be accounted for. There is an expected normal spoilage level that is expressed as a percentage of good units transferred out. Good units transferred out are valued at the calculated cost per unit × (1 + normal spoilage level). Ending work-in-process units are valued only at the calculated cost per unit. Abnormal spoilage units are valued at the calculated unit cost and is immediately expensed. In practice, many firms do not bother with this refinement.

Figure 1D-18 T-Account and Journal Entries for Robusto (Weighted-Average Method)

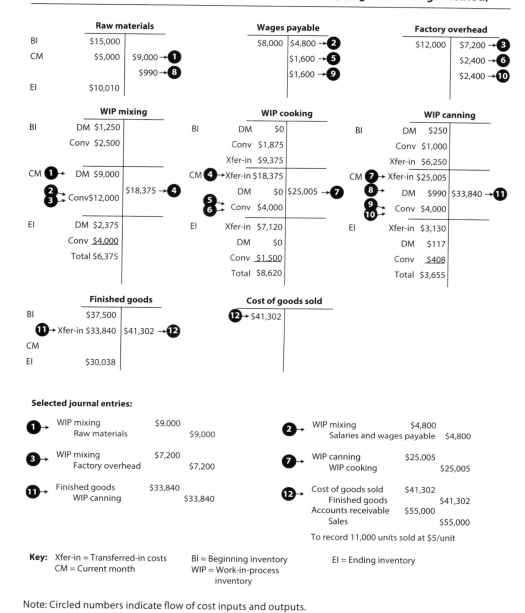

Key: Xfer-in = Transferred-in costs
CM = Current month

BI = Beginning inventory
WIP = Work-in-process inventory

EI = Ending inventory

Note: Circled numbers indicate flow of cost inputs and outputs.

LOS
§1.D.2.e

Benefits and Limitations of Process Costing

Process costing is useful for any highly repetitive flow process, such as mass production of homogeneous items. Conversely, it is not useful for custom orders or other individual jobs. Process costing allocates costs not only by cost per unit but also to specific departments, allowing individual managers to control their own costs.

Activity-Based Costing

Activity-based costing (ABC) is a method of assigning overhead costs to customers, services, and products based on an activity's consumption of resources. ABC is a refinement of the traditional method of assigning overhead costs that is usually based on only one to three allocation bases or cost drivers. This leads to better information about the profitability of its products and services. An **activity** is any type of action, work, or movement performed within an entity. An **activity cost pool** is a logical grouping of activities, actions, movements, or sequences of work that share a common cost driver. A **resource** is an element with economic value that is consumed or applied when performing an activity.

Other terms important to ABC include resource cost drivers and activity cost drivers.

A **resource cost driver** measures the amount of resources consumed by an activity. Resource costs used in an activity are assigned to a cost pool using a resource cost driver. In manufacturing, a resource cost driver could be the amount of rubber required to make a batch of tennis balls. In an engineering services firm, a resource cost driver could be the number of hours used by an engineer to design, build, and maintain a project schedule.

An **activity cost driver** is a measurement of the amount of an activity used by a cost object. Activity cost drivers assign costs in cost pools to cost objects. For example, an activity cost driver is the number of labor hours required for the activity of performing a manufacturing line setup for a particular product.

The basis for ABC is that activities use resources to produce products or services. The resource cost is calculated using a cost driver; the amount of an activity consumed in a period is multiplied by the cost of the activity. The calculated costs are assigned to the product or service.

ABC is especially appropriate for companies that have expanded to multiple products and/or products that use varying amounts of resources. These include not only raw materials and other direct costs, but also indirect costs such as customer service, quality control, and supervision. When each product or product line consumes each of these costs at different rates, a broad brush or uniform cost allocation for all items will make some products appear more profitable and others less profitable than they really are. As a result, products can be overcosted or undercosted: Overcosted items consume few actual resources but are charged as if they had consumed more; undercosted items consume more actual resources than they are charged for.

Strategically, ABC should be used when the cost of making decisions based on inaccurate costing data exceeds the added expense of collecting more information and implementing the system. An effective ABC system can be particularly important to a firm in its decision to drop or add a product line. It can also aid in decisions related to product pricing and where to allocate funds to improve processes.

ABC uses a two-stage approach to allocate costs:

Stage 1: Resource cost assignment of overhead costs to activity cost pools using relevant resource cost drivers

Stage 2: Assignment of activity cost pools to cost objects using relevant activity cost drivers. This measures a cost object's use of an activity.

Key Steps in ABC

The steps for designing an ABC system are: identify activities and resource costs, assign resource costs to activities, and assign activity costs to cost objects.

Step 1. Identify Activities and Resource Costs

An activity analysis identifies the resource costs of performing particular activities by determining the work performed for each activity. The project team makes detailed lists of activities and organizes them into activity centers as well as into these levels:

Unit-level activities include activities that are performed for each unit produced, such as direct materials or direct labor hours. In other words, these are the same as volume-based or unit-based activities.

Batch-level activities include activities that are performed for each batch of units, such as machine setup, purchase orders, batch inspections, batch mixing, or production scheduling.

Product-sustaining activities include activities that are performed to support the production process such as product design, expediting, and implementing engineering changes.

Facility-sustaining activities include activities that support an entire facility that is used for production such as environmental health and safety, security, plant management, depreciation, property taxes, and insurance.

Customer-level activities include activities that are performed to support customer needs such as customer service, phone banks, or custom orders.

Step 2. Assign Resource Costs to Activities

Resource costs are assigned to activities using resource cost drivers. A cause-and-effect relationship must be established between the driver and the activity. Resource cost drivers and the related activity that companies often use include:

Number of employees: personnel activities

Time worked: personnel activities

Setup hours: setup or machine activities

Number or distance of movements: materials-handling activities

Meters: utilities (flow meters, electricity meters, etc.)

Machine hours: machine-running activities

Number of orders: production orders

Square feet: cleaning activities

Amount of value added: general and administrative

Step 3. Assign Activity Costs to Cost Objects

After determining activity costs, the activity costs per unit are measured using an appropriate cost driver. The activity cost driver should have a cause-and-effect relationship or, in other words, be directly related to the rise and fall of the cost.

The activity cost drivers determine the proportion of a cost to allocate to each product or service using the next formula:

$$\text{Rate} = \frac{\text{Cost Pool}}{\text{Driver}}$$

LOS §1.D.2.h

In this example, assume that the company makes two products, A and B. Product A is more complex to make because it has four components and requires more setups. Product B has only two components and requires fewer setups than Product A. Overhead costs for the quarter are $1,000,000. The company will produce 60,000 units of Product A and 40,000 units of Product B. The traditional costing for overhead, based on a total of 100,000 units of output, results in the following:

$1,000,000 / 100,000 = $10/unit

Product A: 60,000 units × $10/unit = $600,000
Product B: 40,000 units × $10/unit = $400,000

If the company decides to use ABC for the allocation of overhead costs, the following would apply:

Cost Pool	$ in Cost Pool (1)	Cost Driver	Total Quantity (2)	Rate (1) / (2)	Product A Quantity × Rate		Product B Quantity × Rate	
Setup Costs	$200,000	# of Setups	20	$10,000	15	$150,000	5	$50,000
Repairs & Maintenance	$300,000	# of Machine Hours	100,000	$3.00	60,000	$180,000	40,000	$120,000
Material Handling	$400,000	# of DM Parts	320,000	$1.25	60,000 × 4 = 240,000	$300,000	40,000 × 2 = 80,000	$100,000
Other	$100,000	# of Units	100,000	$1.00	60,000	$60,000	40,000	$40,000
	$1,000,000			**Total Allocation to Products**		**$690,000**		**$310,000**

By using ABC, the overhead allocation is higher than it would be under the traditional method for Product A: $690,000 as compared to $600,000. This demonstrates that the traditional costing method does not properly allocate costs when there are differences in the complexity of these two products. It results in a simpler product being over-allocated the cost and the more complex product being under-allocated the cost.

When to Use ABC

ABC helps managers understand their costs by highlighting the competitive advantages and weaknesses of their process or product. As more firms adopt ABC, it will become increasingly difficult for companies using a less accurate costing system to compete, because they will find themselves at a competitive disadvantage.

ABC is particularly important for:

- Firms that have high product diversity, complexity, or volume
- Firms that have a high likelihood of cost distortion, such as those with both mass-produced and custom orders, both mature and new products, and both custom delivery and standard delivery channels

ABC was first adopted by manufacturing companies. Now it is also used by service companies such as hospitals, banks, and insurance companies. This is done not only to account for costs, but also to make strategic decisions by analyzing processes, assessing management performance, and assessing profitability.

Differences between ABC and Traditional Costing

The three primary differences between ABC and traditional costing are shown in Figure 1D-19.

Figure 1D-19 ABC versus Traditional Costing

	ABC	Traditional Costing
Cost drivers	Multiple cost drivers: activity and volume-based drivers (whichever fits the cost best)	Up to three cost drivers: only volume-based, chosen for best general fit
Overhead	Overhead assigned to activities and then from activities to products or services	Overhead assigned to departments and then from departments to products or services
Focus	Focus on solving costing and processing issues that cross departmental lines	Focus on assigning responsibility to departmental managers for individual cost and process improvements within their department

Benefits and Limitations of ABC

Benefits of using ABC include these:

- Implementation of ABC may result in some former indirect costs being treated as direct costs when their magnitude and new methods of tracing become apparent and cost effective.
- ABC likely causes more attention to be paid to selling, general, and administrative expenses. Traditional systems typically focus only on manufacturing costs.
- ABC can be used with either a job costing system or a process costing system, the same way traditional cost allocation is used.
- ABC reduces distortions found in traditional cost allocation methods that allocate overhead by department. ABC gives managers access to relevant costs so they can compete better in the marketplace.

- ABC measures activity-driving costs, allowing management to alter product designs and activity designs and know how overall cost and value are affected. This is one example of ABC leading to activity-based management (ABM). ABM uses ABC information to make better management decisions about pricing, product mix, cost reduction, process improvement, and product and process design.
- ABC normally results in substantially greater unit costs for low-volume products than is reported by traditional product costing.

The limitations of ABC include these:

- Notice that there has been no mention of keeping fixed and variable costs separated from one another. This separation is still useful and still important.
- Not all overhead costs can be related to a particular cost driver and some may need to be arbitrarily allocated. This is true when the cost of tracing is greater than the benefit.
- ABC requires substantial development and maintenance time, even when there is available software.
- ABC changes the rules for managers, so resistance to change is common. Without top management support, managers could find ways around using ABC.
- ABC, if viewed only as an accounting initiative, will likely fail.
- ABC generates vast amounts of information. Too much information can mislead managers into concentrating on the wrong data.
- ABC reports do not conform to generally accepted accounting principles (GAAP), so restating financial data adds expense and causes confusion, leaving users unsure as to whether they should rely on the ABC or external data.

Life-Cycle Costing

LOS
§1.D.2.j

Life-cycle costing considers the entire life cycle of a product or service, from concept through sales and warranty service. It is designed to accumulate costs over the life of the product or service.

For example: The life cycle for a pharmaceutical product starts with research and development and moves through multiple stages of testing and approvals, product design, manufacturing, marketing, distribution, and customer service. In this case, the cycle may be defined as the life span of the patent on the product or the life span of its marketability.

LOS
§1.D.2.d

Life-cycle costing is sometimes used on a strategic basis for cost planning and product pricing. It is not a substitute for job costing or process costing systems. It is designed to allow a firm to focus on the overall costs for a product or service. Poor early design could lead to much higher production costs, lower sales, and higher service costs.

LOS
§1.D.2.a

LOS
§1.D.2.b

The projection of costs over the life cycle can be helpful to the firm's management in deciding its pricing strategy and so it is very important. What combination of price and resulting sales quantity is likely to maximize profits over the life cycle? Should the firm choose to employ a skimming price strategy early in the life cycle?

The total costs for a product's life cycle have three phases.

1. Upstream costs: costs that are prior to the manufacturing of the product or sale of the service, such as research and development or design (prototypes, tests, and engineering)
2. Manufacturing costs: costs involved in producing a product or service, such as purchasing and direct and indirect manufacturing costs
3. Downstream costs: costs subsequent to (or coincident with) manufacturing costs, such as marketing, distribution (packaging, shipping and handling, promotions, and advertising), service costs, and warranty costs (defect recalls, returns, and liability)

Life-cycle costing places a strategic focus on managing costs in all three phases. Improving product design is the key to the upstream phase. Improving the manufacturing process and relationships with suppliers is highlighted in the manufacturing phase. Improving the first two phases is the key to lowering downstream costs because actions taken in these phases limit the downstream choices. In other words, life-cycle costing attempts to make managers proactive in the earlier phases so they do not have to be reactive later.

Other Costing Methods

Two other costing methods are **operation costing**—which combines job costing with process costing—and **backflush costing**—which is used in just-in-time production systems.

Operation Costing

Operation costing is a costing system that combines job costing with process costing. Similar to job costing, operation costing assigns direct materials to each job or batch, but direct labor and overhead (conversion costs) are assigned similarly to process costing. This hybrid system is most suitable for manufacturers that have similar processes for high-volume activities, but need to use different materials for different jobs. Clothing manufacturers, for example, have standard operations—choosing patterns, cutting, and sewing—but the fabrics used vary by item, size, color, and price, among other factors. Other industries that are suitable for operation costing include textiles, metalworking, furniture, shoes, and electronic equipment.

For example: A metalworking company produces handrails that are either unfinished (for painting) or chrome-plated. The company uses the metal department to create all of the metal rails and then transfers some to the chrome-plating department.

Assume that the company produced 1,000 unfinished rails and 500 chrome rails during a month. It had no beginning or ending inventory for the month. Operation costing tracks direct materials by job and tracks conversion costs (direct labor and overhead) by department, as shown in Figure 1D-20.

Figure 1D-20 Total Cost Calculation

Direct Materials		
Job 1 — Unfinished Rails (1,000)		$30,000
Job 2 — Chrome Rails (500)		
Materials for Rails in Metal Department	15,000	
Chrome Plating Added to Rails in Chrome Department	10,000	25,000
Total Direct Materials		55,000
Conversion Costs		
Metal Department	45,000	
Chrome Department	10,000	
Total Conversion Costs		55,000
Total Costs		$110,000

The product costs for unfinished rails and chrome rails are calculated in Figure 1D-21. Note that the conversion costs for the metal department groups all rails together because they are all processed the same in that department.

Figure 1D-21 Product Cost Calculation

	Unfinished Rails	Chrome Rails
Direct Materials		
$Job\ 1\left(\dfrac{\$30,000}{1,000}\right)$	$30/Rail	
$Job\ 2\left(\dfrac{\$25,000}{500}\right)$		$50/Rail
$Conversion—Metal\ Department\left(\dfrac{\$45,000}{1,500}\right)$	$30/Rail	$30/Rail
$Conversion—Chrome\ Department\left(\dfrac{\$10,000}{500}\right)$		$20/Rail
Total Cost per Rail	$60/Rail	$100/Rail

Total Product Cost

$$Unfinished\ Rails\ \$60 \times 1,000 = \$60,000$$
$$Chrome\ Rails\ \$100 \times 500 = 50,000$$
$$Total = \$110,000$$

Note that the total cost of $110,000 is the same as in Figure 1D-20, proving that the calculations are correct.

Backflush Costing

Backflush costing is a costing system tailored to just-in-time production systems. A **just-in-time (JIT)** system produces materials just as they are needed for the next step in production. The trigger for manufacturing at a particular work area is the demand from the next station down the line. As a result, organizations using JIT production have very little inventory, making the choice of inventory valuation methods (FIFO or weighted-average) and inventory costing methods (absorption costing or variable costing) irrelevant because the costs flow directly to cost of goods sold during an accounting period.

Backflush costing is in contrast to traditional costing systems that use sequential tracking to record purchases and movements of costs between inventory accounts in the order in which they occur. The sequential tracking of costs goes through a four-stage cycle:

Stage 1: Purchase of direct materials (journal entry in materials inventory)

Stage 2: Production (journal entry in WIP inventory)

Stage 3: Completion of a good finished unit (journal entry in finished goods inventory)

Stage 4: Sale of finished good (journal entry in cost of goods sold)

Each stage is a trigger point that requires a journal entry to be made. Backflush costing omits some or all of the journal entries for the four stages. When the journal entries are omitted from certain stages of the cycle, normal or standard costs are used to work backward to flush out the costs. Then the required journal entries are made for the missing steps that had not been journalized.

Backflush costing skips the journal entry for WIP inventory, because JIT systems reduce the time that materials remain in this stage.

The use of backflush costing may not be in strict accordance with GAAP because backflush costing entries ignore WIP inventory, which still exists and should be recorded as an asset. However, many companies justify the use of backflush costing under JIT production, because the quantity and cost of these items are immaterial. When they are material, these unrecorded costs need to be approximated and adjusting entries made.

Backflush costing can save a company money on accounting. Some critics find the lack of a clear audit trail to be a risk because it limits the ability to pinpoint resources at each stage of the manufacturing process. Many inventories are so low under JIT production, however, that managers can track operations by simple observation and computer monitoring.

Companies that use JIT production systems are prime candidates for using backflush costing. In addition, any industry that has short manufacturing lead times and/or very stable inventory levels can use backflush costing.

Topic Questions:
Costing Systems

Directions: Answer each question in the space provided. Correct answers and explanations appear after the topic questions.

1. The life-cycle costing method is:
    - ☐ **a.** the process for examining the various aspects of a product to identify cost efficiencies.
    - ☐ **b.** the process for managing all costs identified in the value chain.
    - ☐ **c.** a method of costing that minimizes the selling expenses associated with a product.
    - ☐ **d.** a method of costing that focuses on the customer.

2. The costing method that determines product cost by identifying the costs of individual tasks and then assigning these costs to products on the basis of the tasks needed to produce each product is known as:
    - ☐ **a.** activity-based costing.
    - ☐ **b.** job order costing.
    - ☐ **c.** process costing.
    - ☐ **d.** operations costing.

3. A company using job order costing had the following transactions during a calendar year for Job 101.

Date	Transaction	Amount
January 1	Direct materials purchased	£500
February 1	Direct materials used	450
March 1	Direct labor incurred	350
June 1	Overhead applied	50

The company's beginning finished goods inventory on January 1 for Job 101 was £1,500. The company completed and shipped Job 101 on August 1. If the customer paid the company £5,000 for Job 101 on September 1, how much should the company report as cost of goods sold for Job 101 for the year?

    - ☐ **a.** £1,350
    - ☐ **b.** £2,350
    - ☐ **c.** £2,400
    - ☐ **d.** £2,850

Topic Question Answers: Costing Systems

1. The life-cycle costing method is:

    ☐ **a.** the process for examining the various aspects of a product to identify cost efficiencies.

    ☑ **b.** the process for managing all costs identified in the value chain.

    ☐ **c.** a method of costing that minimizes the selling expenses associated with a product.

    ☐ **d.** a method of costing that focuses on the customer.

The life-cycle analysis is concerned with the cost analysis of a product from cradle to grave; therefore, the life-cycle costing method is the process for managing all costs identified in the value chain.

2. The costing method that determines product cost by identifying the costs of individual tasks and then assigning these costs to products on the basis of the tasks needed to produce each product is known as:

    ☑ **a.** activity-based costing.

    ☐ **b.** job order costing.

    ☐ **c.** process costing.

    ☐ **d.** operations costing.

This costing method is known as activity-based costing (ABC). Activity-based costing is a refined version of the traditional method of assigning costs as ABC focuses on breaking down and identifying how costs in an organization are actually consumed. This costing method produces better information about the profitability of its products and services.

3. A company using job order costing had the following transactions during a calendar year for Job 101.

Date	Transaction	Amount
January 1	Direct materials purchased	£500
February 1	Direct materials used	450
March 1	Direct labor incurred	350
June 1	Overhead applied	50

The company's beginning finished goods inventory on January 1 for Job 101 was £1,500. The company completed and shipped Job 101 on August 1. If the customer paid the company £5,000 for Job 101 on September 1, how much should the company report as cost of goods sold for Job 101 for the year?

- ☐ **a.** £1,350
- ☑ **b.** £2,350
- ☐ **c.** £2,400
- ☐ **d.** £2,850

As the name implies, costs under job order costing are assigned to a specific job and they move through the accounting system as a group. The total cost of goods sold for a product equals the sum of all the direct materials used, the direct labor incurred, and the overhead applied. The amount in this company's beginning finished goods inventory account for Job 101 also represent costs related to Job 101; therefore, they also need to be included in the total cost of goods sold. This company should report cost of goods sold of £2,350 (£1,500 + £450 + £350 + £50).

Overhead Costs

MANUFACTURING OVERHEAD COSTS CAN BE very significant for a business. Most often these costs cannot be directly traced to cost objects the way direct materials and direct labor can. This is why manufacturing overhead costs need to be allocated. Overhead costs are product costs, which flow through inventory accounts such as work-in-process inventory and finished goods inventory. Product costs flow to the income statement as cost of goods sold once the product has been sold.

This topic covers fixed and variable overhead, plant-wide versus departmental overhead, and activity-based costing overhead allocation. It also discusses determining an allocation base or cost driver and the allocation of service department costs. It should be pointed out that, while this topic is limited to manufacturing overhead costs, there are instances in which costs other than manufacturing overhead are allocated for management reporting purposes.

 READ the Learning Outcome Statements (LOS) for this topic as found in Appendix A and then study the concepts and calculations presented here to be sure you understand the content you could be tested on in the CMA exam.

Fixed and Variable Overhead Costs

LOS §1.D.3.a

LOS §1.D.3.h

LOS §1.D.3.e

All manufacturing overhead costs are either fixed or variable costs. **Fixed costs** include depreciation on assets, rentals, leasing costs, and indirect labor incurred in manufacturing. These costs do not change during an accounting period, within the relevant range. **Variable costs** include power, water, sewage, engineering support, machine maintenance, and indirect materials. Variable costs change in proportion to the changes in a particular allocation base or cost driver. The cost drivers can be either volume or activity based.

Fixed Overhead Costs

LOS §1.D.3.b

Most fixed costs are set for a certain time period, which is usually for a one-year time period and within the relevant range. So by definition, the day-to-day operations of a business have little effect on fixed costs. The planning of fixed overhead costs has two phases: setting priorities and being efficient in the pursuit of those priorities. Setting priorities means that the firm should determine which fixed overhead costs are needed to obtain strategic and operational goals, which fixed costs do not add value and should be eliminated, and which fixed costs are most important to get right.

The second phase is pursuing efficiency in the fixed overhead costs that are on the list of priorities and determining which costs are most likely to be reduced through more careful planning.

For example: An auto rental company might set its highest fixed cost priority as the purchase of the proper number of rental vehicles for the coming year so that each facility has enough cars to satisfy demand without ending up with too much unused capacity, in the form of too many unrented vehicles. The rental company decides on a cost-effective option by choosing the most trouble-free brands of cars and negotiating the best deals with the auto manufacturers.

Variable Overhead Costs

The planning of variable overhead costs has the same two phases: setting priorities and being efficient in the pursuit of those priorities. Setting priorities for variable costs involves determining which activities add value for customers and which can be eliminated. Unlike fixed costs, variable costs are influenced on a day-to-day basis, so the efficient pursuit of priorities can be an ongoing process.

Some variable overhead rates may be calculated directly. For example, if a delivery truck requires an oil change every 3,000 miles and the average cost of an oil change is $45.00, then $45.00 divided by 3,000 miles is $0.015 per mile. Where this is practical, it is the preferred approach because variable costs are most naturally expressed as dollars per unit of activity.

Sometimes variable costs are based on history and adjusted for how the next period is expected to differ from the current or past period. Consider the cashiering costs in a retail store. We can take the year-to-date cashiering costs for the current year and divide that by the year-to-date sales for the current year to get the first estimate for the budget for the next year. Then we can adjust that for differences expected in the next year. Assume the following:

Year-to-date cashier costs	$350,000
Year-to-date sales	$7,000,000
Expected Wage increase	2%
New labor scheduling system will reduce staffing level by	10%

The calculation:

$350,000 / $7,000,000 = $0.05 per dollar of sales

Cashier costs per dollar of sales	$0.050
Multiply by expected wage increase	1.020
Adjusted rate	$0.051
Multiply by expected reduction in staffing level	0.900
The variable adjusted rate for the next year	$0.046

Note that relying on historical results can produce budgets that institutionalize bad practices if costs were not effectively monitored and controlled during the historical period.

Budgeted Fixed Overhead Cost Allocation Rates

Fixed overhead costs are a lump-sum amount that will not change over the course of a time period even if wide variations occur in activity. The four steps in determining the budgeted fixed allocation rate are:

1. Determine the proper accounting period. An annual basis is preferred over a monthly basis because most companies want to smooth any variations due to seasonality or different numbers of days per month. Using an annual period also keeps managers from having to create a new budget each month.

LOS §1.D.3.i

2. Determine the allocation base (cost driver) to use when allocating fixed overhead that is based on operations. A firm could use a volume- or activity-based cost driver. Although fixed costs do not vary in total, they still must be allocated in proportion to the value they provide to each cost pool.

3. Determine the fixed overhead costs associated with each cost allocation base (cost driver). Fixed overhead costs could be grouped into any number of cost pools based on which allocation base best measures the value provided by those fixed costs.

LOS §1.D.3.j

4. Calculate the rate per unit of each allocation base to be used when allocating fixed overhead costs to cost objects:

$$\text{Fixed Overhead Application Rate} = \frac{\text{Total Cost in Fixed Overhead Cost Pool}}{\text{Total Quantity of Allocation Base}}$$

This results in more of the fixed cost being assigned to the operations that use more of the allocation base than to operations that do not.

For example: A tennis ball manufacturer uses machine hours as its fixed cost driver (Step 2, above). The company budgets 40,000 machine hours annually to produce 200,000 cans of tennis balls.

All fixed manufacturing overhead costs relate to the machine hours allocation base (Step 3, above). The budgeted fixed overhead costs total $1,000,000 for the year. The rate per unit (Step 4, above) is calculated as:

$$\text{Fixed Overhead Application Rate} = \frac{\$1,000,000}{40,000 \text{ Machine Hours}} = \$25/\text{Machine Hour}$$

Common fixed overhead costs include plant leasing costs, machine depreciation costs, and plant manager salaries. Management should select the appropriate allocation base for fixed overhead costs based on operations. Common appropriate allocation bases may include machine hours, labor hours, or labor dollars.

Both fixed and variable overhead are subject to being either over- or underapplied during the year.

Both the fixed overhead spending variance and the production volume variance are reasons why fixed overhead might be underapplied, as a result of unfavorable variances, or overapplied, as a result of favorable variances. (See Section C: Topic 1, Cost and Variance Measures.)

When there is an over-/underapplied overhead balance at the end of the year, it must be disposed of. If the amount is deemed immaterial, it will be charged to cost of goods sold. However, if the amount is material, it will be allocated among cost of goods sold, work-in-process inventory, and finished goods inventory. (See Section D: Topic 1, Measurement Concepts.)

Budgeted Variable Overhead Cost Allocation Rates

The steps and calculations listed for budgeting fixed overhead cost allocation rates are the same for variable rates. Simply substitute "variable" in place of "fixed" in the text to determine how to develop the rate.

$$\text{Variable Overhead Application Rate} = \frac{\text{Total Cost in Variable Overhead Cost Pool}}{\text{Total Quantity of Allocation Base}}$$

LOS §1.D.3.f

Common variable overhead costs include indirect materials, indirect labor, utility costs, maintenance costs, and engineering support. Management should select the appropriate allocation base for variable overhead costs based on operations. Typical appropriate allocation bases include machine hours, labor hours, or labor dollars.

The appropriate cost driver of the variable overhead costs should be selected as the allocation base.

We have illustrated setting overhead rates separately for fixed and variable overhead. When overhead is applied separately it is called the dual-rate method. If overhead is applied in total, it is called the single-rate method. The dual-rate method is preferable, because it enables the income statement to be prepared in a variable costing format.

LOS §1.D.3.k

As was pointed out in Section D: Topic 1, whenever overhead is applied using predetermined standard or normal rates, the actual overhead applied is likely to differ from the actual overhead incurred. The difference is called over-/underapplied overhead and must be disposed of in some manner. Section D: Topic 1, Measurement Concepts discusses this thoroughly and shows how the difference is assigned to cost of goods sold or allocated among work-in-process inventory, finished goods inventory, and cost of goods sold.

High-Low Method

A mixed cost contains both a fixed and variable component. The high-low method is a cost accounting technique used to separate the fixed and variable cost components of a mixed cost. A rental car cost often includes a fixed amount per day plus a variable amount based on miles driven. The method uses, within a relevant range of activity, the highest and lowest amounts of the cost driver (e.g., machine hours) and the highest and lowest respective related cost amounts in order to estimate the variable cost component and the fixed cost component of the cost function. These components are used to determine the cost function, where the slope coefficient is the variable cost component and the constant is the fixed cost component. The formula for this is $y = a + bX$. This formula is discussed in Section B: Topic 3, Forecasting Techniques. By performing a high-low analysis, interested parties gain an initial understanding of the relationship between a cost driver and costs (semivariable cost).

To illustrate the use of the high-low method, consider the next scenario.

Plate, Inc. has the following four months' worth of wage activity associated with production:

Month	Production Activity	Wages
July	2,000 units	$30,000
August	1,800 units	$28,000
September	1,900 units	$29,000
October	2,100 units	$31,000

Begin by selecting the highest and lowest production activity in units from the data provided.

		Units Produced	Wages
October	High	2,100	$31,000
August	Low	1,800	$28,000
	Difference	300	$3,000

Then calculate the variable cost per unit as follows:

$$\text{Variable Cost per Unit} = \text{Wage Difference/Unit Difference}$$
$$\text{VC per Unit} = \$3,000/300 = \$10/\text{unit}$$

The next step is to calculate the total fixed costs. This can be done using either the high production month's or the low production month's data. The results will be the same. To illustrate, August, the low production month's data will be used.

$$\text{Fixed Cost} = \text{Total Cost} - \text{Total Variable Cost}$$
$$\text{Total Variable Cost} = \$10 \times 1,800 = \$18,000$$
$$\text{Fixed Costs} = \$28,000 - \$18,000 = \$10,000$$

The formula for this cost function is:

$$\text{Total Cost} = a + bx$$
$$\text{Total Cost} = \$10,000 + \$10x$$

The advantage of the high-low method is that it is simple to use and, from a logical standpoint, easy to understand. The speed and initial understanding provided about how the cost driver affects indirect manufacturing labor costs is beneficial. The disadvantage is that this method relies on only two observations to estimate a cost function. The method ignores information that may change the results going forward.

Regression Analysis Method

LOS §1.D.3.q

We can also separate the variable and fixed components of a mixed cost using regression analysis. This statistical method is used to determine the impact that one or more variables has on another variable. It provides the best linear equation between the dependent variable (y) and one or more independent variables (x or x's). This type of analysis fits the regression line through a set of data points by minimizing the difference between the prediction line and the actual data points.

Plant-Wide, Departmental, and Activity-Based Overhead Costing

LOS §1.D.3.c

Firms with two or more production departments can assign factory overhead costs to jobs or products in these ways:

- Plant-wide overhead rate
- Departmental overhead rate
- Activity-based overhead costing

LOS §1.D.3.d

Plant-Wide Overhead Rate

A **plant-wide overhead rate** is a single rate used for all overhead costs incurred at a production facility. Not having the overhead rate separated into its fixed and variable components precludes the firm from using variable costing for its management reporting. The total plant factory overhead is determined using the next calculation:

$$\text{Plant-Wide Overhead Rate} = \frac{\text{Total Plant Overhead Costs}}{\substack{\text{Total Units of Cost Driver (Allocation Base)} \\ \text{Common to All Jobs}}}$$

Because plant-wide allocation is, by its nature, very general, it should only be used by facilities that have a strong single cost driver that relates to all the types of production.

If one department in a plant is highly automated and another department is labor-intensive, different cost drivers should be used for each department instead of a plant-wide overhead rate. If not, there will be an over-allocation and under-allocation of manufacturing overhead costs to individual departments and products.

Departmental Overhead Rate

LOS §1.D.3.d

A **departmental overhead rate** is a single overhead rate calculated for a particular department. Departmental overhead rates are more accurate than plant-wide rates.

Each department can have its own rate calculated based on its own cost drivers. As stated for the plant-wide overhead rate, if not separated between fixed and variable overhead, the firm is precluded from using variable costing. The departmental overhead rate is calculated as shown:

$$\text{Departmental Overhead Rate} = \frac{\text{Total Department Overhead Costs}}{\substack{\text{Total Units of Cost Driver Common to All Jobs} \\ \text{for the Department}}}$$

Accounting for each department's overhead amount is tracked by keeping a separate factory actual overhead and applied overhead account for each department. As with the plant-wide rate, the departmental overhead rate is still a general rate, so misallocations of costs can occur if the cost driver chosen does not truly relate to all activities for a department.

Departmental overhead rates should be used only if the department is homogeneous and if a cause-and-effect relationship can be identified between each job or cost-object and the selected cost driver. When this is not true, several sets of cost drivers and associated cost pools should be used. The dangers of improperly allocating costs have been given earlier—that is, certain products will appear less profitable than they really are and vice versa. The risk is mismanagement of the product lines.

Activity-Based Overhead Costing

LOS §1.D.3.d

LOS §1.D.3.l

LOS §1.D.3.m

When the plant-wide and departmental overhead allocation methods are not accurate enough, an **activity-based costing (ABC)** method can be used. ABC assigns factory overhead costs to products or services using multiple cost pools and multiple cost drivers. The cost drivers are selected based on a cause-and-effect relationship and can be both activity based and volume based. For a detailed comparison/contrast discussion of ABC versus traditional costing, see Section D: Topic 2, Costing Systems.

For example: Figure 1D-22 shows the cost pools and cost drivers for a sample production facility.

Figure 1D-22 Cost Pools, Drivers, and Predetermined Overhead Rate

Overhead Cost Pool	Budgeted Overhead Cost	Cost Driver	Quantity	Predetermined Overhead Rate
Utilities	$100,000	Machine hours	10,000	$10/machine hour
Materials handling	120,000	Materials weight (pounds)	40,000	$3/pound
Setups	90,000	Number of setups	300	$300/setup
	$310,000			

In the table, the predetermined overhead rate is calculated by dividing the budgeted overhead cost by the total quantity of the cost driver. The precision in this system is apparent when two or more jobs or products share these costs.

Assume that the facility described has two jobs for the current period. **Job 1** uses 4,000 machine hours, 30,000 pounds in direct materials weight, and has 100 setups. **Job 2** uses 6,000 machine hours, 10,000 pounds in direct materials weight, and has 200 setups. The costs assigned to each job are calculated as shown in Figure 1D-23.

For comparison, if a plant-wide rate had been used with machine hours as the sole cost driver, the total overhead of $310,000 divided by 10,000 machine hours would result in a rate of $31/machine hour. Multiplying this rate by 4,000 hours for job 1 would result in $124,000 and 6,000 hours for job 2 would result in $186,000 being allocated.

Note that the ABC method produces very different costs being allocated to the two products compared to the plant-wide method.

Figure 1D-23 ABC versus Plant-Wide Overhead Allocation

	ABC	Plant-wide	Variance
Job 1 Utilities $10/machine hr. × 4,000 hrs. =	$40,000		
Job 1 Materials handling $3/lb. × 30,000 lbs. =	90,000		
Job 1 Setups $300/setup × 100 setups =	30,000		
Total =	$160,000	124,000	$36,000
Job 2 Utilities $10/machine hr. × 6,000 hrs. =	$60,000		
Job 2 Materials handling $3/lb. × 10,000 lbs. =	30,000		
Job 2 Setups $300/setup × 200 setups =	60,000		
Total =	$150,000	186,000	(36,000)
	$310,000	$310,000	$0

Benefits of Activity-Based Costing

Activity-based overhead allocation may help management identify inefficient products, departments, and activities when it attempts to eliminate activities that do not provide value to products and services. Activity-based overhead allocation may encourage focusing resources on profitable products, departments and activities, and controlling costs. While much of the ABC literature tends to ignore the distinction between variable and fixed costs, maintaining this distinction adds to the value of ABC cost information.

Allocation of Service Department Costs

There are two basic types of departments in a company: production departments and service departments. The production departments have been the focus of the discussion to this point. The service departments do not directly perform operating activities the way the production departments do. Instead, they assist production departments, customers, and employees. Examples of service departments include maintenance, internal auditing, cafeterias, information technology, human resources, purchasing, customer service, engineering, and cost accounting.

The process starts with the preparation of the individual service and production department budgets. It continues with the determination of the appropriate allocation base or cost driver for each service department. Next is the development of the allocation rate for each service department, based on the chosen cost driver. Finally, the allocation of the service department costs can be made to the other departments.

The budgeted allocation uses the predetermined rate and the budgeted quantity of the allocation base. Once the budget is implemented, normal costing is used to apply the costs to the receiving departments using the predetermined rate and the actual quantity of the allocation base.

LOS
§1.D.3.o

Service department costs are allocated because most service departments do not generate any revenue—they are cost centers. When a service department does generate revenue, such as the cafeteria, these revenues offset the costs. Any net cost is then allocated to the production departments. This is essential in order to be compliant with generally accepted accounting principles (GAAP); all manufacturing costs that are direct material, direct labor, and manufacturing overhead need to be included in product inventory valuations through overhead application.

Although a service department may not directly add value to a product, a service department provides a service to other departments within a company that would directly add value to the products and services that the company offers. Management will determine how the service department costs should be allocated back to the operating departments. They will also decide if the dual-rate method will be used to separate the variable costs from the fixed costs.

In the examples that follow, the total of all the department costs equals $780,000. Regardless of which of the following methods is used to allocate the service department costs to the production departments, the total costs in the production departments, after the allocations are made, has to equal $780,000.

LOS
§1.D.3.p

Direct Method

The direct method is the simplest method of allocating service department costs. It allocates the service department costs directly to the production departments. It does not allocate any service department costs to other service departments. This is true even when one service department does perform a service for another service department. This method bypasses such considerations and assigns all costs directly to the production departments. For example, the janitorial service also cleans the HR department. This means that the two production departments are receiving an increased percentage of the janitorial department costs. The direct method concentrates only on the cost drivers attributable to the production departments.

For example: Consider Figure 1D-24, showing four individual departments in a metalworking company.

Figure 1D-24 Department Costs and Cost Drivers

| | Service | | Production | | |
	HR	Janitorial	Metal Department	Chrome Department	Total Cost
Dept. Costs before Allocation	$200,000	$80,000	$400,000	$100,000	$780,000
Labor Hours	10,000	5,000	20,000	5,000	
Space (sq. ft.)	15,000	500	60,000	20,000	

In this example, the human resources (HR) department's costs will be allocated based on labor hours, and the janitorial department's costs will be based on space measurements in square feet, as calculated next:

$$\text{Department Allocation} = \frac{\text{Production Department Quantity}}{\text{Total Qty. for All Production Departments}} \times \text{Department Costs}$$

$$\text{HR Costs to Metal Dept.} = \frac{20,000}{20,000 + 5,000} \times \$200,000 = 0.8 \times \$200,000 = \$160,000$$

$$\text{HR Costs to Chrome Dept.} = 0.2 \times \$200,000 = \$40,000$$

$$\text{Janitorial Costs to Metal Dept.} = \frac{60,000}{60,000 + 20,000} \times \$80,000 = 0.75 \times \$80,000 = \$60,000$$

$$\text{Janitorial Costs to Chrome Dept.} = 0.25 \times \$80,000 = \$20,000$$

This results in the metal department having a total cost of $620,000 ($400,000 + $160,000 + $60,000), and the chrome department having a total cost of $160,000 ($100,000 + $40,000 + $20,000). The new production departments' costs total $780,000 and the service departments will show a total of zero.

Step-Down Method

The step-down method allocates a service department's costs to both service departments and production departments. This method sequentially allocates service department costs, starting with the department that provides the most services to other service departments, and finishing with the department that provides the least services to other service departments. Each successive department's allocation is a step down in costs that need to be allocated.

As with the direct method, only the departments receiving the allocation are included in the calculation of the cost driver proportions.

The following process is used in the step-down method:

Step 1. Determine the service department to be allocated first to the other service and production departments. Calculate the percentage to be used for this allocation based on a cost driver. Then allocate the first service department costs to all the receiving departments.

Step 2. The next service department is allocated to other service and production departments based on a cost driver. Continue this process until all service departments' costs have been allocated to the production departments.

For example: For the metalworking shop, the HR costs would be allocated first, followed by janitorial services.

Figure 1D-25 illustrates the allocation using the step-down method.

Figure 1D-25 Step-Down Method Allocation

| | Service | | Production | | |
	HR	Janitorial	Metal Department	Chrome Department	Total Cost
Dept. Costs before Allocation	$200,000	$80,000	$400,000	$100,000	$780,000
Step 1	(200,000)	33,333	133,334	33,333	
Subtotal	0	113,333	533,334	133,333	
Step 2		(113,333)	85,000	28,333	
Total	$0	$0	$618,334	$161,666	$780,000
Labor Hours	10,000	5,000	20,000	5,000	
Space (sq. ft.)	15,000	500	60,000	20,000	

Some figures are rounded.

The HR department costs are allocated to the three other departments in this way:

Step 1. A factor (or percentage) is created for each of the receiving departments by taking each of the receiving department's labor hours and dividing that number by the total number of labor hours for the three departments that will receive the allocation from the HR department.

- The janitorial department's allocation percentage is calculated by using 5,000 hours as the numerator and 30,000 (5,000 + 20,000 + 5,000 = 30,000) as the denominator. The janitorial department's allocation factor is 5,000/30,000, or 0.167.
- The factors for the metal and chrome departments are 0.667 and 0.167, respectively.
- These factors are then applied to the $200,000 of HR department costs for allocation to the three departments.
- The janitorial department receives an allocation of $33,333 in costs from the HR department.
- The metal department receives an allocation of $133,334 in costs from the HR department.
- The chrome department receives an allocation of $33,333 in costs from the HR department.

Step 2. The new total of $113,333 for the janitorial costs is allocated to the two production departments based on square feet.

Comparing the production departments' total costs to those provided by the direct method, the costs are slightly lower for the metal department and slightly higher for the chrome department when the step-down method is used. The step-down method provides a more accurate measure of how costs should be allocated. However, as can be seen, some costs still can be distorted. For example, janitorial costs still are not allocated to the HR department, even though it has many square feet of space that are cleaned. This can be resolved with the reciprocal method.

As seen using the direct method, the total cost of $780,000 ends up in the production departments.

Reciprocal Method

The reciprocal method fully recognizes all interdepartmental service costs using simultaneous equations. In contrast, the step-down method provides only partial recognition of the support that service departments give one another. Although the reciprocal method is a true recognition method and is most accurate, it is rarely used because of the complexity of its calculations and because the step-down method provides a cost-effective and reasonable approximation of costs. Software applications make the reciprocal method easier to calculate, but most companies still do not use it.

For example: Apply the reciprocal method to the metalworking shop.

Step 1. Set up a system of equations for each of the service departments. Create equations for the HR and Janitorial departments and reduce both to their simplest form:

$$\text{HR} = \$200,000 + \left(\frac{15,000}{15,000 \ + \ 60,000 \ + 20,000} \times \text{Janitorial} \right)$$

$$\text{HR} = \$200,000 + 0.15789(\text{J})$$

$$\text{Janitorial (J)} = \$80,000 + \left(\frac{5,000}{5,000 \ + \ 20,000 \ + 5,000} \times \text{HR} \right)$$

$$\text{J} = \$80,000 + 0.16667(\text{HR})$$

Step 2. Solve for HR's total cost as shown below. Then allocate this amount to the janitorial, metal, and chrome departments based on labor hours.

$$\text{HR} = \$200,000 + 0.15789\left[\$80,000 + 0.16667(\text{HR})\right]$$

$$\text{HR} = \$200,000 + \$12,631.20 + 0.02632(\text{HR})$$

$$1(\text{HR}) - 0.02632(\text{HR}) = \$212,631.20$$

$$0.97368(\text{HR}) = \$212,631.20$$

$$\text{HR} = \frac{\$212,631.20}{0.97368} = \$218,378.93$$

$$\text{HR} \approx \$218,379$$

Step 3. Allocate the new total in janitorial to HR, metal, and chrome departments based on square footage. At this point, all costs end up in the production departments.

	HR Department	Janitorial Department	Metal Department	Chrome Department	Total Cost
Costs	$200,000	$80,000	$400,000	$100,000	$780,000
Step 2	(218,379)*	36,397	145,586	36,397	
Step 3	18,379*	(116,397)	73,514*	24,505*	
	$0	$0	$619,100	$160,902	$780,000*

*Slightly off due to rounding.

Now let's compare the total costs of the two production departments, after the allocation of the service departments' costs, under the three methods.

Method	Metal Department	Chrome Department	Total
Direct	$620,000	$160,000	$780,000
Step-Down	$618,334	$161,666	$780,000
Reciprocal	$619,100	$160,902	$780,000*

*Slightly off due to rounding.

The direct method allocates more of the service department costs to the metal department than to the chrome department. Both the step-down and reciprocal methods result in more accurate allocations and correct for this.

Regardless of the method used, the total cost of $780,000 will end up in the production departments. The service departments will have a zero total balance.

A review of the metal department and chrome department total costs, after the allocations were made under all three methods, resulted in costs that were very close to each other. This is due to the simplicity of the example.

Allocate Production Department Costs to Products

This final allocation is accomplished by the application of manufacturing overhead to cost objects, using the predetermined overhead rate(s) and the appropriate measure of the allocation base. This may be done using the single-rate method or the dual-rate method described next.

Single-Rate Cost Allocation Method

The **single-rate cost allocation method** creates a single allocation base for a production department's combined fixed and variable costs, resulting in a single rate per unit for cost allocation to products. When fixed costs are grouped with variable costs, the entire cost can appear to be a variable cost. A manager might be tempted to outsource to a provider with a lower rate. However, the fixed department costs would be incurred regardless of use, at least in the short term, so outsourcing would cause the department to add new external costs while still continuing to incur the original fixed portion of the internal costs. When the single-rate method is used for the allocation of service department costs to production departments, the single-rate method should also be used to allocate production department costs to products, for consistency. For example:

	Production Department
Variable Cost	$50,000
Fixed Cost	$10,000
Total Cost	$60,000

Assume a single-rate cost allocation method is used based on machine hours:

		Product A	Product B
Machine Hours	120,000	96,000	24,000
	100%	80%	20%
Allocation Amount	$60,000	$48,000	$12,000
Units Produced		100,000	100,000
Rate per Unit		$0.48	$0.12

Dual-Rate Cost Allocation Method

LOS §1.D.3.g

The **dual-rate cost allocation method**, also called the contribution margin cost allocation method, creates separate fixed and variable cost pools for allocation of production department costs to products. Each pool can have its own allocation base, such as labor hours for variable costs and machine hours for fixed costs. Since fixed costs frequently "buy" capacity, the allocation base may very well be a measure of each department's demand for that capacity. An electric utility company bases its charges to industrial customers on peak demand; this same principle can be applied to the internal customers of each service department as a means of allocating the fixed costs of the service department. By using different cost drivers and different rates, as well as standard or actual amounts for each variable, the dual-rate method may produce a different estimate of total costs for a cost object than if the single-rate method were used. For the dual-rate method to be valid, the service department allocations have to use the dual-rate method also.

Now assume that a dual-rate allocation method is used. Variable costs are allocated based on units produced and the fixed costs are allocated based on machine hours.

		Product A	Product B
Units Produced	200,000	100,000	100,000
	100%	50%	50%
Variable Cost	$50,000	$25,000	$25,000
Fixed Cost	$10,000	$8,000	$2,000
Total Cost	$60,000	$33,000	$27,000
Rate per Unit		$0.33	$0.27

Notice the differences in the rate per unit between the two methods. This method should lead to more precise allocation of costs and allow for better managerial decision making. However, it could also result in higher administrative costs due to more complex calculations and the difficulty in determining proper classification of costs.

Much of this topic's material has been about allocations. One must be wary of allocations in general. The development of predetermined overhead rates during the annual planning process is the one time when cost allocations from service departments to production departments are made.

However, in many instances, the harm of management reporting using allocations may outweigh the benefit. If managers are evaluated on the basis of both the costs they are responsible for incurring, as well as the costs that are allocated to them, managers may disregard the entire report on the basis that there are some costs over which they have no control. If there is a compelling reason for the cross-charging of services from a service department to a department using the service, doing that on a basis that is consistent with the annual master budget will keep the department managers using the service feeling responsible for all the costs reported to them. The dual-rate method might prove to be more helpful. It will isolate the variable portion, over which they do have some control, from the fixed portion, over which they do not have control.

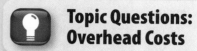

Topic Questions: Overhead Costs

Directions: Answer each question in the space provided. Correct answers and explanations appear after the topic questions.

1. A company manufactures and sells three products. The products are all man-ufactured at the same facility. The controller of the company has decided to accumulate all budgeted overhead costs for the manufacturing facility into a single cost pool. The cost pool is then allocated to the three products based on the direct labor hours used by each product. What type of overhead rate has the controller **most** likely used in this allocation methodology?

    ☐ **a.**   Departmental rate

    ☐ **b.**   Variable rate

    ☐ **c.**   Fixed rate

    ☐ **d.**   Plant-wide rate

2. A company had the following applied fixed overhead balances at the end of the year.

Work-in-process inventory	$100,000
Finished goods inventory	50,000
Cost of goods sold	250,000

    The company is also showing that it has materially under-applied fixed overhead by $30,000. To record the fixed overhead variance, the company should charge:

    ☐ **a.**   work-in-process inventory for $18,750.

    ☐ **b.**   finished goods inventory for $3,750.

    ☐ **c.**   cost of goods sold for $7,500.

    ☐ **d.**   cost of goods sold for $30,000.

3. Which one of the following would **not** be an appropriate cost allocation base for an organization?

    ☐ **a.**   Machine hours

    ☐ **b.**   Direct labor hours

    ☐ **c.**   Square feet of a facility

    ☐ **d.**   Supervisor salaries

Topic Question Answers: Overhead Costs

1. A company manufactures and sells three products. The products are all manufactured at the same facility. The controller of the company has decided to accumulate all budgeted overhead costs for the manufacturing facility into a single cost pool. The cost pool is then allocated to the three products based on the direct labor hours used by each product. What type of overhead rate has the controller **most** likely used in this allocation methodology?

   ☐ **a.** Departmental rate

   ☐ **b.** Variable rate

   ☐ **c.** Fixed rate

   ☑ **d.** Plant-wide rate

The controller most likely used a plant-wide rate in this allocation because he or she decided to accumulate all budgeted overhead costs into a single cost pool.

2. A company had the following applied fixed overhead balances at the end of the year.

Work-in-process inventory	$100,000
Finished goods inventory	50,000
Cost of goods sold	250,000

The company is also showing that it has materially under-applied fixed overhead by $30,000. To record the fixed overhead variance, the company should charge:

   ☐ **a.** work-in-process inventory for $18,750.

   ☑ **b.** finished goods inventory for $3,750.

   ☐ **c.** cost of goods sold for $7,500.

   ☐ **d.** cost of goods sold for $30,000.

Because cost relationships are never perfect, the manufacturing overhead account will typically be either under- or over-applied in a given year. Because the amount of the adjustment is deemed to be material, the company needs to proportionally adjust the ending balance in all "downstream" accounts. The "downstream" accounts consist of the work-in-process, finished goods inventory, and cost of goods sold accounts. The amount of the adjustment for each category is calculated by multiplying the total overhead adjustment by the percent of the total ending balances made up by each account. The calculation for each category is as follows:

	Ending Balances	Weights	× $30,000
Work-in-Process Inventory	100,000	25.00%	7,500
Finished goods inventory	50,000	12.50%	3,750
Cost of Goods Sold	250,000	62.50%	18,750
Total	$400,000	100%	$30,000

3. Which one of the following would **not** be an appropriate cost allocation base for an organization?

☐ **a.** Machine hours

☐ **b.** Direct labor hours

☐ **c.** Square feet of a facility

☑ **d.** Supervisor salaries

Supervisor salaries would not be an appropriate cost allocation base for an organization. A cost allocation base is the basis that a company uses to allocate its overhead costs. Supervisor salaries are a form of indirect labor costs that should be allocated to an organization's products, not a base upon which the costs should be allocated.

Supply Chain Management

A PARADIGM IS AN EXAMPLE OR a model. A paradigm shift refers to a significant change in the model that people use to organize or understand what they are doing. At their inception, supply chain management, lean manufacturing, just-in-time production systems, theory of constraints, and outsourcing all represented paradigm shifts in manufacturing. These manufacturing practices changed the type of information utilized in decision making and the methods used to collect that data. Ultimately, these practices changed the role of the management accountant and improved the efficiency and effectiveness of information reporting. One more paradigm shift is taking place now. Lean manufacturing is being developed to become lean resource management techniques.

This topic looks first at supply chain management and lean resource management techniques. Then it discusses traditional materials requirement planning systems as well as just-in-time, outsourcing systems, enterprise resource planning systems, and the theory of constraints. It also discusses capacity concepts and other production management theories.

READ the Learning Outcome Statements (LOS) for this topic as found in Appendix A and then study the concepts and calculations presented here to be sure you understand the content you could be tested on in the CMA exam.

LOS
§1.D.4.a

Supply Chain Management

Supply chain management (SCM) involves the management of the flow of goods, that includes: the movement and storage of raw materials, work-in-process inventory, and finished goods from the point of origin to the point of consumption. SCM also involves the planning and management of all activities involved in sourcing and procuring raw materials, converting those materials to a finished product, and delivering that finished product to consumers. Coordinating and collaborating with suppliers, intermediaries, third parties, and customers is critical in the execution of these activities.

In essence, the objective of supply chain management is to integrate procurement, operations management, logistics, and information technology while creating value through this chain of key processes and activities.

There have been many supply chain and production methodologies that have been developed and used over the years. Just-in-time (JIT) manufacturing was developed in Japan's post-World War II industries. It is part of the Toyota Production System (TPS) that aimed to reduce flow times within production systems, ranging from supplier response time to customer delivery. Lean resource management techniques were developed from lean manufacturing, that was developed in the late 1980s. This newer technique can be applied to every process within a business organization, as well as to service providers and government. It is not just for manufacturing anymore. The focus is on resource optimization. Some examples of resources include capital, human skills, inventory, information, and production capabilities. JIT as well as lean resource management, materials requirement planning (MRP), and enterprise resource planning (ERP) are described in Figure 1D-26. This figure also includes the operational benefits that can be gotten through the implementation of each method.

Figure 1D-26 Supply Chain and Production Methodologies

Method	Central Purpose	Operational Benefits
Materials Requirement Planning (MRP) (Developed 1960–1970s)	MRP requires production management to plan for what is needed, then "push" the product through production to reach a market. This process ensures that raw materials are available for production and finished goods are available to the customer, regardless of whether there is a demand or not	• Less coordination required between functional areas because everyone follows the master production schedule and the bill of materials • Reduce idle time and machine setup costs due to scheduling improvements • Predictable raw material needs allow purchasing to take advantage of bulk purchasing and other price breaks • More efficient inventory control may reduce raw materials and/or finished goods, which reduces inventory carrying costs
Just-in-Time Manufacturing (JIT) (In US late 1970s)	A comprehensive production and inventory control methodology in which materials arrive exactly as they are needed for each stage in the production process. Need is created by demand for the product. So demand "pulls" a product through the system. Production organized in workcells that group related processes to create the final product. This organization creates multi-skilled workers. It requires strong relationships with reliable suppliers to ensure on-time deliveries of high-quality goods. Uses a **Kanban** system that is a visual record or card to signal the need for a specified quantity of materials or parts to move from one workcell to another, in sequence.	• Creates obvious production priorities • Reduced setup and manufacturing lead time • No overproduction • Improved quality control leads to fewer materials wasted • Easier inventory control due to lower or zero inventory levels • Less paperwork

LOS §1.D.4.d

LOS §1.D.4.e

LOS §1.D.4.f	**Enterprise Resource Planning (ERP) (Developed 1990s)**	ERP evolved from MRP to give organizations an information technology tool to combine and integrate the various systems it uses into one comprehensive system to manage operations. Often includes modules for accounting, human resources, supply chain, and inventory.	• Integrates many business processes to save time and expense • Improved business effectiveness and efficiency • Better and timelier decisions • More flexible and agile organization that can better adapt to change • Improved data integrity and security • Improved collaboration between organizational functions
LOS §1.D.4.b LOS §1.D.4.c	**Lean Resource Management Techniques (Developed 2000s)**	The goal is to maximize customer value while minimizing waste. Any resource used for any goal other than creating customer value is considered waste and should be eliminated. Created the idea of value-added from the customer perspective. Five key steps are in the process: 1. Identify what creates value from the customer's perspective 2. Identify all steps in the value stream (process)—eliminate those that do not create value 3. Make the value-creating steps flow smoothly 4. Make only what is "pulled" by the customer 5. Strive for perfection by continually removing waste.	• Resource optimization • Reduced waste • Improved process flow • Reduced costs • Increased customer value

Outsourcing

LOS §1.D.4.g

Outsourcing describes a company's decision to purchase a product or service from an outside supplier, rather than producing it in house. This allows an organization to concentrate resources on its core business competencies while capitalizing on the expertise of other firms that are more efficient, effective, or knowledgeable at specialized tasks that are peripheral to those core business competencies. Today, many firms outsource significant parts of their support services, such as information technology, customer service, and human resource functions.

The term *make versus buy* is often used in reference to outsourcing. Make-versus-buy analysis examines the relevant costs of keeping activities in-house versus outsourcing to external suppliers. Some firms have extended the idea of outsourcing to **contract manufacturing,** in which another company actually manufactures a portion of the first firm's products. Contract manufacturing can provide a win-win relationship if one firm has excess capacity or expertise and another company lacks capacity or knowledge.

Benefits and Limitations of Outsourcing

There are many strategic reasons an organization may choose to outsource work. For smaller businesses, outsourcing may provide access to resources, expertise, and capabilities that they may not have internally. For larger businesses, outsourcing *can improve* specific functions and provide the following benefits:

- Allows management and employees to focus on core competencies and strategic revenue-generating activities
- Improves efficiency and effectiveness by gaining outside expertise or economies of scale
- Provides access to current technologies at reasonable cost without the risk of obsolescence
- Reduces expenses by gaining capabilities without incurring overhead costs (staffing, benefits, space)
- Improves the quality and/or timeliness of products or services

Despite many attractive advantages, outsourcing is not the answer for all activities or functions. Companies thinking of outsourcing should consider these key cautions:

- May cost more to go outside for specific expertise
- Can result in a loss of in-house expertise and capabilities
- Can reduce process control
- May reduce control over quality
- May lead to less scheduling flexibility (depending on the external supplier)
- May result in less personalized service
- Creates privacy and confidentiality issues
- Can result in giving knowledge away and lead to competitors obtaining expertise, scale, customers, and the like
- Potential for decreased employee morale and loyalty

LOS
§1.D.4.h

Theory of Constraints

In the 1990s, Dr. Eliyahu Goldratt, a physicist turned business management consultant, countered the adage of "A penny saved is a penny earned" with "The goal is not to save money but to make money."

Goldratt developed the **theory of constraints (TOC)** as an overall management philosophy with a basis in the manufacturing environment. The overriding goal of the TOC is to improve speed in the manufacturing process by optimizing throughput, rather than simply measuring output.

The premise behind the TOC is that every system is pursuing a **goal** and that every goal is constrained by a limiting factor. It assumes a system is a series of connecting processes that work together to accomplish some goal. A **constraint** is a limiting factor, bottleneck, or barrier that slows down a product's total cycle time. **Cycle time** is the time it takes to complete a process from beginning to end. Therefore, constraint management is the process of identifying barriers, then analyzing and understanding the barriers to remove them to reduce cycle time and optimize the system's efficiency.

Goldratt maintains that there is only one constraint in a system at any given time and this bottleneck limits the output of the entire system. The remaining components of the system are known as nonconstraints (non-bottlenecks). Overall, the TOC emphasizes fixing the system constraint and temporarily ignoring the nonconstraints. By doing this, the theory has a profound impact on cycle time and process improvement, rather than spreading limited time, energy, and resources across an entire system, which may or may not have tangible results.

However, when one constraint is strengthened, the system does not become infinitely stronger. The constraint simply migrates to a different component of the system and some other factor becomes the bottleneck or barrier. The system is stronger than it was before, but still not as strong as it could be.

Basic Principles in the Theory of Constraints

Inventory, operational expenses, throughput contribution, and the drum-buffer-rope system are the principal concepts underlying the TOC.

Inventory

Inventory refers to all the cost of materials throughout the system in direct materials, work in process, and finished good inventories intended for sale. Depending on how certain costs are allocated to cost of inventory, it may also include the cost of R&D along with buildings and equipment.

> Inventory = (Materials Costs in Direct Materials, Work-in-Process, and Finished Goods Inventories) + (R & D Costs) + (Costs of Equipment and Buildings)

Operational Expenses

In the TOC, *operational or operating expenses* refer to the money the system spends to convert inventory into throughput. Operational expenses include expenditures on direct and indirect labor, supplies, outside contractors, interest payments, and depreciation. Employees are responsible for turning inventory into throughput.

> Operating Expenses = All Costs of Operations, Except Direct Materials

Throughput Contribution

Throughput contribution, also known as throughput margin or simply throughput, is a TOC measure of product profitability. It is the rate at which the entire system generates money through product and/or service sales.

Throughput contribution is calculated using the next formula:

> Throughput Contribution = Sales Revenue – Direct Material Costs

Throughput contribution assumes that the material costs include all purchased components and material handling costs. TOC analysis also assumes that labor is a fixed cost, not a direct and variable cost.

Drum-Buffer-Rope System

The drum-buffer-rope (DBR) system is a TOC method for balancing the flow of production through the constraint. The **drum** connotes the constraint, the **rope** is the sequence of processes prior to and including the constraint, and the **buffer** is the minimum amount of work-in-process input needed to keep the drum busy. The objective of the drum-buffer-rope system is to keep the process flow running smoothly through the constraint, by carefully timing and scheduling the processes in the rope leading up to the constraint.

Theory of Constraints and Throughput Costing

The TOC focuses on improving a company's profits by managing its operating constraints. Companies that employ a TOC approach use a form of variable costing called throughput costing. Throughput costing, also called super-variable costing, is a costing method where the only costs included in inventory are the costs of direct materials. All other costs are classified as period costs. In many companies, it is quite accurate to say that direct labor behaves like a committed fixed cost in the short run and not like a variable cost that adjusts to changes in output. The TOC has a short-term focus, whereby an assumption is made that all operating costs are fixed in the short term and are therefore categorized as fixed costs. Like variable costing, throughput costing is an internal reporting tool.

Steps in the Theory of Constraints

The TOC includes five focusing steps designed to concentrate improvement efforts on the constraint. Figure 1D-27 summarizes the five steps.

Figure 1D-27 Five Focusing Steps of the Theory of Constraints

Step 1 **Identify the system constraint.**

In the first step, an organization identifies which part of the system constitutes the weakest link, or the constraint, and determines whether it is a physical constraint or a policy constraint.

Example: A management accountant works with managers and engineers to flowchart a manufacturing process for a product line. They identify the sequence and the amount of time each step requires. A system constraint is identified where one step in the process is taking too long to complete or is idle too long.

Step 2 **Decide how to exploit the constraint.**

The organization "exploits" the constraint by utilizing every bit of the constraining component without committing to potentially expensive changes and/or upgrades.

Example: Scheduling of key machine time is changed, and employees are redeployed.

Step 3 **Subordinate everything else.**

With a plan in place for exploiting the constraint, an organization adjusts the rest of the system to enable the constraint to operate at maximum effectiveness and then evaluates the results to see if the constraint is still holding back system performance. If it is, the organization proceeds to Step 4. If it is not, it means the constraint has been eliminated and the organization skips ahead to Step 5.

Example: Further analysis looks at actions to maximize flow through the constraint. With a focus on throughput, the review team suggests ways to speed up the process, such as reduced setup times and use of the DBR system. Non-value-added activities are eliminated. The idea is to keep the constraint busy without accumulating inventory or accumulating work in the process.

Step 4 **Elevate the constraint.**

If an organization reaches Step 4, it means that Steps 2 and 3 were not sufficient in eliminating the constraint. At this point, the organization elevates the constraint by taking whatever action is needed to eliminate it. This may involve major changes to the existing system, such as reorganization, divestiture, or capital improvements. Because these typically require a substantial up-front investment, the organization should be certain that the constraint cannot be broken in Steps 1 through 3 before proceeding.

Example: Management considers how to alleviate the constraint to increase capacity of the system. This can be done by adding labor or more/new equipment as needed.

Step 5 **Go back to Step 1, but beware of inertia.**

After a constraint is broken, the organization repeats the steps all over again, looking for the next thing constraining system performance. At the same time, it monitors how changes related to subsequent constraints may impact the constraints that are already broken, thus preventing solution inertia.

Example: The organization considers a strategic response to the constraint. The goal is to improve throughput. The product or the process may be redesigned or hard-to-manufacture products may be eliminated, and so on.

In the theory of constraints, throughput (T), inventory (I), and operating expenses (OE) link operational and financial measures. As discussed in the *Statement on Management Accounting* "Theory of Constraints (TOC) Management System Fundamentals" (Copyright © 1999 Institute of Management Accountants):

- Net profit increases when throughput goes up or operating expenses go down.
- Throughput can go up by increasing sales revenues or reducing variable costs of production.
- Measures that increase net profit increase return on investment—as long as inventory remains the same.
- If inventory can be decreased then return on investment (ROI) will increase even without an increase in net profit.
- Cash flow increases when either throughput goes up or the time to generate throughput is reduced, assuming the time saved is applied toward generating more throughput.

The TOC attempts to maximize throughput contribution while decreasing inventory, operational expenses, and other investments. Unlike traditional performance measures, which focus on direct labor efficiency, unit costs, and how efficiently the company can produce a product, TOC emphasizes how efficiently an organization must manufacture products for optimum market success. The flow of product is dictated by market demand, not by the forces influencing traditional mass production: cheap sources of materials, machine efficiencies, or low direct labor.

Stated another way, T, I, and OE measurements enable a company to understand how much money it is making and how to best leverage capabilities to improve profitability.

Having successfully identified the system constraint, steps can be taken to lessen or eliminate it. The organization may "exploit" the constraint by changing how it uses the constraint without spending more money—such as by reducing setup times to improve efficiency and optimize the activity. The organization may "elevate" the constraint by investing money to increase the capacity of the constrained resources—such as buying another piece of equipment or outsourcing an activity.

Naturally, an organization should spend additional money to elevate a constraint only after exploiting the constraint to the fullest potential.

Theory of Constraints and Activity-Based Costing

Organizations that implement the TOC often use activity-based costing (ABC) as well. TOC and ABC are both used by organizations to assess product profitability. However, there are a few differences in how these two cost management methods are used.

- TOC takes a short-term approach to profitability analysis with an emphasis on materials-related costs. ABC examines long-term costing, including all product costs.

- TOC considers how to improve short-term profitability by focusing on production constraints and plausible short-term product mix adjustments.
- ABC does not consider resource constraints and process capability; it analyzes cost drivers and accurate unit costs for long-term strategic pricing and profit planning decisions.
- ABC is generally used as a tool for planning and control.

The short-term aspects of TOC and the long-range focus of ABC make them complementary profitability analysis methods.

Although the TOC has its roots in the manufacturing environment, applications have been developed for service industries. Measures of speed and cycle time must be defined appropriately for the nature of the enterprise. Additionally, specific TOC implications for management accounting have been assessed to consider the benefits of throughput accounting in business rather than using traditional cost accounting methods.

Using this method, the objective is to maximize throughput contribution while reducing investments and operating costs.

Capacity Concepts

A key issue in costing is choosing the capacity level for computing the allocation of manufacturing overhead. Determining the correct level of capacity to use is a difficult strategic decision for managers. The choice of capacity level used to allocate overhead can have a great effect on product cost information used by managers. If a company has capacity in excess of what it needs, it will incur large costs of unused capacity. Likewise, if a company has too little capacity to meet demand, it may have trouble filling customer orders.

Theoretical capacity (also known as ideal capacity) is the level of capacity that can be achieved under ideal conditions when there are no machine breakdowns, maintenance, delays, or the like. Theoretical capacity represents the largest volume of output possible but is unattainable and unrealistic.

Practical capacity represents the highest level of capacity that can be achieved while allowing for unavoidable losses of production time for machine breakdowns, employee vacations, maintenance, and so on. Unlike theoretical capacity, it is the level of capacity that can realistically be achieved.

Using theoretical capacity when calculating overhead allocations would mean that a large-denominator activity level would be used, resulting in a lower overhead allocation to individual units of product. This would under-allocate costs and provide management with product cost information that is not representative of the actual costs. Practical capacity does not take into consideration the amount of unused capacity when allocating costs. The benefit of this approach is that it encourages managers to focus their attention on the amount of unused capacity, and user departments are not overcharged for a portion of costs related to unused capacity.

Practical capacity is a better choice to use as the denominator activity level for allocating overhead because it is realistic and will generate product costs that accurately reflect the cost of the product. By using practical capacity to calculate product costs, the company is not over- or underallocating costs to each unit of product. Instead, a "practical" or "realistic" amount of overhead is allocated to each unit produced. As a result, many companies prefer to use practical capacity as the denominator to calculate the budgeted or predetermined overhead rate.

Other Production Management Theories

Competitiveness . . . productivity . . . continuous improvement . . . profitability . . .

Organizations constantly strive to improve on what they already do well and to capitalize on growth opportunities. Beyond the manufacturing paradigms previously discussed, organizations have a wide array of other production management techniques to consider in their quest for better, faster, and more profitable operations.

Many organizations have adopted some or all of the approaches listed in Figure 1D-28 in an attempt to reduce costs, increase productivity, improve quality, and increase their overall responsiveness to customers.

Figure 1D-28 Contemporary Productivity Approaches

Technique	Description
Automation/robots	Uses reprogrammable, multifunctional robots (machines) designed to manipulate materials, parts, tools, or specialized devices through variable programmed motions
	Applies robots to the performance of a variety of repetitive tasks
Capacity management and analysis (capacity planning)	Represents an important decision-making area involving strategic, tactical, and operational aspects
	Includes an iterative procedure that:
	• Reviews long-term demand forecasts
	• Translates forecasts into capacity requirements
	• Compares the capacity requirements to present facilities
	• Identifies mismatches between capacity requirements and projected availability
	• Devises plans to overcome mismatches and selects the best alternative
Computer-aided design (CAD)	Uses computers in product development, analysis, and design modification to improve the quality and performance of the product
	Usually entails the drawing or physical layout steps of engineering design
Computer-aided manufacturing (CAM)	Applies the computer to the planning, control, and operation of a production facility

Computer-integrated manufacturing (CIM)	Involves a manufacturing system that completely integrates all factory and office functions within a company via a computer-based information network
	Uses computers to control the integration and flow of information between design, engineering, manufacturing, logistics, warehousing and distribution, customers and suppliers, sales and marketing activities, and accounting
	Facilitates hour-by-hour manufacturing management
Concurrent engineering (simultaneous engineering)	Integrates product or service design with input from all business units and functions throughout a product's or service's life cycle
	Emphasizes upstream prevention versus downstream correction
	Attempts to balance the needs of all parties in product or service design while maintaining customer requirements
Flexible manufacturing system (FMS)	Uses a computerized network of automated equipment that produces one or more groups of parts or variations of a product in a flexible manner

Topic Questions:
Supply Chain Management

Directions: Answer each question in the space provided. Correct answers and explanations appear after the topic questions.

1. The method used to maximize operating income when faced with some bottleneck and some non-bottleneck operations is described as:

   ☐ **a.** sensitivity analysis.

   ☐ **b.** suboptimal decision making.

   ☐ **c.** theory of constraints.

   ☐ **d.** total factory productivity.

2. Enterprise resource planning (ERP) systems integrate:

   ☐ **a.** financial and non-financial information from an organization's business processes.

   ☐ **b.** financial information among different organizations only.

   ☐ **c.** financial and human resources systems only.

   ☐ **d.** financial and non-financial information from an organization's accounting processes.

3. All of the following are benefits of just-in-time manufacturing **except** that it:

   ☐ **a.** can significantly reduce inventory.

   ☐ **b.** helps produce a higher-quality product in less time.

   ☐ **c.** allows for minor defects without shutting down operations.

   ☐ **d.** helps eliminate rework costs.

Topic Question Answers:
Supply Chain Management

1. The method used to maximize operating income when faced with some bottleneck and some non-bottleneck operations is described as:

   ☐ **a.** sensitivity analysis.

   ☐ **b.** suboptimal decision making.

   ☑ **c.** theory of constraints.

   ☐ **d.** total factory productivity.

The goal of the theory of constraints is to improve speed in a process by optimizing throughput, managing constraints, and focusing on continuous improvement. A constraint is a weak link in a chain that will limit the rest of the system. Operating income can be maximized as constraints are identified and eliminated.

2. Enterprise resource planning (ERP) systems integrate:

   ☑ **a.** financial and non-financial information from an organization's business processes.

   ☐ **b.** financial information among different organizations only.

   ☐ **c.** financial and human resources systems only.

   ☐ **d.** financial and non-financial information from an organization's accounting processes.

Enterprise resource planning (ERP) systems integrate financial and non-financial information from an organization's business processes. The goal of an ERP system is to integrate the core processes of an organization into a single system to provide the business with the intelligence that it needs to run efficiently.

3. All of the following are benefits of just-in-time manufacturing **except** that it:

   ☐ **a.** can significantly reduce inventory.

   ☐ **b.** helps produce a higher-quality product in less time.

   ☑ **c.** allows for minor defects without shutting down operations.

   ☐ **d.** helps eliminate rework costs.

Just-in-time manufacturing is a system that focuses on ordering and receiving inventory for production and sales at the time that it is needed to produce the goods. This system does not allow for minor defects without shutting down the company's operations.

Business Process Improvement

BUSINESS PERFORMANCE HAS ORGANIZATIONAL RAMIFICATIONS that go beyond matching or surpassing the competition in your industry. Customers are generally better informed and have virtually unlimited sources of quality goods and services at acceptable prices. Customers today demand more for less than they did in the past. Because of this, organizations are constantly challenged to address these rising customer expectations. The analysis of business process improvement is one way to meet these challenges.

This topic addresses some of the techniques used to analyze business process improvement: value chain analysis, process analysis, process reengineering, benchmarking, activity-based management, continuous improvement, best practice analysis, and cost-of-quality analysis.

 READ the Learning Outcome Statements (LOS) for this topic as found in Appendix A and then study the concepts and calculations presented here to be sure you understand the content you could be tested on in the CMA exam.

Value Chain Analysis

How do organizations make intelligent choices about where to focus their energy and how to best create value in the eyes of their customers? Many organizations have found success through value chain analysis, which has become an integral part of the strategic planning process. Similar to strategic planning, value chain analysis is a continuous process of gathering, evaluating, and communicating information. The basic intent of value chain analysis is to help managers envision an organization's future and implement business decisions to gain and sustain competitive advantage.

The concept underlying this system is **value**, which is generally used to describe the worth, desirability, or utility of a particular asset. It may be applied to an individual product, a service rendered, a group of assets, or to an entire business unit. Value may also be applied as a metric, such as in market value, shareholders' value, and so on.

Value activities describe the collective activities performed by organizations in a given industry. In a manufacturing industry that includes the processing of raw material, to the production and servicing of a final product. Depending on the industry, some firms may be involved in several activities, whereas others may have responsibility for only a single activity. Within an organization, business units may be a further subset. A clothing company, for example, may start with the raw textiles, design and manufacture articles of clothing, contract advertising, and sales to customers. Another clothing company may contract out manufacturing, concentrate on sales and marketing through organizational business units, and rely on retailers for distribution.

A **cost driver** is any factor that causes a change in the cost of an activity. Direct labor hours, machine hours, computer time, and beds occupied in a hospital are all examples of cost drivers. For more meaningful analysis, beyond the total costs of each value-creating activity, the causes for significant costs need to be identified. Firms examine structural cost drivers and executional cost drivers. Structural cost drivers are long-term organizational decisions that determine the economic structure driving the cost of the firm's product or service. Executional cost drivers reflect a firm's operational decisions on how to best use its resources, both human and physical, to achieve organizational goals and objectives.

A **supply chain** is the extended network of suppliers, transporters, storage facilities, and distributors that participate in the design, production, sale, delivery, and use of a company's product or service. During value chain analysis, an organization examines the entire supply chain.

A **value chain** is a system of interdependent activities, each of which is intended to add value to the final product or service from the customer's perspective. Naturally, the development of a value chain depends on the industry. Figure 1D-29 shows a typical value chain for a manufacturing environment. In a service environment, the acquisition of raw materials would be absent, and other activities and operations might vary and/or assume different degrees of importance.

LOS
§1.D.5.a

Value chain analysis (VCA) is a strategic analysis tool organizations use to assess the importance of their customers' value perceptions. It consists of an integrated set of tools and processes that define current costs and performance measures to evaluate where customer value can be increased and where costs can be reduced throughout the value and supply chains.

The distinct benefit of VCA is that it looks at the entire value chain, not just the activities in which the organization participates directly. Suppliers, distributors, and others involved in an organization's value chain each have costs and profit margins that affect the final price to end users and the marketing strategy for the product or service.

Steps in Value Chain Analysis

LOS
§1.D.5.b

The purpose of a VCA is to focus on the total value chain of each product or service to determine which selected part or parts support the firm's competitive advantage and strategy. Theoretically, competitive advantage and competitive strategy cannot be examined meaningfully at the organizational level as a whole or at the business unit level due to the detail required for the analysis. Because a value chain separates the firm into distinct strategic activities, organizations are able to use VCA to determine where in the operations the customers' value can be enhanced and costs

Figure 1D-29 Typical Value Chain for a Manufacturing Environment

Note: In the value chain, marketing includes sales, and customer service includes those services provided after the sale is made. Customer service feeds into research and development. Therefore, the value chain is a continuous cycle.

lowered. In this way, VCA helps to identify sources of profitability and to understand the costs of the related activities and processes.

VCA requires a strategic framework as a starting point for organizing and analyzing internal and external information, as well as for summarizing findings and recommendations.

There is no one standard process to conduct a VCA, and practices will vary among companies. The general steps in VCA discussed on the IMA Web site in the *Statements on Management Accounting*, "Value Chain Analysis for Assessing Competitive Advantage" (Copyright © 1996 Institute of Management Accountants) are summarized in Figure 1D-30.

LOS
§1.D.5.c

Figure 1D-30 Value Chain Approach for Assessing Competitive Advantage

Step 1	Internal cost analysis

This step determines the sources of profitability and the relative cost of internal processes or activities. An internal cost analysis will:

Identify the firm's value-creating processes.

Determine the portion of the total cost of the product or service attributable to each value-creating process.

Identify the cost drivers for each process.

Identify the links between processes.

Evaluate opportunities for achieving relative cost advantages.

(Continued)

Figure 1D-30 (Continued)

Step 2   **Internal differentiation analysis**

During this part of the analysis, sources for creating and sustaining superior differentiation are examined. The primary focus is the customer's value perceptions of the firm's products and services. Similar to Step 1, an internal differentiation analysis first requires identifying internal value-creating processes and cost drivers. With this information, a firm can perform a differentiation analysis to:

> Identify customers' value-creating processes.

> Evaluate differentiation strategies for enhancing customer value.

> Determine the best sustainable differentiation strategies.

Step 3   **Vertical linkage analysis**

Vertical linkage analysis is a broader application of Steps 1 and 2; it includes all upstream and downstream value-creating processes in an industry. Vertical linkage can identify which activities are the most/least critical to competitive advantage or disadvantage. It considers all links, from the source of raw materials to the disposal and/or recycling of a product. A vertical linkage analysis will:

> Identify the industry's value chain and assign costs, revenues, and assets to value-creating processes.

> Diagnose the cost drivers for each value-creating process.

> Evaluate the opportunities for sustainable competitive advantage.

These three steps in the analysis are complementary. Organizations begin by examining their internal operations and then broaden their focus to evaluate their competitive position within their industry.

Typically, a large amount of data is generated during a VCA study. All of the data require careful interpretation to discern the key messages of how to best create customer-perceived value.

Value-Added Concepts and Quality

Quality, like strategy and strategic planning, has many definitions and descriptions and a variety of approaches. The customer ultimately defines what constitutes product or service quality. This is not a static perception. Instead, it is constantly evolving based on factors such as product innovation, market changes, and changes to customers' tastes.

Internal and External Customers

In quality terms, a customer is anyone who is affected by an organization's processes, products, and services. Therefore, a firm has both internal and external customers.

An **internal customer** is an employee, department, or business unit that receives an output in the form of information, a product, or a service from another employee, department, or business unit. Even the next person in a work process is an internal customer. Based on this concept, all work-related activities are considered to be a series of transactions between employees or between internal customers and internal suppliers.

An **external customer** is a person or entity outside of the organization who receives information, a product, or a service. Sometimes, external customers are thought of as being end users outside the organization. An external customer can also be a vendor who manufactures a product for the organization.

Value Chain Analysis and Quality Performance

As organizations strive for quality performance, everyone, from the top executives to an employee on the front line, has a responsibility to create or contribute to the value of the firm's processes, products, and services for the external customer or end user.

Suppliers also have a crucial role. An organization starts with external customer requirements as determined by its industry analysis and/or strategies. The firm proceeds to identify internal customer–supplier relationships and requirements and continues with external suppliers. A chain of operations produces the final product or service. The external customer is best served when every internal customer and supplier receives what they need along the chain.

The concept of **value added** refers to activities that convert resources into products and services consistent with external customer requirements. Non-value-added activities can be eliminated with no deterioration in product or service functionality, performance, or quality in the eyes of the end user. In industries in which product and service parity is prevalent or outputs are perceived as commodities, examples of value-added activities might be some extra fabrication or customization before the sale to a customer or providing more service with the sale. Activities related to materials movement or rework would most likely be non-value-added.

There are instances when an activity, in general terms, is viewed as value added. However, when details are analyzed then it may be questionable. An example of this is quality control and assurance. Quality control in the form of inspections done when raw materials are received from a supplier can be characterized as value added. And it is. However, if every shipment received from a specific supplier is inspected because of high failure rates when the raw materials are used, one can argue that it is non-value added. The remedy for this is to work with that specific supplier to ensure the quality of the raw materials meets the purchaser's quality standard.

The firm would continue to inspect every shipment until the failure rate decreases. Then the inspection rate can be decreased to possibly every other shipment. Constant monitoring of the inspection results, as well as failure in the production process, will indicate whether the efforts have been successful. Further adjustments can be made accordingly, depending on the results.

By removing non-value-added activities, work processes can be more efficient and ultimately yield a better-quality product or service.

Process Analysis

LOS §1.D.5.e

A **process** is an activity or a group of interrelated activities that takes an input of materials and/or resources, adds value to it, and provides an output to internal or external customers. A process often spans several departmental units, such as accounting, sales, production, and shipping.

A firm should recognize and understand the array of business processes that contribute to its business profitability. One way to do this is through process analysis. **Process analysis** refers to a collection of analytic methods that can be used to examine and measure the basic elements for a process to operate. It can also identify those processes with the greatest need for improvement.

Process Characteristics

Three characteristics that help to identify a good process fit are:

1. **Effectiveness.** A process is effective when it produces the desired result and meets or exceeds customers' requirements. Customers perceive an effective process as being of high quality.
2. **Efficiency.** A process is efficient when it achieves results with minimal waste, expense, and/or cycle time. It has a high ratio of output to input.
3. **Adaptability.** A process is adaptable when it is flexible and can react quickly to changing requirements or new competition.

A process needs to address all three areas. A cost-efficient process is of little use if it does not produce an effective product, or if it cannot adapt to changing needs.

An assumption from the early days of quality improvement programs was that process improvements could be gained only at the expense of productivity. Experience has shown that quality improvements usually increase productivity by decreasing waste and the need for rework. The fact is that quality does have a cost, but it is a cost that management can influence and control.

A quality-oriented approach to product design, manufacturing, and service will consider upstream and downstream effects of all decisions. Cost drivers from all the company's departments, plus additional outside costs, must be accurately understood to ensure that sufficient resources are available for the transition to a quality enterprise.

Process Reengineering/Business Process Reengineering

Process improvements and productivity gains achieved through total quality management (TQM) generally are incremental gains achieved by tweaking a system and reducing inputs. In contrast, process reengineering and business process reengineering offer deeper, more sweeping changes and gains.

Process reengineering diagrams a process in detail, evaluates and questions the process flow, and then completely redesigns the process to eliminate unnecessary steps, reduce opportunities for errors, and reduce costs. All activities that do not add value are eliminated.

Business process reengineering (BPR) is the fundamental analysis and radical redesign of business processes within and between enterprises to achieve dramatic improvements in performance (e.g., cost, quality, speed, and service). Michael Hammer and James Champy brought BPR to the forefront in the early 1990s with their book *Reengineering the Corporation* (HarperBusiness, 2003, rev. ed.). BPR promotes the idea that sometimes wiping the slate clean and radically redesigning and reorganizing an enterprise is necessary to lower costs and increase the quality of a product or service.

According to Hammer and Champy, BPR involves changes that are:

Fundamental. BPR forces people to look at tacit rules and assumptions underlying the way they currently do business. Firms must answer two questions: Why do we do what we do? Why do we do it the way we do it?

Radical. BPR is about reinvention, *not* improvement or modification. A radical redesign means disregarding existing processes and inventing a new way of doing work.

Dramatic. BPR is not for the faint of heart. It should be used when "heavy blasting" is needed to alleviate a dire situation. If you need only a slight bump in process improvement, there is no need to reengineer.

Process. BPR is about a process orientation that emphasizes the chain of activities that take input and create output of value to the customer.

The BPR model espouses that process work flow in most large corporations is based on assumptions about technology, people, and organizational goals that are no longer valid. It also maintains that information is a key enabler to achieve radical change.

Figure 1D-31 lists the common tools and tactics underpinning successful BPR efforts.

Figure 1D-31 Fundamentals of Business Process Reengineering

Process orientation	Organizations look at entire processes that cut across organizational boundaries, not narrowly defined tasks with predefined organizational boundaries.
Ambition	Companies aim for breakthroughs, not minor improvements.
Rule breaking	Old traditions and assumptions are deliberately abandoned.
Creative use of technology	Current/state-of-the-art technology serves as an enabler that allows organizations to do work in radically different ways.

Process reengineering and BPR are strong medicine. Many well-intended reengineering efforts have failed for a variety of reasons. In a bit of a backlash to Hammer and Champy's initial foray, reengineering was even accused of being a cover for downsizing and layoffs. Yet, the success stories show that although the boldness has its perils and creates some pain, the resulting gains of reengineering can be dramatic.

Process analysis looks at the linkage of quality, productivity, and process improvements:

1. Productivity implies trying to improve on what already exists.
2. Improving productivity requires continuous quality improvement.
3. Continuous improvement necessitates ongoing organizational learning, process improvements, and reengineering.

These continuous productivity improvements can help an organization be competitive in the long term.

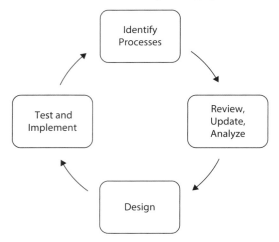

Business Process Reengineering Cycle

LOS
§1.D.5.g

Benchmarking

Benchmarking can be used in coordination with process analysis to develop measures to use in assessing an organization's effectiveness, efficiency, and adaptability. The term **benchmarking** describes a continuous, systematic process of measuring products, services, and practices against the best levels of performance. Many people think of benchmarking as simply capturing best-in-class information, but the practice has a much wider application. Quite often, best-in-class levels are comparisons to external benchmarks of industry leaders. However, they may also be based on internal benchmarking information or measures from organizations outside an industry that have similar processes.

Benchmarking Process Performance

Best-in-class levels may be financial or nonfinancial measures. The IMA *Statement on Management Accounting* "Effective Benchmarking" (Copyright © 1995 Institute of Management Accountants) describes benchmarking as having seven phases with associated activities, as illustrated in Figure 1D-32.

LOS
§1.D.5.h

Benchmarking and Creating Competitive Advantage

The 1990s saw a proliferation in benchmarking studies, but unfortunately many organizations misused benchmarking. Benchmarking studies in various forms, such as best practice, functional, process, and competitive advantage, were freely conducted. Invalid comparisons were often made—for example: 1) comparing the growth of a highly leveraged company to one internally financed from earnings, or 2) comparing the growth of a company in a low-cost environment to one in Silicon Valley. Given such misapplications, most of these benchmarking studies did not give relevant information for improvements to be made.

Figure 1D-32 Benchmarking Phases and Activities

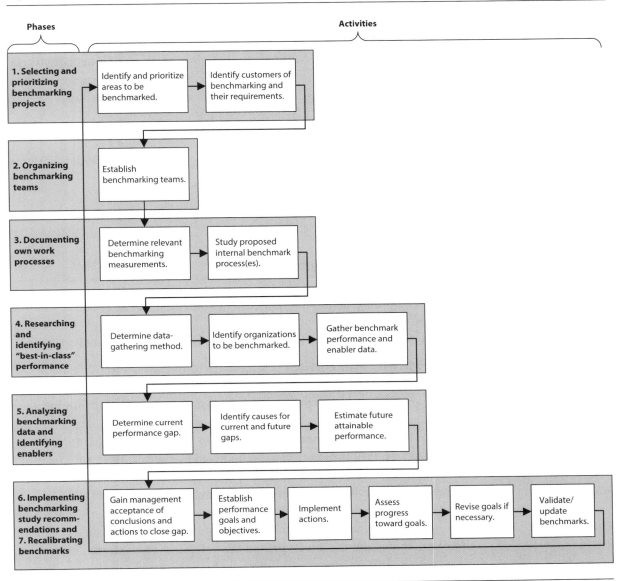

However, well-designed and properly applied benchmarking can be a powerful tool in helping an organization to be competitive. Through benchmarking, a firm identifies best-in-class levels and conducts a study to determine how those levels can be adopted and lead to improved performance. It provides a rational method for setting performance goals and gaining market leadership. Important decisions are based on facts and data rather than on emotions. Because benchmarking is based on what the best are doing, it provides an accurate assessment of what needs to change.

Strategic Benchmarking

Although many benchmarking studies have an operational focus, a benchmarking project may have a strategic focus as well. Strategic benchmarking applies process benchmarking to the level of business strategy by incorporating benchmarking results in the strategic planning process. As such, it helps an organization develop an increased understanding and ability to address strategic business issues such as:

- Building core competencies to help sustain competitive advantage
- Developing a new business line
- Targeting a specific shift in strategy (entering new markets or developing a new service)
- Making an acquisition
- Creating an organization that can quickly respond to uncertainties

Activity-Based Management

Activity-based management is another type of strategic analysis aimed at yielding process improvements.

Activity-based costing and activity-based management are related concepts.

- **Activity-based costing (ABC)** is a measure of the costs and performance of activities, resources, and cost objects. It assigns resources to activities and assigns activities to cost objects. It focuses on a causal relationship between cost drivers and activities.
- **Activity-based management (ABM)** focuses on the management of activities as the way of improving the value received by the customer and the profit achieved by providing this value. ABC provides the data used by ABM for cost driver analysis, activity analysis, and performance measurement.
- While ABC designates and uses cost drivers for each activity, ABM analyzes these cost drivers for their effectiveness in defining the root causes of activity costs. To explain the effects of cost drivers, ABM uses internal interviews, observation, and quality control tools such as theory of constraints, benchmarking, and other analytical tools. The result will be an assessment of how well the cost drivers reflect actual costs and actual areas of profitability.
- Another aspect of ABM is performance measurement. ABM helps make performance evaluation measures relate to the factors that drive the element being measured (cost drivers and revenue drivers). Such measures include revenue, manufacturing cost, nonmanufacturing cost, and profit as well as nonfinancial measures.

The bottom line is that both ABC and ABM are valuable practices for any firm striving to maintain or improve its competitive position. ABC answers the question "What do things cost?" ABM takes a process view and asks, "What causes costs to occur?"

ABM Principles and Process Improvements

ABM is forward-looking and change-oriented. It seeks ways to avoid unnecessary costs and put existing resources to maximum use.

Based on ABM information, organizations generally can:

- Make better decisions.
- Improve performance.
- Increase earnings on total resources deployed.

Overall, ABM supports both process reengineering and BPR by analyzing the organizational processes and by facilitating the measurement of the impact of reengineering efforts. This increases the value created for the resources consumed.

Organizations implement ABM for a variety of reasons. Figure 1D-33 summarizes general situations where a firm can benefit from ABM based on its stage of evolution.

Figure 1D-33 General Applications for ABM

If a firm's operations are . . .	Then ABM can be useful to . . .
Growing	Redeploy non-value-added work.
	Improve processes and activities.
Flat	Identify non-value-added costs.
	Set priorities for improvement and effect improvement.
	Isolate/eliminate cost drivers.
	Determine product/service costs.
Declining	Cut costs.
	Downsize.
	Effect layoffs.
Constrained as to capacity	Determine product/service costs.
	Make product/service decisions.
	Determine activity capacity.
	Identify bottlenecks.

ABM and Quality Improvements

ABM is sometimes erroneously thought of as a replacement for quality improvement efforts, just-in-time systems, process reengineering, BPR, and benchmarking. In fact, ABM supports quality management and the other initiatives by providing an integrated information system that:

- Establishes accountability
- Facilitates measuring of results
- Enables setting of priorities

Specific to quality, an ABM system facilitates quality implementation by:

- Identifying activity costs
- Increasing the visibility of associated costs of quality
- Providing quality cost measures that can be easily incorporated in cost-of-quality reports

Because traditional accounting systems focus on functions (research and design, production, sales and marketing, etc.), collecting data about the costs of quality can be a problem. With ABM, activity costs resulting from poor quality are more readily identifiable.

Advantages and Disadvantages of ABM

ABM has six advantages over traditional cost management techniques:

1. It uses continuous improvement to maintain the firm's competitive advantage.
2. It allocates more resources to activities, products, and customers that add more value, strategically redirecting management focus.
3. It eliminates non-value-added activities.
4. It measures process effectiveness and identifies areas to reduce costs or increase customer value.
5. It works well with just-in-time processes.
6. It ties performance measurement to ABC to provide consistent incentives for using ABC.

ABM has three disadvantages when compared to traditional cost management:

1. Changing to ABC/ABM will result in different product design, process design, manufacturing technology, and pricing decisions. The company must be prepared to support managers who embrace these methods and discourage managers who continue to use the older methods.
2. ABC/ABM is not used for external financial reporting. The need to prepare reports using traditional methods may influence management decision making enough to dilute the impact of ABC/ABM.
3. Implementing ABC/ABM is expensive and time-consuming, so a cost-benefit analysis should be done to identify all hidden costs and benefits.

Continuous Improvement (Kaizen) Concepts

Kaizen is a Japanese term used to describe continuous improvement at all levels in an organization. The premise is that as every process is examined, worked on, and improved, the total enterprise improves. The organization will start with the most important process. Kaizen acknowledges that innovation is valuable. But it also maintains that innovations do not collectively contribute as much as continuous incremental improvements.

The kaizen process is often described as a staircase of improvement. Moving from step to step, an organization uses a continuous process of following an improvement, maintaining an improvement, following an improvement, maintaining an improvement, and so on. Although the steps may be small, each step moves the organization upward toward sustained improvements.

Continuous improvements are often based on standards that become organizational performance expectations and goals. Standards allow an enterprise to identify the cost to manufacture and sell a product or a service and to determine the causes of cost overruns.

Organizations can develop standards based on:

- Activity analysis
- Historical data
- Benchmarking
- Market expectations
- Strategic decisions

Company benchmarking, for example, could be used to compare a firm's current cost structure to that of similar businesses and to develop appropriate standards. Once standards are determined, a series of continuous improvements could be implemented to increase efficiency and effectiveness and minimize any unfavorable variances.

LOS
§1.D.5.f

Best Practice Analysis

The term **best practice** generally refers to a process or technique that has produced outstanding results in one situation and that can be applied and/or adapted to improve effectiveness, efficiency, quality, safety, innovativeness, and/or some other performance measure in another situation. Best practice analysis refers to the collective steps in a gap analysis. A gap analysis is generally described as the difference between the current state and a desired state. It is the space between what is and what an organization hopes to be. The current state is defined by current practices and the desired state is defined by best practices.

Best practice analysis involves assessing how a firm's given performance level measures up to a best practice and then defining the logical next steps in transitioning to the desired performance level.

Typical activities are:

- Defining the gap through a comparison to internal operational data
- Determining the reasons for the gap
- Examining the factors that contribute to the existence of the best practice(s)
- Developing recommendations and an approach to implement the best practice(s)

Techniques and tools for conducting a best practice analysis vary. Qualitative and quantitative tools are used, but most of the tools are common to TQM and kaizen.

It may be said that best practice analysis tools—such as VCA, process analysis, BPR, benchmarking, TQM, and kaizen—are the clout behind business process improvement initiatives. Best practice analysis enables firms to identify and undertake performance improvements.

Costs of Quality Analysis

Process improvement teams need to know the specific costs for each part of the production process in order to determine how changes in a quality design affect profitability. The costs of quality (COQ) are broken down into four categories:

1. **Prevention costs** are the costs of a quality system design, implementation, and maintenance, including audits of the quality system itself. Examples include quality planning, review of new products, surveys of supplier capabilities, team meetings for quality, and training for quality. It also includes the costs related to ensuring the quality or quality improvement of the product: market research and product design.

2. **Appraisal costs** are the costs of auditing processes for quality, including formal and informal measurements and evaluations of quality levels and setting quality standards and performance requirements. Examples include inspection and testing of raw materials, work-in-process and finished goods testing, calibration of equipment, product testing, and audits of operations or services. In addition, they address more externally focused costs, such as monitoring market reaction and competitors' products.

3. **Internal failure costs** include the costs involved with defective products and components that are caught before shipping them to the customer. Examples include scrap, rework, spoilage, retesting, and reinspection. They also include systemic problems, such as the inability to meet the design, manufacturing, and service standards identified for the product.

4. **External failure costs** are the costs involved with shipping a defective product to a customer. Examples include customer complaints, returns, product recalls, and warranty claims. Overall, these costs relate to an inability to meet customer perceptions for product quality and service.

A quality-oriented approach can achieve gains in productivity and profit, but only if the company makes a long-term commitment to implement and sustain the effort.

Case Example—Activity-Based Management

The Midwest Biofuel Company (MBC) experienced a very fast start-up period when the price of fossil fuels was very high and there were various government subsidies available to encourage new biofuel companies. Now that fossil fuel prices have declined and government subsidies are being scaled back, MBC is looking to use

Activity-Based Management Principles and associated process improvements to make better decisions, improve performance, and optimize asset utilization.

MBC's operations are in a flat phase so the company is looking to identify non-value-added costs, set priorities for improvement, isolate/eliminate cost drivers, and determine product/service costs. As the plant controller, you have been tasked to develop a demonstration of the ABM process so you have chosen the company's practice of purchasing custom-painted delivery trucks as a test case.

ABM Review—Custom Painting of Delivery Trucks

Tasks	Item	Cost
Identify non-value-added costs	Custom painting of delivery trucks	$3,000 per vehicle
Set priorities for improvement	Recompute cost of painting process	Task painting contractor for pricing
	Recompute cost of decal alternative	Task decal vendor for pricing
Isolate/eliminate cost drivers	Update cost of painting process	$3,000 per vehicle
	Update cost of decal alternative	$1,500 per vehicle
Determine product /service costs	Painting process	Premium item
	Decal alternative	Industry standard item

Your analysis demonstrates that you can save $1,500 per vehicle using an industry standard decal alternative that will save the company $30,000 with an upcoming fleet replacement of 20 vehicles.

Business Process Improvement in Accounting Operations

The concept of business process improvement goes beyond simply creating efficiencies, improvements, and enhancing quality in the production process. In fact, internal services provided within an organization by "back office" departments and/or "cost centers," such as the accounting and finance department, provide key opportunities for creating efficiencies by focusing on continuous improvement and cost reduction in the activities performed by these departments. This is especially true for routine activities. Through the process of creating efficiencies, organizations can work to identify the root causes for errors in the work flow and eliminate waste and overcapacity. Organizations can pursue these efficiencies by conducting process walk-throughs, process training, reducing the accounting close cycle so as to effect a "fast close," and implementing shared services, where applicable.

Process walk-throughs involve meeting with process owners and gaining an understanding of how their work gets done in order to uncover opportunities for improvement. Through this process, every step performed, every piece of paper created, every input, and every output should be scrutinized. Questions need to be asked, such as "Is this step or process necessary?" "Does it add value?" "Can it be automated?" "Does it take excessive time to complete?" "Is there duplication of effort?" After completing the process walk-throughs, an evaluation of staff training should be made. Most organizations send employees to professional development seminars and provide systems training. Rarely do organizations provide training on how to properly accomplish day-to-day activities. Significant productivity can be achieved through appropriate training.

Organizations can also create efficiencies by identifying ways to reduce the accounting cycle and realize a fast close. While there are a host of ways to do this, organizations should focus on improving and eliminating the time and effort it takes to perform key closing activities. Just a few examples are standardizing the chart of accounts, creating templates for journal entries, and having written accounting policies and procedures. This is especially important for organizations that have multiple locations. The organization could even consolidate local accounting close operations into one centralized location. In addition, using closing checklists and conducting process analyses can also prevent omitting a step in the closing process and/or error oversights.

Finally, organizations can look to implement shared services among routine and often lower-level accounting tasks and activities. This can be done for billing, collections, accounts payable, and payroll processing. This involves grouping employees performing these tasks and activities by business function rather than by business unit. The result is a reduction of costs that would otherwise result from overcapacity having multiple employees performing the same function. It also helps to mitigate errors.

Topic Questions:
Business Process Improvement

Directions: Answer each question in the space provided. Correct answers and explanations appear after the topic questions.

1. Which one of the following statements best describes the concept of continuous improvement when developing standard costs?

   ☐ **a.** Standards become more challenging as time passes.

   ☐ **b.** Standards are developed with zero slack or downtime factored into the calculation.

   ☐ **c.** Standards remain unattainable to encourage employees to strive harder.

   ☐ **d.** Standards are established at an easily attainable level to increase employee morale.

2. A company currently is performing a cost of quality analysis of one of its facilities. The following are costs compiled by the facility accountant:

Inspection	$1,500
Warranty repair	2,800
Testing of new materials	400
Product testing	950
Spoilage	645
Scrap	150
Preventive equipment maintenance	590
Liability claims	1,870
Rework	1,285

   What is the total internal failure cost?

   ☐ **a.** $2,080

   ☐ **b.** $2,785

   ☐ **c.** $4,945

   ☐ **d.** $5,955

3. Which of the following would be the best choice for Timely, Inc., a producer of surface-mount chips (SMC), when it wants to benchmark average call waiting times in its customer service?

☐ **a.** A minimum call waiting time set by a consultant that tracked "best" call waiting times at Timely, Inc.

☐ **b.** The average call waiting time of a competing manufacturer that is a customer service leader

☐ **c.** The average call waiting time for the SMC industry overall

☐ **d.** Internal benchmarks created by reducing current average call waiting time at Timely, Inc.

Topic Question Answers:
Business Process Improvement

1. Which one of the following statements best describes the concept of continuous improvement when developing standard costs?

   ☑ **a.** Standards become more challenging as time passes.

   ☐ **b.** Standards are developed with zero slack or downtime factored into the calculation.

   ☐ **c.** Standards remain unattainable to encourage employees to strive harder.

   ☐ **d.** Standards are established at an easily attainable level to increase employee morale.

The concept of continuous improvement is best described as standards becoming more challenging as time passes. Continuous improvement is often described by the Japanese word, kaizen, which means "improvement" or "good improvement." Under continuous improvement, a company's processes are constantly being evaluated to improve quality, eliminate waste, reduce cost, boost efficiency, and save time. To improve, the standards naturally become more challenging as time passes.

2. A company currently is performing a cost of quality analysis of one of its facilities. The following are costs compiled by the facility accountant:

Inspection	$1,500
Warranty repair	2,800
Testing of new materials	400
Product testing	950
Spoilage	645
Scrap	150
Preventive equipment maintenance	590
Liability claims	1,870
Rework	1,285

What is the total internal failure cost?

   ☑ **a.** $2,080

   ☐ **b.** $2,785

   ☐ **c.** $4,945

   ☐ **d.** $5,955

Internal failure costs are costs that are incurred after the product is produced, but before the product is shipped. The costs that this company would include are the spoilage, scrap, and rework costs; therefore, the total internal failure cost is $2,080 (645 + 150 + 1,285).

3. Which of the following would be the best choice for Timely, Inc., a producer of surface-mount chips (SMC), when it wants to benchmark average call waiting times in its customer service?

   ☐ **a.** A minimum call waiting time set by a consultant that tracked "best" call waiting times at Timely, Inc.

   ☑ **b.** The average call waiting time of a competing manufacturer that is a customer service leader

   ☐ **c.** The average call waiting time for the SMC industry overal

   ☐ **d.** Internal benchmarks created by reducing current average call waiting time at Timely, Inc.

Timely, Inc. should use the average call waiting time of a competing manufacturer that is a customer service leader. Benchmarking is done by identifying and adopting best-in-class levels of performance. Companies can use benchmarking studies to not only improve operations, but also strengthen the organization's strategic focus.

Directions: This sampling of questions is designed to emulate actual exam questions. Read each question and write your response on another sheet of paper. See the "Answers to Section Practice Questions" section at the end of this book to assess your response. Validate or improve the answer you wrote. For a more robust selection of practice questions, access the **Online Test Bank** at www.wileycma.com.

Question 1D1-CQ02

Topic: Measurement Concepts

A company employs a just-in-time (JIT) production system and utilizes back-flush accounting. All acquisitions of raw materials are recorded in a raw materials control account when purchased. All conversion costs are recorded in a control account as incurred, while the assignment of conversion costs are from an allocated conversion cost account. Company practice is to record the cost of goods manufactured at the time the units are completed using the estimated budgeted cost of the goods manufactured.

The budgeted cost per unit for one of the company's products is as shown:

Direct materials	$15.00
Conversion costs	35.00
Total budgeted unit cost	$50.00

During the current accounting period, 80,000 units of product were completed, and 75,000 units were sold. The entry to record the cost of the completed units for the period would be which of the following?

a. Work in Process—Control	4,000,000	
Raw Material—Control		1,200,000
Conversion Cost Allocated		2,800,000
b. Finished Goods—Control	4,000,000	
Raw Material—Control		1,200,000
Conversion Cost Allocated		2,800,000
c. Finished Goods—Control	3,750,000	
Raw Material Control		1,125,000
Conversion Cost Allocated		2,625,000
d. Cost of Goods Sold	3,750,000	
Raw Material—Control		1,125,000
Conversion Cost Allocated		2,625,000

Question 1D1-CQ03

Topic: Measurement Concepts

From the budgeted data shown, calculate the budgeted indirect cost rate that would be used in a normal costing system.

Total direct labor hours	250,000
Direct costs	$10,000,000
Total indirect labor hours	50,000
Total indirect labor-related costs	$5,000,000
Total indirect non-labor-related costs	$7,000,000

☐ **a.** $20/DHL

☐ **b.** $28/DHL

☐ **c.** $40/DHL

☐ **d.** $48/DHL

Question 1D1-CQ06

Topic: Measurement Concepts

Chassen Company, a cracker and cookie manufacturer, has these unit costs for the month of June.

Variable Manufacturing Cost	Variable Marketing Cost	Fixed Manufacturing Cost	Fixed Marketing Cost
$5.00	$3.50	$2.00	$4.00

A total of 100,000 units were manufactured during June, of which 10,000 remain in ending inventory. Chassen uses the first-in, first-out (FIFO) inventory method, and the 10,000 units are the only finished goods inventory at month-end. Using the full absorption costing method, Chassen's finished goods inventory value would be

☐ **a.** $50,000

☐ **b.** $70,000

☐ **c.** $85,000

☐ **d.** $145,000

Question 1D1-CQ12

Topic: Measurement Concepts

During the month of May, Robinson Corporation sold 1,000 units. The cost per unit for May was as shown:

	Cost per Unit
Direct materials	$5.50
Direct labor	3.00
Variable manufacturing overhead	1.00
Fixed manufacturing overhead	1.50
Variable administrative costs	0.50
Fixed administrative costs	3.50
Total	$15.00

May's income using absorption costing was $9,500. The income for May, if variable costing had been used, would have been $9,125. The number of units Robinson produced during May was

- ☐ **a.** 750 units
- ☐ **b.** 925 units
- ☐ **c.** 1,075 units
- ☐ **d.** 1,250 units

Question 1D1-CQ13

Topic: Measurement Concepts

Tucariz Company processes Duo into two joint products, Big and Mini. Duo is purchased in 1,000 gallon drums for $2,000. Processing costs are $3,000 to process the 1,000 gallons of Duo into 800 gallons of Big and 200 gallons of Mini. The selling price is $9 per gallon for Big and $4 per gallon for Mini.

The 800 gallons of Big can be processed further into 600 gallons of Giant if $1,000 of additional processing costs are incurred. Giant can be sold for $17 per gallon. If the net-realizable-value (NRV) method were used to allocate costs to the joint products, the total cost of producing Giant would be:

- ☐ **a.** $5,600
- ☐ **b.** $5,564
- ☐ **c.** $5,520
- ☐ **d.** $4,600

Question 1D1-CQ14

Topic: Measurement Concepts

Tucariz Company processes Duo into two joint products, Big and Mini. Duo is purchased in 1,000 gallon drums for $2,000. Processing costs are $3,000 to process the 1,000 gallons of Duo into 800 gallons of Big and 200 gallons of Mini. The selling price is $9 per gallon for Big and $4 per gallon for Mini.

If the sales value at split-off method is used to allocate joint costs to the final products, the per gallon cost (rounded to the nearest cent) of producing Big is:

- ☐ **a.** $5.63 per gallon
- ☐ **b.** $5.00 per gallon
- ☐ **c.** $4.50 per gallon
- ☐ **d.** $3.38 per gallon

Question 1D1-CQ15

Topic: Measurement Concepts

Tempo Company produces three products from a joint process. The three products are sold after further processing as there is no market for any of the products at the split-off point. Joint costs per batch are $315,000. Other product information is shown next.

	Product A	Product B	Product C
Units produced per batch	20,000	30,000	50,000
Further processing and marketing cost per unit	$0.70	$3.00	$1.72
Final sales value per unit	$5.00	$6.00	$7.00

If Tempo uses the net realizable value method of allocating joint costs, how much of the joint costs will be allocated to each unit of Product C?

- ☐ **a.** $2.10
- ☐ **b.** $2.65
- ☐ **c.** $3.15
- ☐ **d.** $3.78

Question 1D1-CQ16
Topic: Measurement Concepts

Fitzpatrick Corporation uses a joint manufacturing process in the production of two products, Gummo and Xylo. Each batch in the joint manufacturing process yields 5,000 pounds of an intermediate material, Valdene, at a cost of $20,000.

Each batch of Gummo uses 60% of the Valdene and incurs $10,000 of separate costs. The resulting 3,000 pounds of Gummo sells for $10 per pound.

The remaining Valdene is used in the production of Xylo, which incurs $12,000 of separable costs per batch. Each batch of Xylo yields 2,000 pounds and sells for $12 per pound.

Fitzpatrick uses the net realizable value method to allocate the joint material costs. The company is debating whether to process Xylo further into a new product, Zinten, which would incur an additional $4,000 in costs and sell for $15 per pound. If Zinten is produced, income would increase by:

- ☐ **a.** $2,000
- ☐ **b.** $5,760
- ☐ **c.** $14,000
- ☐ **d.** $26,000

Question 1D2-CQ03
Topic: Costing Systems

Loyal Co. produces three types of men's undershirts: T-shirts, V-neck shirts, and athletic shirts. In the Folding and Packaging Department, operations costing is used to apply costs to individual units, based on the standard time allowed to fold and package each type of undershirt. The standard time to fold and package each type of undershirt is shown next.

T-shirt	40 seconds per shirt
V-neck shirt	40 seconds per shirt
Athletic shirt	20 seconds per shirt

During the month of April, Loyal produced and sold 50,000 T-shirts, 30,000 V-neck shirts, and 20,000 athletic shirts. If costs in the Folding and Packaging Department were $78,200 during April, how much folding and packaging cost should be applied to each T-shirt?

- ☐ **a.** $0.5213
- ☐ **b.** $0.6256
- ☐ **c.** $0.7820
- ☐ **d.** $0.8689

Question 1D2-CQ04

Topic: Costing Systems

During December, Krause Chemical Company had these selected data concerning the manufacture of Xyzine, an industrial cleaner.

Production Flow	Physical Units	
Completed and transferred to the next department	100	
Add: Ending work-in-process inventory	10	(40% complete as to conversion)
Total units to account for	110	
Less: Beginning work-in-process inventory	20	(60% complete as to conversion)
Units started during December	**90**	

All material is added at the beginning of processing in this department, and conversion costs are added uniformly during the process. The beginning work-in-process inventory had $120 of raw material and $180 of conversion costs incurred. Material added during December was $540, and conversion costs of $1,484 were incurred. Krause uses the weighted-average process-costing method. The total raw material costs in the ending work-in-process inventory for December are:

- ☐ **a.** $120
- ☐ **b.** $72
- ☐ **c.** $60
- ☐ **d.** $36

Question 1D2-CQ08

Topic: Costing Systems

Oster Manufacturing uses a weighted-average process costing system and has these costs and activity during October:

Materials	$40,000
Conversion cost	32,500
Total beginning work-in-process inventory	$72,500
Materials	$700,000
Conversion cost	617,500
Total production costs—October	$1,317,500
Production completed	60,000 units
Work in process, October 31	20,000 units

All materials are introduced at the start of the manufacturing process, and conversion cost is incurred uniformly throughout production. Conversations with plant personnel reveal that, on average, month-end in-process inventory is 25% complete. Assuming no spoilage, how should Oster's October manufacturing cost be assigned?

	Production Completed	**Work in Process**
☐ a.	$1,042,500	$347,500
☐ b.	$1,095,000	$222,500
☐ c.	$1,155,000	$235,000
☐ d.	$1,283,077	$106,923

Question 1D2-CQ10

Topic: Costing Systems

During December, Krause Chemical Company had these selected data concerning the manufacture of Xyzine, an industrial cleaner:

Production Flow	Physical Units	
Completed and transferred to the next department	100	
Add: Ending work-in-process inventory	10	(40% complete as to conversion)
Total units to account for	110	
Less: Beginning work-in-process inventory	20	(60% complete as to conversion)
Units started during December	**90**	

All material is added at the beginning of processing in this department, and conversion costs are added uniformly during the process. The beginning work-in-process inventory had $120 of raw material and $180 of conversion costs incurred. Material added during December was $540, and conversion costs of $1,484 were incurred. Krause uses the weighted-average process-costing method. The total conversion cost assigned to units transferred to the next department in December was

☐ **a.** $1,664

☐ **b.** $1,600

☐ **c.** $1,513

☐ **d.** $1,484

Question 1D2-CQ12

Topic: Costing Systems

Waller Co. uses a weighted-average process-costing system. Material B is added at two different points in the production of shirts; 40% is added when the units are 20% completed, and the remaining 60% of Material B is added when the units are 80% completed. At the end of the quarter, there are 22,000 shirts in process, all of which are 50% completed. With respect to Material B, the ending shirts in process represent how many equivalent units?

☐ **a.** 4,400 units

☐ **b.** 8,800 units

☐ **c.** 11,000 units

☐ **d.** 22,000 units

Question 1D2-CQ14

Topic: Costing Systems

The Chocolate Baker specializes in chocolate baked goods. The firm has long assessed the profitability of a product line by comparing revenues to the cost of goods sold. However, Barry White, the firm's new accountant, wants to use an activity-based costing system that takes into consideration the cost of the delivery person. Listed are activity and cost information relating to two of Chocolate Baker's major products.

	Muffins	Cheesecake
Revenue	$53,000	$46,000
Cost of goods sold	$26,000	$21,000
Delivery Activity		
Number of deliveries	150	85
Average length of delivery	10 minutes	15 minutes
Cost per hour for delivery	$20.00	$20.00

Using activity-based costing, which one of the following statements is correct?

- ☐ **a.** The muffins are $2,000 more profitable.
- ☐ **b.** The cheesecakes are $75 more profitable.
- ☐ **c.** The muffins are $1,925 more profitable.
- ☐ **d.** The muffins have a higher profitability as a percentage of sales and, therefore, are more advantageous.

Question 1D3-CQ01

Topic: Overhead Costs

During December, Krause Chemical Company had these selected data concerning the manufacture of Xyzine, an industrial cleaner.

Production Flow	Physical Units	
Completed and transferred to the next department	100	
Add: Ending work-in-process inventory	10	(40% complete as to conversion)
Total units to account for	110	
Less: Beginning work-in-process inventory	20	(60% complete as to conversion)
Units started during December	**90**	

All material is added at the beginning of processing in this department, and conversion costs are added uniformly during the process. The beginning work-in-process inventory had $120 of raw material and $180 of conversion costs incurred. Material added during December was $540, and conversion costs of $1,484 were incurred. Krause uses the first-in, first-out (FIFO) process-costing method. The equivalent units of production used to calculate conversion costs for December was:

- ☐ **a.** 110 units
- ☐ **b.** 104 units
- ☐ **c.** 100 units
- ☐ **d.** 92 units

Question 1D3-CQ03

Topic: Overhead Costs

Cynthia Rogers, the cost accountant for Sanford Manufacturing, is preparing a management report that must include an allocation of overhead. The budgeted overhead for each department and the data for one job are shown next.

	Department	
	Tooling	**Fabricating**
Supplies	$ 690	$ 80
Supervisor's salaries	1,400	1,800
Indirect labor	1,000	4,000
Depreciation	1,200	5,200
Repairs	4,400	3,000
Total budgeted overhead	$8,690	$14,080
Total direct labor hours	440	640
Direct labor hours on Job #231	10	2

Using the departmental overhead application rates and allocating overhead on the basis of direct labor hours, overhead applied to Job #231 in the Tooling Department would be:

- ☐ **a.** $44. 00
- ☐ **b.** $197. 50
- ☐ **c.** $241. 50
- ☐ **d.** $501. 00

Question 1D3-CQ05

Topic: Overhead Costs

Atmel Inc. manufactures and sells two products. Data with regard to these products are given next.

	Product A	**Product B**
Units produced and sold	30,000	12,000
Machine hours required per unit	2	3
Receiving orders per product line	50	150
Production orders per product line	12	18
Production runs	8	12
Inspections	20	30

Total budgeted machine hours are 100,000. The budgeted overhead costs are shown next.

Receiving costs	$450,000
Engineering costs	300,000
Machine setup costs	25,000
Inspection costs	200,000
Total budgeted overhead	$975,000

The cost driver for engineering costs is the number of production orders per product line. Using activity-based costing, what would the engineering cost per unit for Product B be?

☐ **a.** $4.00

☐ **b.** $10.00

☐ **c.** $15.00

☐ **d.** $29.25

Question 1D3-CQ08

Topic: Overhead Costs

Logo Inc. has two data services departments (the Systems Department and the Facilities Department) that provide support to the company's three production departments (Machining Department, Assembly Department, and Finishing Department). The overhead costs of the Systems Department are allocated to other departments on the basis of computer usage hours. The overhead costs of the Facilities Department are allocated based on square feet occupied (in thousands). Other information pertaining to Logo is as shown next.

Department	Overhead	Computer Usage Hours	Square Feet Occupied
Systems	$200,000	300	1,000
Facilities	100,000	900	600
Machining	400,000	3,600	2,000
Assembly	550,000	1,800	3,000
Finishing	620,000	2,700	5,000
		9,300	11,600

Logo employs the step-down method of allocating service department costs and begins with the Systems Department. Which one of the following correctly denotes the amount of the Systems Department's overhead that would be allocated to the Facilities Department and the Facilities Department's overhead charges that would be allocated to the Machining Department?

	Systems to Facilities	Facilities to Machining
☐ a.	$0	$20,000
☐ b.	$19,355	$20,578
☐ c.	$20,000	$20,000
☐ d.	$20,000	$24,000

Question 1D3-CQ09
Topic: Overhead Costs

Adam Corporation manufactures computer tables and has this budgeted indirect manufacturing cost information for next year:

| | Support Departments | | Operating Departments | | |
	Maintenance	Systems	Machining	Fabrication	Total
Budgeted Overhead	$360,000	$95,000	$200,000	$300,000	$955,000
Support work furnished					
From Maintenance		10%	50%	40%	100%
From Systems	5%		45%	50%	100%

If Adam uses the direct method to allocate support department costs to production departments, the total overhead (rounded to the nearest dollar) for the Machining Department to allocate to its products would be which of the following?

- ☐ **a.** $418,000
- ☐ **b.** $422,750
- ☐ **c.** $442,053
- ☐ **d.** $445,000

To further assess your understanding of the concepts and calculations covered in Part 1, Section D: Cost Management, practice with the **Online Test Bank** for this section. REMINDER: See the "Answers to Section Practice Questions" section at the end of this book.

Internal Controls (15%)

The Securities and Exchange Commission (SEC) imposes strict requirements over publicly traded companies to deploy internal controls that promote adherence to generally accepted accounting principles (GAAP) and greater transparency in financial reporting. Governance over financial, operational, and other risks that may impede the achievement of company goals and objectives is the driving force of an effective system of internal controls. As such, proper governance and internal control can help both public and private entities alike.

This section examines the appropriate structure and governance necessary for effectively managing actions, policies, and decisions through out an organization. The COSO *Internal Control—Integrated Framework* (2013), COSO *Enterprise Risk Management—Integrating with Strategy and Performance*, and legislative initiatives created to promote greater transparency and reliability of financial reporting are all covered in this section of the CMA body of knowledge.

Governance, Risk, and Compliance

I N 1987, FIVE ORGANIZATIONS—the American Institute of Certified Public Accountants, the Institute of Internal Auditors, the Institute of Management Accountants, the American Accounting Association, and the Financial Executives Institute—formed the Committee of Sponsoring Organizations (COSO). Their goal was to develop an integrated internal control model to guide efforts to articulate and improve accounting controls. COSO now provides guidance related to enterprise risk management, internal control, and fraud deterrence.

An emphasis on controls has grown from several policy and legislative initiatives. The Sarbanes-Oxley Act of 2002 (SOX) created the Public Company Accounting Oversight Board (PCAOB) as a part of the Securities and Exchange Commission. The PCAOB is responsible for the setting of standards for audits of publicly held corporations. The PCAOB has adopted the Committee of Sponsoring Organizations (COSO) internal control model as its guide. The COSO model was originally put into effect in 1992 and is now called the *Internal Control—Integrated Framework* (2013). It contains five primary integrated components of internal control, defines internal control, and establishes the criteria for determining the effectiveness of an internal control system.

In an effort to further address risk management, the original COSO model was expanded in 2004 to incorporate three additional risk-related components. The expanded risk-driven framework was updated in 2013 and called the *Enterprise Risk Management—Integrated Framework* and was updated in 2017 by COSO. It is called *Enterprise Risk Management—Integrating with Strategy and Performance*. The 2017 *Enterprise Risk Management—Integrating with Strategy and Performance* is discussed in Part 2, Section D, which covers risk management topics.

What Is Internal Control?

To paraphrase COSO, a functioning system of internal control is a process which provides reasonable assurance that an entity is achieving its goals related to operations, reporting, and compliance. Figure 1E-1 is the COSO *Internal Control* cube on which this is based:

Figure 1E-1 COSO *Internal Control Cube*

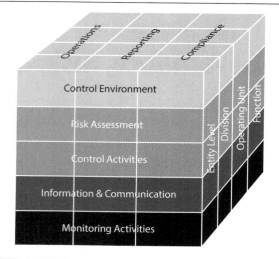

We refer to three dimensions of control systems:

1. Categories of goals or objectives—the following allow organizations to focus on aspects of internal control that may be particularly important to them:

    LOS §1.E.1.b

    a. *Operations*: goals related to the effective and efficient use of organizational resources
    b. *Reporting*: goals related to the reliability, timeliness, and transparency of financial and nonfinancial reporting
    c. *Compliance*: goals relating to compliance with applicable laws and regulations

    These objectives are unique to entities and their operating environments. In some cases, these objectives and controls overlap and support one another. For example, strong controls over cash are likely to increase the reliability of financial reports about cash.

    LOS §1.E.1.u

2. Components to a system of internal control—According to COSO, the five integrated control components to a system of internal control are:

    I. Control environment
    II. Risk assessment
    III. Control activities
    IV. Information and communication
    V. Monitoring activities

3. Organizational structure in the COSO materials describes a structure that is common in large organizations. This third dimension is divided into:

    LOS §1.E.1.c

    a. Organization wide: entity level
    b. Division level: high level or discrete parts of the organization
    c. Operating unit: a separable unit in an organization
    d. Function: accounting, marketing, information technology

These three dimensions capture, with respect to internal control:

- *What* is internal control? The five fundamental components.
- *Why do* we have internal control? The three goals or objectives.
- *Where do* we have internal control? The four units of analysis where we will design, implement, and test internal control.

Types and Limits of Internal Control

Classifying controls is useful in understanding their virtues and limitations. One classification scheme categorizes controls as preventive, detective, corrective, directive, and compensating.

Preventive Controls

Preventive controls help prevent errors and misappropriation of assets. For example, a control may create an obstacle that prevents the processing of a particular type of transaction. Credit checks on existing and potential clients to prevent sales to clients with poor credit risk or guards at exit points to prevent employee theft are other types of preventive controls. Preventive controls in general are usually more cost beneficial than detective controls.

Transactional controls are a specific type of preventive control designed to ensure that every transaction is documented, that false transactions are not entered into the system, and that all valid exchanges are recorded accurately. The types of controls selected depend on the quantity and the nature of the transactions the firm completes.

Preventive controls that depend on functions or people performing their roles effectively may include:

- Separation of duties.
- Supervisory review, such as a supervisor approving a purchase transaction.
- Dual control, such as two authorizations for every transaction above a certain threshold.
- Edit and accuracy checks, such as reconciling invoice amounts against original warehouse receipt records before an invoice is paid.
- Reasonableness checks, such as verifying the total of a transaction against a customer's credit limit. Reasonableness checks often are built into software systems.
- Completeness checks, such as a computer form that will not allow the operator to continue until required fields are completed. For example, if a data entry screen insists on complete fields before it permits processing, the screen itself operates as a preventive control to ensure completeness.

As with internal controls in general, no firm can expect its preventive controls to be foolproof. Thus, it is important for a firm to recognize the dependence of preventive controls on detective controls.

Detective Controls

Detective controls back up preventive controls by detecting errors once they occur. Reconciliation of bank statements is an example of a detective control over cash assets. Detective controls complement preventive controls and are essential components of a well-designed control system. In some cases, detective controls that examine random transactions may be less expensive than preventive controls that must check every transaction.

Corrective Controls

Corrective controls fix problems identified using detective controls. For example, an ordering system's routine edit function may detect an inaccurate account number on a sales order, read the client's name, search the database for the correct account number, and correct the original record. In some cases, if a record cannot be found in the database, the computer may generate an error report, which an employee can use to resolve the discrepancy.

Directive Controls

In contrast to controls that prevent, detect, and correct negative results, directive controls are instructions designed to produce positive results. For example, a firm may have a policy to use local vendors as often as possible. Directive controls may be intended to create a favorable image for the company in the community.

Compensating Controls

Compensating controls, also called mitigating controls, compensate for shortcomings elsewhere in the control structure. For example, having a bank reconciliation done by someone who is independent of accounting and cash handling can compensate for a number of flaws in the controls over cash transactions. Similarly, a hands-on owner-manager's supervision of operations might compensate for a lack of segregation of duties in a small business.

Compensating controls limit risk exposure, which must be analyzed in the context of bad outcomes that could happen, given particular system weaknesses. Compensating controls are sometimes redundant. For example, data entry verification can be achieved by having two entry points, reconciling these records, and generating an exceptions report on any detected differences.

Limitations of Internal Control

Even well-designed control systems can fail. Important threats that may bedevil well-designed systems include management override of controls, employee conflicts of interest, collusion among employees, and collusion between employees and outsiders, such as customers or vendors. Other inherent weaknesses are errors, misunderstandings, mistakes in judgment, and the cost-benefit trade-offs of controls when perfect controls are too expensive to implement.

Management override can threaten any control system. If a well-designed control structure can be overridden at management's discretion, the resulting risk exposure can be the same as having no controls in place. Circumstances sometimes justify management override. However, the control environment can be maintained only if management overrides are monitored and limited. For example, a control may be set in place to trigger an exception report automatically any time management overrides a control procedure.

Employees' conflicts of interest pose a threat to any business. For example, if a purchasing agent for a clothing retailer has a financial interest in a company that manufactures clothing, he or she has a conflict of interest when deciding which supplier to use.

The COSO Control Components: Designing Controls to Address Risks

Five Components of Internal Control

The original COSO framework includes five mutually reinforcing components of internal control that includes 17 principles. These must be integrated with an organization's management processes and adapted to changing conditions. Each component may affect any or all of the others. In 2013, the COSO released revisions and updates to the original 1992 Framework. The new framework, known as the *Internal Control—Integrated Framework* (2013), retains the core definition of internal control and the original five integrated internal control components, but it clarifies the application of the Framework in the current environment with various business models, technology, and related risks. It also codifies the criteria for developing an internal control structure and evaluating its effectiveness, and expands reporting objectives to support financial and nonfinancial reporting, operational, and compliance objectives. The five internal control components of COSO's *Internal Control—Integrated Framework* (2013) and their related 17 Principles include:

I. *Control Environment*:

The control environment refers to the organization's management philosophy and tolerance for risk. It includes an organization's integrity, ethical values, and the environment in which it operates.

#1. *Organizations* must demonstrate a commitment to upholding high standards of ethics and integrity. Management must establish and demonstrate, through actions, an ethical tone at the top. They must adhere to standards of conduct, which should be communicated at all levels of the organization and to outsourced service providers and business partners. They must also commit to prompt and efficient management of ethical failures and deviations from codes of conduct.

LOS §1.E.1.d

#2. *The board of directors* must demonstrate independence from management and oversee the development and monitoring of internal controls. These activities should include a clear statement of the board of directors' oversight responsibilities and independence, and appropriate levels of expertise and training, to enable effective oversight by the board.

LOS §1.E.1.c

#3. *Management* establishes, with board oversight, structures, reporting lines, and appropriate authorities and responsibilities to achieve objectives, including integrating organizational structures and services including outsourced service providers.

LOS §1.E.1.h

#4. *Competence.* The organization demonstrates a commitment to attract, develop, and retain competent individuals consistent with achieving organizational objectives, including to:

- Establish standards, policies, and procedures to attract, develop, and retain competent individual.
- Assess competencies, create development plans to achieve needed skills and competencies, and address deficiencies in skills and competencies through training, hiring, or outsourcing.
- Plan and prepare for turnover and succession.

LOS §1.E.1.h

#5. *Accountability.* The organization holds individuals accountable for internal control responsibilities, including to:

LOS §1.E.1.c

- Enforce accountability through structures, authorities, and responsibilities, including communicating and reinforcing accountabilities at all levels.
- Establish and evaluate performance measures, incentives, rewards, and disciplinary actions for individuals.
- Monitor and consider the potential for excessive performance pressures including unrealistic performance (e.g., earnings) targets and an excessive concern with short-term (e.g., quarterly earnings) targets.

Control Environment Components

The fundamental nature of the control environment recognizes that the core of any organization is its *people*. It is their individual attributes, which include integrity, ethics, and confidence, that primarily determine the organizational environment and culture. Some of the most important components of an ethical control environment are described next.

LOS §1.E.1.c

Tone at the Top

An organization desiring an effective internal control must have ethical top management that proactively works to establish a moral culture. Positive strategies for creating an ethical culture include management emphasizing both the critical role of ethics and integrity in organizational success and the role of mission statements and codes of conduct in promoting integrity. In addition, leading by example is more effective than simply talking the talk of ethical behavior.

Policies and Standards

Explicit development and communication of organizational policies and standards for managing organizational risks is also critical to establishing the desired control environment. For example, some organizations require that a designated team review major proposed projects and activities to assess their risk. Note that the creation of a risk review team is implicit in this recommendation.

Segregation of Duties and Critical Accounting Functions

Designing an effective organizational system of internal control requires particular attention to a set of critical functions. An **event** is an economic transaction that is relevant to the accounting system. Separating responsibilities for critical actions related to events lessens the likelihood of fraud and certain types of errors. Consider four critical activities related to internal control, which should be separated to lessen fraud risk:

1. *Authorizing events*: approving customer credit, authorizing payment of an invoice, approving shipping to a customer
2. *Recording events*: completing source documents, such as a customer invoice or bill of lading, posting events into the general ledger
3. *Safeguarding resources related to events (custody)*: maintaining the cash in a bank vault or the inventory in a store
4. *Reconciling, overseeing, and auditing*: board of director's review, internal and external audits, and reconciling system logs with known system activity

The WorldCom scandal provides a dramatic example of the failure to segregate some of these functions. WorldCom's chief executive officer (CEO), Bernard Ebbers, and chief financial officer (CFO), Scott Sullivan, in a remarkable display of "efficiency," authorized and recorded falsified accounting transactions that inflated revenue by about $11 billion. WorldCom's board of directors approved this system of control and these transactions (lack of oversight). This fraud earned Ebbers and Sullivan a 25-year and a 15-year prison term, respectively.

Bernard Madoff, of Madoff Securities infamy, oversaw one of the largest financial frauds in history at the beginning of the great recession. Mr. Madoff perpetrated the fraud (Ponzi/pyramid scheme), facilitated by maintaining a separate set of books for the company and over which he was the sole overseer. His external auditor was one CPA who was registered with the SEC solely to audit Madoff Securities. Madoff Securities had many employees, but no one seemed to be aware of Mr. Madoff's scheme. Madoff's fraud resulted in more than $66 billion in losses.

Large organizations can and should separate these functions. However, segregation of duties is less feasible, and therefore less likely, in small organizations.

Documenting Control Policies and Procedures

Internal control policies and procedures must be documented. Documentation is needed for training, for audits, and to ensure that systems survive the departure of their creators. At the most detailed level, written job descriptions outline the specific requirements of each job in the firm, including job qualifications, responsibilities, and reporting relationships.

The most common methods used to document control policies and procedures include written narratives accompanied by flowcharts that depict a step-by-step process graphically. Section 404 of the Sarbanes-Oxley Act of 2002 (SOX) requires that publicly held companies document their internal controls.

Four Accounting System Design Principles

Controls are designed to prevent unintentional errors due to carelessness or lack of knowledge. Fraud, however, is intentional, and it is difficult to prevent collusion and management override. No matter how well internal controls are designed, they cannot provide complete assurance against intentional fraud. Moreover, human error, carelessness in executing control procedures, fatigue or stress, and the tendency to let familiarity supersede control procedures can result in errors or fraud. In addition, even a well-designed control system is subject to obsolescence over time if not adjusted to changes in operations. Furthermore, if controls are too lax, they may fail to ensure compliance or to provide reliable information to help management achieve the organization's goals. However, if they are too complex, they increase the difficulty of processing transactions, reducing productivity without adding value.

The four principles of accounting system design can be applied to creating effective controls:

1. *Control principle.* The system helps protect a firm's assets and ensures that data are reliable.
2. *Compatibility principle.* The system's design works with the organizational structure and people in the organization.
3. *Flexibility principle.* The system is flexible; the volume of transactions can grow with the organization.
4. *Cost-benefit principle.* The benefits derived from the system and the information it generates must be equal to or greater than the system's costs, both tangible and intangible. Tangible costs include people, forms, and equipment. Intangible costs include the cost of wrong decisions.

II. Risk Assessment:

The model includes a component for assessing the probability and importance of each risk. Risks are classified as either inherent or residual. Inherent risks exist unless management takes action to avoid or mitigate them, and are the first to be assessed. Residual risks are those that remain after any actions management takes to reduce the inherent risks.

#6. *Objectives.* The organization specifies objectives with sufficient clarity to enable the identification and assessment of risks that threaten the achievement of objectives. In so doing, the organization should consider:

- The precision of the organization's appetite for risk (e.g., can we quantify the risk? To within what range? To which operating units subordinate to the entity as a whole?).
- Materiality in relation to risk assessment. How big is the risk that will threaten the achievement of objectives; a loss of $10,000? $100,000? $1,000,000?
- Risks related to the organization's ability to comply with standards, frameworks, laws, and regulations.
- Risks related to operational and financial performance goals.
- Risks in committing resources.

LOS §1.E.1.v

#7. *Assessment.* The organization identifies risks to the achievement of its objectives across the entity and analyzes risks as a basis to determine how they should be managed. In so doing, the organization should:

- Involve appropriate levels of management in risk assessment.
- Consider risks at multiple levels, as appropriate, including: the entity, subsidiary, division, operating unit, and functional levels.
- Analyze internal and external factors.
- Estimate risk importance.
- Develop appropriate risk responses.

LOS §1.E.1.v

#8. *Fraud.* The organization considers the potential for fraud in assessing risks to the achievement of objectives. In so doing, it:

- Considers fraud risk factors and threats.
- Assesses the potential influences of incentives and pressures on fraud.
- Assesses opportunities that may exist in the organization for fraudsters to commit fraud.
- Assesses attitudes and potential rationalizations that might be used to justify fraudulent actions.

LOS §1.E.1.v

#9. *Change Management.* The organization should identify and assess changes in the external environment, business model, and organizational leadership that could impact the system of internal control. For example, has the organization considered potential implications of changes in business lines, foreign operations, new technologies, and from rapid growth?

III. Control Activities

Policies and procedures are established and implemented to help ensure that the risk responses are carried out effectively. The COSO model lists the following control activities:

a. *Assignment of authority and responsibility* (job descriptions) requires the board of directors to hire the CEO and other managers who will hire, train, and appropriately compensate competent, reliable, ethical employees to accomplish the day-to-day operations of the company.

b. A system of *transaction authorizations* helps to avoid duplicate and fictitious payments, safeguards assets, and generates reliable accounting information. These controls include signatures of approval, reconciliations, and forms that document actions and authorizations.

LOS §1.E.1.m

c. Adequate *documentation and records* provide details of the company's operations. Documents, such as invoices and orders, may be paper or electronic. Prenumbering documents, such as invoices, purchase orders, and checks, reduces theft and inefficiencies by drawing attention to gaps in sequences. In addition, document and system control procedures should specify who is authorized to receive specific documents and to have access to particular portions of accounting systems. For example, who can access employee payroll and salary information.

LOS §1.E.1.i   LOS §1.E.1.h

d. *Security of assets* is enabled by a good system of authorizations and segregation of duties in order to reduce the opportunities for fraud and theft. For example, production activities and sales activities should not be performed by accounting personnel.

LOS §1.E.1.k

e. *Independent verifications* may be internal (such as the internal audit staff) or external (such as an independent certified public accountant who audits financial statements or a regulator who audits regulatory issues).

LOS §1.E.1.l

f. Adequate *separation (segregation) of duties* requires that different employees authorize, execute, record a transaction, and have custody of the assets resulting from the transaction.

For example: A purchase is authorized, perhaps by an assistant controller (i.e., a human), by a purchase requisition originating in inventory control. The purchase is executed by the purchasing agent and is recorded by the information technology department. The receiving department takes possession of the raw materials and validates the receipt to the purchase order by counting, inspecting, and preparing the receiving report. The materials are then released to inventory control.

LOS §1.E.1.v

#10. *Risk Reduction.* Organizational control activities mitigate or reduce the risks to the achievement of objectives to acceptable levels. In so doing, the organization:

- Integrates controls with risk assessments.
- Uses risk reduction analyses to determine which business processes require a control focus.
- Considers how the environment, complexity, nature, and scope of operations influence risk reduction and control activities.
- Evaluates a mix of potential control activity types, including manual and automated preventive and detective controls.
- Segregates incompatible activities, through segregation of duties, and implements alternative controls where segregation is impossible.

#11. *Technology Controls.* The organization selects and implements general controls over technology that support the achievement of its objectives. These activities should include:

- Management understanding of the dependencies among business processes, automated controls, and technology general controls.
- Management establishing controls to ensure the completeness, accuracy, and availability of technology and processing.
- Restricting technology access rights as appropriate.
- Establishing relevant security management process controls.
- Establishing relevant technology acquisition, development, and maintenance process controls.

LOS
§1.E.1.c

#12. *Policies.* The organization's control activities become policies that establish stakeholder expectations of accountability, responsibility, and control. Documented procedures ensure the implementation of these policies. These activities include:

- Establish policies and procedures that support the achievement of management's directives.
- Establish responsibility and accountability for executing policies and procedures.

LOS
§1.E.1.h

- Employ competent personnel to perform control activities in a timely manner and to take corrective action to investigate and act on control problems and issues.
- Periodic management reassessment and revision of policies and procedures to address changing conditions.

LOS
§1.E.1.c

IV. Information and Communication:

The COSO model recognizes that relevant information must be identified, captured, and communicated in a form and time frame that enables people to do their jobs successfully. This assumes that the data communications are secure and accurate.

#13. *Information Quality.* Relevant, high-quality information supports the organization's internal control processes. This activity includes organizational processes that:

- Identify the information needed to support internal control processes, capture internal and external data.
- Transform relevant data into information.
- Produce information that is relevant, timely, current, accurate, verifiable, protected, and retained.
- Consider the costs and benefits of information in relation to organizational objectives.

#14. *Internal Communication.* Internal communication supports internal control processes.

LOS
§1.E.1.h

- Organizational processes communicate required information to enable all personnel to understand and execute their internal control responsibilities.

- Communication between management and the board of directors supports the achievement of organizational objectives.
- Separate communication lines, such as a whistleblower hotline, exist as fail-safe mechanisms to enable anonymous, confidential communication.
- Internal communication methods are sensitive to the timing, audience, and nature of the communication.

#15. *External Communication.* Communication with outsiders supports internal control processes. These organizational processes:

- Communicate relevant and timely information to external parties, including shareholders, partners, owners, regulators, customers, financial analysts, and others.
- Enable inbound communications. Communication channels support the receipt of information from customers, suppliers, external auditors, regulators, financial analysts, and others.
- Separate communication lines, such as a whistle-blower hotline, exist as a fail-safe mechanism to enable anonymous, confidential communication.
- Communicate relevant information resulting from assessments conducted by external parties (e.g., reviews of internal control) to the board of directors.
- Ensure that external communication methods are sensitive to the timing, audience, and nature of the communication and to legal, regulatory, and fiduciary requirements.

LOS §1.E.1.k

V. Monitoring Activities:

All aspects of internal controls are monitored, and modifications are made as necessary. Monitoring is accomplished through ongoing management activities, separate evaluations, or both. Internal auditors, the audit committee, and the disclosure committee, as well as management, may all be involved in monitoring controls.

#16. *Ongoing and Periodic Monitoring.* Ongoing and separate or periodic evaluations to evaluate internal control functioning. These activities include to:

- Consider the mix of ongoing and separate evaluations.
- Benchmark—consider the design and state of the existing system of internal control to establish a baseline understanding for ongoing and separate evaluations.
- Develop and select ongoing and separate evaluations through management consideration of the rate of change of business activities and processes.
- Ensure that personnel have sufficient knowledge to conduct evaluations.

LOS §1.E.1.h

- Integrate ongoing evaluations with business processes and adjusting, as needed, to changing conditions.
- Provid periodic, separate evaluations for objective feedback.
- Adjust the scope and frequency of evaluations based on risk assessments.

LOS §1.E.1.d

#17. *Addressing Deficiencies.* Parties responsible for taking corrective action, including senior management and the board of directors, receive timely communication of internal control deficiencies. These activities include to:

- Assess the results of ongoing and separate evaluations, as appropriate, by management and the board of directors.
- Communicate deficiencies to those responsible for acting on them, to management at least one level above the identified problem, and to senior management and the board of directors, when appropriate.
- Management tracking of the resolution, and its timeliness, of deficiencies.

Enterprise Risk Management Policies and Procedures

In June 2017, COSO issued the new *Enterprise Risk Management—Integrating with Strategy and Performance* that updated both the 2004 *Enterprise Risk Management—Integrated Framework: Executive Summary* and the *Original Framework*. The 2017 ERM and the *Internal Control—Integrated Framework* are meant to complement each other.

It defines risk as the possibility that events will occur and affect the achievement of strategy and business objectives. It defines risk management as "the culture, capabilities, and practices, integrated with strategy-setting and performance, that organizations rely on to manage risk in creating, preserving, and realizing value." ERM focuses on managing risk through:

1. *Recognizing culture.* Culture is developed and shaped by all the people within the entity. ERM helps them to make decisions with an understanding of the role culture plays in shaping the decisions.
2. *Developing Capabilities.* ERM adds to the skills needed to carry out the entity's mission and vision.
3. *Applying Practices.* ERM practices are applied throughout the entity's divisions, business units, and functions.
4. *Managing Risk to Strategy and Business Objectives.* ERM practices provide management and the board of directors with a reasonable expectation that they can achieve the strategy and business objectives. This means the amount of risk is appropriate for the entity and recognizes that there is no absolute precision in predicting risk.
5. *Linking to Value.* The entity must manage risk according to its risk appetite, as expressed in their mission and vision.

Analyzing and Deconstructing Risk

Risk can be usefully analyzed, or deconstructed, into its constituent elements or parts. The two elements or parts include:

1. The *likelihood of a loss.*
2. The *amount of a loss,* should one occur.

The **expected value** of a loss is the likelihood of an estimated range of losses, multiplied by the amount of each estimated loss, should one occur.

A Key Control and Goal: Safeguarding Assets

Internal controls designed to protect the firm's assets are often the most visible controls. Such controls include door locks, security systems, computer passwords, and requirements for dual control of valuable assets. Assets can be stolen, misused, or accidentally destroyed unless protected by adequate controls. Controls for safeguarding assets include segregation of functions in processing transactions. For example, the person who writes up an order should not have access to the assets for fulfillment of the order.

Multiple levels of access controls should be built into an organization's operations and information systems. For example, users with authority to arrange shipments are able to update the inventory system, but sales staff is given read-only access to the data. In addition, the safeguarding of assets is growing increasingly complex in an era where many of an organization's assets (e.g., in the software business) exist primarily in virtual (electronic) form.

"People" (Human Resource) Controls

Competent, motivated, knowledgeable people are essential to systems of internal control. Without them, at least given the current state of artificial intelligence, the system will fail. Hence, hiring and other human resource (HR) policies are central to creating and maintaining effective internal controls. Competent and trustworthy employees, combined with timely and effective training, minimize the need for corrective internal control. Part of the firm's control procedures may relate to methods used to hire, evaluate, and train employees.

Recruiting, Selecting, Hiring, and Supervising Quality People

As a part of their HR controls, organizations should define qualifications for personnel in various positions. Staff are recruited, screened, and hired based on these qualifications, such as educational requirements, work experience, and professional certifications. Hiring practices may include reference and credit checks, security checks, and drug testing. Employers should also screen for conflicts of interest. Organizational structure, lines of authority, and job descriptions are important, but they are no substitute for good employees. Personnel who cannot perform their assigned tasks can threaten even the best-designed internal control policies and procedures.

Most employees require some degree of supervision and facilitation. Supervisory responsibilities include observing the work process and examining the work product. The amount of required supervision and facilitation varies depending on the abilities and experience of the employee and the complexity of the work.

Orientation, Training, Development, and Performance Reviews

Even the most qualified and skilled employees require an orientation to the business's goals, objectives, policies, and procedures. Job orientation should be given at the start of employment. Ongoing training and development is usually desirable, and, in some fields, is required by law or certification requirements. Most organizations recognize the importance of training and development to the overall success of the enterprise, and many provide or compensate employees for attending training sessions.

Periodic reviews help firms assess the performance of individual employees and the achievement of corporate goals and objectives. Most firms provide for regularly scheduled reviews for individual employees, usually conducted by the employee's supervisor. Employee reviews examine the employee's performance in relation to his or her goals and identify areas where the employee could improve. The employee review often sets goals and identifies methods for achieving them. These reviews can also help direct the employee to develop the skills that he or she needs for future organizational positions (e.g., acquiring key certifications or credentials).

Bonding, Rotation, and Vacations

Bonding (not to be confused with that other kind of bonding, like drinking beer together after work) is a type of insurance policy that protects an organization against theft by its employees. Personnel controls often include bonding employees who have custody of money and other assets. Rotation of duties and rotation of shifts can be an important control, especially for personnel with financial responsibilities. Requiring each employee to take vacations is another way to help ensure that an individual has not compromised the controls. Having another employee handle the same tasks during an employee's vacation provides a check on the quality of organizational processes, and on the trustworthiness of the vacationing employee.

Internal Control Monitoring Purpose and Terminology

How Does Monitoring Benefit Corporate Governance?

Monitoring is the core, underlying control component in the COSO ERM model. Its position at the foundation is not accidental and reflects the importance of monitoring to achieving strong internal control and effective risk management.

Why is control monitoring important?

1. People forget, quit jobs, get lazy, or come to work hung over; machines fail. Over time, controls deteriorate. This deterioration is called entropy.
2. Advancements in technology and management techniques demand that internal control and related monitoring processes continually evolve and improve.

Well-designed control monitoring helps lessen the negative effects of entropy and ensure that:

1. Management identifies internal control problems on a timely basis, meaning before they create crises, and addresses them proactively, rather than reactively.
2. Decision makers receive more timely and accurate information.

3. Financial and nonfinancial reports and statements are timely, reliable, and accurate.
4. Certifications of internal control, as required by SOX Section 404, occur on a timely basis.
5. Organizational efficiencies are maximized and costs are reduced.

Audit Risk

Public Company Accounting Oversight Board (PCAOB) Auditing Standard No. 8 now codified in AS 1101: *Audit Risk* discusses both audit risk and the risk of materially misstated financial statements. These are specific types of risk within the broader set of risks presented in the COSO models earlier. The auditing standard states that audit risk is influenced by and consists of two parts:

1. The financial statements are materially misstated.
2. The auditor expresses an inappropriate audit opinion.

Risk of Materially Misstated Financial Statements: Inherent, Control, and Detection Risk

LOS §1.E.1.n

LOS §1.E.1.h

Auditors divide the risk of material misstatement into three types:

1. **Inherent risk (IR)** is the susceptibility of financial statements to material misstatement when there are no internal controls. It is the probability that an error or irregularity (fraud) will occur. Errors are unintentional and relate to the competence of the organization's personnel. Fraud is intentional and relates to the integrity of the organization's personnel. Competence and integrity of personnel are the cornerstones of effective internal control.
2. **Control risk (CR)** is the likelihood that misstatements exceeding an acceptable level will not be prevented or detected by the firm's internal controls. It is the probability of a control failure.
3. **Detection risk (DR)**, also called planned detection risk, is a measure of the risk that audit evidence will fail to detect misstatements exceeding an acceptable audit risk. It is the risk the auditor is willing to take that an error or fraud goes undetected by audit procedures.

Appropriately Low Level of Audit Risk

Appropriately low level of audit risk (AR) is the probability that the auditor will issue an inappropriate audit opinion (often an unmodified opinion) when in fact the financial statements are materially misstated and therefore misleading. It is a function of the three types of risk just defined.

If auditors want greater certainty that the financial statements are not materially misstated, they will lower the AR that the auditor is willing to accept. The lower the audit risk the auditor is willing to accept, the greater will be the need for audit testing.

$$AR = IR \times CR \times DR$$

$$DR = AR / (IR \times CR)$$

where:
AR = audit risk
IR = inherent risk
CR = control risk
DR = detection risk

The auditor assesses the firm's inherent risk and control risk and sets AR in accordance with the auditor's willingness to accept the risk of issuing an inappropriate opinion. The combination of inherent risk and control risk is normally either high or low, based on inherent risk and control risk. If the auditor determines that internal controls are nonexistent or that the controls are entirely ineffective, then more substantive auditor procedures have to be used in order to render an opinion. A lower calculated detection risk means the auditor needs more evidence to support the audit opinion.

External Auditor's Responsibilities

Financial Statement Audit

The primary responsibility of the external auditor is to plan and perform the audit with an attitude of professional skepticism in order to obtain reasonable assurance as to whether the organization's financial statements are free from material error or misstatement. The types of audit opinions an auditor may issue include:

1. An unmodified opinion
2. An unmodified opinion with emphasis-of-matter or other-matter paragraph
3. A modified opinion, which may be a qualified opinion, an adverse opinion, or a disclaimer of opinion

1. An *unmodified opinion* is issued when all of the following conditions have been met:

   - A complete set of general purpose-financial statements (i.e., balance sheet, income statement, statement of cash flows) is included.
   - The three general standards (adequate technical training and proficiency, independence is mental attitude, and due professional care) have been followed in all aspects of the engagement.

- Sufficient appropriate evidence to support the opinion has been obtained.
- The financial statements are prepared, in all material respects and in accordance with the applicable reporting framework (most frequently generally accepted accounting principles [GAAP] in the United States). This implies that adequate financial statement disclosures have been made.
- There are no conditions requiring the addition of an emphasis-of-matter or other-matter paragraph in the audit report.

2. An *unmodified opinion with emphasis-of-matter or other-matter paragraph* meets the criteria of a complete audit with satisfactory results and the financial statements are fairly presented. However, professional standards require that a material matter be brought to the attention of the financial statement users, and the auditor believes it is important to "emphasize" the matter and provide additional information about the matter in the audit report. Some more common situations that would warrant the inclusion of emphasis-of-matter or other-matter paragraphs in the audit report include:

   - Inconsistency in the application of accounting principles (GAAP).
   - Going-concern doubts.
   - Uncertainties, such as whether conclusive audit evidence concerning the outcome of a lawsuit exists at the time of the audit but may occur at some time in the future.
   - A change in opinion for a prior period when reporting on current statements in comparative form.
   - Predecessor auditor's report for a prior period is not presented when reporting on current financial statements in comparative form.
   - Other discretionary circumstances, which might include a catastrophe that affects the audited company's financial position, significant transactions with related parties, or important subsequent events.

3. A *modified opinion* may be any one of the following:

   a. A *qualified opinion* is issued when the auditor concludes that either the financial statements are materially (but not pervasively) misstated (i.e., a specific departure from GAAP) or there is a scope limitation that is not pervasive because the auditor was prevented from obtaining sufficient appropriate audit evidence.
   b. An *adverse opinion* is issued when the auditor concludes that financial statements are materially misstated due to a major GAAP violation or departure and the effects of the misstatements are pervasive.
   c. A *disclaimer of opinion* is issued when the auditor is unable to obtain sufficient appropriate audit evidence and the possible effects are both material and pervasive. A disclaimer states that the auditor does not express an opinion on the financial statements.

LOS
§1.E.1.p

SOX Section 204 requires the public accounting firm that performed the audit to report to the audit committee, on a timely basis, the following:

1. All critical accounting policies and practices that have been used.
2. All alternative treatments of financial information within GAAP.
3. Other material written communications between the external auditing firm and management, such as a management letter.

Reporting on Internal Control

As mentioned previously, Section 404 of SOX also requires the external auditor to attest to and report on the adequacy of an organization's internal controls over financial reporting for issuers/entities whose securities are publicly traded.

LOS §1.E.1.p LOS §1.E.1.q

LOS §1.E.1.r LOS §1.E.1.s

PCAOB Auditing Standard No. 5 requires auditors to follow a risk-based approach to the development of auditing procedures. Auditors are also required to scale the audit to the size of the organization and to follow other prescribed approaches to perform the audit. In addition, Auditing Standard No. 5 provides guidance for the external auditor in complying with Section 404 requirements. It requires auditors to perform their internal control assessment using a top-down, risk assessment (TDRA) approach. TDRA is a hierarchical approach that applies specific risk factors to determine the scope of work (i.e., the controls to test) and evidence required in the assessment of internal controls.

TDRA begins at the financial statement level with the auditor's understanding of the overall risks to internal control over financial reporting. The six steps in TDRA are:

1. Identifying and evaluating entity-level controls that help ensure that management directives pertaining to the entire entity are carried out (e.g., a policies and procedures manual, a whistleblower hotline, a code of conduct).
2. Identifying significant accounts and disclosures (e.g., cash, inventory).
3. Identifying risks of material misstatement within these accounts or disclosures (e.g., theft risk for cash, risk of obsolescence for inventory). Doing this requires the auditor to determine whether an account/disclosure is significant and to rate significant misstatement risks as low, medium, or high. Management must develop a list of assertion-level control objectives for each significant account/disclosure and the risks that have a reasonably possible chance to cause material misstatement risk in the financial statements for each control objective.
4. Determining which entity-level controls sufficiently address the risk.
5. Determining which transaction-based controls compensate for possible entity-level control failures. For each material misstatement risk, the auditor identifies controls (entity-level or transaction-based) that will reduce the risk to a low level.
6. Determining the nature, extent, and timing of tests needed to gather evidence and complete the assessment of the internal controls, based on the assessments in Steps 4 and 5.

The TDRA is a principles-based approach that gives the auditor flexibility in designing the scope of the controls to test and the nature, timing, and extent of testing procedures to be performed.

Corporate Governance and Responsibility

Introduction and Organizational Structure

LOS §1.E.1.f

The term **corporate governance** refers to the system by which a corporation is directed and controlled. The governance structure specifies the distribution of rights and responsibilities among stakeholders, including the board of directors, managers, shareholders, creditors, regulators, and the company's external auditors. The governance structure further specifies the rules and procedures for making decisions about corporate affairs. Governance provides the structure for corporations to establish and pursue their objectives while considering their social, regulatory, and market environments. Governance is a mechanism for monitoring an organization's actions, policies, and decisions.

LOS §1.E.1.e

A corporation's governance structure must comply with a number of federal and state laws. Each state has its own set of laws regulating a corporation's governance. The basic framework of a company's corporate governance structure is designed to meet the laws of its home state and nation. Before a corporation is formed, it must submit several documents to its state, including the company's corporate charter and articles of incorporation. These documents provide a detailed outline of a corporation's planned governance structure and define the hierarchy within it, which includes the means by which authority is communicated and the processes that will be used to maintain the governance structure.

LOS §1.E.1.d

Corporate governance begins with the company's shareholders. The shareholders elect the board of directors, who then appoint the senior management of the corporation, such as the CEO and the CFO. The primary purpose of the board of directors is to oversee and monitor the operation of the corporation. The CEO is the board's agent responsible for managing the corporation on a day-to-day basis. The procedures for making corporate decisions are spelled out in the corporate bylaws.

LOS §1.E.1.c

A company's organizational structure, policies, objectives, and goals, as well as its management philosophy and style, influence the scope and effectiveness of the control environment. The organizational structure defines lines of responsibility and authority. Formal communication about these lines of responsibility and control procedures plays an important role in the organization's overall adherence to internal controls.

Management organizes resources into various functions, such as financial management, production, and so on. Separation of responsibility establishes a structure within which the goals of the business may be accomplished. An organization's structure identifies individual components and the operational and informational interrelationships among the various components. The most common method of documenting organizational structure is through the organizational chart.

The next level of organizational structure outlines the key decisions for which each organizational component is responsible. For example, the controller will determine the financial controls and accounting principles the firm will use. The production manager will be responsible for determining the best means of fulfilling production commitments.

An external, financial statement audit is an additional corporate governance mechanism. Companies that issue public securities must have external, financial statement audits, which are external reviews of financial statements by independent CPA firms. Many firms that do not issue public securities also have annual external audits.

Board of Director and Audit Committee Responsibilities

The board of directors has final responsibility for business practices and results; it sets broad operational goals that guide how control systems should be designed and monitored. The primary responsibility of the board of directors is to ensure that the company operates in the best interest of shareholders. The board is charged with establishing corporate policies and hiring the top officers of the organization who set the organizational tone and manage day-to-day affairs.

For firms that have an internal audit function, the internal auditor provides that assurance to the board of directors by verifying that control procedures are adequate and being followed. The organizational chart should show that the audit director reports directly to the audit committee of the board of directors.

Audit committees have not always been effective. Investors have blamed such committees for lacking the independence or financial expertise to uncover financial reporting failures. Audit committees also have fallen short in cases where a CEO has picked members willing to go with the flow.

Audit committees need independent directors with sophisticated financial backgrounds. SOX requires that the audit committee consists entirely of directors who are independent of the organization, meaning that they cannot accept any consulting, advisory, or other fees from the organization or be affiliated with the organization or any of its subsidiaries. At least one of the audit committee members must qualify as a "financial expert" within the meaning and rules of the Securities and Exchange Commission (SEC), as well as Section 407 of the SOX Act.

Sarbanes-Oxley Act of 2002

Four sections of the SOX Act are relevant to this discussion: sections 404, 201, 203, 302.

Section 404 of SOX requires that public companies establish and maintain a system of internal controls, which is then audited by external auditors. The act requires that corporate officers (CEO and CFO) certify annually that management is responsible for establishing and maintaining adequate internal control over financial reporting and that those internal controls have been tested and assessed as to their effectiveness. This certification is explicitly stated in a report that must accompany financial statements filed with the SEC and must also include notations of any significant defects or material noncompliance found during internal control testing. Additionally, the report must provide a statement regarding the external auditor's attestation on management's assessment of the company's internal control over financial reporting.

Section 201 prohibits registered public accounting firms from providing some nonaudit services (e.g., bookkeeping and accounting systems design) but permits them to provide other nonaudit services, including tax services, with the advance approval of the audit committee.

Section 203 consists of only one sentence. It requires that lead audit partners rotate off engagements every five years (but after one year off, they can return to the engagement).

Finally, Section 302, which is sometimes called the "'bottom on the line'" provision of SOX, mandates that the key executives in a filing company (often the CEO and CFO) attest, under penalty of law, that:

1. They have reviewed the financial statements.
2. To their knowledge, the financial statements do not contain material inaccuracies and fairly present the financial position of the company.
3. They are responsible for internal controls.
4. They have designed internal controls that are adequate to ensure financial reporting integrity.
5. They have evaluated, and opined regarding the effectiveness of, internal control effectiveness within 90 days of the report.
6. They have disclosed, to the auditors and audit committee, significant changes in internal controls, all known frauds, and significant internal control deficiencies and weaknesses.

Foreign Corrupt Practices Act

The Foreign Corrupt Practices Act (FCPA) forbids an American company doing business overseas from paying bribes to a foreign government for obtaining contracts or business.

Firms and/or any officer or director of a firm that violates provisions of the FCPA are subject to criminal and civil penalties. Criminal penalties allow for fines of up to $2 million and imprisonment for up to five years.

Every issuer of securities subject to the FCPA is required to keep detailed records that accurately reflect its transactions and dispositions of its assets. In addition, the issuer must maintain a system of internal accounting controls sufficient to provide reasonable assurances that:

- Transactions are executed in accordance with management's general or specific authorization.
- Transactions are recorded as necessary to permit preparation of financial statements in conformity with GAAP or any other criteria applicable to such statements and to maintain accountability for assets.
- Access to assets is permitted only in accordance with management's general or specific authorization.
- The recorded accountability for assets is compared with the existing assets at reasonable intervals, and appropriate action is taken with respect to any differences.

These objectives should be related to specific internal control procedures in order to evaluate control effectively. Such procedures may include requirements for completion and supervision of expense reports, defining who is authorized to approve expense reports, and obtaining cash and documenting its use. Internal control procedures should include a routine accounting for agreement between totals on expense reports and cash advances.

The SEC is responsible for monitoring compliance with the internal controls provisions of the FCPA.

Topic Questions: Governance, Risk, and Compliance

Directions: Answer each question in the space provided. Correct answers and explanations appear after the topic questions.

1. Internal control can provide only reasonable assurance of achieving entity control objectives because

    ☐ **a.** Management monitors internal control.

    ☐ **b.** The cost of internal control should not exceed its benefits.

    ☐ **c.** The board of directors is active and independent.

    ☐ **d.** The auditor's primary responsibility is the detection of fraud.

2. A company has established policies that emphasize hiring competent people and providing them with professional training. This aligns most closely with which one of the five major components of COSO's internal control framework?

    ☐ **a.** Risk assessment.

    ☐ **b.** Control environment.

    ☐ **c.** Monitoring.

    ☐ **d.** Information and communication.

3. All of the following are internal control provisions under the U.S. Foreign Corrupt Practices Act except a requirement that:

    ☐ **a.** transactions be recorded in a manner that permitted the financial statements to be prepared in conformity with generally accepted accounting principles.

    ☐ **b.** transactions be recorded in such a way that the accountability of assets is maintained.

    ☐ **c.** management does not allow the same accounting firm to complete its audit and tax compliance services.

    ☐ **d.** access to assets is permitted only in accordance with management's general or specific authorization.

Topic Question Answers: Governance, Risk, and Compliance

1. Internal control can provide only reasonable assurance of achieving entity control objectives because

   ☐ **a.** Management monitors internal control.

   ☑ **b.** The cost of internal control should not exceed its benefits.

   ☐ **c.** The board of directors is active and independent.

   ☐ **d.** The auditor's primary responsibility is the detection of fraud.

There is always a tradeoff between internal control effectiveness and the costs that are associated with it. Implementing controls will improve quality and accuracy, but some controls will only improve the assurance slightly and would not justify the associated increase in cost to implement the control.

2. A company has established policies that emphasize hiring competent people and providing them with professional training. This aligns most closely with which one of the five major components of COSO's internal control framework?

   ☐ **a.** Risk assessment.

   ☑ **b.** Control environment.

   ☐ **c.** Monitoring.

   ☐ **d.** Information and communication.

Establishing policies that emphasize hiring competent people and providing them with professional training aligns with the control environment because the control environment component of the framework relates to the company's culture and attitude toward internal controls. To maintain an effective control environment, organizations must ensure that their employees are competent and that they can perform their duties effectively.

3. All of the following are internal control provisions under the U.S. Foreign Corrupt Practices Act except a requirement that:

   ☐ **a.** transactions be recorded in a manner that permitted the financial statements to be prepared in conformity with generally accepted accounting principles.

   ☐ **b.** transactions be recorded in such a way that the accountability of assets is maintained.

   ☑ **c.** management does not allow the same accounting firm to complete its audit and tax compliance services.

   ☐ **d.** access to assets is permitted only in accordance with management's general or specific authorization.

Requiring management to not allow the same accounting firm to complete its audit and tax compliance services is not a requirement of the Foreign Corrupt Practices Act (FCPA). The FCPA requires that an American company doing business overseas must keep detailed records of its transactions and dispositions of assets to ensure that it is not paying bribes to a foreign government to obtain business.

System Controls and Security Measures

LOS
§1.E.2.b

NFORMATION IS A KEY ASSET of any company, and internal controls must protect this asset. Information stored on a computer system is subject to loss or inaccuracy resulting from:

- Computer or network crashes
- Natural disaster
- Human error in input or application
- Manipulation of input data
- Intentional alteration of records or programs
- Sabotage or theft
- Software bugs
- Computer viruses and worms
- Trojan horse programs and other computer system threats

Media reports of computer hacking resulting in information theft or other compromise have become almost routine. Computer hacking occurs not only in relatively unsophisticated systems but also in systems supposedly with the highest level of security. It seems likely that cloud computing will further increase the risk of data theft or compromise.

A company must consider these risks when it establishes internal controls to prevent or minimize losses of sensitive information assets. System controls enhance the accuracy, validity, safety, security and adaptability of system input, processing, output, and storage functions.

This topic deals with the risks associated with information systems and the controls that companies can put in place to reduce these risks, including organizational controls, personnel policies, and systems development controls. It describes some of the network, hardware, and facility controls organizations can utilize; strategies used to help prevent loss of business information and ensure continuing operations in case of a system failure; and accounting controls that are incorporated into computer systems and manual processes. Finally, the topic looks at the use of flowcharting to assess controls and identify gaps.

READ the Learning Outcome Statements (LOS) for this topic as found in Appendix A and then study the concepts and calculations presented here to be sure you understand the content you could be tested on in the CMA exam.

General Information System Controls

Information systems are usually divided into two functions: financial accounting and operating information systems.

1. *Financial accounting information systems* generate an organization's financial statements, budgets, and cost reports for managers.
2. *Operating information systems* gather information relating to various operational activities and generate reports for managers.

Having internal controls to maintain the reliability and integrity of the information system is critical to management's decision-making processes. Protecting the information system and the information in its databases is essential for accurate and reliable financial reports, as well as for the operating reports that managers use to make decisions.

Information system controls consist of general and application controls. *General controls* (also called pervasive controls) are controls related to the computer, technology, or information technology (IT) function. They include:

- Organizational, personnel, and operations controls
- Systems development controls
- Network, hardware, and facility controls
- Backup and disaster recovery controls
- Accounting controls

General system controls include a plan of the information system and the methods and procedures that apply to the system's operations in a business. General controls, as a basis for effective application controls, are vital to protect information systems.

Application controls consist of input, process, and output controls. These controls are covered in greater detail in the discussion of accounting controls later in this topic. As with all controls, the control environment plays a key role in the effectiveness of information system controls. The actions that management and the board of directors take to oversee system controls and the decisions that they make regarding the information systems send clear signals to the rest of the company.

LOS
§1.E.2.b

Risks Associated with Information Systems

Computers and networks give rise to risks that are specific to their nature within the company's operations such as:

- The **audit trail** is less visible because computers reduce or eliminate source documents and other records that auditors use to trace accounting information.

Additional controls must be used to replace the traditional ability to compare output information with hard copy data.

- **Segregation of duties** may be reduced if the system allows functions that were traditionally separated as a control mechanism to be more accessible.
- There may be a lack of **traditional authorization** when transactions are initiated automatically.
- With the **reduction of human involvement**, it is less likely that personnel will identify mistakes that the software may not be designed to catch.
- **Hardware or software** may malfunction *or* systematic errors may occur because of **program design** flaws.

The risks of fraud and information loss are of significant concern because they could result in expensive business interruptions or errors. Stolen personal information can create substantial public relations and financial risks for a company. Threats to an information system can occur either internally or externally:

- Internal threats: From systems personnel including computer maintenance workers, programmers, computer operators, computer and information systems administrators, and data control clerks. Internal threats can come from disgruntled or recently fired employees, and from trusted employees.
- External threats: From intruders.

Hacking is the unauthorized access to or control over a computer network security system for unlawful purposes. Fraud and information loss occurs in a number of ways:

- Sabotage is a deliberate action to weaken an organization through subversion, obstruction, disruption, or destruction. It is often carried out to interrupt operations and destroy software and electronic files.
- Input manipulation is when false or misleading data are input into a computer for a criminal purpose. An example of this is a data processing clerk altering supporting documents and entering inaccurate information into the computer system.
- Output manipulation is when data or software is input into a computer for the purpose of affecting the computer outputs with the intent to commit a crime. One example of this is stealing bank account numbers and personal identification numbers to withdraw money from an ATM.
- Program manipulation is when data or software in a program is altered to commit a crime. For example, a hacker could make unauthorized program changes to divert money to accounts that he or she has created.

Phishing is done to acquire personal or sensitive information such as usernames, passwords, and credit card details, or even to load malware. Often phishing is done through an email that appears to be from a trustworthy entity. These communications often direct users to enter details at a fake website that looks similar to a legitimate site. Consequences of this could be the inability to access an email account or fictitious emails being sent from an account. Another form of phishing is ransomware. This is malicious software that blocks access to the victim's data. It threatens to delete or publish data if the ransom is not paid.

Companies with good internal control systems can prevent these types of fraud by carefully reviewing, testing, approving, and logging all program changes before they are implemented. Direct file alteration is easily prevented by limiting access and encrypting files and databases.

Organization Controls and Personnel Policies

Some general information system controls include personnel policies that apply to the structuring of duties and use of systems.

Segregation of Duties and Functions

LOS
§1.E.2.a

Segregation of information technology (IT) duties and functions begins with the separation of the IT function from the rest of the organization. The head of IT or chief information officer (CIO) should report to the firm's chief executive officer (CEO). IT belongs to the entire organization, not to any one function. Within IT, there needs to be clearly defined responsibilities associated with the accounting and operating subsystems to ensure appropriate segregation of responsibilities. Figure 1E-2 explains segregation of duties as it applies to the IT function.

Figure 1E-2 Segregation of Duties

Department/ Function	Role or Responsibility
IT	Process, store, and disseminate information and data

Within the IT function	Separation of:
	
	 • **Systems development:** application programmers and analysts who select or develop software
	
	 • **Systems operations:** computer operators and input/output function
	
	 • **Systems technical support:**
	
	    • Database administrator
	
	    • Network administrator: all data communication hardware and software, and their usage
	
	    • Security administrator: assignment and control of user access
	
	    • System programmers: for operating and library systems; Systems utilities, such as sorts, merges, compilers, and translators

System user	Data entry and day-to-day processing of transactions. Information and data belongs to the users only.

Any changes made to the master file or transaction files should be authorized by the appropriate accounting personnel before they are implemented. Many firms have control policies that require change request forms to document information about the origin of the change, including the date and a supervisor's approval. Some systems may provide a log of file request changes.

Each application should include functions to track program changes and to control access to the production version of the application. The controls should also include a supervisory review of program maintenance and revisions.

Vacation Rule

Many fraud schemes require constant action by the perpetrator, who manipulates or juggles the accounts to keep the fraud from being detected. For this reason, many firms require personnel in certain positions to take vacations to help detect this or similar types of fraudulent activity.

Computer Access Controls

Only approved users should be allowed to access systems. Administrators can control the rights of individual users, as well as their access to information within the system. System usage can be tracked by time of day, duration of access, and location of access. This tracking provides administrators with information regarding unusual access or use of the system.

Systems Development Controls

Systems development controls begin with an appropriate set of systems development standards that cover the various stages of the systems development life cycle: analysis, design, implementation, and maintenance. The design, development, and implementation of a new computer system or program should be subject to strict controls that will ensure system reliability and data integrity.

A firm planning to purchase or develop a large computer system usually assembles a team to oversee the design, development (or selection), and implementation of the new system. This team should be made up of employees from the information systems department as well as managers and end users of the system.

To support segregation of duties, an auditor who directs the development, installation, and testing of a new information system should be excluded from the team that audits the accounting system and related functional areas.

Analysis

The purpose of analysis is twofold: to understand the system and to develop appropriate design specifications. Team members should study the functionality of the current system, identify needs not met by the current system, and identify other features the new system must or should have.

Design

Design consists of general design (conceptual design) and detailed design (physical design). Detailed design can involve either software selection or software development. Software selection involves purchasing software and using it as is or modifying it, if modifications are permitted by the software vendor, to suit the needs of the organization. The system specifications must be documented in detail before development begins. Having personnel from different areas of the company on the team helps ensure that the new system design incorporates usability, appropriate reporting capabilities, and internal controls.

Prototype

Most development projects include the creation of a prototype that shows the interface design and general features. Changes usually are expected during the prototype stage. This is because making changes to a system or program that is near completion is expensive.

Programming/Development

In the development phase, control policies should ensure that no individual programmer or systems analyst is responsible for the design or development of the complete information system. The design, development, and implementation of a new computer system or program should be subject to strict controls that will ensure system reliability and data integrity.

Quality Assurance

A quality assurance program must test the new system with realistic data to ensure that it functions as expected and is compatible with existing programs and hardware.

Before the entire system is tested, *modular testing* is used to test the system's individual modules to see that they are functioning properly.

End user testing of the system often includes both pilot testing and parallel testing. *Pilot testing*, also called beta testing, is the initial testing of the system by a select group while most of the company continues to use the old software. Pilot testing is conducted when the programming is completed and the system is ready for production. This testing by end users is aimed at identifying both system bugs and usability issues. *Parallel testing* involves inputting and processing the same information on both the old and new systems and comparing the output.

After successful testing, employee training for the individual users of the new system helps ensure a successful implementation. User acceptance should be documented by appropriate user management sign-offs.

Implementation

Once the system has been tested, accepted, and approved for release, the programming staff will convert data from the old system to the new system and provide the system files and documentation to the system administrator for release.

Maintenance

System maintenance involves monitoring the system over time to make sure it is performing at the desired level. Version control software tracks all changes and maintenance to the program. System maintenance and upgrades usually are scheduled for off-peak hours.

Network, Hardware, and Facility Controls

To protect the information on a system, controls must be in place to protect the hardware and the facility that houses it.

Facility and Hardware Controls

Protecting systems and information assets begins with controlling access to the building. Within the building, the data center should be located away from public spaces. Access should be granted only to specifically authorized personnel. Many data centers use individual key codes or biometrics to control entrance to the facility. In addition to the data center being protected from unauthorized entry, computer equipment must also be protected from environmental threats, such as fire and floods, and from human sabotage or attack. Environmental controls, including air conditioning and humidity control, are also required.

Surge protectors and backup power supplies should be used to protect computer equipment from power surges and outages. The system and its supporting network should be designed to handle periods of peak volume. In addition, redundant components should be put in place so the system can switch to a backup unit in the event of hardware failure.

Finally, the controls must extend to the individual users. Software controls can require users to have strong passwords and to change them frequently. However, users must take responsibility for securing their equipment and the information on it. This is especially important with the growing use of laptops, tablets, and smart phones.

Network Controls

The objective of a network is to enable authorized employees to access and work with the firm's data and programs. However, without well-designed and strictly enforced control policies and procedures, unauthorized people within or outside the company may access and alter critical information.

Even the smallest organizations are likely to use *local area networks* (LANs), either wired or wireless, to share data, applications, and other network resources.

Larger organizations may implement a *wide area network* (WAN), a private network connecting multiple LANs over a broad geographic area. Many organizations also use *virtual private networks* (VPNs) that permit secure communications over public or shared network facilities, including the Internet.

The Internet creates risks to computer systems that do not exist on private networks. Threats include increased risk of unauthorized access as the number of hacks has grown and hackers have become more sophisticated in their attacks. The Internet also exposes systems to malware (viruses, worms, spyware, spam, and Trojan horses, etc.). Cloud computing has become very popular, but it may increase the company's risk of data theft or compromise.

Companies must use a variety of controls to protect their systems and data, starting with passwords. Software-based access controls allow the system administrators to manage access privileges. Many firms also encrypt data so that unauthorized users who bypass first-level controls cannot read, change, add to, or remove the data.

Data Encryption and Transmission

Data Encryption

Data encryption converts data from an easily read local language into a code that can be read only by those with the correct decryption key. The data are encoded during the input or transmission stage, then decrypted at output by the person authorized to receive them. Other controls designed to reduce the risk of interception and to detect errors or alterations in data transmissions include routing verification and message acknowledgment.

Routing Verification

Routing verification procedures add assurance that transactions are sent to the correct computer address. A transaction transmitted over a network contains a header label identifying its destination. When the transaction is received, the sending system verifies that the identity of the receiving computer matches the transaction's destination code. Routing verification is assisted by dual transmissions and echo checks. An echo check is a verification by the receiving node that the data was received.

Message Acknowledgment

Message acknowledgment procedures require a trailer message that the receiving computer can use to verify that the entire transmission was received. The receiving computer signals the sending computer of the successful completion of the transmission. If the receiving computer detects an error, data are retransmitted.

Virus Protection and Firewalls

Network information must be protected from both corruption and intruders. Antivirus software scans files to detect viruses and other malicious code. Many companies have policies that prohibit employees from installing any programs not approved by the information systems department. In other systems the end user is not permitted to install any new or updated software. Installations and updates are performed only by IT personnel.

A *firewall*—a combination of hardware and software—is used to help prevent unauthorized access from the Internet. Within the company network, firewalls may be used to prevent unauthorized access to specific systems, such as the payroll or personnel. Multiple firewalls are recommended to improve security.

Several controls or control alerts can be contained within a firewall system. The firewall may include an automated disconnect if a user enters a specified number of incorrect passwords. Change control software provides an audit trail showing the sources of all changes made to files. The network or firewall software may also produce a network control log that lists all transmissions to or from a computer. This log can identify the source of errors or attempts at unauthorized access.

Intrusion Detection System

If someone gains unauthorized access to a company's network, intrusion detection systems analyze network activity for aberrant or unauthorized activity and keep a centralized security event log that includes event logs from servers and workstations and provides alerts to security breaches. Event logs also can be used to detect misuse from internal sources.

Business Continuity Planning

Business continuity planning (BCP) is a strategy that identifies an organization's exposure to internal and external threats and brings its critical resources and assets together in order to protect them and ensure continuing operations and effective recovery in the event of a significant adverse event or disaster.

As part of the BCP process and the development of a *business continuity plan,* organizations implement control policies and procedures to prevent the loss of critical business information and enable the organization to continue operations in the face of a major system failure or facility destruction. Two levels of policies and procedures must be established to protect against these eventualities: data backup and disaster recovery.

Data Backup Policies and Procedures

LOS
§1.E.2.g

LOS
§1.E.2.l

Backup policies and procedures ensure that data that are lost due to malware, natural disasters, hardware failures, theft, deletions, and software malfunctions can be recovered. Most firms back up all network files daily during slow processing times. Backup is normally achieved by copying files to tape or other offline media that may be kept in the data processing center or stored off-site. Off-site storage is preferable because data can be recovered in the event of a disaster that affects the data center. Backup files also can be electronically transferred to off-site locations. This is called electronic vaulting.

Many firms institute a procedure called the grandfather-father-son (GFS) method. With this method, the most recent three generations (e. g., days) of backup files are secured at all times. If data are lost or altered, they may be retrieved from the most recent "clean" backup file.

Firms that employ a master file and transaction files may use the checkpoint procedure, which runs at intervals throughout the day and facilitates recovery from a system failure. In this procedure, the network system temporarily does not accept new transactions while it finishes updating transactions entered since the last checkpoint and then generates a backup copy of all data. If a system failure occurs, the system can be restarted using data from the last checkpoint.

The control policies also should provide for backup of system configurations. Firms lose time if a network must be reformatted and reconfigured to its previous status before backup files can be recovered from storage tapes.

Disaster Recovery Policies and Procedures

Disaster recovery plans are designed to enable the firm to carry on business in the event that an emergency, such as a natural disaster, disrupts normal business operations. Such a plan should define the roles of all members of the business continuance team, including a primary leader and an alternate leader for the process.

The plan should specify backup sites for alternate computer processing. This site may be another location owned by the firm or one leased from another organization.

A *hot site* or *duplex system* is a location that includes a system configured like the firm's production system. This system runs simultaneously with the regular system, and a failure in the main system can trigger an automatic switchover to the backup. A *warm site* is a backup site that has hardware and software available and can be made operational within a short time. A *cold site* is a location where the company can install equipment and personnel on short notice and begin operations using backup files. If a cold site is the designated recovery site, the firm must make additional arrangements for obtaining computer equipment matching the lost system's configuration.

The business continuance/disaster recovery plan should be tested, documented, reviewed, and updated as required. All relevant personnel must be thoroughly trained in these procedures.

Accounting Controls

The accounting system should contain controls that readily test the reliability of recorded data. Types of controls that can be implemented in an accounting system include:

Batch totals—The input preparer reports the total number of records or the total dollar value of all the transactions in the batch. This amount is listed on the cover sheet of the group of transaction documents.

Control accounts—This type of control allows only authorized personnel into particular accounts on the system. For example, a payroll professional should not have access to accounts that do not involve payroll.

Voiding/cancellation—This control involves proper voiding or cancellation of invoices and supporting documents after payment is made.

Feedback controls—Feedback controls provide information about system performance. Diagnostic feedback may consist of written or oral reports, or it may be automated. In all cases, feedback must be delivered quickly so that corrective action can be taken. All monitoring controls are essentially feedback controls, because they collect, analyze, and report data that can be used to determine the success of all other controls.

Feed-forward preventive controls—Feed-forward controls predict future events based on current actions or status and prevent potential problems. They are less common and more complicated to manage than feedback controls. Setting up an off-site location for emergency use is an example of a feed-forward preventive control.

Application and Transaction Controls

LOS
§1.E.2.f

Application and transaction controls are designed to prevent, detect, and correct errors and irregularities in transactions that are processed by accounting systems. These controls can be divided into three categories: input controls, processing controls, and output controls. The purpose of application controls is to provide reasonable assurance that all processing is authorized, complete, and timely.

Input Controls

Input controls are designed to provide a system of checks and balances over the data or transactions entered into the system. Input controls are designed to prevent or detect errors at the time data are entered into the computer system. Often this data entry involves conversion of transaction data into a machine-readable format. The capability of these control procedures to correct errors early helps ensure accuracy and reliability of reporting data.

Among the manual methods used to increase the accuracy of input are:

- Batch controls, including a batch number, record count, control totals, and a hash total (sum of nonsignificant numbers, such as customer numbers, used to detect deletions or insertions in a batch)
- Approval mechanisms
- Dual observation to review data before input
- Supervisory procedure to confirm accuracy of data gathered by the employee before input

Well-designed source documents are an important input control. The input form should be set up to facilitate accurate input. Many accounting systems contain built-in edit tests, such as an accounting input control that requires that debits equal credits before the system will accept a journal entry. A full edit check should be performed on all transactions before they are entered as updates to the master file.

Other input control procedures include redundant data checks, unfound records tests, anticipation checks, preformatted screens, interactive edits, and check digits. These control procedures are explained in Figure 1E-3.

Figure 1E-3 Input Controls

Input Control Procedure	Description	Example
Redundant data checks	Encode repetitious data on a transaction record, enabling a later processing test to compare the two data items for compatibility	A grocery store system may compare the bar code on the product with an alpha description of the item. If they do not match, an exception report is produced
Unfound records test (*aka* validity tests or master file checks)	Any transaction with no master file will be rejected	1. Real-time processing: new account information appears as soon as it is entered, after which the transaction can be input 2. Batch processing: collects data daily and then processes the group of transaction together: operator must wait until new information appears before the transaction can be input
Anticipation checks	Dependence or consistency checks that look for a relationship between two items or conditions	The system could check that sales tax is not included on a sale made to a nonprofit or governmental organization
Preformatted screens	Have logical content groupings and "forced choices" where only certain options are available. Improves efficiency and accuracy of input entry	Preparing a sales invoice with a choice of "taxable" or "non-taxable"
Interactive edits	Performed as data is entered to check that the data in a particular field meets specified requirements	• Character checks: a character in a particular field has to be alphabetic, numeric, or some particular symbol • Completeness checks: all fields requiring characters are filled • Limit, range, or reasonableness checks: values in a field are neither too large nor too small and are reasonable
Check digit	Derived from an operation, such as a sum, performed on all digits in a number	The sum of digits in the account number 5678 would be (5+6+7+8 = 26). The check digit is the last digit of the sum, in this case 6

Processing Controls

Processing controls address the system's manipulation of the data after they are input. Processing controls often are interdependent with input controls and output controls. They involve editing or reentering data and correcting errors. Processing controls include run-to-run totals that help ensure that the output from one application matches the input to an application it feeds. For example, the output of cash disbursements must equal the input to vouchers payable. The sum is meaningless except for the computer's batch control in processing checks. Figure 1E-4 explains different types of processing controls.

Figure 1E-4 Summary of Processing Controls

Processing Control	Description	Example
Mechanization	Consistency is provided by machine processing	Using a calculator to total cash deposits
Standardization	Consistent procedures are developed for all processing	Using a chart of accounts to identify the normal debits and credits for each account
Default option	Automatic use of a predefined value for input transactions that are left blank	Automatically paying salaried employees for 40 hours each week
Batch balancing	A comparison of the items or documents actually processed against predetermined control totals	A cashier balances deposit tickets to control totals of cash remittances
Run-to-run totals	The use of output control totals from one process as input control totals over subsequent processing. The control totals link a sequence of processes over a period of time.	Beginning accounts receivable less payments received, plus new sales should equal ending accounts receivable
Balancing	Procedure that tests for equality between two equivalent sets of data or one set of data and a control total	Balance in the accounts payable subsidiary ledger should equal the balance in the general ledger control account
Matching	Test that compares data from one source with other data from other sources to control the processing of transactions	An accounts payable clerk matches vendor invoices to receiving reports and purchase orders
Clearing account	A zero value should result from processing independent items of equivalent value	Imprest checking should have a zero balance after all paychecks have been cashed by employees for the week
Tickler file	This control file consists of items sequenced by date for processing or follow-up	A tickler file created for invoices received and filed by their due dates
Redundant processing	This includes duplicate processing and comparison of individual results for equality	Two clerks can compute the gross and net pay of each employee for comparison
Trailer label	Provides a control total for comparison with accumulated counts or values of records processed	The last record in a receivable file can be a trailer label that contains a count of the number of records in the file
Automated error correction	This control automatically corrects errors in transactions or records that violate a detective control	The system can send a credit memo automatically when customers overpay their accounts

Output Controls

Output controls are designed to check that input and processing result in accurate and valid output. Output includes data files and reports produced after computer processing is completed. Two types of output controls are required to ensure accuracy and validity of information: controls to validate processing results and controls to regulate the distribution and disposal of the output.

Controls for validating processing results—The validity, accuracy, and completeness of output from accounting systems can be verified by activity reports that provide detailed information about all changes to the master files. File changes can be tracked to the events or documents that initiated the changes, and the accuracy can be verified. If the volume of transactions makes verification using activity reports impractical, exception reports showing material changes to files can be used.

Controls regulating distribution of output—Printed or electronic output from computers must also have controls. Forms controls can be used for printed output along with precautions on who can distribute, store, and dispose of the material and how these processes must be done. Appropriate controls also must be put in place for electronic distribution, including password protection of the document, encryption, controlled distribution lists, and access restrictions.

Figure 1E-5 describes specific output controls.

Figure 1E-5 Summary of Specific Output Controls

Specific Output Control	Description	Example
Reconciliation	This process analyzes differences between the values contained in a detail file and a control total to identify errors	Checking account balance should be reconciled to the bank statement each month
Aging	This process identifies unprocessed or retained items in files, usually according to their transaction date, and classifies the items according to various date ranges	A report that identifies delinquent accounts within 30 days, 60 days, and 90 days or more
Suspense file	This file contains unprocessed or partially processed items that need further action	A file of back-ordered raw materials awaiting receipt
Suspense account	This is a control total for items that need further processing	The total in the accounts payable subsidiary ledger should equal the general ledger control account total
Periodic audit	These files or processes can be verified periodically to detect control problems	The firm can send confirmations to customers and vendors to verify account balances
Discrepancy report	This report contains a list of items that have violated a control and require further investigation	A list of employees who have exceeded overtime limits

Flowcharting to Assess Controls

LOS
§1.E.2.k

Documenting an organization's information system and related control procedures often can be done most effectively through a flowchart that visually depicts the flow of transactions through the process from initiation to storage of data. The process of diagramming the system can help identify gaps or flaws in the controls.

Flowcharts can be useful not only for summarizing the internal auditor's information about processes but also to aid in design, development, and implementation of new accounting information systems or new control procedures.

Standard flowcharting symbols are recognized by the American National Standards Institute and the International Organization for Standardization. A few of the basic symbols are shown in Figure 1E-6.

Figure 1E-6 Flowchart Symbols

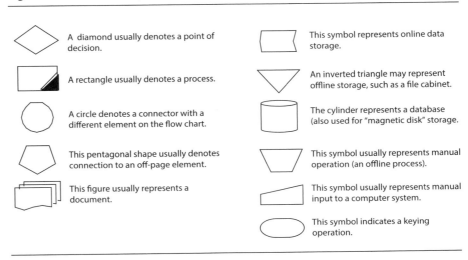

Thus, an internal auditor's flowchart of a transaction process may look something like that shown in Figure 1E-7.

Some computer programs have the ability to create an automated flowchart of a program's functionality and processes.

Flowcharts can help the auditor and managers to analyze a set of internal controls to find their strengths and weaknesses and to develop any new controls needed. Analysis might begin by determining whether the system actually operates as the flowchart describes. Are retail orders actually routed as the flowchart claims, or are there perhaps intervening procedures that are not identified on the chart? At each control point, the auditor might ask, "Is there sufficient oversight by a qualified person?" For example, in Figure 1E-6, transaction orders are input by two different operators, so management may want to examine whether it can improve efficiency by routing all orders to the same input area and then provide the retail and wholesale departments with reports regarding their transactions.

Figure 1E-7 Flowchart of Transaction Process

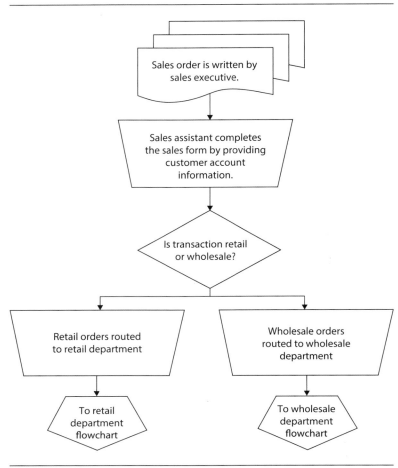

Flowcharts ultimately can be used to depict any process to illustrate relationships between different data elements or to depict the movement of a single document throughout the process.

Topic Questions:
System Controls and Security Measures

Directions: Answer each question in the space provided. Correct answers and explanations appear after the topic questions.

1. Encoding electronic data through the use of an algorithm to make information unreadable to unauthorized individuals is identified as

    ☐ **a.** a firewall.

    ☐ **b.** a worm.

    ☐ **c.** a virus.

    ☐ **d.** encryption.

2. A processing control helps to provide reasonable assurance that

    ☐ **a.** data is entered properly into a computer system.

    ☐ **b.** only authorized users have access to completed data projects.

    ☐ **c.** proper computer programs are used to make data calculations.

    ☐ **d.** finished data products are available on schedule.

3. In an attempt to remain competitive and be more responsive to customers, a company has connected its internal computer networks to outside networks via a host computer. One significant risk of this practice is that

    ☐ **a.** uploaded files may not be properly edited.

    ☐ **b.** data downloaded to the personal computers may not be sufficiently timely.

    ☐ **c.** viruses may gain entry to one or more of the company's systems.

    ☐ **d.** software maintenance on the personal computers may become more costly.

Topic Question Answers: System Controls and Security Measures

1. Encoding electronic data through the use of an algorithm to make information unreadable to unauthorized individuals is identified as

   ☐ **a.** a firewall.

   ☐ **b.** a worm.

   ☐ **c.** a virus.

   ☑ **d.** encryption.

Encryption can help secure data traveling through an organization's network. Encryption converts the data, so it is sent in an unreadable format.

2. A processing control helps to provide reasonable assurance that

   ☐ **a.** data is entered properly into a computer system.

   ☐ **b.** only authorized users have access to completed data projects.

   ☑ **c.** proper computer programs are used to make data calculations.

   ☐ **d.** finished data products are available on schedule.

Processing controls provide reasonable assurance that proper computer programs are used to make data calculations. Processing controls cover how an organization's information system converts data into information that is useful for managers and other users of the information in the organization.

3. In an attempt to remain competitive and be more responsive to customers, a company has connected its internal computer networks to outside networks via a host computer. One significant risk of this practice is that

   ☐ **a.** uploaded files may not be properly edited.

   ☐ **b.** data downloaded to the personal computers may not be sufficiently timely.

   ☑ **c.** viruses may gain entry to one or more of the company's systems.

   ☐ **d.** software maintenance on the personal computers may become more costly.

The risk that viruses may gain entry to one or more of the company's systems is a significant risk of this practice. Although a company can take actions to mitigate this risk, connecting internal networks to outside networks introduces the risk of unauthorized hacking, malware, and viruses.

Directions: This sampling of questions is designed to emulate actual exam questions. Read each question and write your response on another sheet of paper. See the "Answers to Section Practice Questions" section at the end of this book to assess your response. Validate or improve the answer you wrote. For a more robust selection of practice questions, access the **Online Test Bank** at www.wileycma.com.

Question 1E1-CQ01

Topic: Governance, Risk, and Compliance

A firm is constructing a risk analysis to quantify the exposure of its data center to various types of threats. Which one of the following situations would represent the highest annual loss exposure after adjustment for insurance proceeds?

	Frequency of Occurrence (Years)	Loss Amount	Insurance (% coverage)
☐ **a.**	1	$ 15,000	85
☐ **b.**	8	$75,000	80
☐ **c.**	20	$200,000	80
☐ **d.**	100	$400,000	50

Question 1E1-AT12

Topic: Governance, Risk, and Compliance

When management of the sales department has the opportunity to override the system of internal controls of the accounting department, a weakness exists in which of the following?

☐ **a.** Risk management

☐ **b.** Information and communication

☐ **c.** Monitoring

☐ **d.** Control environment

Question 1E1-AT04

Topic: Governance, Risk, and Compliance

Segregation of duties is a fundamental concept in an effective system of internal control. Nevertheless, the internal auditor must be aware that this safeguard can be compromised through:

- ☐ **a.** lack of training of employees.
- ☐ **b.** collusion among employees.
- ☐ **c.** irregular employee reviews.
- ☐ **d.** absence of internal auditing.

Question 1E1-AT05

Topic: Governance, Risk, and Compliance

A company's management is concerned about computer data eavesdropping and wants to maintain the confidentiality of its information as it is transmitted. The company should utilize:

- ☐ **a.** data encryption.
- ☐ **b.** dial-back systems.
- ☐ **c.** message acknowledgment procedures.
- ☐ **d.** password codes.

Question 1E1-AT08

Topic: Governance, Risk, and Compliance

Preventive controls are:

- ☐ **a.** usually more cost beneficial than detective controls.
- ☐ **b.** usually more costly to use than detective controls.
- ☐ **c.** found only in general accounting controls.
- ☐ **d.** found only in accounting transaction controls.

Question 1E1-AT10

Topic: Governance, Risk, and Compliance

Which of the following is **not** a requirement regarding a company's system of internal control under the Foreign Corrupt Practices Act of 1977?

- ☐ **a.** Management must annually assess the effectiveness of its system of internal control.
- ☐ **b.** Transactions are executed in accordance with management's general or specific authorization.
- ☐ **c.** Transactions are recorded as necessary (1) to permit preparation of financial statements in conformity with GAAP or any other criteria applicable to such statements and (2) to maintain accountability for assets.
- ☐ **d.** The recorded accountability for assets is compared with the existing assets at reasonable intervals, and appropriate action is taken with respect to any differences.

Question 1E2-AT11

Topic: System Controls and Security Measures

Which one of the following would **most** compromise the use of the grandfather-father-son principle of file retention as protection against loss or damage of master files?

- ☐ **a.** Use of magnetic tape
- ☐ **b.** Inadequate ventilation
- ☐ **c.** Storing of all files in one location
- ☐ **d.** Failure to encrypt data

Question 1E2-AT12

Topic: System Controls and Security Measures

In entering the billing address for a new client in Emil Company's computerized database, a clerk erroneously entered a nonexistent zip code. As a result, the first month's bill mailed to the new client was returned to Emil Company. Which one of the following would **most** likely have led to discovery of the error at the time of entry into Emil Company's computerized database?

- ☐ **a.** Limit test
- ☐ **b.** Validity test
- ☐ **c.** Parity test
- ☐ **d.** Record count test

Question 1E2-AT07

Topic: System Controls and Security Measures

In the organization of the information systems function, the **most** important separation of duties is:

- ☐ **a.** ensuring that those responsible for programming the system do not have access to data processing operations.
- ☐ **b.** not allowing the data librarian to assist in data processing operations.
- ☐ **c.** using different programming personnel to maintain utility programs from those who maintain the application programs.
- ☐ **d.** having a separate department that prepares the transactions for processing and verifies the correct entry of the transactions.

Question 1E2-AT01

Topic: System Controls and Security Measures

Accounting controls are concerned with the safeguarding of assets and the reliability of financial records. Consequently, these controls are designed to provide reasonable assurance that all of the following take place **except**:

- ☐ **a.** executing transactions in accordance with management's general or specific authorization.
- ☐ **b.** comparing recorded assets with existing assets at periodic intervals and taking appropriate action with respect to differences.
- ☐ **c.** recording transactions as necessary to permit preparation of financial statements in conformity with generally accepted accounting principles and maintaining accountability for assets.
- ☐ **d.** compliance with methods and procedures ensuring operational efficiency and adherence to managerial policies.

Question 1E2-AT05

Topic: System Controls and Security Measures

A critical aspect of a disaster recovery plan or business continuance is to be able to regain operational capability as soon as possible. In order to accomplish this, an organization can have an arrangement with its computer hardware vendor to have a fully operational facility available that is configured to the user's specific needs. This is best known as a(n):

- ☐ **a.** uninterruptible power system.
- ☐ **b.** parallel system.
- ☐ **c.** cold site.
- ☐ **d.** hot site.

To further assess your understanding of the concepts and calculations covered in Part 1, Section E: Internal Controls, practice with the **Online Test Bank** questions for this section. REMINDER: See the "Answers to Section Practice Questions" section at the end of this book.

Technology and Analytics (15%)

One of the most important and primary roles of an accountant is to provide information to owners and managers so that they may make the best possible decisions for their organizations. A well-designed, well-implemented, and properly controlled information system is the principal tool accountants use to capture, process, and produce relevant and reliable information. This section examines the role of technology and analytics in providing and using information. The section covers the role and use of information systems, data governance including COSO and COBIT, and how technology is used in transforming financial data into information. The section concludes by discussing data analytics topics including business intelligence, data mining, analytic tools, and visualization.

Information Systems

In order to provide relevant and reliable information to decision makers, a business requires a formal system of components and procedures to capture and process data and then report information. This formal system is called an information system. This chapter reviews the primary elements of a functional information system.

What Is an Accounting Information System (AIS)?

An accounting information system (AIS) is a specific type of information system (hardware, infrastructure, and software) that exists to capture, process, and report accurate and reliable financial and accounting information about business events to fulfill regulatory obligations, quantify financial performance, and support an organization's management decision-making. An AIS provides relevant information by collecting data when business events occur, and creating, recording, reporting, and summarizing a company's financial transactions related to those business events.

Essentially, the primary model of an AIS is input-process-output data and create reports that convey information to business decision makers. Transactions are created by users or imported into the AIS from another information system, processed and stored in a data repository, and then provided to AIS consumers as procedural output and reports. The data retained by the AIS can then be analyzed and summarized in a manner that is most useful to the decision makers. Summarized information may be as simple as a daily sales report or as complex as the company's financial statements provided to the Securities and Exchange Commission (SEC) on Form 10-K.

Key elements of an AIS are the quality and reliability of data and the timeliness of information. The old computer science adage of garbage in = garbage out certainly applies here. In order to ensure that only clean data is input into an AIS and that data remains clean and accessible during processing and reporting, a properly designed AIS will implement and enforce controls that manage data during all phases of its lifecycle, including data acquisition, data handling, storage, output, and reporting, and even archiving and disposition. Controls ensure that data is acquired properly, stored properly, and is available to authorized individuals when needed.

An AIS is an integral part of an organization's value chain because it enables the organization to efficiently calculate, maintain, and report financial value of each event in which the business is engaged. The value chain is an aggregate of all of an organization's processes, expressed as nine separate but interrelated activities required to deliver value to customers through products or services. The nine value chain activities are grouped separately as five primary and four secondary activities. AIS provides management with visibility and transparency to an organization's business activities, making it easier to establish a common view of the business, make decisions, and identify areas to improve cost effectiveness and efficiency.

Primary value chain activities, which focus on the organization's efforts to create, market, and deliver products and services to its customers, are:

1. Inbound logistics: Handling goods and supplies received from external sources to be used in creating the organization's products or services
2. Operations: Processes to create an organization's products or services
3. Outbound logistics: Distributing products or services to customers
4. Marketing and sales: Efforts to promote customer purchases of the organization's products or services
5. Service: Post-sales maintenance and support to help customers maintain product or service value

Supporting value chain activities, which exist solely to enable and empower the primary activities, are:

6. Infrastructure: Administrative personnel and information systems (including AIS)
7. Technology: Efforts to improve the organization's products, services, and infrastructure
8. Human resources: Processes to hire, manage, and terminate personnel
9. Purchasing: Buying resources needed to produce products or services

A value chain provides a framework that enables organizations to collectively or individually review product and service lines to assess the value they provide to customers. An evaluation of value chain activities, often called value chain analysis, is regularly conducted by organizations to ensure the value generated by these activities exceeds the cost of performing them, or to ensure customer value exceeds production cost.

An AIS is a crucial infrastructure supporting activity that provides management with visibility and transparency to the value and cost of each of these business activities, making it easier to establish a common view of the business, make decisions, and identify areas to elevate value delivery and improve cost effectiveness and efficiency.

Because an AIS stores and maintains all accounting records for an organization—and often some relevant nonfinancial information such as customer and supplier profiles, transportation timing, procurement contract data, and the like—it integrates each primary and secondary activity in the value chain, improving the organization's overall efficiency. This is one of the most important ways AIS delivers value to an organization. Automation provided by an AIS places accurate data at the fingertips of those who need it, often in real-time, boosting confidence in the data and enabling data analytics including simulations and modeling, which are critical to time-sensitive operational decisions.

Connecting to other organizations' value chains enables process alignment and optimization, resulting in interorganizational efficiency. Taking an industry view and linking two or more organizations' value chains (e.g., linking the output of a supplier's value chain to the input of a manufacturer's value chain) creates an industry value chain, also known as a value system or supply chain.

Business Cycles

A properly designed AIS will create, record, report, and summarize all financial data or transactions according to their relevant cycle. A cycle is simply a way of organizing financial transactions according to their purpose. This organization makes it easier to evaluate similar transactions and to calculate metrics to determine how well business processes are operating. Metrics are measurements you can compare to goals to quickly determine process status and assess performance.

For example, suppose your organization's goal is a profit margin of 23% for flashlights you manufacture. If a recent analysis of revenue to cash transactions shows a profit margin of 21.5% for flashlights, that would indicate a problem and should trigger additional investigation.

Metrics don't tell the whole story, but they help identify transactions in specific business cycles that need more attention. Metrics aren't hard limits. If an organization's tolerance is +/– 3% when evaluating profit margin, the previous example of flashlights wouldn't indicate that anything was wrong. An AIS will control an organization's activity, but only as much as the organization is willing to self-impose its own limits.

There are seven primary business cycles:

1. Revenue-to-cash
2. Expenditures
3. Production
4. Human resources and payroll
5. Financing
6. Fixed assets (property, plant, and equipment)
7. General ledger and reporting

Every company divides its transactions across cycles, but not all companies use every cycle. For example, a manufacturing company would likely employ all of the cycles; an advertising agency would not likely use the production cycle, since that cycle is used to track the costs of manufacturing a product. Although most transactions are now typically done entirely online, a manual system is presented below so that the reader may more easily envision the process.

Revenue-to-Cash Cycle

The revenue-to-cash cycle represents a series of key business activities an organization utilizes to convert sales of products or services into cash. The revenue-to-cash cycle can also be presented as a metric that reflects the time, typically presented as a number of days, it takes an organization to progress through the revenue-to-cash process. When joined with other metrics, the revenue-to-cash cycle serves as a quantitative measure of operational and managerial efficiency.

As shown in Figure 1F-1, the typical revenue-to-cash or sales process starts when a company receives a purchase order from a customer. For purchase orders that request to pay on credit, the customer's credit is checked and approved or disapproved by the company's credit manager. Next, inventory control determines whether the requested item(s) is in stock and in sufficient quantity to fill the order. Then a sales order is prepared to internally document the sale. The inventory control department prepares a picking ticket so that personnel in the warehouse may collect, or pick, the items the customer ordered.

After the items are picked, shipping documents, such as the packing list and bill of lading, are prepared to be sent with the items. The items are then packed and shipped to the customer. At the time of shipment, an invoice is sent to the customer, and the customer's account is updated in accounts receivable to record the expected amount that should come from the customer. After a period of time, the customer will send payment for the items listed on the invoice. The payment or cash received is recorded, and the customer account in accounts receivable is updated to reflect the payment.

Figure 1F-1 Revenue-to-Cash Cycle

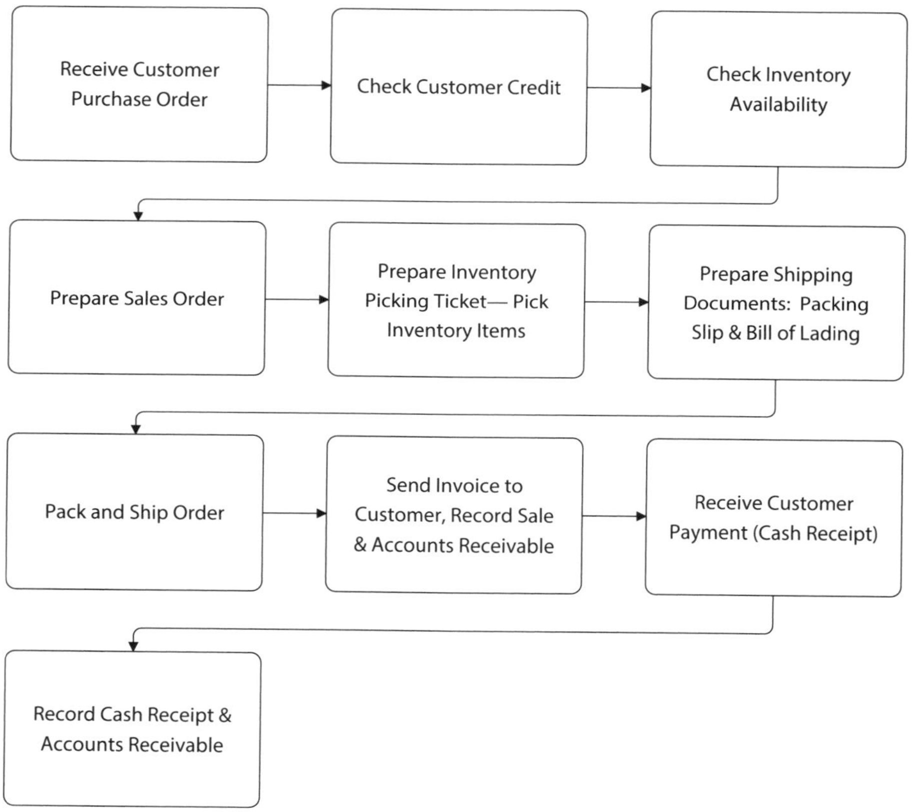

Expenditures Cycle

The expenditures cycle involves the acquisition of and payment for resources needed for the goods and services offered by a business. It is a repetitive process that involves placing orders, receiving purchased materials or services, and disbursing payments. For example, purchasing inventory is a common activity in the expenditure cycle. The expenditure cycle also includes acquiring and paying for resources used in everyday business operations such as office supplies, advertising space, and travel. The expenditures cycle is devoted to purchasing items (mostly inventory) for the operations of the business, whether to simply purchase at wholesale prices and resell at retail prices or to use in the manufacture of a product. Other expenditures include normal business operating activities, such as temporary labor, consulting fees, cloud services, travel costs, and the like.

As presented in Figure 1F-2, the typical expenditure process starts with inventory control identifying a need (insufficient inventory) and preparing a purchase requisition to fill that need. The purchase requisition is sent to the purchasing department, and a purchase order is prepared based on the information from the purchase requisition. The purchase order is sent to the vendor, who fills the order and ships the items to the company. An invoice from the vendor typically follows shortly after the shipment. The shipment from the vendor is received at the receiving department, where items are counted, inspected, and accepted. The receiving department prepares a receiving report to document the receipt of the items. The

Figure 1F-2 Expenditure Cycle

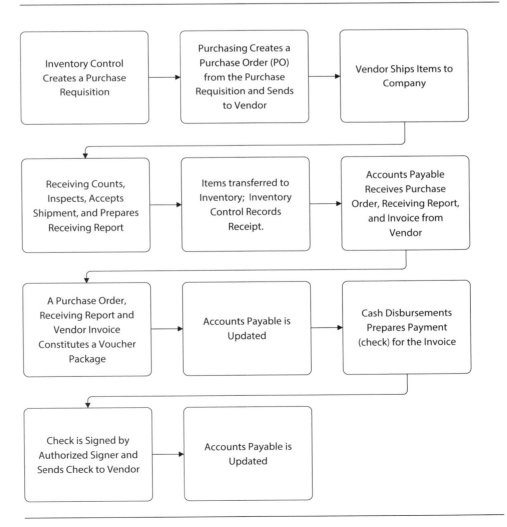

items are then delivered to the warehouse for storage. Inventory control updates the inventory records with the arrival of the items. During this process, accounts payable collects these three documents:

1. Purchase order from purchasing
2. Receiving report from receiving
3. Invoice from vendor

The combination of these three documents constitutes a voucher package. The voucher package provides three essential documents necessary before payment should be made to the vendor: proof of order (purchase order), proof of receipt (receiving report), and proof of billing (invoice). Accounts payable is updated with the purchase and directs cash disbursements to prepare and send payment to the vendor. The payment is typically a check (paper or electronic) that is signed by an authorized signer. After the check is sent, accounts payable is updated with the payment.

Operations (Production) Cycle

The operations (production) cycle is the set of activities through which raw materials are converted to final products. This recurring process begins by designing products and creating a detailed plan for their production. As production is completed, operational and accounting information is generated and recorded. This information creates a feedback loop for the evaluation of operational activities.

The operations (or production) cycle varies by company and by product; however, there is a pattern of accounting data inputs, processes, and outputs that can be used when considering the production cycle. Typically, there are four major activities in the operations cycle:

1. Product design
2. Planning and scheduling
3. Production operations
4. Cost management

As shown in Figure 1F-3, each activity has inputs, processes, and outputs.

Activity 1: Product design incorporates cost management reports as an input into the design process in addition to other relevant sources. Cost information helps guide the design of a product in order to effectively project the cost of the various designs. The output includes the bill of materials (the product ingredients) and the operations list (the product recipe).

Activity 2: Planning and scheduling uses customer orders as the input in determining whether to use manufacturing resource planning (MRP) or lean manufacturing. Specifically, MRP uses customer order forecasts to determine when and how much to manufacture. Lean (just-in-time) manufacturing plans and schedules production based on the actual customer orders, meaning that inventory is ordered, and production is carried out just in time to fill customer orders. The outputs from this activity include the master production schedule, production orders (authorizations to actually start manufacturing the product), material requisitions

Figure 1F-3 Operations Cycle

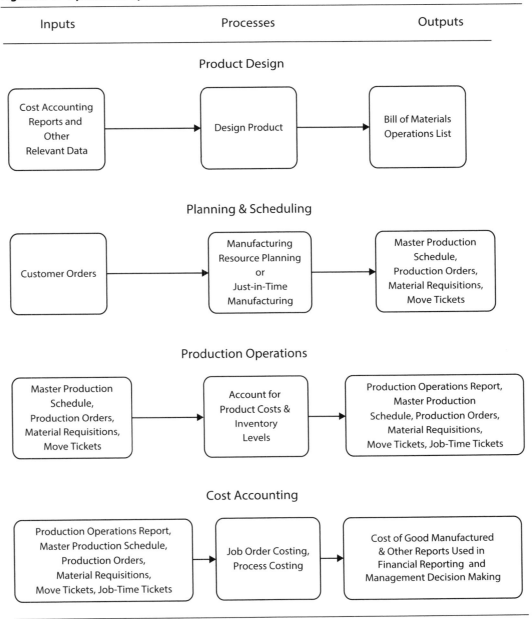

to pull the necessary materials from inventory, and move tickets (authorizations to move products from one stage of the production process to the next).

Activity 3: Production operations utilizes the output documents from Activity 2 for the process of manufacturing the product. The primary accounting function in this activity is to account for production costs and to track relevant inventory levels. The outputs from Activity 3 are the revised and updated input documents plus the job-time tickets used for costing the labor used during production.

Activity 4: Cost accounting includes the output documents from Activity 3. The process uses the data from those documents to determine product costs using either the job order costing or processing costing methods, depending on the nature of the items produced. The final output is the cost of goods manufactured statement and any other relevant and necessary reports that are used in financial reporting and management decision making.

Human Resource and Payroll Cycle

The human resource and payroll cycle is a recurring set of activities that manage and update employee records and subsequently disburse compensation and employment benefits. The cycle begins by updating employment records affected by events such as new hires, promotions, transfers, retirements, and firings. The employment record is then used to process payroll and associated employment benefits. Businesses vary in how often they process payroll; however, the activities within the cycle remain consistent regardless of the payroll cycle length.

The primary role of the human resource cycle is to make sure the business has the people with the right skills in place to carry out its mission. The primary steps in the process are hiring, training, transferring, and firing employees. In addition, the human resource process is the focal point for providing employee benefits, maintaining good morale, and supporting a safe, clean, and productive work environment.

The primary function of the payroll process is to compensate employees for the work they have performed and to take care of taxes related to payroll. The five main steps in the payroll process are:

1. Update master payroll data
2. Record time data
3. Prepare payroll
4. Disburse payroll
5. Disburse taxes and other deductions

Figure 1F-4 presents the payroll process for hourly employees starts with an accurate and up-to-date master file. The master file is updated with relevant payroll-related data from the human resources department, government agencies, insurance companies, and the employees themselves. The human resources department updates the master file with data on new hires, promotions, transfers, and firings. Government agencies provide tax rate data. Insurance companies provide data on the company's assessed insurance rates. Employees provide any updates on their

Figure 1F-4 Payroll Process

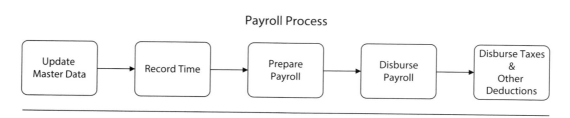

withholdings and deductions, such as the number of claimed exemptions due to changes in their family, such as the birth of a baby or an increase in the amount the employee wishes to contribute to the retirement plan account.

Financing Cycle

The financing cycle is the process through which a business acquires capital for its business operations and makes payments to shareholders and creditors. The two primary sources for acquiring capital are 1) issuing stock and 2) issuing debt. Related to these, the financing cycle involves issuing dividends to shareholders and interest to creditors. Activities related to acquiring capital within the financing cycle tend to occur infrequently. In contrast, the processing of payments to shareholders and creditors occurs on a more regular schedule such as monthly, quarterly, or annually.

Fixed Assets (Property, Plant, and Equipment) Cycle

The property, plant, and equipment (PP&E) cycle is the process by which an organization acquires, maintains, and disposes of long-term, tangible assets. These assets can include land, manufacturing facilities, buildings, vehicles, and machinery. In addition to acquiring and disposing of these assets, the PP&E cycle includes recording depreciation expenses over the useful life of each asset. The PP&E cycle is a key business process due to the significant resources required to acquire and maintain the assets.

The property, plant, and equipment cycle consists of three primary steps (as shown in Figure 1F-5):

1. Acquire assets.
2. Depreciate and maintain assets.
3. Dispose of assets.

Property, plant, and equipment generally represent substantial investments by the company and are expected to last for multiple years. As such, the acquisition or purchase of these assets requires careful planning and analysis. After the assets are acquired, they are maintained and depreciated; their use is then estimated by one of several appropriate methods of depreciation (except property, as it is not a depreciable asset), such as straight line, double declining balance, and units of production for financial and managerial accounting reporting needs. After a fixed asset has served its purpose, it is disposed of by selling or scrapping. Any difference between its net book value and its market value is recorded as a gain or loss, as appropriate. On occasion, an asset may become impaired and should be written down.

Figure 1F-5 Property, Plant & Equipment Cycle

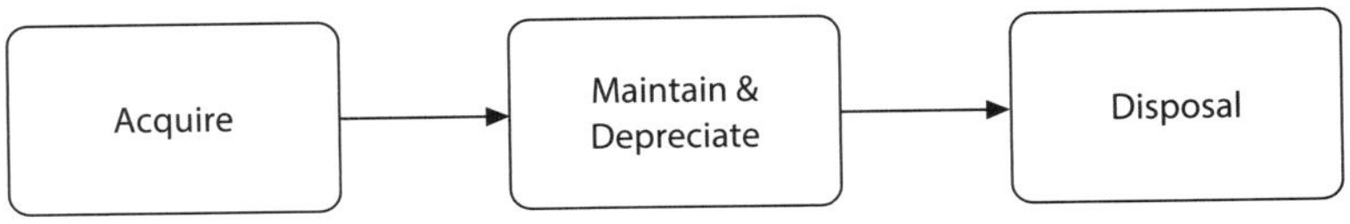

General Ledger and Reporting Process

The general ledger and reporting system cycle is the set of activities that summarizes the economic transactions and financial performance of an organization. The accounting process begins with journal entries to record transactions that are then accumulated in general ledger accounts. At the close of a period, the general ledger is updated and then used to create financial statements and managerial reports. This recurring cycle of information gathering and reporting provides a historical record that is used for a variety of purposes such as performance evaluation, managerial decision-making, firm valuation, and contracting.

The general ledger and reporting process consists of four primary steps (as shown in Figure 1F-6):

1. Update the general ledger.
2. Post adjusting entries.
3. Prepare financial statements.
4. Produce managerial reports.

Journal entries from accounting subledgers and journals as well as the company's treasury department update the general ledger. Adjusting entries originating from the company controller's office are posted to the general ledger. The company's financial statements are prepared from the data maintained in the general ledger. Managerial reports, such as budgets and financial performance reports, are also prepared with data from the general ledger.

Figure 1F-6 General Ledger & Reporting Process

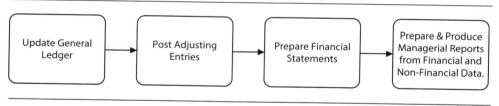

Separate Financial and Nonfinancial Systems

Financial and nonfinancial systems record, track, and report on the health of the business. The difference is that one uses financial metrics and the other uses nonfinancial metrics. In other words, financial and nonfinancial systems measure the same general thing but with different tools and reflect operations that are measured with nonfinancial metrics. The challenge with separate financial and nonfinancial systems is making sure the data is linked accurately in both systems.

When the two systems are separate, the data should be compared to make sure that the systems are measuring the same thing using different metrics. An additional risk comes from transferring data with one set of valid data to another system with limited data.

For example, if the input domain (valid options) for a survey on system A is a value 1–10, but system B interprets survey results on a scale 1–5, a domain mismatch can cause problems. Even if you convert and map the data as it is copied, you lose some precision. If the data the systems draw on is not located in the same place or database, extensive controls must be created and maintained in order for users to have confidence in the quality and reliability of the data and any results of analysis.

Regardless of the storage location, one common constraint of data linked across systems is the time it takes for data to migrate from one system to another. The migration process is rarely immediate and can introduce pauses in the process.

For example, when recording a sale, the financial system records the sale, cash receipt, or receivable, but it does not record other information about the sale, such as the salesperson involved, the time of day, the weather, whether the customer is an individual or a group of people, or how many times the customer inquired about the product (see Figure 1F-7).

Two separate systems would record different data and, based on external sensor information available (i.e. weather-related data), some of the transaction supporting data could be delayed. This could cause a timing issue if a user tries to retrieve data before all of it has been stored.

To mitigate the risk of decision-making based on partial information, controls should be implemented requiring complete data migration prior to providing access to end users, or ensuring partial data is used only when absolutely necessary, with full disclosure provided to end users.

Figure 1F-7 Pre-ERP Processing

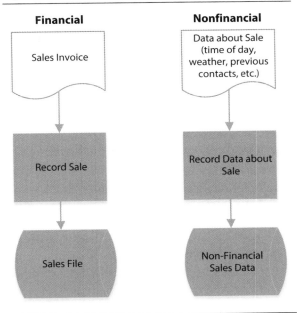

Enterprise Resource Planning (ERP)

LOS §1.F.1.d

LOS §1.F.1.e

Before the days of relational databases and inexpensive computer memory, companies had no alternative but to create separate programs and files to manipulate and maintain data. For example, companies would create a program and data file for daily sales and a second program and data file for accounts receivable. The two files had to be reconciled on a regular basis to ensure data accuracy. Would it not be better to store all company data in one database?

The invention of relational databases and the falling cost of computer memory facilitated the introduction of Enterprise Resource Planning systems (ERP). ERP systems offer the ability to store all company data in one central database. This means the ERP system can store financial and nonfinancial data related to all aspects of the company, from employee health plans, to equipment maintenance records, to customer phone numbers, to capital expenditure budgets, to marketing campaigns—and everything in between. This is the goal of ERP systems but it is not always achieved.

Since ERP systems are designed to manage an entire organization, they can be extremely expensive to purchase, install, configure, and maintain. Many organizations justify the ERP cost by claiming that its benefits are worth the investment. Others do not leverage the ERP as an end-to-end solution, instead strategically choosing the groups of processes they want to manage through the ERP (for example, including inventory and accounting, but excluding human resources and customer relationship management). In either case, ERP implementation projects can be long and tedious, but profitable in the long run.

Invariably, some job roles change when an organization decides to consolidate automation with an ERP system. One of the common issues encountered when implementing ERP is retaining key personnel whose roles may be altered or phased out once the ERP system is up and running. Implementing a new ERP system is often a delicate balancing act that requires technical proficiency and compassionate personnel management to be successful. ERP systems are divided into the typical business cycles as follows (see Figure 1F-8):

1. Order to cash (revenue)
2. Purchase to pay (expenditures)
3. Production
4. Human resources and payroll
5. Financial
6. Project management
7. Customer relationship management
8. Systems tools

Order to cash (revenue cycle) processes order entry, shipping, inventory, cash receipts, and commissions.

Purchase to pay (expenditures cycle) processes purchasing, goods received, inventory and warehouse management, noninventory, and cash disbursements.

Production processes production scheduling, bills of materials, material requirements planning, engineering, work-in-process, quality control, cost management and operations for service companies.

Human resources and payroll maintains and processes human resources, payroll, benefits, time records, training and education, and government reports.

Financial (general ledger and reporting) maintains and processes the general ledger, accounts receivable, fixed assets, cash management, accounts payable, budgeting, financial statements, and other reports.

Figure 1F-8 Enterprise, Resource, Planning (ERP)

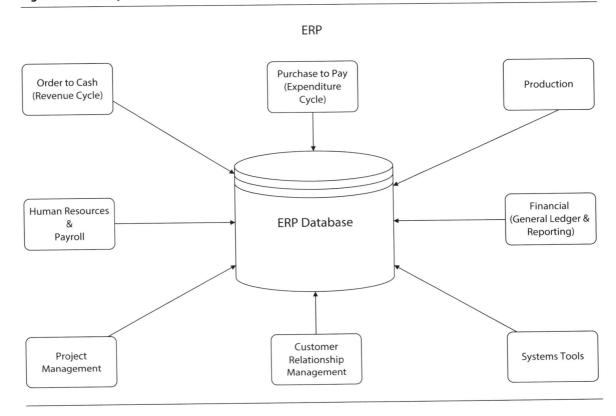

Project management records and maintains billing, costing, time, performance, expenses, and activity management.

Customer relationship management maintains and supports sales, marketing, services, contact with customers, commissions, and call center support. In addition, companies seek to anticipate customer needs through the analysis of big data and the Internet of Things to the extent possible.

System tools are provided to establish and maintain master file data, flow of data, access controls, and others.

The key risks of multiple data sources, delayed data migrations, and decision-making based on inaccurate and partial data that organizations find with separate financial and nonfinancial systems, are all mitigated naturally with an ERP. Consequently, a key advantage of having transaction and supporting data transparent, accessible, and all in one place is that it supports timely and accurate data analysis, which makes comprehensive, real-time reporting of business operations possible and enables agile strategic decision-making. The centralization of data that occurs during ERP implementations gives rise to operational efficiencies as large data migration, reconciliation, and database maintenance teams are longer warranted. This results in lower operational costs, a common tangible benefit that organizations realize from implementing an ERP system

Implementing an ERP can expedite the adoption or implementation of emerging technology. Data analytics, machine learning (ML) algorithms, and artificial intelligence (AI) systems are easier to deploy and maintain with structured input data sourced from a centralized ERP system. Much of the time spent in analytics, ML, and AI model development and deployment is in standardizing, aligning, and cleansing input data. An ERP system helps to provide cleaner data while providing a bird's-eye view of an organization's overall processes, from product or service creation through post-sales support and handling of customer feedback. An ERP system enables organizations to better manage operations and focus on more strategic business goals and outcomes.

ERP implementations do not come without disadvantages. In addition to the significant time and financial commitments required, the magnitude of the investment for an ERP implementation generally obligates an organization not to consider any other comprehensive or niche technological solutions for extended periods of time. Some organizations are effectively married to their ERP vendors and, although better solutions may arise over time, find themselves committed for decades, preventing them from reaping other benefits. Storing all data in one place also increases cyber risk because any data breaches can potentially expose personnel and client files, accounting, and contractual data alike. Therefore, organizations implementing ERPs must also have robust cybersecurity, data access, data backup and data governance processes in place.

Database Management Systems (DBMS)

Centralized data storage is a core feature of most enterprise applications, including AIS and ERP solutions. Enterprise applications share data using a repository with formatted data that multiple clients and users can access. The most common type of data repository in today's applications are databases. A database is a collection of data that is organized into partitions, which each have rules that govern how data gets stored. For example, a product's price field stores different data (numeric) than a customer name (character). A database's design restricts data to specific types.

Users use software applications to read from and write to the database using an interface program called a database management system (DBMS). Figure 1F-9 shows a DBMS and how it provides database access to application software programs.

A DBMS provides the interface for creating, retrieving, updating, and deleting data, often called the CRUD functions. Although there are different types of DBMSs available, the most popular database type for enterprise applications is the relational DBMS, built on top of a relational database. A relational database model was introduced in the 1970s and immediately became very popular for business applications. The relational algebra foundation made relational databases theoretically sound, but the main reason for its popularity is its simplicity.

The relational database model is built on the idea that data of the same type reside in tables. Each table consists of a set of columns that store the attributes of each row, or record. A relational database logically looks like a bunch of spreadsheets. For example, a customer table stores customer data with one customer in

Figure 1F-9 Database Management System (DBMS)

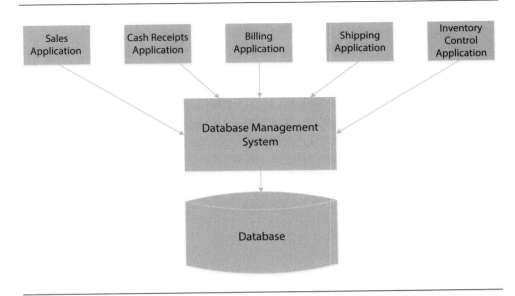

each row. The columns store the attributes, or fields that describe each customer, such as name, address, and credit limit. Storing data logically in tables made it easy to explain database design to others, including nontechnical people. Easy and clear explanations make requests for funding much easier, and relational database systems quickly became the choice for enterprise shared data storage.

Another benefit of the relational model is that the format of each data item (i.e. each field, attribute, or column) is defined and stored in the database schema. The database schema is a data blueprint that defines the database logical structure— the way humans view the data. The schema defines the structure of an entire database, how fields are organized into tables, and what indexes (also called keys) exist to boost data access performance. The DBMS provides a centralized view of the data that can be accessed by many different users from many different locations. Although the database schema provides a central definition of data, it is still possible to design a poorly performing database. Relational database designers use a process of iteratively decomposing, or breaking down, database table definitions into their simplest forms. This process, called normalization, allows designers to create a database schema that provides applications with the best balance of flexibility, performance, and economy of storage space.

The relational DBMS provides an interface between applications and the data, but there still needs to be a way of specifying what data an application requires. A query language provides the ability for an application to issue requests via the DBMS to read or write data. The query language also makes it easy to relate data stored in separate tables (hence the term "relational" database). The ability to "join" tables to access related data is provided by the query language, not the database itself. The most popular query languages for relational databases are Structured Query Language (SQL) and Query by Example (QBE). Both languages were developed in the 1970s to support the relational data model. SQL is an English-like language that many enterprise applications use to interact with a relational database, while QBE is a GUI tool that is mainly used by end users for ad hoc queries. SQL has become the most popular relational DBMS query language and is supported in nearly every DMBS on the market today. The use of a common base query language makes the relational model easy for enterprises to adopt.

Relational DBMSs do much more than just providing shared access to data. An enterprise DBMS also provides protection for data. Since database data is accessed by potentially many users and applications in many locations, the DBMS is responsible for ensuring the integrity, confidentiality, and availability of the enterprise's data. Although data security is a big topic, here are the core ideas behind each tenet of keeping data secure:

- Integrity: Ensuring that only authorized individuals can modify data
- Confidentiality: Ensuring that only authorized individuals can read data
- Availability: Ensuring that authorized individuals can access data whenever they need it

DBMSs offer many features to support the data security core ideas. Data integrity can be enforced using access controls to stop unauthorized changes, and cryptography (such as hashing or check digits) to ensure that no unauthorized changes occurred after data was written to the database. Data confidentiality can be enforced using access controls as well, along with encryption to make data unreadable to unauthorized individuals.

Finally, data availability can be provided with aggressive fault tolerance measures and a solid recovery plan if the database gets damaged. Recovery techniques generally rely on the ability to recover a previously backed-up copy of the database, along with a way to apply (or roll forward) a transaction that occurred after the last backup. Most relational DBMSs use a checkpoint feature to identify transactions that have been completed at a specific point in time. In case a database restore is necessary, the DB admin can restore the last backup, roll forward a transaction that occurred since the backup, and then roll back any transactions that weren't completed when the failure occurred. While this process seems complex, it is standard recovery procedure for enterprise DMBSs and provides unparalleled protection for valuable data.

What Is a Data Warehouse?

A data warehouse is a central data repository that stores summarized and aggregated data from one or more separate data sources. Data stored in a data warehouse is collected and processed periodically from enterprise databases and other sources to be used primarily for analysis rather than processing transactions. Traditional enterprise databases store transaction-based data, also called online transaction processing (OLTP) data. Data that is summarized and aggregated and then stored in a data warehouse is often referred to as online analytics processing (OLAP) or decision support (DS) data. It is essentially a repository or storage location for all of a company's data retrieved from various programs, sources, and OLTP databases. Since OLAP queries tend to involve a large amount of data, running these queries on the same databases that are handling your application's OLTP queries can degrade performance. Building a data warehouse takes effort, lots of disk space, and substantial budget, but can offload the performance penalty of OLAP queries to a nonproduction system.

The periodic process that must be executed to build and maintain a data warehouse is called the extract, transform, and load (ETL) process. Data is first extracted from its source and then transformed or converted into a useful format. An example of transformation is temperature readings taken from multiple countries. Some countries use the Fahrenheit scale and other use the Celsius scale. An ETL process converts all data to a common scale to allow for global comparison and analysis. The final step would be to load the transformed data into the correct table in the data warehouse. Data warehouses are the core driver for business intelligence (BI) functionality, which provides digested measurements to inform management of business performance. Segments of full data warehouses, called data marts, can be defined that present analytics data for a single business unit or line of business. Data marts help functional managers focus on their scoped performance without seeing the entire organization's data. In some enterprise applications, data already exists in a usable form across several databases. Instead of building a complete data warehouse, an enterprise could implement a virtual database. A virtual database is a layer of software that connects to multiple databases but makes the data appear to be in one big database for analysis purposes.

Enterprise Performance Management (EPM)

LOS
§1.F.1.h

LOS
§1.F.1.i

Enterprise performance management (EPM), also known as Corporate Performance Management (CPM) or Business Performance Management (BPM), consists of monitoring and evaluating business performance. EPM consists of all the information systems and data sources an enterprise uses to conduct business, along with the procedures that monitor systems performance across the enterprise. Any enterprise information system components that directly relate to enterprise planning and performance, along with those systems' inputs and outputs, are considered part of EPM. The main goal of EPM software is to automatically consolidate data and measurements to present a single version of the truth without the need for human intervention. EPM software allows enterprise's management to easily collect real-time key performance indicators (KPIs), along with analytics models based on historical data to support planning for future enterprise activity.

EPM is a superset of an enterprise's information systems that allows data analytics to span the entire enterprise and impact both strategic planning and tactical operations. Enterprises can use EPM's analytics capabilities to understand what is happening today, predict what may happen tomorrow, and even suggest tactical changes that could result in desired outcomes. The more common uses of enterprise data analytics are descriptive and predictive models. A descriptive analytics model helps to explain what is happening currently within an organization. Descriptive analytics can help identify similar data and even classify data in ways that may not be obvious. Predictive analytics uses historical data to predict an expected outcome, which can help an enterprise get ready for upcoming activity. The most complex type of analytics is prescriptive analytics. Prescriptive analytics allows an enterprise to set a desired outcome (such as $10 million annual sales) and makes suggestions on variables to change to reach that goal. Prescriptive analytics is difficult because there are often many variables that aren't included in any model, each one of which could affect the desired output. Regardless of how any enterprise uses EPM, it empowers better strategic planning for more efficient operations.

Whereas ERP systems help management with the day-to-day (tactical) operations of a company and is a subset of EPM, EPM is about managing the business at the strategic level through analysis, comprehension, and reporting. EPM supports automation in the enterprise management process. One common management cycle is the Plan-Do-Check-Act (PDCA) cycle. EPM most directly maps to the Check activity, which compares planned metric targets with observed performance. Automating much of the Check activity allows management to focus on planning for and reacting to operational deviations. Although EPM has been around for decades, its methodology has become more and more sophisticated as the tools and software for EPM have improved and evolved.

In its earliest stages, EPM consisted simply of face-to-face meetings and phone calls. The first EPM software applications focused on collecting and providing accounting, budgeting, and financial performance capability. The advent of electronic spreadsheets eliminated the tedious process of creating manual spreadsheets, facilitating more strategic planning, better budgeting, and improved reporting. However, spreadsheets present data in only two dimensions and do not support automatic updating of source data. Although spreadsheets were a step forward, they could not, and still cannot, provide the value of EPM. Later, dedicated EPM software packages were developed that automated much of the financial consolidation and reporting duties of the finance and accounting departments. Windows-based client/server systems have given way to web-based programs. Software as a service (SAAS) applications have been widely adopted, freeing employees to focus on higher-level strategic tasks rather than on managing IT-related concerns.

Topic Questions: Information Systems

Directions: Answer each question in the space provided. Correct answers and explanations appear after the topic questions.

1. An Accounting Information System (AIS) provides value by:
   - ☐ **a.** Improving efficiency.
   - ☐ **b.** Reducing system restore times.
   - ☐ **c.** Reducing the time it would take to find an item.
   - ☐ **d.** Improving the delineation of information along the value chain in order to reduce data integrity problems along the way.

2. Which answer best describes a data warehouse?
   - ☐ **a.** A location where document hard copies can be aggregated and analyzed
   - ☐ **b.** A term to associate multiple sites used for disaster recovery
   - ☐ **c.** A storage of large amounts of information from various databases used for specialized analysis
   - ☐ **d.** A storage commonly used for critical data such as system relationships, data types, formats and sources

3. Which of the following is the primary advantage of automating enterprise resource planning (ERP) functions?
   - ☐ **a.** More time to do departmental tasks
   - ☐ **b.** More time to do strategic tasks
   - ☐ **c.** More time to do operational tasks
   - ☐ **d.** More time to do tactical tasks

Topic Question Answers: Information Systems

1. An Accounting Information System (AIS) provides value by:
   - ☑ **a.** Improving efficiency.
   - ☐ **b.** Reducing system restore times.
   - ☐ **c.** Reducing the time it would take to find an item.
   - ☐ **d.** Improving the delineation of information along the value chain in order to reduce data integrity problems along the way.

Improving efficiency is one of the key strengths of an AIS. It is intended to improve the value chain activities by sharing the knowledge within the system rather than creating separate disparate systems. It is not designed to be a backup and restore system. Finally, while an AIS could reduce search times, search times are more dependent on database maintenance than on the AIS.

2. Which answer best describes a data warehouse?
   - ☐ **a.** A location where document hard copies can be aggregated and analyzed
   - ☐ **b.** A term to associate multiple sites used for disaster recovery
   - ☑ **c.** A storage of large amounts of information from various databases used for specialized analysis
   - ☐ **d.** A storage commonly used for critical data such as system relationships, data types, formats and sources

A data warehouse is a storage of large amounts of information from various databases used for specialized analysis. It is a collection of multiple databases usually containing historical information not usually saved in production systems.

3. Which of the following is the primary advantage of automating enterprise resource planning (ERP) functions?
   - ☐ **a.** More time to do departmental tasks
   - ☑ **b.** More time to do strategic tasks
   - ☐ **c.** More time to do operational tasks
   - ☐ **d.** More time to do tactical tasks

Automation of ERP functions can take less time to complete the departmental, operational, and tactical tasks and can leave more time to do strategic tasks. Efficiencies are gained across the organization's business functions through the automation of ERP functions.

Data Governance

THIS CHAPTER ADDRESSES THE TOPIC of data governance from the standpoint of its definition, frameworks, life cycle, retention policy, and protection.

What Is Data Governance?

Data governance is comprised of the overall management of data within an organization. Concerned primarily with managing the availability, usability, integrity, and security of data, data governance is important because an organization's data holds intrinsic value. However, without a well-designed and functioning data governance program, data can be corrupted, devalued, rendered unusable, lost, or even stolen. A data governance plan should include an oversight body, a set of procedures and controls, and a set of policies or directives to implement the procedures and controls.

During the implementation phase of a data governance plan, data stewards should be selected and trained in their role of responsible caretakers of their assigned data. Data governance is an enterprise-wide endeavor, and requires collaboration and participation across multiple business units. If an organization relies on silos of data and competitive data management practices, such lack of collaboration could be the most difficult part of implementing data governance. Data stewards should be given primary responsibility to ensure that data governance processes are followed and guidelines enforced. The data stewards recommend improvements to data governance processes, thereby managing their data's availability, usability, integrity, and security.

Various controls should be established to aid the stewards in their responsibilities. Input, processing, and output controls aid data stewards in maintaining data quality. Input controls include data entry controls, such as proper data input screen or form design, field checks, limit checks, completeness checks, validity checks, and batch totals. Processing controls include data matching, proper file labels, cross-footing balance tests, and concurrent update controls. Output controls include user review of output, reconciliations, and data transmission controls. Data availability should include proper fault tolerance and redundancies built into information systems (such as a database of replication or filesystem mirroring), uninterruptible power supplies and backup generators, and well-documented critical data backup and recovery procedures. The integrity of data can be preserved by proper segregation of duties, data change management and authorization structures, and independent checks and audits.

Data security can be aided by using a defense-in-depth approach, which includes implementing data security controls throughout the organization at various levels and horizontally across business units; in other words, not relying on just locking the front door, but locking all office and closet doors in case a perpetrator penetrates the front door. In addition, data security depends on employee training on proper data security procedures, authentication controls, authorization controls such as an access control matrix, firewalls and other network security tools, data encryption, and patch management. The best controls in the world can be compromised if one employee accidentally (or intentionally) leaves the data exposed. For this reason, many governing bodies have enacted legislation and regulations to govern data that many types of organizations process and store. Complying with such requirements is often upper management's primary driver when deciding to implement data governance. Of course, there is no way to completely safeguard data from hackers, no matter how much money is spent on safeguards. That is where data risk management comes into play.

Data Governance Frameworks

A data governance framework can provide organizations with a starting point when implementing data governance, especially for the first time. A good framework doesn't just provide procedures for managing data. It provides a structure and guidance umbrella for management activities that empowers upper management to make informed decisions about how to manage data to increase its value and decrease cost, manage risk, and ensure the organization meets all compliance requirements. Two primary data governance frameworks typically are used in the accounting profession. One was developed by the Committee of Sponsoring Organizations (COSO) and the other by the Information Systems Audit and Control Association (ISACA). The COSO framework deals with general data governance; the focus of the ISACA framework is on data governance as it relates to information technology (IT), specifically the Control Objectives for Information and Related Technologies (COBIT) framework.

COSO has published three versions: *COSO Internal Control—Integrated Framework (COSO-ICIF)*, *COSO Enterprise Risk Management* (ERM, 2004), and *COSO Internal Control—Integrated Framework* (2013). COSO-ICIF was published in 1992 to help professionals design and implement effective internal controls, which the COSO framework refers to as processes. The frameworks are designed to break down the task of designing effective internal controls into five areas of focus (also referred to as framework components): Control Environment, Risk Assessment, Control Activities, Information & Communication, and Monitoring. In addition, the frameworks helps users to address internal controls at the operational, financial reporting, and compliance levels and by unit or activity, as shown in Figure 1F-10.

Figure 1F-10 COSO-ICIF Components

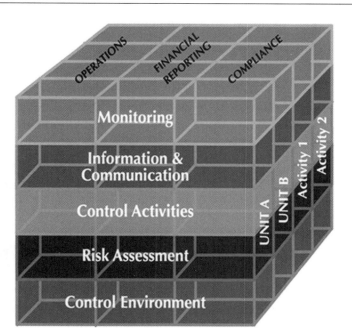

Control Environment

The Control Environment component recognizes that people run businesses and people create a culture or environment for their business. The control environment addresses such factors as the tone at the top (i.e., top management's attitude toward effective internal controls, the integrity and competence of management and employees, and management style). For example, assessing the level of commitment by the organization to data governance.

Risk Assessment

The Risk Assessment component addresses the fact that every entity faces risk from external and internal sources. In order to address risk, first risk must be identified and evaluated as to how it affects business objectives. Then how to manage risk in order to achieve business objectives must be determined. For example, it is important to identify different ways that data can be compromised, likely consequences for each way, and the estimated probability of occurrence. These steps will help prioritize data management improvement initiatives.

Control Activities

The Control Activities component encompasses the policies and procedures employed to achieve business objectives and properly manage risk. For example, how often are employees required to change their passwords? What is the policy regarding sensitive information on employees' laptops?

Information & Communication

The Information & Communication component involves the capture, processing, and reporting of the information needed to manage and control a company's operations. For example, provide periodic training to employees regarding data security practices.

Monitoring

The Monitoring component involves checking to make sure the processes are working properly, to identify deficiencies, and to report those deficiencies so that they may be corrected, and the entire system improved. One method to identify deficiencies in data management processes and security is hiring a consulting firm to perform penetration testing (discussed more later).

COSO Internal Control—Integrated Framework 2013

In 2013 COSO published a revision of the 1992 framework. The original cube remained intact but was enhanced by the addition of 17 principles to better address current business practices and advancements in technology. The 17 principles are building blocks that support effective internal control and are listed next.

Control Environment

1. The organization demonstrates a commitment to integrity and ethical values. It does so, for example, by establishing a code of conduct or creating a process whereby violations of a code of conduct are reported.
2. The board of directors demonstrates independence from management and exercises oversight of the development and performance of internal control by doing such things as creating director roles and responsibilities, policies and practices for director meetings, reviewing management's judgments, etc.
3. Management establishes—with board oversight—structures, reporting lines, and appropriate authorities and responsibilities in the pursuit of objectives by defining roles and reporting lines and levels of authority for different management functions.
4. The organization demonstrates a commitment to attract, develop, and retain competent individuals in alignment with objectives. For example, it creates required levels of skill and expertise, evaluates competence, and selects appropriate service providers.
5. The organization holds individuals accountable for their internal control responsibilities in the pursuit of objectives by clearly defining responsibilities and performance measures and by linking compensation to performance.

Risk Assessment

6. The organization specifies objectives with sufficient clarity to enable the identification and assessment of risks relating to objectives by clearly identifying financial statement accounts, disclosures, assertions, and materiality.

7. The organization identifies risks to the achievement of its objectives across the entity and analyzes risks as a basis for determining how the risks should be managed. Such activities include creating a formal risk identification process, meeting with personnel, assessing the likelihood of risk, and evaluating their risk responses.

8. The organization considers the potential for fraud in assessing risks to the achievement of objectives. For example, the organization could conduct formal fraud risk assessments and consider ways controls could be circumvented or overrode.

9. The organization identifies and assesses changes that could significantly impact the system of internal control. For example, the organization may assess any changes in its external environment or changes in the senior executive team.

Control Activities

10. The organization selects and develops control activities that contribute to the mitigation of risks to the achievement of objectives to acceptable levels. One approach would be to map control activities to identified risks or to implement more careful monitoring of outsourced functions.

11. The organization selects and develops general control activities over technology to support the achievement of objectives. For example, evaluate end-user computing, administer security and access controls, or set up IT infrastructure to support various levels of access to IT depending on functional roles.

12. The organization deploys control activities through policies that establish what is expected and procedures that put policies into action by developing and documenting policies and procedures and conducting regular assessments of control activities.

Information and Communication

13. The organization obtains or generates and uses relevant, quality information to support the functioning of internal control by creating an inventory of information requirements, obtaining information from external sources or non-finance-related managers, or enhancing information quality through a data governance program.

14. The organization internally communicates information, including objectives and responsibilities for internal control, necessary to support the functioning of internal control. For example, the organization should communicate internal control responsibilities, develop policies for communicating with the board of directors, or create a whistleblower program.

15. The organization communicates with external parties regarding matters affecting the functioning of internal control by reviewing external audit communications or surveying relevant external parties.

Monitoring Activities

16. The organization selects, develops, and performs ongoing and/or separate evaluations to ascertain whether the components of internal control are present

and functioning. For example, the organization may establish an appropriate baseline, identify and use monitoring metrics, or employ internal auditors to monitor the operations of the organization.

17. The organization evaluates and communicates internal control deficiencies in a timely manner to those parties responsible for taking corrective action, including senior management and the board of directors, as appropriate. For example, assess and report deficiencies and monitor corrective actions.

Control Objectives for Information and Related Technologies (COBIT)

As the title implies, COBIT is focused on effective internal control as it relates to IT. The COBIT framework provides best practices for effectively managing controls over IT and primarily focuses on security, risk management, and information governance. It is a voluminous and very detailed set of manuals for creating, implementing, and maintaining IT-related controls. The most recent version of the framework, COBIT 5, divides IT activities into 37 separate processes grouped into 5 domains. The 5 domains COBIT defines are Evaluate, Direct, and Monitor (EDM); Align, Plan and Organize (APO); Build, Acquire and Implement (BAI); Deliver, Service and Support (DSS); and Monitor, Evaluate, and Assess (MEA). This organization of IT processes is deliberate to support the core 5 COBIT principles: meeting stakeholder needs, covering the enterprise end-to-end, applying a single integrated framework, enabling a holistic approach, and separating governance from management.

Data Life Cycle

Although there is some debate on the actual number of phases included in the data life cycle, these eight phases represent a general view of the data life cycle: data capture, data maintenance, data synthesis, data usage, data analytics, data publication, data archival, and data purging as shown in Figure 1F-11.

Data Capture/Collection

In order to be analyzed, data must first be collected or captured. Data can be captured through manual entry by hand, scanning with computers, automated entry or uploads leveraging technology, or acquired by sensors. Regardless of the collection method, this process converts real-world observations into their digital representations. The data captured may come from outside or inside the company. Since the volume of data has blossomed far beyond what was conceivable even a few years ago, many organizations implement data capture rules. To avoid capturing redundant data, a valid capture target is data in which at least one data value

Figure 1F-11 Data Life Cycle

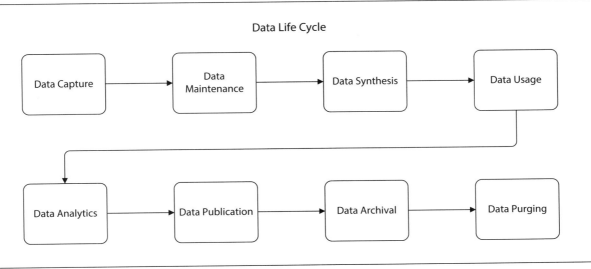

Data Life Cycle

differs from previously stored data and the remaining values satisfy a strategic or analysis requirement. Today's Internet of Things generates huge amounts of data that can potentially be captured.

Data Maintenance

In order to be useful, data must be converted to a usable form. The process of creating usable data may include cleansing, scrubbing, and processing through an extract–transform–load (ETL) methodology. Companies use enterprise resource planning (ERP) systems and other less sophisticated systems for their information needs. ERP and other information systems utilize database technology to organize and query their data. In order for data to be loaded into a database, it must be cleansed and scrubbed of superfluous characters and symbols. Also, it must be checked to ensure that date data fills date fields, numeric data fill numeric fields, and character data fills character fields. Further, data collected from sensors that use different scales, such as recording prices in US dollars and Euros, must be converted to a standard amount. In essence, data cleansing and scrubbing transforms unstructured data into structured data that can be used in an organization's information system.

Data Synthesis

Data synthesis involves the use of statistical methods that combine data from many sources or tests in order to obtain a better overall estimate or answer to the questions being asked of data. One of the concerns of using data to uncover hidden meaning is that it is possible to violate the privacy of the individuals whose data you're analyzing. Many data owners are concerned that private data, such as healthcare data, could be used to divulge private information such as medical conditions.

For this reason, one focus of data synthesis is to find ways to examine sets of data for trends without divulging any individual's identity.

Some term this data modeling or using inductive reasoning to transform data. Others view data synthesis as a subset of data maintenance.

Data Usage

Data usage is simply how data is used to support the mission of the business, such as strategic planning, customer relationship management (CRM), processing invoices, sending purchase orders to vendors, etc. Although there are privacy concerns when carrying out data synthesis activities, most governance and regulatory issues arise during data usage. Most concerns of how data is used relate to privacy, and an increasing number of regulations place restrictions on how organizations can use an individual's data without consent.

Data Analytics

Data analytics is the science of examining data with the purpose of discovering new information and generating business insight. After an organization has gone to the trouble of collecting (data capture) and cleaning its data (data maintenance), building analytics models to uncover hidden trends can be very valuable to strategic decision makers.

It encompasses the skills, technologies, and practices for iterative exploration and investigation of past business performance to gain insight and drive business planning for the future. At its most basic level, it means using data analysis methodologies to answer questions. Some view data analytics as a subset of data usage. Data analytics models can help an organization identify related data, classify their data, make predictions, and even prescribe behavior to create desired results. Clustering methods help an organization identify similar objects, such as similar customers to help target their marketing efforts. Classification methods can help determine the most likely label for an object, such as whether a loan applicant is likely to default on the loan. Predictive models use historical data to make future predictions, such as sales predictions. But the most complex, and often most valuable models are prescriptive models. Prescriptive models let the organization define its desired outcome, such as a 20% increase in sales, and then indicate what the organization must do to reach that goal. Prescriptive models allow organizations to control conditions to create desired outcomes.

Data Publication

Data publication is the act of sending data outside the organization. Although the data can be published for wide consumption, typically data is sent to business partners, such as sending a statement to a customer. Regardless of the level of trust an organization may have with a data publication recipient, the risk for privacy violation is greatest during this phase of data management. Once data leaves an organization's control, internal privacy protections no longer apply.

Data Archival

Data archival is the process of removing data from active use to be stored for potential future use. Archiving data is important because historical data can prove beneficial in future analysis and, in many instances, older data must be retained for regulatory compliance reasons.

Data Purging

Data purging involves deleting data that is no longer useful or needed. Management should create a data retention policy to enforce proper data purging practice. For example, this policy should include governmental and regulatory time frames for data retention, such as the Internal Revenue Service tax return data retention parameters in case of an audit. For internal data, data that has not been accessed for a period of 10 years is purged, for example. Data purging techniques differ depending on the type of media. For traditional magnetic media (hard disks and tapes), degaussing removes the magnetic markers and effectively removes the data. Other technologies, such as optical and Solid State Disks (SSDs), don't respond to degaussing and require other techniques. Although repeated overwriting of media can make it very difficult to recover data, tests have shown that physical device destruction is the most reliable method to purge data.

Record Retention

A competent record retention policy is necessary for every organization. Records must be kept and maintained for internal use as long as they are needed by users to research, analyze and document past events and decisions. In addition, records must be preserved to meet legal and regulatory requirements. For example, the IRS instructs tax payers to retain tax return data for between 2 and 7 years depending on the date of filing or payment and types of deductions the organization claimed.

In fact, more and more regulations, including HIPAA, PCI-DSS, and GDPR, all place specific requirements on organizations to retain data for certain periods of time. Data retention policies are just a start to ensure an organization retains the data to meet their requirements. In spite of the presence of controls, properly educating any personnel that handles data is the main technique to assure data retention compliance. Although there are metrics that help determine whether data retention policy is being followed, in many cases it is easier to identify situations in which data retention policies are lacking or nonexistent. Any time an organization finds that data repositories continue to exhibit growth and use increasing amounts of storage space, it is a good indication that data retention policies, including end-of-life data purging, are lacking. The result of not purging data at end of life is retaining useless data past its useful lifetime. On the other hand, a lack of clear retention policy could result in data being purged too early, which could result in evidence needed for investigations being prematurely removed. A strong data retention policy is necessary to ensure that data is kept long enough, and no longer than it needs to be kept to provide analysis value and comply with legal and regulatory requirements.

Cyberattack Detection and Prevention

All organizations connected to any network, especially to the Internet, are subject to the risk of cyberattack. Malicious attackers conduct cyberattacks using various methods and tactics from email phishing to denial of service (DOS) to SQL injection to zero-day exploits. Most cyber security professionals assert that it is not a question of if a company will be attacked, but when it will be attacked.

Some attacks cause little disruption, while others can cost organizations millions of dollars. Scanning attacks are generally early attack indicators where attackers collect information about an organization's network and its resources. Even before scanning, some attackers look through physical trash to find discarded paperwork with information about an organization and its personnel. This practice is often called dumpster diving. Scanning and dumpster diving are only two attack types used to gather personal information.

Other attack types include skimming (intercepting and saving personal information like credit and debit card information), phishing (sending emails to trick people into clicking on a link that asks for personal information), and pretexting (masquerading as a person in authority, such as a technical support rep, to convince a person to divulge personal information).

Attack techniques also include wiretapping and eavesdropping to intercept messages with personal information. All these attacks are unethical, and even illegal. Some attacks focus on data instead of on people.

For example, a popular attack vector is for an attacker to hijack a user's data by infecting their computer with ransomware. The user's data is encrypted, and the attacker offers the decryption key in exchange for a payment (usually in a hard-to-trace cryptocurrency payment). Still other attacks tend to be less destructive, but still annoying. Adware is a bit of a gray area when it comes to attack types. Technically, adware is more annoying than harmful, but software that forces users to view lots of ads, also called malvertizing (advertising using malware), is still undesirable.

How can companies protect themselves from these attacks? The best approach to security is learning and understanding proven techniques that have stood the test of time to protect IT infrastructure and data. From a data security perspective, as long as you protect data's confidentiality (only authorized users can see data), integrity (only authorized users can modify data), and availability (authorized users can access data on demand), you have provided overall data security. The three tenets of data security are often referred to as the CIA triad (confidentiality, integrity, availability). There is no simple way to secure data. It takes a layered approach, often called "defense in depth" (DiD). DiD means that you place multiple layers of controls between any potential attacker and the resource you're trying to protect. DiD's main goal is to provide organizations with the ability to detect and respond to threats and actual attacks. DiD works best when controls are deployed in layers and partitioned across multiple systems. The idea behind defense in depth is to provide multiple lines of defense that an attacker must compromise to get to a protected resource, such as data. The trick is to provide security and maximum functionality at the same time. That can be quite a balancing act.

Security Controls

Security controls are any countermeasures that are intended to protect one or more resources. A solid DiD plan should include multiple types of controls as well as placing them at different layers. Controls can be administrative (policies and procedures), technical (access controls, firewalls, encryption), or physical (fences, doors with locks, barriers). Most people think of technical controls, sometimes called internal controls, but it takes all types of controls to secure an IT infrastructure. Some types of controls, such as security awareness and training, fit into multiple control categories (preventative and deterrent). You can also classify controls by the function they perform. Looking at control this way, you can group them into preventative controls (controls that prevent an attack before it occurs, like a locked door), detective controls (controls that detect an attack as it occurs, like a burglar alarm), or corrective (also called recovery) controls (controls that repair any damage done after an attack, like switching to an alternate data center or restoring a backup). In some literature you'll see another category of control: compensating controls. Compensating controls are any controls used to augment one or more existing controls. This would be like placing a locked briefcase into a larger box that also has a lock. Any attacker must work harder to compromise multiple controls in a compensating control situation. Compensating controls are often deployed as multiple layers of access controls (you must log in multiple times) or multiple layers of encryption (encrypting something that was already encrypted).

A type of preventative control that is common in today's IT environment are access controls. Access controls limit who can access which resources, and for what purpose. Access controls are crucial for enforcing confidentiality and integrity. Access controls depend on matching a user's identity with a set of permissions. The first step in using access controls is authenticating a user's identity. Anyone can claim to be a specific user, but how can a system be sure the claim is valid? Authentication requires the user to provide an identity (userid) and some additional information. The system compares the additional information with the stored credentials to see if they match. The most common type of authentication is to ask a user for a userid and password. However, this authentication method isn't very secure. All an attacker must do to impersonate a user is to steal or guess that user's password.

There are three types of authentication: Type 1 (something you know, like a password or PIN), Type 2 (something you have, like a token or key), and Type 3 (something you are or something you do, like your fingerprints or iris characteristics). Systems that require only a single response are called single-factor authentication systems. If you must provide two or more responses, such as providing a PIN and presenting a token (including a card with an embedded chip), you are using multifactor authentication. Requiring two responses gives better security than only one response, and requiring three authentication responses is even more secure. As you add authentication requirements, it becomes more difficult for an attacker to acquire all the items and data needed to impersonate another user. Once a user's identity is validated (authenticated), access controls use stored permissions to provide (or deny) authorization to a requested resource.

Biometrics

Biometrics is a specific type of authentication that depends on physical characteristics. Biometrics is a Type 3 authentication control (something you are or something you do) and is popular because it is easy to forget passwords or lose tokens and cards. A fingerprint scanner is a common type of biometric authentication. Many of today's smartphones and tablets have fingerprint readers. Once you register your fingerprints, you can unlock your device with a finger, as opposed to typing a password or passphrase. For shared public resources, fingerprint and other contact-oriented approaches can pass germs and viruses from person to person. That's why other biometrics techniques, such as an iris scanner, are becoming more popular. Scanning a person's iris (or retina) can be done without touching any device—you just look into a camera. Any devices that see a lot of public use, such as ATMs, turnstiles for public transportation or theme parks, or secure doors, all benefit from iris or retina biometrics.

Biometrics are generally considered to be more secure than other types of authentication due to the difficulty of impersonation. An attacker can't just steal a token or guess a password; they must physically impersonate someone else. It isn't impossible, but it is harder than stealing something. On the other hand, biometric controls aren't perfect. They are more expensive to implement than other types of controls and are not 100% accurate. Any biometrics device can be tuned to be more sensitive or less sensitive. When the reader is not sensitive enough, it may exhibit Type I errors (false positives). A Type I error authenticates an imposter. If the reader is too sensitive, it may exhibit a Type II error (false negative). A Type II error fails to authenticate a valid user. The "sweet spot" is to tune the reader to a setting where the Type I error rate and Type II error rate are equal, which is called the crossover error rate.

Firewalls

Firewalls offer another method of detecting and potentially preventing cyberattacks. A firewall is a device or software program that receives a network packet, examines it, and decides whether to forward it along based on a set of rules. The first generation of firewalls looked only at a packet's source address and its destination address and port. These firewalls just filtered packets based on address and port and were called packet-filtering firewalls. All firewalls essentially have three main actions: Accept (send the packet along to its destination), Deny (do not send the packet any further and tell the sender what you've done), and Discard or Drop (silently stop the packet but don't send any notification to the sender). Firewalls can't protect networks and computers from every attack, but they can be very helpful. A firewall generally keeps a log of all traffic it sees, along with source IP and destination IP address, which can be helpful when investigating attack history and origin. Firewalls can limit an organization's exposure to attacks by enforcing a security policy that filters traffic and keeps logs of any attempted violations. Most firewalls, however, don't examine the contents of packets, so if bad traffic comes from a trusted source, most firewalls won't stop it.

Networking applications use a stack of protocols, logically organized into seven separate layers, according to the classic ISO Reference model. The lowest layer, layer 1, represents the physical layer (the wires or radio waves) and the highest layer, layer 7, represents the application layer (your web browser). Most firewalls operate at layer 3. However, newer versions of firewalls have more capabilities to secure communications. Advanced firewalls, also called next-generation firewalls (NGFW), operate closer to the application layer, layer 7, and act more like sophisticated network software that can look at a packet's contents instead of just examining the source and destination addresses and port. Advanced firewalls can do more than filter packets; they can filter applications and the data they use.

Firewalls work best when they separate trust zones and decide what traffic can cross from one zone to another. The most common place for a firewall is between an organization's internal network and the Internet. However, if an organization runs a website on a web server, they want anonymous users to be able to access it, but don't want those users in their network. A common solution is to use two firewalls, with a subnet between them. One firewall is connected to the Internet and the new subnet, and the other firewall is connected to the internal network and the new subnet. The two firewalls can allow Internet users to access resources, such as a web server, in this new subnet but disallow access to the internal network. This approach is called a screened subnet firewall, and the newly created subnet is called a demilitarized zone (DMZ). Even with advanced functionality and creative topology, firewalls alone cannot secure any network. Other devices, such as Intrusion Detection Systems (IDSs) or Intrusion Prevention Systems (IPSs), work together with firewalls to provide a DiD approach to security.

Business Impact Analysis

Deploying the right security controls in the right locations is fundamental to good security. Determining the best placement for controls isn't easy. The best approach is to use a formal method to identify and address vulnerabilities in your environment.

The best place to start is with a Business Impact Analysis (BIA), which identifies all processes that are critical to an organization's operations and risks to those processes. A BIA helps to prioritize efforts to ensure your business processes don't stop. After conducting a BIA, the next step is to create a plan for minor interruptions and major disasters. A Business Continuity Plan (BCP) defines situations that result in temporary business process interruptions and how to address those. The BCP contains recovery controls for as many situations that an organization can think of and are reasonably expected. For example, a temporary interruption could result from a power outage after a storm of construction damage. Larger disruptions from disasters, such as a flood or fire, would be covered in a Disaster Recovery Plan (DRP). A BIA, a BCP, and a DRP are necessary to ensure your business continues regardless of interruptions.

A natural extension of a BIA is to explore security-related threats to critical business processes. Security vulnerability assessments and penetration tests (also called pen tests) can help identify security control placement. The BIA identifies critical processes and the security vulnerability assessment identifies known vulnerabilities associated with each critical process. Both activities can be viewed as preventative controls since their goal is to prevent attacks. A vulnerability assessment, or vulnerability test, searches databases of known vulnerabilities and matches those with hardware devices, firmware in use, and software version installed in your organization to identify potential weaknesses or flaws that an attacker could exploit. A security vulnerability assessment is often confused with a pen test, but the activities are different. A security vulnerability assessment identifies known vulnerabilities that exist in a specific environment and provides a prioritized list of vulnerabilities ranked by severity. It also assesses any existing security controls and identifies gaps in protection. This part of the analysis is called a security controls gap analysis. A security vulnerability assessment doesn't try to exploit any vulnerabilities; it just identifies vulnerabilities that exist. The assessment results help organizations determine which vulnerabilities need controls to address them.

Some organizations take the process another step further. Instead of just identifying vulnerabilities, a pen test tries to carry out exploits against vulnerabilities to attempt to compromise (or break into) one or more systems. If that sounds like a cyberattack, it is. The only difference between a pen test and a cyberattack is that the pen testers have permission from the system owners to carry out the attack. Pen testing can be a lot of fun because the testers themselves get to act like attackers. Pen testers often use the vulnerability assessment report to plan their attack. Since the vulnerability report points to prioritized weaknesses, it makes sense to attack the weakest points first. Pen testing is a specialized skill, and not one that every organization has the budget to support. Many smaller companies retain external specialists to carry out pen tests, and in some cases regulation mandates external resources be used, but some larger organizations use their own internal resources. In fact, the use of teams of professionals to engage in wargames is growing in popularity. The pen testers are the red team, and the defenders are the blue team. Each side tries to defeat the other, and the organization benefits regardless of the winner. The overall goal is to figure out what works and what doesn't, and then fix what doesn't work.

Topic Questions:
Data Governance

Directions: Answer each question in the space provided. Correct answers and explanations appear after the topic questions.

1. Media sanitization work is performed during which of the following stages of the data life cycle?

    ☐ **a.** Data archival

    ☐ **b.** Data purging

    ☐ **c.** Data publication

    ☐ **d.** Data analytics

2. Biometrics and smartcards are forms of what type of control?

    ☐ **a.** Detective

    ☐ **b.** Preventive

    ☐ **c.** Compensating

    ☐ **d.** Corrective

3. Which of the following components exists as part of COSO's Internal Control framework?

    ☐ **a.** Risk Assessment

    ☐ **b.** Risk Response

    ☐ **c.** Objective Setting

    ☐ **d.** Internal Environment

Topic Question Answers: Data Governance

1. Media sanitization work is performed during which of the following stages of the data life cycle?

   ☐ **a.** Data archival

   ☑ **b.** Data purging

   ☐ **c.** Data publication

   ☐ **d.** Data analytics

Data purging is the orderly review of storage and removal of inactive or obsolete data files. It is the removal of obsolete data by erasure, by overwriting of storage, by resetting registers, or by sanitizing the data. It renders stored applications, files, and other information on a system unrecoverable even by laboratory attack methods. Media sanitization is a process to remove information from media such that information recovery is not possible. It includes removing all labels, markings, and activity logs. It changes the content information in order to meet the requirements of the sensitivity level of the network to which the information is being sent. It uses automatic techniques such as processing, filtering, and data blocking during the sanitization process. For example, pulverization is a physically destructive method of sanitizing media; it involves grinding the media to a powder or dust. Data purging is done as the last step at the end of a data life cycle.

2. Biometrics and smartcards are forms of what type of control?

   ☐ **a.** Detective

   ☑ **b.** Preventive

   ☐ **c.** Compensating

   ☐ **d.** Corrective

Biometrics and smartcards are forms of preventive controls. A preventive control is used to stop unwanted and unauthorized access.

3. Which of the following components exists as part of COSO's Internal Control framework?

   ☑ **a.** Risk Assessment

   ☐ **b.** Risk Response

   ☐ **c.** Objective Setting

   ☐ **d.** Internal Environment

Risk Assessment is part of COSO's Internal Control framework. The five components of COSO's Internal Control framework are Control Environment, Risk Assessment, Control Activities, Information & Communication, and Monitoring Activities.

Technology-Enabled Finance Transformation

Management accounting is currently undergoing a transformation—one that is changing the primary role of accounting from business event monitoring and compliance assurance to supporting the organization's strategic decision-making process. As data becomes more of a currency in today's business operations than just an artifact, the effective use of emerging technology will empower management accountants to engage in strategic organizational decisions. This section will feature the key technology topic areas that are viewed as most relevant to the management accounting profession—specifically, systems development life cycle (SDLC), business process analysis, robotic process automation, artificial intelligence, cloud computing, and blockchain technology.

What Is the Systems Development Life Cycle (SDLC)?

The **systems development life cycle (SDLC)** is a structured road map for designing and implementing a new information system. Although there are many versions and variations to SDLC, a basic five-step approach is presented in Figure 1F-12. This five-step approach can be expanded to encompass almost any variation found in the literature. The five steps are:

1. Systems analysis
2. Conceptual design
3. Physical design
4. Implementation and conversion
5. Operations and maintenance

Systems analysis involves identifying the needs of the organization and assembling the information regarding modifying the current system, purchasing a new system, and developing a new system.

Conceptual design (sometimes called planning) involves creating a plan for meeting the needs of the organization. Design alternatives are prepared and detailed specifications are created to provide instruction on how to achieve the desired system.

Figure 1F-12 Systems Development Life Cycle

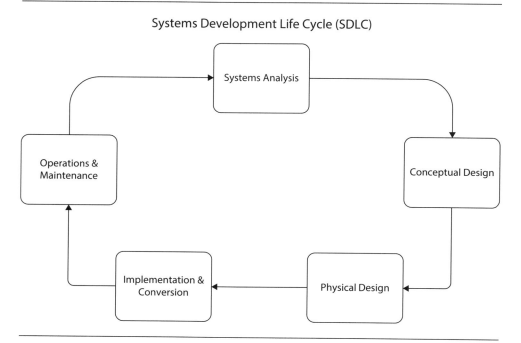

Physical design (also sometimes combined with system analysis to become a single planning step) involves taking the conceptual design and creating detailed specifications for creating the system. The design would include specifications for computer code, inputs, outputs, data file formats, database schemas (definitions and formats), processes and procedures, as well as proper controls.

Implementation and conversion (sometimes called development and testing) involves the installation of the new system including hardware and software. This step is where the project transitions from the planning stage to activities that carry out the work of the project. Although substantial time may have been invested during the design phases, most of the time required for software projects is expended here—in writing the software. The new system is tested and users are trained. New standards, procedures, and controls are instituted.

Operations and maintenance (sometimes just called maintenance) involves running the system, checking performance, making adjustments as necessary, and maintaining the system. Authorization controls are configured here, along with any other controls or configuration settings required to allow end users to interact with the system. Improvements are made and fixes are put in place until the organization determines that the cost of maintaining the old systems does not justify its benefits, and the whole cycle starts over again.

The main purpose of the SDLC is to provide a workflow framework for system development and deployment activities. Experience has shown that a sequential model increases quality and auditability. Although the SDLC process is linear, some organizations allow for emergency deviations from the standard flow. Such "break-the-glass" procedures allow developers to skip normal development and test phases to make changes directly in a production environment. A break-the-glass feature bypasses deliberate safeguards but provides organizations the ability to fix a problem now, such as a bug in a program or database query that is causing slowdowns and get formal approval later.

Moving from one step to the next one requires formal approval and release for promotion. In the first three steps, approval is a management decision. The implementation and conversion step is a little different. Completing this step requires acceptance by the end users after completing the testing process. The testing process ensures that all components are operating as expected and the system satisfies its goals. Although unit testing (testing individual components) occurs early in the implementation and conversion step during development, other types of testing include integration tests to ensure new or updated components function and integrate properly, followed by full-system (also called regression) tests and, finally, user acceptance testing. For integration and systems tests, testers will evaluate how components behave by examining logs of activity, reviewing end-user incident reports, and building test cases to exercise features of specific software versions. Testing requires effective communication and structure. Developers are most comfortable with unit testing, and end users are most familiar with systems and acceptance testing. Integration testing tends to be the type of testing that requires integration specialists since neither developers nor end users tend to understand complex integration issues.

Several different testing approaches are commonly used. The approaches differ based on the amount of internal knowledge a tester possesses of the system being tested. A black-box test is conducted in which the tester has no internal system knowledge. Black-box testing is helpful when the purpose of the test is to validate that a system meets system requirements. A white-box (or glass-box) test is carried out by testers that have access to internal system structure and components. White-box tests evaluate more than just functionality; they also assess how well a system is designed. For software systems testing, white-box tests often include static code analysis, which evaluates program source code to determine if the code meets standards and behaves as intended. Static code analysis most commonly occurs during development, before the code runs. The last main type of tests are gray-box tests, which are a combination of white-box and black-box tests. In a gray-box test, the tester has limited knowledge of system internals, and is helpful when testing power user or administrator functionality. A solid testing strategy helps ensure that a system is functional and secure. Other types of security controls provide first lines of defense, but testing ensures vulnerabilities are minimized in production systems.

Role of Business Process Analysis in Improving System Performance

LOS
1.F.3.b

Because better information should lead to better decisions, the quality of a company's system performance directly impacts the overall performance of the company.

As such, companies always want to find ways to improve—that is, do things better, cheaper, faster, or not at all, to increase profitability. One way to do this is through improved system performance. A company's systems are comprised of a set of business processes. Business processes are simply the way companies run their businesses. They are the tasks, procedures, teams, and communications companies employ every day to provide their products and services and keep the doors open.

In many new and growing businesses, processes were not always developed with an eye to how the processes would fit into the overall structure and objectives of the business. Instead they were created based on the easiest way to get the job done with little thought for long-term consequences. Many times, the easiest way or the path of least resistance is not the best way to accomplish the task. Unfortunately, after a business process is in place, inertia takes over, and it is difficult to change, which can retard growth. A haphazardly designed system is normally ill-prepared to handle business growth and may in turn actually impede business growth.

Business process analysis is a systematic method to study all of a company's business processes to determine how they can be improved. There are four basic steps:

1. *Clearly identify the process, who is involved, and what is currently being done with a clearly defined starting and ending point.* It is best to start with the processes that are most critical to the business. These processes should be directly connected to the company's main product, services, revenues, or expenses.

2. *Conduct a walk-through of the process to document it clearly and fully.* As part of this step, interview key employees to learn what they have to say about the process. Look for gaps in the process where information is lost or misdirected. For example, walking through a production process would allow the analysts to directly observe the process. Direct communication with personnel would help the analyst to fully document the system since the analyst may ask questions of the employees during the walk-through. Visually depicting a process, such as with a decision tree graphic, can help support the process documentation developed in this step. It can also help identify possible improvements to the process.

3. *Examine the current process to identify strong areas and areas that can be improved, such as bottlenecks, friction points, and weaknesses.* Look for ways to add value to the process. A good way to examine a process is to explore its purpose and the value that it is supposed to add. Although not every process has a problem, a root cause analysis is helpful to confirm what a process is supposed to do. Discovering a process root cause, or purpose, can help identify ways to make the process better and more efficient. If a step in the process is not adding value to the company, remove it. As mentioned, direct observation can illuminate areas for improvement. In addition, those working directly in the process have intimate knowledge of its problems and bottlenecks and most likely are in the best position offer solutions to these problems.

4. *Based on the analysis, propose a plan for improvement.* The output from the business process analysis provides one of the inputs to tasks that improve

existing processes or add new ones. Application software developers use the output from this process to design the most effective and efficient software to fulfill the organization's goals.

Robotic Process Automation

Many business processes require professionals to capture and combine data from various sources. For example, for the account reconciliations process, professionals need data from an accounting general ledger package, data tables from an external entity such as a tax authority, and data from the company's human resource system or other data system. Professionals then go through the process of importing or copying and pasting this data into a spreadsheet. This type of work is detailed, time consuming, and subject to human error due to momentary lack of attention or mental fatigue.

Robotic process automation (RPA) provides an effective solution to the risk of human error when performing these tasks. RPA employs software that can reach across various data platforms to capture and record data into one single processing facility, such as a spreadsheet like Excel. RPA robots are able to imitate many user actions, such as logging into programs, copying and pasting data, moving files, and filling in forms. A common entry point for process automation is at the beginning of a data entry process. RPA can fit into many other processing phases, but entering external data into a software application is a popular point of automation. In such cases, RPA handles the preprocessing stage of data entry that occurs before an item is fully processed in the system. Understanding and documenting processes is crucial to best apply RPA. Any time your process analysis identifies repetitive data handling or calculation tasks, consider RPA.

The term "robot," commonly shortened to just "bot," invokes images of walking and talking machines like the droids depicted in science fiction/fantasy movies. However, in this case robots are virtual execution engines carrying out a set of instructions (often according to a schedule) to achieve a specified task. Because using RPA requires minimal knowledge of computer programming, most professionals can be trained to use RPA software to automate desired tasks. For example, suppose an employee is required to copy and paste specific fields of data from a PDF form from a governmental agency's website each week into an Excel spreadsheet so that the data can be analyzed. Instead of manually copying and pasting the data fields, an RPA robot can be programmed to go to the governmental agency's website, retrieve and open the pdf form, open Excel, and move the data from the agency's PDF form to the company's Excel spreadsheet, all while requiring minimal or no modifications to existing software. RPA works with most existing software. Current RPA software utilizes drag-and-drop programming objects in a flowchart-type interface, making the task relatively simple to learn and implement since users are not required to learn a formal programming language.

Not every process is a good candidate for automation, but for the ones that are, RPA can increase efficiency and accuracy, while reducing cost. The best place to find good automation candidates is to identify processes that are suitable for automation—repetitive tasks that require the same action handling data over and over.

RPA is similar to GUI (graphical user interface) testing tools. Both record actions and repeat those actions with changing data. GUI testing tools are used to simulate activity for testing purposes and RPA repeats actions with new data to reduce human workload. Newer RPA products can also incorporate artificial intelligence (AI) into processes, allowing existing software to process data intelligently. One use case for RPA with AI is to respond to input data using natural language responses instead of preprogrammed responses.

RPA has five primary benefits:

1. Quicker completion of monotonous tasks at a lower error rate than humans can perform the tasks.
2. Leaves an audit trail of all of actions and changes to data.
3. 100% consistent in that it performs the programmed functions the same way every time (barring code or data corruption).
4. Frees humans from doing boring and repetitive tasks so that they may focus on more value-added tasks that lead to increased employee morale and productivity.
5. Can work 24 hours a day, 7 days a week without interruption.

Artificial Intelligence and Accounting Data Processing

LOS
1.F.3.d

Manual accounting processes take time and are susceptible to human error. For example, before systems with artificial intelligence (AI), processing purchase orders required that a paper-based purchase order be manually filled out and then manually entered into the company's purchasing system. Then the purchase order was coded, forwarded to the proper party for authorization, and mailed to the vendor. AI systems can now process the full transaction from electronically capturing the purchase order data to processing the data in the company's ERP, including recording and approval, to sending the purchase order electronically to the vendor.

AI can also assess conditions and take actions based on status. For example, AI can respond to real events such as releasing payment to a shipping carrier as soon as the last box is scanned into the receiving system.

In addition to the obvious benefits of greatly increasing efficiency, reducing human intervention, and, over time, improving processing accuracy, using AI systems provides transparency throughout the accounting process, which allows professionals to monitor the process and focus efforts on analyzing the insights drawn from AI implementations.

Two areas where AI can improve accounting processes are in data entry and analysis and in reducing fraud. A significant benefit of AI systems is that they can "learn" from their mistakes and be programmed to not repeat those mistakes.

Intelligent systems can be programmed to identify and interact with customers and vendors; capture, code, and process routine transactions such as invoices and purchase orders; track payment deadlines; and ensure the proper approvals are recorded in a timely manner. AI can increase quality and decrease cost as a result of introducing process stability and consistency that leads to fewer process interruptions. But operations isn't the only benefactor of AI. Management benefits by integrating AI into the overall analysis effort. AI can help standardize acquiring, analyzing, presenting, and interpreting data to help drive strategic decisions. There are currently few commercially available products. Companies often create their own softare, but AI can be expensive to implement due to software development costs and lack of experienced programmers.

Cloud Computing

LOS
1.F.3.e

LOS
1.F.3.f

Computer hardware and software is expensive, requires maintenance, and has a fairly short useful life that requires a relatively frequent capital investment. Thus, many companies have elected to outsource their computing operations. Cloud computing is simply outsourcing computer operations to an outside provider. The term "cloud computing" comes from a network mapping technique that portrayed a cloud between two networks. The "cloud" consists of a number of providers who offer hardware and software for rent. Companies pay the providers to manage their computer processes and store their data. Thus, companies effectively outsource their hardware capital expenditures and their computing obsolescence risk to these providers. They also can derive the tax benefit of directly expensing these costs instead of capitalizing, maintaining, and depreciating the cost of hardware and software over the useful life of the asset.

Cloud computing can support efforts to improve IT efficiency by providing services and applications users can connect to anywhere an Internet connection is available, as well as the flexibility to increase or decrease infrastructure components based on demand. In addition to addressing efficiency, cloud computing is based on renting computing resources, so using (and paying for) only what you need (also referred to as measured service) can reduce operational cost. Many cloud service providers also provide software tools and libraries to manage, interact with, and even carry out advanced analytics on cloud data and resources.

The key technology that makes cloud computing possible and affordable is virtualization. Virtualization is the ability to run multiple virtual machines (software implementations of physical computers) on a single physical computer. With virtualization, one computer can launch and run multiple virtual machines (VMs) based on needs. The effect of virtualization is that physical computers can run as many (or as few) VMs as required, leveraging the investment in hardware. A cloud provider can provide hundreds of VMs on just a few physical servers. To the users, each VM looks and operates like a separate actual computer. Through virtualization, cloud computing makes it easy for users all around the world to connect and work with one another, sharing files working in groups. And for administrators, virtualization simplifies backup and recovery procedures by effortlessly creating and restoring images of entire computers.

However, cloud computing comes with some notable risks, such as the risk that the cloud provider will not provide sufficient security for data and it may be lost, stolen, or corrupted.

Outsourcing computing operations, whether in part or in whole, increases the complexity of any system. Even though maintaining in-house computers and data is expensive, it is simpler and easier to secure than outsourcing to the cloud. On the other hand, cloud service providers have the expertise and personnel to dedicate resources to handling complex security requirements.

Another risk is that the cloud provider may not provide the level of service required to support the operations of the company. The service provider's Service Level Agreement (SLA) contains all of the terms of service performance, including guaranteed uptime. Understanding the SLA before agreeing to it can mitigate any service-related risks. The SLA also specifies the upside of cloud computing, including the ability to provision resources based on changing needs (called dynamic provisioning). Releasing unneeded resources can save substantial cost over maintaining in-house infrastructure. Another approach to balancing security risk with flexibility is in choosing the most appropriate deployment model. The deployment model is based on where the physical computing infrastructure resides. In a public cloud model, the hardware and software are housed in the cloud service provider's data centers.

If an organization wants to retain control over its infrastructure but still offer network services, the private cloud model, in which the hardware and software are housed in the owner's data center, may be a good choice.

The final option is a hybrid cloud model, in which at least one public cloud and one private cloud are used. A hybrid model works well when an organization needs to directly manage the security of part of its application, but wants to leverage the advantages of a public cloud for other parts of its application.

Software as a Service (SaaS) is a common example of cloud computing. Companies can purchase software from a provider and have it delivered through the Internet. Software used to be distributed on tapes, floppy disks, and CDs. Companies had to purchase multiple copies of the software and then purchase upgrades and new editions on these magnetic media. SaaS created a new way to distribute software by allowing customers to use application software that runs in the cloud service provider's cloud infrastructure. Since end users don't need to install any software, all they need is an Internet connection (hopefully secure) and a web browser.

On-premise applications that run on an enterprise's servers require users to access the internal network. With SaaS, users don't need access to any internal enterprise resources. You don't have to buy and install multiple licenses of application software anymore. With SaaS, organizations of all sizes can save money by paying only for what their users need. Companies like this arrangement because it relieves them of the cost of installing and maintaining the software and data on their own computers. SaaS also provides a pay-as-you-go service so companies can pay for the software on a monthly basis. In addition, SaaS allows for easy scaling; customers purchase only what they need and can then add features and users as needed. The software is automatically updated and accessible anytime from anywhere a user can connect to the Internet.

On the risk side, using SaaS makes a company dependent on an SaaS provider for use of the software. SaaS providers may experience service disruptions, impose service changes or alterations to the software that the company does not want, or experience a data breach causing exposure of critical customer data. Additionally, there is a risk of data from one organization being stored with data from another organization. This data contamination is the focus of several types of cloud best-practice controls, but still poses a risk. In addition to making normal operation more confusing and less accurate, a lack of sanitized data (separated by cloud tenant) makes recovering data after an interruption far more difficult.

Blockchain

LOS
1.F.3.g

A contract consists of a verbal or written agreement between parties. Contracts exist to provide legally binding agreements between two or more entities. In the digital world, however, contracts can be difficult to enforce because data can be changed so quickly and conveniently. In the instance of cryptocurrency, who actually owns the currency can be problematic since the currency has no physical manifestation. A person could send cryptocurrency to one party and then immediately send the same cryptocurrency to another party. In essence, the person could pay for goods and services with the same currency, much like a counterfeiter. Thus, in order for contracts to have any force on the engaged parties, parties must be able to lock in their agreement without fear of the contract being altered after the fact. Such a safeguard is known as *nonrepudiation*. Nonrepudiation essentially prevents a party from negating an agreement through denying the authenticity of a signature. However, a nefarious party may attempt to change or invalidate a contract because there are few legitimate copies. However, what if 1,000 legitimate and authentic copies of a contract were separately stored in 1,000 different locations; could a nefarious party change all 1,000 copies? Probably not. How can an authentic copy be stored in 1,000 different locations? Through the use of blockchain technology.

Blockchain technology, or distributed ledger technology in general, is the underlying technology of cryptocurrency such as Bitcoin. Blockchain is one type of distributed ledger. A distributed ledger is a database that is housed in several locations or among several participants; all data and transactions are not processed and validated in one central location. The data is typically not stored until consensus is reached by all parties involved. The files are then timestamped and given a unique and cryptographic signature. Thus, distributed ledger technology provides a verifiable and auditable history of the information stored in that database.

Blockchain is a special kind of database or distributed ledger with individual records or blocks that are linked together in a sequential list called a chain of blocks. These records or blocks are validated by multiple nodes or parties in a peer-to-peer network. The blocks are linked to other blocks, making them immutable or unchangeable. Since the contracts are recorded in these blocks and then linked to other blocks, the possibility of secretly altering a contract is virtually eliminated because the blocks are incorporated into multiple nodes in peer-to-peer networks. The blocks are essentially immutable because an altered block will not be identical to all of the other blocks stored across all of the other nodes in the peer-to-peer network. In other words, if a block is altered, everyone on the network will know that the altered block does not match their copy of the block on their node.

Smart contracts are agreements between parties created by software and embedded in a Blockchain protocol; as such, they take written contracts to another level. Smart contracts are automatically executable software programs that represent an agreement between parties through software code instead of paper. The software code is run and embedded in a blockchain protocol or platform without the need for any type of intermediary, such as a broker or dealer to control the execution of the agreement. The software code represents the terms of the agreement and is immutable since it is incorporated into a block that is part of a chain.

The application of blockchain technology beyond digital currencies can reduce or eliminate intermediary costs, increase transaction transparency, and provide a framework for trustworthy decentralization. The framework also has the potential to detect tax evasion, reduce corruption, track unlawful payments and money laundering, and detect the misappropriation of assets.

As an example, one application of blockchain technology is in the supply chain. The ability of blockchain technology to exchange data seamlessly through decentralized peer-to-peer networks with all transactions immutably stored and available for audit could make the supply chain system much more transparent and reliable.

Every step of a product's journey from origin to consumer would be entered on the blockchain, making product tracking and origin tracing easy for anyone interested in looking at the data. In addition to tracking products, blockchain can track other things, including people. People and even devices have identities. The Internet of Things (IoT) is a growing network of connected devices that are intelligent enough to initiate communication on their own. When devices communicate, just like people, they need a way to identify themselves and track their activities. Once a device or person registers their identity on a blockchain that record is permanent. In the case of people, registering an identity on the blockchain that is associated with a biometric sample means you don't need to carry identification anymore. All you need is a biometric scanner and access to the blockchain. Anyone can verify your identity. Blockchain technology and smart contracts could reduce or eliminate the numerous documents that accompany the international shipment of goods and the time lag required to process international financial transactions.

There are many use cases for blockchain technology, but not every software application should use a blockchain. Currently, blockchain doesn't run as fast as enterprise databases. And every blockchain data access costs a small transaction fee. But in spite of these caveats, blockchain can provide exceptional transparency, auditability, and transaction trust among participants who don't trust one another. Instead of trusting another participant in a transaction, you can trust the technology. As long as your use case can support small transaction fees, blockchain may be a good option. Most transactions in the real world already incur some fees, but be careful of designing applications with high volumes of transactions for a blockchain environment.

The original blockchain implementation, Bitcoin, was a public blockchain. A public blockchain network is one that anyone can join. Anyone can become a node and can download the entire blockchain. Some enterprises want blockchain's benefits but need to store private data. A private blockchain is one that is owned by a person or organization. The owner has to grant permission before any user can access the blockchain. All nodes and copies of the blockchain are controlled by the owner. For some use cases, such as a supply chain blockchain, multiple organizations want access to the data. A tomato supply chain could consist of farmers, co-ops, local markets, carriers, warehouses, distributors, and retailers. All participants in the supply chain want access to the blockchain data, but don't want the competition getting access. This type of blockchain is a form of a private blockchain, called a consortium blockchain. It isn't public, but it isn't purely private either. It is a combination of both. Most consumer-focused apps work best with public blockchains. Internal organization apps are mainly private blockchain apps, and apps that make it easy for groups of organizations to work together are mainly consortium blockchain apps.

Topic Questions:
Technology-Enabled Finance Transformation

Directions: Answer each question in the space provided. Correct answers and explanations appear after the topic questions.

1. During which phase of the systems development life cycle would scanning occur to identify vulnerabilities in the respective system?

    ☐ **a.** Planning

    ☐ **b.** Development

    ☐ **c.** Maintenance

    ☐ **d.** Testing

2. Which of the cloud operating models is **best** described as a service that does not require the customer to maintain servers, operating systems, or applications? The customer is responsible for the data that is uploaded and access to that respective information.

    ☐ **a.** Infrastructure as a Service (IaaS)

    ☐ **b.** Platform as a Service (PaaS)

    ☐ **c.** Software as a Service (SaaS)

    ☐ **d.** Function as a Service (FaaS)

3. Why would an organization adopt a Robotic Process Automation (RPA) solution for financial accounting processing?

    ☐ **a.** To validate the integrity of the financial information being manually inputted

    ☐ **b.** To provide an external audit firm with assurance that processes are being followed

    ☐ **c.** Because accounts payable approval activity is streamlined in the solution by rules-based, auto-approved workflow criteria that limit human involvement to specific approval situations

    ☐ **d.** To give the organization's customers analytical insight into the organization's financial transactions

Topic Question Answers:
Technology-Enabled Finance Transformation

1. During which phase of the systems development life cycle would scanning occur to identify vulnerabilities in the respective system?

    ☐ **a.** Planning

    ☐ **b.** Development

    ☐ **c.** Maintenance

    ☑ **d.** Testing

The system will be tested for vulnerabilities and defects during the testing phase.

2. Which of the cloud operating models is **best** described as a service that does not require the customer to maintain servers, operating systems, or applications? The customer is responsible for the data that is uploaded and access to that respective information.

    ☐ **a.** Infrastructure as a Service (IaaS)

    ☐ **b.** Platform as a Service (PaaS)

    ☑ **c.** Software as a Service (SaaS)

    ☐ **d.** Function as a Service (FaaS)

Software as a Service (SaaS) best describes this cloud operating model. SaaS solutions provide customers the ability to utilize a software solution where the back-end infrastructure (operating system, networking components) is fully managed by the cloud service provider.

3. Why would an organization adopt a Robotic Process Automation (RPA) solution for financial accounting processing?

    ☐ **a.** To validate the integrity of the financial information being manually inputted

    ☐ **b.** To provide an external audit firm with assurance that processes are being followed

    ☑ **c.** Because accounts payable approval activity is streamlined in the solution by rules-based, auto-approved workflow criteria that limits human involvement to specific approval situations

    ☐ **d.** To give the organization's customers analytical insight into the organization's financial transactions

Adopting RPA to streamline accounts payable approval activity correctly describes how the organization would benefit from reduced human interaction for previously manual processes.

Data Analytics

Business Intelligence

Big data is one of those terms that everyone claims to understand, but nobody can provide a definitive definition. Some contend that big data is a data set that will not fit on an Excel spreadsheet. Others say that to be considered big, a data set has to be larger than an exabyte (1 with 18 zeros behind it). The general agreement as to what constitutes Big data is any collection of data that is too big and diverse to be analyzed using traditional analysis techniques. As technology has advanced, more and more data of increasingly different types are able to be collected and stored for analysis. Big data is possible because of significant strides made in the ability of hardware and software to handle very large data sets beyond what normal data processing systems can handle. Big data is commonly analyzed to find patterns or trends in very large data sets. Regardless of your relative view of size, big data presents significant opportunities and challenges. For example, the auditor of a Fortune 100 company could download all of a client's transactions and audit the entire population.

The terms "volume," "variety," "velocity," and "veracity" are typically used to describe big data. Volume, of course, refers to the quantity of data. Variety deals with the types of data, such as numerical, textual, images, audio, and video. Velocity refers to how quickly data can be generated and processed; frequently, big data is available in real time. Veracity is concerned with the quality of the data. Of the four "Vs" of big data, variety is the one that provides the greatest promise of value. The ability to analyze data from many different sources makes it possible to learn more from data than ever before. The opportunities for the use of big data are substantial. Big data can glean data from many sources so that a business can target advertising directly to potential customers who have shown interest in their product by internet searches, social media posts, and demographics. Hospitals can capture data on patients to screen for harmful drug interactions or drug allergies of an incapacitated patient brought into an emergency room. Big data also presents challenges in terms of personal privacy. There is concern about all this data being available to marketers in real time—to say nothing of the cost of data breaches to customers and companies or the risk of the infringement of civil rights in the case of governmental use of big data. Companies also face the challenge of keeping a human touch in interactions with potential customers, who may not appreciate being mere sets of bytes to a company.

LOS 1.F.4.b

Structured data and *unstructured data* are on opposite ends of the spectrum of data. Structured data is data that is organized in such a way that computers can easily work with it. In contrast, unstructured data is not organized in such a way that computers can easily work with the data. *Semi-structured data* lands somewhere in between. A common example of structured data is data that has been placed into a relational database. A relational database is comprised of rows and columns, and data is placed in a cell at the intersection of these rows and columns. The term "relational database" comes from the fact that the design of the way data is stored and accessed is based on relational algebra. Data in a relational database is logically stored as a collection of tables, which makes it very easy to describe to nontechnical people, and the query language makes it easy to relate data across separate tables.

In a structured database, the data can be queried using structured query language (SQL) for any information that may be contained therein. For example, a database may contain two tables: the first one for recorded sales that is linked to a customer table (which means we would have a list of all sales made by the company, and the customers who are associated with these sales). The second table could be for cash receipts; which could also be linked to the customers who have delivered cash payments for purchases. The data is structured so that these data elements could be combined conveniently. If the sales table were combined with the customer table and the cash receipts table, we could easily see which customers have paid and which ones have not. The resulting query of the customers who have not paid comprises the company's uncollected sales—in other words, the company's accounts receivable.

Unstructured data is data that is not organized in such a way that it can easily be queried. Unstructured data can be text, images, video, or audio. Email is an example of unstructured data. Semi-structured data is comprised of varying levels of structured data and unstructured data, such as Extensible Markup Language (XML) files. XML is a self-describing format that supports storing data of many types and in different structures. XML files are sometimes used to store relational data, but they are also used to store and transport dynamic data in flexible formats. XML files are notoriously hard to parse and analyze due to the lack of consistent data structure. When dealing with unstructured and semi-structured data, you often have to extract the raw data and map it into a structure your models can use. Alternatively, text analysis (frequency analysis, sentiment analysis, standard response mapping, etc.) may provide the results without having to build structured versions of raw data. It is estimated that 95% of big data is comprised of unstructured data. Companies that seek to use structured, semi-structured, and unstructured data increase their operational performance to make more personalized product recommendations to customers, find the root cause of problems, identify bottlenecks and defects in their products and processes, and gain a greater understanding of customer habits.

Figure 1F-13 Data Transformation

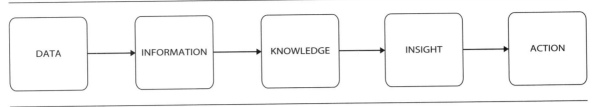

LOS
1.F.4.c

LOS
1.F.4.d

LOS
1.F.4.e

LOS
1.F.4.f

Although the origin of the Data → Information → Knowledge → Insight → Action model is not apparent, the concept provides a useful tool for professionals to understand the progression of data. Data by itself is not very helpful; to be useful, it must be organized into information. Data is composed of numbers, characters, and symbols. Data can be viewed as facts. Organized data creates meaning that can be used as information. Data then can be organized to answer the five basic questions of who, what, where, when, or how. In addition, data can be transformed into information by considering other characteristics, such as intensity, complexity, and relative rank. Knowledge can be thought of as when a person obtains information and competencies by education and experience. In other words, a person takes information and uses his or her own internal processes to convert it to knowledge. Insight is more subjective; in insight, people delve into their knowledge bases to make connections or see patterns that are not readily apparent. Insight can also be thought of as judgment. The true value of data, information, knowledge, and insight is to make informed and rational decisions or to take action.

Before an organization can take action, it has to start with data. An early phase of any analytics project is to identify sources of data already available to you now and find sources of any additional data your model needs. For example, if you're analyzing what products sell the fastest when a hurricane approaches, you'll need to cross-reference your sales history with external weather data. Once you have sources for your data, you can build your models and populate them with data.

One of the biggest challenges in big data analytics is in cleaning and preparing data for analysis. Tasks as simple as aligning all temperature readings to a single scale (Fahrenheit or Celsius) requires time and effort to get right. You'll likely spend more time cleaning your data than in any other phase in your analytics project. Once you have clean data and functional models, you can execute the models, visualize the results to help the recipients of your results interpret those results, and then operationalize your work. However, no analytics model produces good results without ongoing maintenance. One of the most delicate areas of model maintenance is data sourcing. As long as your data sources are constant and don't change anything, all is good. However, data formats and availability changes all the time. It is important to periodically verify all data sources to ensure your models are still getting good data.

The primary focus of business intelligence and artificial intelligence in particular is to create computer programs that can mimic human insight—to take a database of facts and find the connections and the patterns in the data. Business intelligence (BI) is the use of software tools and techniques to transform data into actionable information to help drive strategic decisions and improve efficiency. One of the common ways BI directly affects organizations is through a dashboard. Many BI solutions are implemented specifically to provide filtered, aggregated, and summarized operational data in a graphical format that is easy for management to use, called a dashboard. Dashboards make it easy to see how a business unit is doing in a single screen. Artificial intelligence (AI) is the application of computer algorithms and techniques to simulate human thought in making decisions. When pursued together, AI helps BI produce high-quality actionable results.

The challenge is to capture something as subjective as human insight and decision making and convert it to something as discrete and objective as computer code; lines of detailed instructions that can be programmed into software. In essence, this process creates the thousands of rules necessary to reproduce human decision making. The great opportunity of this work is to capture and preserve expert knowledge, insight, and decision-making skills so that they are not lost to future professionals. In addition, given proper information technology controls, computer programs do not get tired, call in sick, or take vacations. Computer programs can work 24 hours a day, 7 days a week. Programs can acquire and process data faster and in greater volume and detail than a human decision maker.

A company's data is considered one of its most valuable assets. The ability to tap into that asset and make better decisions represents the strategic value of a company's data and its ability to analyze that data. But to leverage the value of data, organizations must ask the right questions. If you're trying to use data to reduce loan defaults in a specific market, a regression model that makes predictions may not be the best model. Perhaps a better approach would be to use clustering or even classification models to discover corroborating reasons for loan defaults. Information learned could then suggest actions to identify high-risk loans and take preemptive action. While the value of data is immeasurable, the value of a team with data science competency can dramatically increases the value of data when it is leveraged to answer the best questions that can drive strategic action. Companies seek to capitalize on the unique insights gleaned from analyzing the data that has been collected over the years. These insights are used to help with customer acquisition and retention, to identify and correct processes that cost more than they benefit the company, to reduce costs through identifying inefficiencies in the company's production or operational processes, and others. Indeed, business intelligence is the use of application, tools, and best practices to transform data into actionable information to capitalize on the strategic and operational value of a company's data.

Data Mining

Data mining consists of using analytic tools on large data sets. In essence, data mining involves querying a lot of data. The idea is to find patterns, relationships, and insights in data that an organization routinely collects but does not use in most operational settings. Data from outside the organization is also typically used. Companies seek to find useful information and identify trends that can lead to increased sales, lower costs, and more effective customer service. A classic and possibly apocryphal example of the use of data mining is finding a significant

LOS 1.F.4.g LOS 1.F.4.h LOS 1.F.4.i LOS 1.F.4.j

correlation between the purchase of beer and diapers (called frequent itemset or market basket analysis). Through data mining techniques, a large retailer found that on Friday afternoons, young fathers who purchase diapers also purchase beer. Thus, the retailer started placing diapers and beer in closer proximity in order to exploit this newly found correlation and increase the sales of both diapers and beer. Another example is credit card fraud. If you have ever received a notice from your credit card company alerting you to suspicious activity on your account, the credit card company has used data mining techniques to identify purchases or purchase location patterns outside of your normal purchasing habits.

Data mining is not an exact science and can be viewed as both an art and a skill. Consider the concept of statistical power or the ability to find relationships among data. One of the major contributing factors of statistical power is that of sample size. In general, the larger the sample size, the greater the chance that a statistically significant relationship can be found among the data in the sample. Just because a statistically significant relationship can be found, however, does not mean that the relation is of any practical significance. For example, some weight-loss programs find a statistically significant difference in the before and after weights of people trying a new diet as opposed to those who do not. However, the difference can be as little as two pounds over three months. Most people would not consider losing two pounds in three months significant. Thus, data mining is a challenging field that should be employed with knowledge, experience, and wisdom. In many cases, data mining is an iterative process. Large data sets are often whittled down as the user refines and adjusts queries to more clearly focus results to provide actionable findings.

Data mining may sound easy, but it does have its challenges. A pervasive problem in data mining is getting good data. Data that resides in disjointed locations is more difficult to acquire on an ongoing basis than data from a single repository. Most data needs cleansing as well. Many data mining algorithms don't handle missing or noisy data well. Ample time must be invested in acquiring and cleansing data before using it. After data mining algorithms reduce large data sets to simple results, another problem often comes into play—privacy. If you're analyzing private data (personal or health data), you have to be careful that your results do not violate any person's privacy by identifying them. For instance, if your data mining efforts results in a list of HIV-infected people by zip code, a zip code with only one infected person can lead to associating an identity with that person. Analysis efforts with private data takes extra effort to maintain individual privacy.

Structured Query Language (SQL) is an established tool used to mine large data sets. The SQL language emerged about the same time as relational databases and quickly became the most popular database language in use. SQL uses an English-like syntax that is built on just a few simple commands. It makes querying database data easy, is flexible enough to handle complex queries, and returns data in an easy-to-use table format. SQL is a favorite of database application developers, and since so much of an organization's sensitive data is stored in databases, it is a favorite tool of attackers as well.

There are three basic commands in SQL:

SELECT
FROM
WHERE

SELECT means to select the data fields that are of interest to the user. In other words, what does the user want to see as a result of the query? *FROM* identifies the tables where the data is located. You can list the fields you want the query to return or you can use the asterisk (*) to tell SQL to return all fields in a table. For example, SELECT * FROM item will return all of the fields in the item table. (The semicolon character [;] tells SQL where the end of a query is.) *WHERE* restricts the data so that it meets certain criteria, such as WHERE Date < December 31. To put it all together, the SQL query SELECT * FROM item WHERE itemnum > 100; returns all fields from the item table that match the WHERE clause (itemnum values ? 100). Other commands—such as mathematical functions, sorting data, joining tables, and so on—are also used in SQL.

Although SQL and relational databases are by far the most popular ways to store and retrieve data, other types of databases work well in big data environments. Databases that are not relational, sometimes called NoSQL databases, store data in key-value pairs that can provide faster performance for large-scale queries. NoSQL databases, such as MongoDB and CouchDB, are optimized for processing large amounts of data and support data mining of larger datasets very well. These fast databases make it easier to analyze vast amounts of data to identify unique or suspicious transaction behavior.

For example, an analyst could explore millions of credit card transactions to create geophysical trajectories of charges over time. Any charge that may appear to be physically impossible, such as several physical purchases made at geographically remote locations in a short period of time, may indicate fraud. Analysts can also examine related traits of customers to help predict future behavior, such as items commonly purchased together or common actions leading up to missed loan payments. Regardless of the nature of the insight an analyst pursues, it all starts with querying existing data to understand past behavior.

Analytic Tools

Due to advances in technology, accountants now have access to powerful data analytic or statistical tools. These tools allow accountants to analyze datasets that before would have required the services of a statistician. However, there is a crucial difference between access to tools and knowing how to effectively use them. These tools are quite adept at fitting a data analytic model to a data set. The problem is that every model is constructed based on a set of criteria which involve certain underlying statistical assumptions. If data analytic models are arbitrarily applied to any given data set, important underlying assumptions may be blindly violated, which may result in flawed analysis, results, and conclusions. For example, many data analytic models rely on the basic assumption that the data set is random and normally distributed (think of a standard bell curve). If the data is not random and normally distributed but is evaluated using a model that depends on the data being normally distributed, the resulting analysis, results, and conclusion will be unreliable.

Likewise, the data you have available and your desired results will drive your decision on selecting the right model. For example, if your goal is to predict a future number of items sold, a linear regression model would be a better choice than logistic regression (logistic regression provides categorical output, such as yes/no, succeed/fail, etc.) Each model handles input data differently as well. Some models handle missing data better than others, so understanding distribution and completeness of your data will impact your model choices.

Descriptive, Diagnostic, Predictive, and Prescriptive Data Analysis

There are four basic types of data analysis:

LOS
1.F.4.m

LOS
1.F.4.u

1. Descriptive
2. Diagnostic
3. Predictive
4. Prescriptive

Descriptive data analysis presents what happened. As the name implies, descriptive analysis presents information that describes the events and operations of an entity. Descriptive data analysis focuses on describing the data using various summary-type measures that help us understand how the data is positioned, how it varies, and how the data distribution may be skewed. Basically, descriptive statistics are all about summarizing and reporting data. Measures that help us see how the data is positioned include the mean (average), median (middle point in the data), mode (how many data points are the same), and percentiles (how the data may be grouped). Measures that help us see how the data is spread out or varies include the range (the highest and the lowest data points), interquartile range (the data points in the middle 50% of the data set), and variance (the average of the squared deviations from the mean or how the data points are dispersed in relation to the mean). Last, the standard deviation is another measure of how the data points are dispersed in relation to the mean. For a standard bell curve, 68% of the data lies within 2 standard deviations of the mean, 95% lies within 4 standard deviations of the mean, and 99.7 lies within 6 standard deviations of the mean. The standard deviation is of more practical use than the variance since the variance is presented as a squared number, and the standard deviation is not. For example, the variance is measured as squared dollars; the standard deviation is measured in dollars. Measures that help us see how symmetrically the data is distributed show whether or to what extent the data is skewed to one side or to another.

Diagnostic data analysis focuses on why something occurred. Companies use historical data to look deeper (drill down) into the data to find patterns and relationships that can provide deeper insight into the issue of interest. For example, a pharmacy wanted to know why a large number of customers had moved their prescriptions to competitors. The pharmacy used diagnostic data analysis on the customer data it had collected over time. It analyzed the cost of customer prescriptions, distance from customer homes to pharmacy, pharmacy nonprescription promotions, customer wait time when picking up prescriptions, and other information. The pharmacy found that the average customer wait time when picking up prescriptions had increased. The problem was diagnosed by analyzing customer data. The next step was to figure out how to reduce customer wait time. This is where predictive and prescriptive data analysis can be employed.

Predictive data analysis seeks to know why something happened and then create a model to forecast what could happen in the future. As such, predictive data analysis attempts to identify what is likely to happen. It essentially attempts to forecast the most likely outcomes based on descriptive and diagnostic data analysis. Predictive analysis seeks to identify future trends and tendencies. For example, investors use descriptive and diagnostic analysis to predict the future performance of certain stocks. In essence, they use predictive analysis to see past the hard-right edge of the stock price chart. Predictive data analysis employs various methods and techniques to generate insights and create recommendations for decision makers. It uses tools such as data mining techniques, big data, statistical modeling, and machine learning to create predictive data models. These models are used to identify patterns and relationships within the data.

For example, many grocery stores host customer loyalty programs that give enrolled customers preferential access to specials and sales discounts. These programs also capture customer buying habit data by recording every purchase a customer makes in their stores. The sales data captured by these loyalty programs can be analyzed to identify customer purchasing patterns so that customers' future purchasing behavior can be predicted. Thus, the grocery store can input data from various scenarios into the model to predict customer purchasing behavior.

For instance, according to the predictive model, do customers purchase more toppings when the price of ice cream is discounted by 10%? Companies use predictive analysis to identify what offers customers would most likely take and also the optimal time to send these targeted offers. Predictive analysis can also provide a good assessment of the lifetime value of a customer, thus allowing a company to know in advance how much to spend on customer acquisition and still achieve an acceptable profit margin per customer.

Prescriptive data analysis works with predictive analysis to determine which of an assortment of actions to take given a future opportunity or future problem. For example, investors use prescriptive analysis to determine investment entry and exit points based on different levels of risk tolerance and economic factors. Prescriptive analysis typically uses artificial intelligence techniques to evaluate the outcomes of many different scenarios of varying probabilities. However, prescriptive analyses are only as good at their underlying models and assumptions. In other words, since no one can see into the future, prescriptive analysis provides an *idea* of what could happen, given the internal and external data employed in the analysis.

Clustering, Classification, and Regression

LOS
1.F.4.n

Three popular data analytic models include clustering, classification, and regression.

Clustering seeks to find similar groups of data points within a data set. Several algorithms or tools are used to find and group similar data points together. Some algorithms use hard clustering, where each data point is assigned to a cluster or group. Others use soft clustering, where each data point belongs to a cluster based on a probability model or the likelihood that a data point should be included in a cluster.

Clustering is most commonly used in market research where a company wants to better understand the preferences of various groups of customers.

Classification seeks to group data points into classifications or categories. The data is discrete. The primary difference between classification and clustering is that classification has set and predefined classifications, also called labels of categories, and seeks to place the data points into those categories. In contrast, clustering seeks to find those categories by analyzing the data. Classification may be used to classify customers by demographic characteristics and their propensity to favor certain products. A classification data model can then be constructed to classify new or potential customers on the likelihood that they will purchase those products.

Regression seeks to predict an outcome based on a model or equation. The input data can be continuous (numerical ranges, such as prices or quantities) or categorical (a value from a list, such as yes/no, a U.S. state, etc.) Users are trying to find the best fit to the data. For example, the regression equation may be used to model or predict the cost of a certain product. A parameter or quantity is input into the equation, and the cost is the calculated output. Regression models are useful for making future predictions, even for data that may be lacking time-series history (e.g., dates or times associated with transactions).

Linear Regression

Linear regression is a tool that help us see how one or more variables affect an outcome. Linear regression is commonly used to provide a set of input variables and make a prediction of an outcome. The variables are the dependent variable (or response variable) and the independent variables (or explanatory variables). Simple regression models only consider a single input value (independent variable) to predict an outcome (dependent variable), while multiple regression analyzes how multiple input values (independent variables) work together to make predictions of an outcome (dependent variable). Basically, we want to see how the independent variables impact the dependent variable. You may think of it like a machine: The independent variables go in one side of the machine and the dependent variable comes out the other side of the machine. The standard regression equation is $y = \beta 0 + \beta 1x + \varepsilon$ where y represents the dependent variable, $\beta 0$ represents the y intercept, $\beta 1$ represents the slope of the regression line, x represents the independent variable, and ε represents error term, also called the *residual* (the expected variance between a predicted value of y and an observed value of y).

The error term represents any variance not explained by the model. Regression models (and time series models) will never provide 100% accuracy because real life always encounters influences that models can't predict. The magnitude of the coefficients ($\beta 1$ in the simple case; multiple regression models will have more coefficients) indicate their effect on the outcome. A larger coefficient has a greater influence on the outcome.

For example, consider a simplified linear equation: $y = 20x + 1$. Each unit increment of x increases y (the outcome) by a value of 20. The x coefficient has a large impact on the value of y (the outcome). To predict a value of y, just plug in a value of x and solve the equation. In the example above, suppose you have a data point with $x = 12$. In that case, y is: $(20 \times 12) + 1 = 241$. For multiple linear regression models, you'll have multiple values of x (x_1, x_2, x_3, etc.), so just substitute each supplied value into the equation and solve. If your equation is $y = 12 + 2x_1 + 3x_2 + 4x_3$, and your values of x_1, x_2, and x_3 are (7, 5, 8), y would be: $12 + (2 \times 7) + (3 \times 5) + (4 \times 8) = 73$.

However, the machine does have some limitations. One limitation is that the dependent variable output does not come out perfectly, causing some variability in the dependent variable (result) called the error term. In addition, there is a term that indicates where the regression line crosses the y axis, better known as the y intercept. In cost-volume-profit analyses, the y intercept equates to fixed costs and the slope of the regression line equates to variable cost per unit. In essence, the regression equation is used to fit a model or line to the data points so that it minimizes the distance between each data point and the regression line.

Regression analysis provides information based on the relationship among various variables based on a sample of data that may not hold for the full population. Such limitations are addressed by various sampling metrics, such the confidence interval, standard error of the estimate, and the goodness of fit. A confidence interval is a measure of the likelihood that the population parameter value will be found within a specified range.

When a sample is selected, typically a point estimate is selected, such as the mean number of defects for a production run for a particular set or sample of products. This point estimate represents the best guess of the average number of product defects for all products (the population) in the production run. A confidence interval is calculated from the sample data to give a range of the number of defects where we will have some confidence that the true number of defects of the entire population will be found. Obviously, the higher the level of confidence, the wider the range in the confidence interval.

To get a better picture of the number of product defects in a production run, it would be best to collect more than one sample. The more samples the better, but it is necessary to stay within budget since sampling does cost time, money, and resources. Say we collect 10 samples. It is probable that the point estimate of each sample will be different; the question is, how different are they? If they are all relatively close, users can feel confident about the point estimate; users will feel less confident if the 10 points estimates are widely different.

To measure the difference in the point estimates, we calculate the standard error of the estimate, which is the standard deviation of the sampling distribution of the estimate. This measures how much the point estimates of the 10 samples vary from each other. To calculate the standard error of the estimate, start with the sum of squared errors (SSE), which is the sum of the squares of each error (the difference between an observed value and the predicted value at each point). Once you have the SSE, the formula for calculating the standard error of the estimate is SQRT(SSE / (N – 2)), where N is the number of samples (data points). For example, if SSE = 143.35 for 75 samples, the standard error of the estimate is SQRT(143.35 / (75 – 2)) = SQRT(1.9637) = 1.40. The relevance of the result depends on the range of your data. If most of your data is in the range 1 to 3, a standard error of the estimate of 1.4 is not good at all. On the other hand, if your data ranges from 0 to 99, 1.4 shows a small expected error. Regardless of the the data ranges, the standard error of the estimate is one way to compare multiple models that use the same data. In that case, a smaller value is better.

Another measure to help us understand the quality of a regression equation is the goodness of fit. There are many accepted models for measuring the goodness of fit based on the distribution of the data, but essentially the goodness of fit measures how closely the model matches or fits the observations or data points in the sample.

Sensitivity analysis is another tool used to determine the reliability of the results of statistical analysis. Statistical models depend on certain assumptions and can change according to variations in the underlying data. Real-life conditions may be a little different from the situation used to build a model. Sensitivity analysis can help determine whether you can trust a model's output of if one feature in sampled data is different than that feature used to build the model, A very sensitive feature in a model wouldn't likely give good results in this case, while a feature with low sensitivity might still be useful. Sensitivity analysis is also useful to determine which features most affect outcomes, helping you reduce the complexity by dropping features that don't contribute heavily to a result. Thus, it is useful to determine how sensitive the results are to changes in assumptions and the data. Changes are made to the assumptions and data to see if the primary results still hold. If so, the results are deemed to be robust to changes in the tools and data; the resulting findings should be pretty strong.

For example, an investment model to purchase a product line from another company is presented. The model includes the use of interest rates and labor rates. Once the data is analyzed, the model recommends pursuing the project and purchasing the product line. Sensitivity analysis would be used to input other interest and labor rates to determine whether the model is too heavily influenced by the standard interest and labor rates or if the model is robust to changes in those rates. As in all data analytic models, sensitivity analysis is subject to the same constraints of the underlying statistical assumptions of samples, distributions, and random selection and thus must never be blindly accepted as the final word.

Although very popular, linear regression models do have limitations. The regression process "boils down" trends in data to a simple representation. The regression line represents an average of outcomes. Since the regression line is an average, there is an expected error for every prediction. Data that contains many outliers will skew the model and reduce its accuracy. Also, linear regression assumes that all independent variables are truly independent, which may not always be the case in real life.

Exploratory Data Analysis

Exploratory data analysis is more of an approach than a set of techniques and tools. Exploratory data analysis uses visual or graphical tools as well as quantitative methods to find patterns in the data, to identify and extract important variables, to find outliers or anomalies included with the data set, to test assumptions and questions about the data, and to gain insight into the data set.

Simulations

If the parameters of a situation are known—for example, the costs and constraints of producing a product—a standard linear regression will forecast the total costs for production runs greater than normal capacity. However, most real-world situations require the use of many variables that are not conveniently available. Thus, to simulate a real-world situation, random input variables are used rather than making constraining assumptions about certain variables. Although it is convenient to think of the simulation inputs as random variables, they are actually based on a range of possible values of the variable of interest and the probability of that value based on a particular probability distribution. The advantage of a simulation model is that the whole range of possible values can be included in running the model instead of a single assumed best-case value. Needless to say, simulations require computer software to switch the full distribution of possible values into and out of the model.

Probably the most commonly known simulation is the Monte Carlo simulation (or probability simulation), which models the probability of possible outcomes given a range of random inputs from a distribution of possible values. The random inputs are designed to imitate the probability of actual occurrences.

For example, suppose your company is considering purchasing a subsidiary from a large multinational corporation because that subsidiary produces a product that complements your primary product. However, your company should consider many variables and unknowns before making an offer for the subsidiary. These unknowns include: can the subsidiary's product be produced cost effectively at your facility, what percentage of the subsidiary's workforce will come with the deal, is there unseen competition for the combination products, what effects may future economic conditions have on the new product, what are interest rate effects on the deal, among others.

A simulation first builds a probability distribution table of its output data by assigning probabilities to each expected output (with all individual probabilities adding up to 1), and then simulates input data by selecting random numbers as input. For each random number selected, the simulation chooses the output with the cumulative probability nearest the random number. For instance, if your simulation selected the random number 0.45433, the output with a cumulative probability closest to 0.45433 in the probability distribution table would be chosen and your cumulative output would be updated with the selected row's value. Then repeat as many times as your simulation requires. The simulated output is the final cumulated value you calculated.

For example, suppose you built the following probability distribution table of cryptocurrency value changes based on recent history (assuming the current price is $100):

Cryptocurrency Price ($)	Probability	Cumulative Probability
$75	.05	.05
$80	.11	.16
$85	.16	.32
$90	.22	.54
$95	.15	.69
$100	.11	.80
$105	.12	.92
$110	.08	1.00

Suppose the simulation selects the following random numbers: 0.3090, 0.9901, 0.2117, 0.8034. The final simulated price would be the increase or decrease applied to the initial price for each selected row. For example, 0.3090 is closest to .32 and the price in that row is $85 ($100 – $85), so the difference would be –$15. Applying this strategy to all selected random numbers, the simulation would calculate a cumulative price this way: $100 – $15 + $10 – $20 + $0 = $75. This distribution is skewed toward a decrease in price, so you'd expect the price to go down more often than up.

A Monte Carlo simulation can take a random value from a range of possible inputs to all of the variables and unknown parameters to calculate a probable output. The result of the simulation is recorded and the process is repeated. A Monte Carlo simulation runs a solution on the model hundreds or even thousands of times using different randomly selected values from the probability distribution. This is also known as what-if or goal-seeking analysis. This approach is also known as prescriptive analysis since the goal is to find inputs that provide a desired output. This is very different from other types of analysis that merely describe current status or predict future outcomes. This type of analysis actively looks for ways to alter behavior to craft an output. As in all data analytic models, simulations are only as good as the quality of their inputs. As the old computer science adage goes, garbage in = garbage out. Thus, the results of simulation tests must never be blindly accepted as the best possible result. The results should be only some of the inputs into an overall decision-making process.

Coefficient of Determination and Correlation

LOS 1.F.4.q

The **correlation coefficient (R)** measures how two variables move together. If they move perfectly together, R = 1 (positive correlation). If they move in the absolute opposite direction, R = –1 (negative correlation). If they do not move together at all, R = 0 (no correlation). Anything in between portrays some level of correlation (positive or negative). For example, R = 0.75 represents as positive correlation in that the two variables move together about 75% of the time.

The R value for any model should be between –1.0 and 1.0 for the model to produce acceptable results. Within that range, higher is generally better. Anything outside this range indicates some interaction between features (variables) your model doesn't consider. If R is less than –1.0 or greater than 1.0, use a different model or different features.

The **coefficient of determination**, more commonly known as R-Squared, tells how well the model performed. Essentially, R^2 explains how much of the variation in the data is explained by the model or rather, how well the model (equation) fits the data.

Values of R-Squared normally range from 0 to 1, with higher values indicating a better model. Sometimes you'll see R-Squared expressed as 0 to 100. The closer you can get to 1 (or 100 if using the alternate scale), the better your model explains dependent variable variations. A value of 1.0 (or 100) indicates perfect correlation (the model was accurate 100% of the time.)

Time Series Analysis

Data can be analyzed either as a cross-sectional data set or as a time series data set. **Cross-sectional data** comes from the observation of many entities at one point in time. For example, the sales revenue of 1,000 companies on the last day of their fiscal year represents a cross section of the sales revenue amounts across all 1,000 companies. With this data set the mean, median, mode, and variance can be calculated for this set of companies. However, say a manager is interested in the cost behavior of a product line over the course of the year. The manager could collect the cost data for each day the product line was in operation. Let's say the product line ran every business day. At the end of the year, the manager would have about 260 data points, one for each business day. This type of data set is called a **time series data set** since the data is collected over a period of time instead of at a single point in time. Time series analysis is often used in conjunction with regression models to smooth time-sensitive data and provide clean predictions. For that reason, time series analysis is often considered to be a type of regression analysis.

The main point of analysis is how the variable changes over time. For example, how do the costs change for the product line over the course of the year? There are four primary measurement components in time series analysis: trend, seasonal, cyclical, and random. If the data steadily increases or decreases, the resulting graph would show an upward- or downward-sloping line known as a linear trend. Other common trends are exponential and S-shaped trends. Time series data may also exhibit seasonal characteristics. For example, a company that specializes in renting mountain bikes earns most of its revenue during the summer season. Thus, a time series graph of this company would show a peak or a spike in sales from June to August. Similar to seasonal characteristics, time series data can exhibit cyclical characteristics in that business conditions tend to cycle over time from growth to recession. Unlike seasonal patterns, business cycles are more difficult to forecast because their time frame is not set. Business cycles vary in length from a year to longer and are difficult to predict. Last, time series data exhibits a random or irregular pattern that some call noise. Irregular patterns represent the unpredictability of events affecting entities, businesses, and the economy in general. Examples include fluctuating oil prices, earthquakes, and financial crises, among others.

The primary use of time series analysis is to identify trends and patterns as well as to forecast the future. Since no one knows the future, we have only past history to help us predict it. For example, time series analysis uses historical data to forecast the future costs of a particular product line.

One common technique used to "smooth out" any cyclic or seasonal variances is to use a moving average. A moving average weighs each data point based on the past few data points. Using a longer time span can affect the results and even hide interesting results. To find a good range of time to use in a moving average, calculate the *Mean Squared Error* (*MSE*) of each range, and then select the smallest one. A smaller MSE means the cumulative error is minimized.

Data Visualization

LOS
1.F.4.bb

LOS
1.F.4.ee

LOS
1.F.4.cc

LOS
1.F.4.ff

Data visualization is one method to convey information to a reader. Data visualization leverages the common adage that a picture is worth a thousand words. Indeed, a well-conceived and constructed image can convey a significant amount of information more quickly and completely than reading text that conveys the same information. Visualizations can make complex data convey simple results. On the other hand, visualizations can oversimplify analytics results. You have to carefully design visualizations to properly convey the true results of analysis, instead of omitting some results to make the picture pretty. The key is the proper design and execution of images that provide information to the viewer. Care must be taken in choosing the most effective data visualization technique to communicate results.

With today's technology, anyone can create pretty pictures and call them visualizations. However, in order to clearly convey the message that is contained in the data, the creators of the visuals must use knowledge of basic statistical principles and assumptions plus judgment in selecting the proper visualization. A poorly designed visual can distort the real story you are trying to tell.

Even with great graphics, any visualization should be presented in an appropriate manner to be effective. Receiving an email with a cool chart about how sales are rapidly declining isn't a good way to break news like that. Bad news often needs a live messenger. Make sure the method you use to communicate is right for the information you're conveying. An email might be great for informal communication, but presenting important information is better either in person or online if you expect questions and want to get feedback. With today's videoconferencing capabilities, it is easy to deliver a live presentation to an audience scattered across the world. Consider your audience as well. A technical presentation may include lots of details, but an executive summary should just include the highlights and high-level findings.

Data tables are the first level of providing information to readers. Tables efficiently use space, are scalable, and can be simple. Due to the prevalence of spreadsheets, most users are familiar with and comfortable making tables and graphs. Software programs can make data tables readily accessible and make it relatively easy to find and manipulate data. Six best practices that can and should be applied to tables and graphs are listed next.

1. *Planning.* Before the first cell receives data, the purpose and content of the table and graph should be planned. Know the audience for the table/graph and plan accordingly.
2. *Focus.* The focus of the table/graph should be the most prominent part of the design so that readers will instantly recognize it.
3. *Alignment.* For tables, text must be aligned or justified on the left of the cell and numerical data must be aligned on the right side of the cell. Column headings must be appropriately placed according to the content.

4. *Size.* Character (text and numeric) size matters. If the text is too small, then it is difficult to read and probably will not be read. In addition, the use of common fonts is recommended; uncommon fonts may focus attention on the font and not the information the designer is seeking to convey.

5. *Clutter.* Clutter is an enemy to every table and graph. Always leave sufficient white space to help the reader focus on the message.

6. *Color.* Color can be a powerful tool in providing depth, focus, and contrast. However, too much or poorly planned color can distract from the message of the table/graph.

A data visualization toolbox contains many tools. Just like a wrench and a screwdriver are useful and have specific purposes, data visualization tools or methods each have their specific purpose. The more common data visualization tools and their purposes are described next. These tools have common uses. Some are better at providing comparisons, others, distributions, still others at relationships and trends. They can also be categorized according to their intended use.

Comparisons

Bar charts are used to compare categories of data or data across time. For example, we could compare the annual gross revenue of 10 different action movies with each bar representing a movie. We could also represent the gross receipts for each month after the release of one movie.

Figure 1F-14 Sample Bar Chart

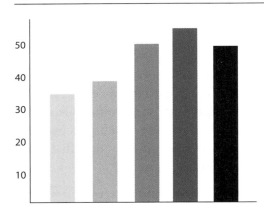

Pie charts can be used to compare the proportion of categories of data. However, most data science experts tend to frown on the use of pie charts unless the proportions are significantly different. Trying to decipher the difference between a 10% pie slice and a 12% pie slice is problematic. Thus, it is best to use only a few slices on your pie chart.

Figure 1F-15 Sample Pie Chart

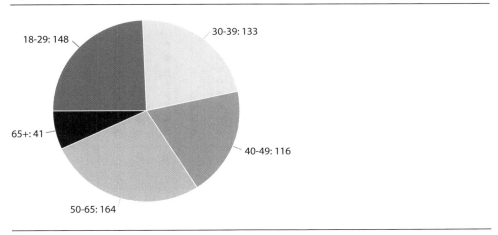

Distributions

Histograms show how many data points fall into a certain range so that the distribution of the data points can be viewed. Histograms can look like bar charts. The main difference is that the histogram displays the distribution (frequency) of one variable where the bar chart displays a comparison based on two variables (i.e., one variable is tracked on the *y*-axis and the other variable is tracked on the *x*-axis). However, histograms are only used with numerical values, and the data points are displayed in an interval rather than the actual values.

Figure 1F-16 Sample Histogram

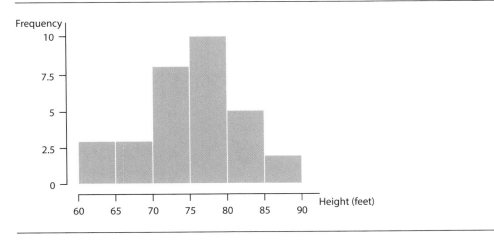

A *dot plot* is similar to a histogram except it uses vertical dots to represent a data distribution rather than a bar. Dot plots are useful for relatively small data sets.

Figure 1F-17 Sample Dot Plot

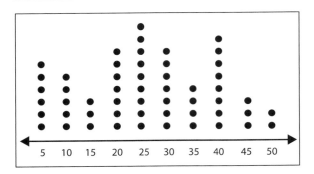

A *box plot* or box-and-whisker plot displays the distribution of a data set using five standard measurements: the minimum data point, the lower quarter of the data points (first quartile), the median or middle point of the data, the third quartile of the data points, and the maximum data point. Box plots do not show individual values and can be skewed, but they are also one of the few techniques that display outliers. They are also useful in showing a comparison among distributions.

Figure 1F-18 Sample Box Plot

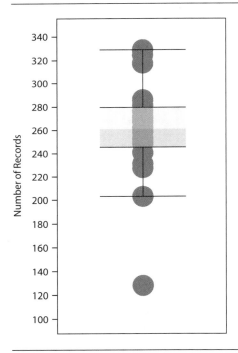

Location

Maps and *filled maps* display geospatial data so that data points can be viewed in relation to their geographical locations. When data relates to geographic locations, such as countries, states, cities, and zip codes, maps and filled maps are powerful tools to visualize data.

Figure 1F-19 Sample GeoChart

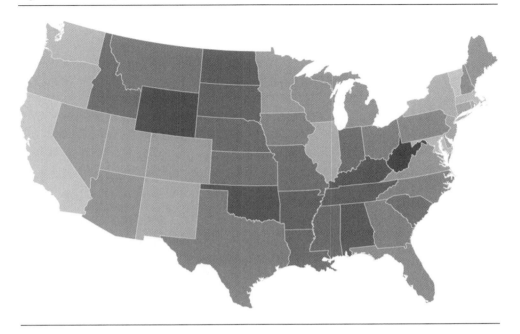

Relationships

A *scatterplot* displays data points as they are plotted according to their relative position to the *x*- and *y*-axis. This technique provides a view of how the data is related or positioned as well as its distribution. However, scatterplots do not show the relation between more than two variables.

Figure 1F-20 Sample Scatterplot

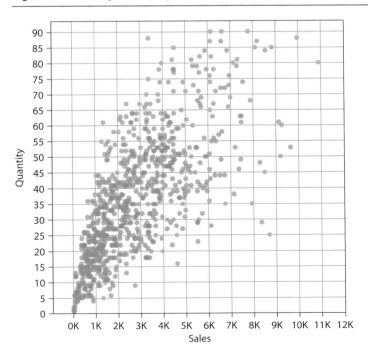

The *bubble chart* is a version of the scatterplot. Here the dots on a scatterplot are consolidated into bubbles, which vary in size to represent the number of data points. Similar to pie charts, bubble charts are best used when the bubble sizes display substantial variation.

Figure 1F-21 Sample Bubble Chart

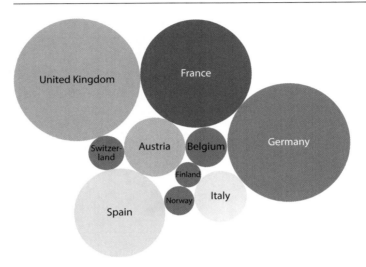

A *heat map* displays a relationship among variables through changes in the intensity of color. Heat maps provide a visual way to see numerical values. In fact, heat maps can show a substantial amount of data without overwhelming readers. Heat maps also facilitate identifying outliers by displaying squares with a color intensity significantly different from the surrounding squares. However, heat maps are less precise than other techniques since distinguishing among various color hues can be difficult.

Figure 1F-22 Sample Heat Map

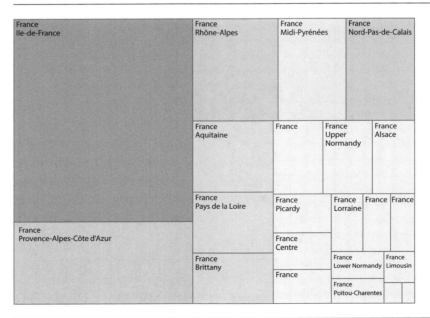

Trend

A *line chart* displays information as series of data points. Line charts are easy to read and interpret. They are also helpful in making comparisons between data sets and for showing changes or trends over time. One limitation is that line charts only show data over time.

Figure 1F.23 Sample Line Chart

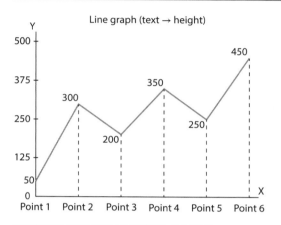

Topic Questions: Data Analytics

Directions: Answer each question in the space provided. Correct answers and explanations appear after the topic questions.

1. All of the following are benefits of using a Monte Carlo simulation **except**:

   ☐ **a.** Provides a sensitivity analysis

   ☐ **b.** Provides a correlation of inputs

   ☐ **c.** Provides analysis with limited data

   ☐ **d.** Provides scenario analysis

2. What type of analysis can be conducted where the data collected is always of a fixed and known period?

   ☐ **a.** Cyclical analysis

   ☐ **b.** Trend analysis

   ☐ **c.** Seasonal analysis

   ☐ **d.** Irregular patterns

3. What is the key difference between structured and unstructured data?

   ☐ **a.** Structured data is comprised of data types whose patterns make them difficult to query; unstructured data is comprised of data that usually is easily searchable, including formats like audio, video, and social media postings.

   ☐ **b.** Structured data is comprised of sometimes-unknown data types whose patterns make them easily searchable; unstructured data is comprised of data that usually is not easily searchable, including formats like audio, video, and social media postings.

   ☐ **c.** Structured data is comprised of clearly defined data types whose patterns make them easily searchable; unstructured data is comprised of data that usually is not easily searchable, including formats like audio, video, and social media postings

   ☐ **d.** Structured data is comprised of clearly defined data types whose patterns make them easily searchable; unstructured data is comprised of data that usually is easily searchable, including formats like audio, video, and social media postings

Topic Question Answers: Data Analytics

1. All of the following are benefits of using a Monte Carlo simulation, **except**:
   - ☐ **a.** Provides a sensitivity analysis
   - ☐ **b.** Provides a correlation of inputs
   - ☑ **c.** Provides analysis with limited data.
   - ☐ **d.** Provides scenario analysis

When data are lacking, the analyst may be forced to use subjective judgment to establish some of the probability distributions. When there is lack of knowledge on correlations, many analysts assume no correlation, i.e., that all variables are independent.

2. What type of analysis can be conducted where the data collected is always of a fixed and known period?
   - ☐ **a.** Cyclical analysis
   - ☐ **b.** Trend analysis
   - ☑ **c.** Seasonal analysis
   - ☐ **d.** Irregular patterns

A seasonal pattern exists when a series is influenced by seasonal factors (e.g., the quarter of the year, the month, or day of the week). Seasonality is always of a fixed and known period. Hence, seasonal time series are sometimes called periodic time series.

3. What is the key difference between structured and unstructured data?
   - ☐ **a.** Structured data is comprised of data types whose pattern makes them difficult to query; while unstructured data is comprised of data that is usually easily searchable, including formats like audio, video, and social media postings
   - ☐ **b.** Structured data is comprised of sometimes unknown data types whose pattern makes them easily searchable; while unstructured data is comprised of data that is usually not easily searchable, including formats like audio, video, and social media postings
   - ☑ **c.** Structured data is comprised of clearly defined data types whose pattern makes them easily searchable; while unstructured data is comprised of data that is usually not easily searchable, including formats like audio, video, and social media postings

☐ **d.** Structured data is comprised of clearly defined data types whose pattern makes them easily searchable; while unstructured data is comprised of data that is usually easily searchable, including formats like audio, video, and social media postings

Structured data is both highly organized and easy to digest, making analytics possible through data mining solutions. Unstructured data sources are made up largely of streaming data coming from multiple platforms such as mobile applications, location services, and Internet of Things technologies.

Practice Questions: Technology and Analytics

Directions: This sampling of questions is designed to emulate actual exam questions. Read each question and write your response on another sheet of paper. See the "Answers to Section Practice Questions" section at the end of this book to assess your response. Validate or improve the answer you wrote. For a more robust selection of practice questions, access the **Online Test Bank** at www.wileycma.com.

Question tb.er.plan.sys.003_1905
Topic: Information Systems

Which of the following economic principles can help an Enterprise Resource Planning (ERP) system to integrate financial systems and nonfinancial systems?

- ☐ **a.** Economies of scale
- ☐ **b.** Economies of scope
- ☐ **c.** Economies of skills
- ☐ **d.** Economies of technology

Question tb.er.plan.sys.011_1905
Topic: Information Systems

Structured query language (SQL) and query by example (QBE) are heavily used as query tools in which of the following database models?

- ☐ **a.** Network data model
- ☐ **b.** Relational data model
- ☐ **c.** Object data model
- ☐ **d.** Hierarchical data model

Question tb.er.plan.sys.017_1905
Topic: Information Systems

Which of the following cases **most closely** fits the characteristics of a data warehouse solution?

- ☐ **a.** A large, centralized, international online retailer that wants real-time analysis of customer interaction for its suggestion engine
- ☐ **b.** A nonprofit organization with three distinct business units, each with its own IT system and infrastructure, and a need to perform periodic analysis of performance across all business units
- ☐ **c.** An association of independently owned convenience stores and gas stations that want to provide members with in-depth statistical analysis of customer trends across the association

☐ **d.** A large organization with a substantial one-year budget to create an analytics platform that will allow users and analysts to build analysis of historical customer activity and, once set up, operate for up to five years after deployment

Question tb.sec.brch.002_1905
Topic: Data Governance

Security controls mitigate a wide variety of information security risks. Security awareness training would **best** fall under which of the following controls?

☐ **a.** Compensating and Corrective

☐ **b.** Preventive and Deterrent

☐ **c.** Preventive

☐ **d.** Corrective

Question tb.sec.brch.011_1905
Topic: Data Governance

Which of the following statements is **true** about a firewall and an intrusion detection system (IDS)?

☐ **a.** Firewalls are a substitute for an IDS.

☐ **b.** Firewalls are an alternative to an IDS.

☐ **c.** Firewalls are a complement to an IDS.

☐ **d.** Firewalls are a replacement for an IDS.

Question tb.sec.brch.022_1905
Topic: Data Governance

Regarding cyberattacks, identity thieves can get personal information through which of the following means?

I. Dumpster diving

II. Skimming

III. Phishing

IV. Pretexting

☐ **a.** I only

☐ **b.** III only

☐ **c.** I and III

☐ **d.** I, II, III, and IV

Question tb. sys.dev.lc.002_1905
Topic: Technology-Enabled Finance Transformation

Which of the following phases of the system development life cycle can be **best** described as the project plan is put into motion and the work of the project is performed?

- ☐ **a.** Maintenance
- ☐ **b.** Design
- ☐ **c.** Implementation
- ☐ **d.** Analysis

Question tb. sys.dev.lc.014_1905
Topic: Technology-Enabled Finance Transformation

Which of the following describes a financial administrative activity that is currently carried out manually that is a candidate for process automation?

- ☐ **a.** The organization's Controller and CFO receive a dashboard containing quarterly results.
- ☐ **b.** The creation of a P&L report is generated using bots rather than humans to allocate and aggregate the data to be presented.
- ☐ **c.** Credit card payment chargebacks are automatically adjusted on monthly sales reports.
- ☐ **d.** Customer data is automatically encrypted upon form entry within the organization's website.

Question tb. proc.au.001_1905
Topic: Technology-Enabled Finance Transformation

A business brings in a new application that performs valuation modeling. Which of the following **best** describes this innovative capability?

- ☐ **a.** The model can calculate the valuation of an asset based on user input.
- ☐ **b.** The model can calculate the valuation of an asset using the 10k or 8k filing.
- ☐ **c.** The model can quickly calculate the valuation of an asset using process automation.
- ☐ **d.** The model can quickly calculate the valuation of an asset using data points around the asset and historical examples.

Question tb.bus.int.001_1905
Topic: Data Analytics

Which of the following would be the **best** answer that describes a business reason to utilize data analytics?

- ☐ **a.** An organization wishes to automate processes such as repetitive data entry that is entered via optical character recognition (OCR) scanning of documents and input into the respective fields.

- ☐ **b.** The CFO and Controller want to see daily reports in the form of dashboards outlining cash flow, accounts receivable, accounts payable, etc.

- ☐ **c.** Internal investigations requests to have the capability to forensically assess data to determine if fraud or corrupt practices are being carried out.

- ☐ **d.** An organization wishes to assess a large volume of data for trends, filtering, and visualization in order to make the information easier to comprehend.

Question tb.bus.int.006_1905
Topic: Data Analytics

Which analytical model would be the **best** choice if a company wishes to test the prediction that is in the form of a quantity?

- ☐ **a.** Intelligence modeling
- ☐ **b.** Regression modeling
- ☐ **c.** Classification modeling
- ☐ **d.** Clustering modeling

Question tb.ana.too.002_1905
Topic: Data Analytics

The makers of home appliances and automobiles are **most** impacted by which of the following components of the time-series data?

- ☐ **a.** Trend component
- ☐ **b.** Cyclical component
- ☐ **c.** Seasonal component
- ☐ **d.** Irregular component

Essay Exam Support Materials

Writing an effective answer to an essay exam question is a special challenge. It tests your written communication skills in addition to your knowledge of the content. Essay questions also test your understanding of how specific pieces of information relate to one another, and your ability to apply your knowledge to real-life situations. The next information is included to help you learn more about how to respond to the exam part content in written essay form.

Preparing for the Essay Portion of the Exam

The essay portion of the CMA exam can draw from any of the LOS and content from Part 1: Financial Planning, Performance, and Analytics. It requires understanding the content and being prepared to evaluate the issues presented as well as making recommendations for the resolution of specific situations.

Your study plan should help you learn the content, learn how to respond to the content in multiple-choice questions, and learn to respond to essay questions presented on the content. This is a significant part of the challenge of the CMA exams. One way to meet this challenge is to break it down into smaller challenges—learn the content first, then practice multiple-choice exam-type questions, then learn how to respond to essay questions.

How to Write Essay Answers

The CMA exam essay questions require you to discuss the main points of a specific topic and then examine their implications. When developing your responses, you must support your answers with evidence of your thinking in order to demonstrate your knowledge and comprehension of a topic and your ability to apply that knowledge via thoughtful analysis.

You will be expected to present written answers that:

- Directly respond to the questions asked.
- Are presented in a logical manner.
- Demonstrate an appropriate understanding of the subject matter.

Clues within the questions can be used to help you formulate and organize your responses. Verbs such as *analyze, apply, explore, interpret,* and *examine* can help delineate the requirements of the question. Using the same verbs within your answer will help ensure that you are responding directly and completely to the specific questions being asked.

Candidates are expected to have a working knowledge and understanding of basic financial statements, time value of money concepts, and elementary statistics. The essay portion of the exam is computer driven. Answers are entered using a text editor similar to Microsoft Notepad.

Writing Skills

The essay section of the CMA exam is a way to assess your ability to analyze, evaluate, and effectively communicate about business situations. Written communication is an important skill required in today's business environment.

The Institute of Certified Management Accountants (ICMA) assesses your writing skills in the essay portion of the CMA exam. The assessment is based on these criteria:

- Use of standard English
- Organization
- Clarity

Use of Standard English

The use of standard English is an integral part of expressing ideas in a business environment. Assessment of the use of clear and concise terminology as is standard to the English language will be administered on the essay portion of the exam.

Organization

When answering essay questions, organizing your answers in a logical manner is important to effective business writing skills. As you read through the question, order your thoughts in a manner that exercises your process of thinking. Make sure that your answer has a clear beginning, outlining what you will be answering, followed by the answer, backed up by CMA content-specific facts, and a summary of what you just described.

Clarity

Being clear in your response is as important as the use of standard English and organization of your response on the CMA exam. Assessors of the essay portion of the CMA exam will look at the answer and critique based on whether the answer is clearly expressed and that the answer is supported by CMA content-specific rationale. When answering, make sure that you read your answer thoroughly to make sure that your response is clear and that the reader will understand how you are attempting to answer the questions.

Using Standard English, Organization, and Clarity in Your Responses to the Essays

When reading through the essay examples, work through the problems as if you were actually answering the questions on the actual CMA exam. When working through the essays, pay close attention to the key words in the question, organize your response, and start writing the answer to the question. When answering, make sure that you are answering the question in a clear and concise manner and make sure that you use standard English. Once complete, compare your answer to the answer provided in the textbook. Pay close attention to the way the answer is organized, the key words that are used, and way the answer is presented. Compare the textbook answer to your answer to see how you did.

Essay Exam Study Tips

On the actual four-hour CMA exam, the essay portion of the exam will begin once you complete the multiple-choice section or after three hours, whichever comes first. This means you will have at least one hour to complete the two essay questions presented.

To make the best use of your time to complete the essay portion:

- Prior to starting the exam in the testing center, take the online tutorial to become familiar with the testing screens. The tutorial is not part of your testing time and may be repeated. However, total tutorial time is limited to 20 minutes.
- Briefly skim through both essay questions and get an idea what each question is asking you to do (i.e., describe, analyze, calculate, etc.)
- You have one hour to complete the full essay exam (more if you have finished the multiple-choice section earlier than the three-hour limit). Determine how much time you will dedicate to each essay question.
- Start with the question you know best. Begin by writing key words, thoughts, facts, figures, and anything else that can be used to answer the question.
- As you answer one question, issues related to the other may occur to you. Write that information next to the appropriate question. This will build your confidence and give you a starting place when you begin the second question.

To answer each question:

- Read the entire question for requirements.
- Be aware of the verb clues that delineate what is being asked. This will help you formulate and organize your answer. Note that you may have more than one task—for example, define abc and interpret its applicability to xyz.
- Write the basic requirements in the answer space so that you are sure to address them.
- Begin your answer with one or two sentences that directly answer the question. If possible, rephrase the question's essential terms in a statement that directly answers the question.
- Use bullet points to show main ideas, and support each point with sufficient detail to show that you understand all the issues relevant to the question.

- Make it as easy as possible for graders to give you points. The goal in grading is to award you points, so show your thinking clearly and effectively. Do not write too little or too much.
- Finish your essay with one or two sentences that summarize your main point(s).
- Proofread your answer for logic, thoroughness, and clarity.
- Keep track of time. Do not spend too much time on one question.
- If you do not have enough time to write a full essay, write an outline of your main points to show what you know in order to get partial credit.

Examples of Essay Question Answers

EACH ESSAY QUESTION ACTUALLY CONSISTS of several related questions based on one scenario. The question as a whole is worth a set number of points and is graded against a scorecard to ensure consistent grading. The scorecard lists appropriate terms, topics, and ideas that address the answer. Presented here are two essay questions drawn from previous exams. The first essay question is followed by an example of an answer that would be awarded maximum points—a "best" answer. How these points are awarded is shown on a scorecard similar to ones used by the Institute of Certified Management Accountants (ICMA).

Following the second essay question are two answers that were awarded fewer points because they do not address all the issues. The "good" answer meets some but not all of the criteria. The "better" answer covers more of the requested information, as shown on the scorecard, and receives more points.

As you will see, the goal of the graders is to give test takers points rather than take them away. If test takers earn more credits than the maximum allowable points, they can be awarded only the maximum allowable number of points.

There are two types of essay questions: questions that ask for a **written response** and questions that ask for a **series of calculations, tables, or charts for a response**.

Note: The questions, answers, and scorecards used in these examples were provided by the ICMA and are used with their permission.

Example Question 1: Amur Company

Amur Company manufactures three lawn care component parts: fuel systems, transmission assemblies, and electrical systems. For the past five years, manufacturing overhead has been applied to products on standard direct labor hours for the units actually produced. The standard cost information is shown next.

Exhibit A shows standard cost information.

Exhibit A Standard Cost Information

	Fuel Systems	Transmission Assemblies	Electrical Systems
Units produced and sold	10,000	20,000	30,000
Standard labor hours	2.0	1.5	1.0
Standard direct material cost per unit	$25.00	$36.00	$30.00
Budgeted and actual manufacturing overhead		$3,920,000	

The current direct labor rate is $10 per hour. New machinery that highly automates the production process was installed two years ago and greatly reduced the direct labor time to produce the three products. The selling price for each of the three products is 125% of the manufacturing cost.

Amur's segment of the lawn care component industry has become very competitive, and the company's profits have been decreasing. Eric West, Amur's controller, has been asked by the president of the company to analyze the overhead allocations and pricing structure. West thinks that future allocations should be based on machine hours and direct labor hours rather than the current allocation method, which is based on direct labor hours only. West has determined the additional product information shown in Exhibit B.

Exhibit B Additional Product Information

	Fuel Systems	Transmission Assemblies	Electrical Systems
Standard machine hours	2.0	4.0	6.0
Manufacturing overhead:			
Direct labor cost		$ 560,000	
Machine cost		$3,360,000	

Questions

1. By allocating all of the budgeted overhead based on direct labor hours, calculate the unit manufacturing cost and unit sales price for each of the three products manufactured at Amur Company.
2. Prepare an analysis for Amur Company using the appropriate cost driver(s) determined by Eric West for manufacturing overhead. Calculate the unit manufacturing cost and unit sales price for each of the three products.
3. Based on your calculations in Questions 1 and 2, prepare a recommendation for the president at Amur Company to increase the firm's profitability.

Sample "Best" Answer for Amur Business Scenario

Question 1

The allocation of all of Amur Company's budgeted manufacturing overhead based on direct labor hours results in the unit manufacturing costs and unit sales prices for its three products is calculated as follows:

Fuel systems

Units: 10,000
Standard labor hour/unit: 2.0
Total standard labor hours: 20,000

Direct material: $25.00
Direct labor at $10/hour: $20.00
Overhead at $49/DLH[1]: $98.00
Total cost: $143.00
Sales price (125% of cost): $178.75

Transmission Assemblies

Units: 20,000
Standard labor hour/unit: 1.5
Total standard labor hours: 30,000

Machine hours per unit: 4.0
Total machine hours: 80,000

Direct material: $36.00
Direct labor at $10/hour: $15.00
Overhead at $49/DLH[1]: $73.50
Total cost: $124.50
Sales price (125% of cost): $155.63

Electrical Systems

Units: 30,000
Standard labor hour/unit: 1.0
Total standard labor hours: 30,000

Direct material: $30.00
Direct labor at $10/hour: $10.00
Overhead at $49/DLH[1]: $49.00
Total cost: $89.00
Sales price (125% of cost): $111.25

Note:

[1] Total manufacturing overhead of $3,920,000 / 80,000 total direct labor hours = $49.00 per direct labor hour.

Question 2

When the cost drivers identified by Eric West are used to allocate manufacturing overhead, the unit manufacturing costs and unit sales prices for the three products manufactured at Amur Company are calculated as follows:

Fuel systems

> Units: 10,000
> Standard labor hour/unit: 2.0

> **Total standard labor hours: 20,000**

> Machine hours per unit: 2.0

> **Total machine hours: 20,000**

> Direct material: $25.00
> Direct labor at $10/hour: $20.00
> Overhead (DLH at $7/hr[1]): $14.00
> Overhead (Machine hrs at $12/hr[2]): $24.00

> **Total cost: $83.00**

> **Sales price (125% of cost): $103.75**

Transmission Assemblies

> Units: 20,000
> Standard labor hour/unit: 1.5

> **Total standard labor hours: 30,000**

> Machine hours per unit: 4.0

> **Total machine hours: 80,000**

> Direct material: $36.00
> Direct labor at $10/hour: $15.00
> Overhead (DLH at $7/hr[1]): $10.50
> Overhead (Machine hrs at $12/hr[2]): $48.00

> **Total cost: $109.50**

> **Sales price (125% of cost): $136.88**

Electrical Systems

> Units: 30,000
> Standard labor hour/unit: 1.0

> **Total standard labor hours: 30,000**

> Machine hours per unit: 6.0

> **Total machine hours: 180,000**

> Direct material: $30.00
> Direct labor at $10/hour: $10.00
> Overhead (DLH at $7/hr[1]): $7.00
> Overhead (Machine hrs at $12/hr[2]): $72.00

Total cost: $119.00

Sales price (125% of cost): $148.75

Notes:

[1] Direct labor overhead of $560,000 / 80,000 total direct labor hours = $7.00 per direct labor hour.

[2] Machine overhead of $3,360,000 / 280,000 total machine hours = $12.00 per machine hour.

Question 3

The summary of the revised margins for each of Amur Company's three products, assuming the sales prices developed in Question 1 (allocation of all manufacturing overhead based on direct labor hours) is compared to revised costs developed in Question 2 (allocation of manufacturing overhead based on cost drivers), is as follows:

Fuel Systems

Current price: $178.75

Revised cost: $83.00

Gross profit (loss): $95.75

Margin: 54%

Transmission Assemblies

Current price: $155.63

Revised cost: $109.50

Gross profit (loss): $46.13

Margin: 30%

Electrical Systems

Current price: $111.25

Revised cost: $119.00

Gross profit (loss): ($7.75)

Margin: NA

Based on this analysis, fuel systems and transmission assemblies are producing a higher return than Amur Company previously thought. Fuel systems are the most profitable (54% gross margin) followed by transmission assemblies; however, electrical systems are losing money on a full-cost basis.

Recommendations for improving profitability include:

- Focus on fuel systems, through actions such as increasing marketing expenditures and reducing the price to increase sales.
- Improve profitability of electrical systems through changes to the manufacturing process to reduce the machine hours required.
- Decrease marketing of this electrical system, and increase the selling price if possible.

Scoring of "Best" Answer for Amur Business Scenario

The Amur question would be graded against a scorecard similar to the one shown next. Note that:

- The scorecard addresses more issues than is required by the question. This is done to accommodate variations between test takers and to provide the greatest opportunity for a maximum score. The goal of the graders is to give test takers points rather than taking them away. If test takers earn more credits than the maximum allowable points, they will be awarded only the maximum allowable points.
- At times, the process is more important than the numeric answers. Test takers should show all work/calculations to earn the maximum allowable points.
- Explanations add points.
- Formatting is not judged. You will be using simple text editing, such as Microsoft Notepad, so you may not be able to make charts and should use dashes for bullets.

Amur Scorecard

Amur—Total allowable points 17

Question 1: Maximum allowable points = 5

Issues to address

Unit manufacturing cost and price (DLH allocation) =

Total labor hrs = Standard hour/Unit × Units for each product

Totals all product labor hrs/ (80,000)

Overhead of $3,920,000/ 80,000 DLH = Overhead rate

Includes unit direct materials cost in product cost

Direct labor = $10 × Standard DLH per unit

OH/Unit for each product = OH rate × standard DLH/Unit

DM + DL + OH = Product cost/ ($143($89)) / ($124.5)

Sales price = 125% × Product cost

Question 2: Maximum allowable points = 5

Unit manufacturing cost and price (Cost driver allocation) =

Total machine hours = (Standard hour / Unit) × Units for each product

Totals all product machine hours / (280,000)

Machine OH = $3,360,000 / 280,000)

DL OH = $560,000 / 80,000 hours / ($7 per DHL)

OH / unit for each product = OH rate × standard MH / unit

OH / unit for each product = OH rate × standard DLH / unit

Includes DM and DLH for each product

Totals all costs / ($83) / ($109.50) / ($119)

Sales price = 125% × Product cost

Question 3: Maximum allowable points = 7

Issues to address

Recommendation

Increase emphasis on fuel systems

    Margin/Profit highest

Increase emphasis on Transmission

    Margin/Profit is high

Increase marketing to generate sales

Decrease price to stimulate sales

Other recommendations to leverage profitability

Decrease emphasis on electrical systems

    Margin is lower/losing money

Improve manufacturing process

Raise price if market will bear it

Other recommendations to deal with electrical systems

Example Question 2: Zylon Corporation

Business Scenario

Jeff Frankie is the chief financial officer of Zylon Corporation, a manufacturer and distributor of electronic security devices primarily suited for residential applications. Frankie is currently in the process of preparing the Y2 annual budget and implementing an incentive plan to reward the performance of key personnel. The final operating plans will then be presented to the board of directors for approval.

Frankie is aware that next year may be very difficult due to announced price increases to major customers. Zylon's president has put pressure on management to achieve the current year's earnings per share amounts. Frankie is, therefore, considering introducing zero-based budgeting in order to bring costs into line with revenue expectations.

Duke Edwards, Zylon's manufacturing director, is attempting to convince Frankie to build budgetary slack into the operating budget. Edwards contends that productivity is burdened by an abnormal amount of product design changes and small lot size production orders that incur costly setup times.

Questions

1. Explain at least three advantages and at least three disadvantages of budgetary slack from the point of view of Zylon Corporation's management group as a whole.

2. Describe how zero-based budgeting could be advantageous to Zylon Corporation's overall budget process.

Sample "Better" Answer for Zylon Business Scenario

Question 1

At least three advantages and three disadvantages of budgetary slack from the point of view of Zylon Corporation's management group as a whole include the following:

Advantages

1. It provides flexibility for operating under unknown circumstances, such as an extra margin for discretionary expenses in case budget assumptions on inflation are incorrect or adverse circumstances arise.
2. Additional slack may be included to offset the costly setups from design changes and/or small lot size orders.
3. The increased pressure to meet Y1 earnings per share targets may result in postponing expenditures into Y2 or aggressively pulling sales into Y1. Budgetary slack in Y2 may compensate for shifting those earnings from Y2 into Y1.

Disadvantages

1. It decreases the ability to highlight weaknesses and take timely corrective actions on problem areas.
2. It decreases the overall effectiveness of corporate planning. Actions such as pricing changes or reduced promotional spending may be taken from a perceived need to improve earnings, when eliminating the budgetary slack could accomplish the same objective without marketplace changes.
3. It limits the objective evaluation of departmental managers and performance of subordinates by using budgetary information.

Question 2

Zero-based budgeting (ZBB) could be advantageous to Zylon Corporation's overall budget process for the following reasons:

- The ZBB process evaluates all proposed operating and administrative expenses as if they were being initiated for the first time. Each expenditure is justified, ranked, and prioritized according to its order of importance to the overall corporation, not just its role in one department.
- The focus is on evaluation of all activities rather than just incremental changes from the prior year. This allows addressing activities that have been ongoing to determine if they are still useful in the current environment. The objectives, operations, and costs of all activities are evaluated, and alternative means of accomplishing the objectives are more likely to be identified.

Scoring of "Better" Answer for Zylon Business Scenario

The Zylon question would be graded against a scorecard similar to the one shown following. Note that:

- The scorecard addresses more issues than is required by the question. This is done to accommodate variations between test takers and to provide the greatest opportunity for a maximum score. The goal of the graders is to give test takers points rather than taking them away. If test takers earn more credits than the maximum allowable points, they can be awarded only the maximum allowable points.

- At times, the process is more important than the numeric answers. Test takers should show all work/calculations to earn the maximum allowable points.
- Explanations add points.
- Formatting is not judged. You will be using simple text editing such as Microsoft Notepad, so you may not be able to make charts and should use dashes for bullets.

Zylon Scorecard

Zylon Total allowable points 12

Question 1: Maximum allowable points = 6

Issues to address

Advantages

Provides flexibility under uncertainty

Extra margin for discretionary expenses

If assumptions wrong or adverse circumstances

Offsets unexpected setup costs

  Design changes

  Small lot sizes

Can compensate for earnings timing shifts

  Pressure to meet EPS

  Postponing expenses or accelerating sales

Other

  Explanation

Disadvantages

Decreases ability to ID weakness and take action

  Expenses are overstated in budget

Decreases effectiveness of overall planning process

Unnecessary actions taken such as

  Price changes or promotional spending cuts

  When eliminating slack would have solved problem

Limits objective evaluation of employees

  Measured against inflated budget

Other

  Explanation

Question 2: Maximum allowable points = 6

Issues to address

Advantages

Each expense is justified and ranked

  Each expense is evaluated as it were first time

Unnecessary activities can be eliminated

  All activities are evaluated

  Ongoing activities must be justified

(Continued)

(Continued)

Slack can be reduced

    Expenses must be grounded in realistic assumptions

Alternative means can be identified

    Are forced to evaluate processes

Other

    With explanation

Sample "Good" Answer for Zylon Business Scenario

A good answer would address enough of the identified three issues on the Zylon scorecard to earn a sore of 70% or 80% of the maximum allowable points. A good answer for the Zylon scenario is shown next. It addresses the issues but does not go beyond the question to provide explanations and clarification.

Question 1

At least three advantages and three disadvantages of budgetary slack from the point of view of Zylon Corporation's management group as a whole include the following:

Advantages

- It provides operating flexibility.
- Additional slack may be included to offset costs.
- Zylon will need to postpone expenditures.

Disadvantages

- It decreases the ability to highlight weaknesses and take timely corrective actions on problem areas.
- It decreases the overall effectiveness of corporate planning.
- It limits the objective evaluation of departmental managers and performance of subordinates.

Question 2

Zero-based budgeting (ZBB) could be advantageous to Zylon Corporation's overall budget process for these reasons:

- The ZBB process evaluates all proposed operating and administrative expenses as if they were being initiated for the first time.
- The focus is on evaluation of all activities.

Practice Essay Questions and Answers

The next essay questions and their answers were adapted from the *Revised CMA Exam, Questions and Answers: Part 4* (2005 and 2008) books supplied by the Institute of Certified Management Accountants and are used with their permission (unless otherwise indicated).

The focus of the questions will be on the test taker's ability to apply concepts presented in the part being tested to a business scenario.

The answers supplied are meant to serve as samples of answers that address 80% or more of the points listed on the question grading guide. There are generally more points on the grading guide than points that can be awarded (i.e., there may be 110 possible points but only 100 that can be awarded in total), so answers scoring 80% may vary among test takers. Thus, the answers presented here represent one possible answer, not a definitive correct answer.

Part 1 Section A Questions*

Question 1A-ES01

It is almost midnight on December 31, 20XX, and the bookkeeping program at Crank-M-Up, Inc. is malfunctioning. Instead of producing an income statement, it keeps printing an alphabetical list of accounts:

Administrative expenses	$215,000
Cost of goods sold	408,500
Income taxes	54,900
Loss on inventory write-down (nonrecurring)	13,000
Gain on foreign currency translation	19,500
Loss from discontinued operations	30,000
Sales	945,000
Selling expenses	145,000

---

*The practice essay questions for Section A are original questions and are not released ICMA questions.

Questions

A. As the new accountant for Crank-M-Up, your first job is to prepare the firm's multiple-step income statement for 20XX with EPS disclosures in accordance with GAAP. Crank-M-Up has 50,000 shares of common stock outstanding and has a 30% federal income tax rate, that also applies to discontinued operations.

B. Mark M. Down, the CEO of Crank-M-Up, is confused about the accounting treatment for irregular items on the income statement and wants you to explain why GAAP requires special treatment for irregular items.

Question 1A-ES02

The accountant at Dark Daze, Inc. suddenly quit on December 31, 2018, leaving behind a mess. You managed to find the following information:

Accum. Depr.—Building	$15,000	Interest Payable	600
Accum. Depr.—Equipment	10,000	Inventory	$102,000
Accounts Receivable	2,000	Land	137,320
Allowance for Bad Debt	140	Notes Payable (due 7/1/18)	14,400
Bonds Payable (due 12/31/22)	78,000	Prepaid Advertising	5,000
Buildings	80,400	Retained Earnings	?
Cash	30,000	Salaries Payable	900
Common Stock	60,000	Taxes Payable	3,000
Equipment	40,000		

Questions

A. Prepare the firm's classified balance sheet for 2018.

B. Ebony Dark, the CEO of Dark Daze, is concerned about the types of disclosures that the firm needs for its balance sheet items. Discuss the disclosures that the firm needs to make for: (1) Inventories; (2) Accounts Receivable; (3) Property, Plant, and Equipment; (4) Bonds Payable; and (5) Common Stock.

Question 1A-ES03

Information for Cash-N-Carry is shown below:

Cash-N-Carry
Comparative Balance Sheet
As of December 31

	2018	2017
Cash	$ 21,500	$120,000
Accounts receivable	195,000	105,000
Inventories	180,000	225,000
Long-term investments	0	60,000
Total assets	$396,500	$510,000
Accounts payable	$ 75,000	$120,000
Operating expenses payable	24,000	15,000
Bonds payable	70,000	100,000
Common stock	125,000	125,000
Retained earnings	102,500	150,000
Total liabilities and stockholders' equities	$396,500	$510,000

Cash-N-Carry
Income Statement
For the year ended December 31, 2018

Sales	$560,000
Cost of goods sold	375,000
Gross profit	185,000
Operating expenses	180,000
Operating income	5,000
Loss on sale of investment	(7,500)
Net loss	$ (2,500)

Other Information
- Accounts payable relate to the purchase of inventory.
- $60,000 of long-term investments were sold for $52,500.
- Cash dividends of $45,000 were declared and paid in 2017.

Questions
A. Prepare the statement of cash flows using the indirect method.
B. Prepare the operating section of the statement of cash flows using the direct method.
C. Buck Spender, the CEO of Cash-N-Carry, is confused about how to classify various types of cash flows. Explain to him which cash flows are classified as operating, investing, and financing.

Question 1A-ES04

On January 1, 2018, Lotsa Loot, Inc. purchased $500,000 of 8%, 5-year bonds for $520,790 for an effective interest rate of 7%. The bonds pay interest on July 1 and January 1, and Lotsa Loot uses the effective-interest method to account for these available-for-sale securities.

				Present	Value of an	Ordinary Annuity				
Period	1%	2%	3%	4%	5%	6%	7%	8%	9%	10%
1	0.990	0.980	0.971	0.962	0.952	0.943	0.935	0.926	0.917	0.909
2	1.970	1.942	1.913	1.886	1.859	1.833	1.808	1.783	1.759	1.736
3	2.941	2.884	2.829	2.775	2.723	2.673	2.624	2.577	2.531	2.487
4	3.902	3.808	3.717	3.630	3.546	3.465	3.387	3.312	3.240	3.170
5	4.853	4.713	4.580	4.452	4.329	4.212	4.100	3.993	3.890	3.791
6	5.795	5.601	5.417	5.242	5.076	4.917	4.767	4.623	4.486	4.355
7	6.728	6.472	6.230	6.002	5.786	5.582	5.389	5.206	5.033	4.868
8	7.652	7.325	7.020	6.733	6.463	6.210	5.971	5.747	5.535	5.335
9	8.566	8.162	7.786	7.435	7.108	6.802	6.515	6.247	5.995	5.759
10	9.471	8.983	8.530	8.111	7.722	7.360	7.024	6.710	6.418	6.145

Questions

A. Record the journal entry for the purchase of the bonds.

B. Record the journal entry for the receipt of interest on July 1, 2018.

C. Record the journal entry to accrue interest on December 31, 2018.

D. Write the entry to recognize the $530,000 fair value of the bonds on December 31, 2018.

E. On January 1, 2019, Lotsa Loot received a check for the interest on the bonds. Immediately after receiving the check, the firm sold the bonds for $530,000. Write the entries for these events.

F. Record the journal entries for the sale of AAA and the purchase of CCC.

G. On December 31, 2020, Lotsa Loot's Trading portfolio of equity securities had the following values:

	Cost	Fair Value at 12/31/20
10,000 shares of BBB Corp. common stock	$182,000	$195,500
600 shares of CCC Corp. common stock	27,550	25,500
	$209,550	$221,000

Record the fair value adjusting entry on December 31, 2020.

H. On January 1, 2021, Lotsa-Loot purchased a 25% interest in the common stock of Gobbled Up Company for $500,000. At that time, Gobbled Up had 1,000,000 shares of its $1 par common stock issued and outstanding.

Lotsa Loot has significant influence over Gobbled Up, and uses the equity method to account for this available-for-sale investment. Record the journal entries for the following events on the books of Lotsa Loot:

1. Purchase of Gobbled Up common stock on January 1, 2021.
2. Gobbled Up paid a total $160,000 cash dividend on July 1, 2021.

3. Net income for Gobbled Up was $360,000 in 2021.
4. What is the balance of Lotsa Loot's investment in Gobbled Up at the end of 2021 before any market fair value adjustment?
   Balance = _____
5. What would these entries have been if Lotsa Loot had been a passive investor that did not have significant influence over Gobbled Up and used the cost method to account for this investment?
6. Gobbled Up paid a $160,000 cash dividend on July 1, 2021.
7. Net income for Gobbled Up was $360,000 in 2021.
8. What would the balance of Lotsa Loot's investment in Gobbled Up have been at the end of 2021 before any market fair value adjustment?
   Balance = _____

Question 1A-ES05

On January 1, 2018, Equi-Tee, Inc. was granted a charter that authorizes issuance of 50,000 shares of 8%, $100 par value, cumulative preferred stock and 150,000 shares of $5 par value common stock.

Questions

Journalize the following transactions for 2018:

A. On January 2, the firm exchanged 8,000 shares of common stock for land valued at $300,000.

B. On January 5, the firm issued 12,000 shares of common stock to the public at $60 per share. The firm also issued 100 shares of common stock to its lawyer for costs associated with the formation of the firm.

C. On February 3, 2018, the firm issued 1,000 bundles of preferred and common stock for $720 each. Each bundle contained 10 shares of common stock and 1 share of 8%, $100 par value preferred stock. On that date, the common stock had a market value of $60 per share, but the preferred stock had no determinable market value.

D. The firm had $200,000 in retained earnings as of June 30, 2018, and the market price for common stock was $60 per share. On that day, the firm declared a 10% stock dividend on common stock.

E. On July 31, the firm issued the shares to fulfill the stock dividend.

F. On August 1, the firm paid $60,000 to reacquire 2,000 shares of its common stock for treasury stock. Equi-Tee uses the cost method to account for treasury stock transactions.

G. On September 1, the firm declared a $20,000 total cash dividend to be paid to preferred and common stockholders on September 30.
   Total preferred stock dividend = _____

   Dividend per share for preferred stockholders = _____

   Total common stock dividend = _____

   Dividend per share for common stockholders = _____

   Journal entry to record the declaration of the dividend:

H. On September 30, the firm paid the cash dividend.

I. On October 1, the firm reissued the treasury stock at $58 per share.

Question 1A-ES06

Hot Stuff, Inc. makes a boutique line of espresso machines that it sells with attached warranties.

Questions

Write the journal entries for the following events:

A. In 2018, Hot Stuff sold 700 espresso machines with attached warranties to restaurants on account for $1,500 each.

B. Hot Stuff estimated that 50% of the machines would need repair during the life of the warranty at a cost of $90 per machine for parts and labor. In 2018, Hot Stuff did warranty repairs on 100 espresso machines.

C. On December 31, 2018, Hot Stuff accrued the liability for future warranty work:

D. If Hot Stuff had sold those 700 espresso machines to restaurants on account for $1,500 each, plus extended warranties for $100 each:

E. Hot Stuff estimated that 50% of the machines would need repair during the life of the warranty at a cost of $90 per machine for parts and labor. In 2018, Pop-Up did warranty repairs on 100 espresso machines.

F. During December 2018, employees at Hot Stuff earned wages of $70,000. Withholdings for these wages included $2,250 for the employees' share of social security (FICA), $7,500 for federal income tax, $2,200 for state income tax, and $500 for union dues. The firm also incurred payroll tax expenses that included $2,250 for its share of FICA, $200 for federal unemployment tax (FUTA), and $700 for state unemployment tax (SUTA). Write the journal entry to record the firm's wage expense for December.

G. Write the journal entry to record the firm's payroll tax expense for December.

H. On December 15, 2018, Pop-Up borrowed $12,000 from the bank on a 7%, 4-month note. Write the following journal entries:
To record the issuance of the note.

I. To accrue interest on the note as of December 31, 2018.

J. To record repayment of the note and interest on April 15, 2019.

Question 1A-ES07

On January 1, 2018, Done-Right Manufacturing issued $10,000,000 of 6%, 5-year bonds when the market interest rate for similar debt is 5%. The bonds pay interest semiannually on July 1 and January 1 and Done-Right uses the effective-interest method to account for long-term debt.

Present Value	2.5%	3.0%	5.0%	6.0%
Single sum for 5 periods	0.88385	0.86261	0.78353	0.74726
Single sum for 10 periods	0.78120	0.74409	0.61391	0.55839
Annuity for 5 periods	4.64583	4.57971	4.32948	4.21236
Annuity for 10 periods	8.75206	8.53020	7.72173	7.36009

Questions

A. Are the bonds issued at a discount or a premium? _____

B. How much cash did the firm get for the bonds? _____

C. Issuance of the bonds on January 1, 2018.

D. Payment of interest on July 1, 2018.

E. Accrual of interest on December 31, 2018.

F. Payment of interest on January 1, 2019.

G. After paying interest on 1/1/19, the firm redeemed the bonds at 98.

H. R. U. Sure, the CEO of Done-Right, has asked you to explain why bonds are sometimes issued at a premium, but sometimes issued at a discount. What would you tell him?

Question 1A-ES08

In 2018, We-Got-Stuff, Inc. purchased some land that it used to build a factory. Expenditures during the year included:

- $100,000 to buy the land
- $5,000 in Realtor fees
- $3,000 in accrued property tax
- $10,000 to demolish an old building on the property
- $2,000 salvage value from the demolished building
- $16,000 for architectural fees
- $54,000 for construction costs
- $7,000 for supervision during construction
- $1,500 for 6 months of insurance during construction
- Construction was completed in 5 months
- $4,400 for shrubs and fences
- $8,000 for office furniture

Questions

A. Cost of the land = _____

B. Cost of the factory = _____

C. We-Got-Stuff is disposing of a truck that originally cost $50,000 and has $40,000 in accumulated depreciation.

Journal entry if We-Got-Stuff sells the truck for $11,000

D. Journal entry if We-Got-Stuff XYZ sells the truck for $6,000

E. Journal entry if We-Got-Stuff scraps the truck

F. Journal entry if the truck had been fully depreciated (accumulated depreciation = acquisition cost) when it was scrapped

G. In 2018, We-Got-Stuff exchanged equipment with Mercury Manufacturing:

	We-Got-Stuff	Mercury Manufacturing
Equipment (cost)	$100,000	$80,000
Accumulated depreciation	50,000	25,000
Fair value (FV)	60,000	50,000
Cash given up		10,000

Value of asset(s) that We-Got-Stuff gives up = _____

H. Value of asset(s) that We-Got-Stuff receives = _____

I. Gain or loss on the exchange for We-Got-Stuff = _____

J. Value of asset(s) that Mercury Manufacturing gives up = _____

K. Value of asset(s) that Mercury Manufacturing receives = _____

L. Gain or loss on the exchange for Mercury Manufacturing = _____

M. Journal entries if the transaction has commercial substance:

    i. On the books of We-Got-Stuff

    ii. On the books of Mercury Manufacturing

N. Journal entries if the transaction lacks commercial substance

    i. On the books of We-Got-Stuff

    ii. On the books of Mercury Manufacturing

Part 1 Section B Questions

Question 1B-ES01

Rein Company, a compressor manufacturer, is developing a budgeted income statement for the calendar year 2019. The president is generally satisfied with the projected net income for 2018 of $700,000 resulting in an earnings per share figure of $2.80. However, next year he would like earnings per share to increase to at least $3. Rein Company employs a standard absorption cost system. Inflation necessitates an annual revision in the standards as evidenced by an increase in production costs expected in 2019. The total standard manufacturing cost for 2018 is $72 per unit produced.

Rein expects to sell 100,000 compressors at $110 each in the current year (2018). Forecasts from the sales department are favorable, and Rein Company is projecting an annual increase of 10% in unit sales in 2019 and 2020. This increase in sales will occur even though a $15 increase in unit selling price will be implemented in 2019. The selling price increase was absolutely essential to compensate for the increased production costs and operating expenses. However, management is concerned that any additional sales price increase would curtail the desired growth in volume.

Standard production costs are developed for the two primary metals used in the compressor (brass and a steel alloy), the direct labor, and manufacturing overhead. The following schedule represents the 2019 standard quantities and rates for material and labor to produce one compressor.

Brass	4 pounds	@	$5.35/pound	$21.40
Steel alloy	5 pounds	@	$3.16/w	15.80
Direct labor	4 hours	@	$7.00/hour	28.00
			Total prime costs	$65.20

The material content of the compressor has been reduced slightly, hopefully without a noticeable decrease in the quality of the finished product. Improved labor productivity and some increase in automation have resulted in a decrease in labor hours per unit from 4.4 to 4.0. However, the significant increases in material prices and hourly labor rates more than offset any savings from reduced input quantities. The manufacturing overhead cost per unit schedule has yet to be completed. Preliminary data is as follows:

	Activity Level (units)		
	100,000	110,000	120,000
Overhead items			
Supplies	$475,000	$522,000	$570,000
Indirect labor	530,000	583,000	636,000
Utilities	170,000	187,000	204,000
Maintenance	363,000	378,000	392,000
Taxes and insurance	87,000	87,000	87,000
Depreciation	421,000	421,000	421,000
Total overhead	$2,046,000	$2,178,000	$2,310,000

The standard overhead rate is based on direct labor hours and is developed by using the total overhead costs from the above schedule for the activity level closest to planned production. In developing the standards for the manufacturing costs, the following two assumptions were made.

- Brass is currently selling at $5.65/pound. However, this price is historically high, and the purchasing manager expects the price to drop to the predetermined standard early in 2019.
- Several new employees will be hired for the production line in 2019. The employees will be generally unskilled. If basic training programs are not effective and improved labor productivity is not experienced, then the production time per unit of product will increase by 15 minutes over the 2019 standards.

Rein employs a LIFO inventory system for its finished goods. Rein's inventory policy for finished goods is to have 15% of the expected annual unit sales for the coming year in finished goods inventory at the end of the prior year. The finished goods inventory at December 31, 2018, is expected to consist of 16,500 units at a total carrying cost of $1,006,500.

Operating expenses are classified as selling, which are variable, and administrative, which are all fixed. The budgeted selling expenses are expected to average 12% of sales revenue in 2019, which is consistent with the performance in 2018. The administrative expenses in 2019 are expected to be 20% higher than the predicted 2018 amount of $907,850.

Management accepts the cost standards developed by the production and accounting department. However, it is concerned about the possible effect on net income if the price of brass does not decrease, and/or the labor efficiency does not improve as expected. Therefore, management wants the budgeted income statement to be prepared using the standards as developed but to consider the worst possible situation for 2019. Each resulting manufacturing variance should be separately identified and added to or subtracted from budgeted cost of goods sold at standard. Rein is subject to a 45% income tax rate.

Questions

A. Prepare the budgeted income statement for 2019 for Rein Company as specified by management. Round all calculations to the nearest dollar.

B. Review the 2019 budgeted income statement prepared for Rein Company and discuss whether the president's objectives can be achieved.

Question 1B-ES02

Gleason Company, a manufacturer of children's toys and furniture, is beginning budget preparation for next year. Jack Tiger, a recent addition to the accounting staff at Gleason, is questioning Leslie Robbins and James Crowe, sales and production managers, to learn about Gleason's budget process.

Crowe says that he incorporates Robbins's sales projections when estimating closing inventories but that the resulting numbers aren't completely reliable because Robbins makes some "adjustments" to her projections. Robbins admits that she does indeed lower initial sales projections by 5% to 10% to give her department some breathing room. Crowe admits that his department makes adjustments not unlike Robbins's; specifically, production adds about 10% to its estimates. "I think everyone here does something similar," he says, and Robbins nods assent.

Questions

A. What benefits do Robbins and Crowe expect to realize from their budgetary practices?

B. What are possible adverse effects of introducing budgetary slack for Robbins and Crowe?

Question 1B-ES03

Matchpoint Racquet Club (MRC) is a sports facility that offers tennis, racquetball, and other physical fitness facilities to its members. MRC owns and operates a large club with 2,000 members in a metropolitan area. The club has experienced cash flow problems over the last five years, especially during the summer months when both court use and new membership sales are low. Temporary bank loans have been obtained to cover the summer shortages.

The owners have decided to take action to improve MRC's net cash flow position. They have asked the club's financial manager to prepare a projected cash budget based on a proposed revised fee structure. The proposal would increase membership fees and replace the hourly tennis and racquetball court fees with a quarterly charge that would allow unlimited usage of the courts. The new rates would remain competitive when compared to the rates of other clubs in the area. Although there will be some members who do not renew because of the increase in price, management believes that the offer of unlimited court time will increase membership by 10%.

The proposed fee structure is shown next, along with the current membership distribution. The membership distribution is assumed to remain unchanged. All members would be required to pay the quarterly court charges.

Proposed Fee Structure

Membership Category	Annual Membership Fees	Quarterly Court Charges
Individual	$300	$50
Student	$180	$40
Family	$600	$90

Membership Distribution		
Individual	60%	
Student	10%	
Family	30%	

Projected Membership Payment Activity

Quarter	New	Renewed	Court Time in Hours	
			Prime	Regular
1	100	700	5,000	7,000
2	70	330	2,000	4,000
3	50	150	1,000	2,000
4	200	600	5,000	7,000

The average membership during the third quarter is projected to be 2,200 people. Fixed costs are $157,500 per quarter, including a quarterly depreciation charge of $24,500. Variable costs are estimated at $15 per hour of total court usage time.

Questions

A. Prepare MRC's cash budget for the third quarter. Assume the opening cash balance is $186,000, that membership at the beginning of the quarter is 2,000, and that the change to the new pricing structure will be implemented. Include supporting calculations where appropriate.

B. How would sensitivity analysis help MRC management in the decision-making process?

C. Identify at least four factors that MRC should consider before implementing this decision.

Question 1B-ES04

Coe Company is a manufacturer of semicustom motorcycles. The company used 500 labor hours to produce a prototype of a new motorcycle for one of its key customers. The customer then ordered three additional motorcycles to be produced over the next six months. Coe estimates that the manufacturing process for these additional motorcycles is subject to a 90% learning curve. Although the production manager was aware of the learning curve projections, he decided to ignore the learning curve when compiling his budget in order to provide a cushion to prevent exceeding the budgeted amount for labor.

Questions

1. By using the cumulative average-time learning curve, estimate the total number of labor hours that are required to manufacture the first four units of product. Show your calculations.
2. Assume the 90% learning curve is realized. Calculate Coe's cost savings in producing the three additional units if the cost of direct labor is $25 per hour. Show your calculations.
3. a. Define *budgetary slack*.
   b. Identify and explain two negative effects that budgetary slack can have on the budgeting process.
4. Assume that Coe actually used 1,740 labor hours to produce the four units at a total cost of $44,805.
   a. If the company ignored the learning curve when creating the budget, for the four units produced, compute Coe's
      1. direct labor rate (price) variance.
      2. direct labor efficiency variance.
   b. How would the above two variances differ if the learning curve had been considered when creating the budget? Show your calculations.
5. Assume that the price variance is unfavorable and the efficiency variance is favorable. Identify and discuss one reason that explains both of these variances.
6. Explain the effect on the direct labor efficiency variance if the manufacturing process was subject to an 80% learning curve.
7. Identify and explain one limitation of learning curve analysis.

Question 1B-ES05

Law Services Inc. provides a variety of legal services to its clients. The firm's attorneys each have the authority to negotiate billing rates with their clients. Law Services wants to manage its operations more effectively, and established a budget at the beginning of last year. The budget included total hours billed, amount billed per hour, and variable expense per hour. Unfortunately, the firm failed to meet its budgeted goals for last year. The results are shown next.

	Actual	Budget
Total hours billed	5,700	6,000
Amount billed/hour	$275	$325

The budgeted variable expense per hour is $50, and the actual total variable expense was $285,000. There is disagreement among the attorneys over the reasons that the firm failed to meet its budgeted goals.

Questions

1. What is the advantage of using a flexible budget as opposed to a static budget to evaluate Law Services' results for last year? Explain your answer.
2. Explain the process of creating a flexible budget for Law Services.
3. Calculate the total static budget revenue variance, the flexible budget revenue variance, and the sales-volume revenue variance. Show your calculations.
4. a. Calculate the variable expense variance. Show your calculations.
   b. Was the variable expense variance a flexible budget variance or a sales volume variance? Explain your answer.

Part 1 Section C Questions

Question 1C-ES01

Handler Company distributes two power tools to hardware stores—a heavy-duty ½-inch hand drill and a table saw. The tools are purchased from a manufacturer where the Handler private label is attached. The wholesale selling prices to the hardware stores are $60 each for the drill and $120 each for the table saw. The 2018 budget and actual results are presented next. The budget was adopted in late 2017 and was based on Handler's estimated share of the market for the two tools.

Handler Company Income Statement for the Year Ended December 31, 2018 (000s omitted)

	Hand Drill		Table Saw		Total		
	Budget	Actual	Budget	Actual	Budget	Actual	Variance
Sales in units	120	86	80	74	200	160	40
Revenue	$7,200	$5,074	$9,600	$8,510	$16,800	$13,584	$(3,216)
Cost of goods sold	6,000	4,300	6,400	6,068	12,400	10,368	2,032
Gross Profit	$1,200	$774	$3,200	$2,442	4,400	3,216	(1,184)
Unallocated costs							
Selling					1,000	1,000	–
Advertising					1,000	1,060	(60)
Administration					400	406	(6)
Income taxes (45%)					900	338	562
Total unallocated costs					3,300	2,804	496
Net income					$1,100	$412	$(688)

During the first quarter of 2018, Handler's management estimated that the total market for these tools actually would be 10% below its original estimates. In an attempt to prevent Handler's unit sales from declining as much as industry projections, management developed and implemented a marketing program. Included in the program were dealer discounts and increased direct advertising. The table saw line was emphasized in this program.

Questions

A. Analyze the unfavorable Gross Profit variance of $1,184,000 in terms of:
1. Sales price variance
2. Cost variance
3. Volume variance

B. Discuss the apparent effect of Handler Company's special marketing program (i.e., dealer discounts and additional advertising) on 2018 operating results. Support your comments with numerical data where appropriate.

Question 1C-ES02

The Jackson Corporation is a large manufacturing company where each division is viewed as an investment center and has virtually complete autonomy for product development, marketing, and production. Performance of division managers is evaluated periodically by senior corporate management. Divisional return on investment is the sole criterion used in performance evaluation under current corporate policy. Corporate management believes return on investment is an adequate measure because it incorporates quantitative information from the divisional income statement and balance sheet in the analysis.

Some division managers complained that a single criterion for performance evaluation is insufficient and ineffective. These managers have compiled a list of criteria that they believe should be used in evaluating division managers' performance. The criteria include profitability, market position, productivity, product leadership, employee development, employee attitudes, public responsibility, and balance between short-range and long-range goals.

Questions

A. Jackson management believes that return on investment is an adequate criterion to evaluate division management performance. Discuss the shortcomings or possible inconsistencies of using return on investment as the sole criterion to evaluate divisional management performance.
B. Discuss the advantages of using multiple criteria versus a single criterion to evaluate divisional management performance.
C. Describe the problems or disadvantages which can be associated with the implementation of the multiple performance criteria measurement system suggested to Jackson Corporation by its division managers.

Question 1C-ES03

George Nickles has recently been appointed vice president of operations for Merriam Corporation. The company's business segments include manufacture of heavy equipment, food processing, and financial services. Nickles has suggested to Merriam's chief financial officer, Karen Schilling, that segment managers should be evaluated on segment data contained in the company's annual report, which presents revenues, earnings, identifiable assets, and depreciation for each segment for a five-year period. Nickles reasons that segment managers may be appropriately evaluated by the same criteria used to evaluate top management. Schilling has doubts about using information from the annual report for that purpose and suggests that Nickles consider other ways of evaluating the segment managers.

Questions

A. What legitimate concerns might Karen Schilling have regarding the evaluation of segment managers using segment information prepared for public reporting?
B. What could the possible behavioral impact be on Merriam Corporation's segment managers if their performance evaluations are based on information published in the annual report?
C. What types of financial information would be more appropriate for George Nickles to use in evaluating the performance of segment managers?

Question 1C-ES04

ARQ Enterprises was formed by the merger of Andersen, Rolvaag, and Quie Corporations. Its three divisions retain the names of the former companies and operate with complete autonomy. Corporate management evaluates the divisions and division management according to return on investment.

The Rolvaag and Quie divisions are currently negotiating a transfer price for a component that Quie manufactures and Rolvaag needs. Quie, which sells the component already into a market that it expects to grow rapidly, currently has excess capacity. Rolvaag could buy the component from other suppliers.

Three transfer prices are under consideration:

1. Rolvaag has bid $3.84 for the component, which is Quie's standard variable manufacturing cost plus a 20% markup.
2. Quie has offered the component to Rolvaag at $5.90, which is its regular selling price in the marketplace ($6.50) minus variable selling and distribution expenses.
3. ARQ management, which has no established policy on transfer pricing, has offered the compromise price of $5.06, which is the standard full manufacturing cost plus 15%.

Both the Quie and Rolvaag divisions have rejected the compromise price. Refer to the pricing chart for a summary of this information.

Pricing Chart	
Regular selling price	$6.50
Standard variable manufacturing cost	$3.20
Standard full manufacturing cost	$4.40
Variable selling and distribution expenses	$0.60
Standard variable manufacturing cost plus 20% ($3.20 × 1.20)	$3.84
Regular selling price less variable selling and distribution expenses ($6.50–$0.6)	$5.90
Standard full manufacturing cost plus 15% ($4.40 × 1.15)	$5.06

Questions

A. What effect might each of the three proposed prices have on the Quie division management's attitude toward intracompany business?
B. Would a negotiation of a price between Quie and Rolvaag be a satisfactory method to establish a transfer price in this situation? Explain your decision.
C. Should ARQ corporate management become involved in resolving this transfer price controversy? Explain your decision.

Question 1C-ES05

Within Sparta Enterprises, the extraction division transfers 100% of its total output of 500,000 units of a particular type of clay to the pet products division, which treats the clay and sells it as cat litter for $42 a unit. The pet products division currently pays a transfer price for the clay of cost plus $1, or $22 a unit. The clay has many other uses and could be sold in the marketplace for $26 in virtually unlimited quantities. If the extraction division did sell the clay into the wider market, it would incur a variable selling cost of $1.50 per unit.

The extraction division recently hired a new manager, Keith Richardson, who immediately complained to top management about the disparity between the transfer price and the market price. For the most recent year, the pet products division's contribution margin on the sale of 500,000 units of cat litter was $5,775,000. The extraction unit's contribution margin on the transfer of an equal number of units of clay to the pet products division was $1,875,000.

Refer to the Unit Cost Structure chart for more information.

	Unit Cost Structure	
	Extraction Division	**Pet Products Division**
Transfer price for clay	—	$22.00
Material cost	$4.00	2.00
Labor cost	6.00	4.00
Overhead	11.00*	7.00†
Total cost per unit	$21.00	$35.00

*Overhead in the extraction division is 25% fixed and 75% variable.
†Overhead in the pet products division is 65% fixed and 35% variable.

Questions

A. Why don't cost-based transfer prices provide an appropriate measure of divisional performance?

B. Using the market price for the clay, what is the contribution margin for the two divisions for the most recent year?

C. What price range for the clay would be acceptable to both divisions if Sparta instituted negotiated transfer pricing and allowed the divisions to buy and sell clay on the open market? Explain your answer.

D. Why should a negotiated transfer price result in desirable behavior from the management of the two divisions?

Question 1C-ES06

4-Cycle, Inc., manufactures small engines for recreational vehicles, motorcycles, boats, and stationary equipment. Each line has its own product manager. The company chief financial officer, Stan Downs, prepares divisional budgets on a per-month basis using a standard cost system. Each product line occupies its own space, with square footage varying considerably among lines. Fixed production costs are allocated on the basis of square feet using a factory-wide rate. Variable factory overhead is based on machine hours. Other costs are based on revenue.

At the company's quarterly meeting, Laura Fleur, the new product manager for marine engines, received an unpleasant surprise. When distributing the performance report (shown next) to each manager, Stan Downs remarked aloud that Fleur would need to see him after the meeting to discuss ways to improve her line's lackluster performance. Since she thought her first quarter's performance was impressive, she was taken aback by Downs's comments. The performance report provided her with no clue to what had gone wrong.

4-Cycle, Inc. Marine Engine Quarterly Performance Report

	Actual	Budget	Variance
Units	10,500	8,500	2,000 F
Revenue	$17,500,000	$14,700,000	$2,800,000 F
Variable production costs			
Direct materials	2,500,000	2,164,750	335,250 U
Direct labor	2,193,000	1,790,000	403,000 U
Machine time	2,300,000	1,950,000	350,000 U
Factory overhead	4,500,000	3,825,000	675,500 U
Fixed production costs			
Indirect labor	925,000	580,250	344,750 U
Depreciation	500,000	500,000	—
Taxes	232,500	220,000	12,500 U
Insurance	437,000	437,000	—
Administrative expense	1,226,000	919,500	306,500 U
Marketing expense	848,000	540,000	308,000 U
Research and development	613,000	460,000	153,000 U
Operating profit	$1,225,000	$1,313,500	$88,500 U

Questions

A. What are at least three weaknesses in 4-Cycle's quarterly performance report? Explain your answer.

B. What are some ways in which 4-Cycle can eliminate the weaknesses in the way it reports quarterly performance to its managers? Revise the quarterly report accordingly.

Question 1C-ES07

SieCo is a sheet metal manufacturer whose customers are mainly in the automobile industry. The company's chief engineer, Steve Simpson, has recently presented a proposal for automating the Drilling Department. The proposal recommended that SieCo purchase from Service Corp. two robots that would have the capability of replacing the eight direct labor workers in the department. The cost savings in the proposal included the elimination of the direct labor costs plus the elimination of manufacturing overhead cost in the Drilling Department as SieCo charges manufacturing overhead on the basis of direct labor costs using a plant-wide rate.

SieCo's controller, Keith Hunter, gathered the information shown in Exhibit 1 to discuss the issue of overhead application at the management meeting at which the proposal was approved.

Exhibit 1

Date	Average Annual Direct Labor Cost	Average Annual Manufacturing Overhead Cost	Average Manufacturing Overhead Rate
Current Year	$4,000,000	$20,000,000	500%

Category	Cutting Department	Grinding Department	Drilling Department
Average Annual Direct Labor	$2,000,000	$1,750,000	$250,000
Average Annual Overhead Cost	11,000,000	7,000,000	2,000,000

Simpson met the chief accountant, Leslie Altman, in the lunchroom and inquired about the status of the proposal. Altman told Simpson that the project had been approved. Simpson said, "That's great. Be sure to make the payment as soon as possible as my brother-in-law owns Service Corp."

Altman was puzzled by the fact that there had been no competitive bidding and spoke to his supervisor, Keith Hunter. Hunter told Altman not to worry; Service Corp will do a great job.

Questions

A. Using the information from Exhibit 1, describe the shortcomings of the system for applying overhead that is currently used by SieCo.

B. Recommend two ways to improve SieCo's method for applying overhead in the Cutting and Grinding Departments.

C. Recommend two ways to improve SieCo's method for applying overhead to accommodate the automation of the Drilling Department.

D. Explain the misconceptions underlying the statement that the manufacturing overhead cost in the Drilling Department would be reduced to zero if the automation proposal were implemented.

E. Referring to the specific standards outlined in IMA's *Statement of Ethical Professional Practice*, identify and discuss the ethical conflicts that Altman needs to resolve.

F. According to IMA's *Statement of Ethical Professional Practice*, identify the steps that Altman should take to resolve this situation

Question 1C-ES08

For many years, Lawton Industries has manufactured prefabricated houses where the houses are constructed in sections to be assembled on customers' lots. The company expanded into the precut housing market in 2019 when it acquired Presser Company, one of its suppliers. In this market, various types of lumber are precut into the appropriate lengths, banded into packages, and shipped to customers' lots for assembly. Lawton decided to maintain Presser's separate identity and, thus, established the Presser Division as an investment center of Lawton.

Lawton uses return on average investment (ROI) as a performance measure the investment defined as operating assets employed. Management bonuses are based in part on ROI. All investments in operating assets are expected to earn a minimum return of 15% before income taxes. Presser's ROI has ranged from 19.3% to 22.1% since it was acquired in 2019. The division had an investment opportunity in the year just ended that had an estimated ROI of 18%, but Presser's management decided against the investment because it believed the investment would decrease the division's overall ROI.

Presser's operating statement for the year just ended is presented next. The division's operating assets employed were $12,600,000 at the end of the year, a 5% increase over the balance at the end of the previous year.

**Presser Division Operating Statement
for the Year Ended December 31
($000 omitted)**

Sales revenue		$24,000
Cost of goods sold		15,800
Gross profit		$8,200
Operating expenses		
Administrative	$2,140	
Selling	3,600	5,740
Income from operations		
before income taxes		$2,460

Questions

A. Calculate these performance measures for the year just ended for the Presser Division of Lawton Industries:

1. Return on average investment in operating assets employed (ROI).
2. Residual income calculated on the basis of average operating assets employed.

B. Would the management of Presser Division have been more likely to accept the investment opportunity it had during the year if residual income were used as a performance measure instead of ROI? Explain your answer.

C. The Presser Division is a separate investment center with Lawton Industries. Identify and describe the items Presser must control if it is to be evaluated fairly by either the ROI or residual income performance measures.

Question 1C-ES09

Klein, Thompson Corporation's CFO, has determined that the Motor Division has purchased switches for its motors from an outside supplier during the current year rather than buying them from the Switch Division. The Switch Division is operating at full capacity and demanded that the Motor Division pay the price charged to outside customers rather than the actual full manufacturing costs, as it has done in the past. The Motor Division refused to meet the price demanded by the Switch Division. The Switch Division contracted with an outside customer to sell its remaining switches, and the Motor Division was forced to purchase the switches from an outside supplier at an even higher price.

Klein is reviewing Thompson Corporation's transfer pricing policy because she believes that suboptimization has occurred. While Klein believes the Switch Division made the correct decision to maximize its divisional profit by not transferring the switches at actual full manufacturing cost, this decision was not necessarily in the best interest of Thompson Corporation.

Klein has requested that the corporate Accounting Department study alternative transfer pricing methods that would promote overall goal congruence, motivate divisional management performance, and optimize overall company performance. The three transfer pricing methods being considered are listed next. One of these methods will be selected and will be applied uniformly across all divisions.

1. Standard full manufacturing costs plus markup
2. Market selling price of the products being transferred
3. Outlay (out-of-pocket) costs incurred to the point of transfer plus opportunity cost per unit

Questions

1. Identify and explain two positive and two negative behavioral implications that can arise from employing a negotiated transfer price system for goods that are exchanged between divisions.
2. Identify and explain two behavioral problems that can arise from using actual full (absorption) manufacturing costs as a transfer price.

3. Identify and explain two behavioral problems **most** likely to arise if Thompson Corporation changes from its current transfer pricing policy to a revised transfer pricing policy that it applies uniformly to all divisions.
4. Discuss the likely behavior of both "buying" and "selling" divisional managers for each of the next transfer pricing methods being considered by Thompson Corporation:
   a. Standard full manufacturing costs plus markup
   b. Market selling price of the products being transferred
   c. Outlay (out-of-pocket) costs incurred to the point of transfer plus opportunity cost per unit

Part 1 Section D Questions

Question 1D-ES01

Many companies recognize that their cost systems are inadequate for today's powerful global competition. Managers in companies selling multiple products are making important product decisions based on distorted cost information, as most cost systems designed in the past focused on inventory valuation. In order to elevate the level of management information, it has been suggested that companies should have as many as three cost systems for (1) inventory valuation, (2) management control of operations, and (3) an activity-based costing system for decision making.

Questions

A. Discuss why the traditional cost system, developed to value inventory, distorts product cost information.
B. 1. Describe the benefits that management can expect from activity-based costing.
   2. List the steps that a company, using a traditional cost system, would take to implement activity-based costing.

Question 1D-ES02

TruJeans, a new start-up company, plans to produce blue jean pants, customized with the buyer's first name stitched across the back pocket. The product will be marketed exclusively via an Internet Web site. For the coming year, sales have been projected at three different levels: optimistic, neutral, and pessimistic. TruJeans does keep inventory on hand but prefers to minimize this investment.

The controller is preparing to assemble the budget for the coming year and is unsure about a number of issues, including:

- The level of sales to enter into the budget
- How to allocate the significant fixed costs to individual units
- Whether to use job order costing or process costing

In addition, the controller has heard of kaizen budgeting and is wondering if such an approach could be used by TruJeans.

Questions

A. How could the use of variable (direct) costing mitigate the problem of how to allocate the fixed costs to individual units?

B. Which cost system seems to make more sense for TruJeans, job order costing or process costing? Explain your answer.

Question 1D-ES03

Sonimad Sawmill Inc. (SSI) purchases logs from independent timber contractors and processes the logs into three types of lumber products:

1. Studs for residential building (e.g., walls, ceilings)
2. Decorative pieces (e.g., fireplace mantels, beams for cathedral ceilings)
3. Posts used as support braces (e.g., mine support braces, braces for exterior fences around ranch properties)

These products are the result of a joint sawmill process that involves removal of bark from the logs, cutting the logs into a workable size (ranging from 8 to 16 feet in length), and then cutting the individual products from the logs, depending on the type of wood (pine, oak, walnut, or maple) and the size (diameter) of the log. The joint process results in the following costs and output of products for a typical month.

Joint production costs	
Materials (rough timber logs)	$500,000
Debarking (labor and overhead)	50,000
Sizing (labor and overhead)	200,000
Product cutting (labor and overhead)	250,000
Total joint costs	$1,000,000

Product yield and average sales value on a per unit basis from the joint process are shown next.

Product	Monthly Output	Fully Processed Sales Price
Studs	75,000	$8
Decorative pieces	5,000	100
Posts	20,000	20

The studs are sold as rough-cut lumber after emerging from the sawmill operation without further processing by SSI. Also, the posts require no further processing. The decorative pieces must be planed and further sized after emerging from the SSI sawmill. This additional processing costs SSI $100,000 per month and normally results in a loss of 10% of the units entering the process. Without this planing and sizing process, there is still an active intermediate market for the unfinished decorative pieces where the sales price averages $60 per unit.

Questions

A. Based on the information given for Sonimad Sawmill Inc., allocate the joint processing costs of $1,000,000 to each of the three product lines using the
   1. Relative sales value method at split-off
   2. Physical output (volume) method at split-off
   3. Estimated net realizable value method
B. Prepare an analysis for Sonimad Sawmill Inc. to compare processing the decorative pieces further, as the company currently does, with selling the rough-cut product immediately at split-off, and recommend which action the company should take. Be sure to provide all calculations.

Question 1D-ES04

Alyssa Manufacturing produces two items in its Trumbull plant: Tuff Stuff and Ruff Stuff. Since inception, Alyssa has used only one manufacturing overhead pool to accumulate costs. Overhead has been allocated to products based on direct labor hours.

Until recently, Alyssa was the sole producer of Ruff Stuff and was able to dictate the selling price. However, last year Marvella Products began marketing a comparable product at a price below the standard costs developed by Alyssa. Market share has declined rapidly, and Alyssa must now decide whether to meet the competitive price or to discontinue the product line. Recognizing that discontinuing the product line would place additional burden on its remaining product, Tuff Stuff, Alyssa is using activity-based costing to determine if it would show a different cost structure for the two products.

The two major indirect costs for manufacturing the products are power usage and setup costs. Most of the power usage is used in fabricating, while most of the setup costs are required in assembly. The setup costs are predominantly for the Tuff Stuff product line. A decision was made to separate the Manufacturing Department costs into two activity centers: (1) fabricating using machine hours as the cost driver (activity base) and (2) assembly using the number of setups as the cost driver (activity base).

		Manufacturing Department	
		Annual Budget Before Separation of Overhead	
	Total	Product Line	
		Tuff Stuff	Ruff Stuff
Number of units		20,000	20,000
Direct labor*		2 hrs./unit	3 hrs./unit
Total direct labor	$800,000		
Direct material		$5.00/unit	$3.00/unit

(Continued)

___

(*Continued*)

Budgeted overhead:	
Indirect labor	$24,000
Fringe benefits	5,000
Indirect material	31,000
Power	180,000
Setup	75,000
Quality assurance	10,000
Other utilities	10,000
Depreciation	15,000

*Direct labor hourly rate is the same in both departments.

Manufacturing Department

Cost Structure after Separation of Overhead into Activity Pools

	Fabrication	Assembly
Direct labor	75%	25%
Direct material	100%	0%
Indirect labor	75%	25%
Fringe benefits	80%	20%
Indirect material	$20,000	$11,000
Power	$160,000	$20,000
Setup	$5,000	$70,000
Quality assurance	80%	20%
Other utilities	50%	50%
Depreciation	80%	20%

Activity Base	Tuff Stuff	Ruff Stuff
Machine hours per unit	4.4	6.0
Number of setups	1,000	272

Questions

A. By allocating overhead based on direct labor hours, calculate the
1. Total budgeted cost of the Manufacturing Department
2. Unit standard cost of Tuff Stuff
3. Unit standard cost of Ruff Stuff

B. After separation of overhead into activity pools, compute the total budgeted cost of the
1. Fabricating Department
2. Assembly Department

C. Using activity-based costing, calculate the unit standard costs for
1. Tuff Stuff
2. Ruff Stuff

D. Discuss how a decision by Alyssa Manufacturing regarding the continued production of Ruff Stuff will be affected by the results of your calculations in Requirement C.

Question 1D-ES05

Inman Inc. is a manufacturer of a single product and is starting to develop a budget for the coming year. Because cost of goods manufactured is the biggest item, Inman's senior management is reviewing how costs are calculated. In addition, senior management wants to develop a budgeting system that motivates managers and other workers to work toward the corporate goals. Inman has incurred the following costs to make 100,000 units during the month of September:

Materials	$400,000
Direct labor	100,000
Variable manufacturing overhead	20,000
Variable selling and administrative costs	80,000
Fixed manufacturing overhead	200,000
Fixed selling and administrative costs	300,000

Inman Inc.'s September 1 inventory consisted of 10,000 units valued at $72,000 using absorption costing. Total fixed costs and variable costs per unit have not changed during the past few months. In September, Inman sold 106,000 units at $12 per unit.

Questions

1. Using absorption costing, calculate:
   a. Inman's September manufacturing cost per unit.
   b. Inman's September 30 inventory value.
   c. Inman's September net income.
2. Using variable costing, calculate:
   a. Inman's September manufacturing cost per unit.
   b. Inman's September 30 inventory value.
   c. Inman's September net income.
3. Identify and explain one reason why the income calculated in the previous two questions might differ.
4. Identify and discuss one advantage of using each of the following:
   a. Absorption costing
   b. Variable costing
5. a. Identify one strength and one weakness each of authoritative budgeting and participative budgeting.
   b. Which of these budgeting methods will work best for Inman Inc.? Explain your answer.
   c. Identify and explain one method the top managers can take to restrict the production manager from taking advantage of budgetary slack.

Question 1D-ES06

Smart Electronics manufactures two types of gaming consoles, Models M-11 and R-24. Currently, the company allocates overhead costs based on direct labor hours; the total overhead cost for the past year was €80,000. Additional cost information for the past year is presented next.

Product Name	Total Direct Labor Hours Used	Units Sold	Direct Costs per Unit	Selling Price per Unit
M-11	650	1,300	€10	€90
R-24	150	1,500	€30	€60

Recently the company lost bids on a contract to sell Model M-11 to a local wholesaler and was informed that a competitor offered a much lower price. Smart's controller believes that the cost reports do not accurately reflect the actual manufacturing costs and product profitability for these gaming consoles. He also believes that there is enough variation in the production process for Models M-11 and R-24 to warrant a better cost allocation system. Given the nature of the electronic gaming market, setting competitive prices is extremely crucial. The controller has decided to try activity-based costing and has gathered the next information:

	Number of Setups	Number of Components	Number of Material Movements
M-11	3	17	15
R-24	7	33	35
Total activity cost	€20,000	€50,000	€10,000

The number of setups, number of components, and number of material movements have been identified as activity-cost drivers for overhead.

Questions

1. Using Smart's current costing system, calculate the gross margin per unit for Model M-11 and for Model R-24. Assume no beginning or ending inventory. Show your calculations.
2. Using activity-based costing, calculate the gross margin for Model M-11 and for Model R-24. Assume no beginning or ending inventory. Show your calculations.
3. Describe how Smart Electronics can use the activity-based costing information to formulate a more competitive pricing strategy. Be sure to include specific examples to justify the recommended strategy.
4. Identify and explain two advantages and two limitations of activity-based costing.

Part 1 Section E Questions

Question 1E-ES01

Superior Co. manufactures automobile parts for sale to major automakers. Superior's internal audit staff is reviewing the internal controls over machinery and equipment and making recommendations for improvements where appropriate.

The internal auditors obtained the information presented next during this review.

- Purchase requests for machinery and equipment normally are initiated by the supervisor in need of the asset. The supervisor discusses the proposed acquisition with the plant manager. A purchase requisition is submitted to the purchasing department when the plant manager determines that the request is reasonable and that there is a remaining balance in the plant's share of the total corporate budget for capital acquisitions.
- Upon receiving a purchase requisition for machinery or equipment, the purchasing department manager looks through the records for an appropriate supplier. A formal purchase order is then completed and mailed. When the machine or equipment is received, it is immediately sent to the user department for installation. This allows the economic benefits from the acquisition to be realized at the earliest possible date.
- The property, plant, and equipment ledger control accounts are supported by lapsing schedules organized by year of acquisition. These lapsing schedules are used to compute depreciation as a unit for all assets of a given type that are acquired in the same year. Standard rates, depreciation methods, and salvage values are used for each major type of fixed asset. These rates, methods, and salvage values were set ten years ago during the company's initial year of operation.
- When machinery or equipment is retired, the plant manager notifies the accounting department so that the appropriate entries can be made in the accounting records.
- There has been no reconciliation since the company began operations between the accounting records and the machinery and equipment on hand.

Question

Identify the internal control weaknesses and recommend improvements that the internal audit staff of Superior Co. should include in its report regarding the internal controls employed for fixed assets. Use the following format in preparing your answer.

Weaknesses	*Recommendations*
1.	1.

Question 1E-ES02

The board of directors of a large corporation recently learned that some members of the senior management team had circumvented the company's internal controls for personal gain. The board appointed a special task force of external auditors and outside legal counsel to investigate the situation.

After extensive review, the task force has concluded that for a period of several years the expenses of the company's chief executive officer, president, and vice president-public relations were charged to an account called the Limited Expenditure Account (LEA). The account was established five years ago and was not subject to the company's normal approval authorization process. Approximately $2,000,000 of requests for reimbursement were routinely processed and charged to LEA. Accounting personnel were advised by the controller to process such requests based on the individual approval of any of the three executives, even when the requests were not adequately documented.

The vice president-public relations and his department were in charge of political fundraising activities. The task force determined, however, that only a small portion of the $1,000,000 raised last year was actually used for political purposes. In addition, departmental resources were used for personal projects of the three identified executives. The task force also uncovered an additional $4,000,000 of expenditures that were poorly documented so that even the amounts for proper business purposes could not be identified.

The task force noted that these payment practices, as well as LEA, were never disclosed in the Internal Audit Department's audit reports even though company disbursements were tested annually. References to these practices and LEA were included on two occasions in recent year's work papers. The director of internal audit, who reports to the controller, advised that she reviewed these findings with the controller who, in turn, advised that he mentioned these findings to the president. The president recommended that they not be included in the internal audit reports. Furthermore, the external auditors, who reviewed the internal audit work papers, did not mention LEA or these payment practices in their recommendations for improved internal control procedures to management or in their external audit reports. The task force also noted that the company did not have a formal, published ethics policy.

Questions

A. Identify at least three internal control weaknesses in the company's internal control system.
B. Identify at least three illegal or improper practices uncovered at the company.
C. Identify at least four important steps the company should take, both procedurally and organizationally, to correct the problems that were uncovered in order to prevent a similar situation in the future.

Question 1E-ES03

Brawn Technology, Inc. is a manufacturer of large wind energy systems. The company has its corporate headquarters in Buenos Aires and a central manufacturing facility about 200 miles away. Since the manufacturing facility is so remote, it does not receive the attention or the support from the staff that the other units do. The president of Brawn is concerned about whether proper permits have been issued for new construction work being done to handle industrial waste at the facility. In addition, he wants to be sure that all occupational safety laws and environmental issues are being properly addressed. He has asked the company's internal auditor to conduct an audit focusing on these areas of concern.

Questions

A. Identify the seven types of internal audits and describe the two most common types of internal audits. Using examples, describe two situations where each type of common audit would be applicable.

B. Referring to Brawn Technology:
   1. Identify the type of audit that would best address the concerns of the president.
   2. Identify the objective of this audit.
   3. Give two reasons why this type of audit would best address the concerns of the president.

C. Recommend two procedures that could be implemented at Brawn's manufacturing plant that would lessen the president's concerns. Explain each of your recommendations.

Question 1E-ES04

Ted Crosby owns Standard Lock Inc., a small business that manufactures metal door handles and door locks. When he first started the company, Crosby managed the business by himself, overseeing purchasing and production as well as maintaining the financial records. The only employees he hired were production workers.

As the business expanded, Crosby decided to hire John Smith as the company's financial manager. Smith had an MBA and ten years of experience in the finance department of a large company. During the interview, Smith mentioned that he was considering an offer from another company and needed to know of Crosby's decision within the next couple of days. Since Crosby was extremely impressed with Smith's credentials, he offered him the job without conducting background checks. Smith seemed to be a dedicated and hard-working employee. His apparent integrity quickly earned him a reputation as an outstanding and trusted manager.

Later in the year, Crosby hired another manager, Joe Fletcher, to oversee the production department. Crosby continued to take care of purchasing and authorized all payments.

Fletcher was highly qualified for the position and seemed to be reliable and conscientious. After observing Fletcher's work for one year, Crosby concluded that he was performing his duties efficiently. Crosby believed that Fletcher and Smith were both good managers whom he could trust and gave them expanded responsibilities.

Fletcher's additional responsibilities included purchasing and receiving; Smith paid all the bills, prepared and signed all checks, maintained records, and reconciled the bank statements.

Soon Crosby began taking a hands-off approach to managing his business. He frequently took long vacations with his family and was not often at the office to check on the business. He was pleased that the company was profitable and expected that it would continue to be profitable in the future under the supervision of two qualified and trusted managers. One year after Crosby left the management of the company to Smith and Fletcher, business began to experience a decline in profits. Crosby assumed that it was due to a cyclical downturn in the economy. When Standard continued to decline even as the economy improved, Crosby began to investigate. He noticed that revenues were increasing but profits were declining. He also discovered that purchases from one vendor had increased significantly as compared to the other five vendors. Crosby is concerned that fraud may be occurring in the company.

Questions

A. Identify and describe four internal control deficiencies within Standard Lock Inc.
B. For each of the internal control deficiencies identified, recommend an improvement in procedures that would mitigate these deficiencies.
C. If the company were to implement an ideal internal control system, can it guarantee that fraud would not occur in future? Explain your answer.

Question 1E-ES05

Sam Pierce is a division controller with Med Direct, Inc., a publicly traded multinational corporation that manufactures large-scale medical equipment and also provides financing services to its customers. Pierce has seen many news stories recently of competitors having severe financial difficulty, including bankruptcy. He has also seen other corporations suffer from regulatory indictments and fines. Pierce not only wants to avoid such problems, but he also wants his company to report stable earnings and a rising stock price. Pierce's goal is to integrate enterprise risk management into the culture and operations of his division, and throughout the whole corporation. He also wants to make sure the company is in compliance with the requirements of the Sarbanes-Oxley Act of 2002.

Questions

A. Identify and explain two risks that a multinational firm such as Med Direct may encounter in each of these three areas:
    1. Buying raw materials from other countries
    2. Selling on credit terms to customers in foreign countries
    3. Developing and manufacturing high-tech equipment
B. Identify two reasons why each of the next three elements is important for a risk assessment and control program to be effective. Provide one example of each element.

1. Understanding your business
2. Implementing checks and balances
3. Developing procedures that set limits or establish standards

C. Explain how a company's organizational policies and management style impact the effectiveness of the control environment and its management of risk.

D. Identify and explain the compliance requirements with respect to internal controls in the Sarbanes-Oxley Act of 2002 (SOX 404).

Question 1E-ES06

Ace Contractors is a large regional general contractor. As the company grew, Eddie Li was hired as the controller and tasked with analyzing the monthly income statements and reconciling all of the accounts formerly handled by Susan Zhao, the sole accounting associate. Li noticed a large amount of demolition expense for February, even though no new projects had started over the past few months. Since Li did not expect such a large amount of demolition expense, nor was any of this type of expense budgeted, Li dug a little deeper. He found that all of those expenses were bank transfers into another bank account. After additional research, it became evident that Zhao had been transferring funds out of the company bank account and into her own and recording fake expenses to make the bank account reconciliation work. While the president kept the prenumbered checks locked up until check run time and signed all of the outgoing checks, he was unaware of the ability to initiate transfers via the Internet. Li had also reviewed the bank reconciliations, which were completed by the office manager, and this fraud was not evident since the ending balance was reasonable.

Questions

1. a. Identify and explain the four types of functional responsibilities that should be segregated properly.
   b. Identify and explain two incompatible duties that Zhao had that allowed her to take company funds.
2. Identify and explain two ways that the company had attempted to safeguard its assets, and suggest two ways to strengthen controls in this area.
3. Refer to COSO's *Internal Control Framework* to answer the next questions.
   a. Identify and describe the three objectives of internal control.
   b. Identify and describe five components of internal controls.
4. Identify and explain three ways internal controls provide reasonable assurance.

Question 1E-ES07

SmallParts is a manufacturer of metal washers, screws, and other parts required in the manufacture of various handmade craft and novelty items. The firm has the ability to custom make virtually any small part, provided the client is able to provide SmallParts with the dimensions and tolerance required of the product. Because of its niche in the market, SmallParts has over 1,000 clients. Unfortunately, many of its small business clients eventually merge or cease operations. One of the company's biggest challenges is the return of shipped product. Usually this is because the small business client has ceased operations. Although most of the product is custom made, SmallParts has found that much of it can be sold to other clients for adapted use. The company's accountant is reviewing the company's internal controls and financial accounting procedures, in particular, with respect to inventory.

Currently, SmallParts has one salesperson responsible for marketing returned product. This salesperson has exclusive and total control over the returned product, including arranging of sales terms, billing, and collection. The salesperson receives the returned product and attempts to find a client who may be able to adapt the product for his or her use. The inventory of returned product is not entered in the accounting records, under the logic that the cost is sunk. Revenue generated from its sale is classified as other revenue on the SmallParts income statement.

Questions

1. Identify and describe the three objectives of a system of internal control.
2. Identify and explain three ways that the procedure for handling returned product violates the internal control system of segregation of duties.
3. Identify four functional responsibilities within an organization that should be separated. Explain why these responsibilities should be separated.
4. Identify and describe three ways that SmallParts can provide for better internal control over its inventory of returned product.
5. The company accountant is concerned about SmallParts' current procedure for accounting for returned product and has turned to the IMA *Statement of Ethical Professional Practice* for guidance.
   a. Identify the ethical principles that should guide the work of a management accountant.
   b. Assume the company's accountant identifies a possible conflict of interest on the part of the salesperson responsible for the returned product.
      (1) Identify and describe the standards that relate to this situation, and explain how they apply.
      (2) Identify the steps the company accountant should take to resolve this situation.

Question 1E-ES08

Michael Hanson is an internal auditor who has been asked to evaluate the internal controls and risks of his company, Consolidated Enterprises Inc. He has been asked to present recommendations to senior management with respect to Consolidated's general operations with particular attention to the company's database procedures. With regard to database procedures, he was specifically directed to focus attention on (1) transaction processing, (2) virus protection, (3) backup controls, and (4) disaster recovery controls.

Questions

1. Define the objectives of
   a. a compliance audit.
   b. an operational audit.
2. For each of the areas shown next, identify two controls that Hanson should review, and explain why.
   a. Transaction processing
   b. Virus protection
   c. Backup controls
3. Identify four components of a sound business continuance plan.
4. During his evaluation of general operations, Hanson found the following conditions:
   a. Daily bank deposits do not always correspond with cash receipts.
   b. Physical inventory counts sometimes differ from perpetual inventory records, and there have been alterations to physical counts and perpetual records.
   c. An unexplained and unexpected decrease in gross profit percentage has occurred.

   For each of these conditions, (1) describe a possible cause of the condition and (2) recommend actions to be taken and/or controls to be implemented that would correct the condition.

Part 1 Section A Answers

Answer to Question 1A-ES01

Answer A:

Crank-M-Up
INCOME STATEMENT
For the Year Ended December 31, 20XX

Sales		$945,000
Cost of goods sold		408,500
Gross profit		536,500
Operating expenses		
Selling expenses	$145,000	
Administrative expenses	215,000	360,000
Income from operations		176,500
Other revenue and gains:		
Gain on foreign currency translation		19,500
		196,000
Other expenses and losses:		
Loss on inventory write-down		13,000
Income from continuing operations before taxes		183,000
Income taxes		54,900
Income from continuing operations		128,100
Loss from discontinued operations, net of $9,000 tax[1]		21,000
Net income		$ 107,100
Earnings per share of common stock—		
Income from continuing operations[2]		$2.56
Discontinued operations loss, net of tax[3]		(0.42)
Net income		$2.14

Supporting Calculations:

1. Loss from discontinued operations = $30,000
   $30,000 loss × 30% tax rate = $9,000 tax shield
   $30,000 loss – $9,000 tax shield = $21,000 loss net of tax
2. EPS: Income from continuing operations = $128,100
   $128,100/50,000 shares = $2.56 per share
3. EPS: Discontinued operations loss, net of tax = $21,000
   $21,000/÷ 50,000 shares = $0.42 per share

Answer B:

External users of financial statements are interested in the income statement because current income is considered to be a predictor of future income. However, not all items on the income statement have the same predictive value. Irregular items (discontinued operations, or expropriation by a foreign government) have little predictive value because they are unrelated to continuing operations and are unlikely to reoccur. Thus, they are separated from income from continuing operations, which is considered to be the most predictive part of net income.

Answer to Question 1A-ES02

Answer A:

<table>
<tr><td colspan="4">Dark Daze, Inc.
BALANCE SHEET
December 31, 2018</td></tr>
<tr><td colspan="4">Assets</td></tr>
<tr><td colspan="4">Current assets</td></tr>
<tr><td>Cash</td><td></td><td>$ 30,000</td><td></td></tr>
<tr><td>Accounts receivable, net of $140 allowance</td><td></td><td>1,860</td><td></td></tr>
<tr><td>Inventory</td><td></td><td>102,000</td><td></td></tr>
<tr><td>Prepaid advertising</td><td></td><td><u>5,000</u></td><td></td></tr>
<tr><td>Total current assets</td><td></td><td></td><td>$ 138,860</td></tr>
<tr><td colspan="4">Property, plant, and equipment</td></tr>
<tr><td>Land</td><td></td><td>137,320</td><td></td></tr>
<tr><td>Building</td><td>$ 80,400</td><td></td><td></td></tr>
<tr><td>Accumulated depreciation—Building</td><td><u>(15,000)</u></td><td>65,400</td><td></td></tr>
<tr><td>Equipment</td><td>40,000</td><td></td><td></td></tr>
<tr><td>Accumulated depreciation—Equipment</td><td><u>(10,000)</u></td><td><u>30,000</u></td><td><u>232,720</u></td></tr>
<tr><td>Total assets</td><td></td><td></td><td>$ 371,580</td></tr>
<tr><td colspan="4">Liabilities and Stockholders' Equity</td></tr>
<tr><td colspan="4">Current liabilities</td></tr>
<tr><td>Notes payable</td><td></td><td>$ 14,400</td><td></td></tr>
<tr><td>Taxes payable</td><td></td><td>3,000</td><td></td></tr>
<tr><td>Salaries payable</td><td></td><td>900</td><td></td></tr>
<tr><td>Interest payable</td><td></td><td><u>600</u></td><td></td></tr>
<tr><td>Total current liabilities</td><td></td><td></td><td>$ 18,900</td></tr>
<tr><td colspan="4">Long-term liabilities</td></tr>
<tr><td>Bond payable</td><td></td><td></td><td><u>78,000</u></td></tr>
<tr><td>Total liabilities</td><td></td><td></td><td>96,900</td></tr>
<tr><td colspan="4">Stockholders' equities</td></tr>
<tr><td>Common stock</td><td></td><td>60,000</td><td></td></tr>
<tr><td>Retained earnings*</td><td></td><td><u>214,680</u></td><td></td></tr>
<tr><td>Total stockholders' equity*</td><td></td><td></td><td><u>274,680</u></td></tr>
<tr><td>Total liabilities and stockholders' equity</td><td></td><td></td><td>$ 371,580</td></tr>
</table>

Supporting Calculations:

Assets = Liabilities + Stockholders' Equities

Assets = $371,580

Liabilities = $96,900

Therefore, Stockholders' Equities = $371,580 – $96,900 = $274,680

Within Stockholders' Equities, Common stock = $60,000

Therefore, Retained Earnings = $274,680 – $60,000 = $214,680

Answer B:

1. For inventories, the firm must disclose the cost flow assumption that it used to value its inventory (FIFO, LIFO, weighted average, or specific identification) and the FIFO equivalent if the firm uses LIFO. In addition, the firm must disclose its valuation basis (net realizable value or lower of cost or market) and any product financing arrangements. Finally, the firm must disclose significant inventory categories:

Service firms	Supplies
Merchandising firms	Supplies
	Purchases
Manufacturing firms	Supplies
	Raw materials
	Work in process
	Finished goods

2. For accounts receivable, the firm must disclose its collection policy, the way that it determined expected future bad debt, and the net realizable value of the receivables.
3. For property, plant, and equipment, the firm must describe the major classifications as well as the valuation basis, depreciation method(s) used, and the accumulated depreciation for each class.
4. For bonds payable, the firm must disclose the face (par) value, the stated and effective interest rates, the maturity date, and any special provisions, such as call provisions or convertibility.
5. For common stock, the firm must disclose the par or stated value of the stock as well as any changes in the number of shares authorized, issued, and outstanding during the period.

Answer to Question 1A-ES03

Answer A:

Cash-N-Carry
Statement of Cash Flows
For the year ended December 31, 2018

Cash flows from operating activities		
Net loss		$ (2,500)
Adjustments to reconcile net income to net		
cash flows from operating activities		
Loss on sale of investments ($60,000 – $52,500)	$ 7,500	
Increase in accounts receivable	(90,000)	
Decrease in inventories	45,000	
Decrease in accounts payable	(45,000)	
Increase in operating expenses payable	9,000	(73,500)

Cash-N-Carry
Comparative Balance Sheet
As of December 31

	2018	2017	
Cash	$ 21,500	$120,000	$98,500 ↓
Accounts receivable	195,000	105,000	90,000 ↑
Inventories	180,000	225,000	45,000 ↓
Long-term investments	0	60,000	60,000 ↓
Total assets	$396,500	$510,000	
Accounts payable	$ 75,000	$120,000	$45,000 ↓
Operating expenses payable	24,000	15,000	9,000 ↑
Bonds payable	70,000	100,000	30,000 ↓
Common stock	125,000	125,000	
Retained earnings	102,500	150,000	47,500 ↓
Total liabilities and stockholders' equities	$396,500	$510,000	

Net cash flows from operating activities		$(76,000)
Cash flows from investing activities		
Sale of long-term investments		52,500
Cash flows from financing activities		
Redemption of bonds	(30,000)	
Payment of cash dividend	(45,000)	
Net cash flows from financing activities		(75,000)
Net decrease in cash		(98,500)
Cash balance, January 1		120,000
Cash balance, December 31		$ 21,500

Answer B:

Cash flows from operating activities		
Cash inflows from customers[1]		$470,000
Cash outflows		
To suppliers for goods[2]	$(375,000)	
For operating expenses[3]	(171,000)	546,000
Net cash flows from operating activities		$(76,000)

(1) Sales Revenue	$560,000	
Less: Increase in Accounts Receivable	– 90,000	
Cash inflow from customers	$470,000	
(2) Cost of Goods Sold	$375,000	
Add: Decrease in Accounts Payable	+ 45,000	
Less: Decrease in Inventories	– 45,000	
Cash outflow to suppliers for goods	$375,000	
(3) Operating Expenses	$180,000	
Less: Increase in operating expenses payable	– 9,000	
Cash outflow for operating expenses	$171,000	

Answer C:

Operating cash flows relate to ordinary firm operations. Operating cash inflows come primarily from customers but may also include cash rent, interest, or dividends received from investments. Operating cash outflows include payments for inventory, operating expenses, or interest on any borrowing.

Investing cash flows come from transactions in long-term assets. Thus, investing cash outflows include cash paid to buy land, buildings, equipment, or to buy patents, trademarks, copyrights, or the stocks and bonds of other firms. Similarly, investing cash inflows come from selling any of these long-term assets.

Financing cash flows come from transactions in long-term liabilities or stockholders' equities. Thus, borrowing money and issuing new bonds or shares of the firm's own stock would be classified as cash inflows from financing activities. By contrast, repaying loans, redeeming bonds, or reacquiring the firm's own stock for treasury stock would be classified as cash outflows from financing activities. In addition, paying cash dividends to shareholders would be classified as a financing cash outflow since it is a transaction with the owners of the firm.

Answer to Question 1A-ES04

Answer A:

1/1/17	Dr. Available-for-sale securities	520,790	
	Cr. Cash		520,790

Answer B:

7/1/17	Dr. Cash[1]	20,000	
	Cr. Interest revenue[2]		18,228
	Cr. Available-for-sale securities[3]		1,772

1. Cash interest = Face value × Stated rate × Fraction of year = $500,000 × 0.08 × ½ year = $\underline{\$20,000}$
2. Carrying value from 1/1/17 = $520,790
   Interest revenue = Carrying value × Effective rate Fraction of year = $520,790 × 0.07 × ½ = $\underline{\$18,228}$
3. Premium amortization = Cash interest – Interest revenue = $20,000 – $18,228 = $\underline{\$1,772}$

New carrying value as of 7/1/17 = Old carrying value – Premium amortized = $520,790 – $1,772 = $519,018

Answer C:

12/31/17	Dr. Interest receivable[1]	20,000	
	Cr. Interest revenue[2]		18,166
	Cr. Available-for-sale securities[3]		1,834

1. Cash interest = Face value × Stated rate × Fraction of year= $500,000 × 0.08 × ½ year = $\underline{\$20,000}$
   Note: Cash interest is due to be received on 1/1/19.
2. Carrying value from 7/1/17 = $519,018
   Interest revenue = Carrying value × Effective rate × Fraction of year = $519,018 × 0.07 × ½ = $\underline{\$18,166}$
3. Premium amortization = Cash interest – Interest revenue = $20,000 – $18,166 = $\underline{\$1,834}$

New carrying value as of 12/31/17 = Old carrying value – Premium amortized = $519,018 – $1,834 = $517,184

Answer D:

12/31/17	Dr. Market FV Adj. – AFS[1]	12,816	
	Cr. Unrealized Holding Gain – Equity		12,816

1. Market fair value adjustment = Fair value – Carrying value= $530,000 – $517,184 = $12,816

Answer E:

1/1/19	Dr. Cash	20,000	
	Cr. Interest receivable		20,000
	Dr. Cash	530,000	
	Cr. Available-for-sale securities		517,184
	Cr. Gain on sale of securities		12,816

Answer F:

2/1/19	Dr. Cash [(5,000 × $31) – $1,500 fees]	153,500	
	Dr. Loss on Sale of Securities	1,500	
	Cr. Trading Securities		155,000
10/1/19	Dr. Trading Securities	27,550	
	Cr. Cash [(600 × $45) + $550 fees]		27,550

Answer G:

12/31/19	Dr. Securities FV Adj. (Trading)	19,450	
	Cr. Unrealized Holding Gain – Income		19,450

Fair Value	$221,000
Cost	– 209,550
Increase in value	$ 11,450

This means that the Securities FV Adj. (Trading) account should have an ending debit balance of $11,450. It currently has an $8,000 credit balance from 12/31/17, so we need to add ($11,450 + $8,000) = $19,450.

Securities FV Adj. (Trading)		**Trading Securities**	
	8,000	209,550	
19,450			
11,450			

$$\text{Fair value} = \text{Cost} + \text{Securities FV Adj. (Trading)}$$
$$= \$209,550 + \$11,450 = \$221,000$$

Answer H:

1. 1/1/20	Dr. Investment in Gobbled Up	500,000	
	Cr. Cash		500,000

2. 7/1/20	Dr. Cash ($160,000 × 25%)	40,000	
	Cr. Investment in Gobbled Up		40,000

| 3. 12/31/20 | Dr. Investment in Gobbled Up | 90,000 | |
| | Cr. Investment revenue ($360,000 × 25%) | | 90,000 |

4. $500,000 + $90,000 − $40,000 = $550,000

| 5. 1/1/20 | Dr. Available-for-sale securities | 500,000 | |
| | Cr. Cash | | 500,000 |

| 6. 7/1/20 | Dr. Cash ($160K × 0.25) | 40,000 | |
| | Cr. Dividend revenue | | 40,000 |

| 7. 12/31/20 | No entry | | |

8. As a passive investor under the cost method, Lotsa Loot does not recognize a portion income earned by Gobbled-Up, so the balance of Lotsa Loot's investment in Gobbled-Up at the end of 2021 before any market fair value adjustment = $500,000.

Answer to Question 1A-ES05

Answer A:

1/2/17	Dr. Land[1]	300,000	
	Cr. Common stock[2]		40,000
	Cr. Additional paid-in capital—common stock[3]		260,000

1. Given
2. Par value of common stock = 8,000 shares × $5/share = $40,000
3. APIC = Difference between market value and par value

Answer B:

1/5/17	Dr. Cash[1]	720,000	
	Cr. Common stock[2]		60,000
	Cr. Additional paid-in capital—common stock[3]		660,000
	Dr. Org. expense[4]	6,000	
	Cr. Common stock[5]		500
	Cr. Additional paid-in capital—common stock[6]		5,500

1. Cash received for shares issued to the public = 12,000 shares × $60/share = $720,000
2. Par value of common stock = 12,000 shares × $5/share = $60,000
3. APIC = Difference between market value and par value

4. Implied value of shares issued to lawyer for organizational work = 100 shares × $60/share = $6,000
5. Par value of shares = 100 shares × $5/share = $500
6. APIC = Difference between market value and par value

Answer C:

2/3/17	Dr. Cash[1]	720,000	
	Cr. Common stock[2]		50,000
	Cr. Additional paid-in capital—common stock[3]		550,000
	Cr. Preferred stock[4]		100,000
	Cr. Additional paid-in capital—preferred stock[5]		20,000

1. 1,000 bundles × $720/bundle = $720,000
2. 1,000 bundles × 10 common shares/bundle = 10,000 shares
   Par value of common stock = 10,000 shares × $5/share = $50,000
3. Market value of preferred stock is unknown, but market value of common stock = 10,000 shares × $60/share = $600,000
   APIC for common stock = Market value of common stock – Par value of common stock = $600,000 – $50,000 = $550,000
4. 1,000 bundles × 1 preferred share/bundle = 1,000 shares
   Par value of preferred stock = 1,000 shares × $100/share = $100,000
5. APIC for preferred stock = Residual value = $720,000 – $50,000 – $550,000 – $100,000 = $20,000

Answer D:

6/30/17	Dr. Retained earnings	180,600	
	Cr. Common stock dividends distributable[2]		15,050
	Cr. Additional paid-in capital—common stock[3]		165,550

1. Dividends always reduce retained earnings. A 10% stock dividend is a small dividend, which is accounted for at market price. Thus, retained earnings is reduced by the number of shares to be issued times the market price per share on the declaration date:

   Shares issued and outstanding as of June 30, 2018:

8,000 shares	1/2/17 for land
12,000 shares	1/5/17 for cash
100 shares	1/5/17 to lawyer
10,000 shares	2/3/17 in bundles
30,100 shares	

   30,100 shares × 10% stock dividend = 3,010 shares for dividend
   Market value = 3,010 shares × $60/share = $180,600

2. The amount credited to common stock dividends distributable on the declaration date is:

   3,010 shares × $5 par value/share = $15,050

3. APIC for common stock = Market value − Par value = $180,600 − $15,050 = $165,550

Answer E:

7/30/17	Dr. Common stock dividends distributable	15,050	
	Cr. Common stock		15,050

Answer F:

8/1/17	Dr. Treasury stock	60,000	
	Cr. Cash		60,000

Answer G:

Total preferred stock dividend = 1,000 shares × $100 par × 8% = $8,000
Preferred stock dividend/share = $8,000/1,000 shares = $8.00/share
Total common stock dividend = $20,000 − $8,000 = $12,000
Common shares outstanding = 30,100 + 3,010 − 2,000 = 31,110 shares
Note: No dividend is paid on treasury stock.
Common stock dividend/share = $12,000/31,110 shares = $0.386/share

9/1/17	Dr. Retained earnings	20,000	
	Cr. Dividends payable—common stock		8,000
	Cr. Dividends payable—preferred stock		12,000

Answer H:

9/30/17	Dr. Dividends payable—preferred stock	8,000	
	Dr. Dividends payable—common stock	12,000	
	Cr. Cash		20,000

Answer I:

10/1/17	Dr. Cash[1]	116,000	
	Cr. Treasury stock[2]		60,000
	Cr. Additional paid-in capital—treasury stock[3]		56,000

1. Cash received = $58/share × 2,000 shares = $116,000
2. In the cost method, the treasury stock account is credited for the same amount that it cost the firm when it acquired those shares.

APIC for treasury stock is the difference between the cash received when the shares are reissued and the cash that was paid when the shares were originally acquired.

Answer to Question 1A-ES06

Answer A:

2018	Dr. Accounts receivable	1,050,000	
	Cr. Sales (700 × $1,500)		1,050,000

Answer B:

2018	Dr. Warranty expense (100 × $90)	9,000	
	Cr. Repair parts, labor, etc.		9,000

Answer C:

12/31/18	Dr. Warranty expense (250 × $90)	22,500	
	Cr. Est. liability under Warranties		22,500

Answer D:

2018	Dr. Accounts receivable	1,120,000	
	Cr. Sales (700 × $1,500)		1,050,000
	Cr. Unearned warranty revenue		70,000

Answer E:

2018	Dr. Warranty expense (100 × $90)	9,000	
	Cr. Repair parts, labor, etc.		9,000
	Dr. Unearned warranty revenue	20,000	
	Cr. Warranty revenue		20,000
	($70,000 × $^{100}/_{350}$)		

Answer F:

12/31/ 2018	Dr. Wage expense	70,000	
	Cr. FICA payable		2,250
	Cr. Federal income tax payable		7,500
	Cr. State income tax payable		2,200
	Cr. Union dues payable		500
	Cr. Wages payable or Cash		57,550

Answer G:

12/31/ 2018	Dr. Payroll tax expense	3,150	
	Cr. FICA payable		2,250
	Cr. FUTA payable		200
	Cr. SUTA payable		700

Answer H:

12/1/18	Dr. Cash	12,000	
	Cr. Notes payable		12,000

Answer I:

12/31/18	Dr. Interest expense	35	
	($12K × 0.7 × $^{0.5}/_{12}$)		
	Cr. Interest payable		35

Answer J:

4/15/19	Dr. Interest expense ($12K × 0.7 × $^{3.5}/_{12}$)	245	
	Dr. Interest payable ($12K × 0.7 × $^{0.5}/_{12}$)	35	
	Dr. Notes payable	12,000	
	Cr. Cash		12,280

Answer to Question 1A-ES07

Answer A:

The bonds are issued at a premium because the 6% stated rate on the bonds is greater than the current market rate of 5% for similar debt.

Answer B:

Interest payments = $10,000,000 × 3% per period = $300,000/payment

PV – OA ($i = 2.5\%$, $n = 10$) = 8.75206 × $300,000 = $2,625,618

Principal = $10,000,000

PV ($i = 2.5\%$, $n = 10$) = 0.78120 × $10,000,000 = $7,812,000

Cash value of the bonds = $2,625,618 + $7,812,000 = $10,437,618

Note: $10,437,618 is the amount of cash that the firm receives when the bonds are issued. It also is the initial carrying value of the bonds. The difference between the cash received and the $10,000,000 face value of the bonds is the premium on the bonds payable. In this case, the premium = ($10,437,618 – $10,000,000) = $437,618. At the end of each interest period, a portion of that premium is amortized away:

Bond interest expense = Carrying value × Market rate × Fraction of a year

Cash interest = Face value × Stated rate × Fraction of a year

Premium amortized = Cash interest – Bond interest expense

New carrying value = Old carrying value – Premium amortized

At the end of 5 years, the premium will be completely amortized, the carrying value will equal the face value, and the bonds will be redeemed for $10,000,000.

Answer C:

1/1/17	Dr. Cash[1]	10,437,618	
	Cr. Bonds payable[2]		10,000,000
	Cr. Premium on bonds payable[3]		437,618

1. See computation above.
2. Face value (given).
3. Premium = Cash value – Face value

Answer D:

7/1/17	Dr. Bond interest expense[1]	260,940	
	Dr. Premium on bonds payable[2]	39,060	
	Cr. Cash[3]		300,000

1. Bond interest expense = Carrying value × Market rate × Fraction of a year = $10,437,618 × 0.05 × ½ = $\underline{\$260,940}$
2. Premium amortized = Cash interest Bond interest expense = $300,000 – $260,940 = $\underline{\$39,060}$
   Remaining premium = Old premium balance – Premium amortized = $437,618 – $39,060 = $\underline{\$398,558}$
   New carrying value = Old carrying value – Premium amortized = $10,437,618 – $39,060 = $\underline{\$10,398,558}$
3. Cash interest = Face value × Stated rate × Fraction of a year = $10,000,000 × 0.05 × ½ = $\underline{\$300,000}$

Answer E:

12/31/17	Dr. Bond interest expense[1]	259,964	
	Dr. Premium on bonds payable[2]	40,036	
	Cr. Bond interest payable[3]		300,000

1. Bond interest expense = Carrying value × Market rate × Fraction of a year = $10,398,558 × 0.05 × ½ = $\underline{\$259,964}$
2. Premium amortized = Cash interest – Bond interest expense = $300,000 – $259,964 = $\underline{\$40,036}$
   Remaining premium = Old premium balance – Premium amortized = $398,558 – $40,036 = $\underline{\$358,522}$
   New carrying value = Old carrying value – Premium amortized = $10,437,618 – $40,036 = $\underline{\$10,358,522}$
3. Cash interest (to be paid on 1/1/19) = Face value × Stated rate × Fraction of a year = $10,000,000 × 0.05 × ½ = $\underline{\$300,000}$

Answer F:

1/1/19	Dr. Bond interest payable	300,000	
	Cr. Cash		300,000

Answer G:

The price of bonds is usually expressed as a percentage of their face value. Therefore, when "the firm redeemed the bonds at 98," it means that the firm paid 98% of the face value to buy the bonds back from the public. $10,000,000 face value × 98% = $9,800,000 cash paid by the firm to reacquire the bonds.

1/1/19	Dr. Bonds payable[1]	10,000,000	
	Dr. Premium on bonds payable[2]	358,522	
	Cr. Gain on redemption of bonds payable[3]		558,522
	Cr. Cash[4]		9,800,000

1. Face value of the bonds redeemed.
2. Remaining unamortized premium: See solution to part E) above.
3. Since the book value of the bonds is greater than the cash paid to redeem them, the firm recognizes a gain for the difference.

Bonds payable	$10,000,000
Unamortized premium	+ 358,522
Book value	$10,358,522
Cash paid	−9,800,000
Gain on redemption	$ 558,522

4. See discussion above.

Answer H:

The stated (face) rate on bonds is determined before the bonds are issued. It represents the contractual interest that the firm must pay annually to bondholders, but it often differs from the market interest rate that investors demand on the issue date.

If the stated rate is lower than the current market interest rate, investors will not buy the bonds at their face value, but they will buy the bonds for less. The resulting discount represents the present value of the difference between the stated rate and the market rate over the life of the bonds. Thus, the effective rate that investors receive is equal to the market rate.

By contrast, if the stated rate is lower than the current market interest rate, the firm will not issue the bonds at their face value, but they will issue the bonds for more. The resulting premium represents the present value of the difference between the stated rate and the market rate over the life of the bonds. Thus, the effective rate that the firm pays is equal to the market rate.

Answer to Question 1A-ES08

Answer A:

$100,000	Purchase of land
+ 5,000	Realtor fees
+ 3,000	Accrued property tax
+ 10,000	Demolishing old building on the property
− 2,000	Salvage from demolished building
$116,000	

Answer B:

$ 16,000	Architectural fees
+ 54,000	Construction costs
+ 7,000	Supervision during construction
+ 1,500	6 months of insurance policy
− 250	1 month of insurance expensed, not capitalized
$ 78,250	

Answer C:

Dr. Cash	11,000	
Dr. Accumulated depreciation	40,000	
Cr. Trucks		50,000
Cr. Gain on disposal		1,000

Answer D:

Dr. Cash	6,000	
Dr. Accumulated depreciation	40,000	
Dr. Loss on disposal	4,000	
Cr. Trucks		50,000

Answer E:

Dr. Accumulated depreciation	40,000	
Dr. Loss on disposal	10,000	
Cr. Trucks		50,000

Answer F:

Dr. Accumulated depreciation	50,000	
Cr. Trucks		50,000

Note: We-Got-Stuff can still use the truck, even if it is fully depreciated, but the firm cannot recognize any additional depreciation expense.

Answer G:

Cost	$100,000
Accumulated depreciation	– 50,000
Book value of asset given up	$ 50,000

Answer H:

FV of new equipment	$ 50,000
Cash received	+ 10,000
FV received	$ 60,000

Answer I:

FV received	$ 60,000
Book value of asset given up	– 50,000
Gain on exchange	$ 10,000

Answer J:

Cost	$ 80,000
Accumulated depreciation	– 25,000
Book value given up	$ 55,000
Cash given up	+ 10,000
Total given up	$ 65,000

Answer K:

Fair value of new equipment	$ 60,000

Answer L:

FV of asset received	$ 60,000
Total given up	– 65,000
Loss on exchange	$ (5,000)

Answer M:

i.

Dr. Equipment (new)	50,000	
Dr. Cash	10,000	
Dr. Accumulated depreciation (old)	50,000	
Cr. Equipment (old)		100,000
Cr. Gain in exchange		10,000

ii.

Dr. Equipment (new)	60,000	
Dr. Accumulated depreciation (old)	25,000	
Dr. Loss on exchange	5,000	
Cr. Equipment		80,000
Cr. Cash		10,000

Answer N:

i.

Dr. Equipment (new)[2]	41,667	
Dr. Cash	10,000	
Dr. Accumulated Depreciation (old)	50,000	
Cr. Equipment (old)		100,000
Cr. Gain in exchange[1]		1,667

1. $10,000/($10,000 + $50,000) = 0.1667$
   $$\$10,000 \times 0.1667 = \underline{\$1,667 \text{ gain recognized}}$$
   $$\$10,000 - \$1,667 \text{ gain recognized} = \$8,333 \text{ gain deferred}$$
2. $50,000$ (FV) $-\$8,333$ gain deferred $= \$41,667$ recorded value

ii.

Dr. Equipment (new)	60,000	
Dr. Accumulated depreciation (old)	25,000	
Dr. Loss on exchange	5,000	
Cr. Equipment		80,000
Cr. Cash		10,000

Note: The journal entry for Mercury Manufacturing is the same regardless of whether the transaction has commercial substance because losses always are recognized when incurred.

Part 1 Section B Answers

Answer to Question 1B-ES01

Answer A:

Rein Company
Budgeted Income Statement
for the Year Ended December 31, 2019

Sales [100,000 × 1.1 × ($110 + 15)]		$13,750,000
Cost of goods sold at standard [110,000 × (65.20 + 19.80)[1]]		9,350,000
Gross margin at standard		$4,400,000
Variances		
Material-brass—unfavorable [(111,650 compressors[2]) × (4 lbs/compressor) × ($.30/lb)]	$(133,980)	
Labor efficiency—unfavorable [(111,650 compressors) × (0.25 hours/compressor) × ($7/hr)]	(195,388)	
Variable overhead efficiency—unfavorable [(111,650 compressors) × (0.25 hrs/compressor) × ($3.30/hour[3])]	(92,111)	
Fixed overhead volume—favorable [(111,650 − 110,000 compressors) × $6.60/compressor[4])]	10,890	(410,589)
Gross margin at actual		$3,989,411

Operating expenses
    Selling expense ($13,750,000 × .12) $1,650,000
    Administrative expense ($907,850 × 1.2)   1,089,420   2,739,420

Income before taxes		$1,249,991
Income tax expense (45%)		562,496
Net income		$687,495
Earnings per share (250,000 shares)		$2. 75

Supporting Calculations

1 Standard cost of compressor

Brass 4 lbs. @ $5.35/lb.	$21.40
Steel alloy 5 lbs. @ $3.16/lb.	15. 80
Direct labor 4 hrs. @ $7.00/hr.	28. 00
Overhead (2,178,000 ÷ 110,000)	19. 80
Total cost per compressor	$85. 00

2 Production schedule

2019 sales	110,000
Desired ending inventory 12/31/19 (110,000 × 1.1 × .15)	18,150
Required inventory	128,150
Beginning inventory 1/1/19 (110,000 × .15)	16,500
2019 production	111,650

3 Determination of the variable overhead rate and total fixed overhead

$$\text{Variable overhead rate per compressor} = \frac{\text{Change in Overhead}}{\text{Change in Activity}}$$

$$\frac{(\$2,178,000 - \$2,046,000)}{110,000 - 100,000} = \frac{\$132,000}{10,000}$$

$$= \$13.20/\text{compressor}$$

$$\text{Variable overhead rate/direct labor hour} = \frac{\$13.20/\text{compressor}}{4 \text{ hrs./compressor}}$$

$$= \$3.30/\text{direct labor hour}$$

Total overhead at 110,000 compressors	$2,178,000
Total variable overhead at 110,000 compressors (110,000 × $13.20)	− 1,452,000
Total budgeted fixed overhead	$726,000

4 Normal activity level and fixed overhead rate

$$\text{Fixed overhead rate} = \frac{\text{Budgeted fixed overhead (See note 3)}}{\text{Normal production activity level}}$$

$$= \frac{\$726,000}{110,000}$$

$$= \$6.60/\text{compressor}$$

Answer B:

Based on the results of the 2019 budgeted income statement, the president's objective cannot be achieved. A review of the statement highlights these circumstances:

- A 2019 income statement prepared using the worst situation gives a net income of $687,495 and earnings per share of $2.75, which is a decrease from the 2018 income of $700,000 and earnings per share of $2.80. These budgeted figures are also considerably below the president's objective of $750,000 net income and $3 earnings per share.
- If the unfavorable variances do not occur, net income will increase by $231,813 after taxes ($421,479 × .55), resulting in an increase in earnings per share of $.927, giving a total earnings per share of $3.677 which is well above the president's objective.
- Manufacturing costs are 65. 5% of the selling price ($72 / $110) in 2018, and 68% of the selling price in 2019. Administrative expenses increased 20% in 2006. Therefore, the 13. 6% sales price increase in 2019 was not sufficient to cover the increases in manufacturing cost and increases in administrative expense.

Answer to Question 1B-ES02

Answer A:

Robbins and Crowe introduce slack into their budgets for these reasons:

- To hedge against uncertainties that might cause actual results to differ markedly from their projections.
- To allow their employees to exceed expectations, show consistent performance, or both. This becomes especially significant if their performance is evaluated by comparing actual results to budget projections.
- To bring the organization's goals into alignment with their own goals by using budgetary slack to improve the organization's assessment of their performance, thus earning higher salaries, better bonuses, or promotions.

Answer B:

Slack might adversely affect Robbins and Crowe in these ways:

- By limiting the usefulness of the budget to motivate top performance from their employees
- By affecting their ability to identify trouble spots and take appropriate corrective action
- By reducing their credibility in the eyes of management

The use of budgetary slack also may affect management decisions, since the budgets will show lower contribution margins (fewer sales, higher expenses). Decisions regarding profitability of product lines, staffing levels, incentives, and other matters could adversely affect Robbins's and Crowe's departments.

Answer to Question 1B-ES03

Answer A:

MRC Cash Budget Proposed	
Third Quarter (only)	
Beginning cash balance (given)	$186,000
Add: Third-quarter cash receipts[1]	200,650
Less: Third-quarter cash expenditures[2]	178,000
Ending cash balance	$208,650

Supporting Calculations

[1] Third-quarter cash receipts.

[2] Cash expenditures.

Fee			Distribution	
Memberships				
Individual	$300	60%	$36,000	[(50 new + 150 renew)×0 .60×$300]
Student	180	10%	3,600	[(50 + 150)×0.10×$180]
Family	600	30%	36,000	[(50 + 150)×0.30×$600]
Total			$75,600	
Court Fees				
Individual	$50	60%	$61,500	[(50 new + 2,000 reg.)×0.60×$50]
Student	40	10%	8,200	[2,050×0.10×$40]
Family	90	30%	55,350	[2,050×0.30×$90]
Total			125,050	
Total Third-Quarter Cash Receipts:			$200,650	

Fixed costs	$157,500	
Less: Depreciation	24,500	
Add: Variable costs	45,000	[(1000 hours + 2000 hours) × $15]
Total Costs:	$178,000	

Answer B:

Sensitivity analysis would help MRC management by testing the assumed projections and seeing how sensitive the cash flows are to changes in the number of members or the distribution of members.

Answer C:

Other factors that MRC should consider include:

- Communication strategy to current members
- Market acceptance of the new pricing strategy
- Cost associated with the change
- Timing of the change
- Effect on the mix of membership class
- Anticipated rate of return for excess cash and the costs of borrowing funds
- Reliability of the projections
- Capacity of the tennis and racquetball courts
- Price elasticity for memberships in similar clubs
- Reaction of the competition
- Quality of its facilities and staff
- Cost of advertising/communicating this price change

Answer to Question 1B-ES04

Answer 1:

Cumulative Number of Units	Cumulative Average Time/Unit	Cumulative of Total Time
1	500	500
2	$500 \times .9 = 450$	$450 \times 2 = 900$
4	$450 \times .9 = 405$	$405 \times 4 = 1620$

Answer 2:

25×500 hours $\times 4$ units $= \$50,000$ with no learning curve

$25 \times 405 \times 4$ units $= \$40,500$ with 90% learning curve

$50,000 - \$40,500 = \$9,500$ savings

Answer 3:

a. Budgetary slack is the practice of underestimating budgeted revenues, or overestimating budgeted costs, to make budgeted targets more easily achievable.

b. Budgetary slack misleads top management about the true profit potential of the company, which leads to inefficient resource planning and allocation as well as poor coordination of activities across different parts of the company.

Answer 4:

a.1. 1. $1,740 \times (25.00 - [44,805/1,740]) = 1,305$ U

a.2. 2. $25.00 \times (1,740 - [4 \times 500]) = 6,500$ F

b. Direct labor rate variance remains the same, but direct labor efficiency variance will become $3000 negative, because actual hours (1740) is more than expected from 90% learning curve (1620).

Answer 5:

A factor that could cause an unfavorable price variance and a favorable efficiency variance is using a higher-skilled labor force that would be paid more per hour but would work more quickly.

Answer 6:

Direct labor efficiency variance would be even more unfavorable if an 80% learning curve were used. The lower number implies more benefit from learning.

Answer 7:

For a new product, the company may have no way of forecasting the amount of improvement (if any) from savings. The company may set up a production method that is more efficient than prototype but will not gain further efficiencies.

Answer to Question 1B-ES05

Answer 1:

A flexible budget allows the attorneys to tell how much of their unfavorable variance is due to lower-than-planned billing hours and how much is due to performance issues, such as the negotiated billed amount or variable expenses. A master budget is static, and any variance must be analyzed further to determine its cause.

Answer 2:

The flexible budget revenues are calculated by multiplying the actual billed hours by the budgeted amount per billed hour. Then the budgeted variable expense per billed hour is multiplied by the actual billed hours. The flexible budget variable expense is subtracted from the flexible budget revenue. The results are compared to the actual results from last year.

Answer 3:

$6,000 \times 325 = \$1,950,000$ static budget revenue

$5,700 \times 275 = \$1,567,500$ actual revenue

$1,950,000 - 1,567,500 = \$382,500$ unfavorable static budget revenue variance

$5,700 \times 325 = \$1,852,500$ flexible budget revenue

$1,852,500 - 1,567,500 = \$285,000$ flexible budget variance

$6,000 \times 5,700 = 300$ hours unfavorable sales volume

$300 \times 325 = \$97,500$ unfavorable sales volume variance

Answer 4:

$6,000 \times 50 = \$300,000$ static budget variable expense

$300,000 - 285,000 = \$15,000$ favorable variable expense variance

$5,700 \times 50 = \$285,000$ flexible budget variable expense

$285,000 - 285,000 = \$0$, so the variance is a sales volume variance

Part 1 Section C Answers

Answer to Question 1C-ES01

Answer A:

Sales Price Variance	Budget Sales Price	Actual Sales Price	Unit Variance	Actual Unit Sales	Sales Price Variance	Total
Hand Drills	$60	$59	$1 U	86,000	$86,000	
Table Saws	$120	$115	$5 U	74,000	$370,000	$456,000 U
Cost Price Variance	**Budgeted Cost**	**Actual Cost**	**Unit Variance**	**Actual Unit Purchases**	**Cost Price Variance**	
Hand Drills	$50	**$50**	$0	86,000	None	
Table Saws	$80	**$82**	$2 U	74,000	$148,000	$148,000 U
Volume Variance	**Budgeted Volume in Units**	**Actual Volume in Units**	**Unit Variance**	**Budgeted[1] Contribution Margin/Unit**	**Volume Variance**	
Hand Drills	120,000	86,000	34,000 U	$10	$340,000	
Table Saws	80,000	74,000	6,000 U	$40	240,000	$580,000 U
Total Gross Margin Variance						**$1,184,000 U**

[1]Budgeted total margin ÷ Budget unit sales	Hand Drills	Table Saws
	$1,200,000	$3,200,000
	120,000	80,000
	$10/unit	$40/unit

Answer B:

The effectiveness of Handler's marketing program is difficult to judge in the absence of actual industry-wide performance data. If the industry estimate of a 10% decline in the market for these tools is used as a basis for comparison, then Handler's gross profit should have fallen to $3,960,000 ($4,400,000 × .9) as summarized next ($000 omitted).

	Hand Drill	**Table Saw**	**Total**
Budgeted gross profit	$1,200	$3,200	$4,400
Budget adjusted for 10% industry decline	$1,080	$2,880	$3,960
Less: Actual gross profit	774	2,442	3,216
Shortage	$ 306	$ 438	$ 744

Handler's gross profit actually fell to $3,216,000, which is $744,000 lower than might have been expected. To have been considered a success, the marketing program should have generated a gross profit above $4,020,000 (the original budget minus the projected industry decline plus the incremental cost of the marketing program, i.e., $4,400 − 440 + 60).

Handler hoped to do better than the industry average by giving dealer discounts and increasing direct advertising. However, to be successful, the discounts and advertising must be offset by an increase in volume. Handler was not successful in this regard in total; sales volume dropped 7.5% in the table saw line as compared to a 28.3% decline in hand drill volume. Note that the table saw price was dropped by 4.2% as against a price decline of only 1.7% on hand drilled. Apparently the discounts and advertising did not generate enough unit sales volume to offset and compensate for the promotion.

Answer to Question 1C-ES02

Answer A:

The shortcomings or possible inconsistencies of using return on investment (ROI) as the sole criterion to evaluate divisional management performance include:

- ROI tends to emphasize short-run performance at the possible expense of long-run profitability.
- ROI is not consistent with cash flow models used for capital expenditure analysis.
- ROI frequently is not controllable by the division manager because many components included in the computation are committed in amount or are the responsibility of others.
- Reliance on ROI as the only measurement indicator could lead to an inaccurate decision or investment at either the divisional or corporate level.

Answer B:

The advantages of using multiple criteria to evaluate divisional management performance include:

- Multiple performance measures provide a more comprehensive picture of performance by considering a wider range of responsibilities.
- Multiple performance measures emphasize both the short-term and long-term results, thereby emphasizing the total performance of the division.
- Multiple performance measures may highlight nonquantitative as well as quantitative-oriented aspects.
- Multiple performance criteria will enhance goal congruence and reduce the importance of the dysfunctional short-run goal of profit maximization.

Answer C:

The problems or disadvantages of implementing a multiple performance criteria measurement system include:

- The measurement criteria are not all equally quantifiable.
- Management may have difficulty applying the criteria on a consistent basis, some criteria may be subjectively more heavily weighted than other criteria, and some criteria may be in conflict with each other.
- A multiple performance measurement system may be confusing to division management.
- Overemphasis on multiple evaluation criteria may lead to diffusion of effort and the failure to perform as well as expected in any one area.

Answer to Question 1C-ES03

Answer A:

Segment information prepared for public reporting may be inappropriate for evaluation of segment managers for these reasons:

- An allocation of common costs incurred for the benefit of more than one segment must be included for public reporting purposes.
- Common costs generally are allocated on an arbitrary basis.
- Segments identified for public reporting may not coincide with actual management responsibilities.
- Information in the annual report does not distinguish between a segment that is a poor investment and one in which the manager has done well despite adverse circumstances.

Answer B:

Segment managers may become frustrated and dissatisfied if their performance is evaluated on the basis of information in the annual financial report. Using that information may lead to their being held responsible for earnings figures that include the arbitrary allocation of common costs and costs that are traceable to them but are not under their control. Such evaluations reduce motivation and may even cause managers to seek other employment.

Answer C:

Merriam Corporation should define responsibility centers that coincide with managers' actual responsibilities rather than using segment rules developed for public reporting. All reports should be prepared using the contribution approach, which separates costs by behavior and assigns costs only to segments that control them. The report should disclose contribution margin, contributions controllable by segment managers, and contribution by each segment after the allocation of common costs.

Answer to Question 1C-ES04

Answer A:

Because Quie's management apparently has excess capacity, it should be positive toward each suggested price in decreasing order. Each price exceeds variable costs and thus will increase Quie's ROI, which is the basis of its evaluation by corporate management.

Answer B:

Negotiating a price between the two divisions is the best method to resolve the controversy in this situation. ARQ is highly decentralized and exhibits all four conditions required for negotiating a transfer price:

1. Outside markets exist to give both parties alternatives to dealing with each other.
2. Both parties have access to market price information.
3. Both parties are free to buy and sell outside the corporation.
4. Top management supports the continuation of the decentralized arrangement.

Answer C:

ARQ management should not become involved in resolving the controversy. This would violate the autonomous relationship of the divisions, which ARQ intends to maintain. Imposing conditions on the pricing will adversely affect the current ROI-based evaluation system, since the two divisions will no longer be in control of their profits. Finally, division management would most likely respond negatively to a loss of the autonomy it is used to exercising.

Answer to Question 1C-ES05

Answer A:

Transfer prices based on cost are not appropriate measures of divisional performance for several reasons, including these:

- The selling division has little incentive to control costs if all costs will be recovered in the transfer price.
- The company as a whole often makes poor decisions when one division is covering another's full costs.

Answer B:

The next table shows the results for both the extraction and pet products divisions of using the market price as the transfer price.

Results of Using Market-Based Transfer Pricing		
	Extraction Division	**Pet Products Division**
Selling price	$26.00	$42.00
Less variable costs		
Material cost	$4.00	$2.00
Labor cost	$6.00	$4.00
Overhead (variable)	$8.25 *	$2.45[†]
Transfer price	—	$26.00
Unit contribution margin	$7.75	$7.55
Volume	× 500,000	× 500,000
Total contribution margin	$3,875,000.00	$3,775,000.00

*Variable overhead = $11 × 75% = $8.25.

[†]Variable overhead = $7 × 35% = $2.45.

Answer C:

If Sparta Enterprises lets its divisions buy and sell in the open market and also allows them to negotiate an acceptable transfer price, the result would be as shown:

- Any price between $24. 50 and $26 will result in an overall benefit to the company.
- The extraction division would prefer to sell its clay to the pet products division at the same price it receives in the market: $26 per unit. But it would be willing to sell at $24. 50, because it saves $1. 50 in selling costs per unit by selling within the company.
- Similarly, the pet products division would like to continue paying $22 per unit for the clay, but if it cannot purchase the clay within the company, it will have to pay the full $26 market price. Therefore, it will be willing to pay the $24.50 transfer price it can negotiate with the extraction division.

Answer D:

Using a negotiated transfer price should result in desirable management behavior because it will:

- Encourage the management of the extraction division to control costs.
- Benefit the pet products division by providing the clay at a below-market price.
- Provide a more realistic measure of divisional performance.

Answer to Question 1C-ES06

Answer A:

The quarterly performance report that 4-Cycle provides to its managers includes at least these three weaknesses:

1. It is based on a static budget. The company should switch to a flexible budget that compares the same levels of activity and shows variances between the actual budget and the flexible budget.
2. The report includes costs that supervisors cannot control, such as fixed production costs and overhead.
3. The report allocates fixed production costs using a single rate for all lines. Since the amount of space occupied by production may not, in fact, determine fixed production costs, the company should select an appropriate base to determine the rate for each product line.

Answer B:

To remove the weaknesses in the performance report, you could recommend that the CFO at 4-Cycle, Inc.:

- Use flexible rather than static budgeting.
- Stop holding product managers responsible for costs they cannot control.
- Include footnotes to make the report easier to understand.

A revised quarterly report that incorporates these suggested changes is shown next.

4-Cycle, Inc.
Marine Engine Quarterly Performance Report

	Actual	Flexible Budget	Flexible Budget Variance
Units	10,500	10,500	
Revenue	17,500,000	$18,158,805[1]	$658,805 U
Variable production costs			
Direct material	2,500,000	2,674,140[2]	174,140 F
Direct labor	2,193,000	2,211,195[3]	18,195 F
Machine time	2,300,000	2,408,805[4]	108,805 F
Factory overhead	4,500,500	4,725,000[5]	224,500 F
Total variable costs	11,493,500	12,019,140	525,640 F
Contribution margin	$6,006,500	$6,139,665	$133,165 U

(1) ($14,700,000 budget ÷ 8,500 budgeted units) × 10,500 actual units
(2) ($2,164,750 budget ÷ 8,500 budgeted units) × 10,500 actual units
(3) ($1,790,000 budget ÷ 8,500 budgeted units) × 10,500 actual units
(4) ($1,950,000 budget ÷ 8,500 budgeted units) × 10,500 actual units
(5) ($3,825,000 budget ÷ 8,500 budgeted units) × 10,500 actual units
Note: All calculations rounded amounts to two decimal places.

Answer to Question 1C-ES07

A. SieCo is currently using a plant-wide overhead rate that is applied on the basis of direct labor costs. In general, a plant-wide manufacturing overhead rate is acceptable only if a similar relationship between overhead and direct labor exists in all departments or the company manufactures products that receive proportional services from each department.

In most cases, departmental overhead rates are preferable to plant-wide overhead rates because plant-wide overhead rates do not provide:

- A framework for reviewing overhead costs on a departmental basis, identifying departmental cost overruns, or taking corrective action to improve departmental cost control
- Sufficient information about product profitability, thus increasing the difficulties associated with management decision making

B. In order to improve the allocation of overhead costs in the Cutting and Grinding Departments, SieCo should:

- Establish separate overhead accounts and rates for each of these departments.
- Select an application basis for each of these departments that best reflects the relationship of the departmental activity to the overhead costs incurred (i.e., machine hours, direct labor hours, etc.).
- Identify, if possible, fixed and variable overhead costs and establish fixed and variable overhead rates for each department.

C. In order to accommodate the automation of the Drilling Department in its overhead accounting system, SieCo should:

- Establish separate overhead accounts and rates for the Drilling Department.
- Identify, if possible, fixed and variable overhead costs and establish fixed and variable overhead rates.
- Apply overhead costs to the Drilling Department on the basis of robot or machine hours.

D. Because SieCo uses a plant-wide overhead rate applied on the basis of direct labor costs, the elimination of direct labor in the Drilling Department through the introduction of robots may appear to reduce the overhead cost of the Drilling Department to zero. However, this change will not reduce fixed manufacturing expenses, such as depreciation, plant supervision, and the like. In reality, the use of robots is likely to increase fixed expenses because of increased depreciation expense. Under SieCo's current method of allocating overhead costs, these costs merely will be absorbed by the remaining departments.

E. Under competence, Altman has a responsibility to "provide decision support information and recommendations that are accurate, clear, concise and timely." It is possible that the decision was made with less than optimal decision support.

Under confidentiality, he must keep information confidential except when disclosure is authorized or legally required, and he must inform his subordinates of the same requirement.

No information is presented that indicates that this standard has been or may be violated.

Under integrity, Altman must "avoid actual or apparent conflicts of interest and advise all appropriate parties of any potential conflict." He must also "refrain from engaging in any activity that would prejudice his ability to carry out his duties ethically." He should also "refrain from engaging in any activity that would discredit the profession." There appears to be a conflict of interest here when Simpson's brother-in-law has won the contract.

Finally, under credibility, Altman must "communicate information both fairly and objectively." He should "disclose fully all relevant information that could reasonably be expected to influence an intended user's understanding of the reports and recommendations presented." The ownership by Simpson's brother-in-law should be disclosed to Hunter.

F. According to the IMA *Statement of Ethical Professional Practice*, Altman should first follow the established policies of the organization he is employed by in an effort to resolve the ethical dilemma. If such policies do not exist or are not effective, he should follow the steps as outlined in "Resolution of Ethical Conflict."

First, he should discuss the problems with his immediate superior. except when it appears the superior is involved. In this case, it is not clear if Hunter is involved. If this step is not successful in solving the dilemma, he should proceed up the chain of command, which in this case would appear to be the president and then the board of directors.

However, he should note that except where legally prescribed, communication of such internal problems should not be discussed with authorities or individuals not employed or engaged by the organization.

Spencer should clarify relevant ethical issues by confidential discussion with an objective advisor (e.g., an IMA ethics counselor) to obtain a better understanding of possible courses of action. He should consult his own attorney as to his legal obligations and rights concerning the ethical conflict.

Answer to Question 1C-ES08

A. 1. Average investment in operating assets employed:

Balance end of current year	$12,600,000
Balance end of previous year*	12,000,000
Total	$24,600,000
Average operating assets employed†	$12,300,000

*$12,600,000 ÷ 1.05
†$24,600,000 ÷ 2

ROI = Income from operations ÷ Average operating assets employed

  = $2,460,000 ÷ $12,300,000

  = .20 or 20%

2. Residual Income:

Income from operations	$2,460,000
Minimum return on assets employed*	1,845,000
Residual income	$615,000

*$12,300,000 × .15

B. Yes, Presser's management probably would have accepted the investment if residual income were used. The investment opportunity would have lowered Presser's ROI because the expected return (18%) was lower than the division's historical returns as well as its actual ROI (20%) for the year just ended. Management rejected the investment because bonuses are based in part on the performance measure of ROI. If residual income was used as a performance measure (and as a basis for bonuses), management would accept any and all investments that would increase residual, including the investment opportunity rejected in the year just ended.

C. Presser must control all items related to profit (revenues and expenses) and investment if it is to be evaluated fairly as an investment center by either the ROI or residual income performance measures. Presser must control all elements of the business except the cost of invested capital, that being controlled by Lawton Industries.

Answer to Question 1C-ES09

Answer 1:

The positive and negative behavioral implications arising from employing a negotiated transfer price system for goods exchanged between divisions include the following:

Positive

- Both the buying and selling divisions have participated in the negotiations and are likely to believe they have agreed on the best deal possible.
- Negotiating and determining transfer prices will enhance the autonomy/ independence of both divisions.

Negative

- The result of a negotiated transfer price between divisions may not be optimal for the firm as a whole and therefore will not be goal congruent.
- The negotiating process may cause harsh feelings and conflicts between divisions.

Answer 2:

The behavioral problems that can arise from using actual full (absorption) manufacturing costs as a transfer price include these:

a. Full-cost transfer pricing is not suitable for a decentralized structure when the autonomous divisions are measured on profitability as the selling unit is unable to realize a profit.

b. This method can lead to decisions that are not goal congruent if the buying unit decides to buy outside at a price less than the full cost of the selling unit. If the selling unit is not operating at full capacity, it should reduce the transfer price to the market price if this would allow the recovery of variable costs plus a portion of the fixed costs. This price reduction would optimize overall company performance.

Answer 3:

The behavioral problems that could arise if Thompson Corporation decides to change its transfer pricing policy to one that would apply uniformly to all divisions including these:

- A change in policy may be interpreted by the divisional managers as an attempt to decrease their freedom to make decisions and reduce their autonomy. This perception could lead to reduced motivation.
- If managers lose control of transfer prices and thus some control over profitability, they will be unwilling to accept the change to uniform prices.
- Selling divisions will be motivated to sell outside if the transfer price is lower than market as this behavior is likely to increase profitability and bonuses.

Answer 4:

The likely behavior of both "buying" and "selling" divisional managers for each of the listed transfer pricing methods being considered by Thompson Corporation include the following:

a. Standard full manufacturing costs plus a markup

The selling division will be motivated to control costs because any costs over standard cannot be passed on to the buying division and will reduce the profit of the selling division.

The buying division may be pleased with this transfer price if the market price is higher. However, if the market price is lower and the buying divisions are forced to take the transfer price, the managers of the buying division will be unhappy.

b. Market selling price of the product being transferred

This creates a fair and equal chance for the buying and selling divisions to make the most profit they can. It should promote cost control, motivate divisional management, and optimize overall company performance. Since both parties are aware of the market price, there will be no distrust between the parties, and both should be willing to enter into the transaction.

c. Outlay (out-of-pocket) costs incurred to the point of transfer, plus opportunity costs per unit.

This method is the same as market price when there is an established market price and the seller is at full capacity. At any level below full capacity, the transfer price is the outlay cost only (as there is no opportunity cost), which would approximate the variable costs of the goods being transferred.

Both buyers and sellers should be willing to transfer under this method because the price is the best either party should be able to realize for the product under the circumstances. This method should promote overall goal congruence, motivate managers, and optimize overall company profits.

Part 1 Section D Answers

Answer to Question 1D-ES01

Answer A:

The traditional cost system, developed to value inventory, distorts product cost information because the cost system:

- Was designed to value inventory in the aggregate and not relate to product cost information.
- Uses a common departmental or factory-wide measure of activity, such as direct labor hours or dollars (now a small portion of overall production costs) to distribute manufacturing overhead to products.
- Deemphasizes long-term product analysis (when fixed costs become variable costs).
- Causes managers, who are aware of distortions in the traditional system, to make intuitive, imprecise adjustments to the traditional cost information without understanding the complete impact.

Answer B:

1. The benefits that management can expect from activity-based costing include:

- It leads to a more competitive position by evaluating cost drivers (e.g., costs associated with the complexity of the transaction rather that the production volume).
- It streamlines production processes by reducing non-value-adding activities (e.g., reduced setup times, optimal plant layout, and improved quality).
- It provides management with a more thorough understanding of product costs and product profitability for strategies and pricing decisions.

2. The steps that a company, using a traditional cost system, would take to implement activity-based costing include these:

- Evaluation of the existing system to assess how well the system supports the objective of an activity-based cost system
- Identification of the activities for which cost information is needed with differentiation between value-adding and non-value-adding activities.

Answer to Question 1D-ES02

Answer A:

Under direct costing, fixed manufacturing costs are expensed rather than being added to the inventoriable cost of each unit. Thus, it is not necessary to determine the allocation of fixed costs to individual units.

Answer B:

At first glance, job order costing appears to make more sense, as each pair of jeans is literally unique, given that the buyer's name is stitched on the back pocket. However, in reality, process costing should be used, because jeans will be produced continually and for cost purposes, costs will be the same for each pair.

Answer to Question 1D-ES03

A. 1. Relative sales value method at split-off:

Product	Monthly Output	Sales Price	Split-Off Value	% of Sales	Allocated Costs
Studs	75,000	$8	$600,000	46.15%	$461,539
Decorative Pieces	5,000	60	300,000	23.08%	230,769
Posts	20,000	20	400,000	30.77%	307,692
Totals			**$1,300,000**	**100%**	**$1,000,000**

A. 2. Physical output (volume) method at split-off:

Product	Monthly Output	% of Output	Allocated Costs
Studs	75,000	75.00%	$ 750,000
Decorative pieces	5,000	5.00%	50,000
Posts	20,000	20.00%	200,000
Totals	**100,000**	**100.00%**	**$1,000,000**

A. 3.   Estimated net realizable value method:

Product	Monthly Output	Sales Price	Split-Off Value	% of Sales	Allocated Costs
Studs	75,000	$ 8	$600,000	44.44%	$444,445
Decorative Pieces	4,500[1]	100	350,000[2]	25.93%	259,259
Posts	20,000	20	400,000	29.63%	296,296
Totals			**$1,350,000**	**100%**	**$1,000,000**

(1) 5,000 monthly units of output − 10% normal spoilage = 4,500 good units

(2) 4,500 good units × $100 = $450,000 − further processing costs of $100,000 = $350,000

B. Presented next is an analysis for Sonimad Sawmill comparing the processing of decorative pieces further versus selling the rough-cut product immediately at split-off. Based on this analysis, it is recommended that Sonimad further process the decorative pieces as this action results in an additional contribution of $50,000.

	Units	Dollars
Monthly unit output	5,000	
Less: Further normal processing shrinkage	500	
Units available for sale	4,500	
Final sales value (4,500 units × $100 each)		$450,000
Less: Sales value at split-off		300,000
Differential revenue		$150,000
Less: Further processing costs		100,000
Additional contribution from further processing		$50,000

Answer to Question 1D-ES04

Answer A:

A. 1.   The total budgeted costs for the Manufacturing Department at Alyssa Manufacturing are presented next.

Direct material		
Tuff Stuff ($5.00/unit × 20,000 units)	$100,000	
Ruff Stuff ($3.00/unit × 20,000 units)	60,000	
Total direct material		$160,000
Direct labor		800,000
Overhead		
Indirect labor	$ 24,000	
Fringe benefits	5,000	
Indirect material	31,000	
Power	180,000	
Setup	75,000	
Quality assurance	10,000	
Other utilities	10,000	
Depreciation	15,000	
Total overhead		350,000
Total budgeted cost		$1,310,000

A. 2 & 3.   The unit standard costs of Tuff Stuff and Ruff Stuff, with overhead allocated based on direct labor hours, are calculated as shown.

Tuff Stuff

Direct material	$5.00
Direct labor ($8.00/hour × 2 hours)*	16.00
Overhead ($3.50hour × 2 hours)*	7.00
Tuff Stuff unit standard cost	$28.00

Ruff Stuff

Direct material	$3.00
Direct labor ($8.00/hour × 3 hours)*	24.00
Overhead ($3.50/hour × 3 hours)*	10.50
Ruff Stuff unit standard cost	$37.50

*Budgeted direct labor hours

Tuff Stuff (20,000 units × 2 hours)	40,000
Ruff Stuff (20,000 units × 3 hours)	60,000
Total budgeted direct labor hours	100,000

Direct labor rate: $800,000 ÷ 100,000 hours = $8.00/hour
Overhead rate: $350,000 ÷ 100,000 hours = $3.50/hour

Answer B:

B. 1 & 2.   The total budgeted cost of the Fabricating and Assembly Departments, after separation of overhead into the activity pools, is calculated as shown.

	Total	Fabricating Percent	Fabricating Dollars	Assembly Percent	Assembly Dollars
Direct material	$160,000	100%	$160,000		
Direct labor	800,000	75%	600,000	25%	$200,000
Overhead					
Indirect labor	24,000	75%	18,000	25%	6,000
Fringe benefits	5,000	80%	4,000	20%	1,000
Indirect material	31,000		20,000		11,000
Power	180,000		160,000		20,000
Setup	75,000		5,000		70,000
Quality assurance	10,000	80%	8,000	20%	2,000
Other utilities	10,000	50%	5,000	50%	5,000
Depreciation	15,000	80%	12,000	20%	3,000
Total overhead	350,000		232,000		118,000
Total budget	$1,310,000		$992,000		$318,000

Answer C:

C. 1 & 2. The unit standard costs of the products using activity-based costing are calculated next.

Fabricating Department	
Total cost	$992,000
Less: Direct material	160,000
Less: Direct labor	600,000
Pool overhead cost for allocation	$232,000
Hours: Tuff Stuff (4.4 hours × 20,000 units)	88,000
Ruff Stuff (6.0 hours × 20,000 units)	120,000
Total machine hours	208,000

Overhead cost/machine hour: $232,000 ÷ 208,000 = $1.1154/hour

Fabrication cost per unit: Tuff Stuff $1.1154 × 4.4 hours = $4.91 per unit
Ruff Stuff $1.1154 × 6.0 hours = $6.69 per unit

Assembly Department

Total cost − Direct labor = Pool overhead cost for allocation
$318,000 − $200,000 = $118,000

Setups = 1,000 (Tuff Stuff) + 272 (Ruff Stuff) = 1,272
Cost per setup: $118,000 ÷ 1,272 = $92.77 per setup

Setup cost per unit:

Tuff Stuff: ($92.77 × 1,000) ÷ 20,000 units = $4.64 per unit
Ruff Stuff: ($92.77 × 272) ÷ 20,000 units = $1.26 per unit

Tuff Stuff Standard Activity-Based Cost

Direct material	$ 5.00
Direct labor	16.00
Fabrication Department overhead allocation	4.91
Assembly Department overhead allocation	4.64
Total cost	$30.55

Ruff Stuff Standard Activity-Based Cost

Direct material	$ 3.00
Direct labor	24.00
Fabrication Department overhead allocation	4.91
Assembly Department overhead allocation	6.69
Total cost	$34.95

Answer D:

When compared to the old standard cost ($37. 50), the new activity-based standard cost for Ruff Stuff ($34. 95) should lead the company to decide to lower the price for Ruff Stuff in order to be more competitive in the market and continue production of the product. Using ABC for allocating overhead costs generally leads to a more accurate estimate of the costs incurred to produce a product, and Alyssa should be able to make better informed decisions regarding pricing and production.

Answer to Question 1D-ES05

Answer 1:

a.

Materials	$400,000
Direct labor	100,000
Variable manufacturing overhead	20,000
Fixed manufacturing overhead	200,000
	$720,000/100,000 = $7.20

b. 10,000 beginning inventory + 100,000 manufactured − 106,000 sold = 4,000 units in ending inventory; 4,000 × $7.20 = $28,800.

c.

Sales (106,000 × $12)		$1,272,000
Cost of Goods Sold:		
Beginning inventory	$ 72,000	
Cost of goods manufactured (100,000 × $7.20)	720,000	
− Ending inventory	(28,800)	763,200
Gross profit		508,800
Less selling and administrative		
Variable costs	80,000	
Fixed costs	300,000	380,000
Income		$ 128,800

Answer 2:

a.

Materials	$400,000
Direct labor	100,000
Variable manufacturing overhead	20,000
	$520,000/100,000 = $5.20

b. 4,000 units × $5.20 = $20,800

c.

Sales		$1,272,000
Less variable costs:		
Manufacturing = $5.20 × 106,000	$551,200	
Selling and administrative	80,000	631,200
Contribution margin		640,800
Less fixed costs:		
Manufacturing	200,000	
Selling and administrative	300,000	500,000
Income		$ 140,800

Answer 3:

The difference in incomes is caused by the treatment of fixed manufacturing overhead. Absorption costing treats this cost as a product cost that is held in inventory until the goods are sold; variable costing treats fixed manufacturing overhead as a period cost, showing it as an expense immediately. Because inventory decreased, absorption costing would expense all of the current month's fixed manufacturing overhead as well as some of the costs that were previously deferred in the prior period's inventory; variable costing would expense only the current month's amount, resulting in a higher income.

Answer 4:

a. The advantages of using absorption costing are:
- It is required for external reporting.
- It matches all manufacturing costs with revenues.

b. The advantages of using variable costing are:
- Data required for cost-volume-profit analysis can be taken directly from the statement.
- The profit for a period is not affected by changes in inventories.
- Unit product costs do not contain fixed costs that are often unitized, a practice that could result in poor decision making.
- The impact of fixed costs on profits is emphasized.
- It is easier to estimate a product's profitability.
- It ties in with cost control measures such as flexible budgets.

Answer 5:

a. Top-down advantage: speed, control top down; disadvantage: little buy-in, top has less information

   Bottom-up advantage: more likely to commit; disadvantage: may set easier targets

b. Best: top-down, cost of products most important, want to focus on control

c. Benchmark with outside examples, mutual learning about problems, balanced scorecard methods of evaluation

Answer to Question 1D-ES06

Answer 1:

Model M-11:

Overhead cost allocated (per unit): [€80,000 / (650 + 150)] × 650 = €65,000

65000 / 1300 = 50

Gross margin per unit: €90 – €10 – €50 = €30

Model R-24:

Overhead cost allocated (per unit): [€80,000 / (650 + 150)] × 150 = €15,000

15,000 / 1500 = 10

Gross margin per unit: €60 – €30 – €10 = €20

Answer 2:

Setups: €20,000 / (3 + 7) = €2,000

Components: €50,000 / (17 + 33) = €1,000

Material Movements: €10,000 / (15 + 35) = €200

Model M-11:

(€2,000 × 3) + (€1,000 × 170) + (€200 15) = €26,000

Overhead cost allocated by ABC (per unit): €26,600 / 1300 = €20.00

Gross margin per unit: €90 – €10 – €20.00 = €60.00

Model R-24:

(€2,000 × 7) + (€1000 × 33) + (€200 × 35) = €54,000

Overhead cost allocated by ABC (per unit): €54,000 / 1,500 = €36.00

Gross margin per unit: €60 – €30 – €36= –€6.00

Answer 3:

Because the products do not all require the same proportionate shares of the overhead resources of setup hours and components, the ABC system provides different results than the traditional system. The traditional method use volume base allocation base, which allocates overhead costs on the basis of direct labor hours. The ABC system considers important differences in overhead resource requirements by using multiple cost drivers and thus provides a better picture of the costs of each product model, provided that the activity measures are fairly estimated.

In the case of Smart Electronics, Model R-24 uses more setups, components, and material movements, which might not be reflected in the labor hours. The following table shows the overhead allocated per unit and profit margin per unit under the current conventional costing system and ABC. As indicated, Model R-24 was previously under-costed and Model M-11 was over-costed.

Overhead Allocated per unit under the current costing system and ABC:

	Current costing system	ABC
Model M-11	€50	€20.00
Model R-24	€10	€36.00

Gross Margin per unit under the current costing system and ABC

	Current costing system	ABC
Model M-11	€30	€60.00
Model R-24	€20	-€6.00

Smart Electronics' management can use the information from the ABC system to make better pricing decisions. After allocating overhead by ABC, it gives a clear cost picture that Model R-24 costs more to manufacture because it uses more setups, components, and material movements. The current price of $60 is inadequate to cover the total cost and results in negative gross margin. Therefore, the company might decide to increase the price of the Model R-24. For Model M-11, the previous overhead was overestimated, given that it was allocated by labor hours. Under ABC, only €60.00 of the overhead was allocated to every unit of Model M-11. Management might reduce the price of Model M-11 to make it more competitive.

Answer 4:

Advantages

The ABC system better captures the resources needed for Model M-11 and Model R-24. It identifies all of the various activities undertaken when producing the products and recognizes that different products consume different amounts of activities. Hence, the ABC system generates more accurate product costs.

Limitations

ABC requires continuously estimating cost drivers and updating and maintaining the system, which make the system relatively costly.

A complicated system is sometimes confusing to top management.

Estimation of cost of activities and selection of cost drivers sometimes may cause estimation errors, which could result in misleading cost information.

Part 1 Section E Answers

Answer to Question 1E-ES01

	Weaknesses	Recommendations
1.	An authorization document that describes the item to be acquired, indicates the benefits to be derived, and estimates its cost is not prepared and reviewed with management.	To obtain approval for the purchase of machinery and equipment, an appropriations request should be prepared, describing the item, indicating why it is needed, and estimating its expected costs and benefits. The document also could include the item's accounting classification, expected useful life, depreciation method and rate, and name the approving company executives.
2.	There is no control over authorized acquisitions. The purchase requisitions and purchase orders for fixed assets are interspersed with other requisitions and purchase orders and handled through normal purchasing procedures.	Authorized acquisitions should be processed using special procedures and purchase orders. These purchase orders should be subjected to numerical control. Copies of purchase orders should be distributed to all appropriate departments so that the acquisition can be monitored.
3.	Plant engineering does not appear to be inspecting machinery and equipment upon receipt.	Purchases of machinery and equipment should be subject to normal receiving inspection routines. In the case of machinery and equipment, plant engineering is usually responsible for reviewing the receipt to make certain the correct item was delivered and that it was not damaged in transit. All new machinery and equipment would be assigned a control number and tagged at the time of receipt.
4.	The lapsing schedules are not reconciled periodically to general ledger control accounts to verify agreement.	At least once each year, machinery and equipment lapsing schedules, which provide information on asset cost and accumulated depreciation, should be reconciled to general ledger control accounts. Furthermore, an actual physical inventory of existing fixed assets should be taken periodically and reconciled to the lapsing schedules and general ledger control account to assure accuracy.
5.	Machinery and equipment accounting policies, including depreciation, have not been updated to make certain that the most desirable methods are being used.	Machinery and equipment accounting procedures, including depreciation, must be updated periodically to reflect actual experience, and changes in accounting pronouncements and income tax legislation.

Answer to Question 1E-ES02

Answer A:

At least three weaknesses in the company's internal control system include:

1. The Limited Expenditure Account (LEA) not being subject to normal accounting controls.
2. The lack of adequate supporting documentation for personal and other expenditures. There is an improper or inadequate identification of the use of these resources, which makes proper accounting classification difficult or impossible. This increases the possibility of illegal use and material misstatements.
3. The Internal Audit Department not reporting its findings in connection with the payment practices and the LEA.

Answer B:

At least three illegal or improper practices uncovered at the company include:

1. Funds raised for political purposes were diverted to other uses. This misappropriation of funds included Public Relations Department resources being used for personal projects and the authorizing of payments to vendors for personal services and goods.
2. Management fraud. Senior management advised the Internal Audit Department to conceal findings; this act is detrimental to the company. There also appears to be a senior management conspiracy.
3. The external auditors not reporting these practices in their recommendations for improved internal control procedures.

Answer C:

At least four important steps that the company should take, both procedurally and organizationally, to correct the problems that were uncovered in order to prevent a similar situation in the future include:

1. Terminating the employment of the chief executive officer, president, vice president-public relations, as well as the controller and director of the Internal Audit Department.
2. Strengthening the company's internal controls, including:

   - The establishment of a company policy that all payments and reimbursements must be supported by appropriate documentation and, also, approved by at least one higher level of authority.
   - Establishing dollar limits that can be approved at each level of authority.

3. Issuing a strong formal company-wide code of ethics.
4. Restructuring the organization so that the Internal Audit Department reports to the audit committee of the board of directors.

Answer to Question 1E-ES03

Answer A:

The seven types of internal audits are financial, operational, performance, information systems, contract, compliance, and special investigation (e.g., fraud). The two most common types of internal audits are operational audits and compliance audits.

An operational audit is a comprehensive review of the varied functions within an enterprise to appraise the efficiency and economy of operations and the effectiveness with which those functions achieve their objective. An example would be an audit to assess productivity. Other examples could include an evaluation of processes to reduce rework, or reduce the time required to process paperwork or goods.

A compliance audit is the review of both financial and operating controls to see how they conform to established laws, standards, regulations, and procedures. An environmental audit would be an example of a compliance audit. Other examples of compliance audits could include the review of controls over industrial wastes or the review of procedures ensuring that proper disclosure is made regarding hazardous materials on site.

Answer B:

1. A compliance audit would best fit the requirements of the president of Brawn.
2. The objective of this compliance audit is to assure the president that the manufacturing facility has appropriate policies and procedures in place for obtaining the needed permits, has obtained all the required permits in accordance with the law, and that environmental and safety issues are being properly addressed.
3. The assignment specifically is to address the proper use of permits, compliance with safety regulations, and compliance with environmental standards. These issues can be properly addressed only by conducting a compliance audit. Although financial and operational areas might be involved, they would be secondary to the compliance issues. For example, a financial impact could result from the evaluation of compliance with safety regulations. The findings might result in additional expenditures for safety precautions or a reduction in the company's risk of being fined for lack of compliance.

Answer C:

To mitigate the president's concern, these activities and procedures could be implemented.

- Set the tone at the top. The president should communicate to all employees that the company expects appropriate business practices on the part of all employees in all divisions.
- Ensure that all employees have the necessary information to perform their duties. Keep the lines of communication open. For example, involve senior mangers from the manufacturing facility in monthly operational meetings for the whole company.
- Conduct regularly scheduled audits of compliance with applicable laws, regulations, and standards.
- Periodically review and update policies, rules, and procedures to ensure that internal controls prevent or help to detect material risks. Make sure all employees have access to the relevant policies and procedures. For example, post the policies and procedures on the company's intranet.

Answer to Question 1E-ES04

Answer A:

1. Crosby, the owner is taking a hands-off approach. He is hardly around to check on the business.
2. The two managers, Smith and Fletcher, have too much control without any independent checks on them.
3. Hiring policies to hire the right kind of employees are lacking; Crosby does not screen the job applicants; he did not check any background references for Smith and Fletcher.
4. Proper internal controls such as segregation of duties, authorizations, independent checks are not in place. Fletcher places purchase orders, and also receives materials. Crosby is in charge of collecting the payments, maintaining records, reconciling the bank accounts, preparing and signing checks, and approving payments. Lack of basic internal controls seems to have opened the door for employees to commit fraud.

Answer B:

Proper internal controls must be in place so that opportunities to commit, and/ or conceal fraud are eliminated. In this case, the internal controls needed are: (1) segregation of duties; (2) system of authorizations; (3) independent checks; and (4) proper documentation. No one department or individual should handle all aspects of a transaction from beginning to end. No one person should perform more than one function recording transactions, and reconciling bank accounts (as done by Crosby in this case). In a similar manner, Fletcher should not authorize purchases, receive inventory, and issue materials for production. The company also should separate the duties of preparing and signing checks, especially because the same person has the authority to approve payment.

There is a failure to enforce authorization controls. Crosby should authorize purchases and approve payments. He might consider hiring another person so that the two tasks, record keeping and bank reconciliation, can be separated.

In addition to that, the company must have better hiring policies in place, may require vacations, conduct internal audits, and have good oversight over employees.

Require vacations, conduct internal audits, owner/board oversight.

Answer C:

Even the best internal controls do not guarantee that fraud will be eliminated. These controls provide reasonable, not absolute, assurance against fraud. Internal controls are not fraud-proof, internal controls never provide absolute insurance that fraud will be prevented. Effectiveness depends on competency and dependability of people enforcing the controls.

Answer to Question 1E-ES05

Answer A:

1. Buying raw materials from other countries will expose the company to market risk, including the exposure to potential loss that would result from changes in market prices or rates. Examples include foreign exchange valuation, interest rate changes, and the volatility of crude oil prices. If a company has a contract to purchase products in a foreign currency, the cost of those products may increase drastically due to depreciation of the home currency. Foreign products may increase in price, or become unavailable, due to political events, such as expropriation or inflation.

2. Credit risk is the economic loss suffered due to the default of a borrower or counterparty. Default can be legal bankruptcy or failure to fulfill contractual obligations in a timely manner, due to inability or unwillingness. Credit risk includes loan default, failure to pay accounts receivable, or the inability of a business partner to fulfill agreed-on actions or payments. These conditions may be worsened when dealing with international counterparties, due to differences in legal systems, accounting systems, and credit reporting services.

3. International companies may have additional operational risk, defined as the risk of direct or indirect loss resulting from inadequate or failed internal processes, people, and systems or from external events. An example is failure to follow quality standards resulting in the shipment of deficient products, customer dissatisfaction, and reputation damage. Other examples include failure to properly monitor financial transactions, the hacking of computer files, and failure to follow loan approval controls.

Answer B:

1. Without a thorough understanding of your business, it is not possible to (1) identify the risks associated with daily operations, (2) understand the external risks associated with elements such as competitors or changes in technology, or (3) to assign individual accountability for risk management. If you do not understand your business position, decisions can be made that would undermine that position. For example, if your customers buy your service or good because of its quality and they don't care about price, you need to know this to mitigate the risk of damaging this relationship.

2. A system of checks and balances (1) prevents any individual or group from gaining the power to take unplanned risks on behalf of an organization, and (2) safeguards assets, and (3) prevents fraudulent activities. Examples include the segregation of duties to safeguard financial transactions and the use of passwords to limit access to records and programs.

3. Procedures that set limits and set standards can (1) prevent inappropriate behavior, and (2) tell a business when to stop. Examples might include standards for sales practices and product disclosures, standards for hiring practices regarding background checks on prospective employees, or termination policies for violation of company policy.

Answer C:

Management should be involved with:

- Setting the tone from the top and building awareness through demonstration of senior management commitment
- Establishing the principles that will guide the company's risk culture and values
- Facilitating open communication for discussing risk issues, escalating exposures, and sharing lessons learned and best practices
- Providing training and development programs
- Selecting appropriate performance measures to promote desired behavior
- Setting compensation policies that reward desired behavior

Answer D:

Management should be involved with:

- Section 404 of the Sarbanes-Oxley Act of 2002 (SOX 404) requires management to "take ownership" of internal controls over financial reporting by assessing and publicly reporting on their effectiveness.
- Each annual report of an issuer (of public securities) will contain an "internal control report." This report contains a statement that management is responsible for maintaining adequate internal controls. The report also contains an assessment of the effectiveness of the internal control structure.
- Each issuer is required to disclose the content of its code of ethics for senior financial officers.
- The auditor's report will evaluate management's assessment of the internal controls and issue an opinion as to the effectiveness of the internal controls.

Answer to Question 1E-ES06

Answer 1:

a. Four types of functional responsibilities that should be performed by different people:
   - Authority to execute transactions
   - Recording transactions
   - Custody of assets and
   - Periodic reconciliations
b. Two incompatible duties Zhao had:

   Zhao could execute transactions by initiating a transfer and could record transactions by entering the joint venture that was erroneous.

Answer 2:

Attempted controls:

- The company had physical controls over its checks.
- The president authorized and signed all checks.
- The company maintained prenumbered check stock.
- The company had a prepared budget to compare to actuals to identify variances.

Ways to strengthen:

- Restrict fund online transferability.
- Randomly select and audit expense transactions on a periodic basis.
- Separate the incompatible duties.

Answer 3:

a. Three internal control objectives
   1. Effectiveness and efficiency of operations—operations should be as efficient as possible
   2. Compliance with applicable laws and regulations—care should be taken to follow and be in compliance with all applicable laws and regulations
   3. Reliability of financial reporting—financial data should be reliable and timely so that it can be useful for management decisions or outside users
b. Five components of internal control.
   1. Control environment—sets the tone of an organization, influencing the control consciousness of its people
   2. Risk assessment—identify and analyze relevant risks as a basis for management
   3. Control activities—the policies and procedures that help ensure that management directives are carried out.
   4. Information and communication
      - Information. Systems support the identification, capture, and exchange of information in a form and time frame that enable people to carry out their responsibilities.
      - Communication. Providing an understanding to employees about their roles and responsibilities.
   5. Monitoring—assesses the quality of internal control performance over time

Answer 4:

Three ways internal controls are designed to provide reasonable assurance.

1. Segregation of duties—assigning different employees to perform functions
2. Reconciliation of recorded accountability with assets
3. Safeguarding controls—limit access to an organization's assets to authorized personnel

Answer to Question 1E-ES07

Answer 1:

A good system of internal control is designed to provide reasonable assurance regarding achievement of an entity's objectives involving effectiveness and efficiency of operations, reliability of financial reporting, and compliance with applicable laws and regulations.

Answer 2:

Segregation of duties requires that no one person have control over the physical custody of an asset and the accounting for it. There is no evidence to suggest Smallparts makes any effort to account for the value of returned product, which may indeed be significant. The one salesperson seems to be in charge of all aspects related to returned product, including authorizing returns, crediting customers, receiving returns, handling physical custody, finding new customers, concluding sales, shipping, billing, and collecting. Most of these duties should be separated.

Answer 3:

A good system of internal control suggests that four functional responsibilities be separated and handled by different individuals: (1) authority to execute transactions, (2) recording transactions, (3) custody of assets involved in the transactions, and (4) periodic reconciliations of the existing assets to recorded amounts. Smallparts might improve its control over the inventory of returned product by separating these responsibilities among four different individuals.

Answer 4:

Separate responsibilities and duties. While the salesman may be assigned to work with customers who return products and find other customers for these products, other staff should post credits to customer accounts following written policy. The products should be received, inventoried, booked, and shipped just like regular products.

Answer 5:

a. The *IMA Statement of Ethical Professional Practice* lists the following four ethical principles: Honesty, Fairness, Objectivity, Responsibility.
b.1. Several standards from the *Statement* apply.
- Credibility: "Each practitioner has a responsibility to disclose deficiencies in internal controls."
- Competence: Duty to maintain an appropriate level of professional expertise relative to standard procedure commonly used in the accounting of firms dealing with returned product.
- Confidentiality: Refrain from using this confidential information for unethical advantage, by not informing firms of the lax controls and availability of steep discounts on returned product.
- Integrity: Mitigating any conflict of interest.
b.2. Steps are outlined in the IMA *Statement of Ethical Professional Practice*.

Answer to Question 1E-ES08

Answer 1:

a. The objective of a compliance audit is to see how financial controls and operating controls conform with established laws, standards, and procedures.

b. The objective of an operational audit is to appraise the efficiency and economy of operations and the effectiveness with which those functions achieve their objectives.

Answer 2:

a. Transaction processing controls include: passwords to limit access to input or change data, segregation of duties to safeguard assets, control totals to ensure data accuracy.

b. Virus protection controls include: ensuring that the latest edition of antivirus software is installed and updated, firewalls are set up to deter incoming risks, Internet access is limited to business-related purposes to reduce chances of viruses.

c. Backup controls include identification of vital systems to be backed up regularly, development of disaster recovery plan, testing of backup communications and resources.

Answer 3:

A sound business continuances plan contains the following components:

- Establish priorities for recovery process.
- Identify software and hardware needed for critical processes.
- Identify all data files and program files required for recovery.
- Store files in off-site storage.
- Identify who has responsibility for various activities, which activities are needed first.
- Set up and check arrangements for backup facilities.
- Test and review recovery plan.

Answer 4:

a. Bank deposits do not always correspond with cash receipts. Cause: Cash received after bank deposits are made. Action: Have a separate individual reconcile incoming cash receipts to bank deposits.

b. Physical inventory counts sometimes differ from perpetual inventory record, and sometimes there have been alterations to physical counts and perpetual records. Cause: Timing differences. Actions: Limit access to physical inventory, require and document specific approvals for adjustments to records,

c. Unexpected and unexplained decrease in gross profit percentage. Causes: Unauthorized discounts or credits provided to customers. Actions: Establish policies for discounts credits, document approvals.

Additional Materials

Answers to Section Practice Questions

Section A: External Financial Reporting Decisions Answers and Explanations

Question 1A1-W001

Topic: Financial Statements

The multistep income statement, with additional income statement items, for Harrington Technologies Inc. is given below.

Net sales	$2,000,000
Less: Cost of goods sold	890,000
Gross profit	1,110,000
Less: Transportation and travel	45,000
Depreciation	68,000
Pension contributions	21,000
Operating income	976,000
Less: Discontinued operations	76,000
Income before taxes	900,000
Less: Tax expense @ 30%	270,000
Net Income	$630,000

Glen Hamilton, a financial analyst, analyzed the company's financial statements and concluded that the real net income should be $683,200 instead of $630,000. Which of the following arguments is **most likely** to support his conclusion?

- ☐ **a.** $53,200 due from a client was written off as irrecoverable after the finalization of accounts for the current period.

- ☐ **b.** The company valued its inventory using the specific identification method, whereas the financial analyst used the LIFO method for the current period.

☐ **c.** The company might have liquidated its LIFO reserve.

☐ **d.** The company has included expenses in relation to discontinued operations as part of income from continued operations.

Explanation: The correct answer is **d**. The company has included expenses in relation to discontinued operations as part of income from continued operations.

Revenue and expenses from discontinued operations do not form part of income from continued operations. In this case, the analyst has excluded discontinued operations since it is a nonrecurring item.

Question 1A1-W003

Topic: Financial Statements

The cash flows and net income from four business segments for Taylor Laboratories Inc. have been provided.

	Segment 1	Segment 2	Segment 3	Segment 4
Cash flow from operations	$3,000	$(250)	$(3,000)	$2,000
Cash flow from investing activities	(4,000)	6,000	8,000	(3,000)
Cash flow from financing activities	1,080	(1,000)	(1,000)	1,080
Net income	1,500	1,750	2,375	1,500

Based on the information, which segment should be discontinued by the company?

☐ **a.** Segment 3, because cash used in operations is high and cash inflow is predominantly from investing activities.

☐ **b.** Segment 1, because net income is lowest and requires high investments.

☐ **c.** Segment 4, because net income and cash inflow from operations are low.

☐ **d.** Segment 2, because cash used in operations is low and cash flow from investing activities is not properly utilized.

Explanation: The correct answer is **a**. Segment 3, because cash used in operations is high and cash inflow is predominantly from investing activities.

Segment 3 should be discontinued because the major portion of income of the segment could be from the sale of its assets.

Question 1A1-W004

Topic: Financial Statements

The cash flow from operations for Charlene Energy Inc. is $25,000 for the current year. If the amortization expense increases by $5,000 and other factors remain the same, under which of the following assumptions will the cash flow from operations remain unaffected?

- ☐ **a.** A change in amortization method will not have a retrospective effect.
- ☐ **b.** The company has an infinite life.
- ☐ **c.** The company is operating in a tax-free environment.
- ☐ **d.** The company can change the depreciation method in between a financial year.

Explanation: The correct answer is **c**. The company is operating in a tax-free environment.

Cash inflow from amortization arises because of the tax shield. In a tax-free environment, change in amortization will not affect the cash flows from operations.

Question 1A1-W005

Topic: Financial Statements

The following information is extracted from the latest financial information of Hines Materials Inc.

Tax rate	30%
Net Income	$15,000
Cash flow from operations	$45,000

Additional information:

1. The tax rate for the coming year is expected to increase by 2%.
2. The company is planning to purchase equipment worth $500,000 in the first quarter of next year.
3. A 15% increase in capacity is expected with the use of new equipment.

Considering the given factors, which of the following would be an ideal strategy to decrease the tax liability for the next year?

- ☐ **a.** Defer the purchase of equipment to next year to take advantage of tax loss carryforward.
- ☐ **b.** Depreciate the asset using the double-declining balance method to show higher cash flows from operations in initial years.
- ☐ **c.** Prepare the cash flow statement using direct method to show lower cash from operations and lower net income.
- ☐ **d.** Defer the purchase of equipment to next year if there is a deferred tax liability can be reasonably estimated.

Explanation: The correct answer is **b**. Depreciate the asset using the double-declining balance method to show higher cash flows from operations in initial years.

Depreciating the equipment using double-declining balance method will result in higher depreciation in the initial years and lower net income. Therefore, net tax liability of the company will decrease.

Question 1A1-W006

Topic: Financial Statements

The financial accountant of Eva Wolfe Corp. has ascertained the cash flows from operations as follows:

Net Income	$15,000
Depreciation on equipment	2,500
Dividend income	2,500
Interest income	5,000
Increases in current assets	8,000
Increases in current liabilities	6,500
Cash flow from operations	$16,000

The management accountant of the company argues that the cash flow from operations should be $8,500. Which of the following statements, if true, will support the management accountant's calculation?

- ☐ **a.** The company operates in a tax-free environment.
- ☐ **b.** The company uses IFRS to ascertain cash flow from operations.
- ☐ **c.** Cash flow from operations is ascertained using direct method.
- ☐ **d.** Depreciation on equipment should not be added back to net income for calculating cash flows from operations.

Explanation: The correct answer is **b**. The company uses IFRS to ascertain cash flow from operations.

The management accountant has followed IFRS for ascertaining cash flows from operations. He has not included dividend income and interest income as part of cash flows from operations. IFRS gives the flexibility of inclusion of dividend income and interest income as part of either operating activities or financing activities. Hence, CFO = $15,000 + $2,500 − ($8,000 − $6,500) − ($2,500 + $5,000) = $8,500.

Question 1A1-W007

Topic: Financial Statements

The management of Arthur Energy recognized a contingent liability of $50,000 in the current year. However, before the annual report was issued, the company resolved the issue making a lump-sum payment of $42,000. The board of directors has decided to incorporate the transaction in the subsequent year's financial statements. Which of the following provisions of US GAAP, if applicable, is likely to prove the management decision wrong?

- ☐ **a.** Loss contingencies must be recognized when it is both probable that a loss has been incurred and the amount of the loss is reasonably estimable.

- ☐ **b.** Whenever GAAP or industry-specific regulations allow a choice between two or more accounting methods, the method selected should be disclosed.

- ☐ **c.** If an event alters the estimates used in preparing the financial statements, then the financial statements should be adjusted.

- ☐ **d.** If an event provides additional evidence about conditions that existed as of the balance sheet date and alters the estimates used, then the financial statements should be adjusted.

Explanation: The correct answer is **d**. If an event provides additional evidence about conditions that existed as of the balance sheet date and alters the estimates used, then the financial statements should be adjusted.

In this case, the amount of contingent liability needs to be revised, as the estimate of the amount of liability had changed. The subsequent event provides evidence regarding conditions present on the balance sheet date. Therefore, the financial statements need to be adjusted.

Question 1A1-W008

Topic: Financial Statements

Shelton Devin Corp. has two stock investments in which it owns 30% of the outstanding stock. The CEO of the company is not in favor of presenting consolidated financial statements. Based on the information, which of the following is **most likely** true?

- ☐ **a.** The decision of the CEO is correct as companies are required to issue consolidated statements only when the ownership exceeds 50%.

- ☐ **b.** The decision of the CEO is wrong as companies are required to issue consolidated statements when the ownership exceeds 20%.

☐ **c.** The decision of the CEO is wrong as companies are required to issue consolidated statements only if it holds more than ten subsidiaries.

☐ **d.** The decision of the CEO is correct as companies are required to issue consolidated statements only when a company has three or more subsidiaries.

Explanation: The correct answer is **a**. The decision of the CEO is correct as companies are required to issue consolidated statements only when the ownership exceeds 50%.

As required by ASC 810, *Consolidation*, all companies with subsidiaries are required to issue consolidated statements including each subsidiary they control, usually meaning 50% or more ownership.

Question 1A2-W002

Topic: Recognition, Measurement, Valuation, and Disclosure

Claire Enterprises has $150,000 in accounts receivable at the end of the current year, and it estimates its bad debts to be 5% of the receivables. Hence, the accountant reports $7,500 as bad debts and the net realizable value as $142,500. Under which of the following circumstances will the amount of bad debts reported **most likely** reduce?

☐ **a.** If the company shortens the credit period allowed

☐ **b.** If the company lengthens the credit period allowed

☐ **c.** If the allowance for doubtful accounts has a credit balance of $1,500

☐ **d.** If the allowance for doubtful accounts has a debit balance of $1,500

Explanation: The correct answer is **c**. If the allowance for doubtful accounts has a credit balance of $1,500.

If there is an existing credit balance in the allowance for doubtful accounts, then the bad debt expense should be adjusted downward from $7,500, as it is necessary to adjust the balance only to the desired level when estimating bad debts as a percentage of receivables. Therefore, the bad debt expense will be $7,500 − $1,500 = $6,000.

Question 1A2-W003

Topic: Recognition, Measurement, Valuation, and Disclosure

The latest financial statements of Darlene Properties show 140,000 outstanding shares, par value $10. The current market value per share is $25. At the beginning of this year, the company reacquired 10,000 shares at $4 per share. The company follows the cost method for the accounting of treasury stock. The current year's books of accounts show the value of outstanding shares as follows:

Common stock, $10 par	$1,400,000
Less: Treasury stock	100,000
Net common stock, $10 par	$1,300,000

The company's CFO did not approve the financial statements. The **most likely** reason for CFO's disapproval is that:

- ☐ **a.** The treasury stock is incorrectly valued based on par value, instead of valuing at the acquisition price.
- ☐ **b.** The treasury stock is incorrectly valued based on par value, instead of valuing at the current market rate.
- ☐ **c.** The par value of the treasury stock should be presented as a deduction from par value of issued shares of the same class
- ☐ **d.** The treasury stock should be reported as an asset.

Explanation: The correct answer is **a**. The treasury stock is incorrectly valued based on par value, instead of valuing at the acquisition price.

In the cost method, the treasury stock account is debited for the cost of the shares reacquired. Therefore, the value of treasury stocks should be $40,000 (10,000 shares × $4), acquired at the acquisition price.

Question 1A2-W004

Topic: Recognition, Measurement, Valuation, and Disclosure

Rogers Electronics is planning to make a market in the company's stock. The company's CFO suggests the reacquisition of shares. Which of the following is **most likely** to happen if the CFO's suggestion is implemented?

- ☐ **a.** The risk of takeovers by competitors will increase.
- ☐ **b.** This will hinder exercise of employee stock options.
- ☐ **c.** The stock price will increase.
- ☐ **d.** This could serve as an indication of the company's negative outlook about its future performance.

Explanation: The correct answer is **c**. The stock price will increase.

Reacquisition of shares reduces the number of shares a company has outstanding without altering the value of the company. Therefore, the stock price of the company will increase.

Question 1A2-W006

Topic: Recognition, Measurement, Valuation, and Disclosure

Calvin Software has invested in the equity stock of BioTech Corp. Its holdings consisted of 35% of the voting stock. The CFO suggests acquiring more stock of BioTech. Based on the information, which of the following will be **true**?

- ☐ **a.** Additional acquisitions beyond 15% will require Calvin Software to issue consolidated financial statements.
- ☐ **b.** Calvin's total value will decrease as incidental costs of acquisition must be subtracted when holding exceeds 35%.
- ☐ **c.** The circumstances leading to the decision to acquire additional shares shall be disclosed in the notes to the financial statements.
- ☐ **d.** Any additional acquisition of assets up to 20% should be classified as held to maturity.

Explanation: The correct answer is **a**. Additional acquisitions beyond 15% will require Calvin Software to issue consolidated financial statements.

Feedback: When an investor acquires an interest in the investee, the acquired percentage of voting stock determines the method of accounting. If the holdings are greater than 50%, the investor company needs to issue consolidated financial statements.

Question 1A2-W007

Topic: Recognition, Measurement, Valuation, and Disclosure

Warner Machines missed recording purchases worth $10,000 in the current year's income statement. While finalizing the financial statements, the company's accountant detected the error and partially corrected it. Under which of the following situations will the company report lower than actual net income?

- ☐ **a.** If the accountant has reduced cash by $10,000
- ☐ **b.** If the accountant has only added the missing purchases worth $10,000 to the cost of goods sold
- ☐ **c.** If the accountant has only increased accounts payable by $10,000
- ☐ **d.** If the accountant has reduced inventory by $10,000

Explanation: The correct answer is **b**. If the accountant has only added the missing purchases worth $10,000 to the cost of goods sold.

When the company misses recording a purchase but includes the purchases as part of cost of goods sold (COGS) in income statement, COGS will be understated and the net income will be overstated. The missing $10,000 should have been included both in purchases and in ending inventory, which will result in the COGS being unaffected.

Question 1A2-W008

Topic: Recognition, Measurement, Valuation, and Disclosure

Sandra Bellucci, a financial analyst, is analyzing inventory of companies from four different industries: consumer goods, sports goods manufacturers, electronics, and aircraft manufacturers. Assuming the inventory valuation methods reflect the actual flow of inventory and the inventory only includes finished goods, which of the following industries will **most likely** have zero LIFO reserve?

- ☐ **a.** Consumer goods
- ☐ **b.** Sports goods manufacturers
- ☐ **c.** Electronics
- ☐ **d.** Aircraft manufacturers

Explanation: The correct answer is **d**. Aircraft manufacturers.

Since this industry deals with high value and customized orders, the production usually starts after receiving the order. Since there will not be any equipment in inventory, the inventory balance will be zero, irrespective of the method of valuation used. Therefore, the balance in LIFO reserve will **most** likely be zero.

Question 1A2-New

Topic: Recognition, Measurement, Valuation, and Disclosure

An entity has determined that a performance obligation within a contract is satisfied over time because the transfer of control of the goods to the customer is satisfied over time. Which of the following is an allowed method to measure an entity's progress toward complete satisfaction of the performance obligation?

- ☐ **a.** Installment input method
- ☐ **b.** Output method
- ☐ **c.** Cost recovery method
- ☐ **d.** Through-put method

Explanation: The correct answer is **b**. Output method.

The new Accounting Standards Update (ASU) 2014-09, Revenue from Contracts with Customers (Topic 606) defines two methods, the output method and the input method, used to measure an entity's progress toward complete satisfaction of a performance obligation that is satisfied over time.

Section B: Planning, Budgeting, and Forecasting Answers and Explanations

Question 1B5-CQ02

Topic: Annual Profit Plan and Supporting Schedules

Troughton Company manufactures radio-controlled toy dogs. Summary budget financial data for Troughton for the current year are shown next.

Sales (5,000 units at $150 each)	$750,000
Variable manufacturing cost	400,000
Fixed manufacturing cost	100,000
Variable selling and administrative cost	80,000
Fixed selling and administrative cost	150,000

Troughton uses an absorption costing system with overhead applied based on the number of units produced, with a denominator level of activity of 5,000 units. Underapplied or overapplied manufacturing overhead is written off to cost of goods sold in the year incurred.

The $20,000 budgeted operating income from producing and selling 5,000 toy dogs planned for this year is of concern to Trudy George, Troughton's president. She believes she could increase operating income to $50,000 (her bonus threshold) if Troughton produces more units than it sells, thus building up the finished goods inventory.

How much of an increase in the number of units in the finished goods inventory would be needed to generate the $50,000 budgeted operating income?

- ☐ **a.** 556 units
- ☐ **b.** 600 units
- ☐ **c.** 1,500 units
- ☐ **d.** 7,500 units

Explanation: The correct answer is: **c.** 1,500 units.

Increasing production over sales allows the company to bury fixed overhead costs in the ending inventory, resulting in an increase in net income. The increase in net income from the extra production can be calculated as shown:

Increase in Net Income = (Fixed Overhead Rate) (Excess of Production over Sales)
= $30,000

Fixed Overhead Rate = (Fixed Manufacturing Costs) /
(Denominator Activity Level)

Fixed Overhead Rate = $100,000 / 5,000 Units = $20 per Unit

Therefore, the increase in production over sales = $30,000 / $20 per unit = 1,500 units.

Question 1B5-CQ04

Topic: Annual Profit Plan and Supporting Schedules

Hannon Retailing Company prices its products by adding 30% to its cost. Hannon anticipates sales of $715,000 in July, $728,000 in August, and $624,000 in September. Hannon's policy is to have on hand enough inventory at the end of the month to cover 25% of the next month's sales. What will be the cost of the inventory that Hannon should budget for purchase in August?

- ☐ **a.** $509,600
- ☐ **b.** $540,000
- ☐ **c.** $560,000
- ☐ **d.** $680,000

Explanation: The correct answer is: **b.** $540,000.

Sales = 1.3 (Cost of Sales), which can also be stated as:

Cost of Sales = (Sales) / 1.3

Expected Ending Inventory for Each Month = 0.25 (Next Month's Sales)

The purchases in a given month can be computed as shown:

Inventory Purchased for a Month = (Sales for the Month / 1.3)
+ (Expected Ending Inventory / 1.3)
− (Expected Beginning Inventory / 1.3)

Inventory Purchased for August = [($728,000) / 1.3] + [(0.25) ($624,000) / 1.3]
− [(0.25) ($728,000) / 1.3]

Inventory Purchased for August = $560,000 + $120,000 − $140,000 = $540,000

Question 1B5-CQ06

Topic: Annual Profit Plan and Supporting Schedules

Tyler Company produces one product and budgeted 220,000 units for the month of August with these budgeted manufacturing costs:

	Total Costs	Cost per Unit
Variable costs	$1,408,000	$6.40
Batch setup cost	880,000	4.00
Fixed costs	1,210,000	5.50
Total	$3,498,000	$15.90

The variable cost per unit and the total fixed costs are unchanged within a production range of 200,000 to 300,000 units per month. The total for the batch setup cost in any month depends on the number of production batches that Tyler runs. A normal batch consists of 50,000 units unless production requires less volume. In the prior year, Tyler experienced a mixture of monthly batch sizes of 42,000 units, 45,000 units, and 50,000 units. Tyler consistently plans production each month in order to minimize the number of batches. For the month of September, Tyler plans to manufacture 260,000 units. What will be Tyler's total budgeted production costs for September?

- ☐ **a.** $3,754,000
- ☐ **b.** $3,930,000
- ☐ **c.** $3,974,000
- ☐ **d.** $4,134,000

Explanation: The correct answer is: **b.** $3,930,000.

September Budgeted Production Costs = (Fixed Costs) + (Variable Costs)
+ (Batch Setup Costs)

Variable Costs = (260,000 Units) ($6.40 per Unit) = $1,664,000

Batch setup costs: 260,000 units require a minimum of 6 batches.

In August, 220,000 units were produced in 5 batches for a
total of $880,000. The cost per batch was $880,000 / 5 = $176,000.

6 Batches at $176,000 per Batch = $1,056,000

September Budgeted Production Costs = ($1,210,000) + ($1,664,000)
+ ($1,056,000) = $3,930,000

Question 1B5-CQ08

Topic: Annual Profit Plan and Supporting Schedules

Savior Corporation assembles backup tape drive systems for home microcomputers. For the first quarter, the budget for sales is 67,500 units. Savior will finish the fourth quarter of last year with an inventory of 3,500 units, of which 200 are obsolete. The target ending inventory is 10 days of sales (based on 90 days in a quarter). What is the budgeted production for the first quarter?

- ☐ **a.** 75,000
- ☐ **b.** 71,700
- ☐ **c.** 71,500
- ☐ **d.** 64,350

Explanation: The correct answer is: **b.** 71,700.

The expected beginning inventory is calculated as shown:

Expected Beginning Inventory = (3,500 Units − 200 Obsolete Units) = 3,300 Units

The expected ending inventory is 10 days' sales, which is calculated as shown:

Expected Ending Inventory = [(67,500 Units) / 90] (10) = 7,500 Units

Therefore, budgeted production = 67,500 Units + 7,500 Units − 3,300 Units
= 71,700 Units.

Question 1B5-CQ09

Topic: Annual Profit Plan and Supporting Schedules

Streeter Company produces plastic microwave turntables. Sales for the next year are expected to be 65,000 units in the first quarter, 72,000 units in the second quarter, 84,000 units in the third quarter, and 66,000 units in the fourth quarter.

Streeter usually maintains a finished goods inventory at the end of each quarter equal to one half of the units expected to be sold in the next quarter. However, due to a work stoppage, the finished goods inventory at the end of the first quarter is 8,000 units less than it should be.

How many units should Streeter produce in the second quarter?

- ☐ **a.** 75,000 units
- ☐ **b.** 78,000 units
- ☐ **c.** 80,000 units
- ☐ **d.** 86,000 units

Explanation: The correct answer is: **d.** 86,000 units.

Budgeted production is calculated as shown:

Budgeted Production = (Expected Sales) + (Expected Ending Inventory)
− (Expected Beginning Inventory)

The expected ending inventory for each quarter equals 50% of the next quarter's expected sales. Since the finished goods inventory at the end of the first quarter is 8,000 less than it should be, the budgeted production for the second quarter is calculated as shown:

Budgeted Production, Second Quarter = 72,000 Units + 0.5(84,000 Units)
− [0.5(72,000 Units) − 8,000 Units]

Budgeted Production, Second Quarter = 72,000 Units + 42,000 Units
− [36,000 Units − 8,000 Units]

Budgeted Production, Second Quarter = 114,000 Units − 28,000 Units
= 86,000 Units

Question 1B5-CQ10

Topic: Annual Profit Plan and Supporting Schedules

Data regarding Rombus Company's budget are shown next.

Planned sales	4,000 units
Material cost	$2.50 per pound
Direct labor	3 hours per unit
Direct labor rate	$7 per hour
Finished goods beginning inventory	900 units
Finished goods ending inventory	600 units
Direct materials beginning inventory	4,300 units
Direct materials ending inventory	4,500 units
Materials used per unit	6 pounds

Rombus Company's production budget will show total units to be produced of:

- ☐ **a.** 3,700
- ☐ **b.** 4,000
- ☐ **c.** 4,300
- ☐ **d.** 4,600

Explanation: The correct answer is: **a.** 3,700.

Budgeted production is calculated as shown:

Budgeted Production = (Expected Sales) + (Expected Ending Inventory) − (Expected Beginning Inventory)

Budgeted Production = 4,000 Units + 600 Units − 900 Units = 3,700 Units

Question 1B5-CQ11

Topic: Annual Profit Plan and Supporting Schedules

Krouse Company is in the process of developing its operating budget for the coming year. Given next are selected data regarding the company's two products, laminated putter heads and forged putter heads, sold through specialty golf shops.

	Putter Heads	
	Forged	**Laminated**
Raw materials		
Steel	2 pounds @ $5/pound	1 pound @ $5/pound
Copper	None	1 pound @ $15/pound
Direct labor	1/4 hour @ $20/hour	1 hour @ $22/hour
Expected sales	8,200 units	2,000 units
Selling price per unit	$30	$80
Ending inventory target	100 units	60 units
Beginning inventory	300 units	60 units
Beginning inventory (cost)	$5,250	$3,120

Manufacturing overhead is applied to units produced on the basis of direct labor hours. Variable manufacturing overhead is projected to be $25,000, and fixed manufacturing overhead is expected to be $15,000.

The estimated cost to produce one unit of the laminated putter head (PH) is:

- ☐ **a.** $42
- ☐ **b.** $46
- ☐ **c.** $52
- ☐ **d.** $62

Explanation: The correct answer is: **c.** $52.

Production Costs = Direct Materials + Direct Labor + Manufacturing Overhead

Direct Materials = (1 Pound Steel) ($5/Pound) + (1 Pound Copper) ($15/Pound)
    = $5 + $15 = $20

Direct Labor = (1 Hour) ($22/Hour) = $22

Manufacturing overhead is calculated as shown:

Manufacturing Overhead = (Total Expected Overhead) /
                (Total Expected Direct Labor Hours)

Manufacturing Overhead = ($25,000 Variable Overhead + $15,000 Fixed
                Overhead) / 4,000 Direct Labor Hours
    = $10

Use the next calculation to determine direct labor hours for the overhead calculation:

Direct Labor Hours = (# Laminated PHs Produced) (# Hours/Laminated PH)
            + (# Forged PHs Produced) (# Hours/Forged PH)

Production of PHs = (Expected Sales) + (Expected Ending Inventory)
            − (Expected Beginning Inventory)

Production of Laminated PHs = 2,000 + 60 − 60 = 2,000 Units

Production of Forged PHs = 8,200 + 100 − 300 = 8,000 Units

Direct Labor Hours = (2,000 Units) (1 Hour/Unit)
            + (8,000 Units) (0.25 Hours/Unit)

Direct Labor Hours = 2,000 Hours + 2,000 Hours = 4,000 Hours

Question 1B5-CQ12

Topic: Annual Profit Plan and Supporting Schedules

Tidwell Corporation sells a single product for $20 per unit. All sales are on account, with 60% collected in the month of sale and 40% collected in the following month. A partial schedule of cash collections for January through March of the coming year reveals these receipts for the period:

	Cash Receipts		
	January	**February**	**March**
December receivables	$32,000		
From January sales	$54,000	$36,000	
From February sales		$66,000	$44,000

Other information includes:

- Inventories are maintained at 30% of the following month's sales in units.
- Assume that March sales total $150,000.

The number of units to be purchased in February is

- ☐ **a.** 3,850 units
- ☐ **b.** 4,900 units
- ☐ **c.** 6,100 units
- ☐ **d.** 7,750 units

Explanation: The correct answer is: **c.** 6,100 units.

The expected unit purchases for any month are calculated as shown:

Expected Purchases = (Expected Sales in Units) + (Expected Ending Inventory) − (Expected Beginning Inventory)

The expected ending inventory for a month is 30% of the next month's expected sales.

Expected sales are calculated as shown:

Expected Sales = (Sales in $) / ($20 Selling Price per Unit)

Number of Units to Be Purchased in February = ($110,000 / $20 per Unit) + [0.3($150,000 / $20 per Unit)] − [0.3($110,000 / $20 per Unit)]

Number of Units to Be Purchased in February = 5,500 Units + [0.3 (7,500 Units)] − [0.3 (5,500 Units)]

Number of Units to Be Purchased in February = 5,500 Units + 2,250 Units − 1,650 Units = 6,100 Units

Question 1B5-CQ13

Topic: Annual Profit Plan and Supporting Schedules

Stevens Company manufactures electronic components used in automobile manufacturing. Each component uses two raw materials, Geo and Clio. Standard usage of the two materials required to produce one finished electronic component, as well as the current inventory, are shown next.

Material	Standard Usage per Unit	Price	Current Inventory
Geo	2.0 pounds	$15/pound	5,000 pounds
Clio	1.5 pounds	$10/pound	7,500 pounds

Stevens forecasts sales of 20,000 components for each of the next two production periods. Company policy dictates that 25% of the raw materials needed to produce the next period's projected sales be maintained in ending direct materials inventory.

Based on this information, what would the budgeted direct material purchases for the coming period be?

	Geo	Clio
☐ **a.**	$450,000	$450,000
☐ **b.**	$675,000	$300,000
☐ **c.**	$675,000	$400,000
☐ **d.**	$825,000	$450,000

Explanation: The correct answer is: **b.** $675,000 and $300,000.

The expected material purchases in units for any month can be calculated as shown:

Expected Material Purchases = (Production Needs for the Month)
        + (Expected Ending Inventory) − (Expected Beginning Inventory)

The expected ending inventory for any month is 25% of the next month's expected sales.

Since 2 pounds of Geo are used per unit, the expected purchase of Geo can be calculated as shown:

Expected Purchases of Geo = (2 Pounds) (20,000) + (0.25) (2 Pounds) (20,000)
        − 5,000 Pounds

Expected Purchases of Geo = 40,000 Pounds + 10,000 Pounds − 5,000 Pounds
        = 45,000 Pounds

Total Cost of Geo = (45,000 Pounds) ($15/Pound) = $675,000

Since 1.5 pounds of Clio are used per unit, the expected purchase of Clio can be calculated as shown:

Expected Purchase of Clio = (1.5 Pounds) (20,000) + (0.25) (1.5 Pounds) (20,000)
$$-7,500 \text{ Pounds}$$

Expected Purchase of Clio = 30,000 Pounds + 7,500 Pounds − 7,500 Pounds
$$= 30,000 \text{ Pounds}$$

Total Cost of Clio = (30,000 Pounds) ($10/Pound) = $300,000

Question 1B5-CQ14

Topic: Annual Profit Plan and Supporting Schedules

Petersons Planters Inc. budgeted these amounts for the coming year:

Beginning inventory, finished goods	$ 10,000
Cost of goods sold	400,000
Direct material used in production	100,000
Ending inventory, finished goods	25,000
Beginning and ending work-in-process inventory	Zero

Overhead is estimated to be two times the amount of direct labor dollars. The amount that should be budgeted for direct labor for the coming year is:

- ☐ **a.** $315,000
- ☐ **b.** $210,000
- ☐ **c.** $157,500
- ☐ **d.** $105,000

Explanation: The correct answer is: **d.** $105,000.

Since there was no change in work-in-process inventory, cost of goods manufactured equals total manufacturing costs.

Cost of goods manufactured is calculated as shown:

Cost of Goods Manufactured = (Ending Finished Goods) + (Cost of Goods Sold)
$$- \text{(Beginning Finished Goods)}$$

Cost of Goods Manufactured = $25,000 + $400,000 − $10,000 = $415,000

Since cost of goods manufactured is equal to total manufacturing costs, use the next formula to solve for direct labor costs:

$$\text{Total Manufacturing Costs} = \text{(Direct Material)} + \text{(Direct Labor)}$$
$$+ \text{(Manufacturing Overhead)}$$

$$\$415{,}000 = \$100{,}000 + \text{Direct Labor} + 2 \text{ (Direct Labor)}$$

$$\$415{,}000 = \$100{,}000 + 3 \text{ (Direct Labor)}$$

$$\$315{,}000 = 3 \text{ (Direct Labor)}$$

$$\text{Direct Labor} = \$105{,}000$$

Question 1B5-CQ15

Topic: Annual Profit Plan and Supporting Schedules

Over the past several years, McFadden Industries has experienced the costs shown regarding the company's shipping expenses:

Fixed costs	$16,000
Average shipment	15 pounds
Cost per pound	$0.50

Shown next are McFadden's budget data for the coming year.

Number of units shipped	8,000
Number of sales orders	800
Number of shipments	800
Total sales	$1,200,000
Total pounds shipped	9,600

McFadden's expected shipping costs for the coming year are:

- ☐ **a.** $4,800.
- ☐ **b.** $16,000.
- ☐ **c.** $20,000.
- ☐ **d.** $20,800.

Explanation: The correct answer is: **d.** $20,800.

Total shipping costs include both fixed and variable shipping costs.

$$\text{Total Shipping Costs} = \text{Fixed Shipping Cost} + \text{Variable Shipping Cost}$$

$$\text{Total Shipping Costs} = \$16{,}000 + (\$0.50) \text{ (Number of Pounds Shipped)}$$

$$\text{Total Shipping Costs} = \$16{,}000 + (\$0.50) \text{ (9,600 Pounds)}$$

$$\text{Total Shipping Costs} = \$16{,}000 + \$4{,}800 = \$20{,}800$$

Question 1B5-CQ18

Topic: Annual Profit Plan and Supporting Schedules

In preparing the direct material purchases budget for next quarter, the plant controller has this information available:

Budgeted unit sales	2,000
Pounds of materials per unit	4
Cost of materials per pound	$3
Pounds of materials on hand	400
Finished units on hand	250
Target ending units inventory	325
Target ending inventory of pounds of materials	800

How many pounds of materials must be purchased?

- ☐ **a.** 2,475
- ☐ **b.** 7,900
- ☐ **c.** 8,700
- ☐ **d.** 9,300

Explanation: The correct answer is: **c.** 8,700.

The direct material purchases budget is calculated as shown:

Direct Materials Purchases = (Production Requirement) + (Expected Ending Inventory in Pounds) − (Expected Beginning Inventory in Pounds)

Direct Materials Purchases = 8,300 Pounds + 800 Pounds − 400 Pounds = 8,700 Pounds

Production Requirement = (4 Pounds per Unit) (Expected Production)

Production Requirement = (4 Pounds per Unit) (2,075 Units) = 8,300 Pounds

Expected Production = (Sales) + (Expected Ending Finished Goods Inventory) − (Expected Beginning Finished Goods Inventory)

Expected Production = 2,000 Units + 325 Units − 250 Units = 2,075 Units

Question 1B5-CQ22

Topic: Annual Profit Plan and Supporting Schedules

Given the next data for Scurry Company, what is the cost of goods sold?

Beginning inventory of finished goods	$100,000
Cost of goods manufactured	700,000
Ending inventory of finished goods	200,000
Beginning work-in-process inventory	300,000
Ending work-in-process inventory	50,000

- ☐ **a.** $500,000
- ☐ **b.** $600,000
- ☐ **c.** $800,000
- ☐ **d.** $950,000

Explanation: The correct answer is: **b.** $600,000.

Cost of goods sold is calculated as shown:

Cost of Goods Sold = (Cost of Goods Manufactured) + (Beginning Finished Goods Inventory) − (Ending Finished Goods Inventory)

Cost of Goods Sold = $700,000 + $100,000 − $200,000

Cost of Goods Sold = $600,000

Question 1B5-CQ23

Topic: Annual Profit Plan and Supporting Schedules

Tut Company's selling and administrative costs for the month of August, when it sold 20,000 units, were:

	Cost per Unit	Total Cost
Variable costs	$18.60	$372,000
Step costs	4.25	85,000
Fixed costs	8.80	176,000
Total selling and administrative costs	$31.65	$633,000

The variable costs represent sales commissions paid at the rate of 6.2% of sales.

The step costs depend on the number of salespersons employed by the company. In August there were 17 persons on the sales force. However, 2 members have taken early retirement effective August 31. It is anticipated that these positions will remain vacant for several months.

Total fixed costs are unchanged within a relevant range of 15,000 to 30,000 units per month.

Tut is planning a sales price cut of 10%, which it expects will increase sales volume to 24,000 units per month. If Tut implements the sales price reduction, the total budgeted selling and administrative costs for the month of September would be:

☐ **a.** $652,760

☐ **b.** $679,760

☐ **c.** $714,960

☐ **d.** $759,600

Explanation: The correct answer is: **a.** $652,760.

Total budgeted selling and administrative costs in this problem can be calculated as shown:

Total Budgeted Selling and Administrative Costs = (Variable Costs)
+ (Step Costs) + (Fixed Costs)

Total Budgeted Selling and Administrative Costs = $401,760 + $75,000
+ $176,000

Total Budgeted Selling and Administrative Costs = $652,760

Rearrange the next formula to determine sales for August, then sales price per unit.

Variable Costs = (6.2%) (Sales)

Sales = (Variable Costs) / (0.062) = $372,000 / 0.062 = $6,000,000

Sales Price per Unit = (Sales) / (# Units Sold) = $6,000,000 / 20,000 = $300

Expected Sales in September = (90%) (August Sales Price per Unit)
(September Sales Volume)
= (0.9) (($300) (24,000) = $6,480,000

Budgeted Variable Costs = (0.062) ($6,480,000) = $401,760

Step Costs per Salesperson = $85,000 / 17 Salespeople = $5,000

Due to the retirement of two salespeople, the budgeted step costs are reduced and are calculated as shown:

Budgeted Step Costs = (15 Salespeople) ($5,000 Cost per Salesperson)
= $75,000

Total Budgeted Selling and Administrative Costs = $401,760 + $75,000
+ $176,000

Total Budgeted Selling and Administrative Costs = $652,760

Question 1B5-CQ36

Topic: Annual Profit Plan and Supporting Schedules

Data regarding Johnsen Inc. 's forecasted dollar sales for the last seven months of the year and Johnsen's projected collection patterns are shown next.

Forecasted Sales

June	$700,000
July	600,000
August	650,000
September	800,000
October	850,000
November	900,000
December	840,000

Types of Sales

Cash sales	30%
Credit sales	70%

Collection pattern on credit sales (5% determined to be uncollectible)

During the month of sale	20%
During the first month following the sale	50%
During the second month following the sale	25%

Johnsen's budgeted cash receipts from sales and collections on account for September are:

- ☐ **a.** $635,000
- ☐ **b.** $684,500
- ☐ **c.** $807,000
- ☐ **d.** $827,000

Explanation: The correct answer is: **b.** $684,500.

The budgeted cash receipts from sales and collections on account for September are calculated as shown:

Budgeted Cash Receipts from Sales and Collections on Account, September
= (September Cash Sales) + (Collections from September Credit Sales)
+ (Collections from August Sales) + (Collections from July Sales)

September Cash Sales = (30%) (September Sales)
= (0.3) ($800,000) = $240,000

Collections from September Credit Sales = (20%) (70%) (September Sales)

Collections from September Credit Sales = (0.2) (0.7) ($800,000) = $112,000

Collections from August Sales = (50%) (70%) (August Sales)

Collections from August Sales = (0.5) (0.7) ($650,000) = $227,500

Collections from July Sales = (25%) (70%) (July Sales)

Collections from July Sales = (0.25) (0.7) ($600,000) = $105,000

Budgeted Cash Receipts from Sales and Collections on Account, September
    = $240,000 + $112,000 + $227,500 + $105,000
    = $684,500

Question 1B5-CQ37

Topic: Annual Profit Plan and Supporting Schedules

The Mountain Mule Glove Company is in its first year of business. Mountain Mule had a beginning cash balance of $85,000 for the quarter. The company has a $50,000 short-term line of credit. The budgeted information for the first quarter is shown next.

	January	February	March
Sales	$60,000	$40,000	$50,000
Purchases	$35,000	$40,000	$75,000
Operating costs	$25,000	$25,000	$25,000

All sales are made on credit and are collected in the second month following the sale. Purchases are paid in the month following the purchase while operating costs are paid in the month that they are incurred. How much will Mountain Mule need to borrow at the end of the quarter if the company needs to maintain a minimum cash balance of $5,000 as required by a loan covenant agreement?

- ☐ **a.** $0
- ☐ **b.** $5,000
- ☐ **c.** $10,000
- ☐ **d.** $45,000

Explanation: The correct answer is: **c.** $10,000.

The projected cash balance, without borrowing, at the end of the quarter is calculated as shown:

Projected Cash Balance, Without Borrowing, End of Quarter
    = (Beginning Cash Balance) + (Projected Cash Receipts)
        – (Projected Cash Disbursements)

Beginning Cash Balance for the Quarter = $85,000

Projected cash receipts for the quarter are equal to the January sales amount, because all sales are made on credit and are collected in the second month following business.

Projected Cash Receipts for the Quarter = $60,000

Projected cash disbursements for the quarter will include the purchases from January and February (March purchases are not included, because they will be paid for in April), plus the operating costs for the months of January, February, and March.

$$\text{Projected Cash Disbursements} = \$35,000 + \$40,000 + \$25,000 \\ + \$25,000 + \$25,000 \\ = \$150,000$$

The projected cash balance, without borrowing, for the end of the quarter can be calculated as shown:

$$\text{Projected Cash Balance, Without Borrowing, End of Quarter} \\ = \$85,000 + \$60,000 - \$150,000 \\ = -\$5,000$$

Therefore, $10,000 will have to be borrowed to maintain a minimum cash balance of $5,000.

Question 1B3-CQ05

Topic: Forecasting Techniques

Aerosub, Inc. has developed a new product for spacecraft that includes the manufacture of a complex part. The manufacturing of this part requires a high degree of technical skill. Management believes there is a good opportunity for its technical force to learn and improve as it becomes accustomed to the production process. The production of the first unit requires 10,000 direct labor hours. If an 80% learning curve is used, the cumulative direct labor hours required for producing a total of eight units would be:

- ☐ **a.**   29,520 hours
- ☐ **b.**   40,960 hours
- ☐ **c.**   64,000 hours
- ☐ **d.**   80,000 hours

Explanation: The correct answer is: **b.** 40,960 hours.

Using a cumulative average time learning curve, as the cumulative output doubles, the cumulative average direct labor hours per unit becomes the learning curve percentage times the previous cumulative average direct labor hours per unit. So, if the direct labor hours for the first unit are 10,000 and an 80% learning curve is used, the cumulative average direct labor hours for 2 units would be calculated as shown:

Cumulative Average Direct Labor Hours for 2 Units
= 0.8 (10,000 Direct Labor Hours)
= 8,000 Direct Labor Hours

When output doubles to 4 units, the cumulative average direct labor hours would be calculated as shown:

Cumulative Average Direct Labor Hours for 4 Units = 0.8 (8,000 Direct Labor Hours)
= 6,400 Direct Labor Hours

When output doubles again, this time to 8 units, the cumulative average direct labor hours would be calculated as shown:

Cumulative Average Direct Labor Hours for 8 Units = 0.8 (6,400 Direct Labor Hours)
= 5,120 Direct Labor Hours

Therefore, the cumulative direct labor hours for 8 units = (5,120 direct labor hours) (8 units) = 40,960 direct labor hours.

Question 1B3-CQ18

Topic: Forecasting Techniques

Scarf Corporation's controller has decided to use a decision model to cope with uncertainty. With a particular proposal, currently under consideration, Scarf has two possible actions: invest or not invest in a joint venture with an international firm. The controller has determined this information:

Action 1: Invest in the Joint Venture

    Events and Probabilities:
        Probability of success = 60%
        Cost of investment = $9.5 million
        Cash flow if investment is successful = $15.0 million
        Cash flow if investment is unsuccessful = $2.0 million
        Additional costs to be paid = $0
        Costs incurred up to this point = $650,000

Action 2: Do Not Invest in the Joint Venture

Events:
Costs incurred up to this point = $650,000
Additional costs to be paid = $100,000

Which one of the next alternatives correctly reflects the respective expected values of investing versus not investing?

- ☐ **a.** $300,000 and ($750,000)
- ☐ **b.** ($350,000) and ($100,000)
- ☐ **c.** $300,000 and ($100,000)
- ☐ **d.** ($350,000) and ($750,000)

Explanation: The correct answer is: **c.** $300,000 and ($100,000).

The expected value of not investing is ($100,000), since this is the additional cost that would be incurred if no investment is made.

The expected value of investing can be calculated by adding together the expected value of when the investment is successful and adding to it the expected value of when the investment is unsuccessful and then subtracting the initial investment cost.

Expected Value of Investing = (Expected Value When Successful) + (Expected Value When Unsuccessful) – (Initial Investment Cost)

Expected Value of Investing = (0.6) ($15,000,000) + (0.4) ($2,000,000) – $9,500,000

Expected Value of Investing = $9,000,000 + $800,000 – $9,500,000

Expected Value of Investing = $300,000

Note that the $650,000 in costs incurred up to this point are sunk costs and are irrelevant to the analysis.

Section C: Performance Management Answers and Explanations

Question 1C1-CQ16

Topic: Cost and Variance Measures

The following performance report was prepared for Dale Manufacturing for the month of April.

	Actual Results	**Static Budget**	**Variance**
Sales units	100,000	80,000	20,000 F
Sales dollars	$190,000	$160,000	$30,000 F
Variable costs	125,000	96,000	29,000 U
Fixed costs	45,000	40,000	5,000 U
Operating income	$20,000	$ 24,000	$ 4,000 U

Using a flexible budget, Dale's total sales-volume variance is:

- ☐ **a.** $4,000 unfavorable.
- ☐ **b.** $6,000 favorable.
- ☐ **c.** $16,000 favorable.
- ☐ **d.** $20,000 unfavorable.

Explanation: The correct answer is: **c.** $16,000 favorable.

The sales-volume variance is the difference between the static budget profit of $24,000 and the flexible budget profit at the actual volume of 100,000 sales units.

Flexible Budget Profit at 100,000 Units = Budgeted Sales – Budgeted Variable Costs – Budgeted Fixed Costs all at 100,000 Units.

Budgeted Sales = (Budgeted Price) (Actual Sales in Units)

Budgeted Sales = ($160,000 / 80,000 Units) (100,000 Units)

Budgeted Sales = $200,000

Budgeted Variable Costs = (Unit Variable Cost) (Actual Sales in Units)

Budgeted Variable Costs = ($96,000 / 80,000 Units) (100,000 Units)

Budgeted Variable Costs = $120,000

Budgeted Fixed Costs = $40,000 at Any Volume in the Relevant Range.

Flexible Budget Profit = $200,000 – $120,000 – $40,000
= $40,000

Total Sales-Volume Variance = $24,000 – $40,000
= $(16,000), or $16,000 Favorable

Question 1C1-CQ17

Topic: Cost and Variance Measures

MinnOil performs oil changes and other minor maintenance services (e. g. , tire pressure checks) for cars. The company advertises that all services are completed within 15 minutes for each service.

On a recent Saturday, 160 cars were serviced resulting in the following labor variances: rate, $19 unfavorable; efficiency, $14 favorable. If MinnOil's standard labor rate is $7 per hour, determine the actual wage rate per hour and the actual hours worked.

		Wage Rate	Hours Worked
☐	a.	$6.55	42.00
☐	b.	$6.67	42.71
☐	c.	$7.45	42.00
☐	d.	$7.50	38.00

Explanation: The correct answer is: **d.** $7.50 and 38.00.

The labor efficiency variance of $(14), or $14 favorable, is used in the next formula to determine the actual hours (AH):

Labor Efficiency Variance = (Standard Rate) (Actual Hours – Standard Hours)

$$-\$14 = (\$7) [AH - (160 \text{ Units}) (1/4 \text{ Hour per Unit})]$$

$$-\$14 = \$7(AH - 40)$$

$$-\$14 = \$7AH - \$280$$

$$-\$14 = \$7AH - \$280$$

$$\$266 = \$7AH$$

$$AH = 38$$

The labor rate variance of $19, or $19 unfavorable, is used in the next formula to determine the actual wage rate (AR):

Labor Rate Variance = (Actual Hours) (Actual Wage Rate − Standard Wage Rate)

$$\$19 = (38 \text{ Hours})(AR - \$7)$$

$$\$19 = (38 \text{ Hours})(AR - \$7)$$

$$\$19 = 38AR - \$266$$

$$\$285 = 38AR$$

$$AR = \$7.50$$

Question 1C1-CQ18

Topic: Cost and Variance Measures

Frisco Company recently purchased 108,000 units of raw material for $583,200. Three units of raw materials are budgeted for use in each finished good manufactured, with the raw material standard set at $16.50 for each completed product.

Frisco manufactured 32,700 finished units during this period and used 99,200 units of raw material. If management is concerned about the timely reporting of variances in an effort to improve cost control and bottom-line performance, the materials purchase price variance should be reported as

- ☐ **a.** $6,050 unfavorable.
- ☐ **b.** $9,920 favorable.
- ☐ **c.** $10,800 unfavorable.
- ☐ **d.** $10,800 favorable.

Explanation: The correct answer is: **d.** $10,800 favorable.

The material purchase price variance is calculated as shown:

Material Purchase Price Variance = (Actual Quantity Purchased) (Actual Price) − (Actual Quantity Purchased) (Standard Price)

Material Purchase Price Variance = ($583,200) − (108,000 Units) ($16.50 / 3 Units)

Material Purchase Price Variance = $583,200 − $594,000 = $(10,800) Favorable

Question 1C1-CQ19

Topic: Cost and Variance Measures

Christopher Akers is the chief executive officer of SBL Contracting. Actual and budget information relating to the materials for a job include:

	Purchased and Used	Budget
Bricks—number of bundles	3,000	2,850
Bricks—cost per bundle	$7.90	$8.00

Which one of the following is a **correct** statement regarding the stadium job for SBL?

- ☐ **a.** The price variance was $285 favorable.
- ☐ **b.** The price variance was $300 favorable.
- ☐ **c.** The efficiency variance was $1,185 unfavorable.
- ☐ **d.** The flexible budget variance was $900 favorable.

Explanation: The correct answer is: **b.** The price variance was favorable by $300.

The material price variance is calculated as shown:

Material Price Variance = (Actual Quantity Purchased)
(Actual Price – Standard Price)

Material Price Variance = (3,000) ($7.90 – $8.00) = $(300) favorable.

The other available answer choices are incorrect. Note that the flexible budget variance is the variance between the actual results and flexible budget amount, which equals $900 unfavorable.

Question 1C1-CQ20

Topic: Cost and Variance Measures

A company isolates its raw material price variance in order to provide the earliest possible information to the manager responsible for the variance. The budgeted amount of material usage for the year was computed as shown:

150,000 Units of Finished Goods × 3 Pounds/Unit × $2.00/Pound = $900,000

Actual results for the year were the following:

Finished goods produced	160,000 units
Raw materials purchased	500,000 pounds
Raw materials used	490,000 pounds
Cost per pound	$2.02

The raw material price variance for the year was

- ☐ **a.** $9,600 unfavorable.
- ☐ **b.** $9,800 unfavorable.
- ☐ **c.** $10,000 unfavorable.
- ☐ **d.** $20,000 unfavorable.

Explanation: The correct answer is: **c.** $10,000 unfavorable.

The raw material price variance is calculated as shown:

Raw Material Price Variance = (Actual Quantity Purchased) (Actual Price − Standard Price)

Raw Material Price Variance = (500,000) ($2.02 − $2.00)
= $10,000 Unfavorable.

Question 1C1-CQ21

Topic: Cost and Variance Measures

At the beginning of the year, Douglas Company prepared this monthly budget for direct materials.

Units produced and sold	10,000	15,000
Direct material cost	$15,000	$22,500

At the end of the month, the company's records showed that 12,000 units were produced and sold and $20,000 was spent for direct materials. The variance for direct materials is:

- ☐ **a.** $2,000 favorable.
- ☐ **b.** $2,000 unfavorable.
- ☐ **c.** $5,000 favorable.
- ☐ **d.** $5,000 unfavorable.

Explanation: The correct answer is: **b.** $2,000 unfavorable.

The variance for direct materials is calculated as shown:

Variance for Direct Materials = (Actual Direct Material Cost)
  − (Budgeted Direct Material Cost at
  Actual Level of Production)

Variance for Direct Materials = ($20,000) − (12,000 Units)
  ($15,000 / 10,000 Units)

Variance for Direct Materials = $20,000 − $18,000
  = $2,000 unfavorable

Question 1C1-CQ22

Topic: Cost and Variance Measures

Cordell Company uses a standard cost system. On January 1 of the current year, Cordell budgeted fixed manufacturing overhead cost of $600,000 and production at 200,000 units. During the year, the firm produced 190,000 units and incurred fixed manufacturing overhead of $595,000. The production volume variance for the year was:

- ☐ **a.** $5,000 unfavorable.
- ☐ **b.** $10,000 unfavorable.
- ☐ **c.** $25,000 unfavorable.
- ☐ **d.** $30,000 unfavorable.

Explanation: The correct answer is: **d.** $30,000 unfavorable.

The fixed overhead volume variance is calculated as shown:

Fixed Overhead Volume Variance (FOVV) = (Fixed Overhead Rate) (Normal
  Base Level of Production
  − Actual Production Level)

Fixed Overhead Rate = SRF

FOVV = (SRF) (200,000 Units − 190,000 Units)

FOVV = 10,000 SRF

The fixed overhead rate (SRF) is equal to the budgeted fixed overhead of $600,000, divided by the normal (budgeted) base of 200,000 units, which comes to $3.00 per unit.

Therefore, the FOVV = (10,000) ($3) = $30,000 unfavorable.

Question 1C1-CQ23

Topic: Cost and Variance Measures

Harper Company's performance report indicated this information for the past month:

Actual total overhead	$1,600,000
Budgeted fixed overhead	$1,500,000
Applied fixed overhead at $3 per labor hour	$1,200,000
Applied variable overhead at $0.50 per labor hour	$200,000
Actual labor hours	430,000

Harper's total overhead spending variance for the month was:

- ☐ **a.** $100,000 favorable.
- ☐ **b.** $115,000 favorable.
- ☐ **c.** $185,000 unfavorable.
- ☐ **d.** $200,000 unfavorable.

Explanation: The correct answer is: **b.** $115,000 favorable.

The overhead spending variance is calculated as shown:

Overhead Spending Variance (OSV) = (Actual Overhead) − (Budgeted Overhead at Actual Direct Labor Hours Used)

OSV = ($1,600,000) − (Budgeted Overhead at Actual Direct Labor Hours Used)

Budgeted Overhead at the Actual Direct Labor Hours Used = (Fixed Overhead) + (Actual Direct Labor Hours) (Rate of Labor Hours Used to Apply Variable Overhead)

Budgeted Overhead at the Actual Direct Labor Hours Used = $1,500,000 + (430,000 Hours × $0.50 per Direct Labor Hour)

Budgeted Overhead at the Actual Direct Labor Hours Used = $1,500,000 + $215,000 = $1,715,000

OSV = $1,600,000 − $1,715,000 = $(115,000) Favorable

Question 1C1-CQ24

Topic: Cost and Variance Measures

The JoyT Company manufactures Maxi Dolls for sale in toy stores. In planning for this year, JoyT estimated variable factory overhead of $600,000 and fixed factory overhead of $400,000. JoyT uses a standard costing system, and factory overhead is allocated to units produced on the basis of standard direct labor hours. The denominator level of activity budgeted for this year was 10,000 direct labor hours, and JoyT used 10,300 actual direct labor hours.

Based on the output accomplished during this year, 9,900 standard direct labor hours should have been used. Actual variable factory overhead was $596,000, and actual fixed factory overhead was $410,000 for the year. Based on this information, the variable overhead spending variance for JoyT for this year was:

   ☐ **a.** $24,000 unfavorable.

   ☐ **b.** $2,000 unfavorable.

   ☐ **c.** $4,000 favorable.

   ☐ **d.** $22,000 favorable.

Explanation: The correct answer is: **d.** $22,000 favorable.

The variable overhead spending variance is calculated as shown:

Variable Overhead Spending Variance (VOSV) = (Actual Variable Overhead) − (Budgeted Variable Overhead at the Actual Level of Direct Labor Hours Used)

VOSV = ($596,000) − (Budgeted Variable Overhead at the Actual Level of Direct Labor Hours Used)

The budgeted variable overhead at the actual level of direct labor hours used is calculated as shown:

Budgeted Variable Overhead at the Actual Level of Direct Labor Hours Used = (Variable Overhead Rate, or SRV) (Actual Direct Labor Hours Used)

Budgeted Variable Overhead at the Actual Level of Direct Labor Hours Used = (SRV) (10,300 Direct Labor Hours)

SRV = (Estimated Variable Overhead) / (Budgeted Direct Labor Hours)

SRV = ($600,000) (10,000 Budgeted Direct Labor Hours) = $60 per Direct Labor Hour

Budgeted Variable Overhead at the Actual Level of Direct Labor Hours = $60 (10,300 Hours)

Budgeted Variable Overhead at the Actual Level of Direct Labor Hours
= $618,000

VOSV = $596,000 − $618,000 = −$22,000, or $22,000 Favorable

Question 1C1-CQ25

Topic: Cost and Variance Measures

Johnson Inc. has established per unit standards for material and labor for its production department based on 900 units normal production capacity as shown.

3 pounds of direct materials @ $4 per pound	$12
1 direct labor hour @ $15 per hour	15
Standard cost per unit	$27

During the year, 1,000 units were produced. The accounting department has charged the production department supervisor with the next unfavorable variances.

Material Quantity Variance		**Material Price Variance**	
Actual usage	3,300 pounds	Actual cost	$4,200
Standard usage	3,000 pounds	Standard cost	4,000
Unfavorable	300 pounds	Unfavorable	$200

Bob Sterling, the production supervisor, has received a memorandum from his boss stating that he did not meet the established standards for material prices and quantity and corrective action should be taken. Sterling is very unhappy about the situation and is preparing to reply to the memorandum explaining the reasons for his dissatisfaction.

All of the following are valid reasons for Sterling's dissatisfaction **except:**

☐ **a.** The material price variance is the responsibility of the purchasing department.

☐ **b.** The cause of the unfavorable material usage variance was the acquisition of substandard material.

☐ **c.** The standards have not been adjusted to the engineering changes.

☐ **d.** The variance calculations fail to properly reflect that actual production exceeded normal production capacity.

Explanation: The correct answer is: **d.** The variance calculations fail to properly reflect that actual production exceeded normal production capacity.

Production variances (cost, spending, and efficiency variances) are based on *actual production volumes*. They are not based on normal production, capacity production, budgeted production, estimated production, projected production, expected production, or any other measure of production. Therefore, the difference between actual production and any other measure of production is irrelevant.

Question 1C3-AT35
Topic: Cost and Variance Measures

Teaneck Inc. sells two products, Product E and Product F, and had these data for last month:

	Product E		Product F	
	Budget	**Actual**	**Budget**	**Actual**
Unit sales	5,500	6,000	4,500	6,000
Unit contribution margin (CM)	$4.50	$4.80	$10.00	$10.50

The company's sales mix variance is:

- ☐ **a.** $3,300 favorable.
- ☐ **b.** $3,420 favorable.
- ☐ **c.** $17,250 favorable.
- ☐ **d.** $18,150 favorable.

Explanation: The correct answer is: **a.** $3,300 favorable.

CM = Contribution Margin
Budgeted mix:
55% E × $4.50 CM	$2.475
45% F × $10.00 CM	4.500
Per unit CM	$6.975

Actual mix:
50% E × $4.50 CM	$2.250
50% F 3 $10.00 CM	5.000
Per unit CM	$7.250

Increase in CM 0.275 × Actual Units of 12,000 = $3,300 favorable

Question 1C2-CQ17
Topic: Responsibility Centers and Reporting Segments

Manhattan Corporation has several divisions that operate as decentralized profit centers. At the present time, the Fabrication Division has excess capacity of 5,000 units with respect to the UT-371 circuit board, a popular item in many digital applications. Information about the circuit board is presented next.

Market price	$48
Variable selling/distribution costs on external sales	$5
Variable manufacturing cost	$21
Fixed manufacturing cost	$10

Manhattan's Electronic Assembly Division wants to purchase 4,500 circuit boards either internally or else use a similar board in the marketplace that sells for $46. The Electronic Assembly Division's management feels that if the first alternative is pursued, a price concession is justified, given that both divisions are part of the same firm. To optimize the overall goals of Manhattan, the minimum price to be charged for the board from the Fabrication Division to the Electronic Assembly Division should be:

- ☐ **a.** $21.
- ☐ **b.** $26.
- ☐ **c.** $31.
- ☐ **d.** $46.

Explanation: The correct answer is: **a.** $21.

The optimal transfer price is calculated as shown:

Optimal Transfer Price, T(o) = (Manufacturing Division's Opportunity Cost of Production) + (Any Avoidable Fixed Costs) + (Any Forgone Contribution from Manufacturing the Product)

The Manufacturing Division's opportunity cost of production is equal to its relevant unit variable cost per unit, or $21 in this case.

Since the Fabrication Division has excess capacity, the forgone contribution is $0.

There is no mention of avoidable fixed costs.

T(o) = $21 + $0 + $0 = $21

Question 1C3-CQ12

Topic: Performance Measures

Performance results for four geographic divisions of a manufacturing company are shown next.

Division	Target Return on Investment	Actual Return on Investment	Return on Sales
A	18%	18.1%	8%
B	16%	20.0%	8%
C	14%	15.8%	6%
D	12%	11.0%	9%

The division with the **best** performance is:

- ☐ **a.** Division A.
- ☐ **b.** Division B.
- ☐ **c.** Division C.
- ☐ **d.** Division D.

Explanation: The correct answer is: **b.** Division B.

Division B exceeded its target return on investment (ROI) by 25%, which is calculated as shown:

Percent of ROI Achieved = (Actual ROI − Target ROI) / (Actual ROI)

Percent of ROI Achieved = (20 − 16) / 16
= 25%

Divisions A and C exceeded their targets by much less. Division D's actual ROI was lower than its target ROI.

Question 1C3-CQ13

Topic: Performance Measures

KHD Industries is a multidivisional firm that evaluates its managers based on the return on investment (ROI) earned by its divisions. The evaluation and compensation plans use a targeted ROI of 15% (equal to the cost of capital), and managers receive a bonus of 5% of basic compensation for every one percentage point that the division's ROI exceeds 15%.

Dale Evans, manager of the Consumer Products Division, has made a forecast of the division's operations and finances for next year that indicates the ROI would be 24%. In addition, new short-term programs were identified by the Consumer Products Division and evaluated by the finance staff as shown.

Program	Projected ROI
A	13%
B	19%
C	22%
D	31%

Assuming no restrictions on expenditures, what is the optimal mix of new programs that would add value to KHD Industries?

- ☐ **a.** A, B, C, and D
- ☐ **b.** B, C, and D only
- ☐ **c.** C and D only
- ☐ **d.** D only

Explanation: The correct answer is: **b.** B, C, and D only.

KHD would want to invest in any project whose ROI exceeds the corporate target of 15%. Programs B, C, and D all have ROI's that exceed 15%.

Question 1C1-AT03

Topic: Cost and Variance Measures

Franklin Products has an estimated practical capacity of 90,000 machine hours, and each unit requires two machine hours. The next data apply to a recent accounting period.

Actual variable overhead	$240,000
Actual fixed overhead	$442,000
Actual machine **hours** worked	88,000
Actual finished **units** produced	42,000
Budgeted variable overhead at 90,000 machine hours	$200,000
Budgeted fixed overhead	$450,000

Of the following factors, the production volume variance is **most** likely to have been caused by:

- ☐ **a.**   acceptance of an unexpected sales order.
- ☐ **b.**   a wage hike granted to a production supervisor.
- ☐ **c.**   a newly imposed initiative to reduce finished goods inventory levels.
- ☐ **d.**   temporary employment of workers with lower skill levels than originally anticipated.

Explanation: The correct answer is: **c.** a newly imposed initiative to reduce finished goods inventory levels.

Volume variances are caused by a difference in the budgeted fixed overhead and the amount allocated on the basis of actual output. A newly imposed initiative to reduce finished goods inventory levels is consistent with the change in production compared to budget.

A wage hike would affect the spending variance, not the volume variance.

Since the volume variance in this case is unfavorable (amount allocated less than budget), acceptance of an unexpected sales order would not be correct because an unexpected sales order would increase the amount allocated.

Question 1C3-AT19

Topic: Performance Measures

Which one of the following **best** identifies a profit center?

- ☐ **a.** A new car sales division for a large local auto agency
- ☐ **b.** The Information Technology Department of a large consumer products company
- ☐ **c.** A large toy company
- ☐ **d.** The Production Operations Department of a small job-order machine shop company

Explanation: The correct answer is: **a.** A new car sales division for a large local auto agency.

A profit center is a responsibility center whose manager is responsible for revenues as well as costs. Profit is used to measure performance of a new car sales division of a local auto agency, which best identifies a profit center as it has its own costs and revenues.

Question 1C3-AT21

Topic: Performance Measures

The balanced scorecard provides an action plan for achieving competitive success by focusing management attention on key performance indicators. Which one of the following is **not** one of the key performance indicators commonly focused on in the balanced scorecard?

- ☐ **a.** Financial performance measures
- ☐ **b.** Internal business processes
- ☐ **c.** Competitor business strategies
- ☐ **d.** Employee innovation and learning

Explanation: The correct answer is: **c.** Competitor business strategies.

The critical success factors used in the balanced scorecard are:

- Financial performance
- Customer satisfaction
- Internal business processes
- Innovation and learning

Section D: Cost Management
Answers and Explanations

Question 1D1-CQ02

Topic: Measurement Concepts

A company employs a just-in-time (JIT) production system and utilizes back-flush accounting. All acquisitions of raw materials are recorded in a raw materials control account when purchased. All conversion costs are recorded in a control account as incurred, while the assignment of conversion costs are from an allocated conversion cost account. Company practice is to record the cost of goods manufactured at the time the units are completed using the estimated budgeted cost of the goods manufactured.

The budgeted cost per unit for one of the company's products is as shown:

Direct materials	$15.00
Conversion costs	35.00
Total budgeted unit cost	$50.00

During the current accounting period, 80,000 units of product were completed, and 75,000 units were sold. The entry to record the cost of the completed units for the period would be which of the following?

a. Work-In-Process—Control	4,000,000	
Raw Material—Control		1,200,000
Conversion Cost Allocated		2,800,000
b. Finished Goods—Control	4,000,000	
Raw Material—Control		1,200,000
Conversion Cost Allocated		2,800,000
c. Finished Goods—Control	3,750,000	
Raw Material Control		1,125,000
Conversion Cost Allocated		2,625,000
d. Cost of Goods Sold	3,750,000	
Raw Material—Control		1,125,000
Conversion Cost Allocated		2,625,000

Explanation: The correct answer is:

b. Finished Goods—Control	4,000,000	
Raw Material—Control		1,200,000
Conversion Cost Allocated		2,800,000

With JIT, there is no work-in-process inventory. To record the cost of the completed units during the period, the next entries would be made:

Credit the Raw Material—Control account for $1,200,000 (80,000 units @ $15 direct materials each) to show the transfer of raw materials to finished goods. The offsetting debit would go to the Finished Goods—Control account.

Credit the Conversion Cost Allocated account for $2,800,000 (80,000 units @ $35 conversion costs each) to show the transfer of conversion costs to finished goods. The offsetting debit would go to the Finished Goods—Control account.

In total, the Finished Goods—Control account would receive a debit in the amount of $4,000,000, which is made up of $1,200,000 of raw materials and $2,800,000 of conversion costs.

Question 1D1-CQ03

Topic: Measurement Concepts

From the budgeted data shown, calculate the budgeted indirect cost rate that would be used in a normal costing system.

Total direct labor hours	250,000
Direct costs	$10,000,000
Total indirect labor hours	50,000
Total indirect labor-related costs	$ 5,000,000
Total indirect non-labor-related costs	$ 7,000,000

- ☐ **a.** $20/DHL
- ☐ **b.** $28/DHL
- ☐ **c.** $40/DHL
- ☐ **d.** $48/DHL

Explanation: The correct answer is: **d.** $48.

The budgeted indirect cost rate per direct labor hour is calculated as shown.

Budgeted Indirect Labor Cost Rate per Direct Labor Hour
    = (Budgeted Indirect Costs) / (Budgeted Direct Labor Hours)

Budgeted Indirect Labor Cost Rate per Direct Labor Hour
    = ($5,000,000 + $7,000,000) / $250,000

Budgeted Indirect Labor Cost Rate per Direct Labor Hour
    = $12,000,000 / $250,000

Budgeted Indirect Labor Cost Rate per Direct Labor Hour
    = $48 per Direct Labor Hour

Question 1D1-CQ06

Topic: Measurement Concepts

Chassen Company, a cracker and cookie manufacturer, has these unit costs for the month of June.

Variable Manufacturing Cost	Variable Marketing Cost	Fixed Manufacturing Cost	Fixed Marketing Cost
$5.00	$3.50	$2.00	$4.00

A total of 100,000 units were manufactured during June, of which 10,000 remain in ending inventory. Chassen uses the first-in, first-out (FIFO) inventory method, and the 10,000 units are the only finished goods inventory at month-end. Using the full absorption costing method, Chassen's finished goods inventory value would be

- ☐ **a.** $50,000
- ☐ **b.** $70,000
- ☐ **c.** $85,000
- ☐ **d.** $145,000

Explanation: The correct answer is: **b.** $70,000.

The full absorption cost inventory consists of variable and fixed manufacturing costs per unit multiplied by the number of units in the inventory.

$$\text{Full Absorption Cost Inventory} = (\$5 + \$2)\,(10{,}000\ \text{Units})$$
$$= \$7(10{,}000\ \text{Units}) = \$70{,}000$$

Question 1D1-CQ12

Topic: Measurement Concepts

During the month of May, Robinson Corporation sold 1,000 units. The cost per unit for May was as shown:

	Cost per Unit
Direct materials	$ 5.50
Direct labor	3.00
Variable manufacturing overhead	1.00
Fixed manufacturing overhead	1.50
Variable administrative costs	0.50
Fixed administrative costs	3.50
Total	$15.00

May's income using absorption costing was $9,500. The income for May, if variable costing had been used, would have been $9,125. The number of units Robinson produced during May was

☐ **a.**   750 units

☐ **b.**   925 units

☐ **c.**   1,075 units

☐ **d.**   1,250 units

Explanation: The correct answer is: **d.** 1,250 units.

Use the next formula to solve for the production units:

Full Absorption Cost Operating Income = (Variable Cost Operating Income) + (Fixed Manufacturing Cost per Unit) (Production Units – Sales Units)

Full absorption cost operating income is given as $9,500.

Variable cost operating income is given as $9,125.

$9,500 = $9,125 + ($1.50) (Production Units – 1,000 Units)

$9,500 = $9,125 + $1.50 (Production Units) – $1,500

$9,500 = $7,625 + $1.50 (Production Units)

$1,875 = $1.50 (Production Units)

1,250 = Production Units

Question 1D1-CQ13

Topic: Measurement Concepts

Tucariz Company processes Duo into two joint products, Big and Mini. Duo is purchased in 1,000 gallon drums for $2,000. Processing costs are $3,000 to process the 1,000 gallons of Duo into 800 gallons of Big and 200 gallons of Mini. The selling price is $9 per gallon for Big and $4 per gallon for Mini.

The 800 gallons of Big can be processed further into 600 gallons of Giant if $1,000 of additional processing costs are incurred. Giant can be sold for $17 per gallon. If the net-realizable-value (NRV) method was used to allocate costs to the joint products, the total cost of producing Giant would be:

☐ **a.** $5,600

☐ **b.** $5,564

☐ **c.** $5,520

☐ **d.** $4,600

Explanation: The correct answer is: **a.** $5,600.

The NRV of a product at split-off is its market value less the costs to complete and dispose of the product.

The NRV of Giant at split-off is calculated as shown:

NRV of Giant at Split-Off = (Market Value) – (Separable Processing Costs)

Market Value of Giant = (600 Gallons) ($17 Each) = $10,200

NRV of Giant at Split-Off = $10,200 – $1,000 = $9,200

The NRV of Mini at split-off is calculated as shown:

NRV of Mini at Split-Off = (Market Value) – (Separable Processing Costs)

NRV of Mini at Split-Off = (200 Gallons) ($4 Each) = $800

NRV of Giant and Mini = $9,200 + $800 = $10,000

Therefore, Giant's share of the joint costs is ($9,200 / $10,000) ($5,000) = $4,600.

Cost of Using NRV at Split-Off, Giant = (Separable Costs)
                          + (Share of Joint Processing Costs)

Cost of Using NRV at Split-Off, Giant = $1,000 + $4,600 = $5,600

Question 1D1-CQ14
Topic: Measurement Concepts

Tucariz Company processes Duo into two joint products, Big and Mini. Duo is purchased in 1,000 gallon drums for $2,000. Processing costs are $3,000 to process the 1,000 gallons of Duo into 800 gallons of Big and 200 gallons of Mini. The selling price is $9 per gallon for Big and $4 per gallon for Mini.

If the sales value at split-off method is used to allocate joint costs to the final products, the per gallon cost (rounded to the nearest cent) of producing Big is:

- ☐ **a.** $5.63 per gallon
- ☐ **b.** $5.00 per gallon
- ☐ **c.** $4.50 per gallon
- ☐ **d.** $3.38 per gallon

Explanation: The correct answer is: **a.** $5.63 per gallon.

The per gallon cost of Big, using the relative sales value at split-off method, is calculated by finding Big's share of the joint costs and dividing it by the 800 gallons produced.

Sales Value of Big at Split-Off = (800 Gallons) ($9) = $7,200

Sales Value of Mini at Split-Off = (200 Gallons) ($4) = $800

Total Sales Value (Big + Mini) at Split-Off = $7,200 + $800 = $8,000

Big's Share of the Joint Costs = ($7,200/$8,000) ($5,000) = $4,500

Big's Cost per Gallon = $4,500 / 800 Gallons = $5.625, or $5.63 rounded

Question 1D1-CQ15

Topic: Measurement Concepts

Tempo Company produces three products from a joint process. The three products are sold after further processing as there is no market for any of the products at the split-off point. Joint costs per batch are $315,000. Other product information is shown next.

	Product A	Product B	Product C
Units produced per batch	20,000	30,000	50,000
Further processing and marketing cost per unit	$0.70	$3.00	$1.72
Final sales value per unit	$5.00	$6.00	$7.00

If Tempo uses the net realizable value method of allocating joint costs, how much of the joint costs will be allocated to each unit of Product C?

- ☐ **a.** $2.10
- ☐ **b.** $2.65
- ☐ **c.** $3.15
- ☐ **d.** $3.78

Explanation: The correct answer is: **d.** $3.78.

The joint cost per unit assigned to Product C using the net realizable value (NRV) at split-off method is calculated by taking the product's share of the joint costs of $315,000 and dividing it by the 50,000 units produced.

NRV at Split-Off for Product A = (Product A Market Value) − (Separable Costs)

NRV at Split-Off for Product A = (20,000 Units) ($5 per Unit)
                          − (20,000) ($0.70 per Unit)

NRV at Split-Off for Product A = $100,000 − $14,000 = $86,000

NRV at Split-Off for Product B = (Product B Market Value) − (Separable Costs)

NRV at Split-Off for Product B = (30,000 Units) ($6 per Unit) − (30,000 Units) ($3.00 per Unit)

NRV at Split-Off for Product B = $180,000 − $90,000 = $90,000

NRV at Split-Off for Product C = (Product C Market Value) − (Separable Costs)

NRV at Split-Off for Product C = (50,000 Units) ($7 per Unit) − (50,000 Units) ($1.72 per Unit)

NRV at Split-Off for Product C = $350,000 − $86,000 = $264,000

Sum of the Three NRVs = $86,000 + $90,000 + $264,000 = $440,000

Product C's Share of Total Costs = ($264,000 / $440,000) ($315,000) = $189,000

Product C's Cost per Unit Using NRV at Split-Off Method = $189,000/50,000 Units

Product C's Cost per Unit Using NRV at Split-Off Method = $3.78

Question 1D1-CQ16

Topic: Measurement Concepts

Fitzpatrick Corporation uses a joint manufacturing process in the production of two products, Gummo and Xylo. Each batch in the joint manufacturing process yields 5,000 pounds of an intermediate material, Valdene, at a cost of $20,000.

Each batch of Gummo uses 60% of the Valdene and incurs $10,000 of separate costs. The resulting 3,000 pounds of Gummo sells for $10 per pound.

The remaining Valdene is used in the production of Xylo, which incurs $12,000 of separable costs per batch. Each batch of Xylo yields 2,000 pounds and sells for $12 per pound.

Fitzpatrick uses the net realizable value method to allocate the joint material costs. The company is debating whether to process Xylo further into a new product, Zinten, which would incur an additional $4,000 in costs and sell for $15 per pound. If Zinten is produced, income would increase by:

- ☐ **a.** $2,000
- ☐ **b.** $5,760
- ☐ **c.** $14,000
- ☐ **d.** $26,000

Explanation: The correct answer is: **a.** $2,000.

The increase in income from producing Zinten is calculated by taking the $30,000 market value of Zinten (2,000 pounds at $15 per pound) and subtracting both the $24,000 market value of Xylo (2,000 pounds at $12 per pound) and the $4,000 in additional processing costs.

Increase in Income = $30,000 – $24,000 – $4,000 = $2,000

The joint costs and their allocation are sunk and are therefore irrelevant.

Question 1D2-CQ03

Topic: Costing Systems

Loyal Co. produces three types of men's undershirts: T-shirts, V-neck shirts, and athletic shirts. In the Folding and Packaging Department, operations costing is used to apply costs to individual units, based on the standard time allowed to fold and package each type of undershirt. The standard time to fold and package each type of undershirt is shown next.

T-shirt	40 seconds per shirt
V-neck shirt	40 seconds per shirt
Athletic shirt	20 seconds per shirt

During the month of April, Loyal produced and sold 50,000 T-shirts, 30,000 V-neck shirts, and 20,000 athletic shirts. If costs in the Folding and Packaging Department were $78,200 during April, how much folding and packaging cost should be applied to each T-shirt?

- ☐ **a.** $0.5213
- ☐ **b.** $0.6256
- ☐ **c.** $0.7820
- ☐ **d.** $0.8689

Explanation: The correct answer is: **d.** $0.8689.

The folding and packaging cost applied to each T-shirt can be calculated as shown.

Folding and Packaging Cost Applied = (40 Seconds) (Cost Rate per Second)

Cost Rate per Second = ($78,200) / (Total Seconds)

Cost Rate per Second = ($78,200) / [(50,000 T-Shirts) (40 Seconds per Shirt) + (30,000 V-Neck Shirts) (40 Seconds per Shirt) + (20,000 Athletic Shirts) (20 Seconds per Shirt)]

$$\text{Cost Rate per Second} = (\$78,200) / (2,000,000 \text{ Seconds} + 1,200,000 \text{ Seconds} + 400,000 \text{ Seconds})$$

$$\text{Cost Rate per Second} = \$78,200 / 3,600,000 \text{ Seconds}$$

$$\text{Cost Rate per Second} = \$0.0217222 \text{ per Second}$$

$$\text{Cost Applied to Each T-Shirt} = (40 \text{ Seconds}) (0.0217222 \text{ per Second}) = \$0.8689$$

Question 1D2-CQ04

Topic: Costing Systems

During December, Krause Chemical Company had these selected data concerning the manufacture of Xyzine, an industrial cleaner.

Production Flow	Physical Units
Completed and transferred to the next department	100
Add: Ending work-in-process inventory	10 (40% complete as to conversion)
Total units to account for	110
Less: Beginning work-in-process inventory	20 (60% complete as to conversion)
Units started during December	**90**

All material is added at the beginning of processing in this department, and conversion costs are added uniformly during the process. The beginning work-in-process inventory had $120 of raw material and $180 of conversion costs incurred. Material added during December was $540, and conversion costs of $1,484 were incurred. Krause uses the weighted-average process-costing method. The total raw material costs in the ending work-in-process inventory for December are:

- ☐ **a.** $120
- ☐ **b.** $72
- ☐ **c.** $60
- ☐ **d.** $36

Explanation: The correct answer is: **c.** $60.

The total raw material cost in the ending inventory is calculated by taking the equivalent units of raw material in the ending inventory and multiplying it by the raw material costs per equivalent unit.

Total Raw Material Cost, Ending Inventory = (Equivalent Units, Raw Material Ending Inventory) (Raw Material Costs per Equivalent Unit)

The weighted-average method assumes that all units and costs are current (i.e., there is no beginning inventory). Therefore, 110 equivalent units of raw material are required to yield a transfer-out of 100 units and 10 units in the ending inventory.

Raw Material Cost per Equivalent Unit = (Total Material Cost) / (Equivalent Units)

Raw Material Cost per Equivalent Unit = ($120 + $540) / (110 Equivalent Units)

Raw Material Cost per Equivalent Unit = $660 / 110 Units
$$= \$6 \text{ per Unit}$$

Therefore, the total raw material cost, ending inventory = (10 equivalent units) ($6 per unit) = $60.

Question 1D2-CQ08

Topic: Costing Systems

Oster Manufacturing uses a weighted-average process costing system and has these costs and activity during October:

Materials	$40,000
Conversion cost	32,500
Total beginning work-in-process inventory	$72,500
Materials	$700,000
Conversion cost	617,500
Total production costs—October	$1,317,500
Production completed	60,000 units
Work-in-process, October 31	20,000 units

All materials are introduced at the start of the manufacturing process, and conversion cost is incurred uniformly throughout production. Conversations with plant personnel reveal that, on average, month-end in-process inventory is 25% complete. Assuming no spoilage, how should Oster's October manufacturing cost be assigned?

	Production Completed	**Work in Process**
☐	**a.** $1,042,500	$347,500
☐	**b.** $1,095,000	$222,500
☐	**c.** $1,155,000	$235,000
☐	**d.** $1,283,077	$106,923

Explanation: The correct answer is: **c.** $1,155,000 and $235,000.

The cost of the units completed is calculated as shown:

Cost of Units Completed = (Number of Units) (Total Cost per Equivalent Unit)

Cost of Units Completed = (60,000 Units) (Total Cost per Equivalent Unit)

Because all materials are introduced at the start of the manufacturing process, the equivalent units of material for October consist of the completed units and the work-in-process units.

$$
\begin{aligned}
\text{Equivalent Units of Material for October} &= \text{(Completed Production Units)} \\
&\quad + \text{(Work-in-Process Units)} \\
&= 60,000 + 20,000 = 80,000.
\end{aligned}
$$

The Equivalent Units for Conversion are calculated by adding together the units that were started and finished to the equivalent units that were in work-in-process inventory.

$$
\begin{aligned}
\text{Equivalent Units for Conversion} &= \text{(Units Started and Finished)} \\
&\quad + \text{(\% Complete for Conversion) (Ending} \\
&\quad \text{Work-in-Process Inventory)}
\end{aligned}
$$

$$
\begin{aligned}
\text{Equivalent Units for Conversion} &= (60,000) + (0.25)\,(20,000) \\
&= 65,000 \text{ Equivalent Units for Conversion}
\end{aligned}
$$

$$
\text{Cost per Equivalent Unit for Materials} = (\$40,000 + \$700,000)\,/\,80,000 \text{ Equivalent Units}
$$

$$
\begin{aligned}
\text{Cost per Equivalent Unit for Materials} &= \$740,000\,/\,80,000 \text{ Equivalent Units} \\
&= \$9.25
\end{aligned}
$$

$$
\text{Cost per Equivalent Unit for Conversion} = (\$32,500 + \$617,500)\,/\,65,000 \text{ Equivalent Units}
$$

$$
\begin{aligned}
\text{Cost per Equivalent Unit for Conversion} &= \$650,000\,/\,65,000 \text{ Equivalent Units} \\
&= \$10
\end{aligned}
$$

$$
\text{Total Cost per Equivalent Unit} = (\$9.25 + \$10) = \$19.25
$$

The cost of the 60,000 units completed would be calculated as shown:

$$
\text{Cost of Units Completed} = (60,000 \text{ Units})\,(\$19.25) = \$1,155,000
$$

$$
\begin{aligned}
\text{Cost of the Ending Inventory} &= \text{(Equivalent Units for Materials)} \\
&\quad \text{(Materials Cost per Equivalent Unit)} + \\
&\quad \text{(Equivalent Units for Conversion} \\
&\quad \text{Costs) (Conversion Cost per Equivalent Unit)}
\end{aligned}
$$

$$
\begin{aligned}
\text{Cost of the Ending Inventory} &= (20,000 \text{ Equivalent Units for Materials}) \\
&\quad (\$9.25 \text{ per Unit}) + (5,000 \text{ Equivalent Units for} \\
&\quad \text{Conversion}) (\$10 \text{ per Unit}) \\
&= \$235,000
\end{aligned}
$$

Question 1D2-CQ10

Topic: Costing Systems

During December, Krause Chemical Company had these selected data concerning the manufacture of Xyzine, an industrial cleaner:

Production Flow	Physical Units
Completed and transferred to the next department	100
Add: Ending work-in-process inventory	10 (40% complete as to conversion)
Total units to account for	110
Less: Beginning work-in-process inventory	20 (60% complete as to conversion)
Units started during December	**90**

All material is added at the beginning of processing in this department, and conversion costs are added uniformly during the process. The beginning work-in-process inventory had $120 of raw material and $180 of conversion costs incurred. Material added during December was $540, and conversion costs of $1,484 were incurred. Krause uses the weighted-average process-costing method. The total conversion cost assigned to units transferred to the next department in December was

- ☐ **a.** $1,664
- ☐ **b.** $1,600
- ☐ **c.** $1,513
- ☐ **d.** $1,484

Explanation: The correct answer is: **b.** $1,600.

The total conversion cost assigned to the units transferred to the next department can be calculated as shown:

Total Conversion Cost Assigned to Units Transferred to Next Department
= (Number of Units Transferred) (Conversion Cost per Equivalent Unit)

Number of Units Transferred = 100

The weighted-average method assumes that all units and costs are current (i.e., there is no beginning inventory).

Therefore, the Equivalent Units for Conversion Cost
= (Units Completed) + (Units in Ending Inventory) (% Complete).

Equivalent Units for Conversion Cost = (100) + (10) (40%) = 104

Conversion Cost per Equivalent Unit = ($180 + $1,484) / 104 Equivalent Units

Conversion Cost per Equivalent Unit = $1,664 / 104 = $16 per Equivalent Unit

Total Conversion Cost Assigned to the Units Transferred to the Next Department
= (100 Units) ($16) = $1,600

Question 1D2-CQ12

Topic: Costing Systems

Waller Co. uses a weighted-average process-costing system. Material B is added at two different points in the production of shirts; 40% is added when the units are 20% completed, and the remaining 60% of Material B is added when the units are 80% completed. At the end of the quarter, there are 22,000 shirts in process, all of which are 50% completed. With respect to Material B, the ending shirts in process represent how many equivalent units?

- ☐ **a.** 4,400 units
- ☐ **b.** 8,800 units
- ☐ **c.** 11,000 units
- ☐ **d.** 22,000 units

Explanation: The correct answer is: **b.** 8,800 units.

The ending inventory of 22,000 shirts is only 50% complete. Therefore, the inventory units have only 40% of the Material B.

This equates to 8,800 equivalent units, which is calculated by multiplying the number of units in ending inventory (22,000) by the percent of Material B (40%).

$$\text{Equivalent Units, Shirts} = (22{,}000 \text{ Units})(0.4) = 8{,}800 \text{ Units}$$

Question 1D2-CQ14

Topic: Costing Systems

The Chocolate Baker specializes in chocolate baked goods. The firm has long assessed the profitability of a product line by comparing revenues to the cost of goods sold. However, Barry White, the firm's new accountant, wants to use an activity-based costing system that takes into consideration the cost of the delivery person. Listed are activity and cost information relating to two of Chocolate Baker's major products.

	Muffins	**Cheesecake**
Revenue	$53,000	$46,000
Cost of goods sold	$26,000	$21,000
Delivery Activity		
Number of deliveries	150	85
Average length of delivery	10 minutes	15 minutes
Cost per hour for delivery	$20.00	$20.00

Using activity-based costing, which one of the following statements is correct?

☐ **a.**   The muffins are $2,000 more profitable.

☐ **b.**   The cheesecakes are $75 more profitable.

☐ **c.**   The muffins are $1,925 more profitable.

☐ **d.**   The muffins have a higher profitability as a percentage of sales and, therefore, are more advantageous.

Explanation: The correct answer is: **c.** The muffins are $1,925 more profitable.

The gross profit for muffins after assigning delivery costs would be calculated as shown:

Gross Profit, Muffins = Revenue – Cost of Goods Sold – Assigned Delivery Costs

Gross Profit, Muffins = $53,000 – $26,000 – Assigned Delivery Costs

Gross Profit, Muffins = $27,000 – Assigned Delivery Costs

The assigned delivery costs are calculated as shown:

Assigned Delivery Costs, Muffins = (Number of Deliveries) (Cost per Delivery)

Assigned Delivery Costs, Muffins = (150 Deliveries) (10 Minutes / 60 Minutes) ($20 per Hour)
= $500

Gross Profit for Muffins = $27,000 – $500 = $26,500.

The gross profit for cheesecake after assigning delivery costs would be calculated as shown:

Gross Profit, Cheesecake = Revenue – Cost of Goods Sold – Assigned Delivery Costs

Gross Profit, Cheesecake = $46,000 – $21,000 – Assigned Delivery Costs

Gross Profit, Cheesecake = $25,000 – Assigned Delivery Costs

The assigned delivery costs are calculated as shown:

Assigned Delivery Costs, Cheesecake = (Number of Deliveries) (Cost per Delivery)

Assigned Delivery Costs, Cheesecake = (85 Deliveries) (15 Minutes/ 60 Minutes) ($20 per Hour)
= $425

Gross Profit for Cheesecake = $25,000 − $425 = $24,575

The gross profit for cheesecake is $1,925 less than the gross profit for muffins.

$26,500 − $24,575 = $1,925

Question 1D3-CQ01
Topic: Overhead Costs

During December, Krause Chemical Company had these selected data concerning the manufacture of Xyzine, an industrial cleaner.

Production Flow	Physical Units
Completed and transferred to the next department	100
Add: Ending work-in-process inventory	10 (40% complete as to conversion)
Total units to account for	110
Less: Beginning work-in-process inventory	20 (60% complete as to conversion)
Units started during December	**90**

All material is added at the beginning of processing in this department, and conversion costs are added uniformly during the process. The beginning work-in-process inventory had $120 of raw material and $180 of conversion costs incurred. Material added during December was $540, and conversion costs of $1,484 were incurred. Krause uses the first-in, first-out (FIFO) process-costing method. The equivalent units of production used to calculate conversion costs for December was:

- ☐ **a.** 110 units
- ☐ **b.** 104 units
- ☐ **c.** 100 units
- ☐ **d.** 92 units

Explanation: The correct answer is: **d.** 92 units.

FIFO follows the actual flow of the units through the process. Therefore, the equivalent units of production used to calculate conversion costs for December can be calculated as shown:

Equivalent Units, Conversion Costs = (Units in Beginning Inventory)
(1 − Completion Rate at the Beginning of the Period) + (Units Started and Finished) + (Units in Ending Inventory) (Completion %)

Equivalent Units, Conversion Costs = (20 Units) (1 − 0.6) + (80 Units)
+ (10 Units) (0.4)

Equivalent Units, Conversion Costs = 8 Units + 80 Units + 4 Units = 92 Units

Question 1D3-CQ03

Topic: Overhead Costs

Cynthia Rogers, the cost accountant for Sanford Manufacturing, is preparing a management report that must include an allocation of overhead. The budgeted overhead for each department and the data for one job are shown next.

	Department	
	Tooling	**Fabricating**
Supplies	$ 690	$ 80
Supervisor's salaries	1,400	1,800
Indirect labor	1,000	4,000
Depreciation	1,200	5,200
Repairs	4,400	3,000
Total budgeted overhead	$8,690	$14,080
Total direct labor hours	440	640
Direct labor hours on Job #231	10	2

Using the departmental overhead application rates and allocating overhead on the basis of direct labor hours, overhead applied to Job #231 in the Tooling Department would be:

- ☐ **a.** $44.00
- ☐ **b.** $197.50
- ☐ **c.** $241.50
- ☐ **d.** $501.00

Explanation: The correct answer is: **b.** $197.50.

The overhead applied to Job #231 in the Tooling Department is calculated as shown:

Tooling Overhead Applied, Job #231 = (Tooling Overhead Rate) (Number of Direct Labor Hours Used by Job #231)

Tooling Overhead Rate = (Total Tooling Overhead Costs) / (Total Direct Labor Hours Used in Tooling Department)

Tooling Overhead Rate = ($8,690) / (440 Direct Labor Hours)
= $19.75 per Direct Labor Hour

Tooling Overhead Applied, Job #231 = ($19.75) (10 Direct Labor Hours)
= $197.50

Question 1D3-CQ05

Topic: Overhead Costs

Atmel Inc. manufactures and sells two products. Data with regard to these products are given next.

	Product A	Product B
Units produced and sold	30,000	12,000
Machine hours required per unit	2	3
Receiving orders per product line	50	150
Production orders per product line	12	18
Production runs	8	12
Inspections	20	30

Total budgeted machine hours are 100,000. The budgeted overhead costs are shown next.

Receiving costs	$450,000
Engineering costs	300,000
Machine setup costs	25,000
Inspection costs	200,000
Total budgeted overhead	$975,000

The cost driver for engineering costs is the number of production orders per product line. Using activity-based costing, what would the engineering cost per unit for Product B be?

☐ **a.** $4.00

☐ **b.** $10.00

☐ **c.** $15.00

☐ **d.** $29.25

Explanation: The correct answer is: **c.** $15.00.

The engineering cost per unit for Product B is calculated as shown:

Engineering Cost per Unit, Product B
= [(Engineering Cost per Production Order) (Number of Production Orders for Product B)] / (Number of Units of Product B)

Engineering Cost per Production Order = ($300,000) / 30 Total Production Orders

Engineering Cost per Production Order = $10,000 per Production Order

Engineering Cost per Unit, Product B = [($10,000) (18)] / (12,000 Units)
= $15 per Unit

Question 1D3-CQ08

Topic: Overhead Costs

Logo Inc. has two data services departments (the Systems Department and the Facilities Department) that provide support to the company's three production departments (Machining Department, Assembly Department, and Finishing Department). The overhead costs of the Systems Department are allocated to other departments on the basis of computer usage hours. The overhead costs of the Facilities Department are allocated based on square feet occupied (in thousands). Other information pertaining to Logo is as shown next.

Department	Overhead	Computer Usage Hours	Square Feet Occupied
Systems	$200,000	300	1,000
Facilities	100,000	900	600
Machining	400,000	3,600	2,000
Assembly	550,000	1,800	3,000
Finishing	620,000	2,700	5,000
		9,300	11,600

Logo employs the step-down method of allocating service department costs and begins with the Systems Department. Which one of the following correctly denotes the amount of the Systems Department's overhead that would be allocated to the Facilities Department and the Facilities Department's overhead charges that would be allocated to the Machining Department?

	Systems to Facilities	**Facilities to Machining**
☐ **a.**	$0	$20,000
☐ **b.**	$19,355	$20,578
☐ **c.**	$20,000	$20,000
☐ **d.**	$20,000	$24,000

Explanation: The correct answer is: **d.** $20,000 and $24,000.

The amount of the Systems Department's overhead that would be allocated to the Facilities Department is calculated as follows:

Systems Department Overhead Allocated to Facilities Department
= [(Number of Facilities Computer Usage Hours) (Systems Department Overhead Cost)] / (Number of Computer Usage Hours Used by All Departments Except System)

System's Department Overhead Allocated to Facilities Department
= [(900 Hours) ($200,000)] / (9,000 Hours) = $20,000

The Facilities Department now has $120,000 to allocate to the three production departments.

The Facilities Department's overhead charges that would be allocated to the Machining Department are:

Facilities Department Overhead to Be Allocated to Machining Department
= ($120,000) (2,000 Square Feet Occupied by Machining) / (10,000 Square Feet Occupied by the Three Production Departments)

Facilities Department Overhead to Be Allocated to Machining Department
= $24,000

Question 1D3-CQ09

Topic: Overhead Costs

Adam Corporation manufactures computer tables and has this budgeted indirect manufacturing cost information for next year:

	Support Departments		Operating Departments		
	Maintenance	Systems	Machining	Fabrication	Total
Budgeted Overhead	$360,000	$95,000	$200,000	$300,000	$955,000
Support work furnished					
From Maintenance		10%	50%	40%	100%
From Systems	5%		45%	50%	100%

If Adam uses the direct method to allocate support department costs to production departments, the total overhead (rounded to the nearest dollar) for the Machining Department to allocate to its products would be which of the following?

- ☐ **a.** $418,000
- ☐ **b.** $422,750
- ☐ **c.** $442,053
- ☐ **d.** $445,000

Explanation: The correct answer is: **d.** $445,000.

The direct method of cost allocation assumes service departments serve production only. There are no interservice department services. Therefore, the total overhead for the Machining Department to allocate to its products is calculated as:

Total Overhead, Machining Department
= (Machining Department Overhead) + (Machining Department Share of Maintenance Overhead) + (Machining Department Share of Systems' Overhead)

Total Overhead, Machining Department

$$= (\$200,000) + [(0.50) / (0.50 + 0.40)] (\$360,000) + [(0.45) / (0.45 + 0.50)] (\$95,000)$$

$$\text{Total Overhead, Machining Department} = \$200,000 + \$200,000 + \$45,000 = \$445,000$$

Section E: Internal Controls Answers and Explanations

Question 1E1-CQ01

Topic: Governance, Risk, and Compliance

A firm is constructing a risk analysis to quantify the exposure of its data center to various types of threats. Which one of the following situations would represent the highest annual loss exposure after adjustment for insurance proceeds?

		Frequency of Occurrence (years)	Loss Amount	Insurance (% coverage)
☐	**a.**	1	$ 15,000	85
☐	**b.**	8	$75,000	80
☐	**c.**	20	$200,000	80
☐	**d.**	100	$400,000	50

Explanation: The correct answer is: **a.** 1, $15,000, 85.

The exposure is the same as the expected loss, which is calculated by dividing 1 by the "Frequency of Occurrence," multiplying it by the loss amount, and then multiplying that by 1 minus the "Insurance % coverage" rate.

Expected Loss = (Frequency of Occurrence) (Loss Amount)
(1 – % Insurance Coverage)

For answer a, the Expected Loss = (1/1) ($15,000) (1– 0.85) = $2,250.

For answer b, the Expected Loss = (1/8) ($75,000) (1– 0.8) = $1,875.

For answer c, the Expected Loss = (1/20) ($200,000) (1– 0.8) = $2,000.

For answer d, the Expected Loss = (1/100) ($400,000) (1– 0.5) = $2,000.

Answer a represents the highest annual loss exposure after adjusting for insurance proceeds.

Question 1E1-AT12

Topic: Governance, Risk, and Compliance

When management of the sales department has the opportunity to override the system of internal controls of the accounting department, a weakness exists in which of the following?

☐ **a.** Risk management

☐ **b.** Information and communication

☐ **c.** Monitoring

☐ **d.** Control environment

Explanation: The correct answer is: **d.** Control environment. The control environment includes attitude of management toward the concept of controls.

Question 1E1-AT04

Topic: Governance, Risk, and Compliance

Segregation of duties is a fundamental concept in an effective system of internal control. Nevertheless, the internal auditor must be aware that this safeguard can be compromised through

☐ **a.** lack of training of employees.

☐ **b.** collusion among employees.

☐ **c.** irregular employee reviews.

☐ **d.** absence of internal auditing.

Explanation: The correct answer is: **b.** collusion among employees.

Effective segregation of duties means that no single employee has control over authorization, recording, and custody. If two or more employees are in collusion, these controls can be overridden.

Question 1E1-AT05

Topic: Governance, Risk, and Compliance

A company's management is concerned about computer data eavesdropping and wants to maintain the confidentiality of its information as it is transmitted. The company should utilize:

☐ **a.** data encryption.

☐ **b.** dial-back systems.

☐ **c.** message acknowledgment procedures.

☐ **d.** password codes.

Explanation: The correct answer is: **a.** data encryption.

Data encryption, which uses secret codes, ensures that data transmissions are protected from unauthorized tampering or electronic eavesdropping.

Question 1E1-AT08

Topic: Governance, Risk, and Compliance

Preventive controls are:

☐ **a.** usually more cost beneficial than detective controls.

☐ **b.** usually more costly to use than detective controls.

☐ **c.** found only in general accounting controls.

☐ **d.** found only in accounting transaction controls.

Explanation: The correct answer is: **a.** usually more cost beneficial than detective controls.

The three types of controls designed into information systems are preventive, detective, and corrective. Preventive controls are designed to prevent threats, errors, and irregularities from occurring. They are more cost beneficial than detecting and correcting the problems that threats, errors, and irregularities can cause.

Question 1E1-AT10

Topic: Governance, Risk, and Compliance

Which of the following is **not** a requirement regarding a company's system of internal control under the Foreign Corrupt Practices Act of 1977?

☐ **a.** Management must annually assess the effectiveness of its system of internal control.

☐ **b.** Transactions are executed in accordance with management's general or specific authorization.

☐ **c.** Transactions are recorded as necessary (1) to permit preparation of financial statements in conformity with GAAP or any other criteria applicable to such statements, and (2) to maintain accountability for assets.

☐ **d.** The recorded accountability for assets is compared with the existing assets at reasonable intervals, and appropriate action is taken with respect to any differences.

Explanation: The correct answer is: **a.** Management must annually assess the effectiveness of its system of internal control.

Management's annual assessment of internal control is not a requirement of the Foreign Corrupt Practices Act. It became a requirement with the passage of the 2002 Sarbanes-Oxley Act.

Question 1E2-AT11

Topic: System Controls and Security Measures

Which one of the following would **most** compromise the use of the grandfather-father-son principle of file retention as protection against loss or damage of master files?

- ☐ **a.** Use of magnetic tape
- ☐ **b.** Inadequate ventilation
- ☐ **c.** Storing of all files in one location
- ☐ **d.** Failure to encrypt data

Explanation: The correct answer is: **c.** Storing of all files in one location.

Storing all files in one location undermines the concept of multiple backups inherent in the grandfather-father-son principle.

Question 1E2-AT12

Topic: System Controls and Security Measures

In entering the billing address for a new client in Emil Company's computerized database, a clerk erroneously entered a nonexistent zip code. As a result, the first month's bill mailed to the new client was returned to Emil Company. Which one of the following would **most** likely have led to discovery of the error at the time of entry into Emil Company's computerized database?

- ☐ **a.** Limit test
- ☐ **b.** Validity test
- ☐ **c.** Parity test
- ☐ **d.** Record count test

Explanation: The correct answer is: **b.** Validity test.

A validity test compares data against a master file for accuracy. Data that cannot possibly be correct (e. g. , a nonexistent zip code) would be discovered at that time.

Question 1E2-AT07

Topic: System Controls and Security Measures

In the organization of the information systems function, the **most** important separation of duties is:

☐ **a.** ensuring that those responsible for programming the system do not have access to data processing operations.

☐ **b.** not allowing the data librarian to assist in data processing operations.

☐ **c.** using different programming personnel to maintain utility programs from those who maintain the application programs.

☐ **d.** having a separate department that prepares the transactions for processing and verifies the correct entry of the transactions.

Explanation: The correct answer is: **a.** assuring that those responsible for programming the system do not have access to data processing operations.

The information technology (IT) function should be separate from the other functional areas in the organization. In addition, within IT, there should be a separation between programmers/analysts, operations, and technical support.

Question 1E2-AT01

Topic: System Controls and Security Measures

Accounting controls are concerned with the safeguarding of assets and the reliability of financial records. Consequently, these controls are designed to provide reasonable assurance that all of the following take place **except**:

☐ **a.** executing transactions in accordance with management's general or specific authorization.

☐ **b.** comparing recorded assets with existing assets at periodic intervals and taking appropriate action with respect to differences.

☐ **c.** recording transactions as necessary to permit preparation of financial statements in conformity with generally accepted accounting principles and maintaining accountability for assets.

☐ **d.** compliance with methods and procedures ensuring operational efficiency and adherence to managerial policies.

Explanation: The correct answer is: **d.** compliance with methods and procedures ensuring operational efficiency and adherence to managerial policies.

An internal control system is concerned with safeguarding assets, accuracy and reliability of records, operational efficiency, adherence to policy, and compliance with laws and regulations. The first two are called accounting controls. The latter three are referred to as administrative controls.

Question 1E2-AT05

Topic: System Controls and Security Measures

A critical aspect of a disaster recovery plan is to be able to regain operational capability as soon as possible. In order to accomplish this, an organization can have an arrangement with its computer hardware vendor to have a fully operational facility available that is configured to the user's specific needs. This is **best** known as a(n)

- ☐ **a.** uninterruptible power system.
- ☐ **b.** parallel system.
- ☐ **c.** cold site.
- ☐ **d.** hot site.

Explanation: The correct answer is: **d.** hot site.

A hot site is a backup site in another location that has the company's hardware and software and is ready to run on a moment's notice.

Section F: Technology and Analytics Questions and Answers

Question tb.er.plan.sys.003_1905

Topic: Information systems

Which of the following economic principles can help an Enterprise Resource Planning (ERP) system to integrate financial systems and nonfinancial systems?

- ☐ **a.** Economies of scale
- ☐ **b.** Economies of scope
- ☐ **c.** Economies of skills
- ☐ **d.** Economies of technology

Explanation: The correct answer is **b.** Economies of scope

Economies of scope refers to gaining efficiencies with the integration of the number of products, services, systems, functions, and activities in an organization. For example, integrating financial systems with nonfinancial systems is an example of economies of scope. Similarly, integrating all business functions such as manufacturing, marketing, accounting, finance, and human resources is another example of economies of scope. Basically, economies of scope refers to the ability of a firm to produce multiple products or render multiple services more inexpensively in combination than separately.

Question tb.er.plan.sys.011_1905

Topic: Information systems

Structured query language (SQL) and query-by-example (QBE) are heavily used as query tools in which of the following database models?

- ☐ **a.** Network data model
- ☐ **b.** Relational data model
- ☐ **c.** Object data model
- ☐ **d.** Hierarchical data model

Explanation: The correct answer is **b.** Relational data model

Structured query language (SQL) is a data manipulation language that is heavily used in relational database management systems. SQL statements are written in the form of SQL scripts without using a graphical user interface. SQL is used to enter (insert), modify database. Similarly, query-by-example (QBE), which is a graphical query language, is also heavily used in relational database management systems. The QBE language, which is an intermediary step, is converted into SQL language for final execution of user queries in the background. In the QBE, user queries are shown to the database as user examples to tell the system what the user really wants the database to do. Hence, the relational data model heavily uses the SQL and QBE as query tools.

Question tb.er.plan.sys.017_1905

Topic: Information systems

Which of the following cases most closely fits the characteristics of a data warehouse solution?

☐ **a.** A large, centralized, international online retailer that wants real-time analysis of customer interaction for its suggestion engine.

☐ **b.** A non-profit organization with three distinct business units, each with its own IT system and infrastructure, and a need to perform periodic analysis of performance across all business units.

☐ **c.** An association of independently owned convenience stores and gas stations that want to provide members with in-depth statistical analysis of customer trends across the association.

☐ **d.** A large organization with a substantial one-year budget to create an analytics platform that will allow users and analysts to build analysis of historical customer activity and, once set up, operate for up to five years after deployment.

Explanation: The correct answer is **b.** A non-profit organization with three distinct business units, each with its own IT system and infrastructure, and a need to perform periodic analysis of performance across all business units.

A data warehouse does provide a centralized location for collected data and supports periodic analysis of historical data.

Question tb.sec.brch.002_1905

Topic: Data governance

Security controls mitigate a wide variety of information security risks. Security Awareness Training would **best** fall under which of the following controls?

☐ **a.** Compensating and Corrective

☐ **b.** Preventive and Deterrent

☐ **c.** Preventive

☐ **d.** Corrective

Explanation: The correct answer is **b.** Preventive and Deterrent

Security Awareness training is both a Preventive and Deterrent control where as a Preventive control it stops unauthorized or unwanted activity from occurring and as a Deterrent control it discourages the same type of activities.

Question tb.sec.brch.011_1905

Topic: Data governance

Which of the following statements is **true** about a firewall and an intrusion detection system (IDS)?

- [ ] **a.** Firewalls are a substitution for an IDS.
- [ ] **b.** Firewalls are an alternative to an IDS.
- [ ] **c.** Firewalls are a complement to an IDS.
- [ ] **d.** Firewalls are a replacement for an IDS.

Explanation: The correct answer is **c.** Firewalls are a complement to an IDS.

An intrusion detection system (IDS) should be used as a complement to a firewall, not as a substitute, alternative, or replacement for it. Together, they provide a synergistic strong effect. A firewall is a hardware or software providing protection against outside attackers by shielding a user's computer or network from malicious or unnecessary network traffic. Firewalls can also prevent malicious software (malware) from accessing a computer or network via the Internet. Firewalls can be configured to block data from certain locations using computer network addresses, applications, or ports while allowing relevant and necessary data through using rules.

An IDS is a hardware or software product that gathers and analyzes information from various areas within a computer or a network to identify possible security breaches, which include intrusions (hacker attacks from outside the organization) and misuse (employee attacks from within the organization).

Question tb.sec.brch.022_1905

Topic: Data governance

Regarding cyberattacks, identity thieves can get personal information through which of the following means?

I. Dumpster diving

II. Skimming

III. Phishing

IV. Pretexting

- [ ] **a.** I only
- [ ] **b.** III only
- [ ] **c.** I and III
- [ ] **d.** I, II, III, and IV

Explanation: The correct answer is **d.** I, II, III, and IV

Identity thieves get personal information by stealing records or information while they are on the job, bribing an employee who has access to these records, hacking electronic records, and conning information out of employees. Sources of personal information include dumpster diving, which includes rummaging through personal trash, a business's trash, or public trash dumps. Skimming includes stealing credit card or debit card numbers by capturing the information in a data storage device. Phishing and pretexting deal with stealing information through email or phone by posing as legitimate companies and claiming that you have a problem with your account. This practice is known as phishing online or pretexting (social engineering) by phone respectively.

Pretext callers who are fraudsters use pieces of a customer's personal information to impersonate an account holder to gain access to that individual's account information. Armed with personal information, such as an individual's name, address, and Social Security number, a pretext caller may try to convince a bank's employee to provide confidential account information. While pretext calling may be difficult to spot, there are measures banks can take to reduce the incidence of pretext calling, such as limiting the circumstances under which customer information may be disclosed by telephone. A bank's policy could be that customer information is disclosed only through email, text message, a letter, or in-person meeting.

Question tb. sys.dev.lc.002_1905

Topic: Technology-enabled finance transformation

Which of the following phases of the System Development Lifecycle can be **best** described as the project plan is put into motion and the work of the project is performed?

- ☐ **a.** Maintenance
- ☐ **b.** Design
- ☐ **c.** Implementation
- ☐ **d.** Analysis

Explanation: The correct answer is **c.** Implementation

The Implementation Phase involves putting the project plan into action. The activities required to build each deliverable will be clearly specified within the project requirements document and project plan.

Question tb. sys.dev.lc.014_1905

Topic: Technology-enabled finance transformation

Which of the following describes a financial administrative activity that is currently carried out manually that is a candidate for process automation?

- ☐ **a.** The organization's Controller and CFO receive a dashboard containing quarterly results.
- ☐ **b.** The creation of a P&L report is generated using bots rather than humans to allocate and aggregate the data to be presented.
- ☐ **c.** Credit card payment chargebacks are automatically adjusted on monthly sales reports.
- ☐ **d.** Customer data is automatically encrypted upon form entry within the organization's website.

Explanation: The correct answer is **b.** The creation of a P&L report is generated using bots rather than humans to allocate and aggregate the data to be presented.

Typically the process to create a P&L report has been traditionally manual, whereas the utilization of bots can automate the entire report creation process.

Question tb. proc.au.001_1905

Topic: Technology-enabled finance transformation

A business brings in a new application that performs valuation modeling. Which of the following **best** describes this innovative capability?

- ☐ **a.** The model can calculate the valuation of an asset based on user input.
- ☐ **b.** The model can calculate the valuation of an asset using the 10k or 8k filing.
- ☐ **c.** The model can quickly calculate the valuation of an asset using process automation.
- ☐ **d.** The model can quickly calculate the valuation of an asset using data points around the asset and historical examples.

Explanation: The correct answer is **d.** The model can quickly calculate the valuation of an asset using data points around the asset and historical examples.

Valuation modeling enables an organization to obtain near-accurate valuations based on historical data and industry trends.

Question tb.bus.int.001_1905

Topic: Data analytics

Which of the following would be the **best** answer that describes a business reason to utilize Data Analytics?

- ☐ **a.** An organization wishes to automate processes such as repetitive data entry that are entered via OCR scanning of documents and input into the respective fields.
- ☐ **b.** The CFO and Controller want to see daily reports in the form of dashboards outlining cash flow, accounts receivable, accounts payable, etc.
- ☐ **c.** Internal investigations requests to have the capability to forensically assess data to determine if fraud or corrupt practices are being carried out.
- ☐ **d.** An organization wishes to assess a large volume of data for trends, filtering, and visualization in order to make the information easier to comprehend.

Explanation: The correct answer is **d.** An organization wishes to assess a large volume of data for trends, filtering, and visualization in order to make the information easier to comprehend.

Data analytics will empower the business to intake a large amount of data to make intelligent decisions based on the trends identified.

Question tb.bus.int.006_1905

Topic: Data analytics

Which analytical model would be the **best** choice if a company wishes to test the prediction that is in the form of a quantity?

- ☐ **a.** Intelligence modeling
- ☐ **b.** Regression modeling
- ☐ **c.** Classification modeling
- ☐ **d.** Clustering modeling

Explanation: The correct answer is **b.** Regression modeling

A regression problem requires the prediction of a quantity; the regression can have real-valued or discrete input variables.

Further, a regression problem where input variables are ordered by time is called a time series forecasting problem.

Question tb.ana.too.002_1905

Topic: Data analytics

The makers of home appliances and automobiles are **most** impacted by which of the following components of the time-series data?

- ☐ **a.** Trend component
- ☐ **b.** Cyclical component
- ☐ **c.** Seasonal component
- ☐ **d.** Irregular component

Explanation: The correct answer is **b.** Cyclical component

The makers of home appliances and automobiles are most impacted by the cyclical component of the time-series data. Cyclical fluctuations repeat themselves in a general pattern in the long term, but occur with differing frequencies and intensities. Thus, they can be isolated, but not totally predicted.

Time-series analyses use past data points to project future data points and have four components: trends (upward or downward data movement), cycles (data patterns that occur every several years that tie into the business cycles), seasonality (data pattern that repeats itself periodically in weeks and months), and random variation (no data patterns shown as bumps or blips in the data that are caused by chance and unusual conditions and hence cannot be predicted). This random variation is called the irregular component.

ICMA Learning Outcome Statements—Part 1

(Content Specification Outline effective January 2020, revised June 2020)

PART 1—Financial Planning, Performance, and Analytics

Section A. External Financial Reporting Decisions (15%—Levels A, B, and C)

Part 1—Section A.1. Financial statements

For the balance sheet, income statement, statement of changes in equity, and the statement of cash flows, the candidate should be able to:

a. identify the users of these financial statements and their needs
b. demonstrate an understanding of the purposes and uses of each statement
c. identify the major components and classifications of each statement
d. identify the limitations of each financial statement
e. identify how various financial transactions affect the elements of each of the financial statements and determine the proper classification of the transaction
f. demonstrate an understanding of the relationship among the financial statements
g. demonstrate an understanding of how a balance sheet, an income statement, a statement of changes in equity, and a statement of cash flows (indirect method) are prepared

With respect to integrated reporting, the candidate should be able to:

h. define integrated reporting (IR), integrated thinking, and the integrated report and demonstrate an understanding of the relationship between them
i. identify the primary purpose of IR
j. explain the fundamental concepts of value creation, the six capitals, and the value creation process
k. identify elements of an integrated report; i.e., organizational overview and external environment, governance, business model, risks and opportunities, strategy and resource allocation, performance, outlook, basis of preparation, and presentation
l. identify and explain the benefits and challenges of adopting IR

Part 1—Section A.2. Recognition, measurement, valuation, and disclosure

The candidate should be able to:

Asset valuation

  a. identify issues related to the valuation of accounts receivable, including timing of recognition and estimation of the allowance for credit losses
  b. distinguish between receivables sold (factoring) on a with-recourse basis and those sold on a without-recourse basis, and determine the effect on the balance sheet
  c. identify issues in inventory valuation, including which goods to include, what costs to include, and which cost assumption to use
  d. identify and compare cost flow assumptions used in accounting for inventories
  e. demonstrate an understanding of the lower of cost or market rule for LIFO and the retail inventory method and the lower of cost and net realizable value rule for all other inventory methods
  f. calculate the effect on income and on assets of using different inventory methods
  g. analyze the effects of inventory errors
  h. identify advantages and disadvantages of the different inventory methods
  i. recommend the inventory method and cost flow assumption that should be used for a firm given a set of facts
  j. demonstrate an understanding of the following debt security types: trading, available-for-sale, and held-to-maturity
  k. demonstrate an understanding of the valuation of debt and equity securities
  l. determine the effect on the financial statements of using different depreciation methods
  m. recommend a depreciation method for a given set of data
  n. demonstrate an understanding of the accounting for impairment of long-term assets and intangible assets, including goodwill

Valuation of liabilities

  o. identify the classification issues of short-term debt expected to be refinanced
  p. compare the effect on financial statements when using either the assurance warranty approach or the service warranty approach for accounting for warranties

Income taxes (applies to Assets and Liabilities subtopics)

  q. demonstrate an understanding of interperiod tax allocation/deferred income taxes
  r. distinguish between deferred tax liabilities and deferred tax assets
  s. differentiate between temporary differences and permanent differences and identify examples of each

Leases (applies to Assets and Liabilities subtopics)

  t. distinguish between operating and finance leases
  u. recognize the correct financial statement presentation of operating and finance leases

Equity transactions

  v. identify transactions that affect paid-in capital and those that affect retained earnings
  w. determine the effect on shareholders' equity of large and small stock dividends, and stock splits

Revenue recognition

  x. apply revenue recognition principles to various types of transactions
  y. demonstrate an understanding of revenue recognition for contracts with customers using the five steps required to recognize revenue
  z. demonstrate an understanding of the matching principle with respect to revenues and expenses and be able to apply it to a specific situation

Income measurement

  aa. define gains and losses and indicate the proper financial statement presentation
  bb. demonstrate an understanding of the treatment of gain or loss on the disposal of fixed assets
  cc. demonstrate an understanding of expense recognition practices
  dd. define and calculate comprehensive income
  ee. identify the correct treatment of discontinued operations

GAAP–IFRS differences

Major differences in reported financial results when using GAAP vs. IFRS and the impact on analysis

  ff. identify and describe the following differences between U.S. GAAP and IFRS: (i) expense recognition, with respect to share-based payments and employee benefits; (ii) intangible assets, with respect to development costs and revaluation; (iii) inventories, with respect to costing methods, valuation, and write-downs (e.g., LIFO); (iv) leases, with respect to lessee operating and finance leases; (v) long-lived assets, with respect to revaluation, depreciation, and capitalization of borrowing costs; and (vi) impairment of assets, with respect to determination, calculation, and reversal of loss

Section B. Planning, Budgeting, and Forecasting (20%—Levels A, B, and C)

Part 1—Section B.1. Strategic planning

The candidate should be able to:

a. discuss how strategic planning determines the path an organization chooses for attaining its long-term goals, vision, and mission, and distinguish between vision and mission
b. identify the time frame appropriate for a strategic plan
c. identify the external factors that should be analyzed during the strategic planning process and understand how this analysis leads to recognition of organizational opportunities, limitations, and threats
d. identify the internal factors that should be analyzed during the strategic planning process and explain how this analysis leads to recognition of organizational strengths, weaknesses, and competitive advantages
e. demonstrate an understanding of how the mission leads to the formulation of long-term business objectives such as business diversification, the addition or deletion of product lines, or the penetration of new markets
f. explain why short-term objectives, tactics for achieving these objectives, and operational planning (master budget) must be congruent with the strategic plan and contribute to the achievement of long-term strategic goals
g. identify the characteristics of successful strategic plans
h. describe Porter's generic strategies, including cost leadership, differentiation, and focus
i. demonstrate an understanding of the following planning tools and techniques: SWOT analysis, Porter's 5 forces, situational analysis, PEST analysis, scenario planning, competitive analysis, contingency planning, and the BCG Growth-Share Matrix

Part 1—Section B.2. Budgeting concepts

The candidate should be able to:

a. describe the role that budgeting plays in the overall planning and performance evaluation process of an organization
b. explain the interrelationships between economic conditions, industry situation, and a firm's plans and budgets
c. identify the role that budgeting plays in formulating short-term objectives and planning and controlling operations to meet those objectives
d. demonstrate an understanding of the role that budgets play in measuring performance against established goals
e. identify the characteristics that define successful budgeting processes
f. explain how the budgeting process facilitates communication among organizational units and enhances coordination of organizational activities

g. describe the concept of a controllable cost as it relates to both budgeting and performance evaluation

h. explain how the efficient allocation of organizational resources are planned during the budgeting process

i. identify the appropriate time frame for various types of budgets

j. identify who should participate in the budgeting process for optimum success

k. describe the role of top management in successful budgeting

l. demonstrate an understanding of the use of cost standards in budgeting

m. differentiate between ideal (theoretical) standards and currently attainable (practical) standards

n. differentiate between authoritative standards and participative standards

o. identify the steps to be taken in developing standards for both direct material and direct labor

p. demonstrate an understanding of the techniques that are used to develop standards such as activity analysis and the use of historical data

q. discuss the importance of a policy that allows budget revisions that accommodate the impact of significant changes in budget assumptions

r. explain the role of budgets in monitoring and controlling expenditures to meet strategic objectives

s. define budgetary slack and discuss its impact on goal congruence

Part 1—Section B.3. Forecasting techniques

The candidate should be able to:

a. demonstrate an understanding of a simple regression equation

b. define a multiple regression equation and recognize when multiple regression is an appropriate tool to use for forecasting

c. calculate the result of a simple regression equation

d. demonstrate an understanding of learning curve analysis

e. calculate the results under a cumulative average-time learning model

f. list the benefits and shortcomings of regression analysis and learning curve analysis

g. calculate the expected value of random variables

h. identify the benefits and shortcomings of expected value techniques

i. use probability values to estimate future cash flows

Part 1—Section B.4. Budget methodologies

For each of the budget systems identified (annual/master budgets, project budgeting, activity-based budgeting, zero-based budgeting, continuous (rolling) budgets, and flexible budgeting), the candidate should be able to:

a. define its purpose, appropriate use, and time frame

b. identify the budget components and explain the interrelationships among the components

   c. demonstrate an understanding of how the budget is developed

   d. compare and contrast the benefits and limitations of the budget system

   e. evaluate a business situation and recommend the appropriate budget solution

   f. prepare budgets on the basis of information presented

   g. calculate the impact of incremental changes to budgets

Part 1—Section B.5. Annual profit plan and supporting schedules

The candidate should be able to:

   a. explain the role of the sales budget in the development of an annual profit plan

   b. identify the factors that should be considered when preparing a sales forecast

   c. identify the components of a sales budget and prepare a sales budget

   d. explain the relationship between the sales budget and the production budget

   e. identify the role that inventory levels play in the preparation of a production budget and define other factors that should be considered when preparing a production budget

   f. prepare a production budget

   g. demonstrate an understanding of the relationship between the direct materials budget, the direct labor budget, and the production budget

   h. explain how inventory levels and procurement policies affect the direct materials budget

   i. prepare direct materials and direct labor budgets based on relevant information and evaluate the feasibility of achieving production goals on the basis of these budgets

   j. demonstrate an understanding of the relationship between the overhead budget and the production budget

   k. separate costs into their fixed and variable components

   l. prepare an overhead budget

   m. identify the components of the cost of goods sold budget and prepare a cost of goods sold budget

   n. demonstrate an understanding of contribution margin per unit and total contribution margin, identify the appropriate use of these concepts, and calculate both unit and total contribution margin

   o. identify the components of the selling and administrative expense budget

   p. explain how specific components of the selling and administrative expense budget may affect the contribution margin

   q. prepare an operational (operating) budget

   r. prepare a capital expenditure budget

   s. demonstrate an understanding of the relationship between the capital expenditure budget, the cash budget, and the pro forma financial statements

   t. define the purposes of the cash budget and describe the relationship between the cash budget and all other budgets

   u. demonstrate an understanding of the relationship between credit policies and purchasing (payables) policies and the cash budget

   v. prepare a cash budget

Part 1—Section B.6. Top-level planning and analysis

The candidate should be able to:

    a. define the purpose of a pro forma income statement, a pro forma balance sheet, and a pro forma statement of cash flows, and demonstrate an understanding of the relationship among these statements and all other budgets

    b. prepare pro forma income statements based on several revenue and cost assumptions

    c. evaluate whether a company has achieved strategic objectives based on pro forma income statements

    d. use financial projections to prepare a pro forma balance sheet and a pro forma statement of cash flows

    e. identify the factors required to prepare medium- and long-term cash forecasts

    f. use financial projections to determine required outside financing and dividend policy

Section C. Performance Management (20%—Levels A, B, and C)

Part 1—Section C.1. Cost and variance measures

The candidate should be able to:

    a. analyze performance against operational goals using measures based on revenue, manufacturing costs, non-manufacturing costs, and profit depending on the type of center or unit being measured

    b. explain the reasons for variances within a performance monitoring system

    c. prepare a performance analysis by comparing actual results to the master budget, calculate favorable and unfavorable variances from the budget, and provide explanations for variances

    d. identify and describe the benefits and limitations of measuring performance by comparing actual results to the master budget

    e. analyze a flexible budget based on actual sales (output) volume

    f. calculate the sales-volume variance and the sales-price variance by comparing the flexible budget to the master (static) budget

    g. calculate the flexible-budget variance by comparing actual results to the flexible budget

    h. investigate the flexible-budget variance to determine individual differences between actual and budgeted input prices and input quantities

    i. explain how budget variance reporting is utilized in a management by exception environment

    j. define a standard cost system and identify the reasons for adopting a standard cost system

    k. demonstrate an understanding of price (rate) variances and calculate the price variances related to direct material and direct labor inputs

l. demonstrate an understanding of efficiency (usage) variances and calculate the efficiency variances related to direct material and direct labor inputs

m. demonstrate an understanding of spending and efficiency variances as they relate to fixed and variable overhead

n. calculate a sales-mix variance and explain its impact on revenue and contribution margin

o. calculate and explain a mix variance

p. calculate and explain a yield variance

q. demonstrate how price, efficiency, spending, and mix variances can be applied in service companies as well as manufacturing companies

r. analyze factory overhead variances by calculating variable overhead spending variance, variable overhead efficiency variance, fixed overhead spending variance, and production volume variance

s. analyze variances, identify causes, and recommend corrective actions

Part 1—Section C.2. Responsibility centers and reporting segments

The candidate should be able to:

a. identify and explain the different types of responsibility centers

b. recommend appropriate responsibility centers given a business scenario

c. calculate a contribution margin

d. analyze a contribution margin report and evaluate performance

e. identify segments that organizations evaluate, including product lines, geographical areas, or other meaningful segments

f. explain why the allocation of common costs among segments can be an issue in performance evaluation

g. identify methods for allocating common costs such as stand-alone cost allocation and incremental cost allocation

h. define transfer pricing and identify the objectives of transfer pricing

i. identify the methods for determining transfer prices and list and explain the advantages and disadvantages of each method

j. identify and calculate transfer prices using variable cost, full cost, market price, negotiated price, and dual-rate pricing

k. explain how transfer pricing is affected by business issues such as the presence of outside suppliers and the opportunity costs associated with capacity usage

l. describe how special issues such as tariffs, exchange rates, taxes, currency restrictions, expropriation risk, and the availability of materials and skills affect performance evaluation in multinational companies

Part 1—Section C.3. Performance measures

The candidate should be able to:

a. explain why performance evaluation measures should be directly related to strategic and operational goals and objectives; why timely feedback is critical; and why performance measures should be related to the factors that drive the element being measured, e.g., cost drivers and revenue drivers

b. explain the issues involved in determining product profitability, business unit profitability, and customer profitability, including cost measurement, cost allocation, investment measurement, and valuation

c. calculate product-line profitability, business unit profitability, and customer profitability

d. evaluate customers and products on the basis of profitability and recommend ways to improve profitability and/or drop unprofitable customers and products

e. define and calculate return on investment (ROI)

f. analyze and interpret ROI calculations

g. define and calculate residual income (RI)

h. analyze and interpret RI calculations

i. compare and contrast the benefits and limitations of ROI and RI as measures of performance

j. explain how revenue and expense recognition policies may affect the measurement of income and reduce comparability among business units

k. explain how inventory measurement policies, joint asset sharing, and overall asset measurement policies may affect the measurement of investment and reduce comparability among business units

l. define key performance indicators (KPIs) and discuss the importance of these indicators in evaluating a firm

m. define the concept of a balanced scorecard and identify its components

n. identify and describe the perspectives of a balanced scorecard, including financial, customer, internal process, and learning and growth

o. identify and describe the characteristics of successful implementation and use of a balanced scorecard

p. demonstrate an understanding of a strategy map and the role it plays

q. analyze and interpret a balanced scorecard and evaluate performance on the basis of the analysis

r. recommend performance measures and a periodic reporting methodology given operational goals and actual results

Section D. Cost Management (15%—Levels A, B, and C)

Part 1—Section D.1. Measurement concepts

The candidate should be able to:

   a. calculate fixed, variable, and mixed costs and demonstrate an understanding of the behavior of each in the long and short term and how a change in assumptions regarding cost type or relevant range affects these costs
   b. identify cost objects and cost pools and assign costs to appropriate activities
   c. demonstrate an understanding of the nature and types of cost drivers and the causal relationship that exists between cost drivers and costs incurred
   d. demonstrate an understanding of the various methods for measuring costs and accumulating work-in-process and finished goods inventories
   e. identify and define cost measurement techniques such as actual costing, normal costing, and standard costing; calculate costs using each of these techniques; identify the appropriate use of each technique; and describe the benefits and limitations of each technique
   f. demonstrate an understanding of variable (direct) costing and absorption (full) costing and the benefits and limitations of these measurement concepts
   g. calculate inventory costs, cost of goods sold, and operating profit using both variable costing and absorption costing
   h. demonstrate an understanding of how the use of variable costing or absorption costing affects the value of inventory, cost of goods sold, and operating income
   i. prepare summary income statements using variable costing and absorption costing
   j. determine the appropriate use of joint product and by-product costing
   k. demonstrate an understanding of concepts such as split-off point and separable costs
   l. determine the allocation of joint product and by-product costs using the physical measure method, the sales value at split-off method, constant gross profit (gross margin) method, and the net realizable value method; describe the benefits and limitations of each method

Part 1—Section D.2. Costing systems

For each cost accumulation system identified (job order costing, process costing, activity-based costing, life-cycle costing), the candidate should be able to:

   a. define the nature of the system, understand the cost flows of the system, and identify its appropriate use
   b. calculate inventory values and cost of goods sold
   c. demonstrate an understanding of the proper accounting for normal and abnormal spoilage

    d. discuss the strategic value of cost information regarding products and services, pricing, overhead allocations, and other issues

    e. identify and describe the benefits and limitations of each cost accumulation system

    f. demonstrate an understanding of the concept of equivalent units in process costing and calculate the value of equivalent units

    g. define the elements of activity-based costing such as cost pool, cost driver, resource driver, activity driver, and value-added activity

    h. calculate product cost using an activity-based system and compare and analyze the results with costs calculated using a traditional system

    i. explain how activity-based costing can be utilized in service firms

    j. demonstrate an understanding of the concept of life-cycle costing and the strategic value of including upstream costs, manufacturing costs, and downstream costs

Part 1—Section D.3. Overhead costs

The candidate should be able to:

    a. distinguish between fixed and variable overhead expenses

    b. determine the appropriate time frame for classifying both variable and fixed overhead expenses

    c. demonstrate an understanding of the different methods of determining overhead rates, e.g., plant-wide rates, departmental rates, and individual cost driver rates

    d. describe the benefits and limitations of each of the methods used to determine overhead rates

    e. identify the components of variable overhead expense

    f. determine the appropriate allocation base for variable overhead expenses

    g. calculate the per unit variable overhead expense

    h. identify the components of fixed overhead expense

    i. identify the appropriate allocation base for fixed overhead expense

    j. calculate the fixed overhead application rate

    k. describe how fixed overhead can be over- or under-applied and how this difference should be accounted for in the cost of goods sold, work-in-process, and finished goods accounts

    l. compare and contrast traditional overhead allocation with activity-based overhead allocation

    m. calculate overhead expense in an activity-based costing setting

    n. identify and describe the benefits derived from activity-based overhead allocation

    o. explain why companies allocate the cost of service departments such as Human Resources or Information Technology to divisions, departments, or activities

p. calculate service or support department cost allocations using the direct method, the reciprocal method, the step-down method, and the dual allocation method

q. estimate fixed costs using the high-low method and demonstrate an understanding of how regression can be used to estimate fixed costs

Part 1—Section D.4. Supply chain management

The candidate should be able to:

a. explain supply chain management

b. define lean resource management techniques

c. identify and describe the operational benefits of implementing lean resource management techniques

d. define materials requirements planning (MRP)

e. identify and describe the operational benefits of implementing a just-in-time (JIT) system

f. identify and describe the operational benefits of enterprise resource planning (ERP)

g. explain the concept of outsourcing and identify the benefits and limitations of choosing this option

h. demonstrate a general understanding of the Theory of Constraints

i. identify the five steps involved in Theory of Constraints analysis

j. define throughput costing (super-variable costing) and calculate inventory costs using throughput costing

k. define and calculate throughput contribution

l. describe how capacity level affects product costing, capacity management, pricing decisions, and financial statements

m. explain how using practical capacity as the denominator for the fixed cost allocation rate enhances capacity management

n. calculate the financial impact of implementing the above-mentioned methods

Part 1. D.5. Business process improvement

The candidate should be able to:

a. define value chain analysis

b. identify the steps in value chain analysis

c. explain how value chain analysis is used to better understand a firm's competitive advantage

d. define, identify, and provide examples of a value-added activity and explain how the value-added concept is related to improving performance

e. demonstrate an understanding of process analysis and business process reengineering, and calculate the resulting savings

f. define best practice analysis and discuss how it can be used by an organization to improve performance

g. demonstrate an understanding of benchmarking process performance

h. identify the benefits of benchmarking in creating a competitive advantage

i. apply activity-based management principles to recommend process performance improvements

j. explain the relationship among continuous improvement techniques, activity-based management, and quality performance

k. explain the concept of continuous improvement and how it relates to implementing ideal standards and quality improvements

l. describe and identify the components of the costs of quality, commonly referred to as prevention costs, appraisal costs, internal failure costs, and external failure costs

m. calculate the financial impact of implementing the above-mentioned processes

n. identify and discuss ways to make accounting operations more efficient, including process walk-throughs, process training, identification of waste and overcapacity, identifying the root cause of errors, reducing the accounting close cycle (fast close), and shared services

Section E. Internal Controls (15%—Levels A, B, and C)

Part 1—Section E.1 Governance, risk, and compliance

The candidate should be able to:

a. demonstrate an understanding of internal control risk and the management of internal control risk

b. identify and describe internal control objectives

c. explain how a company's organizational structure, policies, objectives, and goals, as well as its management philosophy and style, influence the scope and effectiveness of the control environment

d. identify the board of directors' responsibilities with respect to ensuring that the company is operated in the best interest of shareholders

e. identify the hierarchy of corporate governance; i.e., articles of incorporation, bylaws, policies, and procedures

f. demonstrate an understanding of corporate governance, including rights and responsibilities of the CEO, the board of directors, the audit committee, managers and other stakeholders; and the procedures for making corporate decisions

g. describe how internal controls are designed to provide reasonable (but not absolute) assurance regarding achievement of an entity's objectives involving (i) effectiveness and efficiency of operations, (ii) reliability of financial reporting, and (iii) compliance with applicable laws and regulations

   h. explain why personnel policies and procedures are integral to an efficient control environment
   i. define and give examples of segregation of duties
   j. explain why the following four types of functional responsibilities should be performed by different departments or different people within the same function: (i) authority to execute transactions, (ii) recording transactions, (iii) custody of assets involved in the transactions, and (iv) periodic reconciliations of the existing assets to recorded amounts
   k. demonstrate an understanding of the importance of independent checks and verification
   l. identify examples of safeguarding controls
   m. explain how the use of pre-numbered forms, as well as specific policies and procedures detailing who is authorized to receive specific documents, is a means of control
   n. define inherent risk, control risk, and detection risk
   o. define and distinguish between preventive controls and detective controls
   p. describe the major internal control provisions of the Sarbanes-Oxley Act (Sections 201, 203, 204, 302, 404, and 407)
   q. identify the role of the PCAOB in providing guidance on the auditing of internal controls
   r. differentiate between a top-down (risk-based) approach and a bottom-up approach to auditing internal controls
   s. identify the PCAOB preferred approach to auditing internal controls as outlined in Auditing Standard #5
   t. identify and describe the major internal control provisions of the Foreign Corrupt Practices Act
   u. identify and describe the five major components of COSO's Internal Control - Integrated Framework (2013)
   v. assess the level of internal control risk within an organization and recommend risk mitigation strategies
   w. demonstrate an understanding of external auditor responsibilities, including the types of audit opinions the external auditors issue

Part 1—Section E.2 System controls and security measures

The candidate should be able to:

   a. describe how the segregation of accounting duties can enhance systems security
   b. identify threats to information systems, including input manipulation, program alteration, direct file alteration, data theft, sabotage, viruses, Trojan horses, theft, and phishing
   c. demonstrate an understanding of how systems development controls are used to enhance the accuracy, validity, safety, security, and adaptability of systems input, processing, output, and storage functions

    d. identify procedures to limit access to physical hardware

    e. identify means by which management can protect programs and databases from unauthorized use

    f. identify input controls, processing controls, and output controls and describe why each of these controls is necessary

    g. identify and describe the types of storage controls and demonstrate an understanding of when and why they are used

    h. identify and describe the inherent risks of using the internet as compared to data transmissions over secured transmission lines

    i. define data encryption and describe why there is a much greater need for data encryption methods when using the internet

    j. identify a firewall and its uses

    k. demonstrate an understanding of how flowcharts of activities are used to assess controls

    l. explain the importance of backing up all program and data files regularly, and storing the backups at a secure remote site

    m. define business continuity planning

    n. define the objective of a disaster recovery plan and identify the components of such a plan including hot, warm, and cold sites

Part 1—F. Technology and Analytics (15%—Levels A, B, and C)

Part 1—Section F.1 Information systems

The candidate should be able to:

    a. identify the role of the accounting information system (AIS) in the value chain

    b. demonstrate an understanding of the accounting information system cycles, including revenue to cash, expenditures, production, human resources and payroll, financing, and property, plant, and equipment, as well as the general ledger (GL) and reporting system

    c. identify and explain the challenges of having separate financial and nonfinancial systems

    d. define enterprise resource planning (ERP) and identify and explain the advantages and disadvantages of ERP.

    e. explain how ERP helps overcome the challenges of separate financial and nonfinancial systems, integrating all aspects of an organization's activities

    f. define relational database and demonstrate an understanding of a database management system

    g. define a data warehouse and data mart

    h. define enterprise performance management (EPM) (also known as corporate performance management (CPM) or business performance management (BPM))

    i. discuss how EPM can facilitate business planning and performance management

Part 1—Section F.2 Data governance

The candidate should be able to:

a. define data governance; i.e., managing the availability, usability, integrity, and security of data

b. demonstrate a general understanding of data governance frameworks, such as COSO's Internal Control and Enterprise Risk Management frameworks and ISACA's COBIT (Control Objectives for Information and Related Technologies)

c. identify the stages of the data life cycle; i.e., data capture, data maintenance, data synthesis, data usage, data analytics, data publication, data archival, and data purging

d. demonstrate an understanding of data preprocessing and the steps to convert data for further analysis, including data consolidation, data cleaning (cleansing), data transformation, and data reduction

e. discuss the importance of having a documented record retention (or records management) policy

f. identify and explain controls and tools to detect and thwart cyberattacks, such as penetration and vulnerability testing, biometrics, advanced firewalls, and access controls

Part 1—Section F.3 Technology-enabled finance transformation

The candidate should be able to:

a. define the systems development life cycle (SDLC), including systems analysis, conceptual design, physical design, implementation and conversion, and operations and maintenance

b. explain the role of business process analysis in improving system performance

c. define robotic process automation (RPA) and its benefits

d. evaluate where technologies can improve efficiency and effectiveness of processing accounting data and information (e.g., artificial intelligence (AI))

e. define cloud computing and describe how it can improve efficiency

f. define software as a service (SaaS) and explain its advantages and disadvantages

g. recognize potential applications of blockchain, distributed ledger, and smart contracts

Part 1—Section F.4 Data analytics

The candidate should be able to:

Business intelligence

a. define Big Data, explain the four Vs: volume, velocity, variety, and veracity, and describe the opportunities and challenges of leveraging insight from this data

b. explain how structured, semi-structured, and unstructured data is used by a business enterprise

c. describe the progression of data, from data to information to knowledge to insight to action

d. describe the opportunities and challenges of managing data analytics

e. explain why data and data science capability are strategic assets

f. define business intelligence (BI); i.e., the collection of applications, tools, and best practices that transform data into actionable information in order to make better decisions and optimize performance

Data mining

g. define data mining

h. describe the challenges of data mining

i. explain why data mining is an iterative process and both an art and a science

j. explain how query tools (e.g., Structured Query Language (SQL)) are used to retrieve information

k. describe how an analyst would mine large data sets to reveal patterns and provide insights

Analytic tools

l. explain the challenge of fitting an analytic model to the data

m. define the different types of data analytics, including descriptive, diagnostic, predictive, and prescriptive

n. define the following analytic models: clustering, classification, and regression; determine when each would be the appropriate tool to use

o. identify the elements of both simple and multiple regression equations

p. calculate the result of regression equations as applied to a specific situation

q. demonstrate an understanding of the coefficient of determination (or R squared)

r. demonstrate an understanding of time series analyses, including trend, cyclical, seasonal, and irregular patterns

s. identify and explain the benefits and limitations of regression analysis and time series analysis

t. define standard error of the estimate, goodness of fit, and confidence interval

u. explain how to use predictive analytic techniques to draw insights and make recommendations

v. describe exploratory data analysis and how it is used to reveal patterns and discover insights

w. define sensitivity analysis and identify when it would be the appropriate tool to use

x. demonstrate an understanding of the uses of simulation models, including the Monte Carlo technique

y. identify the benefits and limitations of sensitivity analysis and simulation models

z. demonstrate an understanding of what-if (or goal-seeking) analysis

aa. identify and explain the limitations of data analytics

Visualization

bb. utilize table and graph design best practices to avoid distortion in the communication of complex information

cc. evaluate data visualization options and select the best presentation approach (e.g., histograms, boxplots, scatter plots, dot plots, tables, dashboards, bar charts, pie charts, line charts, bubble charts)

dd. understand the benefits and limitations of visualization techniques

ee. determine the most effective channel to communicate results

ff. communicate results, conclusions, and recommendations in an impactful manner using effective visualization techniques

Practice Multiple Choice Questions and Answers

PART 1—Financial Planning, Performance, and Analytics

The following multiple-choice questions are retired ICMA questions and are used with their permission. The explanations are original answers and are not released from the ICMA but are supplied as further explanations to help further understand the question.

Section A. External Financial Reporting Decisions (15%—Levels A, B, and C)

1. An accountant is preparing the statement of cash flows using the indirect method. She found on the balance sheet that the prior year's balance of equipment was $295,700 and the current year's balance of equipment is $304,000. Depreciation expense during the current year was $22,400. During the year, the company sold equipment for $40,000, resulting in a gain of $21,600. On the statement of cash flows, what is the cash outflow for the purchase of equipment this year?
   a. $4,300.
   b. $49,100.
   c. $52,300.
   d. $70,700.

   Explanation: The correct answer is **b.** $49,100.

   The book value for the equipment sold for the year must first be calculated. The book value can be calculated as cash received less any gain recognized on the sale. In this case, the book value of the equipment sold during the year equals $18,400 ($40,000 − $21,600).
   The formula to calculate the current year's balance of equipment is the prior year's balance minus depreciation minus book value of any equipment sold plus purchases. Rearranging this formula, the cash outflow for the purchase of equipment equals $49,100 ($304,000 − $295,700 + $22,400 + $18,400).

2. Majesty Amusement Park recently installed a new thrill ride. Although this attraction has an average life of 40 years, Majesty estimates that the ride will be popular for 15 years, at which point it will be disassembled and replaced with a different ride. Park attendance is based upon the local economy, which is difficult to predict. The method Majesty should use to depreciate this ride is
   a. declining balance.
   b. straight-line with a 15-year life.
   c. straight-line with a 40-year life.
   d. units-of-output.

   Explanation: The correct answer is **b.** straight-line with a 15-year life.

   Depreciation is recognized over the period of time that long-term assets provide benefit to the organization. Straight-line depreciation recognizes an equal amount of depreciation over the asset's useful life. Because Majesty estimates that the ride will be replaced in 15 years, and it can be assumed that it will provide an equal amount of benefit each year, Majesty should use the straight-line method with a 15-year life.

Section B. Planning, Budgeting, and Forecasting (20%—Levels A, B, and C)

3. In strategic planning, PEST analysis is best described as evaluating which of the following factors?
   a. Political, economic, social, and technological.
   b. People, environment, sustainability, and tactics.
   c. Process, efficiency, scale, and timing.
   d. Products, employees, strengths, and threats.

   Explanation: The correct answer is **a.** Political, economic, social, and technological.

   The PEST analysis is a specific tool used to analyze external and internal conditions. The acronym stands for Political, Economic, Social, and Technological.

4. Which one of the following best describes a reason why a company's budgeting should be based on the company's strategic plans?
   a. Helps control costs so that products can be sold profitably.
   b. Identifies resources needed to reach strategic goals.
   c. Identifies the external factors that have changed from the prior year and those that remain the same.
   d. Establishes standards to measure employee performance.

   Explanation: The correct answer is **b.** Identifies resources needed to reach strategic goals.

A budget that is based on the company's strategic plans can help the company identify resources needed to reach strategic goals because the money that an organization spends and resources the organization invests represents the organization's strategy; therefore, an effective budget can identify spending that will help the company meet their goals and spending that is not effective to implementing their strategy.

5. An accountant estimated the repair costs for the company's plant facilities for next year's operating budget. The accountant has determined the following probability distribution after analyzing historical repair costs.

Probability	Repair costs
15%	$2,000,000
45%	2,500,000
30%	3,500,000
10%	5,000,000

What is the estimated repair cost that the accountant should project for next year's operating budget?

    a. $1,850,000.
    b. $1,925,000.
    c. $2,975,000.
    d. $3,250,000.

Explanation: The correct answer is **c.** $2,975,000.

The formula for the expected value of a set of possible outcomes is: $EV = \Sigma(rp)$ where r = result of the outcome, and p = probability of the outcome. The expected value of the repair costs in this scenario equals $2,975,000 ((15% × $2,000,000) + (45% × $2,500,000) + (30% × 3,500,000) + (10% × $5,000,000)).

6. Which one of the following types of budgets will allow management to best assess how costs will change based on changes in cost drivers such as direct labor hours or machine hours?
    a. Rolling budget.
    b. Activity-based budget.
    c. Production budget.
    d. Cost budget.

Explanation: The correct answer is **b.** Activity-based budget.

Activity-based budgeting results in a more sophisticated and detailed view of the many activities that drive costs in most organizations. Core activities are identified and used throughout the organization to assign costs based on actual consumption relationships which results in more accurate cost planning, control, and evaluation results for management.

7. A steel company manufactures heavy-duty brackets for the shelving industry. The company has budgeted for the production and sale of 1,000,000 brackets, and has no beginning or ending inventory. Relevant operational, revenue, and cost data is as follows.

Unit selling price of a bracket	$22.50
Direct material required per unit	4 pounds
Direct labor required per unit	0.15 hours
Cost of material per pound	$1.75
Direct labor cost per hour	$9.00
Total variable selling costs	$2,250,000
Total fixed costs	$1,500,000

Based on the data provided, what is the unit contribution margin per bracket?

   a. $14.15.
   b. $11.90.
   c. $10.60.
   d. $10.40.

Explanation: The correct answer is **b.** $11.90.

   The unit contribution margin is calculated as sales price per units less total variable costs per unit. In this example the total variable costs per unit consist of direct materials of $7.00 per unit (4 pounds × $1.75), direct labor of $1.35 per unit (0.15 hours × $9.00), and total variable selling costs of $2.25 per unit ($2,250,000 ÷ 1,000,000 units). The unit contribution margin equals $11.90 ($22.50 − ($7.00 + $1.35 + $2.25)).

8. A company makes one product that it sells for €125 per unit. The product has a contribution margin of 35% of sales. Direct materials account for 10% of sales. Variable manufacturing overhead is 5% of sales. Fixed costs are €200,000 per year. The controller wants to create a pro forma income statement where the sales increase from 10,000 units to 12,000 units. The average income tax rate is 25.71%. What is the change in operating income as a result of the increase in unit sales?
   a. €50,000.
   b. €65,000.
   c. €75,000.
   d. €87,500.

Explanation: The correct answer is **d.** €87,500.

   The operating income is the income before interest and taxes. One way to calculate the change in operating income from the increase in unit sales is to multiply the increase in units of 2,000 units (12,000 − 10,000) by the unit contribution margin which is €43.75 (€125 × 35%). This formula can be used because the fixed costs of €200,000 will remain the same whether 10,000 or 12,000 units are produced; therefore, the increase in operating income will be €87,500 (2,000 units × €43.75).

Section C. Performance Management (20%—Levels A, B, and C)

9. A company's master budget projected the following information.

Sales (25,000 units)	$250,000
Manufacturing costs (1/3 fixed)	120,000
Other operating costs (all fixed)	100,000

If the company actually sold 27,500 units, the operating income when using a flexible budget would be

  a. $33,000.
  b. $43,000.
  c. $47,000.
  d. $51,000.

Explanation: The correct answer is **c.** $47,000.

The operating income is calculated as sales minus all operating costs before interest and taxes. When using a flexible budget, the sales price per unit and variable cost per unit must first be calculated in order to calculate the operating income. The sales price is $10 per unit ($250,000 ÷ 25,000 units) and the variable manufacturing costs per unit equal $3.20 because only 2/3 of the costs are variable (($120,000 × (2 ÷ 3)) ÷ 25,000 units). The total sales if the company actually sold 27,500 units would be $275,000 (27,500 units × $10), the total variable costs would be $88,000 (27,500 units × $3.20), the total fixed manufacturing costs would be $40,000 ($120,000 × (1 ÷ 3)) and the other operating costs would equal $100,000 because they are all fixed; therefore, the operating income would be $47,000 ($275,000 − ($88,000 + $40,000 + $100,000).

10. The maintenance department of a hotel would be considered a (n)
  a. cost center.
  b. revenue center.
  c. profit center.
  d. investment center.

Explanation: The correct answer is **a.** cost center.

A cost center is an organizational unit whose manager is responsible only for costs. Cost centers often include service or staff departments that do not generate revenue. The maintenance department of a hotel is an example of a department that does not generate revenue.

11. On a balanced scorecard, each of the following is an example of the customer perspective measure except
    a. economic value-added.
    b. customer retention.
    c. time taken to fulfill orders.
    d. number of customer complaints.

    Explanation: The correct answer is **a.** economic value-added.

    The customer perspective is the performance related to targeted customer and market segments. Economic value-added fits in the internal business processes perspective.

Section D. Cost Management (15%—Levels A, B, and C)

12. A dairy farm produces the following products jointly during the fiscal year for a total joint cost of €9,000,000.

Product	Kilograms
Milk	1,170,000
Butter	570,000
Yogurt	330,000
Cheese	930,000

    Based on the information, which one of the following is most accurate regarding the allocation of the joint cost under the physical measure method?
    a. The milk product line should be allocated €1,710,000 of the joint costs.
    b. The butter product line should be allocated €990,000 of the joint costs.
    c. The yogurt product line should be allocated €3,510,000 of the joint costs.
    d. The cheese product line should be allocated €2,790,000 of the joint costs.

    Explanation: The correct answer is **d.** The cheese product line should be allocated €2,790,000 of the joint costs.

    The allocation of the total joint cost to the four products is based on the percentage of kilograms of each product compared to the total amount of kilograms produced for all products. The total amount produced is 3,000,000 kilograms (1,170,000 + 570,000 + 330,000 + 930,000). The joint costs allocated to the cheese product line equals €2,790,000 (€9,000,000 × (930,000 ÷ 3,000,000)).

13. The life-cycle costing method is
    a. the process for examining the various aspects of a product to identify cost efficiencies.
    b. the process for managing all costs identified in the value chain.
    c. a method of costing that minimizes the selling expenses associated with a product.

d. method of costing that focuses on the customer.

Explanation: The correct answer is **b.** the process for managing all costs identified in the value chain.

The life-cycle analysis is concerned with the cost analysis of a product from cradle to grave; therefore, the life-cycle costing method is the process for managing all costs identified in the value chain.

14. A company manufactures and sells three products. The products are all manufactured at the same facility. The controller of the company has decided to accumulate all budgeted overhead costs for the manufacturing facility into a single cost pool. The cost pool is then allocated to the three products based on the direct labor hours used by each product. What type of overhead rate has the controller **most** likely used in this allocation methodology?
    a. Departmental rate.
    b. Variable rate.
    c. Fixed rate.
    d. Plant-wide rate.

    Explanation: The correct answer is **d.** Plant-wide rate.

The controller most likely used a plant-wide rate in this allocation because he or she decided to accumulate all budgeted overhead costs into a single cost pool.

15. The method used to maximize operating income when faced with some bottleneck and some non-bottleneck operations is described as:
    a. Sensitivity analysis.
    b. Suboptimal decision making.
    c. Theory of Constraints.
    d. Total factory productivity.

    Explanation: The correct answer is **c.** Theory of Constraints.

The goal of the theory of constraints is to improve speed in a process by optimizing throughput, managing constraints, and focusing on continuous improvement. A constraint is a weak link in a chain that will limit the rest of the system. Operating income can be maximized as constraints are identified and eliminated.

Section E. Internal Controls (15%—Levels A, B, and C)

16. Internal control can provide only reasonable assurance of achieving entity control objectives because
    a. management monitors internal control.
    b. the cost of internal control should not exceed its benefits.
    c. the board of directors is active and independent.

d. the auditor's primary responsibility is the detection of fraud.

Explanation: The correct answer is **b.** the cost of internal control should not exceed its benefits.

There is always a tradeoff between internal control effectiveness and the costs that are associated with it. Implementing controls will improve quality and accuracy, but some controls will only improve the assurance slightly and would not justify the associated increase in cost to implement the control.

17. Which of the following types of audits is used to determine if a company has met regulatory or legal obligations?
    a. Operational.
    b. Productivity.
    c. Performance.
    d. Compliance.

Explanation: The correct answer is **d.** Compliance.

Each type of audit is designed to review specific controls to determine whether specific business functions are controlled and managed well. Compliance audits focus on reviewing controls specifically related to ensuring compliance with laws, regulations, and company policies.

18. Encoding electronic data through the use of an algorithm to make information unreadable to unauthorized individuals is identified as
    a. a firewall.
    b. a worm.
    c. a virus.
    d. encryption.

Explanation: The correct answer is **d.** encryption.

Encryption can help secure data traveling through an organization's network. Encryption converts the data, so it is sent in an unreadable format.

Bibliography and References

American Institute of Certified Public Accountants, www.aicpa.org.

Anderson, David R., Dennis J. Sweeney, Thomas A. Williams, Jeff Camm, and R. Kipp Martin. *Quantitative Methods for Business*, 11th ed. Mason, OH: South-Western, 2010.

Arens, Alvin A., Randal J. Elder, and Mark S. Beasley. *Auditing and Assurance Services: An Integrated Approach*, 13th ed. Upper Saddle River, NJ: Prentice-Hall, 2009.

Bergeron, Pierre G. *Finance: Essentials for the Successful Professional*. Independence, KY: Thomson Learning, 2002.

Bernstein, Leopold A., and John J. West. *Financial Statement Analysis: Theory, Application, and Interpretation*, 6th ed. Homewood, IL: Irwin, 1997.

Blocher, Edward J., David E. Stout, Paul E. Juras, and Gary Cokins. *Cost Management: A Strategic Emphasis,* 6th ed. New York: McGraw-Hill, 2013.

Bodnar, George H., and William S. Hopwood. *Accounting Information Systems*, 10th ed. Upper Saddle River, NJ: Prentice-Hall, 2010.

Brealey, Richard A., Stewart C. Myers, and Franklin Allen. *Principles of Corporate Finance*, 10th ed. New York: McGraw-Hill, 2011.

Brigham, Eugene F., and Michael C. Ehrhardt. *Financial Management: Theory and Practice*, 14th ed. Mason, OH: Cengage, 2013.

Campanella, Jack, ed. *Principles of Quality Costs: Principles, Implementation, and Use,* 3rd ed. Milwaukee: ASQ Quality Press, 1999.

Committee of Sponsoring Organizations of the Treadway Commission (COSO), www.coso.org

Committee of Sponsoring Organizations of the Treadway Commission (COSO). Enterprise Risk Management—Integrated Framework, 2004.

COSO. Enterprise Risk Management—Integrating with Strategy and Performance (2017), https://www.coso.org/Pages/ERM-Framework-Purchase.aspx

Daniels, John D., Lee H. Radebaugh, and Daniel Sullivan. *International Business: Environments and Operations*, 14th ed. Upper Saddle River, NJ: Prentice-Hall, 2012.

Evans, Matt H. Course 11: The Balanced Scorecard, www.exinfm.com/training/pdfiles/course11r.pdf

Flesher, Dale. *Internal Auditing: Standards and Practices*. Altamonte Springs, FL: Institute of Internal Auditors, 1996.

Financial Accounting Standards Board, www.fasb.org

Financial Accounting Standards Board. *Statements of Financial Accounting Concepts*. Norwalk, CT: Author.

Forex Directory. "U. S. Dollar Charts," www.forexdirectory.net/chartsfx.html

Garrison, Ray H., Eric W. Noreen, and Peter Brewer. *Managerial Accounting*, 14th ed. Boston: McGraw-Hill/Irwin, 2011.

Gelinas, Ulric J. Jr., Richard B. Dull, and Patrick Wheeler. *Accounting Information Systems*, 9th ed. Cincinnati: South-Western College Publishing, 2011.

Gibson, Charles H. *Financial Reporting and Analysis*, 13th ed. Mason, OH: South-Western Cengage Learning, 2013.

Goldratt, Elihayu M., and Jeff Cox. *The Goal: A Process of Ongoing Improvement*, 25th anniversary revised ed. Great Barrington, MA: North River Press, 2011.

Grant Thorton, LLP, www.grantthornton.ca

Greenstein, Marilyn, and Todd M. Feinman. *Electronic Commerce: Security, Risk Management, and Control.* Boston: McGraw-Hill Higher Education, 2000.

Hildebrand, David K., R. Lyman Ott, and J. Brian Gray. *Basic Statistical Ideas for Managers*, 2nd ed. Belmont, CA: Thomson Learning, 2005.

Hilton, Ronald W., Michael W. Maher, and Frank H. Selto. *Cost Management: Strategies for Business Decisions,* 4th ed. Boston: McGraw-Hill Irwin, 2007.

Horngren, Charles T., Srikant M. Datar, and Madhav Rajan. *Cost Accounting: A Managerial Emphasis*, 14th ed. Upper Saddle River, NJ: Prentice-Hall, 2012.

Hoyle, Joe B., Thomas F. Schaefer, and Timothy S. Doupnik. *Advanced Accounting,* 10th ed. Boston: McGraw-Hill Irwin, 2010.

Institute of Internal Auditors. *International Standards for the Professional Practice of Internal Auditing,* https://na.theiia.org/standards-guidance/mandatory-guidance/Pages/Standards.aspx

Institute of Management Accountants, www.imanet.org

Institute of Management Accountants. *Enterprise Risk Management: Frameworks, Elements, and Integration.* Montvale, NJ: Author, 2006.

Institute of Management Accountants. *Enterprise Risk Management: Tools and Techniques for Effective Implementation.* Montvale, NJ: Author, 2007.

Institute of Management Accountants. *IMA Statement of Ethical Professional Practice.* Montvale, NJ: Author, 2005.

Institute of Management Accountants. *Managing Quality Improvements.* Montvale, NJ: Author, 1993.

Institute of Management Accountants. *Value and Ethics: From Inception to Practice.* Montvale, NJ: Author, 2008.

International Accounting Standards Board, www.ifrs.org

Investopedia.com, *www.investopedia.com*

Kaplan, Robert S., and David P. Norton. *The Balanced Scorecard: Translating Strategy into Action.* Boston: Harvard Business School Press, 1996.

Kaplan, Robert S., and David P. Norton. *The Strategy-Focused Organization: How Balanced Scorecard Companies Thrive in the New Business Environment.* Boston: Harvard Business School Press, 2001.

Kaplan, Robert S., and David P. Norton. "Using the Balanced Scorecard as a Strategic Management System." *Harvard Business Review* (January–February 1996).

Kieso, Donald E., Jerry J. Weygandt, and Terry D. Warfield. *Intermediate Accounting*, 14th ed. Hoboken, NJ: John Wiley & Sons, 2012.

Larsen, E. John. *Modern Advanced Accounting*, 10th ed. New York: McGraw-Hill, 2006.

Laudon, Kenneth C., and Jane P. Laudon. *Management Information Systems*, 11th ed. Upper Saddle River, NJ: Pearson Prentice Hall, 2010.

Mackenzie, Bruce, Danie Coetsee, Tapiwa Njikizana, Raymond Chamboko, Blaise Colyvas, and Brandon Hanekom. *Interpretation and Application of International Financial Reporting Standards.* Hoboken, NJ: John Wiley & Sons, 2012.

McMillan, Edward J. *Not-for-Profit Budgeting and Financial Management.* Hoboken, NJ: John Wiley & Sons, 2010.

Moeller, Robert R., *COSO Enterprise Risk Management*, 2nd ed. Hoboken, NJ: John Wiley & Sons, 2011.

Moyer, R. Charles, James R. McGuigan, and Ramesh P. Rao. *Contemporary Financial Management*, 13th ed. Mason, OH: Cengage, 2014.

MSN Money, "Currency Exchange Rates," http://investing.money.msn.com/investments/exchange-rates/

Nicolai, Loren A., John D. Bazley, and Jefferson P. Jones. *Intermediate Accounting*, 11th ed. Mason, OH: Cengage, 2010.

Olve, Nils-Göran, and Anna Sjöstrand. *The Balanced Scorecard*, 2nd ed. Oxford, UK: Capstone, 2006.

Hartgraves , Al L., and Wayne J. Morse. *Managerial Accounting*, 6th ed. Lombard, IL: Cambridge Business, 2012.

Rosenberg, Jerry M. *The Essential Dictionary of International Trade*. New York: Barnes & Noble, 2004.

Sarbanes-Oxley, www.sarbanesoxleysimplified.com/sarbox/compact/htmlact/sec406.html

Sawyer, Lawrence B., Mortimer A. Dittenhofer, and Anne Graham, eds. 2003. *Sawyer's Internal Auditing: The Practice of Modern Internal Auditing*, 5th ed. Altamonte Springs, FL: Institute of Internal Auditors, 2003.

Securities and Exchange Commission, www.sec.gov/rules/final/33-8177.htm

Shim, Jae K., and Joel G. Siegel. *Schaum's Outlines: Managerial Accounting*, 2nd ed. New York: McGraw-Hill, 2011.

Siegel, Joel G., Jae K. Shim, and Stephen W. Hartman. *Schaum's Quick Guide to Business Formulas: 201 Decision-Making Tools for Business, Finance, and Accounting Students*. New York: McGraw-Hill, 1998.

Simkin, Mark G., Jacob M. Rose, and Carolyn S. Norman. *Core Concepts of Accounting Information Systems*, 12th ed. Hoboken, NJ: John Wiley & Sons, 2012.

Stiglitz, Joseph E. *Globalization and Its Discontents*. New York: Norton, 2002.

Subramanyam, K. R., and John L. Wild, *Financial Statement Analysis*, 10th ed. New York: McGraw-Hill, 2009.

U.S. Department of Justice. Foreign Corrupt Practices Act, Antibribery Provisions, www.usdoj.gov/criminal/fraud/fcpa/guide.pdf

U.S. Securities and Exchange Commission, www.sec.gov

Van Horne, James C., and John M. Wachowicz Jr. *Fundamentals of Financial Management*, 13th ed. Harlow, UK: Pearson Education, 2008.

Warren, Carl S., James M. Reeve, and Jonathan Duchac. *Financial and Managerial Accounting*, 12th ed. Mason, OH: Cengage, 2013.

Wessels, Walter J. *Economics*, 5th ed. New York: Barron's, 2012.

XE.com, www.xe.com

Index of Learning Outcome Statements

Index

This index identifies the page on which a key term or concept is introduced in context. It is not meant as a comprehensive index of all references to that term or concept.

795